Abstracts
of
Probate Records
for
The District *of* Stafford
in
Fairfield, County Connecticut

- 1803-1848 -

Compiled By:
Spencer P. Mead, L.L.B.

Southern Historical Press, Inc.
Greenville, South Carolina

This volume was reproduced
from a personal copy located in
the Publishers private library

All rights reserved. No part of this publication may be reproduced,
stored in a retrieval system, transmitted in any form, posted
on the web in any form or by any means without the
prior written permission of the publisher.

Please direct all correspondence and book orders to:
SOUTHERN HISTORICAL PRESS, Inc.
1071 Park West Blvd.
Greenville, SC 29611

Published 1924 by:
  Spencer P. Mead
ISBN #978-1-63914-652-9
Printed in the United States of America

RECORDS HERETOFORE ABSTRACTED BY THE AUTHOR.

Births, Marriages, and Deaths of the Town of Greenwich, Connecticut, from the earliest Town and Land Records to June, 1847

Every Known Tombstone in the Town of Greenwich, Connecticut, Also in the Cemetery at Middle Patent, Westchester County, New York, where many residents of the Town of Greenwich, have been buried.

Church Records of the Town of Greenwich, Connecticut, from the earliest records extant to 1850.

Church Records of the Town of Darien, Connecticut, from the earliest records extant to 1850.

Probate Records for the District of Stamford, Fairfield County, Connecticut, from 1729 to 1802.

CONTENTS.

	Page.
Volume 10,	2.
Volume 11,	44.
Volume 12,	101.
Volume 13,	138.
Volume 14,	179.
Volume 15,	233.
Volume 16,	302.
Volume 17,	347.
Miscellaneous papers not copied,	390.
Index to Estates,	408.
Index to Persons,	423.

STAMFORD PROBATE RECORDS.

Abstract of Probate Records for the District of Stamford from the 1st day of January, 1803, to the 24th of July, 1848. This Probate District during the above period included the Towns of Greenwich, Stamford and Darien.
That part of the Town of New Canaan, which was set off from the Town of Stamford in 1801, came under the jurisdiction of the Probate Court for the District of Norwalk in May, 1802. The Probate Court for the District of Greenwich was created by an Act of the General Assembly, passed July 4, 1853.

VOLUME 10, 1803-1815.

Addington, Thomas, late of Greenwich, Mch. 7, 1807, letters of administration on his estate granted to John Addington, who was ordered to advertise for claims, page 493. Inventory taken Mch. 9, 1807, by Nehemiah Mead and Isaac Weed, and filed Mch. 14, 1807, page 493.
Apl. 2, 1810, the court appointed John Addington guardian of Caroline Addington, about nine years of age, and Lemuel Addington, about ten years of age, children of decedent, page 505[1].

Anderson, Matthias, late of Greenwich, Apl. 6, 1813, letters of administration on his estate granted to Hannah Anderson, who was ordered to advertise for claims, page 522.
Dec. 7, 1813, Henry Anderson, about fifteen years of age, a son of decedent, made choice of Jared Strang to be his guardian; and the court appointed Hannah Anderson guardian of Sally Ann, Matthias, Polly, Priscilla, and John, other children of decedent, page 507.
Dec. 7, 1813, and Mch. 1, 1814, the application of Jared Strang, guardian of William Henry Anderson, and Hannah Anderson, guardian of the other minor children of decedent, for leave to sell the real estate of said minors, page 461.
June 13, 1814, report of sale filed, page 461.

STAMFORD PROBATE RECORDS.
Volume 10, 1803-1815.

Avery, John, late of Greenwich, May 30, 1812, letters of administration on his estate granted to Zophar Avery, who was ordered to advertise for claims, page 523.

Bates, David, late of Stamford, will dated Apl. 21, 1800, probated Mch. 9, 1809, mentions his wife Lavina, and nephew Ezra Raymond. Executrix his wife. Witnesses Samuel Mather and David Maltbie, page 86.
Inventory taken Mch. 21, 1809, by Charles Whiting and Nathaniel Slason, and filed May 2, 1809, page 87.

Bates, David, late of Stamford, Apl. 6, 1809, letters of administration on his estate granted to Lavina Bates, who was ordered to advertise for claims, page 91.

Bates, Gershom, late of Stamford, will dated June 29, 1810, probated Jan. 16, 1811, mentions his wife Martha, and children Elizabeth, Martha, Gershom, Sarah Talmage, Mary Waterbury, John, Ebenezer, and Lewis Smith Bates. Executors his wife and son John. Witnesses Nathan Weed, Nancy Selleck, and Polly Crissy, page 139.
Jan. 16, 1811, letters with the will annexed granted to Gershom Bates, who was ordered to advertise for claims, page 139.
Inventory taken Jan. 22, 1811, by Cary Leeds and Nathaniel Waterbury, and filed Feb. 5, 1811, pages 141 and 143.
1811, estate ordered distributed to his children Betsy Bates, Gershom Bates, Sarah Talmage, Mary Waterbury, John Bates, Lewis Smith Bates, Ebenezer Bates, and Martha Bates, page 144.
Dec. 5, 1811, estate distributed accordingly, page 144.

Bates, James, late of Stamford, will dated Oct. 8, 1805, probated Jan. 7, 1806, all to his wife Mary with reservations. Executor Gershom Scofield. Witnesses Gershom Scofield, Warren Percival, and Nathaniel Waterbury, 2nd, page 22.
Inventory taken Jan. 16, 1806, by Nathan Weed and Isaac Pencyer, and filed Mch. 1, 1806, page 24.
Mch. 1, 1806, order to advertise for claims, page 25.

Bates, Lewis Smith, late of Stamford, Feb. 12, 1812, letters of administration on his estate granted to Gershom Bates, who was ordered to advertise for claims, page 465.
Inventory taken Mch. 4, 1812, by Nathaniel Waterbury and Cary Leeds, and filed Apl. 4, 1812, page 465.

STAMFORD PROBATE RECORDS.
Volume 10, 1803-1815.

Bates, Lewis Smith, continued :
    Jan. 5, 1813, estate ordered distributed to his brothers and sisters, Sarah wife of John Tallmage, Polly wife of Isaac Waterbury, Betsy Bates, Martha wife of John Bacon, Gershom Bates, John Bates, and Ebenezer Bates, page 466.
    Mch. 31, 1813, estate distributed accordingly, page 467.

Bates, Mary, late of Stamford, will dated Aug. 16, 1810, probated Jan. 29, 1811, mentions her children Hannah wife of Samuel Waterbury, Selleck Bates, Mary Bates, and Sarah Bates, Executor Joseph Silliman. Witnesses John Jarvis, Seely Bates, and Rebecca Hoyt, page 88.
    Jan. 29, 1811, order to advertise for claims, page 90.
    Inventory taken Jan. 14, 1811, by James Wardwell and Seely Bates, and filed Jan. 14, 1811, page 90.

Bates, Mary, late of Stamford, will dated Mch. 23, 1811, probated June 2, 1812, mentions her deceased husband James Bates, all to her black girl Zalpha Johnson, who is given her freedom. Executor Warren Percival. Witnesses Nathaniel Waterbury, 2nd, Abigail Waterbury, and Mary Weed, page 136.
    Inventory taken June 16, 1812, by Gershom Scofield and Jeremiah Andreas, and filed July 7, 1812, page 138.

Bayeux, Thomas, Dr., late of Greenwich, July 12, 1811, letters of administration on his estate granted to Joseph Wood of Stamford, who was ordered to advertise for claims, page 498.
    Inventory taken July 24, 1811, by William Knapp and Jabez Mead, and filed Sept. 3, 1811, page 498.
    Mch. 21, 1812, estate ordered distributed to his widow, Priscilla Bayeux, and children Priscilla wife of Epenetus Lockwood, Elizabeth A. wife of Oliver L. Ford, Maria Bayeux, and Sally Bayeux, page 502.
    July 28, 1813, estate distributed accordingly, page 515.

Bell, Francis, late of Stamford, will dated Apl. 6, 1795, probated May 5, 1806, mentions Leah Bell wife of Stephen Bell, and the children of said Stephen Bell, viz: Frederick, and Hannah Bell. Executor Thaddeus Hoyt. Witnesses David Webb, John Davenport, Jr., and Caty Webb, page 12.
    Inventory taken Apl. 6, 1806, by Jeremiah Andreas and Cary Leeds, and filed May 8, 1806, page 13.
    Apl. 20, 1807, account filed, and distribution ordered to Leah Bell wife of Stephen Bell, Frederick Bell a son

STAMFORD PROBATE RECORDS.
Volume 10, 1803-1815.

Bell, Francis, continued :
of said Stephen Bell, Deborah Scofield, widow of Samuel Scofield, Hannah Scofield wife of Thaddeus Scofield, sisters of deceased, and to Noah Bell a brother of deceased, page 15.
Apl. 27, 1807, estate distributed accordingly, page 15.

Bell, Isaac, late of Stamford, will dated Aug. 23, 1799, probated Jan. 12, 1809, mentions his wife Susannah, and children James, Isa-ac, Hannah wife of Fitch Rogers, and Catharine wife of Nehemiah Rogers. Executors his wife and son-in-law Nehemiah Rogers. Witnesses Samuel Mills, Abijah Bishop, and Alexander Bishop, page 389.
Inventory taken Feb. 20, 1809, by Isaac Holly, Jr., and Seymour Jarvis, and filed Aug. 24, 1809, page 390.

Bell, James, formerly of Stamford, but now of Warwick, Orange County, N. Y., father of Julia Bell and Thaddeus Bell, minors, Apl. 2, 1811, asked for leave to sell the real estate of said minors, page 522.
June 4, 1811 order authorizing sale, page 522.

Bell, Thaddeus, late of Stamford, will dated May 8, 1801, probated Apl. 7, 1807, mentions his children Thaddeus, John, Cary, and Mary wife of Ebenezer Seely. Executors his sons Thaddeus, John and Cary. Witnesses Gershom Scofield, Ira Scofield, and Rua Scofield, page 19.
Inventory taken June 2, 1807, by Doctor Brown and John Waterbury, and filed June 2, 1807, page 22.
Apl. 7, 1807, order to advertise for claims, page 21.

Bellamy, Isaac, late of Stamford, Sept. 13, 1813, the court appointed Seth Weed of Stamford guardian of John Bellamy, a son of decedent, page 506.

Betts, Frederick, of Greenwich, May 1, 1810, guardian of Henrietta Betts, Caroline Betts, Daniel Betts, Mary Betts, Hannah Betts, and Filo Betts, minor children of said Frederick Betts, asked leave to sell the real estate of said minors, page 303.
July 10, 1810, order authorizing sale, page 304.

Betts, Nathaniel William, late of Greenwich, Apl. 13, 1811, Eliza Ann Betts, a daughter of decedent, made choice of Burwell Betts to be her guardian, page 506.

STAMFORD PROBATE RECORDS.
Volume 10, 1803-1815.

Bishop, Abijah, late of Stamford, Jan. 2, 1810, letters of administration on his estate granted to Ellen Bishop, who was ordered to advertise for claims, page 92.
Inventory taken Jan. 12, 1810, by Cary Leeds and Joseph Bishop, and filed Feb. 6, 1810, page 92.
Aug. 7, 1810, account filed, and real estate ordered sold to pay debts, page 492.

Bishop, Alexander, late of Stamford, will dated May 9, 1807, probated Sept. 26, 1807, mentions his wife Hannah, and children Charles F., John K., David H., now deceased, Levina, and niece Susannah Holly Bishop. Executors his wife and sons Charles F., and John K. Witnesses Abijah Bishop, Newman Holly, and Abijah Bishop, Jr., page 34.
Inventory taken by Abijah Bishop, and Cary Leeds, and filed Oct. 6, 1807, page 37.
Oct. 6, 1807, order to advertise for claims, page 39.

Bishop, Andrew, a minor about 15 years of age, Sept. 5, 1814, made choice of Joseph B. Cock, Jr., of Danbury to be his guardian, page 512.

Bishop, Silas, late of Stamford, May 21, 1806, letters of administration on his estate granted to Joseph Bishop, who was ordered to advertise for claims, page 31.
Inventory taken May 23, 1806, by Samuel Hoyt, Jr. and Jeremiah Andreas, and filed May 27, 1806, page 31.
May 17, 1807, account filed, page 33.

Bostwick, Samuel, late of Bedford, Mch. 29, 1809, Stephen Bostwick, about 16 years of age, a son of decedent, made choice of Daniel Bostwick to be his guardian, page 505.

Briggs, Hannah, widow of Reuben Briggs, late of Stamford, May 22, 1806, letters of administration on her estate granted to Nathaniel June of Stamford, who was ordered to advertise for claims, page 42.
Inventory taken June 30, 1806, by Daniel Nichols and Solomon Clason, and filed July 5, 1806, page 42.
Jan. 5, 1808, account filed, and real estate ordered sold to pay debts, page 44.
Feb. 2, 1808, estate ordered distributed to Hannah wife of Nathaniel June, a daughter; Jemima wife of Hezekiah Wood, a daughter; Ezra Briggs, a son; John Briggs and Prudence Stratton the legal representatives of John Briggs, a deceased son, page 44.
Feb. 11, 1808, estate distributed accordingly, page 45.

STAMFORD PROBATE RECORDS.
Volume 10, 1803-1815.

Brown, Bezaleel, late of Greenwich, will dated Jan. 3, 1805, probated July 27, 1805, mentions his wife Rachel, and children Levi, Nathaniel, Josiah, Bezaleel, Rachel wife of Hardy Mead. Executors son Bezaleel and Jabez Fitch Witnesses Andrew Mead, Ira Mead, and John Lockwood, page 25.
July 27, 1805, order to advertise for claims, page 28.
Inventory taken Aug. 22, 1805, by Abraham Husted and Peter Mead, and filed Sept. 6, 1805, page 29.
May 15, 1810, dower of his widow set out, page 520.

Brown, David, late of Greenwich, will dated Mch. 19, 1812, probated Apl. 6, 1813, mentions his children James, David, Robert, Sarah wife of Levi Brown, Deborah wife of Jonathan Rundle, Phebe wife of Shadrach Rundle, Martha wife of John Knapp, Margaret, Elizabeth, Clara, Anna, William, and grandson Elihu Marshall. Executors son Robert and son-in-law Jonathan Rundle. Witnesses James Brown, Gilbert Peck, and Ebenezer Mead, page 516.
Apl. 14, 1813, order to advertise for claims, page 518.
Inventory taken Apl. 19, 1813, by Ebenezer Mead and Abraham Close, and filed May 4, 1813, page 518.

Brown, Doctor, late of Stamford, Apl. 6, 1813, letters of administration on his estate granted to Elizabeth Brown, who was ordered to advertise for claims, page 523.

Brown, James, late of Stamford, Dec. 3, 1805, letters of administration on his estate granted to Henry Brown, who was ordered to advertise for claims, page 40.
Inventory taken Dec. 27, 1805, by Jeremiah Andreas and Joseph Bishop, and filed Jan. 7, 1806, page 40.
July 1, 1806, account filed, page 41.

Brown, James, late of Greenwich, Apl. 19, 1813, letters of administration on his estate granted to Gideon Close, who was ordered to advertise for claims, page 436.
Inventory taken Apl. 22, 1813, by Elias Peck and Nathaniel Palmer, and filed May 4, 1813, page 436.

Brown, John, of Stamford, a son of Hannah Brown, a free black woman, about 15 years of age, made choice of Rufus Scofield to be his guardian, page 509.

Brown, Nehemiah, late of Greenwich, June 21, 1810, letters of administration on his estate granted to Major Brown and Gilbert Close, who were ordered to advertise for claims, page 521.

STAMFORD PROBATE RECORDS.
Volume 10, 1803-1815.

Brown, Nehemiah, continued :
    Inventory taken June 27, 1810, by Phinehas Rundle and Seymour Hobby, and filed Aug. 7, 1810, page 521.

Brown, Rebecca, late of Stamford, Aug. 17, 1814, letters of administration on her estate granted to John Brown of Stamford, who was ordered to advertise for claims, page 512.

Brundige, James, late of Greenwich, will dated July 16, 1806, probated Sept. 10, 1806, mentions his children Sarah and James, son-in-law Jotham Wilson, grandson Jotham Wilson, Jr., and greatgranddaughter Mary Wilson. Executors Jared Strang of Greenwich and Jonah Brundige of Rye. Witnesses Silas Carpenter, Charles Willson and Jared Strang, page 1.
    Inventory taken Sept. 19, 1806, by William Anderson and Nehemiah Willson, and filed Oct. 7, 1806, page 3.
    Oct. 7, 1806, commissioners appointed to adjust claims of creditors, page 3.
    Apl. 7, 1807, report of commissioners filed, page 4.
    Apl. 9, 1807, account filed, and creditors ordered paid page 5.

Brush, Shubal, late of Greenwich, inventory taken Mch. 28, 1800, by David Wood and Benjamin Brush, and filed Oct. 26, 1800, page 149.
    Apl. 5, 1811, account filed, and real estate ordered sold to pay debts, page 151.
    May 22, 1811, commissioners appointed to set out the share of decedent's widow, Christina Brush, now Christina Finch, page 152.
    Apl. 2, 1811, widow's share set out, page 152.
    Apl. 15, 1811, estate ordered distributed to the children of deceased, Samuel, Benjamin, Jr., James, John, Edward, Anne Hobby, Mary Brush, Christina Brush, and Betsy(Elizabeth)Brush, page 154.
    Apl. 18, 1811, estate distributed accordingly, page 154.

Bunnell, David, late of Stamford, Nov. 2, 1813, letters of administration on his estate granted to Ezra Lockwood, who was ordered to advertise for claims, page 507.
    June 7, 1814, Lockwood Bunnell, about 15 years of age, a son of decedent, made choice of Charles Knapp to be his guardian, page 510.

STAMFORD-PROBATE RECORDS.
Volume 10, 1803-1815.

Bush, Deborah, widow, late of Greenwich, 1804, letters of administration on her estate granted to Richard Mead, page 55.
Inventory taken Apl. 7, 1804, by Ebenezer Mead and Isaac Weed, and filed Apl. 10, 1804, pages 55 and 57.
Feb. 1, 1805, account filed, and estate ordered distributed to Joseph Mead, a son; to the legal representatives of Mary wife of Abraham Hobby, a deceased daughter; to Hannah wife of Robert Calwell, page 57.
Mch. 18, 1805, estate distributed to Rebecca wife of John R. Cozine, Hannah wife of John Calwell, legal representatives of Mary wife of Abraham Hobby, a deceased daughter, and to Joseph Mead, page 58.

Buxton, Ezra, late of Stamford, Mch. 10, 1812, letters of administration on his estate granted to Abigail Buxton, widow of deceased, page 273.
Inventory taken Mch. 11, 1812, by Benjamin Scofield and Warren Scofield, and filed Mch. 13, 1812, page 273.
Mch. 13, 1812, commissioners appointed to adjust claims of creditors, page 274.
Oct. 21, 1812, report of commissioners filed, page 275.
Nov. 5, 1812, commissioners appointed to set out the dower of his widow, Abigail Buxton, page 275.
Nov. 16, 1812, dower set out, page 275.
Nov. 16, 1812, Hoyt Scofield on behalf of Abigail Buxton, administratrix, filed account, and real estate ordered sold to pay debts, page 275.
Dec. 15, 1812, account filed, and creditors ordered paid, page 275.

Buxton, Isaac, late of Stamford, will dated Feb. 25, 1812, prebated May 20, 1812, mentions his wife Rachel, and children Mary, Esther wife of Nathaniel Webb, Jr., James Newman, Seth, John, Munson, Betsy, and Sally. Executor Titus Lockwood, page 469.
May 22, 1812, the executor refused to qualify and letters with the will annexed granted to Seth Buxton, who was ordered to advertise for claims, page 470.
Inventory taken May 26, 1812, by Benjamin Scofield and Warren Scofield, and filed June 2, 1812, page 470.
Dec. 2, 1812, account filed, and real estate ordered sold to pay debts, page 471.
Dec. 12, 1812, report of sale filed, page 472.

Clason, Stephen, late of Stamford, will dated Aug. 25, 1807, probated Nov. 7, 1809, mentions his wife Martha, and

STAMFORD PROBATE RECORDS.
Volume 10, 1803-1815.

Clason, Stephen, continued:
children Isaac, Seth, Solomon, Ard, Benjamin, Stephen, if living, and if dead to his daughter Edee, daughter Abigail Jessup, and granddaughter Olive Clason. Executor his son Benjamin. Witnesses Jacob Bates, Eber Smith, and Daniel Nichols, page 119.
Inventory taken Dec. 5, 1809, by Daniel Lockwood, Jr., and Daniel Nichols, and filed Dec. 5, 1809, pages 121 and 126.
Dec. 5, 1809, order to advertise for claims, page 126.

Clock, Albert, late of Stamford, Mch. 5, 1805, that part of his estate set off to his widow for her dower, and also the estate of Albert Clock a son of said deceased, being a minor, distributed to Nathaniel Clock, and to the heirs of Abraham Clock, and Henry Clock, children of said deceased, page 519.

Clock, Jonas, late of Stamford, June 5, 1810, letters of administration on his estate granted to John Weed, page 127.
Inventory taken June 13, 1810, by Nathan Weed and William Walmsley, and filed June 13, 1810, pages 127 and 129.
1811, estate ordered distributed, page 129.
Mch. 20, 1811, estate distributed to the legal representatives of Nancy wife of James Bell, a deceased daughter; Sally wife of Hezekiah Weed, a daughter of deceased; and Jacob W. Clock, a son of deceased, page 130
June 9, 1810, Jacob Weed Clock, about 17 years of age, a son of decedent, made choice of Frederick Weed to be his guardian, page 505^3.
Mch. 12, 1811, Jacob Weed Clock, made choice of William Shaw of New York City, to be his guardian in place of Frederick Weed, page 506.

Close, Gideon, Sr., late of Greenwich, Feb. 3, 1809, letters of administration on his estate granted to Edward Close, page 202.
Inventory taken Feb. 23, 1809, by Charles Smith and Benjamin Brush, and filed Mch. 7, 1809, page 202.
Mch. 7, 1809, account filed, and real estate ordered distributed to the brothers and sisters of deceased, viz: Edward Close, Shadrach Close, Odle Close, Elizabeth Close, and Hannah Close, page 203.
Mch. 29, 1810, estate distributed accordingly, page 203.

STAMFORD PROBATE RECORDS.
Volume 10, 1803-1815.

Close, Jonathan, late of Greenwich, June 2, 1812, letters of administration on his estate granted to Gideon Close, who was ordered to advertise for claims, page 485.
Inventory taken June 10, 1812, by Elnathan Husted and Amos Husted, and filed Aug. 4, 1812, page 485.
Mch. 20, 1813, account filed, and real estate ordered sold to pay debts, page 487.
Apl. 5, 1813, report of sale filed, page 487.

Close, Odle, Jr., late of Greenwich, June 5, 1804, letters of administration on his estate granted to Gideon Close and Edward Close, page 47.
Inventory taken June 6, 1804, by Benjamin Brush and Charles Smith, and filed Aug. 7, 1804, pages 47 and 49.
Apl. 2, 1805, account filed, and real estate ordered sold to pay debts, page 49.
Nov. 5, 1805, report of sale filed, and estate ordered distributed to his widow Hannah Close, and children Edward, Shadrach, Gideon, Odle, Elizabeth, and Hannah, page 50.
Dec. 11, 1805, estate distributed accordingly, page 50.
Apl. 3, 1810, the court appointed Gideon Close guardian of Odle Close, about 12 years of age; and also appointed Edward Close guardian of Hannah Close, about 9 years of age, children of decedent, page 505^1.

Crissy, John, late of Stamford, Dec. 4, 1810, Polly Crissy, about 15 years of age, a daughter of decedent, made choice of David Stevens of New Canaan to be her guardian, and the court appointed said David Stevens guardian of John Crissy, about 12 years of age, a son of decedent, page 505^3.

Davenport, Elizabeth, late of Stamford, will dated June 17, 1802, probated Oct. 27, 1808, mentions Sarah Davenport, a daughter of her nephew John Davenport; Theodora wife of William Davenport; niece Catharine Davenport; Jerusha wife of Ebenezer Davenport; the present wife of her nephew John Davenport; Catharine Maltbie, a daughter of David Maltbie, and nephew Abraham Davenport, a son of Silas Davenport, a deceased brother. Executor said Abraham Davenport. Witnesses John Davenport, Jr., Elizabeth Smith, and Mary W. Davenport, page 308.
Codicil dated Feb. 6, 1808, page 310.

Davenport, Hannah, late of Stamford, inventory taken May 1, 1810, by Nathaniel Waterbury and Cary Leeds, and filed May 1, 1810, by the administrator, page 415.

STAMFORD PROBATE RECORDS.
Volume 10, 1803-1815.

Davenport, Mehitable, widow of James Davenport, late of Stamford, will dated Sept. 22, 1803, probated Dec. 4, 1804, mentions her children Abigail Fitch Davenport, Mary Ann Davenport, and Frances Louisa Davenport; Elizabeth Cogswell Davenport a daughter of my deceased husband; Alice Cogswell a niece of my deceased husband; niece Mehitable Cogshall a daughter of my deceased brother William; Mary Stiles Holly and Elizabeth King Holly daughters of my sister Martha wife of David Holly,; sister Eunice Cogshall the widow of my deceased brother William Cogshall and their children, viz: Mehitable, George, Robert, Charles, James, and Frances; nephew William Cogshall; owned property at Milford, Conn. Executor John Davenport, Jr., a brother of my deceased husband. Witnesses Daniel Smith, Azariah Scofield, and John Andreas, page 329.
Codicil dated Oct. 22, 1803, page 330.
Inventory taken Feb. 1804, by Jeremiah Andreas and Abraham Davenport, and filed Nov. 13, 1805, page 331.

Demill, Peter, late of New York City, Nov. 9, 1810, Elizabeth S. Demill and Mary R. Demill, children of decedent, made choice of Richard Mead to be their guardian, and the court appointed said Richard Mead guardian of Thomas A. William S. , Richard M., Frances S., Peter E., and Cornelia A., other children of decedent, page 505[3].

Demill, Sarah, widow of Joseph Demill, late of Stamford, will dated Nov. 28, 1809, probated Jan. 27, 1810, legacies to Annie Rogers, John Melanchton Holly, William Welles Holly, Abigail Elizabeth Holly, and Alfred Apollos Holly, children of John W. Holly; John Hudson a grandson of said John W. Holly; niece Sarah wife of James Weed; brother Newman Holly; and niece Elizabeth wife of David Waterbury. Executor John William Holly. Witnesses Elizabeth Wooster, Hannah Hoyt, and Ebenezer Davenport, page 93.
Jan. 27, 1810, order to advertise for claims, page 95.
Inventory taken Jan. 27, 1810, by Joseph Bishop and Isaac Holly, Jr., and filed page 95.
Sept. 1810, estate distributed to Newman Holly, a brother of deceased; Sarah Weed, a niece, and Elizabeth Waterbury, a niece, page 131.

Edwards, John, a soldier in the 25th Regiment, U. S. A. , late of Stamford, will dated May 3, 1814, probated June 5, 1815, all to Betsy Hoyt, widow of Benjamin Hoyt, late

STAMFORD PROBATE RECORDS.
Volume 10, 1803-1815.

Edwards, John, continued :
of Stamford. No executor. Witnesses Jesse Beach, Sally Beach, and Sally Hoyt. Letters of administration with the will annexed granted to Elizabeth Hoyt, page 13.
June 5, 1815, order to advertise for claims, page 13.

Ferris, Clauson, late of Greenwich, Apl. 7, 1814, Hanford Ferris, about 15 years of age, a son of decedent, made choice of Eliphalet St. John of New Canaan to be his guardian, page 508.

Ferris, David, Jr., late of Greenwich, Dec. 1, 1810, Lemuel Ferris, about 16 years of age, a son of decedent, made choice of Betsy Ferris, his mother, to be his guardian, page 5054.

Ferris, Ebenezer, late of Greenwich, July 27, 1813, letters of administration on his estate granted to David Wood, who was ordered to advertise for claims, page 234.

Ferris, Nathaniel, late of Greenwich, will dated Oct. 10, 1807 probated Oct. 3, 1809, mentions his children Ebenezer, Oliver, Sarah, Mary Ann wife of Levi Mead of North Castle, and Jemima wife of James Palmer of Greenwich. Executor his son Benjamin. Witnesses Nathaniel Ingersoll, Tompkins Close, and Benjamin Reynolds, page 270.
Inventory taken Nov. 2, 1809, by David Wood, Jr., and Jonathan Finch, and filed Dec. 5, 1809, page 416.
Oct. 3, 1809, order to advertise for claims, page 271.
Apl. 6, 1813, estate ordered distributed to Ebenezer Ferris, Mary Ann Mead, Jemima Palmer, and Sally Chapman, children of deceased, page 273.
Apl. 24, 1813, estate distributed to Ebenezer Ferris, Mary Ann Mead, Jemima Palmer, and Sally wife of John Chapman, being the legal representatives of Oliver Ferris, deceased, page 272.

Ferris, Oliver, late of Greenwich, inventory taken Apl. 24, 1813, by Jared Smith and David Brundage, and filed May 4, 1813, by the administrator, page 415.

General Assembly, Oct. 1806, appointed John Davenport, Jr., Judge of Probate for the special purpose of settling the estate of Elizabeth Davenport, late of Stamford, page 308.

STAMFORD PROBATE RECORDS.
Volume 10, 1803-1815.

George, Prince, late of Greenwich, Apl. 18, 1814, letters of
administration on his estate granted to Justus L. Bush,
who was ordered to advertise for claims, page 464.

Gray, Philip, late of Stamford, will dated Mch. 8, 1814, probated Apl. 5, 1814, mentions his wife Hannah, and children Mary, Eleanor, John A., and Alfred. Executor Samuel Whiting. Witnesses Gershom Scofield, Nathaniel Slason, and Josiah Whitney, page 440.
Inventory taken Apl. 9, 1814, by Joshua Scofield and Josiah Whitney, and filed May 3, 1814, page 442.
Apl. 5, 1814, the court appointed Josiah Whitney guardian of Alfred Gray, about 11 years of age, a son of decedent, page 508.
May 11, 1814, the court appointed Joel Hurlbutt guardian of John A. Gray, a son of decedent, page 509.

Green, Charles, Jr., late of North Castle, will dated Mch. 7, 1808, probated Mch. 18, 1814, mentions his wife Thankful, and children Reuben, Elizabeth, Abraham, Nathan, and Elisha. Executors Joshua Knapp and John Ferris, Jr. Witnesses Solomon Haviland, John Ferris, and Ferris Lyon, page 299.
Inventory taken Mch. 1814, by Silas Sutherland and Benjamin Knapp, and filed Mch. 18, 1814, page 300.

Griffin, Charles, a minor of Greenwich, about 16 years of age, Nov. 2, 1813, made choice of Simeon Minor to be his guardian, page 507.

Grigg, Walter, late of Greenwich, Feb. 2, 1813, letters of administration on his estate granted to Ebenezer Mead, who was ordered to advertise for claims, page 434.
Inventory taken Mch. 11, 1813, by Richard Mead and Samuel Bush, and filed Apl. 6, 1813, page 435.
Feb. 1, 1814, account filed, and realestate ordered sold to pay debts, page 435.

Hait, David, late of Stamford, will dated June 18, 1805, probated Aug. 7, 1810, mentions his wife Ann, and children Mary Ann, Hannah Coggswell, Sally Cowdre, Esther Mead, and Frederick, grandsons Nathaniel Palmer, William Palmer, and Henry Hait. Executors his wife and son. Witnesses Margaret Mackay, John Mackay, and John Mackay Jr., page 98.
Aug. 7, 1810, order to advertise for claims, page 99.
Inventory taken Aug. 13, 1810, by Joel Waring and Seth Smith, and filed Oct. 6, 1810, page 99.

STAMFORD PROBATE RECORDS.
Volume 10, 1803-1815.

Hait, John, late of Stamford, will dated Dec. 20, 1794, probated Nov. 7, 1809, mentions his wife Jemima, and children John, Reuben, Henry, and Jemima. Executor his son John Hait, 4th. Witnesses Ezekiel Seely, Jesse Crissy, and Reuben Scofield, page 105.
Codicil dated Feb. 23, 1796, page 106.
Inventory taken Nov. 1, 1809, by Nathaniel Waterbury and Reuben Scofield, and filed Jan. 2, 1810, page 106.

Hait, Ruth, late of Stamford, will dated 1799, probated Jan. 21, 1808, mentions her children Thankful Hait, Ruth Hait, Elizabeth Hait, and Mary Hait; granddaughter Lydia wife of Daniel Hubbard; others Jesse Hait, Joel Hait, Seth Hait, Nehemiah son of Seth Hait, and Stephen Hait. Executors son Seth Hait and daughter Thankful Hait. Witnesses Charles Smith, Benjamin Smith, and Sally Smith, page 474.

Hait, Sarah, widow of Jonathan Hait, late of Stamford, will dated Sept. 24, 1799, probated May 6, 1806, mentions her son Jonathan Hait, and granddaughter Sarah Hait, a daughter of Ezra Hait, a deceased son. Executor Cary Hait. Witnesses Samuel Webb, Nathaniel Waterbury, Jr., and Jonathan Weed, Jr., page 73.
Inventory taken June 26, 1806, by Hanford Hoyt and Cary Leeds, and filed July 1, 1806, page 74.

Halleck, George, late of Greenwich, will dated Aug. 20, 1803, probated Jan. 18, 1812, all to his wife Amy H., for life, remainder to her daughter Amy Wollis. Executrix his wife. Witnesses Elijah Reynolds, Hobby Reynolds, and Peter A. Burtus, page 296.
Inventory taken Feb. 3, 1812, by John Adams, Jr., and Jabez Mead, and filed Feb. 3, 1812, page 423.
Feb. 14, 1812, order to advertise for claims, and on Mch. 3, 1812, commissioners appointed to adjust claims of creditors, page 424.
Oct. 6, 1812, report of commissioners filed, page 465.
Feb. 15, 1813, and Feb. 14, 1814, accounts filed, and creditors ordered paid, pages 403 and 430.
Nov. 13, 1812, dower of his widow, Anna Halleck, set out, page 430.

Hawley, Elijah, Deacon, late of Stamford, will dated Aug. 11, 1800, probated Feb. 16, 1807, mentions his wife Hannah, and children Hannah and Polly. Executrix his daughter Hannah. Witnesses James Lounsbury, Reuben Scofield, and Jared Lounsberry, page 76.

STAMFORD PROBATE RECORDS.
Volume 10, 1803-1815.

Hawley, Elijah, Deacon, continued:
    Feb. 16, 1807, the executrix refused to qualify, and letters with the will annexed granted to Hanford Hoyt, page 76.
    Inventory taken Mch. 30, 1807, by Ezra Knapp and Uzal Knapp, and filed, page 77.

Haxton, Charlotte, late of Stamford, will dated Apl. 16, 1810, probated Sept. 21, 1810, all to her husband Dyer Haxton for life, remainder to child to be born, if any, otherwise to her brothers Asahel Weed, Amos Weed, Jonathan Weed, Abishai Weed, and sisters Mary wife of Josiah Hays, Prudence wife of Nezer Hoyt, and Hannah wife of Epenetus Hoyt. Executor her husband. Witnesses Benjamin Perine, Sarah Perine, and Joseph Wood, page 157.
    Inventory taken Oct. 10, 1810, by Henry Hoyt, Jr., and Isaac Holly, Jr., and filed Oct. 10, 1810, page 159.

Hendrie, William, late of Greenwich, will dated May 21, 1804, probated Nov. 26, 1804, mentions his wife Hannah, and children Mary wife of Phinehas Lockwood, Jane wife of Edward Reed, Anne Hendrie, Alexander and Charles. Executrix his wife. Witnesses Samuel Sturges, Thomas Bayeux, and Ebenezer Davenport, page 344.
    Inventory taken Dec. 4, 1804, by Silvanus Knapp and Enos Lockwood, and filed Dec. 1805, page 346.
    Dec. 10, 1808, estate ordered distributed to his widow, and to his children Alexander and Charles, page 349.
    Dec. 29, 1808, estate distributed accordingly, page 349.

Hitchcock, Joseph, late of Greenwich, July 16, 1810, letters of administration on his estate granted to Samuel L. Hitchcock, who was ordered to advertise for claims, page 267.
    Inventory taken Aug. 25, 1810, by Nehemiah Mead, Jr., and John Timpany, and filed Aug. 27, 1810, page 267.

Hitchcock, Thomas, late of Greenwich, will dated Feb. 12, 1811, probated Jan. 22, 1814, mentions his wife Hannah, and children John, William R., Mary Silkman, Sarah Raymond, Thyrza Ritch, Cyrus, Adaline, Louisa, and Thomas J. Executors his wife and son John. Witnesses Oliver Ferris, Justus L. Bush, and Esther R. Knapp, page 257.

Hobby, Amy, late of Greenwich, will dated June 21, 1804, probated July 6, 1813, mentions her children Ebenezer

STAMFORD PROBATE RECORDS.
Volume 10, 1803-1815.

Hobby, Amy, continued :
Mead and Enoch Mead; grandchildren children of her daughter Hannah wife of Elkanah Mead, viz: Hannah wife of David Husted, Sally wife of Benjamin Smith, and Amos Mead; her sons Benjamin Hobby and Squire Hobby; granddaughter Amy Mead, a daughter of said Ebenezer Mead; granddaughters Amy Hobby, a daughter of said Benjamin Hobby and Amy Hoby, a daughter of said Squire Hobby; her daughters Sally wife of Amos Hobby and Amy wife of Andrew Mead. Executor her son-in-law Andrew Mead. Witnesses Samuel M. Fitch and Jabez Fitch, page 265.
July 6, 1813, order to advertise for claims, page 267.
Inventory taken Aug. 3, 1813, by Jabez Fitch and Ebenezer Hobby, and filed Aug. 3, 1813, page 419.

Hobby, Benjamin, late of Greenwich, May 13, 1813, letters of administration on his estate granted to Maria Hobby, who was ordered to advertise for claims, page 489.
Inventory taken May 25, 1813, by Elkanah Mead and Isaac Peck, and filed June 1, 1813, page 421.
Mch. 24, 1814, the court appointed Nehemiah Brown, Jr., of Rye, guardian of Philander, Nehemiah B., Benjamin, Amy, Samuel S., and Abby Jane, children of dedecent, page 503.
Mch. 24, 1814, and June 9, 1814, petition of Nehemiah Brown, Jr., guardian of the aforesaid minors for leave to sell their realestate, pages 304 and 489.
June 18, 1814, date of report of sale, shows other persons interested to be Lydia Hobby and Maria Hobby, page 489.
June 7, 1814, account filed, and realestate ordered sold to pay debts, page 489.
June 18, 1814, report of sale filed, page 489.

Hobby, Squire, late of Greenwich, inventory taken May 14, 1811, by Andrew Mead and Ebenezer Hobby, and filed May 16, 1811, by the administrator, page 117.

Holly, Nathan, late of Stamford, inventory taken Oct. 10, 1810, by Henry Hoyt, Jr., and Robert Scofield, and filed Nov. 6, 1810, by the administrator, page 115.

Holly, Sarah, wife of Newman Holly, late of Stamford, will dated Jan. 19, 1814, probated Feb. 7, 1814, mentions her husband Newman Holly, and children Josiah, Hannah, David, deceased, John, Joseph, and granddaughter Abigail. Executor son Josiah. Witnesses Levina Bishop, Sally Weed, and Samuel Webb, page 432.

STAMFORD PROBATE RECORDS.
Volume 10, 1803-1815.

Holly, Sarah, continued :
Inventory taken Feb. 7, 1814, by Isaac Holly, Jr., and Rufus Newman, and filed Feb. 7, 1814, page 434.

Holmes, Benjamin, late of Greenwich, Sept. 26, 1809, letters of administration on his estate granted to Jemima Holmes, page 167.
Inventory taken Sept. 28, 1809, by Ebenezer Mead and Jabez Fitch, and filed Oct. 3, 1809, and commissioners appointed to adjust claims of creditors, pages 167 and 169.
May 11, 1810, report of commissioners filed, page 169.
Oct. 10, 1809, personal estate ordered sold to pay debts, page 169.
Mch. 5, 1811, account filed, and realestate ordered sold to pay debts, page 171.

Holmes, Isaac, Jr., late of Greenwich, Nov. 29, 1809, on the application of Richard Mead, administrator de bonus non, realestate ordered sold to pay debts, page 395.

Holmes, Reuben, late of Greenwich, will dated Jan. 28, 1804, probated Apl. 20, 1808, mentions his children Susannah Dally, Molly wife of Lewis Hine, Ruth Hobby, Absalom, Benjamin, Jotham, Stephen, Silas, Reuben, and the children of my son Israel, late of Waterbury; grandson Walter Knapp, a son of my said daughter Susannah; granddaughter Polly wife of Justus B. Mead, and daughter of my said daughter Susannah. Executor son Reuben. Witnesses Samuel M. Fitch, Sarah Fitch, and Jabez Fitch, page 351.
Inventory taken Apl. 21, 1808, by Peter Mead and Robert Mead, and filed Apl. 22, 1808, page 352.
Apl. 12, 1809, receipt for legacies by Polly wife of Justus B. Mead, Walter Knapp, Hannah Holmes, as administratrix of the estate of Stephen Holmes, Benjamin Holmes, Lewis Hine, Absalom Holmes, Jotham Holmes, Ruth Hobby, Silas Holmes, Sarah Holmes, Susannah Dally, and the heirs of Israel Holmes, page 77.

Hose, Henry G., late of Stamford, Aug. 3, 1813, letters of administration on his estate granted to Simeon H. Minor who was ordered to advertise for claims, page 408.

Howe, David, late of Stamford, June 3, 1809, his widow Rebecca, now deceased, and the residuary legatee, Jacob Howe, now deceased, distribution of estate of said Jacob Howe ordered to Elizabeth Howe, widow of said deceased Jacob Howe, her dower, and the remainder

STAMFORD PROBATE RECORDS.
Volume 10, 1803-1815.

Howe, David, continued :
to his children Mary wife of David Fansher, Selleck Howe, Henry Howe, David Howe, Jacob Howe, Betsy Howe, Catharine wife of Justus Onderdonk, Sally Howe, and Raymond Howe, page 372.
June 7, 1809, estate distributed accordingly, page 372.

Howe, Rebecca, late of Stamford, will dated July 18, 1805, probated Jan. 18, 1809, mentions her children Bowers Howe, Abigail wife of William Crissy, Rebecca wife of Benjamin Socfield, Betsy wife of Thaddeus Bell, Sarah wife of Jeremiah Andreas; and granddaughter Betsy a daughter of Jacob Howe, deceased. Executor said Jeremiah Andreas. Witnesses John Davenport, Jr., Samuel Lockwood and Benjamin H. Olmstead, page 380.
Inventory taken Feb. 14, 1809, by William Walmsley and Benjamin Weed, Jr., and filed Feb. 15, 1809, page 381.

Hoyt, Benjamin, late of Stamford, Dec. 7, 1813, letters of administration on his estate granted to Elizabeth Hoyt, and Simeon H. Minor, who were ordered to advertise for claims, page 409.
July 22, 1814, account filed, and creditors ordered paid, page 479.

Hoyt, Ezra, late of Rhinebeck, Dutchess County, N. Y., Feb. 25, 1809, letters of administration on his estate granted to Silas Hoyt, Jr., page 297.
Inventory taken Mch. 6, 1809, by Jeremiah Andreas and Frederick Webb, and filed Mch. 7, 1809, and commissioners appointed to adjust claims of creditors, page 297.
Sept. 14, 1809, report of commissioners filed, page 298

Hoyt, Jared, late of Stamford, May 11, 1812, letters of administration on his estate granted to Epenetus Hoyt, who was ordered to advertise for claims, page 428.
Inventory taken May 16, 1812, by Deodate Davenport and Philo Weed, and filed May 16, 1812, page 425.
Oct. 29, 1812, order to advertise, and on Nov. 3, 1812, commissioners appointed to adjust claims of creditors, page 428.
June 5, 1813, real estate ordered sold to pay debts, pages 408 and 430.
June 3, 1813, report of commissioners to adjust claims filed, page 431.

Hoyt, Joel, late of Stamford, July 2, 1805, letters of administration on his estate granted to Abigail Hoyt, widow

STAMFORD PROBATE RECORDS.
Volume 10, 1803-1815.

Hoyt, Joel, continued :
of deceased, page 374.
Inventory taken Jan. 24, 1793, by Aaron Peck and Benjamin Brush, and filed July 8, 1805, page 374.
May 5, 1807, estate ordered distributed to his widow, Abigail Hoyt, her dower, and to his children Mehitable and Freeman, part having been sold to pay debts, page 376.
June 9, 1807, estate distributed accordingly, page 376.

Hoyt, Jonah, late of Stamford, Sept. 6, 1814, letters of administration on his estate granted to Timothy Reynolds, of Stamford, page 512.

Hoyt, Joseph, late of Stamford, Nov. 7, 1809, Benjamin Hoyt, a son of decedent, about 18 years of age, made choice of Amos Weed to be his guardian, page 505^1.

Hoyt, Josiah, late of Stamford, will dated Mch. 27, 1801, probated July 2, 1811, mentions his wife Elizabeth, and children Josiah, Isaac, Rhoda, Anna, and Mercy. Executors his sons. Witnesses Ebenezer Lockwood, Ellen Bates, and Hannah Lyman, page 101.
July 2, 1811, order to advertise for claims, page 103.
Inventory taken by Jonathan Bates and Noyes Richards, and filed Sept. 3, 1811, page 103.

Hoyt, Nathan, late of Stamford, Mch. 6, 1810, letters of administration on his estate granted to Jonas Scofield, page 489.
Inventory taken July 24, 1810, by Cary Leeds and Frederick Hoyt, and filed Aug. 7, 1810, page 489.
Oct. 11, 1810, estate ordered distributed to his children Esther, widow of Jacob White, and Sarah wife of Jonas Scofield, page 491.
Oct. 12, 1810, estate distributed accordingly, page 492.

Hoyt, Nezer, late of Stamford, Apl. 2, 1811, letters of administration on his estate granted to John Augur and William Hoyt, Jr., decedent's widow having renounced, who were ordered to advertise for claims, page 160.
Inventory taken June 4, 1811, by Reuben Scofield and Benjamin Scofield, and filed June 4, 1811, page 160.
Mch. 21, 1812, estate ordered distributed to Prudence Hoyt, widow of deceased, and to his children William Hoyt, Jr., Nancy wife of Dr. John Augur, and Prudence Hoyt, page 161.
Apl. 6, 1812, estate distributed accordingly, page 162.

STAMFORD PROBATE RECORDS.
Volume 10, 1803-1815.

Hoyt, Peter, late of Stamford, will dated Oct. 21, 1807, probated Sept. 4, 1810, mentions his children Betsy, Sally wife of Jonathan Waterbury, Peter, Enoch, and Salmon; and granddaughter Sarah H. Waterbury, a daughter of Jonathan Waterbury. Executors his sons Enoch and Salmon. Witnesses Joseph Gray, Sarah Scofield, and Reuben Scofield, page 111.
Sept. 4, 1810, order to advertise for claims, page 111.
Inventory taken Sept. 25, 1810, by Cary Leeds and Henry Hoyt, Jr., and filed Oct. 2, 1810, page 114.

Hoyt, Ruth, widow, late of Stamford, inventory taken Jan. 22, 1808, by Jonathan Hoyt and Seth Smith, and filed Feb. 2, 1808, by Seth Hoyt, executor, page 424.

Hoyt, Salmon, late of Stamford, Dec. 5, 1809, letters of administration on his estate granted to Enoch Hoyt and Cary Leeds, page 479.
Inventory taken Dec. 12, 1809, by Nathan Weed and Henry Hoyt, Jr., and filed Dec. 19, 1809, page 479.
Dec. 30, 1809, commissioners appointed to adjust claims of creditors, page 481.
July 2, 1810, report of commissioners filed, page 481.
Sept. 6, 1810, account filed, and real estate ordered sold to pay debts, page 483.
Sept. 24, 1810, report of sale filed, page 483.
Oct. 2, 1810, estate ordered distributed to his widow, Hannah Hoyt, and children James Harvey Hoyt, Hannah Hoyt, and Amos Hoyt, page 484.
Oct. 11, 1810, estate distributed accordingly, page 484.
Sept. 29, 1810, the court appointed Hannah Hoyt, widow of deceased, guardian of James Harvey, Amos, and Hannah children of deceased, page 5022.

Hoyt, Samuel, late of Stamford, Nov. 1, 1814, letters of administration on his estate granted to John Leeds, who was ordered to advertise for claims, page 513.

Hoyt, Samuel, late of Stamford, June 7, 1814, on the application of Samuel Hoyt, executor, estate ordered distributed to his children Hanford Hoyt, Sarah wife of Seymour Tallmadge, Abigail wife of Uzal Knapp, Nancy wife of Frederick Weed, and Samuel Hoyt, page 473.
June 22, 1814, estate distributed accordingly, page 473.

Hoyt, Uriah, late of Stamford, June 5, 1810, letters of administration on his estate granted to Jane Hoyt, page 171.

STAMFORD PROBATE RECORDS.
Volume 10, 1803-1815.

Hoyt, Uriah, continued :
Inventory taken June 8, 1810, by Nathaniel Waterbury and Reuben Scofield, and filed July 3, 1810, page 171.
Mch. 5, 1811, account filed, and real estate ordered sold to pay debts, page 173.
1811, estate ordered distributed to Jane Hoyt, widow of deceased, and to his children Uriah Hoyt, Samuel Hoyt, Hannah Stevens, Sally Bostwick, and Salome Hoyt, page 173.
Apl. 13, 1811, estate distributed accordingly, page 173.

Husted, Sarah, late of Greenwich, Jan. 3, 1815, letters with the will annexed on her estate granted to Ira Lockwood, of Greenwich, page 514.

Ireland, Job, late of Greenwich, will dated Apl. 6, 1805, probated Apl. 2, 1807, mentions his wife Martha, Israel Reynolds, so-called, a bastard son of Prudence Ireland, so-called; Job Ireland, a son of Abraham Ireland; and Levi Ireland, a son of Gilbert Ireland. Executors John Palmer and Josiah Field. Witnesses Uriah Field, Aaron Field, and Nehemiah Mason, pages 369, 371, and 392.
Inventory taken Apl. 3, 1807, and filed June 10, 1809, page 370.
July 13, 1809, receipts for legacies by Job Ireland; and Levi Ireland by his father and guardian Gilbert Ireland, pages 79 and 80.

Jeffery, Mercy, late of Stamford, will dated Apl. 1, 1807, probated Dec. 1, 1809, mentions her daughters Martha Jeffery, Rebecca wife of John Hoyt, Jr., Hannah wife of Isaac Smith, and Mercy wife of Ezra Hoyt. Executor Isaac Smith. Witnesses Sarah Scofield, Sally Scofield, and Samuel Webb, page 399.
Dec. 1, 1809, the executor refused to qualify, and letters with the will annexed granted to John Hoyt, who was ordered to advertise for claims, page 400.

Jeffery, Samuel, late of Stamford, 1807, letters of administration on his estate granted to Isaac Smith, Jr., who was ordered to advertise for claims, page 240.
Inventory taken May 1, 1807, by Joseph Gray and Cary Leeds, and filed May 5, 1807, pages 240 and 242.
Mch. 1, 1808, account filed, and estate ordered distributed to Mercy Jeffery, widow of deceased, and to his children Rebecca wife of John Hoyt, Jr., Hannah

STAMFORD PROBATE RECORDS.
Volume 10, 1803-1815.

Jeffery, Samuel, continued :
    wife of Isaac Smith, Jr., Mercy wife of Ezra Hoyt, and
    Martha Jeffery, page 242.
    Apl. 2, 1808, estate distributed accordingly, page 243.

Jessup, Abigail, late of Stamford, Apl. 6, 1813, letters of administration on her estate granted to Cary Leeds,
    page 476.
    Inventory taken Apl. 10, 1813, by Joseph Gray and Nathaniel Waterbury, and filed Apl. 10, 1813, page 416.
    Apl. 10, 1813, account filed, and real estate ordered
    sold to pay debts, page 476.
    Apl. 12, 1813, report of sale filed, page 476.
    In 1813, estate ordered distributed to her children
    Isaac Jessup, Joseph Jessup, John Jessup, Joram Jessup,
    Jonathan Jessup, George Jessup, Elizabeth Jessup, Sarah
    wife of Wodlsey Webb, and Hannah wife of Samuel Hoyt,
    page 476.
    Apl. 20, 1813, estate distributed accordingly, page 477.

Jezup, Jonathan, late of Greenwich, will dated Apl. 9, 1805,
    probated June 4, 1805, mentions his wife Anne, and children Jonathan, Edward, James, Anne wife of Jeremiah
    Rundle, Mary wife of William Peacock, Hannah wife of
    Peter Lockwood, Sarah wife of Daniel Lockwood, 3rd,
    deceased sons Peter and Gershom; grandson Samuel Jessup
    a son of my daughter Mary. Executors his wife and son
    Jonathan. Witnesses Stephen Ferris, Stephen Ferris,
    Jr., and Ebenezer Davenport, page 63.
    Inventory taken May 23, 1805, by Ebenezer Peck and Silvanus Knapp, and filed June 11, 1805, pages 65 and 66.
    Apl. 15, 1807, account filed, and estate ordered distributed to Ann Jessup, his widow, and to Jonathan
    Jezup, Ebenezer Jesup, James Jezup, Edward Jezup, Timothy Jezup, Anne wife of Jeremiah Rundle, Mary wife of
    William Peacock, Hannah wife of Peter Lockwood, Sarah
    wife of Daniel Lockwood, 3rd, legal representatives of
    Peter Jezup, and to the legal representatives of Gershom Jezup, page 67.
    May 6, 1807, estate distributed accordingly, page 68.

Jessup, Joram, late of Stamford, July 18, 1814, letters of administration on his estate granted to Sarah Jessup of
    New York City, page 472.
    Inventory taken July 19, 1814, by John Leeds and Josiah
    Lockwood, and filed July 19, 1814, page 472.
    July 19, 1814, account filed, and real estate ordered
    sold to pay debts, page 473.

STAMFORD PROBATE RECORDS.
Volume 10, 1803-1815.

Jesup, Peter, late of Greenwich, Oct. 6, 1807, on the application of Paris Robbins of Greenwich, guardian of Samuel, Jonathan, Peter, Susan, and Mary, minor children of deceased, his estate was ordered partitioned between said minors, and Jabez Mead, as assignee of Elijah Reynolds, page 229.
Oct. 23, 1807, partition made accordingly, page 229.

Jesup, Timothy, late of Stamford, will dated Apl. 7, 1808, probated May 3, 1808, mentions his wife Sally and children Peter, Sally, and Maria. Executors William Waterbury, son of David Waterbury, and Daniel Lockwood, Jr. Witnesses Ezra Knapp, Joshua Knapp, and Samuel Webb, page 221.
Codicil dated Apl. 10, 1808, mentions his father Jonathan Jessup, late of Greenwich, and mother Ann Jessup, page 223.
May 3, 1808, the executors refused to qualify, and letters with the will annexed granted to his widow, Sally Jesup, who was ordered to advertise for claims, page 224.
Inventory taken July 4, 1808, by Jeremiah Andreas and George Mills, and filed July 5, 1808, page 225.
Aug. 1808, commissioners apppinted to adjust claims of creditors, pages 226 and 227.
Mch. 2, 1809, report of commissioners filed, page 227.

Jones, Isaac, late of Stamford, Nov. 1, 1814, letters of administration on his estate granted to Selleck Jones, who was ordered to advertise for claims, page 514.

Knapp, Abel, late of Stamford, Oct. 11, 1809, letters of administration on his estate granted to Charity Knapp, who was ordered to advertise for claims, page 429.
Inventory taken Oct. 12, 1809, by Isaac Smith and William Knapp, Jr., and filed Oct. 7, 1809, page 412.

Knapp, Abel, late of Stamford, Oct. 21, 1814, commissioners appointed to adjust claims of creditors, page 447.
May 22, 1815, report of commissioners filed, page 447.

Knapp, Abigail, late of the Town of Washington, N. Y., inventory taken by Nehemiah Brown, Jr., and David D. Husted, and filed Jan. 25, 1810, by Isaac Peck, 3rd, administrator, page 410.

STAMFORD PROBATE RECORDS.
Volume 10, 1803-1815.

Knapp, Bethia, late of Stamford, will dated Mch. 21, 1796 probated May 5, 1807, mentions her brothers Epenetus Knapp Gideon Knapp, Silvanus Knapp, and Hezekiah Knapp, and the heirs of Charles Knapp, a deceased brother; sisters Sarah Mead and Hannah Lockwood; Bethia Davis a daughter of my sister Sarah Mead; Bethia Knapp; a daughter of my brother Hezekiah Knapp; Gideon Clock and Phebe Selleck two children of my sister Hannah Lockwood; Charles Knapp and Sarah St. John, two children of my brother Silvanus Knapp. Executor brother Hezekiah Knapp. Witnesses Sarah Lockwood, Benjamin Weed, 3rd, and William Walmsley, page 335.
Inventory taken and filed Nov. 21, 1808, page 337.
Nov. 21, 1808, account filed, and estate ordered distributed to Epenetus Knapp, Silvanus Knapp and Hezekiah Knapp, brothers of deceased; Hannah Lockwood a sister of deceased; William Knapp, Jr., Sarah wife of Alexander Mills, and Elizabeth wife of John Bedient, children of Charles Knapp, a deceased brother; Nehemiah Mead, Jr., Bethia Davis, Rachel Weed, Clara Mead, and Lucy Howe, children of Sarah Mead, a deceased sister; and Sophia Demill a grandchild of said Sarah Mead, deceased; Bethia Knapp a daughter of Hezekiah Knapp; Gideon Clock and Phebe Selleck; Charles Knapp and Sarah St. John. Gideon Knapp, one of the legatees predeceased the testatrix, page 339.
Dec. 6, 1808, estate distributed accordingly, page 340.

Knapp, Daniel, late of Stamford, July 9, 1812, letters of administration on his estate granted to Samuel Germonds, who was ordered to advertise for claims, page 135. Inventory taken July 9, 1812, by Henry Hoyt, and Henry Close, and filed July 9, 1812, page 136.

Knapp, David, late of Greenwich, Oct. 25, 1814, letters of administration on his estate with the will annexed granted to Abigail Knapp and Lemuel Ferris, who were ordered to advertise for claims, page 513.

Knapp, Gideon, late of Stamford, will dated Jan. 13, 1806, probated Sept. 3, 1806, mentions the heirs of his brother Charles Knapp; sisters Sarah Mead, Hannah Lockwood, and Bethia Knapp; brothers Epenetus Knapp, Hezekiah Knapp, and Silvanus Knapp; Gideon Clock, a son of his sister Hannah; and Charles Knapp, a son of his brother Silvanus Knapp. Executor said Charles Knapp, a son of Silvanus Knapp. Witnesses Sally Jessup,

STAMFORD PROBATE RECORDS.
Volume 10, 1803-1815.

Knapp, Gideon, continued :
    Billy Hoyt, and Samuel Webb, page 288.
    Nov. 12, 1808, appeal from probate taken by William
    Knapp, page 289.
    Inventory taken Oct. 23, 1806, by George Mills and Will
    iam Waterbury, 4th, and filed Oct. 27, 1806, page 290.

Knapp, Gideon, late of Stamford, will dated Jan. 30, 1793, pxx
    probated Nov. 1807, mentions his brothers and sisters
    Charles Knapp, Sarah Mead, Hannah Lockwood, Bethia
    Knapp, Epenetus Knapp, Hezekiah Knapp, and Silvanus
    Knapp; and Charles Knapp, a son of said Silvanus Knapp.
    Executor his brother Silvanus Knapp. Witnesses Will-
    iam Waterbury, Molly Waterbury, and Mary Bulkley,
    page 207.
    Appeal taken by William Knapp, Jr., from said pro-
    bate, page 209.
    Feb. 5, 1808, probate affirmed, page 209.
    Inventory taken Feb. 17, 1808, by Jeremiah Andreas and
    George Mills, and filed Mch. 1, 1808, page 209.
    Sept. 5, 1808, account filed, and estate ordered dis-
    tributed to the legal representatives of Sarah Mead,
    a deceased sister; legal representatives of Charles
    Knapp, a deceased brother; legal represenatives of
    Bethia Knapp a deceased sister; and Hannah Lockwood,
    a sister. The legacies to Epenetus Knapp and Gideon
    Clock having been paid, page 211.
    Oct. 4, 1808, estate distributed accordingly, page 211.

Knapp, James, late of Stamford, will dated Feb. 17, 1803, pro-
    bated Nov. 27, 1809, mentions his wife Prudence. Exec-
    utor Ezra Lockwood. Witnesses Ebenezer Peck, Reuben
    Mead, and Nathan Mead, page 494.
    Inventory taken Jan. 2, 1810, by Joseph Bishop and
    Jeremiah Palmer, and filed Jan. 2, 1810, page 413.
    Nov. 27, 1809, order to advertise for claims, page 495.
    Aug. 23, 1810, account filed and estate ordered dis-
    tributed to his widow, and children James, Daniel, John,
    Reuben, and Hannah Hoyt, page 496.
    Mch. 27, 1811, estate distributed accordingly, page 496.

Knapp, James, late of Stamford, Jan. 5, 1813, letters of ad-
    ministration on his estate granted to Frederick Smith,
    who was ordered to advertise for claims, page 429.
    Inventory taken Feb. 2, 1813, by Isaac Smith, Jr., and
    Ezra Lockwood, and filed Feb. 2, 1813, page 410.

STAMFORD PROBATE RECORDS.
Volume 10, 1803-1815.

Knapp, Joel, late of Greenwich, Jan. 5, 1813, letters of administration on his estate granted to Benjamin Knapp, who was ordered to advertise for claims, page 429.
Jan. 14, 1814, account filed, page 265.

Knapp, Joshua, late of Stamford, 1813, letters of administration on his estate granted to Augustus Lockwood, page 254.
Inventory taken May 3, 1813, by Ezra Lockwood and Isaac Lockwood, and filed May 4, 1813, page 254.
1813, commissioners appointed to set out the dower of his widow, Susannah Knapp, page 256.
Dec. 26, 1813, dower set out, page 256.

Knapp, Peter, late of Stamford, will dated, Feb. 1, 1811, probated Mch. 5, 1811, mentions his wife Sarah and children Mary wife of Warren Hoyt, Sarah wife of Abraham Hoyt, Abigail, Lydemia, Jonathan, Peter, and Ezra. Executors his sons Jonathan and Peter. Witnesses Thaddeus Hoyt, Abigail Palmer, and Ruth Knapp, page 213.
Inventory taken Mch. 4, 1811, by Isaac Lockwood and Samuel Hoyt, Jr., and filed Mch. 14, 1811, page 215.
Mch. 5, 1811, order to advertise for claims, page 214.

Knapp, Samuel, late of Stamford, will dated Apl. 29, 1805, probated Feb. 7, 1811, mentions his wife Susannah, and children Abigail wife of David Knapp of Greenwich, Polly wife of John Nichols of Stamford, Prudence wife of Ebenezer Waterbury, Jr., Susannah wife of Ralph Newman of New York, Nancy Knapp, Jacob Knapp, Joshua Knapp Isaac Knapp, Stephen Knapp; Fanny Knapp, and Clara Knapp daughters of Samuel Knapp, a deceased son. Executors his sons Jacob and Joshua. Witnesses Henry Weeks, Elizabeth Weeks, and Samuel Weeks, page 292.
Inventory taken Feb. 7, 1811, by Isaac Lockwood and Ezra Lockwood, and filed Feb. 7, 1811, pages 294 and 296.
Feb. 7, 1811, order to advertise for claims, page 293.
Apl. 25, 1812, estate ordered distributed to his widow, Susannah Knapp, and children Jacob, Joshua, Isaac, and Stephen, subject to rights of Nancy Knapp in accordance with said will, page 443.
May 11, 1812, estate distributed accordingly, page 444.

Knapp, Sylvanus, late of Stamford, will dated Apl. 28, 1806, probated Aug. 18, 1810, mentions his wife Abigail, and children Sarah St. John, and Charles. Executor his son. Witnesses Molly Webb, Henry W. Webb, and Samuel Webb, page 108.

STAMFORD PROBATE RECORDS.
Volume 10, 1803-1815.

Knapp, Sylvanus, continued:
    Aug. 18, 1810, order to advertise for claims, page 109.
    Inventory taken Aug. 23, 1810, by William Waterbury, 4th and Jeremiah Andreas, and filed Sept. 4, 1810, page 108.

Lane, Abraham, late of Rye, will dated July 12, 1813, probated Apl. 5, 1814, all to his wife Deborah, who is appointed executrix. Witnesses John Haviland, Wilson Merritt, and John Brown, page Ex 437.
    July 12, 1813, order to advertise for claims, page 438.

Leeds, Elisha, late of Stamford, May 4, 1813, letters of administration on his estate granted to Cary Leeds and Sarah Leeds, who were ordered to advertise for claims, page 334.
    Apl. 2, 1814, the court appointed Sarah Leeds guardian of Charles S., William E., Eliza, and Caty Leeds, children of decedent, page 511.

Lockwood, Daniel, late of Stamford, will dated Aug. 25, 1806, probated Feb. 2, 1808, mentions his wife Mary, and children Daniel, 3rd, Sarah wife of Ebenezer Jones, Martha wife of Dr. Walter Hough, Mary wife of Daniel Smith, Betsy wife of Joseph Chapman, a daughter of Abigail Hutton, a deceased daughter, granddaughter Deborah Frost, a daughter of Elizabeth, a deceased daughter. Executor his son Daniel. Witnesses Mary Davenport, Alexander Bishop, and Ebenezer Davenport, page 318.
    Feb. 2, 1808, order to advertise for claims, page 319.
    Inventory taken by Ezra Lockwood and Solomon Clason, and filed Feb. 2, 1809, page 319.
    June 7, 1808, additional inventory filed, page 324.
    Jan. 3, 1809, account filed and commissioners appointed to set out widow's dower, page 324.
    Jan. 16, 1809, dower set out to Mary Lockwood, the widow of deceased, page 324.

Lockwood, Jeremiah, Jr., late of Stamford, Nov. 2, 1814, letters of administration on his estate granted to Frederick Waterbury, who was ordered to advertise for claims, page 514.

Lockwood, Joseph, late of Greenwich, May 5, 1807, letters of administration on his estate granted to Ebenezer Webb and Jared Lockwood, page 205.
    Inventory taken May 9, 1807, by Frederick Lockwood and Joshua Ferris, and filed May 11, 1807, page 205.

STAMFORD PROBATE RECORDS
Volume 10, 1803-1815.

Lockwood, Joseph, continued:
    June 2, 1807, order to advertise for claims, page 207.
    June 7, 1807, account filed, and real estate ordered sold to pay debts, page 207.

Lounsberry, Elijah, late of Stamford, May 23, 1805, letters of administration on his estate granted to John Lounsberry, who was ordered to advertise for claims, pages 189 and 366.
    Inventory taken June 7, 1805, by Reuben Scofield and Seth Weed, and filed, page 366.
    Feb. 2, 1808, account filed, and real estate ordered sold to pay debts, and report of sale, page 367.
    Apl. 5, 1808, estate ordered distributed to his widow, Martha or Hannah, and to his children Elijah, Clarissa or Clara, Benjamin, Anna, Elizabeth, Ezra, and Martha, part having been sold to pay debts, page 404.
    Apl. 19, 1808, estate distributed accordingly, page 404.

Lounsberry, James, late of Stamford, June 8, 1814, letters of administration on his estate granted to Nathaniel Webb, Jr., who was ordered to advertise for claims, page 510.

Lounsberry, Jared, late of Stamford, May 27, 1814, letters of administration on his estate granted to Munson Buxton, and commissioners appointed to adjust claims of creditors, page 269.

Lyon, Gilbert, Jr., late of Greenwich, Apl. 19, 1808, letters of administration on his estate granted to Thomas Lyon, page 314.
    Inventory taken May 4, 1808, by James Banks and Nehemiah Mead, and filed June 23, 1808, pages 314 and 315.

Lyon, Martha, widow of James Lyon, late of Greenwich, Apl. 9, 1807, letters of administration on her estate granted to Nehemiah Willson of Greebwich, page 365.
    Inventory taken Apl. 14, 1807, by Ebenezer Mead and Timothy Walker, and filed Apl. 17, 1807, page 365.
    Apl. 17, 1807, account filed, and real estate ordered sold to pay debts, and report of sale, page 365.
    Apl. 30, 1807, the petition of Nehemiah Willson, guardian of Augustus Lyon and Elizabeth Lyon, grandchildren of decedent, for an order distributing estate to her children, viz: Sarah wife of James Banks, Elizabeth wife of Abraham Merritt, David Lyon, Daniel Lyon, Mary wife of Daniel Banks, and Benjamin Lyon, and to the legal representatives of James Lyon, Jr., a deceased son,

STAMFORD PROBATE RECORDS.
Volume 10, 1803-1815.

Lyon, Martha, continued:
viz: Lewis Lyon, James Lyon, Augustus Lyon, Sarah Lyon, Elizabeth Lyon, and the wife of Drake Husted, page 365. July 1, 1807, estate distributed to her children Sarah wife of James Banks, David Lyon, Daniel Lyon, Benjamin W. Lyon, Mary wife of Daniel Banks, Elizabeth wife of Abraham Merritt, and to the heirs of James Lyon, deceased, viz: Lewis Lyon, James Lyon, Samuel Lyon, Augustus Lyon, Nancy wife of Drake Husted, Sally wife of Daniel Merritt, and Elizabeth Lyon, all his heirs by his wife Susannah, now the wife of James Green, page 383.

Lyon, Mary, of Rye, Dec. 5, 1809, parent of Sarah Budd Lyon, Elizabeth Jane Lyon, and Mary Underhill Lyon, minors, asked for leave to sell the real estate of said minors in Greenwich conveyed to said Mary Lyon, Harriet Halsted Lyon, and said minors by Andrew Lyon of Rye, page 401.

Marshall, Ezra, late of Greenwich, Nov. 1, 1814, letters of administration on his estate granted to Ebenezer Mead, and on Nov. 5, 1814, commissioners were appointed to adjust claims of creditors, page 513.

Mather, Moses, Rev., late of Stamford, will dated Dec. 26, 1793, probated Nov. 4, 1806, mentions his children Joseph, Hannah wife of Jesse Raymond, Noyes, Samuel, and Isaac. Executor his son Joseph. Witnesses Jeremiah Andreas, Thaddeus Bell, Jr., and Deddate Waterbury, page 80.
Oct. 7, 1806, order to advertise for claims, page 82.
Inventory taken Oct. 29, 1806, by Gershom Scofield and Charles Whiting, and filed Nov. 4, 1806, page 82.
June 1, 1807, estate distributed to his children Joseph, Noyes, Samuel, and Hannah Raymond, page 83.

Mather, Noyes, late of New York City, May 6, 1808, letters of administration on his estate granted to John Weed, Jr. page 387.
June 7, 1808, commissioners appointed to adjust claims of creditors, page 387.
Jan. 3, 1809, report of commissioners filed, page 387.
Inventory taken July 4, 1808, by Gershom Scofield and Joshua Scofield, and filed July 5, 1808, deceased was a son of Rev. Moses Mather, page 388.
Jan. 3, 1809, real estate ordered sold to pay debts, and report of sale filed Feb. 16, 1809, page 388.

STAMFORD PROBATE RECORDS.
Volume 10, 1803-1815.

Mather, Noyes, continued :
>Feb. 16, 1809, account filed, and creditors ordered paid, page 389.

Mead, Angelina A., a minor of Greenwich, about 6 years of age, the court appointed Ebenezer Mead to be her guardian, Mch. 11, 1814, page 508.

Mead, David, late of Greenwich, will dated Apl. 8, 1808, probated Oct. 1808, mentions Allen Peck son of Samuel Peck rest of his estate to his wife Anna Mead. Executors his wife and Samuel Peck of Greenwich. Witnesses Obadiah Mead, Evert Denton, and Enoch Youngs, page 305.
Oct. 1808, order to advertise for claims, page 306.
Inventory taken Oct. 11, 1808, by Israel Peck and Jehiel Mead, Jr., and filed Nov. 1, 1808, page 307.

Mead, Israel, late of Greenwich, 1807, letters of administration on his estate granted to Shadrach Mead, who was ordered to advertise for claims, page 184.
Inventory taken Dec. 1, 1807, by Job Lyon and Gideon Close, and filed Jan. 5, 1808, pages 184 and 185.
Dec. 22, 1807, commissioners appointed to adjust claims of creditors, page 185.
Sept. 6, 1808, report of commissioners filed, and real estate ordered sold to pay debts, pages 187 and 189.
Jan. 5, 1808, on the application of Nathaniel Mead, 3rd guardian of Major, Betsy, and Eli Mead, minor children of decedent, estate ordered distributed, page 185.
Mch. 1, 1808, estate distributed to the aforesaid Nathaniel Mead, 3rd, guardian of Major, Betsy, and Eli Mead, and Mary Mead, widow of deceased, page 186.

Mead, Joshua, late of Greenwich, inventory taken July 4, 1812, by Ambrose Reynolds and Isaac Holly, and filed July 7, 1812, page 418.
Aug. 4, 1812, the court appointed Hannah Mead guardian of Solomon Mead, a son of decedent, page 506.

Mead, Martha, late of Stamford, Apl. 7, 1812, letters of administration on her estate granted to Jeremiah Andreas, who was ordered to advertise for claims, page 523.

Mead, Mary, late of Greenwich, June 1, 1813, letters of administration on her estate granted to Justus B. Mead, who was ordered to advertise for claims, page 523.

STAMFORD PROBATE RECORDS.
Volume 10, 1803-1815.

Mead, Silas, Jr., late of Greenwich, Aug. 2, 1814, the court
appointed Jabez Mead of Greenwich guardian of Sarah,
Silas H., and Francis, children of decedent, page 511.

Merritt, Jotham, late of Greenwich, Mch. 7, 1814, letters of
administration on his estate granted to Mary W. Merritt
and Eliza Merritt, who were ordered to advertise for
claims, page 511.
Apl. 7, 1814, the court appointed Nehemiah Brown, Jr.,
of Rye, guardian of Caroline and Jotham children of decedent, page 509.

Miller, James, late of New York City, Oct. 21, 1813, letters
of administration on his estate granted to Timothy Reynolds, who was ordered to advertise for claims, page 409.

Miller, Westover, late of Greenwich, Feb. 20, 1810, letters
of administration on his estate granted to Hannah Miller, who was ordered to advertise for claims, page 429.

Mills, Samuel, late of Greenwich, will dated Mch. 23, 1791,
probated Dec. 6, 1808, mentions his wife Abigail, and
children Samuel, John, Abigail Seymour, Sarah wife of
Jonathan Lockwood, Jr., Mary wife of Simeon Lyon, Hannah wife of Abraham Lyon, Clemence and Lydia. Refers
to a deed of trust to his son Samuel. Executor son
Samuel. Witnesses Moses Husted, Jr., Roda Close, and
Jabez Fitch, page 60.

Morehouse, Gershom, late of Stamford, will dated May 2, 1812,
probated Dec. 25, 1812, mentions his wife Phebe, and
children Betsy Penoyer, deceased, Joshua, Elizabeth
Weed, and granddaughter Mary Morehouse. Executor Jonathan Bates. Witnesses Jonathan Bates, Samuel Mather,
and Raymond Mather, page 448.
Dec. 25, 1812, order to advertise for claims, page 450.
Inventory taken Jan. 25, 1813, by Justus Barnum and
Jeremiah Andreas, and filed Feb. 2, 1813, page 450.

Munday, Sarah, late of Stamford, will dated Feb. 12, 1807,
probated Aug. 20, 1809, mentions her brother Seymour
Jarvis; nephew Samuel Odell Jarvis a son of said Seymour Jarvis; brother Samuel Jarvis and his wife Elizabeth Jarvis; nieces Martha Jarvis Todd and Levina Harrison Todd, daughters of Rev. Ambrose Todd; sister Hannah wife of John Ingersoll; sister Lavinia wife of Rev.
Ambrose Todd; niece Sarah Munday Beardsley, a daughter
of my sister Mary Dibble, and niece Margaret Beedle;
and nephew William King. Executors Seymour Jarvis,

STAMFORD PROBATE RECORDS.
Volume 10, 1803-1815.

Munday, Sarah, continued:
William King, and Nathaniel Webb. Witnesses Frederick Scofield, Jeremiah Andreas, and Samuel Webb, page 462.
Aug. 20, 1809, Nathaniel Webb refused to qualify and letters were issued to the other executors, who were ordered to advertise for claims, page 464.

Murphy, Joseph B., late of Greenwich, Jan. 6, 1807, letters of administration on his estate granted to Robert Murphy, page 455.
Inventory taken Feb. 5, 1807, by Edmond Knapp and Henry Knapp, and filed Sept. 1, 1807, page 455.
Mch. 7, 1809, account filed, and real estate ordered sold to pay debts, page 456.

Nichols, Abraham, late of Stamford, Feb. 2, 1813, letters of administration on his estate granted to Catharine Nichols, who was ordered to advertise for claims, page 457.
Inventory taken Mch. 1, 1813, by Solomon Clason and Drake Studwell, and filed Mch. 20, 1813, page 457.
Sept. 7, 1813, account filed, and on Sept. 14, 1813, commissioners appointed to adjust claims of creditors, page 459.
Mch. 15, 1814, report of commissioners filed, page 459.
Apl. 5, 1814, account filed, and creditors ordered paid, page 460.

Nichols, Elizabeth, late of Stamford, June 7, 1809, letters of administration on her estate granted to Daniel Nichols of Stamford, page 378.
Inventory taken July 5, 1809, by Jonathan Smith and Solomon Clason, and filed July 5, 1808, page 378.
May 2, 1809, account filed, and real estate ordered sold to pay debts, page 379.

Palmer, Ferris, late of Stamford, July 6, 1813, letters of administration on his estate granted to Simeon H. Minor, who was ordered to advertise for claims, page 269.
Feb. 15, 1814, commissioners appointed to adjust claims of creditors, page 268.

Palmer, Justus, late of Greenwich, July 7, 1812, letters of administration on his estate granted to John Lane, who was ordered to advertise for claims, page 132.

STAMFORD PROBATE RECORDS.
Volume 10, 1803-1815.

Palmer, Messenger, late of Greenwich, (no date), executors deed, according to his will to his daughter Esther Sackett and her children Peter Sackett and James Sackett, of land in Dutchess County, N. Y., approved, page 402.

Peck, Gideon, late of Greenwich, 1813, letters of administration on his estate granted to Samuel Brown and Gideon Peck, who were ordered to advertise for claims, page 259.
Inventory taken Feb. 10, 1813, by Ebenezer Mead and Platt Mead, and filed Feb. 16, 1813, page 259.
Oct. 5, 1813, account filed, and real estate ordered sold to pay debts, page 262.
Nov. 2, 1813, estate ordered distributed to Jerusha Peck widow of deceased, and to his children Gideon, Theophilus, Clara wife of Elias Peck, Fanny wife of Samuel Brown, Mary Peck, Elizabeth Peck, and Eunice Peck, page 262.
Jan. 1, 1814, estate distributed accordingly, page 263.

Quenett, Hannah, late of Stamford, Oct. 4, 1813, letters of administration on her estate granted to Amos Weed, who was ordered to advertise for claims, page 408.

Quintard, Peter, 3rd, late of Stamford, Nov. 14, 1809, letters of administration on his estate granted to Isaac Quintard and Seymour Jarvis, who were ordered to advertise for claims, page 403.
Apl. 2, 1811, letters of Seymour Jarvis cancelled, page 511.

Quintard, Peter, late of Stamford, Oct. 5, 1813, letters of administration on his estate granted to Ruth Quintard, who was ordered to advertise for claims, page 409.

Raymond, Ezra, late of Stamford, July 7, 1812, letters of administration on his estate granted to William White, and commissioners appointed to adjust claims of creditors, page 132.
Aug. 4, 1812, estate ordered sold, page 149.

Raymond, Isaac, late of New York City, will dated June 5, 1809 probated Nov. 4, 1809, mentions his uncle David Bates, late of Middlesex; children Robert and Josiah. Mary the woman with whom I now live and consider my wife to bring up the children I have had by her, viz: Ezra Freeman, Hiram Mitcher, and Jane Benedict. Executrix said Mary Raymond. Witnesses Stephen M. Wilmut, Jacob

STAMFORD PROBATE RECORDS.
Volume 10, 1803-1815.

Raymond, Isaac, continued :
    Stevens, and Joseph Smith, page 392.
    Inventory taken Nov. 6, 1809, by Nathaniel Slason and
    Charles Whiting, and filed Nov. 6, 1809, page 395.

Reynolds, Horton, late of Greenwich, Mch. 7, 1814, letters of
    administration on his estate granted to Abigail Reynolds
    and Shadrach Mead, who were ordered to advertise for
    claims, page 510.

Roberts, Josiah, a minor about 18 years of age, Oct. 27, 1813,
    made choice of Thaddeus Bell to be his guardian,
    page 507.

Rundle, Eli, late of Greenwich, Jan. 27, 1808, on the appli-
    cation of Mary, widow of Israel Mead, daughter of de-
    ceased, her share of decedent's estate ordered set out,
    page 187.
    Feb. 18, 1808, set out accordingly, page 187.

Rundel, Reuben, late of Greenwich, May 2, 1815, letters of ad-
    ministration on his estate granted to Jonathan Rundel,
    the widow having refused, who was ordered to advertise
    for claims, page 515.

St. John, Hannah, late of Stamford, May 3, 1808, letters of
    administration on her estate granted to Ezra St. John
    of Stamford, page 363.
    Inventory taken July 1, 1808, by Jeremiah Andreas and
    Augustus Lockwood, and filed July 1, 1808, page 363.

St. John, Lewis, late of Wilton, Aug. 2, 1814, the court ap-
    pointed Josiah Hays of Stamford guardian of Daniel St.
    John, a son of decedent, page 512.

Scofield, Epenetus, late of Stamford, will dated Feb. 28, 1812
    probated Apl. 7, 1812, mentions his wife Abigail, and
    children Epenetus, Nehemiah, Hezekiah, Rhaa wife of
    Ezra St. John, Susannah wife of Solomon Scofield, and
    Hannah wife of Isaac Blackman. Executor Reuben Sco-
    field. Witnesses Silvanus Scofield, John Scofield,
    and Samuel Webb, page 439.
    Apl. 7, 1812, order to advertise for claims, page 440..
    Inventory taken Apl. 3, 1812, by Thaddeus Hoyt and John
    Scofield, and filed Apl. 7, 1812, page 440.

STAMFORD PROBATE RECORDS.
Volume 10, 1803-1815.

Scofield, Isaac, late of Stamford, will dated Feb. 10, 1814, probated Apl. 11, 1814, mentions his friends David Scofield, John Scofield, Mary wife of Reuben June, and Betsy, a daughter of said Mary, and my two sisters Abigail Whelpley and Sally Holly. Executor William White Witnesses Seth Hait, Elizabeth June, and Silas June, page 453.
Apl. 11, 1814, order to advertise for claims, page 454.
Inventory taken Apl. 9, 1814, by Timothy Reynolds and Seth Hait, and filed Apl. 11, 1814, page 455.

Scofield, Jane, late of Stamford, Feb. 3, 1807, letters of administration on her estate granted to Joseph Lockwood, page 232.
Inventory taken Feb. 4, 1807, by Amos Weed and Daniel Provost, and filed Apl. 7, 1807, page 232.
Feb. 6, 1808, commissioners appointed to adjust claims of creditors, page 232.
Sept. 6, 1808, report of commissioners filed, page 232.
Apl. 4, 1809, account filed, and creditors ordered paid, page 234.

Scofield, Nathan, late of Stamford, will dated Jan. 8, 1805, probated Sept. 24, 1807, mentions his wife Marcy, and children Sarah Curtis, Elizabeth wife of Samuel Weed, X Jr., and Seth. Executor his son Seth. Witnesses Daniel Scofield, Samuel Scofield, and Reuben Scofield. Codicil dated July 16, 1807, appointed Reuben Scofield executor in place of Seth Scofield, page 361.
Inventory taken Sept. 1, 1807, by Benjamin Scofield and Warren Scofield, and filed May 3, 1808, page 362.

Scofield, Seth, late of Stamford, Oct. 8, 1810, Elihu Scofield a son of decedent, about 17 years of age, made choice of Obadiah Scofield to be his guardian, page 5054.

Seward, Phebe, widow, late of Stamford, will dated Aug. 17, 1807, probated Sept. 1, 1807, mentions her sisters Hannah Smith, Sarah Seely, Elizabeth wife of Samuel Waring; nephew John Gorum, a son of my brother Daniel Gorum, and niece Charity Gorum, a daughter of by brother George Gorum. Executor John Weed, Jr. Witnesses John Clock, Sarah Bishop, and Martin Clock, page 326.
Inventory taken Sept. 7, 1807, by John Clock and Samuel Pencyer, and filed June 7, 1808, page 328.

STAMFORD PROBATE RECORDS.
Volume 10, 1803-1815.

Skelding, John, formerly of New York City, now of Stamford, Oct. 26, 1808, petitioner on behalf of Samuel Skelding and George Skelding, minor children of said petitioner for the sale of their real estate, page 302.

Slason, Nathan, late of Stamford, will dated Apl. 3, 1798, probated Apl. 2, 1811, mentions his mother Elizabeth Provost to whom he leaves his estate for life, remainder to his friend Jonathan Bishop. Executor Jonathan Bishop. Witnesses Jeremiah Mead, Peter Hubbell, and Sarah Hubbell, page 178.
Inventory taken Dec. 27, 1811, by Gershom Scofield and John Clock, and filed Jan. 7, 1812, page 179.

Smith, Ezekiel, late of Stamford, Oct. 5, 1813, letters of administration on his estate granted to Peter Smith, Jr., who was ordered to advertise for claims, page 409.

Smith, Isaac, Dr., late of Stamford, Mch. 27, 1809, Philander Smith, a son of decedent, about 20 years of age, made choice of Silvanus Marshall of Stamford to be his guardian, page 505.
Dec. 2, 1809, Alba Smith, a son of decedent, about 16 years of age, made choice of Timothy Reynolds to be his guardian, page 505^1.

Smith, Simeon, late of Stamford, will dated Apl. 30, 1805, probated Apl. 1, 1806, all to his wife Hannah for life, and remainder to his children, if any, if none then to Drake Studwell of Greenwich, brother of testator's wife or to testator's brother Isaiah Smith's children. Executrix his wife. Witnesses Daniel Nichols, James Studwell, and Eber Smith, page 6.
Inventory taken Apl. 29, 1806, by Solomon Clason and Abraham Davis, and filed May 6, 1806, and commissioners appointed to adjust claims, pages 7 and 9.
May 2, 1807, account filed by Elijah Scofield, executor in the right of his wife Hannah Scofield, formerly Hannah Smith, page 10.
Dec. 11, 1806, real estate ordered sold to pay debts, page 11.

Smith, Stephen, late of Stamford, May 1, 1810, account filed by Jared Smith, administrator, and real estate ordered sold to pay debts, page 234.
May 4, 1810, estate ordered distributed to Mary Smith, widow of deceased, and to his children Isaac, Stephen,

STAMFORD PROBATE RECORDS.
Volume 10, 1803-1815.

Smith, Stephen, continued :
Shadrach, Charlotte wife of Silas Hoyt, Jr., Mary Smith
Anne Smith, Electa Smith, Harriet Smith, and Julia Ann
Smith, page 235.
Apl. 4, 1811, estate distributed accordingly, page 235.
May 14, 1814, the court appointed William Husted guardian of Julia Ann, a daughter to decedent, page 510.

Stevens, Obadiah, late of Stamford, will dated Mch. 1, 1811,
probated Mch. 25, 1811, mentions his wife Mary, and
children Edward, Obadiah, William, deceased, Seth, Sarrah, Jane, and Lydia. Executors his son Obadiah and
Joseph Silliman of New Canaan. Witnesses Joseph Smith
Henry Marshall, and Seely Lounsbury, page 276.
Mch. 25, 1811, order to advertise for claims, page 286.
Inventory taken Mch. 22, 1811, by Nathaniel Waterbury,
and Gilbert Scofield, and filed Mch. 25, 1811, page 279.
Apl. 2, 1811, estate ordered distributed to his widow,
Mary Stevens, and children Edward, Obadiah, Seth, children of William, deceased, Sarah wife of William Tucker,
Jane, and Lydia, page 282.
Apl. 25, 1811, estate distributed accordingly, page 283.

Sutherland, Mary, late of Greenwich, widow of Roger Sutherland
Will dated Sept. 3, 1810, probated Mch. 1, 1808, mentions her daughter Sarah Ingersoll, stepdaughter Hannah Canfield, grandson Amos Weed, grandchildren Lydia
Sutherland and Samuel Fikes (Feeks). Executor Benjamin Brush. Witnesses Charles Green and John Mackay,
page 311.
Mch. 1, 1808, order to advertise for claims, page 312.
Inventory taken Mch. 2, 1808, by David Weed, Jr., and
Charles Smith, and filed Mch. 5, 1808, page 315.313.
Nov. 1, 1808, account filed, and distribution ordered
according to her will, page 314.

Thorp, Charles, late of Stamford, May 3, 1814, on the application of Cary Leeds, administrator, the time to settle estate extended, page 509.

Todd, John, late of Stamford, May 2, 1814, the court appointed
Timothy Reynolds guardian of Henry and Gabriel, children of decedent, page fxx 509.

Tooker,(or Tucker) Daniel, late of Greenwich, will dated
Apl. 3, 1809, probated June 3, 1809, mentions his mother Deborah Tompkins, sisters Elizabeth wife of Char-

STAMFORD PROBATE RECORDS.
Volume 10, 1803-1815.

Tooker, (or Tucker) Daniel, continued:
les Feeks, Nancy Tompkins, and Sarah Tompkins. Executor Nehemiah Willson. Witnesses James Willson, Desire Willson, and Nehemiah Willson, page 193.
Inventory taken June 9, 1809, by Isaac Anderson and Jotham Merritt, and filed Aug. 11, 1809, page 195.

Tryon, Samuel, late of Stamford, Nov. 1, 1808, letters of administration on his estate granted to Cary Leeds, pages 303 and 385.
Inventory taken Jan. 2, 1809, by Nathan Weed and Joseph Bishop, and filed Jan. 2, 1809, page 385.
Feb. 7, 1809, order to advertise for claims, page 385.
Aug. 14, 1809, account filed, and real estate ordered sold to pay debts, page 386.

Van Bun Schoten, John E., late of Poughkeepsie, Oct. 6, 1807, letters of administration on his estate granted to James Sackett of Bedford, page 18.
Inventory taken Oct. 27, 1807, by Benjamin Holmes and Justus Sackett, Jr., and filed Oct. 26, 1807, page 18.

Waring, Jonathan, late of Stamford, will dated Jan. 7, 1804, probated Aug. 22, 1805, legacies to the heirs of Michael Waring, deceased; son Jonathan Waring; heirs of Samuel Waring, a deceased son; viz: Hezron, Jotham, Betsy, and Alfred; daughters Rebecca, Elizabeth, Mary, and Abigail; Joel Waring, the eldest son of Joel Waring deceased; heirs of Jesse Waring, a deceased son; son Abraham Waring; heirs of Noah Waring, a deceased son, viz: Nancy, Betsy, Marilda, and Noah; and son James Waring. Executors his son-in-law Samuel Kellogg, and son James. Witnesses Joseph Waring, Walter Keeler, and Hannah Keeler, page 216.
Inventory taken Sept. 10, 1805, by Elnathan Todd and Joseph Waring, and filed Oct. 1, 1805, page 219.

Waring, Noah, late of Stamford, July 3, 1810, the court appointed David Tupper guardian of Noah Waring, about 14 years of age, and Marilda Waring, about 6 years of age, children of decedent, page 502.

Waterbury, Benjamin, late of Stamford, May 2, 1808, letters of administration on his estate granted to Deodate Waterbury of Stamford, page 368.
Inventory taken May 14, 1808, by Frederick Hoyt, Jr., and Henry Weed, and filed June 7, 1808, page 368.

STAMFORD PROBATE RECORDS.
Volume 10, 1803-1815.

Waterbury, David, late of Stamford, will dated May 25, 1805, probated May 18, 1812, mentions his wife Jemima, and children Sarah, Moses, Phebe wife of William Bates, Elizabeth wife of Charles Lockwood; and grandson William Weed Waterbury. Executor his only son Moses. Witnesses Uriah Waterbury, Hezekiah Weed, Jr., and Nathan Weed, page 246.
May 18, 1812, order to advertise for claims, page 249.
Inventory taken May 25, 1812, by Isaac Pencyer and John Clock, and filed June 2, 1812, page 349.
Apl. 6, 1812, account filed, and estate ordered distributed to Jemima Waterbury, his widow, and to his children Sarah Waterbury, Phebe wife of William Bates, Elizabeth wife of Charles Lockwood, and Moses Waterbury, page 251.
Apl. 6, 1813, estate distributed accordingly, pages 252 and 253.

Waterbury, James, late of Stamford, Apl. 7, 1807, letters of administration on his estate granted to Elizabeth Waterbury, who was ordered to advertise for claims, page 219.
Inventory taken Apl. 9, 1807, by Alexander Bishop and Henry Brown, and filed May 22, 1807, page 220.

Waterbury, Nathaniel, late of Stamford, May 14, 1814, account filed by Abigail Waterbury, administratrix, and real estate ordered sold to pay debts, page 447.

Webb, David, late of Stamford, will dated June 28, 1805, probated July 13, 1805, mentions his wife Sarah, and children Catharine wife of Rev. Daniel Smith, Samuel, and Sarah wife of Isaac Wooden. Executors son Samuel and Rev. Daniel Smith. Witnesses John Davenport, Jr., Ebenezer Webb, Jr., and Alice Coggswell, page 355.
Inventory taken Sept. 7, 1805, by Jeremiah Andreas and Eliphalet St. John, and filed Sept. 7, 1805, page 356.

Weed, Jesse, late of Stamford, Jan. 3, 1815, letters of administration on his estate granted to Seth Weed, who was ordered to advertise for claims, page 514.

Weed, John, 3rd, late of Stamford, Feb. 3, 1807, letters of administration on his estate granted to Samuel Webb, who was ordered to advertise for claims, page 196.
Inventory taken Feb. 6, 1807, by Thaddeus Waring, and John Tompson, and filed Sept. 17, 1807, pages 196 and 198.

STAMFORD PROBATE RECORDS.
Volume 10, 1803-1815.

Weed, Jonas, late of Stamford, Aug. 7, 1810, Henry Weed, a
son of decedent, about 17 years of age, made choice of
Deborah Weed, to be his guardian, page 502.

Weed, Mary, late of Stamford, Dec. 6, 1808, letters of administration on her estate granted to Smith Weed of Stamford, who was ordered to advertise for claims, pages
59 and 395.
Inventory taken Jan. 25, 1809, by Nathaniel Waterbury
and Elisha Leeds, and filed Feb. 7, 1809, page 395.
Sept. 5, 1809, account filed and real estate ordered
sold to pay debts, and report of sale filed, page 396.
Nov. 3, 1809, estate distributed to her brother Joseph
or Jesse Weed, mother Mary Weed, brother James Weed,
brother Smith Weed, Jr., and sister Susannah Weed,
page 396.

Weed, Sylvanus, Jr., late of Stamford, Dec. 20, 1809, distribution of that part of his estate set off to his widow,
Mary Weed, as her dower, to his children Sylvanus, Peter, Sarah wife of David Foster, and Alva Scofield, a
son of Mary Scofield, a deceased daughter, page 401.

Weeks, Bartholomew, late of Stamford, will dated Feb. 21, 1803
probated Nov. 21, 1806, mentions his wife Hannah, and
children Elizabeth wife of Elijah Hoyt, Mary wife of
Elisha Scofield, Hannah, Anne, Henry, William and John.
Executor Ebenezer Davenport. Witnesses Ebenezer Davenport, Jerusha Davenport, and Mary Davenport, page 198
Nov. 21, 1806, the executor having renounced, letters
with the will annexed were granted to Ezra Lockwood,
who was ordered to advertise for claims, page 200.
Inventory taken Jan. 19, 1807, by John Nichols and Thomas Lounsbury, and filed Jan. 19, 1807, page 201.
Mch. 15, 1808, account filed, and real estate ordered
sold to pay debts, page 202.

Welles, William, late of Stamford, Dec. 18, 1805, letters of
administration on his estate granted to John Davenport,
Jr., page 180.
Inventory taken by Samuel Webb and Nathan Weed, and
filed Sept. 1807, page 180.
Nov. 19, 1806, account filed, and commissioners appointed to adjust claims of creditors, page 181.
Aug. 19, 1807, report of commissioners filed, page 181.
Sept. 7, 1807, estate ordered distributed to Benjamin
Welles, Noah Welles, Melanchton W. Welles, John Welles,
Mary S. Davenport, and Rebecca Holly, brothers and sis-

STAMFORD PROBATE RECORDS.
Volume 10, 1803-1815.

Welles, William, continued:
ters of deceased, and to the legal representatives of Sarah Livingston, a deceased sister of deceased, page 182.
Sept. 10, 1807, estate distributed accordingly, page 182

White, Jacob, late of Stamford, Nov. 1, 1804, estate distributed to his widow, and heirs, viz: Jacob White, Esther White, Anne Miller, Nathan White, Sarah White, Hannah White, Henry White, and Mariah White, page 1.

Willson, Daniel, late of Greenwich, will dated June 4, 1812, probated July 7, 1812, all to his wife Hannah Willson until youngest child becomes of age, and remainder to his children. Executrix his wife. Witnesses Drake Willson, Monmouth Willson, and William Knapp, Jr., page 133.

Willson, Joseph, late of Rye, will dated May 30, 1810, probated Apl. 15, 1814, mentions his wife Susannah, and children Mary Green, Susannah Merritt, Nehemiah; grandsons Samuel Brown and Wilson Merritt, reserved a parcel of land for the use of the Baptist Church, and also a burial plot. Executor his son Nehemiah. Witnesses Thomas Willson, Drake Seymour, and Thomas M. Willson, page 451.

Willson, Jotham, late of Greenwich, Dec. 4, 1811, letters of administration on his estate granted to Nehemiah Willson, page 230.
Inventory taken Dec. 5, 1811, by Nathan Peck and Isaac Howe, and filed Jan. 7, 1812, page 230.

Willson, Thomas, a minor of Greenwich, about 19 years of age, Feb. 7, 1814, made choice of Nehemiah Peck to be his guardian, page 508.

Wilmut, Francis, late of Stamford, July 18, 1812, letters of administration on his estate granted to Esther Wilmut, who was ordered to advertise for claims, page 403.

Youngs, Abraham, late of Stamford, will dated May 1, 1801, probated Sept. 1, 1807, only son Richard, daughters Phebe Burr, Sarah Hoyt, Susannah Squire, and Hannah Sanford. Executor his son Nathan Weed, Jr. Witnesses Alexander Bishop, John Clock, and Uriah Waterbury, page 189.
Codicil dated Dec. 29, 1803, page 192.

STAMFORD PROBATE RECORDS.
Volume 10, 1803-1815.

Youngs, Abraham, continued :
    Inventory taken Aug. 17, 1807, by Stephen Jarvis and
William Walmsley, and filed Sept. 1, 1807, page 192.

STAMFORD PROBATE RECORDS.
Volume 11, 1803-1819.

Ambler, Isaac, late of Danbury, Ohio, Sept. 30, 1818, letters
of administration on his estate granted to Cary Leeds,
who was ordered to advertise for claims, page 572.

Ambler, Joseph, late of Stamford, May 29, 1819, estate ordered
distributed to his widow, and to Jonathan Weed in right
of the children of Hannah, deceased, late wife of Ebenezer Weed, deceased; 1/2 to Erastus H. Weed, Daniel A.
Weed, Sarah Weed, Lydia A. wife of Harris Scofield, and
Thirza wife of Anson Hoyt of Salem, N. Y., the remainder having been given by said will to Henry R. Weed,
late of Stamford, deceased, whose estate is insolvent,
page 554.

Anderson, Isaac, late of Greenwich, will dated Jan. 28, 1813,
probated Nov. 7, 1815, mentions his wife Hannah, and
children seven daughters and five sons, among them are
mentioned Dolly, Rebecca, and Prue; James Anderson, a
son of Elizabeth Banks wife of Joseph Banks, Jr., and
a daughter of testator. Executors sons Israel and
Purdy. Witnesses Sarah Willson, Nehemiah Willson,
Eunice Peck, Jared Strang, and Augustus Lyon, page 507.
Inventory taken Nov. 17, 1815, by Jared Strang and Nehemiah Sherwood, and filed Dec. 2, 1815, page 508.

Anderson, Matthias, late of Greenwich, inventory taken Apl. 8,
1813, by Isaac How and Nehemiah Wilson, and filed Apl.
8, 1813, by Hannah Anderson, administratrix, page 5.
Nov. 2, 1813, account filed, and real estate ordered
sold to pay debts, page 7.
Apl. 16, 1814, report of sale filed, page 8.
Mch. 1, 1814, order authorizing sale of the real estate
of John, Sally Ann, Priscilla, Polly, and Matthias,
minor children of decedent, page 7.
Apl. 16, 1814, report of sale filed, page 7.
Jan. 22, 1818, John Anderson, a son of decedent, about

STAMFORD PROBATE RECORDS.
Volume 11, 1803-1819.

Anderson, Matthias, continued :
14 years of age, made choice of Jared Strang to be his guardian, page 436.

Avery, John, late of Greenwich, inventory taken June 2, 1812, by Ebenezer Mead and Richard Mead, and filed Aug. 12, 1812, by Zophar Avery, administrator, page 92.

Banks, Daniel, late of Greenwich, will dated Sept. 12, 1811, probated Feb. 1, 1814, mentions Mary, a daughter of Ephraim Mead, and said Ephraim Mead. Executor said Ephraim Mead. Witnesses Timothy Walker, Reumah Walker and Nancy E. Walker, page 71.
Inventory taken Feb. 17, 1814, by Jonas Mead and Noah Mead, and filed Mch. 31, 1814, page 72.
Feb. 1, 1814, order to advertise for claims, page 72.

Bates, Jonathan, late of Stamford, will dated Sept. 1, 1813, probated Aug. 6, 1816, mentions his children Hannah wife of Benjamin Brown, Henry and his wife Fanny, lot to the Ecclesiastical Society of Middlesex for a burial ground; William Henry, Richard, and Walter children of my said son. Executor son. Witnesses Ebenezer Davenport, David Nash, and David N. Camp, page 242.
Codicil dated Apl. 28, 1813, page 243.
Inventory taken July 4, 1816, by Jonathan Bates and Samuel Whiting, and filed Aug. 6, 1816, page 244.
Aug. 6, 1816, order to advertise for claims, page 244.
Apl. 28, 1817, the household furniture ordered distributed to Henry Bates and Hannah wife of Benjamin Brown, according to his will, page 335.

Bates, William, of Nelson in Upper Canada, Mch. 4, 1817, perent and natural guardian of Henry Bates of said Nelson, asked for leave to sell the real estate of said minor, which was devised to him by David Waterbury, late of Stamford, page 287.
May 31, 1817, sale authorized, page 350.
May 31, 1817, sale made, page 350.

Bayeux, Priscilla, late of Greenwich, Jan. 25, 1816, letters of administration on her estate granted to Oliver L. Ford and Henry Lockwood, who were ordered to advertise for claims, page 97.
Inventory taken Mch. 21, 1816, by Enos Lockwood and Ebenezer Peck, and filed Apl. 2, 1816, page 190.

STAMFORD PROBATE RECORDS.
Volume 11, 1803-1819.

Bayeux, Thomas, Dr., late of Greenwich, Feb. 16, 1816, distribution ordered of that part of his estate set off to his widow, Priscilla Bayeux, as her dower, to his children, viz: Priscilla wife of Epenetus Lockwood, Elizabeth wife of Oilver L. Ford, Maria wife of Henry Lockwood, and Sally Bayeux, page 184.
Mch. 22, 1816, estate distributed accordingly, page 230.

Bellamy, Isaac, late of Stamford, June 11, 1817, the court appointed William Hoyt, Jr., guardian of Edwin Bellamy, a son of decedent, about 15 years of age, page 352.

Bishop, Abijah, late of Stamford, Aug. 17, 1810, account filed by Ebenezer Bishop, administrator, and real estate ordered sold to pay debts, page 141.

Bishop, Abijah, late of Stamford, will dated Feb. 18, 1815, probated Apl. 4, 1815, mentions his wife Hannah, and son Ezra H. Executrix his wife. Witnesses John Weed, Jr., and Samuel Webb, page 228.
Apl. 4, 1815, order to advertise for claims, page 228.
Inventory taken July 4, 1815, by John Weed, Jr., and William Webb, and filed July 4, 1815, page 229.
Jan. 20, 1819, Hannah Bishop was appointed by the court guardian of Her son Ezra H. Bishop, about 17 years of age, page 544.

Bishop, Hannah, late of Stamford, Apl. 6, 1819, letters of administration on her estate granted to John K. Bishop, who was ordered to advertise for claims, page 581.

Brown, Deborah, late of Greenwich, Apl. 2, 1816, letters of administration on her estate granted to Benjamin Brush of Greenwich, who was ordered to advertise for claims, page 190.

Brown, Doctor, late of Stamford, inventory taken Apl. 14, 1813, by Joseph Gray and Cary Leeds, and filed July 6, 1813, page 222.
Dec. 7, 1813, account filed, and real estate ordered sold to pay debts, page 224.
Dec. 30, 1813, report of sale filed, page 224.
Sept. 5, 1815, estate ordered distributed to his widow, Elizabeth, and children Polly Wilmut, Elizabeth L., Rebecca, Sally, Hannah, William Henry, Julia Ann, Charles, and Emeline, page 225.

STAMFORD PROBATE RECORDS.
Volume 11, 1803-1819.

Brown, Peter, late of Stamford, will dated July 9, 1818, probated Aug. 3, 1818, mentions his wife Martha, legacy to his daughter Jerusha, and remainder to the rest of his children. No executor. Witnesses Rufus Newman and Isaac Holly, page 531.
Aug. 3, 1818, letters with the will annexed to Martha Brown and Peter Brown, who were ordered to advertise for claims, page 531.
Inventory taken Sept. 2, 1818, by Samuel Hoyt and Isaac Holly, and filed Sept. 21, 1818, page 532.

Brown, Rachel, late of Greenwich, widow of Bezaleel Brown, will dated June 18, 1814, probated Feb. 6, 1816, all to her son Bezaleel Brown, and appointed him executor. Witnesses Sarah W. Knapp, Susan J. Knapp, and Maria Rogers, page 516.

Brown, Rebecca, late of Stamford, inventory taken Jan. 2, 1815, by William Walmsley and John Waterbury, and filed Jan. 3, 1815, page 424.
May 2, 1815, account filed, and estate ordered distributed to her children John Brown, Adam Brown, Noah Brown, Abigail Brown, Rebecca Brown, Jonathan Brown, the legal representatives of Doctor Brown, deceased, and the legal representatives of Francis Brown, deceased, page 424.
Estate distributed accordingly, page 424.

Brown, Samuel, 3rd, late of Greenwich, Oct. 1, 1816, letters of administration on his estate granted to Timothy Walker, who was ordered to advertise for claims, page 257.
Inventory taken Oct. 11, 1816, by Ebenezer Mead and William Knapp, and filed Nov. 5, 1816, page 270.
May 1, 1817, order to advertise for claims, page 348.
May 6, 1817, commissioners appointed to adjust claims of creditors, page 348.

Brush, James, late of Greenwich, will dated Mch. 8, 1811, probated Aug. 4, 1812, mentions his wife Martha, and children Edward, James, David, Sarah wife of Henry Van Cleck, and Rachel. Executors sons Edward and James. Witnesses Clark Reynolds, Alexander Lockwood, and David Wood, Jr., page 498.
Aug. 4, 1812, order to advertise for claims, page 500.
Inventory taken July 30, 1812, by Reuben Finch and Jared Smith, and filed Aug. 4, 1812, page 500.

STAMFORD PROBATE RECORDS.
Volume 11, 1803-1819.

Brush, James, continued :
    June 11, 1813, the dower of his widow, Martha Brush, set out, page 501.

Bunnell, David, late of Stamford, inventory taken Dec. 7, 1813, by John Weed, Jr/, and Hezekiah Weed, and filed Dec. 7, 1813, page 426.
    June 7, 1814, order to advertise for claims, page 428.
    June 14, 1814, commissioners appointed to adjust claims of creditors, page 428.
    Jan. 16, 1815, report of commissioners filed, page 429.
    Feb. 15, 1815, account filed by Ezra Lockwood, administrator, and creditors ordered paid, page 431.

Buxton, John, late of Stamford, Apl. 7, 1818, letters of administration on his estate granted to Cary Leeds, page 471.
    Inventory taken Apl. 10, 1818, by Warren Scofield and Abishai Scofield, and filed Apl. 13, 1818, page 471.
    Apl. 13, 1818, account filed, and ordered to advertise for claims, page 471.
    Apl. 18, 1818, commissioners appointed to adjust claims of creditors, page 485.
    Dec. 7, 1818, account filed, and realestate ordered sold to pay debts, page 541.
    Dec. 15, 1818, date of sale, page 541.
    Nov. 2, 1818, commissioners appointed to set out the dower of his widow, Emmy Buxton, now Emmy Waterbury, page 541.
    Nov. 25, 1818, dower set out, page 541.
    Dec. 7, 1818, report of commissioners to adjust claims filed, page 542.
    Dec. 16, 1818, account filed, and creditors ordered paid, page 543.

Buxton, Samuel, late of Stamford, inventory taken Sept. 10, 1812, by Reuben Scofield and Joseph Gray, and filed Sept. 11, 1812, page 399.
    Sept. 11, 1812, order to advertise for claims, page 399
    Sept. 16, 1812, commissioners appointed to adjust claims of creditors, page 400.
    Apl. 19, 1812, report of commissioners filed, page 400.

Carringcross, George, also spelled Carncross, late of Greenwich, Sept. 5, 1815, letters of administration on his estate granted to Andrew Mead of Greenwich, page 70.
    Inventory taken Oct. 2, 1815, by Ebenezer Hobby and Aaron Clark, and filed Oct. 3, 1815, page 401.

STAMFORD PROBATE RECORDS.
Volume 11, 1803-1819.

Close, Aaron, late of Stamford, Apl. 3, 1815, letters of administration of his estate granted to Sarah Close, widow of deceased, and Joseph Wood, both of Stamford, who were ordered to advertise for claims, page 54.
Inventory taken Apl. 5, 1815, by Josiah Smith and Nathaniel Mills, and filed June 12, 1815, page 237.
Nov. 7, 1815, his widow, Sarah Close, appointed guardian of Elizabeth F., Oliver F., and Eliza, children of deceased, page 70.

Close, Jonathan, late of Greenwich, Jan. 6, 1818, estate ordered distributed to his widow, Rebecca Close, and children Gilbert, Horace, Elizabeth wife of Cyrus Mead, William, Jonathan A., and Mary Rebecca, page 485.
Mch. 31, 1818, estate distributed accordingly, page 486.

Cornell, John, late of Greenwich, will dated 1st day, 9th month, 1806, probated June 12, 1813, mentions his wife ----, Samuel Cornell, Joshua Cornell, John Cornell, Sarah Cornell, Mary Cornell, Phebe Hallet, Quimby Cornell, James Cornell, William Cornell, Daniel Cornell, Josiah Cornell, Matthew Dayton, and Benjamin Forweling. Executors Thomas Clapp, John Griffin, and Josiah Field. Witnesses Aaron Field, James Field, and Charles Field, page 11.
Codicil dated 3rd day, 4th month, 1812, mentions Susannah wife of John Reynolds and her son Cornelius, page 11.
Inventory taken 2nd day, 8th month, 1813, by Thomas Carpenter and James Field, and filed Aug. 3, 1813, page 14.
June 12, 1813, order to advertise for claims, page 13.

Crabb, Ely, a minor of Stamford, about 16 years of age, and David Crabb of Stamford, a minor about 18 years of age, Apl. 13, 1818, made choice of Elisha Crabb of Stamford to be their guardian, page 468.

Dan, John, late a soldier in the service of the United States, July 6, 1815, letters of administration on his estate granted to Charles W. Dan of Stamford, page 69.

Dan, Nathan, late of Stamford, Dec. 11, 1805, letters of administration on his estate granted to Alexander Mills of Stamford, page 123.
Inventory taken Dec. 27, 1805, by Nathaniel Webb and Joseph Gray, and filed Dec. 28, 1805, and commissioners appointed to adjust claims of creditors, page 123.

STAMFORD PROBATE RECORDS.
Volume 11, 1803-1819.

Dan, Nathan, continued :
    July 28, 1806, report of commissioners filed, page 124.

Davenport, Hannah, late of Stamford, Mch. 6, 1810, letters of administration on her estate granted to William Scofield, Jr., of Stamford, page 35.

Davenport, James, late of Stamford, Aug. 15, 1812, John Davenport, Jr., guardian of Frances L. Davenport, a daughter of deceased, asked leave to sell the realestate of said minor, page 1.
Dec. 1812, order authorizing sale, page 1.

Davis, Abraham, late of Stamford, will dated Feb. 10, 1816, probated Apl. 2, 1816, mentions his wife Mary, and children Aaron, Polly wife of James Jarman, Catharine, Mehitable wife of Lewis Knapp, and Levina. Executor son Aaron. Witnesses Daniel Nichols, Jonathan Smith, and William June, page 186.
Apl. 2, 1816, order to advertise for claims, page 186.
Inventory taken by Daniel Nichols and Solomon Clason, and filed June 4, 1816, page 448.
Mch. 4, 1817, estate ordered distributed to his children Aaron Davis, Catharine Nichols, Levina Davis, Polly wife of James Jarman, and the legal representatives of Mehitable Knapp, page 448.
Mch. 14, 1817, estate distributed accordingly, page 449.

Davis, Elisha, late of Greenwich, will dated Mch. 16, 1813, probated Apl. 24, 1813, mentions his wife Ann, and children Nancy, Thomas, Walter, Silas, Elizabeth Jarman, Johanna Benson, Sally Betts, Esther Riker, and Clarissa wife of Butler Hubbard; and John a son of my daughter Nancy. Executors son Silas and Jonas Mead. Witnesses David Mead, Griffin Finch, and William Knapp, page 434.
Inventory taken Apl. 29, 1813, by Henry Grigg and Goold John Selleck, and filed May 4, 1813, page 436.

Dayton, David, late of North Castle, Westchester County, N.Y., Sept. 19, 1814, letters of administration on his estate granted to Jared Smith of Greenwich, who was ordered to advertise for claims, page 517.
Inventory taken Oct. 22, 1814, by Calvin Mead and Josiah Field, and filed Feb. 24, 1815, page 517.

STAMFORD PROBATE RECORDS.
Volume 11, 1803-1819.

Denton, Samuel, late of Greenwich, Feb. 4, 1817, letters of administration on his estate granted to Humphrey Denton, who was ordered to advertise for claims, page 279. Inventory taken Mch. 31, 1817, by John Sackett and Aaron Husted, and filed Apl. 1, 1817, page 288.

Dibble, George, late of Stamford, will dated Jan. 31, 1812, probated July 5, 1813, mentions his wife Phebe, and children Samuel, John, Josiah, Jonathan, Mary Ann, Grace, Sarah Waring, Deborah Ames, Abigail Feeks, and Elizabeth Ingersoll. Executors Benjamin Isaacs of Bedford, and Jared Smith of Greenwich. Witnesses Benjamin Brush, Benjamin S. Brush, and Anne Smith, page 514.
July 5, 1813, order to advertise for claims, page 515.
Inventory taken June 7, 1813, by David Wood and Reuben Finch, and filed July 5, 1813, page 516.

Dunham, John, late of Stamford, Oct. 20, 1817, Esther Dunham, a daughter of decedent, about 20 years of age, made choice of Gilbert Scofield to be her guardian, page 401.

Fancher, David, late of Stamford, Apl. 1, 1817, letters of administration on his estate granted to Jeremiah Andreas, page 348.
Apl. 14, 1817, order to advertise for claims, page 348.
Inventory taken Apl. 5, 1817, by Samuel Whiting and Joshua Scofield, and filed June 10, 1817, page 351.
May 17, 1817, estate ordered distributed to his children David, Sarah wife of John Clock, Rebecca wife of Cary Bell, the legal representatives of Hannah deceased wife of Peter Weed, and Martha wife of Enos Tuttle, page 354.
July 1, 1817, estate distributed accordingly, page 354.

Ferris, David, Jr., late of Greenwich, July 3, 1810, letters of administration on his estate granted to Nathaniel Adams and Betsy Ferris, who were ordered to advertise for claims, page 35.
Inventory taken July 13, 1810, by Enos Knapp and Jabez Mead, and filed Aug. 7, 1810, page 36.
Feb. 5, 1811, commissioners appointed to set out the dower of his widow, Betsy Ferris, page 38.
Mch. 4, 1811, dower set out, page 41.
Feb. 5, 1811, account filed, and realestate ordered sold to pay debts, page 38.

STAMFORD PROBATE RECORDS.
Volume 11, 1803-1819.

Ferris, Ebenezer, late of Greenwich, inventory taken July 29, 1813, by Reuben Finch and Jared Smith, and filed Aug. 3, 1813, page 1 and 3.
Apl. 30, 1814, account filed by David Wood, administrator, and real estate ordered sold to pay debts, page 2.
June 7, 1812,1814, report of sale filed, page 3.
June 10, 1814, estate distributed to Mary Ann wife of Levi Mead, a sister of deceased; Jemima wife of James Palmer, a sister of deceased, and Sally wife of John Chapman, page 3.

Ferris, James, late of Greenwich, will dated Feb. 25, 1807, probated Sept. 1, 1812, mentions his wife Mary, and children Mary Palmer, Sarah Lockwood, James, deceased, Hannah Palmer, deceased, Asa, Abel, and Shadrach; granddaughters Sybil W. Palmer and Hetty Palmer, daughters of John Wood Palmer, deceased. Executors sons Asa, Abel, and Shadrach. Witnesses Enos Knapp, Enos Lockwood, and Elias Peck, Jr., page 23.
Sept. 1, 1812, order to advertise for claims, page 25.
Inventory taken by Alexander Hendrie and Stephen Ferris, Jr., and filed Oct. 1812, page 26.

Ferris, James, Jr., late of Greenwich, Dec. 5, 1815, estate ordered distributed to his children Mary wife of Israel Mead, Nathaniel Ferris, Jr., Hannah widow of Nathaniel Rundle, Amy wife of Edward Mead, Betsy wife of Abraham Merrill, Deborah wife of Abraham Conn, and Lemuel Ferris, page 425.
Jan. 10, 1816, estate distributed accordingly, page 425.

Ferris, Jeduthan, late of Greenwich, will dated Aug. 24, 1807, probated July 14, 1809, mentions his children John, Jeduthan, Ethan, Phebe, Ann Stiles, Eliphalet, Joseph, Andrew, Mary Peck, and the children of a deceased daughter Deborah. Executor son Ethan. Witnesses Sarah Fitch, and Elizabeth Fitch, page 20.
July 14, 1809, order to advertise for claims, page 21.
Inventory taken July 16, 1809, by Joshua Ferris and William Skidmore, and filed July 29, 1809, page 22.

Ferris, Jeremiah, late of Greenwich, Dec. 5, 1795, estate distributed to his widow Nancy Ferris, and children Joseph Jr., Abigail, Sarah, Ruth, Charles and Betsy, page 135.

Ferris, Mary, late of Stamford, July 6, 1816, letters of administration on her estate granted to Calvin Hoyt, page 218.

STAMFORD PROBATE RECORDS.
Volume 11, 1803-1819.

Ferris, Mary, continued:
Inventory taken July 25, 1816, by Nathan White and David Smith, 3rd, and filed Aug. 29, 1816, page 247.

Ferris, Oliver, late of Greenwich, Feb. 10, 1813, letters of administration on his estate granted to David Wood, who was ordered to advertise for claims, page 42.
Nov. 13, 1813, account filed, and real estate ordered sold to pay debts, page 42.
Dec. 15, 1813, estate distributed to the legal representatives of Ebenezer Ferris, viz: Mary Ann wife of Levi Mead, Jemima wife of James Palmer, and Sally wife of John Chapman, page 42.

Ferris, Shadrach, late of Stamford, Nov. 7, 1815, letters of administration on his estate granted to Henry Close of Stamford, who was ordered to advertise for claims, page 70.
Nov. 4, 1815, inventory taken Nov. 4, 1815, by Isaac Lockwood, Jr., and Asahel Palmer, and filed Nov. 17, 1815, page 239.
Apl. 5, 1816, on the application of Maria Ferris, widow of deceased, commissioners were appointed to set out her dower, page 188.
Apl. 24, 1816, dower set out, page 240.
July 2, 1816, account filed, and real estate ordered sold to pay debts, page 217.

Field, Uriah, late of Greenwich, will dated 19th day, 5th month, 1812, probated Dec. 5, 1814, mentions his wife, Mary, father Robert Field, children Abigail wife of Richard Mott, Elizabeth wife of John Carpenter, Sarah wife of John J. Griffin, Mary wife of Daniel Griffin, Anne wife of John Haviland, Hannah Field, Aaron, Josiah, Robert, James; grandsons Uriah Carpenter, Uriah Field, a son of Robert Field, and Charles Field. Executors sons Robert and James. Witnesses Daniel Mathews, Gilbert Sherwood, and Oliver Mathews, page 511.
Dec. 5, 1814, order to advertise for claims, page 512.
Inventory taken 12th month, 15th day, 1814, by Daniel Mathews and Thomas Carpenter, and filed Jan. 7, 1815, page 513.

Flanagan, Daniel, late of Greenwich, Aug. 7, 1816, letters of administration on his estate granted to James Green, Jr. who was ordered to advertise for claims, page 246.
Inventory taken Sept. 2, 1816, by Joseph Green and Platt Mead, and filed Oct. 1, 1816, page 252.

STAMFORD PROBATE RECORDS.
Volume 11, 1803-1819.

Flanegan, Daniel, continued :
    Oct. 1, 1816, order to advertise for claims, page 262.
    Oct. 5, 1816, commissioners appointed to adjust claims of creditors, page 262.
    June 6, 1817, report of commissioners filed, page 351.
    Oct. 1, 1816, all his estate ordered sold to pay debts, page 350.

Fletinbourgh, -----, a minor of Greenwich, about 15 years of age, and a son of the wife of James Prendergest, Sept. 3, 1816, the court appointed said James Prendergest his guardian, page 247.

Gray, Philip, late of Stamford, additional inventory filed, Nov. 1, 1814, page 451.
    Nov. 14, 1814, his personal estate distributed to Mary Gray, Elianor Gray, John Anson Gray, and Alfred Gray, page 452.
    Oct. 5, 1818, his estate ordered distributed to his children Mary wife of Thaddeus Seely, Elinor Gray, John A. Gray, and Alfred Gray, page 561.
    Oct. 23, 1818, estate distributed accordingly, page 561.

Green, John, Captain, late of Greenwich, Feb. 20, 1816, letters of administration on his estate granted to Thomas Green, who was ordered to advertise for claims, page 151
    Inventory taken Mch. 24, 1816, by Platt Mead and Joseph Green, and filed Apl. 15, 1816, page 336.

Green, Mercy, widow, late of Stamford, June 4, 1805, letters of administration on her estate granted to Cary Hoyt, who was ordered to advertise for claims, page 19.
    Inventory taken June 21, 1805, by Cary Leeds and Nathaniel Waterbury, and filed July 2, 1805, page 19.

Grigg, Walter, late of Greenwich, Apl. 22, 1814, additional inventory filed, page 8.
    Mch. 14, 1814, estate ordered distributed to his brothers and sister, viz: John, Henry, and Ann Lockwood, page 8.
    May 2, 1814, estate distributed to his brothers James, John, to the heirs of Alexander, Henry, and sister Ann Lockwood, page 9.

Haggerty, John, late of Greenwich, Aug. 3, 1818, letters of administration on his estate granted to James Green, Jr who was ordered to advertise for claims, page 550.

STAMFORD PROBATE RECORDS.
Volume 11, 1803-1819.

Haggerty, John, continued :
    Inventory taken Aug. 8, 1818, by Platt Mead and Samuel Brown, and filed Aug. 10, 1818, and all his property ordered sold to pay debts, page 550.
    Aug. 17, 1818, sale made, page 551.
    Aug. 10, 1818, commissioners appointed to adjust claims of creditors, page 550.
    Feb. 3, 1819, report of commissioners filed, page 548.

Hait, Frederick, late of Stamford, inventory taken Oct. 10, 1814, by Joel Waring, and Henry Hait, 3rd, and filed Oct. 10, 1814, page 290.

Hait, Jonah, late of Stamford, inventory taken Oct. 1, 1814, by Seth Smith and Seth Hait, and filed Oct. 10, 1814, page 438.

Hait, Seth, late of Stamford, will dated Apl. 20, 1815, probated Sept. 5, 1815, mentions his wife Sarah, and children Lucy Ann wife of Seth Wood, Nehemiah, Seth, and John, others not named. Executor son Nehemiah. Witnesses Platt Buffett, Hannah Buffett, and Elouisa Buffett, page 302.
    Sept. 5, 1815, order to advertise for claims, page 304.
    Inventory taken by Solomon Clason and Seth Smith, and filed Sept. 5, 1815, page 304.

Hitchcock, Rufus, a minor of Greenwich, about 18 years of age, Dec. 2, 1815, made choice of Elizabeth Hitchcock to be his guardian, page 74.

Hitchcock, Thomas, late of Greenwich, inventory taken Feb. 24, 1814, by Eliakim Lockwood and Lustus L. Bush, and filed Feb. 26, 1814, page 315.
    Apl. 5, 1816, Cyrus Hitchcock, a son of decedent, about 19 years of age, made choice of John Hitchcock of New York City to be his guardian, page 186.

Hobby, Amy, late of Greenwich, Feb. 15, 1819, her estate ordered distributed to Amy wife of Andrew Mead, and Sally wife of Amos Hobby, in accordance with her will, page 572.

Hobby, Cynthia, of Greenwich, Apl. 15, 1818, chosen guardian of her children Amy M. Hobby, ae. 20; Sally Hobby, ae. 17; and Caroline Hobby, ae. 15, page 497.
    Apl. 15, 1818, appointed guardian of her children

STAMFORD PROBATE RECORDS.
Volume 11, 1803-1819.

Hobby, Cynthia, continued:
    George E. Hobby, ae 12; William Hobby, ae 10; and
    Eunice Rebecca Hobby, ae. 8, page 519.

Hobby, Ebenezer, late of Greenwich, Oct. 2, 1806, commissioners
    appointed to set out the dower of his widow Mary Hubby, page 453.

Hobby, Mills, late of Greenwich, Jan. 31, 1817, Mills Hobby,
    a son of decedent, made choice of Thomas Close to be
    his guardian; and the court appointed Ruth Hobby guardian of Sarah Hobby, about 18 years of age, and Mary
    Hobby, about 20 years of age, daughters of said decedent, page 279.
    Jan. 31, 1817, the guardians asked for leave to sell
    the real estate of said minors, page 278.
    Apl. 25, 1817, order authorizing sale, and report of
    sale filed, page 335.

Hobby, Squire, late of Greenwich, Apl. 15, 1818, his estate
    ordered distributed to his widow, Cynthia Hobby, and
    his children Husted, Elisa, Andrew, Lucy Close, Amy M,
    Sally, Caroline, George E., William, and Eunice R.,
    page 522.
    Apl. 24, 1818, estate distributed accordingly, page 522.

Hobson, Allen, a minor of Greenwich, about 19 years of age,
    June 6, 1815, made choice of Samuel Ferris of Greenwich to be his guardian, page 68.

Holly, Increase, late of Stamford, inventory taken July 28,
    1806, by Gilbert Scofield and Peter Husted, and filed
    July 29, 1806, by Enoch Holly, administrator, page 289.

Holly, Isaac, late of Stamford, will dated Jan. 15, 1816, probated Feb. 6, 1816, all to his wife Deborah for life,
    and remainder to his children. Executor Jeremiah Curtis. Witnesses Reuben Scofield, Enoch Stevens, and
    Amy Stevens, page 317.
    Feb. 6, 1816, order to advertise for claims, page 318.
    Inventory taken Feb. 2, 1816, by Enoch Stevens and
    Jacob Stevens, Jr., and filed Feb. 6, 1816, page 318.

Holly, Mersey, late of Stamford, will dated May 2, 1811, probated June 5, 1818, all to sister Elizabeth Holly for
    life, and remainder to the Town of New Canaan. Executor Joseph Silliman of New Canaan. Witnesses Ebenezer Ferris, Abigail Ferris, and Joseph Wood, page 519.

STAMFORD PROBATE RECORDS.
Volume 11, 1803-1819.

Holly, Mersey, continued:
    June 5, 1818, order to advertise for claims, page 520.
    Inventory taken June 5, 1818, by Rowland Tryon and
    James Webb, and filed June 5, 1818, page 521.

Holly, Newman, late of Stamford, Mch. 5, 1805, on the application of Abijah Bishop on his behalf as purchaser from Alexander Bishop and Hannah his wife of her right in the real estate of said decedent, and in behalf of the minor children of Susannah Bishop, late of Stamford deceased, as father and natural guardian of said minors for an order of distribution of the remainder of the real estate of said decedent, as devised to said Hannah and Susannah, daughters of said deceased. Distribution ordered accordingly, page 313.
    Mch. 5, 1805, estate distributed accordingly, page 314.

Holly, Rheuama, late of Stamford, Nov. 5, 1812, letters of administration on her estate granted to Samuel Holly of Stamford, page 78.
    Inventory taken Jan. 18, 1813, by Daniel Provost and Reuben Scofield, and filed Jan. 21, 1813, page 79.
    Dec. 9, 1816, account filed, and exceptions thereto filed by Mercy Holly, widow, Elizabeth Burtis, and Rhoda wife of Gideon Leeds, and an appeal taken, page 277.
    Dec. 1816, order of the lower court overruled, page 393.

Holmes, Jabez, late of Greenwich, will dated June 29, 1815, probated Oct. 7, 1815, mentions his children Gideon, Mary, and Betsy Mead. Executor son Gideon; Witnesses Gilbert Close, Isaac Peck, 3rd, and Isaac Knapp, page 509.
    Oct. 7, 1815, order to advertise for claims, page 509.
    Inventory taken Nov. 2, 1815, by Gilbert Close and Seymour Hobby, and filed Nov. 7, 1815, page 510.

Hopkins, Thomas, late of North Castle, Westchester County, N.Y. will dated 3rd day, 1st month, 1812, probated Feb. 8, 1815, mentions his wife Zeruiah, and children Mary, Pine, James, Samuel, Thomas, Elizabeth Cock, Mary Hopkins; granddaughter Elizabeth, a daughter of my son Samuel; grandson Thomas Cook. Executors sons James, Thomas, and Pine. Witnesses Samuel Mellis, John H. Smith, and John Smith, page 438.
    Inventory taken Feb. 8, 1815, by John Smith and Robert Leonard, and filed Feb. 8, 1815, page 440.

STAMFORD PROBATE RECORDS.
Volume 11, 1803-1819.

Hose, Henry G., late of Stamford, Aug. 3, 1813, inventories taken by Joseph Gray and Henry Close, and filed Sept. 27, 1813, page 454.

Hoyt, Anna, late of Stamford, wife of Colonel Joseph Hoyt, Mch. 4, 1817, letters of administration on her estate granted to Henry Weeks of Stamford, who was ordered to advertise for claims, page 287.

Hoyt, Benjamin, late of Stamford, inventory taken Dec. 9, 1813, by Isaac Holly, Jr., and Jonathan Brown, and filed Dec. 13, 1813, page 330.
Dec. 13, 1813, order to advertise for claims, page 332.
Dec. 20, 1813, commissioners appointed to adjust claims of creditors, page 333.
July 21, 1814, report of commissioners filed, page 333.

Hoyt, Benjamin, a minor of New York City, about 15 years of age, Nov. 25, 1817, made choice of his mother Elizabeth Hoyt of New York City to be his guardian, page 420.

Hoyt, Deodate, late of Stamford, June 3, 1817, that part of his estate set off to his widow for her dower, ordered distributed to his brothers and sisters, to the legal representatives of Abigail Hoyt, deceased, to the legal representatives of William Hoyt, deceased, to the legal representatives of Nezer Hoyt, deceased, to the legal representatives of Hannah Smith, deceased, and Susannah wife of Abishai Weed, page 410.
July 3, 1817, estate distributed accordingly, but no part to Susannah wife of Abishai Weed, page 410.

Hoyt, Elijah, late of Stamford, Dec. 12, 1815, letters of administration on his estate granted to Elizabeth Hoyt, and Cary Leeds, both of Stamford, who were ordered to advertise for claims, page 75.
Inventory taken Dec. 19, 1815, by Joseph Gray and John Leeds, and filed Jan. 2, 1816, page 79.
Mch. 11, 1816, commissioners were appointed to set out the dower of his widow, Elizabeth Hoyt, page 209.
Apl. 16, 1816, dower set out, page 209.
Dec. 4, 1817, that part of his estate set off to his widow for her dower, ordered distributed to his children Jonah, Elizabeth Scofield, Elihu, Anne, and Ziba, and to the legal representatives of Catharine, page 420.
Dec. 24, 1817, distributed accordingly to his children Jonah, Elizabeth Scofield, Elihu, Anna, and Ziba(son), page 468.

STAMFORD PROBATE RECORDS.
Volume 11, 1803-1819.

Hoyt, Elizabeth, late of Stamford, Oct. 7, 1817, letters of administration on her estate granted to Cary Leeds, who was ordered to advertise for claims, page 387.
Deceased the widow of Elijah Hoyt.
Inventory taken Dec. 2, 1817, by John Leeds and Rowland Tryon, and filed Dec. 4, 1817, page 423.

Hoyt, Enoch, late of Stamford, Apl. 26, 1819, letters of administration on his estate granted to Philip Lockwood, of Greenwich, who was ordered to advertise for claims, page 553.
May 3, 1819, commissioners appointed to adjust claims of creditors, page 554.
Inventory taken Apl. 26, 1819, by Ebenezer Webb, Jr., and Sturges P. Thorp, and filed May 3, 1819, page 554.
May 18, 1819, account filed, page 554.

Hoyt, Frederick, late of Stamford, Oct. 4, 1814, letters of administration on his estate granted to William White, who was ordered to advertise for claims, page 63.
Apl. 6, 1815, the court appointed Phebe Hoyt, widow of deceased, guardian of David Newton Hoyt, a son of decedent, page 54.
Apl. 11, 1815, account filed, and estate ordered distributed to his widow, and to the legal representatives of Hannah Reynolds, a deceased daughter of deceased; Sarah wife of Isaac Ayres, and David Newton Hoyt, children of deceased, page 298.
May 4, 1815, estate distributed accordingly, page 299.

Hoyt, Hanford, late of Stamford, Oct. 1, 1816, letters of administration on his estate granted to Ezra Knapp of Stamford, who was ordered to advertise for claims, page 257.
Inventory taken Oct. 4, 1816, by Nathaniel Waterbury and John Husted, and filed Oct. 5, 1816, page 257.
Oct. 5, 1816, commissioners appointed to adjust claims of creditors, page 260.
Oct. 5, 1816, real estate ordered sold to pay debts, page 345.
Oct. 17, 1816, sale made, page 345.
June 3, 1817, report of commissioners to adjust claims filed, page 352.
June 3, 1817, account filed, and creditors ordered paid, page 350.

STAMFORD PROBATE RECORDS.
Volume 11, 1803-1819.

Hoyt, John, late of Stamford, Dec. 3, 1816, the court appointed John Hoyt guardian of Joseph Warren Hoyt, a son of decedent, about 15 years of age, page 274.

Hoyt, Joseph, late of Stamford, Apl. 5, 1814, account filed by Amos Weed, executor, in right of his wife Hannah, formerly Hannah Hoyt, and distribution of his estate ordered to the children of deceased, viz: Benjamin, Harvey, and Joseph, and to the widow of deceased, now Hannah Weed, page 459.
Estate distributed accordingly, page 460.

Hoyt, Samuel, late of Stamford, inventory taken Nov. 18, 1814, by Cary Leeds and Nathaniel Waterbury, and filed Dec. 6, 1814, page 513.
Apl. 12, 1813, account filed by John Leeds, administrator, and real estate ordered sold to pay debts, page 514.

Hoyt, Samuel, Jr., late of Stamford, May 22, 1818, account filed by Hannah Hoyt, administratrix, and creditors ordered paid, page 527.

Hoyt, Seth, late of Stamford, June 4, 1816, on the application of Nehemiah Hoyt, executor, the moveable estate was ordered distributed to his widow, and children, viz: Mary Ann, Rachel, Ruth, Rebecca, Seth, Nehemiah, and John, page 254.
Sept. 2, 1816, estate distributed accordingly, page 254.

Hoyt, Sylvanus, late of Stamford, Nov. 5, 1816, letters of administration on his estate granted to Cary Leeds, and Sally Hoyt, who were ordered to advertise for claims, page 271.
Inventory taken Dec. 3, 1816, by John Leeds and Augustus Lockwood, and filed Dec. 3, 1816, page 275.
Dec. 3, 1816, commissioners appointed to set out the dower of his widow, Sally Hoyt, page 277.
Feb. 4, 1817, dower set out, page 281.
Dec. 17, 1816, the court appointed Sarah Hoyt, guardian of Eliza Hoyt, a daughter of decedent, about 18 years of age, page 278.
July 1, 1817, account filed, and real estate ordered sold to pay debts, page 360.
July 24, 1817, date of sale, page 360.

STAMFORD PROBATE RECORDS.
Volume 11, 1803-1819.

Hubbard, Nathaniel, Dr., late of Stamford, Mch. 23, 1818, that part of his estate set off to his widow for her dower, ordered distributed. Nathaniel Hubbard, Isaac Hubbard William Hubbard, and Margaret D. Webber having forfeited their rights in said estate, and the same having been sold as escheats, and Frederick Webb has purchased the same; therefore 4/7 was ordered distributed to said Webb, and the remainder to the legal representatives of Elizabeth Townsend, a deceased daughter of deceased; to Nancy wife of Samuel Bush, and to the widow Mary Saunders, children of said deceased, page 518.
May 9, 1818, estate distributed accordingly, page 518.

Heusted, Isaac, late of Greenwich, Sept. 6, 1818, letters of administration on his estate granted to Samuel Heusted, page 380.
Inventory taken Oct. 6, 1817, by Alexander Hendrie and Enos Lockwood, and filed Jan. 6, 1818, page 447.
Jan. 6, 1818, account filed, and real estate ordered sold to pay debts, page 447.

Heusted, Sarah, late of Greenwich, will dated Apl. 18, 1796, probated Jan. 3, 1815, mentions her children Benjamin Heusted, and Nathaniel Heusted,; children of a daughter Rachel Delevan, deceased, late wife of John Delevan of Salem, Westchester County, N. Y.; children of a daughter Sarah wife of Titus Reynolds of said Salem; children of a daughter Deborah wife of Nathaniel Reynolds of Greenwich; children of a daughter Martha wife of James Brush of Greenwich; children of a daughter Mary Mead, deceased, late wife of Jonah Mead of Greenwich; and children of a daughter Azuba wife of Stephen Palmer of Westchester County, N. Y. Executor David Wood. Witnesses William Seward, Sarah Mead, and Rebecca Ann Seward, page 89.
Jan. 3, 1815, the executor being now deceased letters with the will annexed granted to Ira Lockwood, who was ordered to advertise for claims, page 91.
Inventory taken Jan. 9, 1815, by David Wood and Charles Rundle, and filed Jan. 20, 1815, page 91.
Jan. 20, 1816, account filed, and Edward Brush appointed administrator de bonus non, page 89.

Jeffery, Mercy, late of Stamford, inventory taken Jan. 17, 1810, by Cary Leeds and Joseph Bishop, and filed Mch. 6, 1810, page 48.

STAMFORD PROBATE RECORDS.
Volume 11, 1803-1819.

Jesup, Samuel, late of Stamford, will dated Nov. 17, 1812, probated Dec. 1, 1812, all to his daughter Elizabeth Jesup. Executors Joseph Gray and Cary Leeds. Witnesses Abram Leeds, Benjamin Tryon, and Rowland Tryon, page 455.
Dec. 1, 1812, order to advertise for claims, page 455.
Dec. 5, 1812, real estate ordered sold to pay debts, page 455.
Inventory taken Dec. 2, 1812, by Joseph Gray and Abram Leeds, and filed Dec. 5, 1812, page 456.
July 6, 1813, report of commissioners to adjust claims filed, page 456.
July 6, 1813, real estate ordered sold to pay debts, page 456.

Jones, Isaac, late of Stamford, inventory taken Dec. 13, 1814, by Nathan Weed and Isaac Pencyer, and filed Dec. 14, 1814, page 309.
Nov. 11, 1815, estate distributed to his children Selleck Jones, Abigail wife of Samuel Gorham, Isaac Jones, and Benjamin Jones, page 311.

Jones, Isaac, late of Stamford, May 11, 1818, letters of administration on his estate granted to Selleck Jones, who was ordered to advertise for claims, page 485.
Inventory taken by Samuel Waring and Uriah Waterbury, and filed Oct. 6, 1818, page 560.

Jones, Smith, late of Stamford, June 6, 1809, letters of administration on his estate granted to Lewis S. Lockwood page 44.
Inventory taken June 21, 1809, by Jeremiah Curtis and John Seely, and filed July 5, 1809, pages 44 and 45.
Aug. 10, 1809, order to advertise for claims, page 45.
Mch. 27, 1810, account filed, and estate ordered distributed to his sisters and brothers, viz: Abigail wife of Seth Stevens, Hannah wife of Lewis S. Lockwood, Sally wife of Joseph Allen, Isaac Jones, and Smith Jones, a son of Amos Jones, a deceased brother, page 45.
Apl. 7, 1810, estate distributed accordingly, page 46.

Knapp, Abel, late of Stamford, Nov. 8, 1816, the court appointed Isaac Bell guardian of Noah Knapp, a son of decedent, about 14 years of age, page 272.

Knapp, Anna, Apl. 24, 1815, guardian of Silas Knapp and Esther M. Knapp, asked for leave to sell the real estate of said minors, page 494, and sale authorized, page 495

STAMFORD PROBATE RECORDS.
Volume 11, 1803-1819.

Knapp, Daniel, late of Stamford, Oct. 14, 1816, the court appointed David Holly guardian of Sally Knapp, a daughter of decedent, about 14 years of age, page 260.

Knapp, David, late of Greenwich, will dated June 27, 1812, probated Feb. 2, 1813, mentions his wife Elizabeth, and children David B., Abby L., and Nehemiah. Executor Jabez Mead. Witnesses Frederick Betts, Peter Horton, and Nathaniel Olcott, page 495.
Feb. 2, 1813, the executor refused to qualify and letters with the will annexed granted to Elizabeth Knapp, page 495.
Inventory taken Apl. 20, 1813, by Nathaniel Olcott and John Adams, 3rd, and filed Nov. 1, 1814, page 496.
July 4, 1815, account filed, and real estate ordered sold to pay debts, page 497.

Knapp, Edward, late of Stamford, a soldier in the United States Army, Nov. 27, 1815, letters of administration on his estate granted to John Brown, Jr., who was ordered to advertise for claims, page 73.

Knapp, Israel, late of Greenwich, Feb. 20, 1813, that part of his real estate set off to his widow for her dower, ordered distributed to Sally wife of David Wood, Betsy wife of John McKay, Anna wife of William Thorn, Cornelia wife of David Reed; to Charles K. Thompson and William A. Thompson, the legal representatives of Fanny Thompson, deceased; to Adaline Thompson, Margaret Thompson, Cornelia Thompson, Caroline Thompson, Harriet Thompson, and James Thompson, the legal representatives Amy Thompson, deceased, page 476.
May 4, 1813, estate distributed to Sally W. wife of David Wood, a daughter; Elizabeth McKay, a daughter; Charles K. Thompson and William A. Thompson, children of Fanny Thompson, a deceased daughter; Ann wife of William Thorn, a daughter; Cornelia wife of David Reed, a daughter; Adeline Palmer, Margaret Thomson, Cornelia Thompson, Caroline Thompson, Harriet Thompson, and James Thompson, page 476.

Knapp, John, late of Greenwich, will dated Jan. 5, 1814, probated Nov. 7, 1815, mentions his wife Rosannah, William Knapp, Jr., and Samuel Close, a son of Henry Close, deceased. Executors Abraham Close and Samuel Close. Witnesses Hervey Close, Nathaniel Mead, and Daniel Peck, page 466.
Nov. 7, 1815, Abraham Close refused to qualify and let-

STAMFORD PROBATE RECORDS.
Volume 11, 1803-1819.

Knapp, John, continued :
tters with the will annexed granted to Samuel Close, who was ordered to advertise for claims, page 467. Inventory taken Dec. 5, 1815, by Gilbert Close and Daniel Peck, and filed Dec. 5, 1815, page 467.

Knapp, Joshua, late of Stamford, Jan. 19, 1814, account filed by Augustus Lockwood, administrator, and real estate ordered sold to pay debts, page 464.

Knapp, Mary, widow, late of Greenwich, inventory taken July 4, 1815, by Isaac Holly, Jr., and William Keeler, and filed July 4, 1815, page 477.

Knapp, Mercy, late of Stamford, widow of Nathaniel Knapp, June 6, 1815, letters of administration on her estate granted to Abraham Lockwood, who was ordered to advertise for claims, page 68.

Knapp, Nathan, late of Stamford, May 9, 1815, that part of his estate set off to his widow for her dower, ordered distributed to Mary S. wife of Abraham Lockwood, a daughter of deceased; Nathan Knapp, a son; to the legal representatives of Adam Knapp, deceased, and to the legal representatives of Abel Knapp, deceased, page 464. Estate distributed accordingly, page 464.

Lane, Abraham, late of Rye, inventory taken Apl. 18, 1814, by Shubal Reynolds, Daniel Carpenter, Jr., George Lockwood, and Nathaniel Olcott, and filed May 3, 1814, page 437.

Leeds, Elisha, late of Stamford, inventory taken May 14, 1813, by Nathan Weed and Nathaniel Waterbury, and filed July 6, 1813, page 320.
Sept. 22, 1814, estate distributed to his widow, Sarah Leeds, and his children Sarah Weed, Polly Brown, Elisa Leeds, Charles Thorp Leeds, William Edward Leeds, and Caty Leeds, page 323.

Lewis, Amzi, Rev., late of Stamford, will dated Jan. 30, 1819, probated Apl. 12, 1819, mentions his wife Huldah, grandson Nathan W. Lewis, a son of my son Amzi Lewis, deceased; daughter Sally A. wife of Rev. Robert G. Armstrong; children of my daughter Clarissa, deceased, wife of Benjamin Howard of New Town, L. I.; children of my daughter Rachel, deceased, wife of Edward McLaughlin of New York City, excepting Edward A. McLaugh-

STAMFORD PROBATE RECORDS.
Volume 11, 1803-1819.

Lewis, Amzi, continued :
lin, one of the above children, and excepting William L
McLaughlin; grandson William Howard. Executors William Davenport and Abishai Scofield. Witnesses John
Augur, Seth Weed, and Ralph Hoyt, Jr., page 574.
Apl. 12, 1819, order to advertise for claims, page 576.
Inventory taken Apl. 14, 1819, by Reuben Scofield and
Warren Scofield, and filed Apl. 19, 1819, page 577.

Lewis, Beal N., late of New York City, Apl. 9, 1817, letters
of administration on his estate granted to Isaac Lewis
of Westchester County, Zachariah Lewis and Roswell W.
Lewis of New York City, who were ordered to advertise
for claims, page 309.

Lewis, Nathaniel B., late of New York City, inventory taken
May 1, 1817, of his property in Greenwich, by Ebenezer
Mead and Timothy Walker, and filed June 10, 1817,
page 390.

Lockwood, Amos, late of Greenwich, will dated June 2, 1812,
probated Apl. 10, 1816, mentions his friend Phebe Brown
niece Harriet Lockwood, both of Greenwich. Executrix
Phebe Brown. Witnesses David Mead, Sarah Peck, and
Shadrach Mead, page 510.
Apl. 10, 1816, order to advertise for claims, page 510.
Inventory taken Apl. 15, 1816, by Samuel Peck and Gideon Close, and filed June 4, 1816, page 214.

Lockwood, Bethiah, late of Stamford, widow of Edmond Lockwood,
will dated Oct. 10, 1815, probated Feb. 9, 1818, all to
Natte Schofield, the eldest son of her brother Jonathan
Schofield, and born of his first wife, called Natte or
Nathaniel. Executor said Nathaniel Schofield. Witnesses Elizabeth Studwell and Daniel Nichols, page 463.
Inventory taken Feb. 5, 1818, by Enos Waterbury and
Jonathan Weed, and filed, page 464.

Lockwood, Frederick, late of Greenwich, inventory taken Apl.
26, 1808, by Enos Lockwood and Joshua Ferris, and filed
June 7, 1808, page 207.

Lockwood, Gilbert, late of Greenwich, will dated Mch. 19, 1811
probated June 7, 1811, mentions his brothers Richard,
Andrew, Noah, sisters Tamer wife of Aaron Clark, and
Ruth and her son William. Executor William Waterbury, 4th. Witnesses Asa Ferris, Letitia Hendrie, and

STAMFORD PROBATE RECORDS.
Volume 11, 1803-1819.

Lockwood, Gilbert, continued:
    Samuel Webb, page 193.
    June 7, 1811, order to advertise for claims, page 194.
    Inventory taken July 1, 1811, by Asa Ferris and Alexander Hendrie, and filed July 2, 1811, page 194.
    Aug. 4, 1812, account filed, and distribution of his estate ordered to his brothers and sisters Richard, Andrew, Noah, Tamar Clark, and Ruth Lockwood, page 196.
    Sept. 17, 1812, estate distributed accordingly, page 197.

Lockwood, Gilbert, Sr., late of Greenwich, Mch. 3, 1812, that part of his estate set off to his widow as her dower, ordered distributed to his children Richard, Noah, Andrew, Elnathan, Edward, Amos, Ruth, Tamer, the legal representatives of Gilbert and Solomon, deceased, page 195.
    Mch. 1812, estate distributed to his children Tamar Clark, Ruth Lockwood, Noah, Andrew, Richard, Elnathan, Edward, and Amos, and to the legal representatives of Gilbert and Solomon, deceased, page 195.

Lockwood, Isaac, late of Stamford, will dated May 9, 1805, probated Nov. 5, 1816, mentions his children Isaac, Peter, Augustus, Frederick, Mary wife of Peter Selleck, Abigail wife of Frederick Hoyt, Betsy wife of Rev. Samuel Sturges, and Rebecca wife of Thaddeus Hoyt, Jr. Executors sons Isaac and Frederick. Witnesses Jerusha Davenport, Mary Davenport, and Ebenezer Davenport, page 263.
    Nov. 5, 1816, order to advertise for claims, page 265.
    Inventory taken Nov. 5, 1816, by Samuel Hoyt and Ezra Lockwood, and filed Nov. 5, 1816, page 265.
    Jan. 24, 1806, antinuptial agreement between said Isaac Lockwood and Mary Waring, widow of Samuel Waring, both of Stamford, page 263.

Lockwood, Jeremiah, Jr., late of Stamford, inventory taken Nov. 28, 1814, by Nathaniel Waterbury and John Waterbury, and filed Dec. 30, 1814, page 438.

Lockwood, Jonathan, late of Greenwich, 1811, letters of administration on his estate granted to Amelia Lockwood, page 191.
    Inventory taken June 11, 1811, by Enos Lockwood and Joshua Ferris, and filed Apl. 4, 1812, page 191.
    Apl. 7, 1812, estate ordered distributed to his widow, Amelia Lockwood, and his children David, Nancy wife of Ananias Lockwood, Hannah, and Clara, page 191.
    Estate distributed accordingly, page 192.

STAMFORD PROBATE RECORDS.
Volume 11, 1803-1819.

Lockwood, Jonathan, late of Greenwich, will dated Apl. 25, 1817, probated Sept. 9, 1817, mentions his wife Sarah and children Elizabeth, Sarah, Hannah, Lydia, Mary, Deborah, Alla, Edmond, Mills, and William; granddaughter Mariah Ferris. Executors sons Mills and William. Witnesses Hannah Smith, John Mackay, and David Wood, page 377.
Sept. 9, 1817, order to advertise for claims, one of the executors, William, now a minor, page 378.
Inventory taken Aug. 22, 1817, by Jared Smith and Ira Lockwood, and filed Sept. 9, 1817, page 378.

Lockwood, Stephen, late of Stamford, Nov. 14, 1814, his estate ordered distributed to his widow, Elizabeth Lockwood, and his children Henry, Oliver, Elizabeth Knapp, Mary, and Stephen, page 483.
Dec. 3, 1814, estate distributed accordingly, page 483.

Lockwood, Titus, late of Stamford, will dated Nov. 30, 1815, probated Jan. 15, 1816, mentions his wife Hannah, and children Peter, Isaac, Daniel, Ebenezer, Clarissa Warding, and grandson Andrew Mead, a son of my daughter Betsy Mead. Executors sons Daniel and Ebenezer. Witnesses Reuben Scofield, Hezekiah Bishop, and Thomas Close, page 77.
Jan. 15, 1816, order to advertise for claims, page 78.
Inventory taken Feb. 24, 1816, by Shadrach Lockwood and Silas Hoyt, Jr., and filed Feb. 26, 1816, page 164.
Mch. 31, 1817, dispute among his children as to advancements, page 309.

Lounsbury, Enos, Jr., late of Stamford, a soldier in the United States Army, Nov. 9, 1815, the court appointed Jesse Hoyt guardian of Sherman, Anne, and Charles, children of deceased, page 71.

Lounsberry, James, late of Stamford, inventory taken June 29, 1814, by Warren Scofield and Titus Lockwood, and filed July 5, 1814, page 477.
Feb. 7, 1815, account filed by Nathaniel Webb, Jr., administrator, and real estate ordered sold to pay debts, page 55.
Apl. 5, 1815, report of sale filed, page 56.
Apl. 4, 1815, estate ordered distributed to his widow, and children, and to the legal representatives of Jared Lounsberry, deceased; Isaac Lounsberry; Hannah widow of Abijah Bishop, Betsy Lounsberry, Samuel Lounsberry, and Sally Lounsberry, page 478.
Apl. 29, 1815, estate distributed accordingly, page 478.

STAMFORD PROBATE RECORDS.
Volume 11, 1803-1819.

Lounsbury, Jared, late of Stamford, inventory taken June 3,
1814, by Reuben Scofield and Warren Scofield, and filed
June 7, 1814, page 480.
May 2, 1815, real estate ordered sold to pay debts,
page 480.
Jan. 9, 1815, report of commissioners to adjust claims
of creditors filed, page 480.
May 2, 1815, commissioners appointed to set out the
dower of his widow, page 482.
May 12, 1815, dower set out, page 482.
June 6, 1815, account filed, and creditors ordered
paid, page 483.

Lounsberry, Lemuel, late of Stamford, Sept. 19, 1816, letters
of administration on his estate granted to Nehemiah
Lounsberry of Stamford, page 69.

Lounsberry, Thomas, late of Stamford, inventory taken by Nathaniel Waterbury and Jonathan Knapp, and filed Mch.
28, 1812, page 198.
Dec. 1, 1812, account filed by Josiah Smith and Uzal
Knapp, administrators, and real estate ordered sold to
pay debts, page 184.
Mch. 9, 1816, estate ordered distributed to his children Samuel, William, Edwin, Sally Ann, Polly, and Betsy
Ann, page 184.
Mch. 15, 1816, estate distributed accordingly, page 185.

Lyon, Andrew, late of Rye, will dated May 14, 1808, probated
Oct. 3, 1809, mentions the children of my late daughter
Sarah Halsted; grandson William Bush, a son of my
daughter Mary Bush; daughter Tamar wife of Roger Purdy;
granddaughters Sally Lyon Bush and Rebecca Bush; and
daughter-in-law Mary Lyon. Executors grandson William
Bush and Jared Peck. Witnesses William Coleman, John
Brown, and James Gray, page 200.
Codicil dated Aug. 13, 1809, mentions my grandchildren,
the children of my deceased son Underhill Lyon and
wife Mary, page 202.
Inventory taken Oct. 5, 1809, by Ebenezer Mead and Nehemiah Willson, and filed Dec. 7, 1809, page 203.

Lyon, Benjamin Woolsey, late of Greenwich, will dated July 6,
1810, probated Sept. 4, 1810, mentions his wife Phebe,
and children Mary Husted, Sarah, Woolsey, James, Daniel
and Thomas. Executrix his wife. Witnesses Mary
Banks, Catharine Banks, and Thomas Huggeford, Page 203.
Sept. 4, 1810, order to advertise for claims, page 204.

STAMFORD PROBATE RECORDS.
Volume 11, 1803-1819.

Lyon, Benjamin Woolsey, continued:
Inventory taken Sept. 13, 1810, by Ebenezer Mead and Joshua Lyon, and filed Nov. 6, 1810, page 205.

Lyon, Daniel, late of Greenwich, will dated Aug. 16, 1817, probated Sept. 15, 1817, mentions his children Hannah wife of Daniel Merritt, Lavinia wife of Henry S. Brooks Loretta wife of John Huter; grandchildren, the children of my daughter Elizabeth wife of Abraham Banks, both deceased, viz: Mary wife of Daniel Baker, Daniel Banks, and Joseph Banks. Executors said Henry S. Brooks and John Huter. Witnesses Henry Strang, Hannah Miller and Rivers Morrell, page 379.
Sept. 17, 1817, order to advertise for claims, page 379
Inventory taken Sept. 15, 1817, and filed Sept. 15, 1817, page 380.

Lyon, Gilbert, late of Greenwich, will dated Aug. 28, 1809, probated June 5, 1816, mentions his children Abraham, Gilbert, deceased, Joshua, Andrew, Deborah Merritt, Sarah Miller, Abigail Purdy, and Elizabeth Lyon; grandson Thomas Lyon; granddaughters Betsy Lyon and Anne Lyon; children of granddaughter Jane Hubbs; father Thomas Lyon; brother Jonathan Lyon; Mary widow of Simeon Lyon. Executors son Joshua Lyon and son-in-law Samuel Lyon. Witnesses Jabez Fitch, Jacob Fletcher, and Elizabeth Fitch, page 210.
June 5, 1816, order to advertise for claims, page 213.
Inventory taken May 30, 1816, by Ebenezer Mead and Benjamin Peck, and filed June 4, 1816, page 213.

McEntire, John, late of Stamford, Sept. 26, 1818, letters of administration on his estate granted to Jeremiah Andreas, who was ordered to advertise for claims, page 572
Inventory taken Sept. 30, 1818, by John Bell and Cary Bell, and filed Nov. 2, 1818, page 572.

Madden, Amos, late of Greenwich, Jan. 18, 1819, letters of administration on his estate granted to Aaron Sherwood, the widow having refused to qualify, who was ordered to advertise for claims, page 571.
Inventory taken Jan. 20, 1819, by Hezekiah Tracy and Jabez Mead, and filed Feb. 4, 1819, page 571.

Marshall, Eliza, a minor of Greenwich, about 13 years of age, Apl. 10, 1819, made choice of Eliakim Lockwood of Greenwich to be her guardian, page 551.

STAMFORD PROBATE RECORDS.
Volume 11, 1803-1819.

Marshall Ezra, late of Greenwich, inventory taken Nov. 7,
   1814, by Ebenezer Mead, Jr., and Robert Mead, and filed Nov. 8, 1814, pages 403 and 404.
   June 7, 1815, report of commissioners to adjust claims of creditors filed, page 404.
   July 4, 1815, account filed, and real estate ordered sold to pay debts, page 404.
   July 14, 1815, date of sale, page 405.

Mead, Abner, late of Greenwich, will dated July 29, 1808, probated June 12, 1810, mentions his brothers Silas, Jr., Aaron, Calvin, sister Mary wife of Jonah Mead. Executor brother Silas Mead, Jr. Witnesses Harrison June, William Finch, Jr., and Zophar Mead, Jr., page 159.
   Inventory taken June 20, 1810, by Gilbert Close and Darius Mead, and filed July 3, 1810, page 161.

Mead, Amos, late of Greenwich, May 6, 1808, on the application of Richard Mead, administrator, commissioners were appointed to set out the dower of his widow, Martha Mead, page 159.

Mead, Angelina A., a minor of Greenwich, Mch. 17, 1814, petition by her guardian Ebenezer Mead for leave to sell the real estate of said minor, page 10.
   June 15, 1814, order authorizing sale, page 10.
   Mch. 3, 1818, then about 11 years of age, the court appointed Timothy Walker of Greenwich to be her guardian, page 451.

Mead, Benjamin, late of Greenwich, will dated May 13, 1809, probated Mch. 14, 1815, mentions his wife Mary, and children Anne widow of David Mead, Theodosia late wife of Edmund Mead, Mary wife of Samuel Peck, Phebe wife of Jehiel Mead, Jr., grandsons Brochurst Mead and Obadiah Mead, sons of said Edmund Mead. Executor Samuel Peck. Witnesses James Nash, Enoch Youngs, and Permila Rowell, page 492.
   Mch. 14, 1815, the executor refused to qualify and letters with the will annexed granted to Obadiah Mead, who was ordered to advertise for claims, page 494.
   Inventory taken Mch. 16, 1815, and filed Apl. 4, 1815, page 494.

Mead, Charity, late of Greenwich, inventory taken by Nathaniel Heusted and Isaac How, and filed June 6, 1815, page 422.
   Nov. 9, 1816, estate ordered distributed to her chil-

STAMFORD PROBATE RECORDS.
Volume 11, 1803-1819.

71.

Mead, Charity, continued :
    dren Jasper Mead, Charity wife of Joshua Knapp, Rebecca wife of Shubal Knapp, Nathaniel Mead, William Mead, Betsy Mead, and Anna wife of Gilbert Totten, page 272. Nov. 15, 1816, estate distributed accordingly, page 274.

Mead, Ebenezer, late of Greenwich, will dated Mch. 15, 1817, probated Mch. 3, 1818, mentions his wife Nancy, and children Marilda wife of Samuel Bouton, Ebenezer, Reuma wife of Timothy Walker, and Jabez; granddaughter Angelina Amy Mead. Executors son Ebenezer and Timothy Walker. Witnesses Jabez Mead, John Mead, Jr., and Joseph Wright, page 457.
    Mch. 3, 1818, order to advertise for claims, page 459.
    Inventory taken Mch. 25, 1818, by Isaac Holly and Jabez Mead, and filed Apl. 7, 1818, page 473.
    Apl. 6, 1819, additional inventory filed, page 551.

Mead, Eliphalet, late of Greenwich, May 5, 1818, letters of administration on his estate granted to Darius Mead, who was ordered to advertise for claims, page 484.
    Inventory taken July 4, 1818, and filed July 7, 1818, pages 527 and 528.
    July 7, 1818, order to advertise for claims, and real estate ordered sold to pay debts, page 528.
    July 25, 1818, date of sale, page 528.
    Aug. 3, 1818, commissioners appointed to adjust claims of creditors, page 529.
    Feb. 9, 1819, report of commissioners filed, page 549.

Mead, Elkanah, late of Greenwich, will dated Jan. 16, 1804, probated July 2, 1816, mentions his children Hannah, Sally, and Amos. Executor son Amos. Witnesses Clark Sanford, Frederick Lockwood, and Enos Lockwood, page 221.
    July 2, 1816, order to advertise for claims, page 222.
    Inventory taken July 8, 1816, by Charles Smith and Benjamin Brush, and filed Aug. 6, 1816, page 241.

Mead, Jeremiah, late of Greenwich, Feb. 23, 1815, inventory taken by Nathaniel Ferris and Charles Smith, and filed Mch. 17, 1815, page 454.

Mead, Joshua, late of Greenwich, June 15, 1812, letters of administration on his estate granted to Jonathan Mead, Jr., and Darius Mead, Jr., who were ordered to advertise for claims, page 338.
    May 6, 1813, estate distributed to his widow Hannah Mead, and to his children Jonathan, Joshua, Prudence,

STAMFORD PROBATE RECORDS.
Volume 11, 1803-1819.

Mead, Joshua, continued :
David, Mary, Rachel, Darius, and Solomon, page 339.

Mead, Martha, late of Stamford, inventory taken Apl. 13, 1812, by David Holly and Frederick Scofield, and filed Apl. 13, 1812, page 158.

Mead, Mary, Mrs., late of Greenwich, inventory taken July 1, 1813, by Samuel Bush and Jared Mead, and filed Aug. 3, 1813, page 337.

Mead, Mary, late of Greenwich, Apl. 2, 1816, on the application of Justus B. Mead, administrator, estate ordered distributed to her children Betsy Brown, Ruth Bouton; children of Mary Grigg, deceased; Anna Denton, Rebecca Moore, Charity Howell, Sarah Fancher, Pamela Marshall, Matthew Mead, Justus B. Mead, Amos Mead, and Bush Mead, page 219.
Apl. 24, 1816, estate distributed accordingly, page 219.

Mead, Nathaniel, 3rd, late of Greenwich, will dated Mch. 12, 1804, probated Apl. 11, 1814, mentions his wife Martha, and children Martha Lockwood, Prudence Bradwell, Nehemiah, Nathaniel, William, Walter, Tyler, Harvey, Anna Sutton, Hannah Steut(?), and Betsy. Executrix his wife Witnesses Annis Hubby, Sarah Fitch, and Shadrach Mead, page 401.
Apl. 11, 1814, order to advertise for claims, page 402.
Nov. 15, 1814, account filed, and real estate ordered sold to pay debts, page 403, and inventory page 402.
Nov. 18, 1814, date of sale, page 403.

Mead, Nathaniel, late of Greenwich, inventory taken by Nathaniel Heusted and Isaac How, and filed Apl. 4, 1815, page 421.
June 19, 1816, account filed by Nathaniel Knapp, administrator, and real estate ordered sold to pay debts, page 422.
Nov. 9, 1816, estate ordered distributed to his children Jasper, Charity wife of Joshua Knapp, Rebecca wife of Shubal Knapp, Nathaniel, William, Betsy, and Anna wife of Gilbert Totten, page 272.
Nov. 15, 1816, estate distributed accordingly, page 274.

Mead, Nathaniel, Jr., late of Greenwich, will dated Dec. 16, 1805, probated Sept. 29, 1818, mentions his wife Elizabeth, and children Smith, Josiah, Hannah, Abigail Denton, Nathaniel, John, Betsy Palmer, and Thomas. Ex-

STAMFORD PROBATE RECORDS.
Volume 11, 1803-1819.

Mead, Nathaniel, Jr., continued :
    ecutor son Thomas. Witnesses Joseph Morrell, Elizabeth Fitch and Jabez Fitch, page 536.
    Sept. 29, 1818, order to advertise for claims, page 538.
    Inventory taken Oct. 19, 1818, by Peter Mead and William Husted, and filed Nov. 3, 1818, page 555.

Mead, Polly, late of Stamford, Nov. 5, 1816, letters of administration on her estate granted to Augustus Lockwood who was ordered to advertise for claims, page 272. Inventory taken Dec. 3, 1816, by Ezra Lockwood and Isaac Lockwood, and filed Dec. 3, 1816, page 276.

Mead, Riley, a minor of Greenwich, June 10, 1816, made choice of Hezekiah Tracy to be his guardian, page 215.

Mead, Sarah, late of Greenwich, widow of Nehemiah Mead, will dated Feb. 1804, probated Sept. 1808, mentions her children Nehemiah Mead, Lucy wife of Isaac Howe, Rachel wife of Charles Weed, Bethiah wife of Stephen Davis, and Clarinda wife of Isaac Mead, Jr.; granddaughter Sophia wife of Peter Demill of New York City. Executor son Nehemiah. Witnesses Robert Mead, Rachel Mead, and Prudence Mead, page 342.

Mead, Silas, Jr., late of Greenwich, June 29, 1813, letters of administration on his estate granted to Jabez Mead, who was ordered to advertise for claims, page 502. Inventory taken July 9, 1813, by Calvin Mead and Zophar Mead, Jr., and filed Aug. 3, 1813, page 502.
Feb. 25, 1815, petition of Jabez Mead, guardian of Sarah, Silas H., and Francis, minor children of decedent, for leave to sell the real estate of said minors, page 502, also another petition on page 43, dated Dec. 6, 1814, and order authorizing sale, dated Feb. 21, 1815, page 44.
Apl. 1, 1816, estate distributed to Silas H. Mead, Sarah Mead, and Francis Mead, page 235.

Mead, Titus, late of Greenwich, will dated May 8, 1812, probated Sept. 25, 1812, mentions his wife Tamise, and children Andrew, Hardy, Titus, deceased, Jabez, Ira, and his wife Nancy, daughters not named. Executor his son Shadrach. Witnesses Justus Sackett, Jr., Henry Knapp, and Hannah Banks, page 153.
Sept. 25, 1812, order to advertise for claims, page 155.
Inventory taken Sept. 22, 1812, by Samuel Peck and Isaac Holly, and filed Sept. 28, 1812, page 155.

STAMFORD PROBATE RECORDS.
Volume 11, 1803-1819.

Merritt, Joseph, late of Harrison, Westchester County, N. Y., will dated Aug. 10, 1807, probated June 12, 1813, mentions his wife Wilmot Merritt, and children Susannah, Elizabeth, Henry, John, and James; brother James Merritt; sister Mary; father Nathan Merritt. Executors William Field, Joseph Carpenter, and Thomas Clapp. Witnesses John Hallsted, William Hallsted, and Daniel Hallsted, page 406.
Codicil dated Mch. 17, 1809, mentions his brother Jotham Merritt, and sister Mary Manna, page 407.
Inventory taken 8th month, 23rd day, 1813, by Thomas Carpenter and James Field, and filed Dec. 7, 1813, page 408.

Merritt, Jotham, late of Greenwich, inventory taken Mch. 8, 1814, by Ebenezer Mead and Platt Mead, and filed Apl. 7, 1814, pages 502 and 503.
Apl. 7, 1814, estate ordered distributed to his widow, Mary W. Merritt, and to his children Elizabeth, Harriet, Caroline, and Jotham, page 503.
Apl. 28, 1814, estate distributed accordingly, page 504.
Apl. 15, 1815, account filed, and May 8, 1815, the residue of his estate distributed in accordance with the foregoing order, page 506.

Miller, Anna, Oct. 22, 1814, parent of Eliza Ann Miller, Elbert Alonzo Miller, and Maria Emeline Miller, asked for leave to sell the real estate of said minors, page 463.
Feb. 7, 1815, order authorizing sale, page 54.
Apl. 5, 1815, report of sale filed, page 55.

Miller, James, late of New York City, inventory taken Oct. 29, 1813, by Frederick Hait and Joel Waring, and filed Nov. 27, 1813, and Apl. 10, 1814, page 462.
Feb. 7, 1815, account filed by Timothy Raynolds, administrator, and real estate ordered sold to pay debts, page 55.
Apl. 5, 1815, report of sale filed, page 55.

Miller, Westover, late of Greenwich, inventory taken Feb. 22, 1810, by Ebenezer Mead and Nehemiah Willson, and filed Feb. 22, 1810, page 99.

Moore, George, late of Greenwich, will dated in 1809, but probate refused Jan. 18, 1813, all to his wife Sarah. Executor Nehemiah Willson. Witnesses Joshua Banks, Jared Ritch, and Obadiah Banks, Jr., page 162.

STAMFORD PROBATE RECORDS.
Volume 11, 1803-1819.

Moore, George, continued :
    Jan. 18, 1813, letters of administration on his estate
    granted to Peter Mead, page 163.
    Inventory taken Jan. 20, 1813, by William Husted and
    Zaccheus Mead, and filed Jan. 21, 1813, page 163.
    Mch. 7, 1814, account filed, and real estate ordered
    sold to pay debts, page 164.
    Apl. 5, 1814, report of sale filed, page 164.

Morehouse, Andrew, late of Stamford, Dec. 2, 1817, letters of
    administration on his estate granted to Solomon Clason
    and Mary Morehouse, who were ordered to advertise for
    claims, page 420.
    Inventory taken Dec. 22, 1817, by Daniel Lockwood, Jr.,
    and Caleb Knapp, and filed, page 433.
    Jan. 6, 1818, account filed, and real estate ordered
    sold to pay debts, page 433.
    Jan. 17, 1818, commissioners appointed to adjust claims
    of creditors, page 441.
    Aug. 4, 1818, report of commissioners filed, page 543.
    Dec. 15, 1818, account filed, and creditors ordered
    paid, page 543.

Nichols, Elizabeth, late of Stamford, Apl. 7, 1812, estate or-
    dered distributed to her children Elizabeth wife of
    John Scofield, Daniel Nichols, John Nichols, Joseph
    Nichols, Ruth wife of Joshua Knapp, Mary wife of Will-
    iam June, Robert Nichols, Abraham Nichols, and David
    Nichols, page 180.
    Apl. 16, 1812, estate distributed accordingly, page 180.

Nichols, James, late of Stamford, inventory taken June 1, 1807
    by Isaac Lockwood and Ezra Lockwood, and filed June 1,
    1807, page 134.

Nichols, Robert, late of Stamford, Sept. 6, 1814, estate or-
    dered distributed to his heirs Elizabeth wife of John
    Scofield, Daniel Nichols, Joseph Nichols, John Nichols,
    Ruth Knapp, Mary wife of William June, Robert Nichols,
    the heirs of Abraham Nichols, deceased, and David
    Nichols, page 405.
    Nov. 2, 1814, estate distributed accordingly, page 178.

Olcott, Nathaniel, Jan. 2, 1816, his son William Olcott, made
    choice of Lemuel Ferris of Greenwich to be his guardi-
    an, page 79.

STAMFORD PROBATE RECORDS.
Volume 11, 1803-1819.

Palmer, Alva, Dec. 7, 1817, guardian of Samuel Palmer, Seely Palmer, and Linus Palmer, all of Greenwich, asked leave to sell the real estate of said minors, page 421.
Feb. 13, 1818, order authorizing sale, page 450.

Palmer, Ferris, late of Stamford, Oct. 10, 1814, account filed by Simeon H. Minor, administrator, and real estate ordered sold to pay debts, page 39.
Aug. 22, 1814, report of commissioners to adjust claims of creditors filed, page 39.
1815, on the application of Simeon H. Minor, administrator, estate ordered distributed to his brothers and sisters Messenger, Ralph, Oliver, Asa, Sybil W. wife of Joseph Ferris, and Hetty wife of Waite Webb, page 177.
Apl. 11, 1815, estate distributed accordingly, page 177.

Palmer, Gilbert, late of North Castle, will dated Aug. 22, 1799, probated Mch. 22, 1810, mentions his wife ----, and children John, Mary Tripp, Hannah Doughty, Sarah Hopkins, Phebe Disco, and Margery Robbins; granddaughters Charlotte Palmer and Elizabeth Palmer; and Harrison Aikins, a son of said Hannah Doughty. Executors his wife, his son John, and son-in-law Daniel Tripp. Witnesses Daniel Tripp, John Tripp, and Samuel Tripp, page 16.
Inventory taken Feb. 26, 1810, by Silas Mead, Jr., and David D. Heusted, and filed Mch. 22, 1810, page 19.

Palmer, John, late of North Castle, will dated Apl. 12, 1817, probated Apl. 5, 1819, mentions his wife Phanny; John Tripp; John Hopkins, a son of my sister Sarah Hopkins; sisters Mary Tripp, Hannah Doty, Sarah Hopkins, and Margery Robbins, nieces Elizabeth Tolaton and Charlotte Palmer. Executors Oliver Green and Samuel H. Tripp. Witnesses William Bowron, John Hoag, and Mary Bowron, page 579.
Apl. 5, 1819, order to advertise for claims, page 580.
Inventory taken by James Nash and Benjamin Husted, Jr., and filed May 28, 1819, page 581.

Palmer, Justus, late of Greenwich, 1812, letters of administration on his estate granted to John Lane, who was ordered to advertise for claims, page 167.
Inventory taken July 27, 1812, by Lemuel Ferris and Jabez Mead, and filed Sept. 1, 1812, page 168.

STAMFORD PROBATE RECORDS.
Volume 11, 1803-1819.

Palmer, Lockwood, about 19 years of age, and Nathaniel Palmer, about 18 years of age, Feb. 21, 1818, made choice of Nathan Palmer of Poundridge to be their guardian, page 459.

Palmer, Phebe, late of Greenwich, will dated Jan. 30, 1812, probated Dec. 2, 1817, mentions her children Winas Palmer, Elizabeth Ferris, and Anna Reynolds. Mentions notes payable to Winas Palmer, Mercy wife of William Jordon, and Anna Reynolds. Executors Silas Sutherland Jr., and James Palmer. Witnesses John B. Sutherland and Silas Sutherland, page 422.
Dec. 2, 1817, order to advertise for claims, page 423.
Aug. 3, 1818, account filed, and distribution ordered t to her children Winas Palmer and Elizabeth Ferris. Anna Reynolds died before testatrix, her share to her legal representatives, said Winas Palmer and Elizabeth Ferris, Jonathan Palmer, Benjamin G. Palmer, and to the legal representatives of Mercy Jordon, children of testatrix, pages 535 and 536.

Palmer, Samuel, late of Greenwich, will dated Apl. 15, 1813, probated May 12, 1813, mentions his wife Mary, and children William, Rundle, David, Alva, Marcus, Seely, Samuel, Linus, Delia, and Hannah. Executors my faithful brother Levi Palmer, and my beloved son William. Witnesses Levi Palmer, William Knapp, 3rd, and Elisha R. Belcher, page 118.
May 12, 1813, order to advertise for claims, page 119. Inventory taken my Tompkins Close and Isaac Peck 3rd, and filed July 6, 1813, page 120.

Palmer, Seely, a minor, about 20 years of age/ Dec. 1, 1817, made choice of Alva Palmer to be his guardian, his former guardian, Tompkins Close, having been discharged, page 420.

Palmer, Winas, late of Greenwich, Dec. 23, 1817, estate ordered distributed to his children Winas, Jonathan, Benjamin G., Elizabeth wife of Solomon Ferris, the legal representatives of Marcy Jordon, deceased, and of Anna Reynolds, deceased, page 431.
Jan. 3, 1818, estate distributed accordingly, page 432.

Parketing, Abraham, a minor of Stamford, about 16 years of age, Apl. 7, 1811, the court appointed Hanford Hoyt to by his guardian, page 40. Cary Leeds appointed guardian in place of Hanford Hoyt, Feb. 15, 1815, page 40.

STAMFORD PROBATE RECORDS.
Volume 11, 1803-1819.

Parkston, Rodney, a minor of Greenwich, about 16 years of age, Feb. 3, 1817, made choice of Daniel Haight of Greenwich to be his guardian, page 279.

Peck, Blackman, and Ralph, minors of Greenwich, Mch. 18, 1816, made choice of Sally Peck to be their guardian, page 164

Peck, Hannah, widow, late of Greenwich, will dated Aug. 17, 1816, probated Oct. 1, 1816, mentions her grandson Robert Peck, Jr., son of Robert Peck, Jr., deceased; granddaughter Anna Peck, a daughter of Robert Peck, Jr., deceased; daughter Anna Knapp widow of Silas Knapp, deceased, of Washington, Dutchess County, N. Y.; daughter Esther wife of Seth Lawton of said Washington; grandson Silas Knapp, a son of Silas Knapp, deceased, of said Washington; grandchildren, the children of Jonathan Knapp of said Washington, viz: Levina, Hannah, Jonathan, Sally Ann, Amanda, and Alanson; son Abraham Peck of the State of Ohio. Executor Samuel Peck. Witnesses Thomas M. Wilson, Bethiah Davis, and Israel Peck, page 249.
Oct. 1, 1816, the executor refused to qualify, and letters with the will annexed granted to Isaac Peck, 3rd, who was ordered to advertise for claims, page 251.

Peck, Israel, late of Greenwich, will dated Dec. 31, 1818, probated Feb. 1, 1819, mentions his wife Levina, and children Israel, Nehemiah, Rachel, and Levina wife of Nathan Brown of the State of New York. Executors sons Nehemiah and Israel. Witnesses Elisha Belcher, Daniel Peck, and Jonas Howe, page 564.
Feb. 1, 1819, order to advertise for claims, page 570.
Inventory taken Feb. 17, 1819, by Gilbert Close and Isaac How, and filed Nov. 5, 1819, page 570.

Peck, Jerusha, late of Greenwich, Nov. 16, 1818, letters of administration on her estate granted to Aaron Husted, who was ordered to advertise for claims, page 562.
Inventory taken Nov. 20, 1818, by Andrew Mead and William Husted, and filed Dec. 1, 1818, page 563.

Peck, Samuel, late of Stamford, Apl. 5, 1815, letters of administration on his estate granted to Abigail Peck, widow of deceased, who was ordered to advertise for claims, page 54.
Inventory taken by Enos Knapp and Ebenezer Peck, and filed Dec. 5, 1815, page 513.

STAMFORD PROBATE RECORDS.
Volume 11, 1803-1819.

Peck, Solomon, late of Greenwich, Aug. 20, 1816, letters of administration on his estate granted to Mary Peck, who was ordered to advertise for claims, page 246.
Inventory taken Oct. 5, 1816, by Jonathan Ferris and Jeduthan Ferris, and filed Oct. 19, 1816, page 261.
Oct. 28, 1816, the court appointed Mary Peck guardian of John F., about 2; Jeduthan, about 6; Emeline, about 11; and Solomon, about 14; children of decedent, page 262.
Oct. 28, 1816, it appearing that the deceased was the owner in common with Ethan Ferris and Samuel Ferris of certain Real Estate, partition thereof was ordered, page 262.
Dec. 9, 1816, partition accordingly made, page 283.
Oct. 28, 1816, estate ordered distributed to his widow, Mary Peck, and children Solomon, Emeline, Jeduthan, and John F., page 283.
Jan. 23, 1817, estate distributed accordingly, page 284.
Feb. 4, 1817, petition for leave to sell the real estate of said minors, page 285.
Feb. 6, 1818, order authorizing same, page 453.

Perry, Sturges, late of Stamford, inventory taken Mch. 12, 1806, by Jeremiah Andreas and Joseph Bishop, and filed Mch. 19, 1806, by the administrator, page 128.

Peterson, Frederick, late of Stamford, May 15, 1812, letters of administration on his estate granted to Amos Roberts page 172.
Inventory taken May 16, 1812, by Noyes Richards and Isaac Hoyt, Jr., and filed May 22, 1812, page 172.
May 22, 1812, commissioners appointed to adjust claims of creditors, page 172.
Dec. 23, 1812, report of commissioners filed, page 173.

Provost, Salmon, late of Stamford, Nov. 18, 1815, letters of administration on his estate granted to Samuel Provost, page 73.

Purdy, Daniel, late of Greenwich, will dated Apl. 14, 1817, probated May 6, 1817, mentions his wife Abigail, and children John, Nehemiah, Daniel, William, Rebecca Townsend, and Hannah Matthias. Executrix wife and sons John and Nehemiah. Witnesses Jesse Slawson, Gilbert Totten, and Elisha Belcher, page 346.
May 6, 1817, order to advertise for claims, page 346.
Inventory taken May 13, 1817, by Ebenezer Mead and Joshua Lyon, and filed May 22, 1817, page 349.

STAMFORD PROBATE RECORDS.
Volume 11, 1803-1819.

Purdy, Daniel, continued :
 Apl. 25, 1818, estate ordered distributed to his widow, and children Nehemiah, Daniel, and William, according to his will, page 521.
 Apl. 28, 1818, estate distributed accordingly, page 521.

Quenett, Hannah, late of Stamford, 1813, letters of administration on her estate granted to Amos Weed, who was ordered to advertise for claims, page 174.
 Inventory taken Oct. 5, 1813, by Benjamin Weed and William Hoyt, and filed Oct. 16, 1813, page 174.
 May 5, 1814, estate distributed to her brother Peter Mead, sister Jerusha Smith, sister Sarah Town, sister Mary Lockwood, and to the legal representatives of Abigail Bayard, a deceased sister, page 176.

Quintard, Peter, 3rd, late of Stamford, inventory taken by S. H. Minor and Isaac Ambler, and filed Dec. 25, 1809, by the administrator, page 165.

Quintard, Peter, late of Stamford, inventory taken Oct. 25, 1813, by Jeremiah Andreas and Jonathan Bishop, and filed Nov. 2, 1813, page 397.

Quintard, Peter, late of Stamford, will dated Aug. 5, 1814, probated June 13, 1817, mentions his wife Elizabeth, and children Polly White, Isaac, Fanny Hennesy, and Abraham. Executor son Isaac. Witnesses James Stevens, Stephen White, and Samuel Webb, page 353.
 June 13, 1817, the executor refused to qualify and letters with the will annexed granted to testator's widow, page 353.
 Inventory taken June 19, 1817, by Samuel Hoyt and Samuel Webb, and filed July 1, 1817, page 357.

Raymond, Ezra, late of Stamford, inventory taken July 28, 1812 by Frederick Hait and Joel Waring, and filed Aug. 4, 1812, by the administrator, page 381.
 Apl. 5, 1813, report of commissioners to adjust claims filed, page 382.

Raymond, Ira, late of Stamford, will dated Feb. 22, 1816, probated Apl. 2, 1816, mentions his wife Thirza, and children Samuel Lewis, and Sally Ann. Executor Jeremiah Curtis. Witnesses Stephen Bishop, Enoch Stevens, and Gould Raymond, page 188.
 Apl. 2, 1816, order to advertise for claims, page 188.
 Inventory taken Mch. 29, 1816, by Enoch Stevens and

STAMFORD PROBATE RECORDS.
Volume 11, 1803-1819.

Raymond, Ira, continued :
    Jacob Stevens, and filed Apl. 2, 1816, page 189.
    Feb. 5, 1817, account filed, and real estate ordered
    sold to pay debts, page 282.

Reynolds, Horton, late of Greenwich, inventory taken Mch. 9/
    1814, by Gideon Close and Samuel Peck, and filed Mch.
    12, 1814, page 394.
    Feb. 7, 1815, the court appointed Joseph Ingersoll
    guardian of James Horton Reynolds and John Ingersoll
    Reynolds, children of decedent; and on Feb. 8, 1815,
    the court appointed Abigail Reynolds guardian of Abi-
    gail Jane Reynolds and Emeline Reynolds, other chil-
    dren of decedent, page 40.
    Mch. 18, 1815, estate ordered distributed to his widow,
    Abigail Reynolds, now the wife of Shadrach Mead, and
    children James H., Abigail J., Emeline, and John I.,
    page 361.
    Apl. 17, 1815, estate distributed accordingly, page 361.

Reynolds, Isaac P., late of New York City, Dec. 7, 1818, the
    court appointed Deborah Reynolds of Greenwich guardian
    of Nathaniel and George, sons of decedent, page 571.

Reynolds, Joseph, late of Greenwich, will dated Mch. 31, 1812,
    probated Nov. 7, 1815, mentions his daughters Semantha
    Brush, and Sarah Holly; grandson Joseph Brush; and
    granddaughter Semantha R. Holly. Executors sons-in
    law Benjamin Brush and Isaac Holly. Witnesses Richard
    Studwell, Phebe Lockwood, and David Wood, page 395.
    Inventory taken Oct. 25, 1815, by Charles Smith and
    James Smith, and filed Nov. 7, 1815, page 396.

Reynolds, Lydia, late of Greenwich, will dated Mch. 30, 1801,
    probated Aug. 3, 1812, mentions her children Horton Rey-
    nolds, Charity Platt, Lydia Belcher, Bethiah Sackett,
    Rachel Sanford, Ruth Knapp, Anna Hobby, and Polly War-
    ing; granddaughter Lydia K. Belcher. Executor son-in-
    law Elisha Belcher. Witnesses Stephen Waring, Alla
    Belcher, and Polly Belcher, page 383.
    Codicil dated Feb. 10, 1808, daughter Charity Platt,
    now deceased, page 383.
    Aug. 3, 1812, order to advertise for claims, page 384.
    Inventory taken Sept. 2, 1812, by Job Lyon and David
    Mead, and filed Nov. 16, 1812, page 385.

Reynolds, Timothy, late of Stamford, will dated Aug. 12, 1815,
    probated Feb. 20, 1816, all to his only child Samuel
    Hoyt Reynolds. If he died without issue than to the

STAMFORD PROBATE RECORDS.
Volume 11, 1803-1819.

Reynolds, Timothy, continued :
    children of Sarah Ayres the sister of my late wife ; brothers Jared, Abel, George, Asa, Elijah, and sister Abigail Peck. Executors Seth Smith and brother Abel Reynolds. Witnesses David Smith, 3rd, Silvanus Marshall, and Joseph Smith, 4th, page 151.
    Feb. 20, 1816, order to advertise for claims, page 152.
    Inventory taken Feb. 24, 1816, by Joseph Waring and Smith Clason, and filed Feb. 24, 1816, page 395.
    Feb. 24, 1816, the court appointed Seth Smith guardian of Samuel Hoyt Reynolds, a son of decedent, about five years of age, page 158.

Reynolds, William, of Chester, Warren County, N. Y., Jan. 6, 1818, parent and natural guardian of William P. Reynolds and Allen Reynolds, asked leave to sell the real estate of said minors, page 431.
    June 24, 1818, order authorizing sale, page 529.

Rundle, Amy, late of Greenwich, Sept. 16, 1816, letters of administration on her estate granted to Levi Palmer and Elizabeth Wood, page 249.
    Inventory taken Sept. 28, 1816, by Gideon Holmes and Isaac Peck, 3rd, and filed Oct. 1, 1816, page 253.

Rundle, Nathaniel, late of Greenwich, Feb. 7, 1815, letters of administration on his estate granted to Hannah Rundle, who was ordered to advertise for claims, page 40.
    Mch. 3, 1815, inventory taken by Jonathan Rundel and Job Lyon, and filed Apl. 4, 1815, page 52.

Rundel, Reuben, late of Greenwich, inventory taken May 5, 1815 by Abraham Close and Gilbert Close, and filed June 5, 1815, page 362.
    Feb. 6, 1816, estate ordered distributed to his widow, Amy Rundle, and children the legal representatives of Amy Peck, deceased; Reuben, Deborah wife of Gilbert Peck, Samuel, Hannah wife of Isaac Finch, Jonathan, and Shadrach, page 362.
    Feb. 13, 1816, estate distributed accordingly, page 363.

Rundell, Samuel, late of Greenwich, will dated July 14, 1800, probated Mch. 5, 1811, mentions his wife Hannah, and children Phinehas, Ruth, and Hannah, grandsons Samuel Rundell, James Smith, Benjamin Brush, Samuel Brush, James Brush, and granddaughter Ruth Smith. Executors wife and son Phinehas. Witnesses John McKay, Jr., Edward Brush, and Margaret McKay, page 385.

STAMFORD PROBATE RECORDS.
Volume 11, 1803-1819.

Rundell, Samuel, continued :
    Mch. 5, 1811, order to advertise for claims, page 386.
    Inventory taken Jan. 30, 1811, by Gilbert Close and Nehemiah Brown, and filed Mch. 5, 1811, page 386.
    Nov. 2, 1814, estate ordered distributed to Phinehas Rundle, a son; Samuel Brush, Benjamin Brush, Jr., and James Brush, children of Ruth Brush, a deceased daughter; James Smith and Ruth Knapp, children of Hannah Smith, a deceased daughter, page 387.

Rundle, William, late of Greenwich, Oct. 1, 1816, that part of his estate set off to his widow for her dower, ordered distributed to his children Elizabeth Wood, Sarah wife of Levi Palmer, Abigail wife of Levi Mead, Rachel widow of Samuel Banks, Anna wife of Abraham Reynolds, Charity wife of Joshua Smith, and to the legal representatives of Amy Palmer, deceased, page 280.
    Oct. 15, 1816, estate distributed accordingly, page 280.

Sackett, Joseph, late of Greenwich, Mch. 1, 1803, letters of administration on his estate granted to James Sackett, w who was ordered to advertise for claims, page 125.
    Inventory taken Mdh. 25, 1803, by Andrew Mead and Justus Sackett, and filed Apl. 11, 1803, page 125.
    Dec. 27, 1803, commissioners appointed to adjust claims of creditors, page 126.
    Jan. 1, 1805, report of commissioners filed, page and an appeal taken therefrom by Hannah wife of Frederick Betts, a daughter of said deceased, page 126.

St. John, Hannah, late of Stamford, will dated Sept. 5, 1814, probated Oct. 4, 1814, mentions her sons John St. John, and Ezra St. John; granddaughter Betsy wife of Oliver Weed. Executor her son Ezra. Witnesses Polly Scofield and Abigail Hoyt, page 364.
    Inventory taken Sept. 30, 1814, by Samuel Hoyt and Henry R. Weed, and filed Dec. 6, 1814, page 365.

Scofield, Abraham, late of Stamford, will dated May 14, 1812, probated May 27, 1812, mentions his children Ezra, Phinehas, Sarah Hoyt, Esther Lounsbury, and Abigail. Executors sons Ezra and Phinehas. Witnesses Reuben Scofield, Jonathan Miller, and Jared Lounsbury, page 29.
    May 27, 1812, order to advertise for claims, page 301.
    Inventory taken by Seth Weed and Reuben Scofield, and filed June 2, 1812, page 301.

STAMFORD PROBATE RECORDS.
Volume 11, 1803-1819.

Scofield, Daniel, late of Stamford, will dated May 7, 1812, probated Feb. 2, 1813, conditional devise of land to the North or New Baptist Church of about fifty acres; Samuel Weed, Jr., to have my wood land, if he desires it, and other land. Executors Samuel Weed, Jr., and Reuben Scofield. Witnesses Reuben Scofield, Israel Scofield, and John Weed, a son of Miles Weed, page 58. Feb. 2, 1813, order to advertise for claims, page 60. Inventory taken Dec. 17, 1812, by Warren Scofield and Abishai Scofield, and filed Feb. 2, 1813, page 60.

Scofield, Daniel, late of Stamford, Nov. 1815, on the application of Reuben Scofield, executor, his estate was ordered distributed to the legal representatives of Nathan Scofield, a deceased brother; to the legal representatives of Israel Scofield, a deceased brother; and to the legal representatives of Mary Bishop, a deceased sister, page 75.
Nov. 9, 1815, estate distributed accordingly, pages 76 and 444.

Scofield, Daniel, late of Stamford, Dec. 1817, appeal from decree dated Nov. 9, 1815, heard, and decree affirmed, page 446.

Scofield, Gilbert, of Stamford, Oct. 20, 1817, guardian of Esther Dunham, asked leave to sell the real estate of said minor, who is the owner in common with said Gilbert Scofield and James Scofield, of land in Stamford, page 399.

Scofield, Hannah, widow, late of Stamford, will dated Apl. 2, 1810, probated Oct. 2, 1810, mentions Hezekiah Bishop, Mary wife of Reuben Knapp, and Hannah Bishop, children of my sister Mary Bishop, deceased. Executor Reuben Scofield. Witnesses Gideon Scofield, Israel Scofield, and Reuben Scofield, page 391.
Inventory taken by Abishai Scofield and Samuel Weed, Jr and filed Oct. 2, 1810, page 392.

Scofield, James, late of Stamford, Feb. 4, 1812, letters of administration on his estate granted to William White, who was ordered to advertise for claims, page 67. Inventory taken Feb. 6, 1812, by Timothy Reynolds and David Smith, 3rd, and filed Apl. 2, 1812, page 67. Sept. 24, 1814, estate ordered distributed to his children David, John, Isaac, Mary wife of Reuben June, Abigail wife of Amos Whelpley, and Sally wife of Richard Kelly, page 62.

STAMFORD PROBATE RECORDS.
Volume 11, 1803-1819.

Scofield, James, continued:
Sept. 28, 1814, estate distributed accordingly, page 109

Scofield, Robert, late of Stamford, will dated Apl. 21, 1817, probated Aug. 5, 1817, mentions his wife Hannah, and children Darius, George, James B., Holly, Oliver, Rebert, Eliza, Sally, Emily, and Hannah; brothers John Scofield, Jr., Silas Scofield, and James Scofield, Jr. Executors his wife, and father-in-law Thaddeus Bell. Witnesses Sally Gay, Asel Johnson, and Samuel Webb, page 359.
Aug. 5, 1817, order to advertise for claims, page 359.
Inventory taken Oct. 2, 1817, by Isaac Wardwell and James Scofield, Jr., and filed Oct. 7, 1817, page 393. May 9, 1818, the land owned in common with John Scofield, and Silas Scofield, partitioned, part to the widow and heirs of deceased, and remainder to said Silas Scofield and John Scofield, Jr., page 485.

Scofield, Seth, late of Stamford, inventory taken Oct. 22, 1813, by Reuben Scofield and John Blanchard, and filed Feb. 1, 1814, by the executor, page 411.

Secor, William, a minor of Greenwich, about 3 years of age, June 20, 1816, the court appointed Jonathan Secor to be his guardian, page 215.

Seely, Abijah, late of Stamford, Sept. 16, 1801, agreement between his widow and children in regard to her estate, viz: Lydia Seely, widow, Ezekiel Stone, Sally Stone, Peter Buxton, Susannah Buxton, Jared Seymour, Abigail Seymour, Jacob How, Jr., Elizabeth How, Mercy Seely, Thomas Seely, and Simeon Seely, page 182.

Seely, James, late of Stamford, inventory taken Oct. 11, 1813, by Simeon H. Minor and Seymour Jarvis, and filed Oct. 11, 1813, by the administrator, page 374.

Sellick, Daniel, late of Stamford, will dated Dec. 5, 1818, probated Mch. 15, 1819, all to his two sons Isaac and Thomas, and appointed them executors. Witness Clark Bissell, page 556.
Mch. 15, 1819, order to advertise for claims, page 557.
Inventory taken Mch. 16, 1819, by Samuel Whiting and Stephen Ferris, and filed Apl. 29, 1819, page 557.

Selleck, Edward, late of Stamford, will dated Mch. 17, 1813,

STAMFORD PROBATE RECORDS.
Volume 11, 1803-1819.

Selleck, Edward, continued :
    probated May 7, 1813, mentions his wife Hannah, and children Kilbourn, Nanne wife of Isaac Hoyt, Jr., and Catharine Selleck, granddaughter Elizabeth Reed, a daughter of my eldest daughter Phebe, deceased, late wife of John Reed, Jr. of Norwalk. Executor son Kilbourn. Witnesses Wyx Seely, Nancy Waterbury, and Nathan Weed, page 368.
    May 7, 1813, order to advertise for claims, page 367.
    Inventory taken May 8, 1813, by Joshua Scofield and Samuel Whiting, and filed June 1, 1813, page 369.
    June 24, 1813, account filed, and estate ordered distributed to Kilbourn Selleck, Nanne wife of Isaac Hoyt, Jr., and Catharine Selleck, his children; and to Elizabeth Reed, a granddaughter, page 370.
    Estate distributed accordingly, page 370.

Selleck, James, late of Stamford, Aug. 5, 1817, letters of administration on his estate granted to Charlotte Selleck of Stamford, who was ordered to advertise for claims, page 360.
    Inventory taken Sept. 1, 1817, by Jeremiah Andreas and Richard Bell, and filed Oct. 7, 1817, page 393.
    Aug. 7, 1818, the court appointed Charlotte Selleck guardian of James Bell Selleck, a son of decedent, about one year of age, page 467.

Seymour, Drake, late of Greenwich, Mch. 17, 1819, letters of administration on his estate granted to Mary Seymour and Delia R. Seymour, who were ordered to advertise for claims, page 563.
    Inventory taken Apl. 6, 1819, by John Sackett and Alvan Mead, and filed Apl. 12, 1819, page 563.

Seymour, Samuel, late of Greenwich, will witnessed Sept. 5, 1816, probated Apl. 18, 1818, mentions his wife Abigail and children Drake, Hannah wife of Nathaniel Mead, Subrina Bush, Polly wife of Nehemiah Brown of Rye; grandchildren the children of my daughter Elizabeth Marshall; the three sons of my son William deceased; the two youngest sons of my daughter Rhoda Hobby, viz: Nehemiah B. Hobby and Samuel S. Hobby; and grandson Samuel Seymour Hobby. Executors his wife and son Drake. Witnesses Hezekiah Tracy, Reuben Holmes, and David Holmes, Jr., page 488.
    Apl. 18, 1818, order to advertise for claims, page 490.
    Inventory taken in Apl. 1818, by John Sackett and Alan Mead, and filed May 5, 1818, page 490.

STAMFORD PROBATE RECORDS.
Volume 11, 1803-1819.

Seymour, Samuel, continued :
    Mch. 24, 1819, letters of administration de bonus non granted to Mary Seymour and Delia R. Seymour, both of Greenwich, page 561.

Sherwood, Matthew, late of Stamford, will dated Aug. 21, 1812, probated Jan. 18, 1813, mentions his wife Thankful, and children Nathan, Matthew, John, Amy, Hannah, Rachel, Mary, Prudence, and Thankful. Executor his son Matthew. Witnesses Reuben Scofield, William Y. Knapp, Jr and Earle Smith, page 32.
Jan. 18, 1813, order to advertise for claims, page 33.
Inventory taken Jan. 21, 1813, by Timothy Reynolds and David Smith, 3rd, and filed Mch. 21, 1813, page 34.
Aug. 31, 1813, account filed, and real estate ordered sold to pay debts, page 35.

Skidmore, Henry, late of Stamford, Dec. 7, 1818, letters of administration on his estate granted to Samuel B. Warren, who was ordered to advertise for claims, page 548.
Jan. 4, 1819, commissioners appointed to adjust claims of creditors, page 548.

Skilden, John, late of New York City, will dated June 26, 1812 probated Aug. 25, 1813, mentions his children Samuel and George, and sister Prudence Lockwood. Executor John Aikman of New York City. Witnesses Nathaniel Hubbard, Samuel Wheaton, and David Wood, page 411.
Aug. 25, 1813, order to advertise for claims, page 412.
Inventory taken Aug. 19, 1813, by Joseph Gray and S. H. Minor, and filed Aug. 25, 1813, page 413.

Slason, Deliverance, late of Stamford, will dated Apl. 11, 1775, probated Oct. 1, 1811, mentions his wife Hannah, and children Ebenezer, Nathaniel, Gershom, Amos, Hannah, Abigail, Millecent; grandson Jonathan, a son of my eldest son Jonathan, who is supposed to be deceased. Executor son Nathaniel. Witnesses Mary James, Hannah Mather, and Moses Mather, page 344.
Codicil dated Mch. 10, 1789, legacy to Sally wife of John Dibble, and a daughter of my daughter Hannah, page 344.

Slason, Nathan, late of Stamford, additional inventory taken Feb. 18, 1812, and filed Mch. 3, 1812, by Gershom Scofield, and John Clock, page 376.

STAMFORD PROBATE RECORDS.
Volume 11, 1803-1819.

Slawson, Abraham, late of Stamford, June 23, 1815, letters of administration on his estate granted to Samuel Whiting, of Stamford, who was ordered to advertise for claims, page 70.
Inventory taken July 4, 1815, by Joshua Morehouse and Rufus Scofield, and filed July 4, 1815, page 365.

Smith, Abel, late of North Castle, will dated 5th day, 7th month, 1810, probated Apl. 10, 1811, mentions his wife -----, and children John, Benjamin, Abel, James, Sarah, Charity Matthews, Deborah Clapp, Jerusha Shute, Barthsheba Baker, and Abigail Gales; Abel S. Clapp, a son of James Clapp; Smith Baker, a son of Jeremiah Baker; and granddaughter Phebe S. Kipp. Executors Daniel Tripp and John Palmer. Witnesses Elisha Belcher, James Merritt, and John Griffin, page 26.
Inventory taken Apl. 10, 1811, by David D. Husted and Robert Leonard, and filed Apl. 10, 1811, page 29.

Smith, Amos, late of Stamford, will dated Dec. 7, 1818, probated Apl. 15, 1819, mentions his wife Deborah, and children Hannah, Sarah, Mary, Abigail; son-in-law Messenger Palmer. Executor Abel Reynolds. Witnesses Josiah Smith, Catharine Palmer, and Samuel Webb, page 573.
Apl. 15, 1819, order to advertise for claims, page 573.
Inventory taken Apl. 22, 1819, by Abishai Weed and Thaddeus Handford, and filed Apl. 24, 1819, page 574.
Apl. 24, 1819, personal estate ordered sold to pay debts, page 574.

Smith, Elizabeth, late of Stamford, will dated May 30, 1815, probated Nov. 12, 1816, mentions her sister Elizabeth Smith of New Haven; Martha Hazard of Smithtown; Rebecca Hillhouse, Theodosia Woolsey, and Mary Wright, all of New Haven; Abigail Coggshall of Lloyds Neck and Mary S. Davenport; and Rebecca Holly of Stamford; Peggy Hazard and nephew William Smyth Babcock. Executor nephew William Smyth Babcock. Witnesses Ann R. Davenport, and Samuel Webb, page 273.
Nov. 12, 1816, the executor refused to qualify and letters with the will annexed granted to Theodore Davenport, page 273.

Smith, Ezekiel, late of Stamford, inventory taken Nov. 30, 1812, by Samuel Hoyt, Jr., and Seymour Jarvis, and filed Dec. 7, 1813, pages 405 and 406.

STAMFORD PROBATE RECORDS.
Volume 11, 1803-1819.

Smith, Isaiah, late of Stamford, inventory taken Apl. 14, 1812 by Daniel Nichols and Solomon Clason, and filed May 5, 1812, page 375.

Smith, John, late of Stamford, May 3, 1805, to Jan. 25, 1814, several receipts for legacies from Elizabeth Newman, Henry Hubbard, Polly Newman, Susannah Smith, John Newman, Eber Smith, Zetty Newman, Prudence Reed, Mary Whitney, Henry Newman, Martha Smith, and Elizabeth Smith, page 216.

Smith, Mary, late of Stanwich in Stamford, will dated Apl. 5, 1790, probated May 5, 1810, mentions her children Ebenezer, Seth, Noah, John, and two daughters. Executors none named. Witnesses Daniel Nichols, Jr., John Smith Jr., and Silas June, page 302. (30?)
May 5, 1810, letters of administration with the will annexed granted to Noah Smith of Ridgefield, page 31. Inventory taken May 18, 1810, by Seth Hait and Solomon Clason, and filed May 21, 1810, page 31.

Smith, Mary, widow, late of Stamford, inventory taken Nov. 5, 1811, by Seth Hait and Seth Smith, and filed Nov. 5, 1811, page 374.

Smith, Nathaniel, late of Stamford, will dated June 28, 1803, probated June 18, 1812, mentions his wife Sarah; widow Abigail Smith; daughter Susannah wife of William White; son Daniel Smith; granddaughter Mary wife of Reuben June; grandchildren Abigail, David, Sarah, Isaac, and John, the children of James Scofield; granddaughter Permellia wife of Jared Sherwood; granddaughter Mary wife of Sylvanus Marshall; grandchildren Ruth, Elizabeth, Caleb, Isaac, Philander, Alva, Edwin, and Jesse, children of my son Isaac Smith, deceased. Executor William White. Witnesses William June, Jr., John Brush, and John Mackay, Jr., page 295.
June 18, 1812, order to advertise for claim, page 296.
Inventory taken May 12, 1812, by Timothy Reynolds and David Smith, 3rd, and filed June 24, 1812, page 297.
July 7, 1812, commissioners appointed to adjust claims of creditors, page 297.
Feb. 8, 1813, report of commissioners filed, page 298.

Smith, Samuel, late of Stamford, July 7, 1818, letters of administration on his estate granted to George Smith of Stamford, who was ordered to advertise for claims, page 530.

STAMFORD PROBATE RECORDS.
Volume 11, 1803-1819.

Smith, Samuel, continued:
Inventory taken Aug. 19, 1818, by Charles Knapp and Samuel Hoyt, and filed Aug. 19, 1818, page 530.

Smith, Stephen, late of Stamford, July 7, 1803, letters of administration on his estate granted to Jared Smith, who was ordered to advertise for claims, page 131.
Inventory taken July 9, 1803, by Seth Smith and Seth Hoyt, and filed July 11, 1803, page 131.

Stevens, Edward, late of Stamford, inventory taken May 7, 1812 by David Stevens and John Hoyt, Jr., and filed May 12, 1812, page 365.
Nov. 30, 1812, on the application of Obadiah Stevens, administrator, estate ordered distributed to his brothers and sisters, viz: Obadiah Stevens, Seth Stevens, Sarah wife of William Tucker, Jane wife of Elisha Stevens, and Lydia wife of Samuel Stevens, and the legal representatives of William H. Stevens, a deceased brother, subject to the dower rights of deceased's mother, page 366.
estate distributed accordingly, page 367.

Stevens, Hellenah, late of Stamford, will dated Dec. 19, 1809, probated Nov. 5, 1811, all to Levina Bishop, Hellenah Bishop and Susannah Holly Bishop, children of my son-in-law Abijah Bishop, deceased. Executor Joseph Bishop. Witnesses Jerusha Davenport, and Ebenezer Davenport, page 375.
Inventory taken Dec. 2, 1811, by Isaac Holly, Jr., and Henry Brown, and filed Dec. 3, 1811, page 376.

Sturges, Strong, of New York City, Mch. 26, 1811, father of Harriet Sturges, Elizabeth R. Sturges, Mary Ann Sturges and George W. Sturges, asked leave to sell the real estate of said minors, and sale ordered, page 389.

Taber, Charles, late of Stamford, a soldier in the United States Army, Nov. 27, 1815, letters of administration on his estate granted to Joseph Wood, who was ordered to advertise for claims, page 74.

Taylor, Isaac, a minor of Greenwich, about 17 years of age, Feb. 5, 1818, made choice of Nehemiah Sherwood of Greenwich to be his guardian, page 450.

Thorp, Charles, late of Stamford, 1813, letters of administration on his estate granted to Cary Leeds, who was ordered to advertise for claims, page 168.

STAMFORD PROBATE RECORDS.
Volume 11, 1803-1819.

Thorp, Charles, continued :
  Inventory taken May 14, 1813, by Nathan Weed and Nathaniel Waterbury, and filed July 6, 1813, pages 168 and 169.

Timpany, Mary, late of Greenwich, widow of Michael C. Timpany, will dated Feb. 7, 1815, probated Apl. 5, 1815, mentions her daughter Elizabeth wife of Philo Clark, grandsons Cyrus Hitchcock, a son of Thomas Hitchcock, Robert J. Clark, Darius Clark, and Edward J. Clark, sons of Philo Clark. Executor Jabez Mead. Witnesses Ephraim Lane, Lot Palmer, and Fanny Bross, page 56.
  Apl. 5, 1815, the executor refused to qualify and letters with the will annexed granted to Philo Clark, who was ordered to advertise for claims, page 57.
  Inventory taken by William Skidmore and Lemuel Ferris, and filed June 6, 1815, page 413.

Todd, Harvey, about 18 years of age, and Gabriel H. Todd, about 15 years of age, both of Stamford, made choice of Selleck Scofield of Stamford, to be their guardian on May 4, 1819, page 529.

Todd, John, Jr., late of Stamford, inventory taken Aug. 23, 1810, by Frederick Hait and Joel Waring, and filed Sept. 4, 1810, and Oct. 6, 1810, page 390.
  Feb. 3, 1812, account filed, and real estate ordered sold to pay debts, page 391.
  Report of sale filed, page 391.

Todd, John, late of Stamford, will dated May 20, 1811, probated Sept. 6, 1814, mentions his wife Jemima, and children Noah, John, Elnathan, Washington, Deborah Benedict, Hannah Webb, Phebe Webb, and Mary Bouton. Executors Elnathan Todd, and Ebenezer Webb, Jr. Witnesses Joseph N. Smith, Samuel Weed, Jr., and Reuben Scofield, page 141.
  Sept. 6, 1814, order to advertise for claims, page 142.
  Inventory taken Oct. 4, 1814, by Joseph Waring and Joel Waring, and filed Oct. 10, 1814, page 143.

Todd, John, late of Stamford, July 11, 1816, the court appointed Washington Todd guardian of Harvey Todd, about 15 years of age, and Gabriel Hubbard Todd, about 11 years of age, sons of deceased, page 218.

STAMFORD PROBATE RECORDS.
Volume 11, 1803-1819.

Todd, Washington, late of Stamford, May 4, 1819, letters of administration on his estate granted to Benjamin Husted, Jr., of Greenwich, and Charlotte Todd of Stamford, who were ordered to advertise for claims, page 577.
May 18, 1819, personal estate ordered sold to pay debts, page 577.
July 5, 1819, commissioners appointed to adjust claims of creditors, page 578.
Inventory taken by Joel Waring and John Husted, and filed May 18, 1819, page 578.

Totton, Anna, late of Rye, wife of Gilbert Totton, will dated May 3, 1818, probated Nov. 3, 1818, mentions her children Charity, Esther, Rebecca, and Betsy. Executor her husband Gilbert Totton. Witnesses Elisha R. Belcher, Samuel Totton, Jr., and Moses Totton, page 555.
Nov. 3, 1818, order to advertise for claims, page 556.
Inventory taken Dec. 5, 1818, by Samuel Close and Daniel Peck, and filed Dec. 7, 1818, page 556.

Tryon, Samuel, formerly of Stamford, but late of Havanna, May 16, 1809, letters of administration on his estate granted to Benjamin Tryon and Rowland Tryon, page 83.
Inventory taken Apl. 18, 1810, by John Hoyt and Cary Leeds, and filed Apl. 6, 1812, page 81.
Apl. 7, 1812, order to advertise for claims, page 81.
Apl. 13, 1812, commissioners appointed to adjust claims of creditors, page 81.
Apl. 28, 1812, order to sell all the property of deceased, page 83.
Nov. 13, 1812, report of commissioners to adjust claims filed, page 82.

Vail, Abigail, late of Greenwich, Sept. 15, 1817, letters of administration on her estate granted to James Field, who was ordered to advertise for claims, page 380.
Inventory taken 11th month, 3rd day, 1817, by William Sutton and Thomas Carpenter, and filed Nov. 4, 1817, page 409.

Waldrum, Nicholas, late of Stamford, a soldier of the 25th Regiment, United States Army, Apl. 15, 1815, letters of administration on his estate granted to Cynthia Waldrum, page 191.
June 14, 1816, inventory taken by John Mackay and Benjamin Peck, and filed June 21, 1816, page 215.

STAMFORD PROBATE RECORDS.
Volume 11, 1803-1819.

Waring, Michager, late of Greenwich, Nov. 17, 1804, letters of administration on his estate granted to Catharine Waring, page 116.
Inventory taken Dec. 17, 1804, by Enos Knapp and Drake Lockwood, and filed Jan. 1, 1805, and order to advertise for claims, page 116.

Waring, Samuel, late of Stamford, Nov. 26, 1805, letters of administration on his estate granted to Nathan Weed, who was ordered to advertise for claims, page 110.
Inventory taken Dec. 7, 1805, and filed Dec. 7, 1805, page 110.
Mch. 31, 1806, account filed, and distribution ordered to his widow, Mary now the wife of Isaac Lockwood, and his children Samuel, John, Silvanus, Elizabeth widow of Abraham Clock, Hannah wife of David Lyon, Mary wife of Joseph Washburn, Sarah Waring, Mary Ann wife of Marshall Washburn, and James Waring, page 112.
May 3, 1806, estate distributed accordingly, page 112.
(Note distribution of the part set off to the widow as her dower, Mch. 14, 1827, Volume 13, page 134.)

Waters, John, late of Stamford, Oct. 25, 1817, letters of administration on his estate granted to Lewis S. Lockwood, who was ordered to advertise for claims, page 403

Waterbury, Bethiah, late of Stamford, will dated Jan. 25, 1810 probated July 3, 1810, mentions her nephew Nathaniel Waterbury; sister Abigail Waterbury, widow of my deceased brother Benjamin Waterbury; Sarah Waterbury, widow of my deceased brother James Waterbury; Sarah Waterbury, widow of my deceased brother Josiah Waterbury; Sarah Waterbury, widow of my deceased brother Ebenezer Waterbury; Abigail wife of my said nephew Nathaniel Waterbury; Nancy Waterbury and Reuma Waterbury, children of my said nephew Nathaniel Waterbury; Bethiah Waterbury, a daughter of said Benjamin Waterbury, deceased. Executor Deodate Waterbury, one of my nephews. Witnesses Nathan Weed, Ezra Waterbury, and Mary Weed, page 95.
July 3, 1810, order to advertise for claims, page 97.
Inventory taken by Isaac Holly and Frederick Hoyt, Jr., and filed Sept. 4, 1810, page 98.

Waterbury, Jonathan, late of Stamford, Mch. 3, 1812, letters of administration on his estate granted to Sally Waterbury, who was ordered to advertise for claims, page 86.
Inventory taken Apl. 15, 1812, by Cary Leeds and John

STAMFORD PROBATE RECORDS.
Volume 11, 1803-1819.

94.

Waterbury, Jonathan, continued :
    Weed, Jr., and filed May 5, 1812, page 86.
    Apl. 6, 1815, account filed, and real estate ordered sold to pay debts, page 181.
    Mch. 11, 1816, estate ordered distributed to his widow, Sally Waterbury, and children Sarah Hoyt Waterbury, Abigail wife of Lockwood Lounsbury, Betsy Waterbury, Nathaniel, Amos H., Nancy, Cornelia, Apollos W., Sylvester E., and Charles E., page 232.
    Apl. 4, 1816, estate distributed accordingly, page 233.
    Jan. 27, 1817, Sally Waterbury, parent and natural guardian of Nancy, Amos H., Cornelia, and Apollos W., children of decedent, asked for leave to sell the real estate of said minors, page 278.
    May 26, 1817 petition for leave to sell the real estate of Sylvester, a minor son of decedent, and sale authorized, pages 349, 282, and 283.
    May 26, 1817, sale made, page 349.

Waterbury, Nathaniel, Jr., late of Stamford, June 1, 1813, letters of administration on his estate granted to Abigail Waterbury, who was ordered to advertise for claims, page 146.
    Inventory taken July 2, 1813, by Isaac Holly and Nathan Weed, and filed July 6, 1813, page 146.

Waterbury, Samuel, Jr., late of Stamford, Apl. 5, 1811, letters of administration on his estate granted to Ebenezer Waterbury, who was ordered to advertise for claims page 144.
    Inventory taken Apl. 8, 1811, by Cary Leeds and Nathaniel Waterbury, and filed May, 1811, page 144.
    July 9, 1811, account filed, and on July 15, 1811, commissioners appointed to adjust claims of creditors, page 145.
    Feb. 15, 1812, report of commisioners filed, page 145.

Waterbury, Samuel, late of Stamford, Nov. 1, 1814, estate ordered distributed to his children Joseph, Thaddeus, Samuel, Sarah Hoyt, Huldah Platt, to the legal representatives of Hannah Weed, deceased, Ruth Waterbury, a daughter of deceased died before coming of age, unmarried and intestate, page 418.
    Feb. 7, 1815, estate distributed accordingly, page 418.

Webb, Nathaniel, late of Stamford, will dated Feb. 21, 1791, probated Jan. 4, 1819, mentions his wife Hannah, and children Nathaniel, Elisha, Hannah wife of Nathaniel

STAMFORD PROBATE RECORDS.
Volume 11, 1803-1819.

Webb, Nathaniel, continued:
Waterbury, Jr., Jerusha, wife of John Lounsbury, and Rebecca Webb. Executors sons Nathaniel and Elisha. Witnesses David Maltbie, Elihu P. Smith, and Smith Weed, page 544.
Codicil dated Sept. 5, 1810, executors son Nathaniel and son-in-law Nathaniel Waterbury, page 544.
Jan. 4, 1819, order to advertise for claims, page 545.
Inventory taken Jan. 14, 1819, by John Brown and Jonathan Knapp, and filed Jan. 18, 1819, page 546.
Jan. 10, 1795, antenuptial agreement with Abigail Marshall of Stamford, recorded Jan. 29, 1819, page 546.
Apl. 26, 1819, estate ordered distributed to his children Nathaniel, Elisha of New Rochelle, N. Y., Hannah wife of Nathaniel Waterbury, Jerusha wife of John Lounsbury, and Rebecca wife of Zadoc Newman of said New Rochell, page 557.
Apl. 29, 1819, estate distributed accordingly, page 558

Webb, Seth, late of Stamford, Jan. 6, 1818, letters of administration on his estate granted to Ann Webb, who was ordered to advertise for claims, page 432.
Inventory taken Jan. 26, 1818, by Isaac Holly and William Keeler, and filed Feb. 4, 1818, page 451.
May 18, 1819, account filed, and real estate ordered sold to pay debts, page 553.
May 18, 1819, commissioners appointed to set out the dower of his widow, Ann Webb, page 553.

Weed, Abigail, late of Stamford, Aug. 2, 1811, Strong Sturges, administrator, released from all claims of our deceased sister's estate by Ebenezer W. Weed, Joseph A. Weed, and Hannah A. Weed, page 389.

Weed, Amos, late of Stamford, will dated May 11, 1815, probated June 6, 1815, mentions his wife Hannah, and children Abigail, Mercy wife of John Lockwood, Philo, and Amos. Executor son Philo. Witnesses Seth Weed, John Augur, and William Hoyt, Jr., page 413.
June 6, 1815, order to advertise for claims, page 414.
Inventory taken June 8, 1815, by Jeremiah Curtis and Samuel Dean, and filed Aug. 1, 1815, page 414.

Weed, David, late of Southbury, New Haven County, Conn., will dated Jan. 15, 1813, probated June 7, 1814, mentions his wife Jerusha, and children Sally, Mary, Betsy, and Rebecca. Executrix his wife. Witnesses Ebenezer Lockwood, Clarissa Cook, and Ebenezer Lockwood, Jr.,

STAMFORD PROBATE RECORDS.
Volume 11, 1803-1819.

Weed, David, continued :
    page 356.
    Jan. 15, 1813, order to advertise for claims, page 357.
    Inventory taken June 16, 1814, by John Augur and Reuben
    Scofield, and filed June 18, 1814, page 357.
    Aug. 7, 1817, estate distributed to his widow Jerusha
    Weed, and children Rebecca, Betsy wife of Jonathan B.
    Waterbury, Mary, and Sally wife of Ezra Lockwood,
    page 525.

Weed, Ebenezer P., late of Stamford, Mch. 24, 1818, that part
    of his estate set off to his widow for her dower, or-
    dered distributed to his children Smith Weed, Jesse
    Weed, James Weed, Susannah Weed, and to the legal rep-
    resentatives of Mary Weed, deceased, page 472.
    Apl. 7, 1818, estate distributed accordingly, but to
    Susannah Leeds, a daughter of deceased, also, page 472.

Weed, Enos, late of Stamford, now in New Canaan, Nov. 5, 1801,
    account filed by Seth Weed, executor, and estate order-
    ed distributed to his widow, and children Seth Weed,
    Mary St. John, and Rachel Gray, according to his will,
    page 83.
    Mch. 14, 1810, estate distributed to his widow, and
    children Stephen Weed, Mary wife of Reuben Scofield,
    and to the heirs of Rachel Gray, page 83.

Weed, Hannah, late of Stamford, wife of Ebenezer Weed, will
    dated Apl. 28, 1795, probated Feb. 18, 1813, all to
    Damaras wife of Asa Fitch. Executor my honored Uncle
    Daniel Bouton of Stamford. Witnesses Eleazer Bouton,
    Jr., Mary Bouton and Daniel Bouton, 3rd, page 93.
    Inventory taken Feb. 3, 1813, by Daniel Weed and Reuben
    Scofield, and filed Apl. 9, 1813, page 95.

Weed, Henry R., late of Stamford, will dated Apl. 10, 1818,
    probated July 7, 1818, all to his father Jonathan Weed.
    Executors his father and Strong Sturges. Witnesses
    John Augur, William Hoyt, Jr., and Elizabeth Ambler,
    page 540.
    July 7, 1818, order to advertise for claims, page 540.
    Jan. 26, 1819, account filed, and ordered to advertise
    for claims, page 551.
    Mch. 1, 1819, commissioners appointed to adjust claims
    of creditors, page 552.
    Inventory taken Aug. 27, 1818, by Enos Waterbury and
    Hezekiah Hoyt, and filed Dec. 1, 1818, page 552.

STAMFORD PROBATE RECORDS.
Volume 11, 1803-1819.

Weed, James, late of Stamford, Dec. 5, 1815, letters of administration on his estate granted to Lydia Weed, and James B. Weed, who were ordered to advertise for claims, page 74.
Inventory taken Dec. 11, 1815, by Thaddeus Bell and Thaddeus Hoyt, Jr., and filed Jan. 2, 1816, page 440.
Apl. 6, 1816, on the application of Lydia Weed, his widow, estate ordered distributed to said widow, and his children James B., Mary Andreas, Clarissa Holmes, Hezekiah, Ebenezer, and Catharine, pages 190 and 441.
Apl. 19, 1816, estate distributed to his widow Lydia Weed, and his children James B., Mary wife of William Andreas, Clarissa wife of Latham Holmes, Hezekiah, Ebenezer, and Catharine, page 441.
Apl. 22, 1816, Hezekiah, 3rd, and Ebenezer, sons of decedent, made choice of Darius Hoyt to be their guardian, page 193.

Weed, Jesse, late of Stamford, inventory taken Jan. 3, 1815, by John Augur and Amos Weed, and filed June 6, 1815, by the administrator, page 153.
Jan. 2, 1816, account filed by Seth Weed, administrator and real estate ordered sold to pay debts, page 127.

Weed, Joel, late of Stamford, Mch. 4, 1817, letters of administration on his estate granted to Cary Leeds, who was ordered to advertise for claims, page 286.
Mch. 10, 1817, commissioners appointed to adjust claims of creditors, page 286.
Oct. 7, 1817, report of commissioners filed, page 388.
Inventory taken Mch. 10, 1817, by Henry Webb, Jr., and Nathaniel Waterbury, and filed Mch. 10, 1817, page 287.
Additional inventory taken Oct. 2, 1817, and filed Oct. 7, 1817, page 388.
Oct. 7, 1817, account filed, and real estate ordered sold to pay debts, page 409.

Weed, John, 3rd, late of Stamford, July 2, 1816, Henry Weed, a son of decedent, about 14 years of age, made choice of Samuel Webb to be his guardian, page 218.

Weed, Jonas, 3rd, late of Stamford, Aug. 25, 1809, letters of administration on his estate granted to Deborah Weed, page 49.
Inventory taken Aug. 31, 1809, by Nathan Weed and Charles Whiting, and filed Sept. 5, 1809, page 49.
Aug. 7, 1810, estate ordered distributed to his widow,

STAMFORD PROBATE RECORDS.
Volume 11, 1803-1819.

Weed, Jonas, 3rd, continued:
Deborah Weed, and children Charlotte and Henry, page 63.
Aug. 15, 1810, estate distributed accordingly, page 63.

Weed, Lucy Ann, late of Stamford, will dated July 15, 1818, probated Aug. 17, 1818, legacy to the church in Stamwich, and in North Stamford, mentions her husband Seth Weed; brother Benjamin Brush; Hannah Ann Knapp, a daughter of Jona Knapp; Henry Hoyt; Lucy Ann Down; Sarah Cowdrey Hoyt; Genet Ann Hoyt; Elihu Smith; widow Ann Smith; Rachel wife of Benjamin Brush; and Polly Abbott and Abigail Bishop my sister's daughters. Executor her husband. Witnesses William Hoyt, Philo Weed, and Abiahai Weed, Jr., page 538.
Aug. 17, 1818, order to advertise for claims, page 538.

Weed, Miles, late of Stamford, Jan. 2, 1810, letters of administration on his estate granted to Reuben Scofield, page 121.
Inventory taken Mch. 27, 1810, by Benjamin Scofield and Hezekiah Bishop, and filed Mch. 10, 1810, page 121.
Mch. 10, 1810, account filed, and real estate ordered sold to pay debts, page 122.
Aug. 7, 1810, report of sale filed, page 122.

Weed, Peter, of Warwick, Orange County, N. Y., July 11, 1817, parent and natural guardian of Mary Weed, Darius Weed, Sylvanus Weed, Martha Weed, and Sally Weed, asked leave to sell the realestate of said minors, page 388.
Oct. 8, 1817, order authorizing sale, page 447.

Weed, Scudder, Jr., late of Stamford, Oct. 3, 1815, letters of administration on his estate granted to Thaddeus Bell, who was ordered to advertise for claims, page 69.
Oct. 16, 1815, inventory taken by Jonathan Bates and Jeremiah Andreas, and filed Apl. 2, 1816, page 186.

Weed, Scudder, late of Stamford, Aug. 21, 1816, his personal estate distributed to his widow, Elizabeth Weed, and to his heirs George Weed, Mary Scofield, Esther Smith, Sally Weed, and Naomi Weed, page 248.

Weed, Silvanus, late of Stamford, Oct. 3, 1815, letters of administration on his estate granted to Thaddeus Bell, who was ordered to advertise for claims, page 69.

Weeks, William, late of Greenwich, May 13, 1812, letters of administration on his estate granted to Jabez Mead, who

STAMFORD PROBATE RECORDS.
Volume 11, 1803-1819.

Weeks, William, continued:
was ordered to advertise for claims, page 148.
Inventory taken June 11, 1812, by Joshua Ferris and Nehemiah Mead, Jr., and filed June 11, 1812, pages 148 and 158.
July 6, 1813, petition of Hannah Weeks guardian of Charles D., William A., Phebe M., John V., and William W., children of decedent for leave to sell the real estate of said minors, page 99.
Oct. 1, 1813, order authorizing sale, page 99.

Willson, Daniel, late of Greenwich, inventory taken Aug. 10, 1812, by James Green and Platt Mead, and filed Sept. 1, 1812, page 138.

Willson, Nehemiah, late of Greenwich, will dated Jan. 20, 1814, probated Mch. 14, 1814, mentions his wife Sarah, father Joseph Willson, and children Desire Haight, Eunice Peck, James Bowne and Elizabeth Bowne, children of Thomas Bowne, late of Rye. Executors sons-in-law Daniel Haight and Elias Peck, Jr. Witnesses Jotham Merritt, Eliza Merritt, and John Brown, page 415.
Codicil dated Jan. 23, 1814, page 415.
Mch. 14, 1814, order to advertise for claims, page 417.
Inventory taken Mch. 3, 1814, by Ebenezer Mead and Peter Mead, and filed Mch. 15, 1814, page 417.

Willson, Uriah, late of Greenwich, will dated May 17, 1810, probated Sept. 4, 1810, all to his wife Johanna. Executor Nehemiah Willson. Witnesses Nathaniel Finch, Jr., Sally Finch, and Elizabeth Smith, page 136.
Inventory taken Aug. 20, 1810, by Isaac How and Gilbert Close, and filed Sept. 4, 1810, page 137.

Wilmut, Francis, late of Stamford, July 18, 1812, letters of administration on his estate granted to Esther Wilmut of Stamford, page 139.
Inventory taken July 28, 1812, by John Waterbury, Jr., and Cary Leeds, and filed Aug. 14, 1812, page 140.
Feb. 19, 1813, account filed, and real estate ordered sold to pay debts, page 140.

Wood, David, late of Greenwich, will dated Feb. 10, 1810, probated Nov. 5, 1811, mentions his wife Sarah, and children David, Martha Dayton, Rebecca Smith, Sarah Hoyt, Hannah Wood, and Joseph. Executors his sons David and Joseph. Witnesses Charles Rundle, Benoni Rundle, and

STAMFORD PROBATE RECORDS.
Volume 11, 1803-1819.

Wood, David, continued :
    Charles Rundle, Jr., page 100.
    Inventory taken by Charles Rundle and Stephen Lockwood, and filed Feb. 4, 1812, page 101.
    Partition agreement dated July 15, 1812, between Sarah Wood, David Wood, and Joseph Wood, filed Nov. 3, 1812, page 106.

Worden, Isaac, late of Greenwich, June 4, 1816, letters of administration on his estate granted to Hannah Worden, who was ordered to advertise for claims, page 209. Inventory taken by Amos Hobby and Edmund Knapp, and filed Oct. 1, 1816, page 251.

STAMFORD PROBATE RECORDS.
Volume 12, 1819.

Adams, Eli, late of Stamford, Dec. 6, 1819, letters of administration on his estate granted to Abraham Adams, who was ordered to advertise for claims, page 37. Inventory taken Dec. 21, 1819, by Isaac Holly and Erastus H. Weed, and filed Dec. 21, 1819, page 37. Dec. 6, 1820, time for final settlement extended to June 6, next, page 107.

Ambler, Joseph, late of Stamford, Aug. 19, 1819, estate distributed to Johnathan Weed, Erastus H. Weed, Daniel A. Weed, Sarah Weed, Lydia A., wife of Harris Scofield, and Thirza wife of Anson Hoyt, subject to the dower of Elizabeth Ambler, widow of deceased, page 11.

Anderson, William, of ----, May 10, 1823, appointed guardian of his son William Anderson, page 330.

Banks, James, Jr., late of North Castle, will dated Jan. 4, 1820, probated Feb. 13, 1821, mentions his wife Anna, son George, and provided for an unborn child. Executors John Mead of Somers and Guy B. Hobby of North Castle. Witnesses Henry Brown, William Finch, and Nelson Banks, page 127.
Feb. 13, 1821, order to advertise for claims, page 127.
Inventory taken Mch. 12, 1821, by Benjamin Brush and James Smith, and filed Apl. 9, 1821, page 128.
Jan. 7, 1822, commissioners appointed to adjust claims of creditors, page 195.
Aug. 10, 1822, report of commissioners filed, page 230.
June 3, 1822, time for final settlement extended to Aug. 24, 1822, page 230.

Banks, Samuel, late of North Castle, Sept. 11, 1822, letters of administration on his estate granted to Rachel Banks who was ordered to advertise for claims, page 304.

STAMFORD PROBATE RECORDS.
Volume 12, 1819.

Banks, Samuel, continued :
Inventory taken by Edward Close and Aaron Peck, and filed Apl. 23, 1823, page 304.
Apl. 23, 1823, estate ordered distributed to his widow, Rachel Banks, and children ; to the legal representatives of James Banks, Jr., William R. Banks, Nelson Banks, to the legal representatives of Deborah Lounsbury, and Rachel wife of William Finch, page 304.
May 9, 1823, estate distributed accodingly, page 305.

Barmore, Walter, late of New York City, will dated Apl. 22, 1823, probated June 30, 1823, mentions his wife Mary, and children Mary Barmore and Ann Barmore; nephew and niece Philip Agnew and Susan Agnew; and Abraham C. Barmore. Executors his wife, Eldad Holmes, and Thomas Hyatt. Witnesses John H. Smith, David Munson, Elisha R. Belcher, and Augustus Lyon, page 296.
June 30, 1823, order to advertise for claims, page 296.
Inventory taken by Samuel Bush and Zabed Finch, and filed June 30, 1823, page 298.

Bates, Gershom, late of Stamford, Dec. 9, 1822, letters of administration on his estate granted to Hannah Bates and Cary Leeds, who were ordered to advertise for claims, page 263.
Inventory taken Feb. 11, 1823, by Samuel Hoyt and John Leeds, and filed Feb. 25, 1823, page 263.
Apl. 22, 1823, John Bates of Darien appointed guardian of Lewis H. and Samuel G., sons of decedent, and Hannah Bates appointed guardian of Mary J., Hannah E., William H., and Martha S., other children of decedent, page 330.
Mch. 26, 1824, John Bates guardian of Lewis H. Bates, asked leave to sell the real estate of said minor in Stamford, and sale ordered, page 354.
May 20, 1824, real estate sold to Richard Fox, and report of sale filed, page 354.

Bell, Betsy, of Stamford, Dec. 6, 1819, appointed guardian of her daughter -------, about four years of age, page 32.

Bell, Jonathan, Jr., late of Stamford, Apl. 6, 1819, letters of administration on his estate granted to Betsy Bell, who was ordered to advertise for claims, page 31.
Inventory taken June 7, 1819, by Thaddeus Bell and John Bell, and filed Dec. 6, 1819, page 31.

STAMFORD PROBATE RECORDS.
Volume 12, 1819.

Bell, Jonathan, Jr., continued:
    Dec. 6, 1819, dower of his widow, Betsy Bell, ordered set out; account filed; and distribution ordered to his widow, and Sally Ann Bell, only child, page 85.
    Aug. 19, 1820, estate distributed accordingly, page 86.

Bell, Noah, late of Stamford, will dated Feb. 19, 1822, probated Mch. 11, 1822, mentions his wife Prudence, and children Noah, John, Sally wife of James Sniffin, Mary wife of Henry Webb, Jared, Ezekiel, Francis, Prudence Bell and Rebecca Bell. Executors his sons Ezekiel and Francis. Witnesses Frederick Bell, Rowland Tryon, and Abigail Webb, page 205.
    Ezekiel Bell declined to act, page 206.
    Inventory taken Mch. 18, 1822, by Rowland Tryon and Jonas Scofield, and filed Mch. 18, 1822, page 207.

Bishop, Alexander, late of Stamford, Apl. 6, 1819, letters of administration with the will annexed granted to John K. Bishop, page 65.
    Inventory taken May 27, 1819, by Isaac Wardwell and Henry Brown, and filed Feb. 18, 1820, page 65.

Bishop, Jonathan, late of Darien, Oct. 29, 1821, letters of administration on his estate granted to John Holmes, who was ordered to advertise for claims, page 188.
    Inventory taken Oct. 31, 1821, by John Clock and John Bell, and filed Nov. 8, 1821, page 188.

Brown, Charles, late of Stamford, Feb. 15, 1820, letters of administration on his estate granted to Jacob Lockwood, Jr., who was ordered to advertise for claims, page 76.
    Inventory taken Feb. 21, 1820, by Isaac Penoyer and Phineahas Waterbury, and filed Apl. 3, 1820, page 76.
    Apl. 24, 1820, commissioners appointed to adjust claims of creditors, page 77.
    May 5, 1820, personal property ordered sold to pay debts, and same sold on May 18, 1820, page 100.
    Nov. 6, 1820, report of commissioners to adjust claims filed, page 100.

Brown, Peter, late of Stamford, July 31, 1819, Martha Brown and Peter Brown, administrators with the will annexed, time for final settlement extended to Feb. 3, 1820,

STAMFORD PROBATE RECORDS.
Volume 12, 1819.

Brown, Peter, continued:
   page 40.
   Feb. 25, 1820, estate distributed to Martha Brown, his widow, and children Jerusha, Peter, and Patty, page 93.

Brundage, Charity, late of Greenwich, Mch. 29, 1823, letters of administration on her estate granted to Aaron Field, who was ordered to advertise for claims, page 291. Inventory taken Apl. 16, 1823, by William Sutton and John Carpenter, and filed May 19, 1823, page 291.

Brush, Benjamin, late of Stamford, will dated Feb. 19, 1822, probated Jan. 6, 1823, mentions his wife Rebekah, and children Rebekah, Benjamin S., Ard, Jonathan, Rachel, Mary Ann, Abigail Knapp, Anne Smith, and Lucy Ann Downs Executors Benjamin Brush, Jr., and Benjamin S. Brush. Witnesses John Dibble, Alexander Lockwood, and David Wood, page 275.
   Jan. 6, 1823, order to advertise for claims, page 276. Inventory taken Jan. 24, 1823, by Jared Smith and Edward Brush, and filed Feb. 11, 1823, page 277.
   Mch. 13, 1823, necessaries set out to his widow, page 277.
   Jan. 5, 1824, time for final settlement extended to July 6, 1824, page 352.
   Apl. 19, 1824, account filed, and reale state ordered sold to pay debts, page 352.
   May 7, 1824, reale state sold to Edward Brush and Benjamin S. Brush, and report of sale filed, page 352.

Cannon, Charles Ogilvie, late of Norwalk, will dated Oct. 18, 1817, probated July 7, 1819, mentions his mother Sally Cannon, brothers John C., and George, sister Esther Mary wife of Solomon Townsend, now of Albany, lands in Ohio, sister Antoinette Cannon, brother-in-law Thaddeus Betts interest in store at Norwalk in company with Willaim M. Betts. Executor brother-in-law Thaddeus Betts. Witnesses Samuel Daskam, John Daskam, and Henry Street, page 38.

Carhart, William, late of Rye, July 7, 1823, letters of administration on his estate granted to Abraham Close of Greenwich, and commissioners appointed to adjust claims of creditors, page 329.
   Mch. 1, 1824, report of commissioners filed, page 330.

STAMFORD PROBATE RECORDS.
Volume 12, 1819.

Clason, Martha, late of Stamford, will dated Apl. 15, 1815, probated June 16, 1820, mentions her granddaughter Adah Clason, son Benjamin Clason, granddaughter Martha Clason a daughter of her son Solomon, children Isaac Clason, Solomon Clason, Ard Clason, and Abigail Jessup. Executor her son Solomon. Witnesses Daniel Nichols, Samuel June, and William June. page 91.
June 16, 1820, order to advertise for claims, page 91.
Inventory taken July 10, 1820, by Daniel Lockwood, and Stephen Bishop, and filed Aug. 7, 1820, page 91.

Clock, Martin, late of Darien, will dated May 23, 1822, probated Aug. 3, 1822, mentions his wife Patty, and children Hetty Bell, Rebecca Bell, Hiram, Samuel, Oliver, Nelly Clock, Harriet Clock, Sally Clock, and Betsy Clock. Executor John Weed, Jr. Witnesses Warren Percival, John Dibble, Jr., and Morris Tuthill, page 347.
Aug. 3, 1822, order to advertise for claims, page 348.
Inventory taken Aug. 8, 1822, by Isaac Gray and Daniel Chadayne, and filed Jan. 30, 1823, page 348.
Oct. 13, 1823, account filed, and real estate ordered sold to pay debts, page 349.
Dec. 3, 1823, real estate sold to John Reed, Jr., and report of sale filed, page 349.
Dec. 27, 1823, petition of Martha Clock guardian of Sarah and Elizabeth, children of decedent, for leave to sell the real estate of said minors, and sale ordered, page 353.
Also petition of Enos Wilmot guardian of Oliver and Harriet, other children of decedent, for leave to sell the real estate of said minors, and sale ordered, page 353.
June 10, 1823, Oliver and Harriet, children of decedent, made choice of Enos Wilmot of Darien to be their guardian, and the court also appointed Martha Clock guardian of Sarah and Elizabeth, other children of decedent, page 302.

Close, Gideon, late of Greenwich, will dated Nov. 20, 1819, probated Dec. 15, 1819, mentions his wife Bethiah, nephews Jonathan Allen Close, Gilbert Close, Horace Close, and William Close. Executor nephew Edward Close Witnesses Anna N. Peck, Samuel Peck, and Shadrach Mead, page 52.
Dec. 15, 1819, order to advertise for claims, page 52.
Inventory taken Dec. 29, 1819, by Elias Peck and Samuel Peck, and filed July 7, 1820,

STAMFORD PROBATE RECORDS.
Volume 12, 1819.

Close, Jonathan, of Greenwich, about 17 years of age, Apl. 3, 1820, made choice of Elias Peck to be his guardian, page 79.

Close, Mary R., of Greenwich, Mch. 1, 1824, made choice of Job Lyon to be her guardian, page 331.

Comstock, James B., of Stamford, Apl. 3, 1821, William Knapp, Jr., appointed his guardian, page 119.
Mch. 29, 1823, made choice of William Knapp, Jr., to be his guardian, page 253.

Crennell, Abigail J., late of Stamford, Aug. 29, 1821, letters of administration on her estate granted to Cary Leeds, who was ordered to advertise for claims, page 190.

Davenport, John, late of Stamford, will dated Aug. 11, 1819, probated Mch. 6, 1820, mentions his wife Sarah, and children Sally wife of Abraham Bates, Julia Ann wife of Jotham Hoyt, William, and James; grandchildren children of his daughter Theodosia deceased wife of William Davenport, viz: Hezekiah R., Dorfus, and Mary A. Executors sons William and James. Witnesses Ebenezer Weed, Reuben Scofield, and Ephraim Jones, page 56.
Mch. 6, 1820, order to advertise for claims, page 58.
Inventory taken Mch. 8, 1820, by Reuben Scofield and David Stevens, and filed Mch. 20, 1820, page 58.

Davis, Walter, late of Rye, Feb. 24, 1821, letters of administration on his estate granted to Ruth Davis of Rye, who was ordered to advertise for claims, page 126.
Inventory taken Feb. 7, 1821, by Abraham Lyon and John Lyon, and filed Feb. 26, 1821, page 126.
Dec. 3, 1821, commissioners appointed to adjust claims of creditors, page 192.
July 6, 1822, report of commissioners filed, page 230.
July 6, 1822, account filed, and real estate ordered sold to pay debts, page 231.
July 29, 1822, real estate sold to Elnathan Mead, and report of sale filed, page 231.

Denton, Daniel, late of Greenwich, Aug. 30, 1823, letters of administration on his estate granted to John M. Denton, who was ordered to advertise for claims, page 331.
Inventory taken Oct. 24, 1823, by Hezekiah Tracy and John Sackett, and filed Oct. 28, 1823, page 331.

STAMFORD PROBATE RECORDS.
Volume 12, 1819.

Dixon, Sarah A., and Catherine Dixon, both over 12 years of age, Apl. 4, 1823, made choice of Isaac Wardwell of Stamford to be their guardian, page 254.

Ferris, Clarissa, and William Ferris, of Greenwich, June 4, 1821, Edmond Mead and Nathaniel Ferris, Jr., respectively appointed their guardians, page 182.

Ferris, Nathaniel, late of Greenwich, Oct. 18, 1823, letters of administration on his estate granted to Gideon Ferris, who was ordered to advertise for claims, page 321. Inventory taken Dec. 13, 1823, by Enos Lockwood and Alexander Hendrie, and filed Dec. 13, 1823, page 321. Mch. 9, 1824, estate ordered distributed to his widow, Mary Ferris, and children John, George, Gideon, Ann wife of Andrew Ferris, Elizabeth wife of David Kimberly, and Esther wife of Samuel Ferris, page 342.
Apl. 20, 1824, estate distributed accordingly, page 342.

Ferris, Solomon, late of Greenwich, (Stanwich), Feb. 28, 1820, letters of administration on his estate granted to Ira Lockwood, who was ordered to advertise for claims, page 68.
Inventory taken Mch. 1, 1820, by Jared Smith and Jonathan Finch, and filed Apl. 1, 1820, page 68.
Apl. 3, 1820, Jared Smith, James Smith, and Seth Lyon, all of Greenwich, were appointed to set off widow's dower, page 68.
Apl. 13, 1820, dower set off to Lavina Ferris, widow of deceased, page 68.
Jan. 8, 1821, estate ordered distributed to his children Solomon, Andrew, Joseph, Lewis, Benjamin, Deborah, Anna, Levina, Ruth, Clarry, and Amy, page 154.
May 7, 1821, estate distributed accordingly, subject to the widow's right of dower, page 154.

Finch, Nathaniel, late of Greenwich, will dated Dec. 18, 1815, probated May 6, 1823, mentions his wife Anna, and children Zabed and Sophia. Executor his son Zabed. Witnesses Sarah Morrell, Reumah Walker, and Timothy Walker, page 302.
May 6, 1823, order to advertise for claims, page 303.
Inventory taken June 17, 1823, by Caleb Husted and Lucknor Mead, and filed July 3, 1823, page 303.

Gorum, Daniel, late of Stamford, Feb. 24, 1820, letters of administration on his estate granted to Samuel B. Warren, who was ordered to advertise for claims,

STAMFORD PROBATE RECORDS.
Volume 12, 1819.

Gorum, Daniel, continued :
page 122.
Inventory taken Feb. 29, 1820, by Barnabas Marvin and Henry Bates, and filed Mch. 21, 1821, page 122.
Mch. 30, 1821, time for final settlement extended to Aug. 24, next, page 125.

Gorum, Daniel, late of Darien, Dec. 20, 1822, estate distributed to his widow, Jane Gorum, and children Samuel, Daniel, Joseph, George, Alfred, Henry, Polly wife of Isaac Gray, Charlotte Gorum, and Phebe wife of Benjamin Gray, page 237.

Gray, Benjamin, late of Darien, June 2, 1823, letters of administration on his estate granted to Alfred Gorum, who was ordered to advertise for claims, page 298.
Inventory taken July 30, 1823, by Isaac Penoyer and Abram Clock, and filed July 30, 1823, page 298.

Green, John, late of Darien, Jan. 26, 1822, letters of administration on his estate granted to Henry Weed, Jr., and commissioners appointed to adjust claims of creditors, page 190.
Inventory taken Jan. 31, 1822, by James Stevens and Nathaniel Waterbury, and filed Feb. 6, 1822, page 190.
Feb. 9, 1822, necessaries allowed to his widow, Elizabeth Green, page 191.
Jan. 23, 1823, time for final settlement extended to June 26, 1823, page 316.
May 2, 1823, report of commissioners to adjust claims filed, page 316.
May 10, 1823, account filed, and real estate ordered sold to pay debts, page 317.
May 20, 1823, real estate sold to John Leeds, Warren Hoyt, and James Webb, and report of sale filed, page 317.

Grigg, Alexander, late of Greenwich, Jan. 21, 1822, on the application of Caleb Husted in right of his wife Mary, one of the children of deceased, estate ordered distributed to Betsy Grigg, Ann wife of Edmond Brown of the City of New York, John Grigg of the West Indies, Letty wife of William Blair of Scotland, Mary Husted, and Walter Grigg, children of decedent, page 216.
Mch. 22, 1822, estate distributed accordingly, page 217.

Hawley, Electer, of Stamford, May 1, 1820, appointed guardian of her children Sarah E. Hawley, about 6 years of age,

STAMFORD PROBATE RECORDS.
Volume 12, 1819.

109.

Hawley, Elector, continued:
and Charles S. Hawley, about 3 years of age, page 66.

Hawley, Elisha, late of Stamford, Oct. 4, 1819, letters of administration on his estate granted to Joseph Wood and Elector Hawley, who were ordered to advertise for claims, page 40.
Inventory taken by Isaac Holly and Frederic Webb and filed Dec. 6, 1819, page 39.

Haxton, Dyer, late of Stamford, will dated May 9, 1811, probated Oct. 23, 1820, all to his wife Sarah. Executrix his wife. Witnesses Ebenezer Ferris, Abigail Ferris, and Joseph Wood, page 120.
Inventory taken Oct. 26, 1820, by Cary Leeds and Isaac Holly, and filed Dec. 12, 1820, page 121.

Haxton, Louisa C., late of Stamford, Sept. 4, 1820, letters of administration on her estate granted to Jonathan Weed, Jr., who was ordered to advertise for claims, page 102.
Inventory taken Sept. 6, 1820, by Isaac Holly and Shadrach Hoyt, page 102.

Hebbard, Nathaniel, late of Greenwich, will dated Aug. 11, 1820, probated June 4, 1822, mentions his wife ----, and children Esther Hebbard, Ruth wife of Obadiah Mead, and Polly wife of Esben Husted; grandchildren Charles Mead and Hannah H. Mead children of daughter Hannah, deceased wife of Jonas Mead, and nephew Nathaniel Hebbard son of Jonathan Hebbard; owned land in Greenwich, Ohio. Executors Obadiah Mead and Jonas Mead. Witnesses Amos Husted, William Husted, and Caleb Husted, page 256.
June 4, 1822, order to advertise for claims, page 257.
Inventory taken by William Husted and Caleb Husted, and filed July 1, 1822, page 257.

Hobby, Mary, late of Greenwich, Apl. 29, 1819, letters of administration on her estate granted to Ebenezer Hobby of Greenwich, who was ordered to advertise for claims, page 40.

Holly, Abraham, late of Stamford, will dated Nov. 15, 1815, probated Sept. 3, 1821, mentions his children Mary, Rebecca, Lucy, Chloe, Jared, and Abraham, children of his daughter Elizabeth, and John a son of Elnathan a deceased son. Executor his son Jared. Witnesses

STAMFORD PROBATE RECORDS.
Volume 12, 1819.

Holly, Abraham, continued :
Sarah Scofield, Anna Scofield, and Reuben Scofield, page 159.
Sept. 3, 1821, order to advertise for claims, page 160.
Inventory taken Sept. 17, 1821, by William Scofield and Hezron Scofield, and filed Sept. 20, 1821, page 182
Apl. 11, 1822, account filed and real estate ordered sold to pay debts, page 210.
Sale on Apl. 25, 1822, of salt meadow to William Scofield, and of land at Hunting Ridge to William Youngs, page 210.
May 4, 1822, estate ordered distributed to Stephen, Jared, Mary Pardee, Rebecca Hobby, Lucy Smith, and Cloe Ingersoll, children of deceased, and to Electa Simmons, Samuel Coley, and Hannah Coley, the only children of Elizabeth Coley, a deceased daughter, according to his will, page 222.
May 24, 1822, estate distributed accordingly, page 223.

Holly, Mercy, late of Stamford, June 9, 1819, Joseph Silliman, executor, Elizabeth Burtis, sister of deceased, acknowledged the receipt of the whole of decedent's estate, page 38.

Holly, Samuel, late of Stamford, will dated Dec. 26, 1808, probated Aug. 11, 1821, all to his wife Phebe. Executrix his wife. Witnesses Thomas Lounsbury, Henry Wilmot, and Samuel Webb, page 147.
Inventory taken by James Webb and Alpheus Scofield, and filed Aug. 29, 1821, page 147.
Aug. 29, 1821, commissioners appointed to adjust claims of creditors, and personal property ordered sold page 148.
Apl. 8, 1822, report of commissioners filed, page 210.
Apl. 8, 1822, account filed, and real estate ordered sold to pay debts, page 211.

Holmes, John, late of Stamford, Feb. 22, 1820, letters of administration on his estate granted to John Holmes, who was ordered to advertise for claims, page 66.

Holmes, John, late of Darien, will dated June 20, 1822, probated Aug. 9, 1822, mentions his wife Nancy, and children John, Jr., Sarah Catharine, Rebekah, Mary and Hannah Elizabeth. Executrix his wife. Witnesses Mary Holmes, Alba Holmes, and Samuel Webb, page 251.
Aug. 9, 1822, order to advertise for claims, page 252.

STAMFORD PROBATE RECORDS.
Volume 12, 1819.

Holmes, John, continued:
    Inventory taken Aug. 21, 1822, by Nathaniel Waterbury and John Leeds, and filed Nov. 6, 1822, page 252.

Hoyt, Abraham, late of Stamford, Nov. 4, 1822, letters of administration on his estate granted to Ezra Knapp, and Sarah Hoyt, who were ordered to advertise for claims, page 261.
    Inventory taken Nov. 7, 1822, by Shadrach Hoyt, Jr., and William Keeler, and filed Dec. 10, 1822, page 261.

Hoyt, Anna, late of Stamford, July 3, 1820, letters of administration on her estate granted to Augustus Scofield, who was ordered to advertise for claims, page 101.
    Inventory taken July 3, 1820, by Jonathan Scofield and Jacob Knapp, and filed Sept. 4, 1820, page 101.
    May 1, 1821, estate ordered distributed to Jonah Hoyt, and Elihu Hoyt, brothers of deceased; to Horace Scofield only child of Betsy Scofield a deceased sister, and to the heirs-at-law of Ziba Hoyt, a deceased brother, page 153.
    May 19, 1821, estate distributed accordingly, page 153.

Hoyt, Betsy, late of Stamford, Dec. 7, 1820, letters of administration on her estate granted to John Tillman, who was ordered to advertise for claims, and commissioners appointed to adjust claims of creditors, pages 106, and 180.
    Inventory taken Dec. 7, 1820, by Isaac Lockwood and Isaac Holly, and filed Jan. 1, 1821, page 106.
    Aug. 31, 1821, letters of administration de bonus non on her estate granted to Stephen B. Provost (former administrator John Tillman, now deceased), page 181.
    July 28, 1821, report of commissioners to adjust claims of creditors filed, page 181.

Hoyt, Edwin, of -----, Dec. 10, 1822, made choice of his mother Sarah Hoyt, to be his guardian, page 263.

Hoyt, Enoch, late of Stamford, Oct. 18, 1819, report of commissioners to adjust claims filed, page 40.

Hoyt, Hannah, of Stamford, Oct. 8, 1822, appointed guardian of her son Philip L. Hoyt, page 246.

Hoyt, Hervey, late of Stamford, Mch. 6, 1820, letters of administration on his estate granted to Benjamin Hoyt and Joseph S. Hoyt, who were ordered to advertise for

STAMFORD PROBATE RECORDS.
Volume 12, 1819.

Hoyt, Hervey, continued :
    claims, page 72.
    Inventory taken Apl. 5, 1820, by Jotham Hoyt and Luther Weed, and filed Mch. 6, 1820, page 72.

Hoyt, Josiah, late of Stamford, Mch. 9, 1819, Isaac Hoyt only acting executor, real estate ordered distributed to Isaac, son 1/2, and other 1/2 to the legal representatived of Josiah Hoyt, late of Norwalk, and personal property to said Isaac Hoyt, Rhoda wife of Gilbert Woolsey of Stamford, Anna wife of Gideon Weed of New Canaan, Mary or Mercy wife of Selleck Weed of Stamford, and to the legal representatives of Josiah Hoyt, late of Norwalk, page 28.
    Aug. 2, 1819, estate distributed accordingly, page 28.

Hoyt, Josiah, late of Stamford, Jan. 22, 1821, letters of administration on his estate granted to Cary Leeds, who was ordered to advertise for claims, page 113.
    Inventory taken Jan. 26, 1821, by Jonas Scofield and Benjamin Tryon, and filed Jan. 20, 1821, page 113.

Hoyt, Nathaniel, late of Darien, will dated Aug. 23, 1819, probated May 2, 1822, mentions his wife Sarah, and children Ralph Hoyt and Martha wife of John Reed, Jr. Executors his son, and Barnabas Marvin of Norwalk. Witnesses Noyes Richards, Isaac Hoyt, and Henry Bates, page 258.
    May 2, 1822, order to advertise for claims, page 258.
    Inventory taken June 25, 1822, by Thomas Reed and Henry Bates, and filed Dec. 20, 1822, page 259.

Hoyt, Seth, late of Stamford, Nov. 3, 1818, Nehemiah Hoyt, executor and one of the devisees, dower of his widow ordered to be set out, and realestate ordered distributed to Nehemiah, Seth, John, Mary Ann, Rachel, Ruth, and Rebecca, children of deceased, according to his will, page 32.
    May 1, 1819, distribution made accordingly, page 32.
    June 12, 1819, Mary Ann, Rachel, and Ruth, daughters of decedent, made choice of Nehemiah Hoyt to be their guardian, who was also appointed guardian of Rebecca, about 10 years of age, another daughter of decedent, page 32.

Hoyt, Ziba, late of Stamford, Feb. 7, 1820, letters of administration on his estate granted to John Brown, Jr., who was ordered to advertise for claims, page 111.

STAMFORD PROBATE RECORDS.
Volume 12, 1819.

Hoyt, Ziba, continued :
    Inventory taken Dec. 19, 1820, by Rowland Tryon and Nehemiah Scofield, and filed Dec. 19, 1820, page 111.
    Apl. 10, 1820, commissioners appointed to adjust claims of creditors, page 112.
    Dec. 19, 1820, report of commissioners confirmed, page 112.
    May 1, 1821, estate ordered distributed to Jonah Hoyt and Elihu Hoyt, brothers of deceased, and to Horace Scofield only child of Betsy Scofield, a deceased sister, page 153.
    May 19, 1821, estate distributed accordingly, page 154.

Husted, Abraham, late of Greenwich, will dated May 16, 1819, probated June 18, 1819, mentions his wife Hannah, and children David, Hannah Waterbury, Drake, Sally, and William. Executors his sons Drake and William. Witnesses Israel K. Avery, Isaac Ferris, and George Platt, pages 1 and 79.
    Inventory taken by Hezekiah Tracy and Peter Mead, and filed June, 1819, pages 3 and 81.
    Dec. 3, 1819, on the application of Thomas Waterbury of Greenwich, in right of his wife Hannah, a daughter of deceased, an appeal was taken from the probate of the will of said deceased, page 83.

Husted, Peter, late of Greenwich, will dated Mch. 27, 1815, probated May 2, 1821, mentions his wife Eunice, and children Aaron, Caleb, Amos, Peter, Elnathan, Moses, Cynthia widow of Squire Hobby, and Eunice Husted. Executors his wife and son Elnathan. Witnesses Richard Mead, Ebenezer Mead, Jr., and Ebenezer Mead, page 139.
    Letters granted to his son Elnathan, the widow having renounced, page 139.
    May 2, 1821, order to advertise for claims, page 139.
    Inventory taken by Drake Husted and William Husted, and filed June 19, 1821, page 162.

Jarvis, Stephen, late of Darien, May 14, 1822, letters of administration on his estate granted to Jeremiah Andreas of Darien, who was ordered to advertise for claims, page 224.
    Inventory taken May 20, 1822, by Joshua Scofield and Samuel Whiting, and filed July 1, 1822, page 224.

Jessup, Samuel, about 15 years of age, Aug. 17, 1820, made choice of Sarah Jessup to be his guardian, page 83.

STAMFORD PROBATE RECORDS.
Volume 12, 1819.

Jessup, Timothy, late of ---- Nov. 26, 1823, Peter, Sarah, and Martha, children of decedent, made choice of Philip Lockwood of Greenwich to be their guardian, page 301.

Jones, Isaac, Jr/, late of Stamford, June 7, 1819, Selleck Jones, administrator, distribution of the real estate ordered to Selleck Jones, eldest brother, and personal property to said Selleck Jones, Benjamin Jones, and Abigail, wife of Samuel Gorum, brothers and sister of deceased, page 14.
June 11, 1819, estate distributed accordingly, page 14.

Jones, James, late of Stamford, now Darien, Aug. 7, 1820, letters of administration on his estate granted to Selleck Jones, who was ordered to advertise for claims, page 97
Inventory taken Oct. 23, 1820, by Uriah Waterbury and John Bell, and filed Oct. 23, 1820, page 97.
Oct. 8, 1821, personal property ordered distributed to Selleck Jones, Benjamin Jones, and Abigail Gorum wife of Samuel Gorum, all of Darien, his only heirs-at-law, page 152.
Oct. 19, 1821, estate distributed accordingly, page 152

Jones, Katharine, late of Stamford, Aug. 7, 1820, letters of administration on her estate granted to Selleck Jones, who was ordered to advertise for claims, page 180.
Inventory taken Feb. 28, 1821, by John Bell, Deby Bell, and Richard Bell, and filed May 14, 1821, page 180.

Judson, John, late of Stamford, will dated Sept. 26, 1818, probated Sept. 17, 1822, mentions his wife Charity, and children John, Jr., Sarah wife of Benjamin Perine, Molly wife of Solomon Smith, Charity wife of Isaac Bell, Lewis, Amos, Rebecca Raymond, and James. Executors his wife and son Lewis. Witnesses Susan Webb, Betsy Webb, and Samuel Webb, page 273.
Sept. 17, 1822, order to advertise for claims, page 274.
Inventory taken by Isaac Holly and Peter Smith, and filed Oct. 12, 1822, page 274.

Keeler, William, late of Stamford, Dec. 22, 1823, letters of administration on his estate granted to Charles Hawley and Debby Keeler, both of Stamford, and commissioners appointed to adjust claims of creditors, page 306.
Inventory taken Jan. 24, 1823, by Isaac Lockwood and James F. Palmer, and filed Feb. 4, 1823, page 306.
Additional inventory filed Sept. 15, 1823, page 308.

STAMFORD PROBATE RECORDS.
Volume 12, 1819.

Keeler, William, continued:
Jan. 27, 1823, personal property ordered sold, page 310.
Oct. 10, 1823, report of commissioners to adjust claims filed, page 308.
Oct. 21, 1823, necessaries set out to his widow, Debby Keeler, page 310.
Nov. 26, 1823, dower of his widow ordered set out, page 311.
Nov. 26, 1823, dower set out to his widow, Deborah Keeler, page 311.
Nov. 26, 1823, real estate lying in Norwalk, and other real estate sold, and report of sale filed, page 312.
Jan. 21, 1824, account filed, and creditors ordered paid forty five cents on the dollar, page 313.

Knapp, Edmund, late of Greenwich, July 7, 1823, letters of administration on his estate granted to Abraham Close, who was ordered to advertise for claims, page 293. Inventory taken by Drake Mead and Isaac Holly, and filed Sept. 1, 1823, page 293.
Mch. 26, 1824, additional inventory filed, and necessaries allowed to his widow, page 357.
Mch. 26, 1824, account filed, and real estate ordered sold to pay debts, page 358.

Knapp, Hannah, about 17 years of age, Jan. 24, 1824, made choice of David L. Palmer to be her guardian, page 301.

Lewis, Amzi, Rev., late of Stamford, Oct. 30, 1819, commissioners appointed to adjust claims of creditors, page 35.
Dec. 6, 1819, report of commissioners filed, page 35.

Lewis, Daniel, late of Greenwich, will dated July 1, 1817, probated Jan. 24, 1820, mentions his wife Martha, and children Benjamin, Daniel, David, Calvin, Nehemiah, Silvanus, Sally wife of Monmouth Wilson, Elizabeth wife of Isaac Maby, Nancy wife of Benjamin Lyon, and Hetty wife of Joseph Horton; to Susannah Brown formerly the wife of Ebenezer Brown of Hogpen Ridge a legacy. Executors his sons Daniel and David. Witnesses John Mackay, Charity W. Brown, and James Green, Jr., page 75. David Lewis renounced his executor-ship.
Jan. 24, 1820, order to advertise for claims, page 75.
Inventory taken Jan. 25, 1820, by Solomon Peck and Charles Wilson, and filed Jan. 31, 1820, page 75.
Mch. 21, 1821, account filed, and real estate ordered sold to pay debts, page 144.

STAMFORD PROBATE RECORDS.
Volume 12, 1819.

116.

Lewis, Daniel, continued :
- Mch. 27, 1821, dower set out to his widow, Martha Lewis, page 143.
- Apl. 17, 1821, part of the real estate sold to Benjamin Green, and report of sale confirmed on May 9, 1821, page 144.
- May 9, 1821, estate ordered distributed to his children Daniel, David, Calvin, Nehemiah, Sylvanus, Sally Wilson, Elizabeth Maby, Nancy Lyon, and Hetty Horton, page 144.
- Estate distributed accordingly, page 145.
- Jan. 19, 1821, time for final settlement extended to July 24, next, page 107.

Lockwood, Edward, Jr., late of Greenwich, Jan. 14, 1822, letters of administration on his estate granted to Lydia Lockwood and Edward Close, who were ordered to advertise for claims, page 186.
- Inventory taken Jan. 16, 1822, by Benjamin Brush and Shadrach Close, and filed Jan. 22, 1822, page 186.
- Feb. 4, 1822, necessaries allowed to his widow, Lydia Lockwood, page 188.
- Feb. 22, 1823, account filed, and real estate ordered sold to pay debts, page 256.

Lockwood, Edward, late of Greenwich, Aug. 5, 1822, letters of administration on his estate granted to William P. Lockwood, who was ordered to advertise for claims, page 255.
- Inventory taken Sept. 18, 1822, and an additional inventory taken by Benjamin Brush and Shadrach Close, and filed Feb. 23, 1822, page 255.
- Jan. 28, 1822, time for final settlement extended to July 14, next, page 256.

Lockwood, Ezra, late of Stamford, Mch. 19, 1821, letters of administration on his estate granted to Charles Knapp and Samuel Lockwood, who were ordered to advertise for claims, page 135.
- Inventory taken Mch. 21, 1821, by Erastus H. Weed and Daniel Lockwood, and filed Mch. 31, 1821, page 136.
- Inventory of estate in Watertown taken Apl. 10, 1821, by Ebenezer Bates and Theophilus Baldwin, and filed Apl. 20, 1821, page 138.
- Mch. 28, 1821, necessaries allowed his widow, page 138.
- Aug. 9, 1822, additional inventory filed, page 232.
- Mch. 4, 1822, account filed and real estate ordered sold to pay debts, page 233.

STAMFORD PROBATE RECORDS.
Volume 12, 1819.

Lockwood, Ezra, continued:
    Mch. 25, 1822, real estate sold, and report of sale filed, page 233.
    Aug. 9, 1822, account filed, shows real estate in Watertown, Litchfield County, and estate ordered distributed to the legal representatives of Ezra Lockwood, late of said Watertown, William Lockwood of Green, N. Y., Rufus Lockwood, Polly Bunnell, Elizabeth wife of said Charles Knapp, Samuel Lockwood, Lewis Lockwood, and Davis Lockwood, the only heirs-at-law of deceased, page 233.
    Aug. 14, 1822, estate distributed accordingly, page 234.

Lockwood, Frederick, late of Greenwich, Sept. 25, 1813, estate distributed to Deborah Lockwood widow of deceased, and to his children Seymour, Frederic, Ezekiel, Alfred, Luke, Uriah, Lot, Fanny, Deborah, and Sally, page 18.

Lockwood, Jonathan, late of Stamford, will dated June 1, 1810, probated Dec. 23, 1822, mentions his wife Hannah, and children Charlotte wife of Isaac Miles, Isaac, Smith, and Jonathan. Executor his son Isaac. Witnesses Samuel Wheaton, Daniel Nichols, and Zadock Newman, page 278.
    Dec. 23, 1822, order to advertise for claims, page 278.
    Inventory taken by Aaron Davis and Abel Reynolds, and filed May 1, 1823, page 279.
    Aug. 13, 1823, account filed, and real estate ordered sold to pay debts, page 279.
    Oct. 22, 1823, real estate sold to Nathaniel Hubbard and Nehemiah Hoyt, and report of sale filed, page 283.

Lockwood, Josiah, late of Stamford, Feb. 7, 1820, letters of administration on his estate granted to Harvy Lockwood, and Isaac Knapp, Jr., who were ordered to advertise for claims, page 64.
    Inventory taken Feb. 12, 1820, and filed Feb. 14, 1820, page 64.

Lockwood, Maurice, late of Greenwich, Dec. 7, 1819, letters of administration on his estate granted to Enos B. Lockwood, who was ordered to advertise for claims, page 82.
    Inventory taken by Charles Hendrie and Samuel Husted, and filed Mch. 6, 1820, page 82.

Lockwood, Thaddeus, late of Greenwich, will dated Mch. 30, 1808, probated Feb. 1, 1822, mentions his wife Sarah, and children William, Amy Armstrong, Isabel James,

STAMFORD PROBATE RECORDS.
Volume 12, 1819.

118.

Lockwood, Thaddeus, continued :
Anne Gales, Sarah Baxter, Deborah Lockwood, Mary Briggs, Thaddeus, Ira, Edmond, Dennison, and the children of his daughter Abigail Smith. Executors his sons Thaddeus and Edmond. Witnesses Samuel M. Fitch, Sarah Fitch, and Elizabeth Fitch, page 193.
Feb. 19, 1822, inventory taken by Jared Smith and Jonathan Smith, and filed Feb. 25, 1822, page 204.
Mch. 18, 1822, estate ordered distributed to his children Edmond and Denison, according to his will, page 205.

Lounsbury, Sherman, of ----, about 15 years of age, Mch. 9, 1824, made choice of Ezekiel Scofield to be his guardian, page 331.

Lounsbury, William, late of Stamford, Oct. 25, 1819, letters of administration on his estate granted to Edwin Lounsbury, who was ordered to advertise for claims, page 97. Inventory taken June 26, 1820, by Isaac Lockwood, and Frederick Lockwood, and filed Oct. 24, 1820, page 97.

Lyon, Charles F., of ---- about 20 years of age, Mch. 19, 1822, made choice of John D. Lounsbury to be his guardian, page 203.

Lyon, Thomas, late of Greenwich, will dated Nov. 20, 1821, probated Dec. 14, 1821, mentions his wife Abigail, and children Polly, Katharine, Armenia, Elisha, and Charles F. Executors his wife, son Elisha, and Seth Lyon. Witnesses Daniel Sherwood, Jared Strang, and Caleb Knapp, page 174.
Dec. 14, 1821, order to advertise for claims, page 176. Inventory taken Dec. 17, 1821, by James Green and Platt Mead, and filed Jan. 19, 1822, page 176.

Madden, Amos, late of Greenwich, Jan. 10, 1820, time for final settlement extended to July 18, next, page 40.
Aug. 30, 1820, application of Henry Nelson of Milford, Worcester County, Mass., as guardian of Africa Madden, Sally Madden, and Michael Europe Madden; and Otis Parkhurst of said Milford as guardian of America Madden, Mary Ann Madden, Ezekiel Madden, and William R. Madden, for leave to sell the real estate of said minors lying in Greenwich, page 125.

STAMFORD PROBATE RECORDS.
Volume 12, 1819.

Mead, Abraham, late of Greenwich, Apl. 28, 1821, that part of
his estate set off to his widow, as her dower, ordered
distributed to his children, page, 185.
May 11, 1821, said estate distributed to his children
Daniel, Jotham, Eunus, 3rd, son, Samuel, Isaac, Job,
Zebulon, Nancah, Eunice Weed, and Ruth wife of Major
Brown, page 185.

Mead, Andrew, late of Greenwich, May 8, 1821, letters of administration on his estate granted to Amy Mead, who
was ordered to advertise for claims, page 172.
Inventory taken by Charles Smith and Hezekiah Tracy,
and filed June 7, 1821, page 172.
June 7, 1821, dower ordered set out to his widow,
Amy Mead, page 174.
June 7, 1821, dower set out, page 222.
Mch. 11, 1822, necessaries allowed his widow, page 212.
Mch. 23, 1822, account filed, and real estate ordered
sold to pay debts, page 212.
Additional inventory taken Mch. 13, 1822, and filed
Mch. 18, 1822, page 201.

Mead, Angeline A., June 9, 1821, Ebenezer Mead, appointed her
guardian, page 146.

Mead, Nancy, late of Greenwich, will dated Sept. 15, 1818,
probated Feb. 13, 1821, mentions her children Marilda
Bouton, Ebenezer, Rheuma Walker, Jabez, granddaughters
Nancy Elisa Walker, and Angelina A. Mead. Executor
Timothy Walker. Witnesses Reuben Holmes, Walter K.
Mead, and Lewis Ferris, page 130.
Feb. 13, 1821, order to advertise for claims, page 131.
Inventory taken Feb. 9, 1821, by Richard Mead and Alvan
Mead, and filed Feb. 13, 1821, page 131.

Mead, Nathaniel, late of Greenwich, Mch. 21, 1823, dower of
his widow, Elizabeth Mead, ordered set out, page 292.
Apl. 21, 1823, dower set out, page 292.

Mead, Ruth, late of Greenwich, May 2, 1821, at the request of
Jonathan Mead, letters of administration on her estate
were granted to Peter Mead, who was ordered to advertise for claims, page 141.
Inventory taken May 8, 1821, by Nathaniel Palmer and
Isaac Howe, and filed Nov. 1, 1822, page 260.
Oct. 7, 1822, time for final settlement extended to
Nov. 4, next, page 259.

STAMFORD PROBATE RECORDS.
Volume 12, 1819.

Miles, John, late of Greenwich, Oct. 5, 1819, letters of administration on his estate granted to Reuben R. Finch, of Greenwich, page 34.
    Inventory taken Oct. 1819, by Alvah Smith and Jared Smith, and filed Nov. 12, 1819, page 34.

Moore, Charles, late of Greenwich, Feb. 25, 1822, letters of administration on his estate granted to James Green, Jr and commissioners appointed to adjust claims of creditors, page 207.
    Inventory taken Feb. 25, 1822, by Joseph Green and S. Brown, and filed Mch. 18, 1822, page 208.
    Sept. 18, 1822, report of commissioners to adjust claims filed, page 244.
    Sept. 18, 1822, account filed, and personal property and part of real estate ordered sold to pay debts, page 245.
    Oct. 1, 1822, real estate sold, and report of sale filed, page 245.

Morehouse, Joshua, late of Darien, Dec. 3, 1822, letters of administration on his estate granted to Rufus Bell of Darien, and commissioners appointed to adjust claims of creditors, page 328.
    Inventory taken Dec. 1822, by Barnabas Marvin and John Bell, and filed Dec. 20, 1822, page 328.
    Oct. 18, 1823, report of commissioners to adjust claims filed, page 329.

Nash, David, late of Stamford, will dated Feb. 10, 1819, probated Sept. 6, 1823, mentions his wife Rachel, and child Elizabeth wife of Isaac Camp of Windham, Green County, N. Y., granddaughter Susannah R. Camp, a daughter of said Elizabeth Camp, nephew Edward a son of William Nash of Norwalk. Executor grandson David N. Camp. Witnesses Samuel Hoyt, Isaac Lockwood, and S. H. Minor, page 318.
    Sept. 6, 1823, order to advertise for claims, page 319.
    Inventory taken Sept. 8, 1823, by Erastus H. Weed and Isaac Holly, and filed Feb. 10, 1823, page 320.

Newman, Allen, of Greenwich, about 18 years of age, Jan. 24, 1822, made choice of Shadrach Finch to be his guardian, page 180.

Newman, Nathaniel, late of Stamford, Oct. 17, 1820, letters of administration on his estate granted to Solomon Clason, who was ordered to advertise for claims, page 103.

STAMFORD PROBATE RECORDS.
Volume 12, 1819.

Newman, Nathaniel, continued :
    Inventory taken Oct. 23, 1820, by Daniel Lockwood and Seth Smith, and filed Dec. 11, 1820, page 103.
    Dec. 16, 1820, necessaries to widow, page 105.
    May 15, 1821, dower of his widow, Thankful Newman, set out, page 184.
    Oct. 27, 1821, time for final settlement extended to Apl. 17, 1822, page 184.

Nichols, Robert, late of Stamford, Oct. 20, 1820, letters of administration on his estate granted to Isaac Lockwood, 3rd, who was ordered to advertise for claims, page 102.
    Inventory taken by Eber Smith and Drake Studwell, and filed Jan. 15, 1821, page 102.
    May 7, 1821, commissioners appointed to adjust claims of creditors, page 170.
    Dec. 10, 1821, report of commissioners filed, page 171.
    Dec. 1, 1821, account filed, and real estate ordered sold to pay debts, page 170.
    Jan. 1, 1822, sale made, and order of confirmation, page 171.

Palmer, Denham, late of Greenwich, will dated Mch. 18, 1817, probated Sept. 1, 1819, mentions his wife Ann, and children Edmond and Henry, and grandchildren William Doty, John Doty, and Lue Ann Doty. Executor William Knapp. Witnesses William Cornwall, Sarah W. Knapp, and Susan J. Knapp, page 25.
    Inventory taken Oct. 29, 1819, by Timothy Walker and Amos Hobby, and filed Dec. 6, 1819, page 27.

Park, Eunice, late of Greenwich, will dated Mch. 21, 1820, probated Jan. 1, 1821, mentions her son John Knapp, daughter Rachel Mead, granddaughters Clarissa Ferris, Marilda Ferris, and Catharine Ferris, grandson William Ferris, and daughter-in-law Sarah Knapp. Executors her son John Knapp and son-in-law Edmond Mead. Witnesses William Kinch, Nathaniel Husted, Jr., and Elisha Belcher, page 116.
    Inventory taken Jan. 4, 1821, by Charles Smith and Nathaniel Knapp, and filed Jan. 23, 1821, page 117.
    July 2, 1821, account filed, page 168.

Peck, Joseph, late of Greenwich, Jan. 24, 1823, letters of administration on his estate granted to Asahel Palmer, who was ordered to advertise for claims, page 324.
    Inventory taken Jan. 27, 1823, by Joseph Ferris and Alexander Hendrie, and filed Jan. 29, 1823, page 324.

STAMFORD PROBATE RECORDS.
Volume 12, 1819.

Peck, Joseph, continued :
Nov. 15, 1823, estate ordered distributed to Joseph Peck, Jesse Peck, Betsy wife of John Johnson, Prue wife of Solomon Close, Catherine wife of Robert Barnard, Polly wife of Andrew Newman, to the legal representatives of Solomon Peck, his only heirs at law, page 324.
Dec. 15, 1823, estate distributed accordingly, page 325.

Peck, Stephen, late of the City of New York, Jan. 25, 1822, letters of administration on his estate granted to Asahel Palmer of Greenwich, decedent's father Isaac Peck having renounced, and commissioners appointed to adjust claims of creditors, page 199.
Inventory taken Jan. 29, 1822, by Ethan Ferris and Jabez Mead, and filed Feb. 4, 1822, page 200.
Aug. 21, 1822, report of commissioners to adjust claims filed, page 254.
Sept. 2, 1822, account filed, and real estate ordered sold to pay debts, page 254.
Oct. 29, 1822, real estate sold and report of sale filed, page 254.
Dec. 3, 1822, creditors ordered paid ten cents on the dollar, page 255.

Penoyer, Henry, late of Darien, Dec. 6, 1820, letters of administration on his estate granted to Isaac Penoyer and Hannah Penoyer, who were ordered to advertise for claims, page 107.
Inventory taken Dec. 22, 1820, by Nathaniel Waterbury and Anson D. Penoyer, and filed Dec. 25, 1820, page 107.
Oct. 13, 1821, additional inventory filed, page 189.
Nov. 2, 1822, necessaries allowed his widow, Hannah Penoyer, page 244.
Nov. 28, 1821, time for final settlement extended to June 6, next, page 189.
Nov. 6, 1822, account filed, and real estate ordered sold to pay debts, page 245.
Oct. 17, 1823, Isaac Penoyer of Darien appointed guardian of James H. and Smith, sons of decedent, page 330.
Nod. 28, 1823, petition of Isaac Penoyer guardian of James H. Penoyer, about 8 years of age, and Smith Penoyer, about 5 years of age, for leave to sell the real estate of said minors, and sale ordered, page 354.
Feb. 17, 1824, real estate sold to Alfred Penoyer, and report of sale filed, page 355.

Pierce, Daniel, late of Greenwich, Feb. 12, 1822, letters of administration on his estate granted to Phebe Pierce,

STAMFORD PROBATE RECORDS.
Volume 12, 1819.

Pierce, Daniel, continued :
and commissioners appointed to adjust claims of creditors, page 217.
Inventory taken Feb. 15, 1822, by Asahel Palmer and Lemuel Ferris, and filed Mch. 4, 1822, page 218.
Mch. 4, 1822, necessaries allowed his widow, Phebe Pierce, and personal property ordered sold, page 218.
Sept. 2, 1822, report of commissioners to adjust claims filed, page 219.
Sept. 21, 1822, dower of his widow, Phebe Pierce, ordered set out, page 246.
Sept. 27, 1822, dower set out, page 246.
Oct. 8, 1822, account filed, and real estate ordered sold to pay debts, page 247.
Nov. 4, 1822, real estate sold, and report of sale filed, pages 247 and 248.

Quintard, Peter, Jr., late of Stamford, Feb. 5, 1821, Ruth Quintard, administratrix, proceedings for the appointment of commissioners to adjust claims of creditors, page 228.

Quintard, Ruth, late of Stamford, will dated Feb. 9, 1815, probated June 12, 1821, mentions her children Rebecca Raymond of New York City, Lewis Y. Quintard, and Clarissa Mott. Executor her son. Witnesses Nathan Beers, Debe Keeler, and Reed Haveland, page 141.
June 12, 1821, order to advertise for claims, page 142.
Inventory taken June 8, 1821, by Isaac Gray and John Weed, Jr., and filed June 12, 1821, page 142.
June 3, 1822, time for final settlement extended to Dec. 5, next, page 230.

Reynolds, Jared, late of Greenwich, Mch. 9, 1822, letters of administration on his estate granted to Abel Reynolds of Stamford, who was ordered to advertise for claims, page 214.
Inventory taken Mch. 23, 1822, by Stephen Bishop and Drake Studwell, and filed Mch. 25, 1822, and necessaries allowed his widow, page 215.
Mch. 19, 1823, account filed, and real estate ordered sold to pay debts, page 278.

Reynolds, Nathaniel, late of Greenwich, will dated June 12, 1820, probated July 6, 1822, mentions his wife Deborah, and children Nathaniel, Rebecca wife of Austin Smith, Husted, Ard, and Harriet Reynolds, grandsons Allen and Nathaniel, children of Zadoc, a deceased son. Exec-

STAMFORD PROBATE RECORDS.
Volume 12, 1819.

Reynolds, Nathaniel, continued :
utor his son Ard. Witnesses Ezekiel Reynolds, Jr.,
Joseph Morrell, and Jabez Mead, page 248.
Codicil dated Apl. 3, 1822, page 250.
July 6, 1822, order to advertise for claims, page 250.
Inventory taken July 29, 1822, by Amos Mead and Ephraim Marshall, and filed Aug. 5, 1822, page 250.

Sanford, Clark, Dr., late of Greenwich, will dated June 4,
1819, probated Sept. 20, 1819, mentions his wife Anna,
and children Nancy Mariah, Pamela, Rhoda, Henry Horace,
and John Clark Sanford. Executors his son John Clark
Sanford, William Knapp, and Jared Strang of Greenwich,
and Oliver H. Hicks of the City of New York. Witnesses Hezekiah Tracy, Lydia K. Mead, and Darius Mead, Jr.,
page 20.
Inventory taken Sept. 21, 1819, by Platt Mead and
Darius Mead, Jr., and filed Dec. 6, 1819, page 38.
Sept. 20, 1819, Henry H. Hicks, made choice of Oliver H
Hicks to be his guardian, page 79.

Scofield, Abigail, late of Stamford, Jan. 18, 1822, letters of
administration on her estate granted to Ezra Scofield,
Jr., who was ordered to advertise for claims, page 189.
Inventory taken by Warren Scofield and Abishai Scofield, and filed Feb. 16, 1822, page 200.

Scofield, Benjamin, late of Stamford, Apl. 20, 1822, letters
of administration on his estate granted to Selleck Scofield and Isaac Scofield, who were ordered to advertise
for claims, page 228.
Inventory taken Apl. 22, 1822, by Warren Scofield and
Peter Scofield, and filed June 5, 1822, page 229.
Dec. 30, 1822, account filed, and real estate ordered
sold to pay debts, page 246.

Scofield, Betsy, late of Stamford, June 7, 1820, letters of
administration on her estate granted to Augustus Scofield, who was ordered to advertise for claims, page 92.
Inventory taken June 7, 1820, by Jacob Knapp and Jonathan Scofield, and filed July 3, 1820, page 92.
Mch. 16, 1821, additional inventory taken, and filed
Apl. 2, 1821, page 119.

Scofield, Henry, late of Stamford, Nov. 1, 1819, letters of
administration on his estate granted to Samuel Whiting,
who was ordered to advertise for claims, page 41.
Inventory taken by Jeremiah Andreas and Joshua Scofield

STAMFORD PROBATE RECORDS.
Volume 12, 1819.

Scofield, Henry, continued :
and filed Dec. 20, 1819, page 42.
Nov. 6, 1820, time for final settlement extended to May 5, next.

Scofield, Henry, late of Darien, Sept. 7, 1821, personal property distributed to Henry Scofield, Joseph Scofield, James Scofield, Mary Scofield, Ann Eliza Scofield, Mercy or Nancy Scofield, and Margaret Scofield, page 149.

Scofield, Israel, late of Stamford, June 7, 1822, letters of administration on his estate granted to Erastus H. Weed who was ordered to advertise for claims, page 231.
Inventory taken June 7, 1822, by Isaac Holly and Silas Hoyt, and filed June 7, 1822, page 231.
May 10, 1823, estate ordered distributed to Gideon Scofield, Ezra Scofield, Amos Scofield, Hannah widow of Miles Weed, Mercy Scofield, and to the legal representatives of Jacob Scofield, deceased, page 287.
June 9, 1823, estate distributed accordingly, page 288.

Scofield, Jacob, late of Stamford, will dated Dec. 22, 1819, probated May 6, 1822, mentions his wife Abigail, and children Frederic, William Wardwell, Betsy wife of Solomon Garnsey, Abigail Scofield, and Hannah Scofield. Executrix his wife. Witnesses Lydia Lounsbury, Patty Lounsbury, and Samuel Webb, page 226.
May 6, 1822, order to advertise for claims, page 227.
Inventory taken by John Scofield, Jr., and Silas Scofield, and filed May 28, 1822, page 227.

Scofield, James, about 11 years of age, Aug. 28, 1820, Joseph Scofield appointed his guardian, page 94.

Scofield, John, 3rd, late of Stamford, Oct. 18, 1819, letters of administration on his estate granted to Ebenezer E. Scofield, who was ordered to advertise for claims, page 37.
Inventory taken Dec. 17, 1819, by Thaddeus Hoyt, Jr., and William Andreas, and filed Dec. 17, 1819, page 37.

Scofield, Margaret, Aug. 28, 1820, Warren Percival appointed her guardian, page 94.

Scofield, Obadiah, late of Stamford, May 2, 1823, letters of administration on his estate granted to Polly Scofield and Erastus H. Weed, who were ordered to advertise for claims, page 294.

STAMFORD PROBATE RECORDS.
Volume 12, 1819.

Scofield, Obadiah, continued :
    May 10, 1823, proceedings for the appointment of commissioners to adjust claims, page 295.
    Inventory taken by Isaac Lockwood and Jonathan Brown, and filed July 2, 1823, page 295.

Scofield, Phinehas, late of Stamford, Mch. 27, 1820, letters of administration on his estate granted to Hiram Scofield, who was ordered to advertise for claims, page 72.
    Inventory taken Apl. 1, 1820, by Luther Weed and Jotham Hoyt, and filed Apl. 4, 1820, page 72.
    Nov. 10, 1820, necessaries allowed his widow, Mercy Scofield, page 118.
    Nov. 14, 1820, account filed, and real estate ordered sold to pay debts, pages 119 and 132.
    Dec. 21, 1820, real estate sold to John Weed, 2nd, page 132.
    Mch. 28, 1821, estate ordered distributed to Mary or Mercy Scofield, his widow, and to his children Hiram, Nathaniel, Mary, and Lydia, page 133.
    Apl. 30, 1821, estate distributed accordingly, page 133.

Scofield, Sally, of Darien, Jan. 24, 1821, appointed guardian of her children Mary A. Scofield, and John D. Scofield, page 101.
    Petitions, Jan. 26, 1821, and Apl. 2, 1821, for leave to sell the real estate of said minors in Stamford, and sale ordered, pages 126 and 180.
    May 23, 1821, real estate sold to Hoyt Scofield, and sale confirmed, page 180.

Selleck, Henry, late of Darien, Feb. 16, 1822, letters of administration on his estate granted to John Bell, Jr., and commissioners appointed to adjust claims, page 202.
    Inventory taken May 7, 1822, by Samuel Whiting and Thaddeus Bell, and filed May 17, 1822, page 209.
    May 17, 1822, personal property ordered sold to pay debts, page 209.
    May 17, 1822, necessaries allowed his widow, Sally Selleck, page 209.
    Nov. 30, 1822, report of commissioners to adjust claims filed, page 355.
    July 16, 1823, account filed, and real estate ordered sold to pay debts, and report of sale filed, page 356.
    Nov. 5, 1823, creditors ordered paid eight and seven tenths cents on the dollar, page 357.
    Jan. 25, 1823, time for final settlement extended to Aug. 16, next, page 259.

STAMFORD PROBATE RECORDS.
Volume 12, 1819.

Selleck, James, late of Stamford, Nov. 17, 1819, estate distributed to Charlotte Selleck, widow of deceased, and James B. Selleck, a son of deceased, page 16.

Selleck, Molly, late of Darien, will dated Dec. 21, 1822, probated Feb. 17, 1823, all to her son Gould Selleck, now of New York. Executor Thomas Reed of Norwalk. Witnesses Samuel Richards, John Reed, Jr., and Roswell Reed, page 300.
Feb. 17, 1823, order to advertise for claims, page 301.
Inventory taken Aug. 23, 1823, by Barnabas Marvin and Roswell Reed, and filed Aug. 23, 1823, page 301.

Selleck, Uriah, late of Darien, May 7, 1821, letters of administration on his estate granted to Henry Selleck, who was ordered to advertise for claims, page 189.

Selleck, Uriah, late of Darien, Feb. 16, 1822, letters of administration on his estate granted to John Bell, Jr., of Darien, and commissioners appointed to adjust claims of creditors, page 203.
May 7, 1822, inventory taken by Samuel Whiting and Thaddeus Bell, and filed May 17, 1822, page 208.
May 17, 1822, personal property ordered sold to pay debts, page 209.
Nov. 30, 1822, report of commissioners to adjust claims filed, page 272.
Jan. 25, 1823, time for final settlement extended to Aug. 16, next, page 272.
Apl. 14, 1823, account filed, and real estate ordered sold to pay debts, page 272.

Shaw, William, late of Stamford, Apl. 23, 1821, letters of administration on his estate granted to John Silliman, who was ordered to advertise for claims, page 160.
Inventory taken Apl. 21, 1821, by Henry Close and David Hoyt, and filed May 24, 1821, page 160.
Dec. 10, 1821, letters de bonus non granted to Joseph Wood, page 162.
Dec. 17, 1822, Isaac Quintard, Jr., appointed guardian of Mariah, Nancy E., Caroline, and Eliza, children of decedent, page 245.

Sherwood, Jabez, late of Greenwich, May 7, 1821, letters of administration on his estate granted to Daniel Sherwood, Jr., the widow having renounced, page 196.
June 4, 1821, commissioners appointed to adjust claims of creditors, page 196.

STAMFORD PROBATE RECORDS.
Volume 12, 1819.

Sherwood, Jabez, continued :
    Inventory taken June 1, 1821, by S. Moulton and Platt Mead, and filed June 4, 1821, and an allowance made to his widow, page 197.
    Feb. 25, 1822, additional inventory taken and filed, page 213.
    Feb. 25, 1822, report of commissioners to adjust claims filed, and real estate ordered sold to pay debts, and report of sale, pages 213 and 214.

Sherwood, Matthew, late of Stamford, Aug. 7, 1820, account filed by Matthew Sherwood, executor, and real estate ordered sold to pay debts, page 83.
    May 21, 1820, report of sale filed, pages 83 and 87.

Sherwood, Nathan, late of Stamford, Apl. 21, 1823, letters of administration on his estate granted to Selleck Scofield who was ordered to advertise for claims, page 289.
    Inventory taken Apl. 23, 1823, by Isaac Ayres and Jared Holly, and filed Apl. 25, 1823, page 289.

Skidmore, Henry, late of Stamford, inventory taken Jan. 20, 1819, by Barnabas Marvin, and filed Aug. 21, 1819, page 41.
    Aug. 21, 1819, report of commissioners to adjust claims filed, page 41.

Smith, Amos, late of Stamford, July 31, 1819, account filed by Abel Reynolds, executor, and real estate ordered sold to pay debts, page 77.
    Dec. 22, 1819, account filed, and real estate ordered sold to pay debts, page 78.
    Apl. 27, 1820, account filed, and real estate ordered sold to pay debts, page 78.
    May 4, 1820, report of sale filed, page 78.
    Apl. 15, 1820, time for final settlement extended for six months.
    May 6, 1820, Nathaniel Hubbard, Benjamin Smith and Solomon Clauson, Jr., all of Stamford, were appointed to set out the dower of Deborah Smith, widow ff deceased, and distribute the remainder to his children Hannah Mills, Sarah Smith, Mary Marvin, and Abigail Palmer, according to his will, page 79.
    Sept. 5, 1820, estate distributed accordingly, page 98.
    Oct. 20, 1820, order confirming sale of real estate of deceased on May 5, 1820, to Joseph Smith, 3rd, page 101.

STAMFORD PROBATE RECORDS.
Volume 12, 1819.

Smith, David, late of Stamford, will dated Mch. 7, 1815, probated Apl. 24, 1820, mentions his daughter-in-law Hannah Smith, widow of his deceased son Ezra, and their daughter Elizababeth Smith. Executrix his daughter-in-law. Witnesses Daniel Nichols, Jonathan Smith, and Anne Nichols, page 61.
Apl. 24, 1820, order to advertise for claims, page 61.
Inventory taken May 4, 1820, by Daniel Nichols and Abel Reynolds, and filed May 4, 1820, page 62.
Jan. 18, 1821, petition of Hannah Smith, as guardian of Elizabeth Smith, for leave to sell the real estate of said minor in Stamford, page 132.
Apl. 2, 1821, sale ordered, and sale made on Apl. 5, 1821, page 132.
Dec. 16, 1820, Elizabeth Smith, about 16 years of age, made choice of Hannah Smith, her mother, to be her guardian, page 101.

Nov. 14, 1823, estate ordered distributed to Hannah Smith, his widow, and Elizabeth Smith, his daughter, according to his will, page 333.
Dec. 4, 1823, estate distributed accordingly, page 333.

Smith, John, late of Stamford, Sept. 1819, letters of administration on his estate granted to Seth Smith, who was ordered to advertise for claims, page 66.
Inventory taken Sept. 17, 1819, by Solomon Clason and Nehemiah Hait, Jr., and filed Oct. 18, 1819, page 66.

Smith, John, late of Stamford, Feb. 24, 1821, David Miller appointed guardian of William, Emeline, Abigail, and Betsy Ann, children of decedent, all under 12 years of age, page 119.
Mch. 28, 1821, estate ordered distributed to his widow, Betsy Smith, and to his children William, Emeline, Abigail, and Betsy Ann, page 157.
Apl. 30, 1821, estate distributed accordingly, page 157.

Smith, Joseph, late of Stamford, June 7, 1819, Nancy Smith, about 17 years of age, made choice of Abraham Smith to be her guardian; Rebecca Smith, about 15 years of age made choice of George Smith to be her guardian; the court also appointed Joseph Smith, Jr., guardian of Alexander Smith, about 12 years of age, and Joseph J. Smith, about 10 years of age, all children of said Joseph Smith, page 32.

STAMFORD PROBATE RECORDS.
Volume 12, 1819.

Smith, Samuel, late of Stamford, June 7, 1819, George Smith, administrator, estate ordered distributed to George Smith, Abraham Smith, Alexander Smith, Joseph J. Smith, brothers of deceased, Abigail Smith, Polly Smith, Nancy Smith, and Rebecca Smith, sisters of deceased, page 31.

Smith, Reuben, late of Stamford, Mch. 3, 1823, letters of administration on his estate granted to John Auger, who was ordered to advertise for claims, page 313.
Inventory taken Mch. 7, 1823, by Abishai Weed and Jacob Stevens, Jr., and filed Mch. 21, 1823, page 313.
Nov. 12, 1823, account filed, and real estate ordered sold to pay debts, page 314.
Dec. 2, 1823, part of his real estate sold to James Stevens. and report of sale filed, page 314.
Dec. 6, 1823, estate ordered distributed to William Smith, James Smith, Sarah wife of Elisha Waters, Mary wife of George Deal, Rhoda wife of Hezekiah Wood, and to the legal representatives of Abigail Walton, his heirs-at-law, page 352.
Jan. 21, 1824, estate distributed to William Smith, Mary wife of George Deal, Sarah wife of Elisha Waters, James Smith, Rhoda wife of Hezekiah Wood, and to the heirs of Abigail the deceased wife of Thomas Walton, page 314.

Stevens, Darius, about 16 years of age, Dec. 20, 1820, made choice of Ashbel Scofield to be his guardian, page 101.

Stevens, Lavinia, late of Darien, Jan. 28, 1823, letters of administration on her estate granted to Abigail Stevens who was ordered to advertise for claims, page 331.
Inventory taken Apl. 7, 1823, by John Hoyt, 2nd, and Gilbert Scofield, and filed Aug. 16, 1823, page 332.
Aug. 16, 1823, account filed, and real estate ordered sold to pay debts, page 332.
Sept. 22, 1823, part of her real estate sold to Seth Scofield, and report of sale filed, page 332.

Stevens, Obadiah, late of Darien, Oct. 16, 1820, letters of administration on his estate granted to Joseph Silliman of New Canaan, who was ordered to advertise for dlaims, page 113.
Inventory taken Nov. 14, 1820, by John Hoyt and Gilbert Scofield, and filed Nov. 15, 1820, page 114.
Oct. 16, 1820, Abigail Stevens, appointed guardian of Lavina and Leonidas, children of decedent, page 115.
Nov. 15, 1820, necessaries allowed his widow, page 115.

STAMFORD PROBATE RECORDS.
Volume 12, 1819.

Stevens, Obadiah, continued :
  Nov. 15, 1820, dower ordered set out to his widow, Abigail Stevens, page 115.
  Feb. 25, 1822, additional allowance to his widow, Abigail Stevens, page 202.
  Sept. 13, 1821, additional inventory filed, page 168.
  May 21, 1821, commissioners appointed to adjust claims of creditors, page 168.
  Oct. 10, 1821, dower of his widow, Abigail Stevens, set out, page 169.
  Jan. 14, 1822, report of commissioners to adjust claims filed, and proceedings of commissioners reviewed, page 283.
  May 14, 1823, account filed, and real estate ordered sold to pay debts, page 285.
  May 27, 1822, real estate sold to Charles G. Smith, Leander Slason, George Weed, Ashbel Scofield, and to Abigail Stevens, widow of deceased, and report of sale filed, page 285.
  June 5, 1822, estate ordered distributed to his children Lavinia and Leonidas his only heirs-at-law, page 285.
  June 12, 1822, estate distributed accordingly, page 286.

Taylor, Nathaniel, late of Greenwich, Oct. 13, 1823, letters of administration on his estate granted to Joseph Taylor, Jr., who was ordered to advertise for claims, page 304.
  Inventory taken by Platt Mead and John C. Sanford, and filed Nov. 3, 1823, page 304.

Thorp, Sturges, Pl, late of Stamford, Jan. 16, 1822, letters of administration on his estate granted to David B. Thorp and Silas Hoyt, Jr., and commissioners appointed to adjust claims, page 197.
  Inventory taken by Isaac Lockwood and James Stevens, and filed Feb. 6, 1822, page 198.
  Additional inventory filed Feb. 15, 1822, page 202.
  Feb. 15, 1822, personal property ordered sold to pay debts, page 202.
  Aug. 21, 1822, report of commissioners to adjust claims filed, page 220.
  Aug. 23, 1822, account filed, and real estate ordered sold to pay debts, page 253.
  Oct. 24, 1822, part of his real estate sold to Isaac Banks, and on Dec. 4, 1823, part sold to David Holly, and report of sale filed, page 253.

STAMFORD PROBATE RECORDS.
Volume 12, 1819.

Tillman, John, late of Stamford, May 29, 1821, letters of administration on his estate granted to Anne S. Tillman and Stephen B. Provost, who were ordered to advertise for claims, page 162.
Sept. 7, 1821, letters granted to Andrew P. Tillman jointly with the aforesaid administrators, page 162.
Inventory taken Aug. 31, 1821, by Isaac Lockwood and Charles Hawley, and filed Nov. 16, 1821, page 163.
Dec. 2, 1821, Anne S. Tillman appointed guardian of her children Mary C. and Elizabeth Tillman, page 167.
Oct. 4, 1821, dower of Anne S. Tillman, widow of deceased, ordered set out, page 202.
May 15, 1822, dower set out, page 211.
May 3, 1822, petition of Anne S. Tillman for leave to sell the real estate in Stamford of her minor children Mary C., Elizabeth and John H. Tillman, and sale ordered, page 247.
Sept. 13, 1823, account filed, and estate ordered distributed to his widow Ann S. Tillman, and children Mary C., Elizabeth, and John H., page 335.
Sept. 15, 1823, estate distributed accordingly, page 336

Todd, Washington, late of Stamford, May 18, 1819, Benjamin Husted and Charlotte Todd, administrators, personal property ordered sold to pay debts; report of sale, and order of confirmation of Feb. 28, 1820, pages 108 and 109.
Report of Commissioners to adjust claims of creditors, and order of confirmation of Jan. 4, 1820, page 109.
July 3, 1820, dower ordered set out to Charlotte Todd, widow of deceased, and time for final settlement extended to Nov. 4, next, page 110.
Aug. 29, 1820, dower set out, page 110.
Oct. 2, 1820, William Todd, made choice of Charlotte Todd to be his guardian, page 95.

Totten, Ann, late of Rye, Nov. 6, 1820, order confirming report of sale on Nov. 25, 1818, of real estate in Greenwich to William Mead by Gilbert Totten, executor, page 96.

Waterbury, Apollos W., Sept. 10, 1823, made choice of Sally Waterbury to be his guardian, page 318.

Waterbury, Elizabeth, late of Stamford, Mch. 6, 1820, letters of administration on her estate granted to Henry Waterbury, who was ordered to advertise for claims, page 196.
Inventory taken by Henry Brown, page 196.

STAMFORD PROBATE RECORDS.
Volume 12, 1819.

Webb, Frederic, late of Stamford, Oct. 7, 1823, letters of administration on his estate granted to Charles Knapp and Charles Hawley, who were ordered to advertise for claims, page 350.
Inventory taken Oct. 8, 1823, by Isaac Lockwood and Jonathan Brown, and filed Oct. 23, 1823, page 350.

Webb, Mary, late of Stamford, widow of Joseph Webb, will dated Dec. 19, 1816, probated Apl. 2, 1821, mentions her children Deborah Webb, Polly Webb, Abigail widow of Samuel Buxton, Joseph Webb, grandson William Erastus son of Joseph Webb, greatgrandson James Breadsley son of her granddaughter Nancy W. Comstock, deceased. Executors Frederick Smith and William Knapp. Witnesses Sally Smith, Mary Smith, and Jane Smith, page 128.
Apl. 2, 1821, order to advertise for claims, page 128.
Inventory taken Apl. 3, 1821, by Isaac Smith and William Keeler, and filed Apl. 3, 1821, page 129.
Nov. 5, 1821, account filed, page 168.

Webb, Nathaniel, late of Stamford, Dec. 6, 1819, account filed Nathaniel Webb and Nathaniel Waterbury, executors, and personal estate ordered distributed according to his will to said Nathaniel, Elisha, Hannah wife of said Nathaniel Waterbury, Jerusha wife of John Lounsbury, and Rebecca wife of Zadoc Newman, children of decedent, page 22.
Dec. 11, 1819, estate distributed accordingly, page 23.

Webb, Seth, late of Stamford, Aug. 12, 1819, Nancy Webb, administratrix, distribution ordered of the real estate of deceased, not heretofore sold, to Andrew, Walter, Albert, Sally Brown, Mary Ann Merritt, Caty Webb, and Rheua Webb, children of decedent, page 5.
Estate distributed accordingly, together with dower to his widow, Nancy Webb, page 5.

Weed, Ananias, late of North Stamford, will dated Aug. 19, 1818, probated Jan. 31, 1820, mentions his wife Sally, and children Cynthia, Darius, Thaddeus, and Samuel. Executors his sons Darius, Thaddeus, and Samuel. Witnesses ----. Will accepted by his widow, Sally Weed, and only surviving children Thaddeus, Samuel, Darius, Cynthia Barnum, and Horace Barnum, page 70.
Inventory taken Feb. 1, 1820, by Luther Weed and Thaddeus Hanford, and filed Mch. 20, 1820, page 71.

STAMFORD PROBATE RECORDS.
Volume 12, 1819.

Weed, Benjamin, late of Stamford, will dated Feb. 19, 1821, probated Apl. 30, 1821, mentions his wife Eunice, and children Benjamin M., Elizabeth Weed, Lucretia Weed, Clarissa wife of Ezra Dibble, and Ruth wife of Walter Dibble, the latter two of Danbury. Executor his son. Witnesses Daniel Provost, Abishai Weed, and John Augur, page 140.
Apl. 30, 1821, order to advertise for claims, page 141.
Inventory taken May 30, 1821, by Abishai Weed and Thaddeus Hanford, and filed July 2, 1821, page 177.
Apl. 12, 1822, estate ordered distributed to his widow, Eunice Weed, and children Benjamin M., Elizabeth, Lucretia, Clarissa wife of Ezra Dibble of Danbury, and Ruth wife of Walter Dibble of Danbury, children of deceased, according to his will, page 234.
Apl. 18, 1822, estate distributed accordingly, page 235.

Weed, Gideon, late of Stamford, will dated Nov. 28, 1817, probated Jan. 24, 1820, mentions his wife Abigail, and children Jonas, Daty, Abigail Waterbury, Gideon, Selleck, Abraham, Isaac, Hannah Wardwell, Jacob, and Martha Lounsbury. Executor son Daty Weed. Witnesses Nathan Weed, Mary Weed, and David Barnum, page 54.
Jan. 24, 1820, order to advertise for claims, page 55.
Inventory taken Jan. 26, 1820, by John Bell and Thaddeus Hoyt, Jr., and filed Jan. 31, 1820, page 56.
Mch. 7, 1820, estate ordered distributed to Abigail Weed, his widow, and children Daty, Gideon, Selleck, Abraham, Isaac, Jacob, widow Abigail Waterbury, Hannah wife of James Wardwell, and Martha wife of Epenetus Lounsbury, page 87.
Aug. 19, 1820, estate distributed accordingly, page 88.

Weed, Henry R., late of Stamford, Dec. 4, 1819, Jonathan Weed, one of the executors, order extending time of final settlement, and real estate ordered sold to pay debts, page 10.
Dec. 4, 1819, report of commissioners to adjust claims filed, page 11.

Weed, James H., late of Darien, May 14, 1822, letters of administration on his estate granted to Jeremiah Andreas of Darien, who was ordered to advertise for claims, page 232.
Inventory taken May 20, 1822, by Joshua Scofield and Samuel Whiting, and filed July 1, 1822, page 232.

Weed, John, of Darien, Apl. 1, 1822, his daughters Mariah E. and Hannah made choice of John Bell, Jr., to be their

STAMFORD PROBATE RECORDS.
Volume 12, 1819.

Weed, John, continued:
    guardian, page 216.

Weed, Jonas, late of Darien, will dated Aug. 6, 1822, probated Feb. 6, 1823, mentions his wife Rebekah, and children Jonas, 3rd, Paul, Mary, Annah, and Sarah wife of Alfred Webb. Executors his sons Jonas, 3rd, and Paul. Witnesses Thaddeus Bell, Warren Percival and Isaac Howe page 280.
Feb. 6, 1823, order to advertise for claims, page 281.
Inventory taken Mch. 5, 1823, by Cary Bell and Azariah Waterbury, and filed Mch. 22, 1823, page 281.

Weed, Joseph, of Darien, about 19 years of age, Aug. 28, 1820, made choice of John Weed to be his guardian, page 94.

Weed, Nathan, late of Stamford, will dated July 15, 1818, probated Dec. 6, 1819, mentions his wife Mary, and children Debby Bell, Anne Richards, Mary Weed, Joseph Weed, William Franklin Weed, and sister Ann St. John. Executrix his wife. Witnesses John Weed, Jr., David Barnum, and Betsy Barnum, page 45.
Codicils, dated Sept. 11, 1819, and Oct. 5, 1819, page 48.
Inventory taken Dec. 15, 1819, by Jeremiah Andreas and Gershom Scofield, and filed Feb. 7, 1820, page 49.
June 5, 1820, dower of his widow, Mary Weed, ordered set out, and also the share of his daughter Mary Weed so long as she remains unmarried, page 84.
June 13, 1821, dower and share set off, page 84.

Weed, Raymond, late of Darien, Apl. 1, 1822, letters of administration on his estate granted to Henry Weed, 3rd, of Darien, who was ordered to advertise for claims, page 256.

Weed, Seth, late of Stamford, will dated Dec. 16, 1822, probated Jan. 6, 1823, mentions his wife Abigail, and children Betsy wife of Thaddeus Hanford, Deborah wife of Ralph Hoyt, Mary wife of Israel White, and Sarah wife of Ezra Scofield. Decedent was the owner of two soldiers' rights of land in Illinois purchased from Samuel Provost and Seymour Weed. Executors Thaddeus Hanford and Ralph Hoyt. Witnesses Benjamin M. Weed, Samuel Miller, and Charles Hawley, page 265.
Jan. 6, 1823, order to advertise for claims, page 267.
Inventory taken Jan. 7, 1823, by Jacob Stephens, Jr., and Peter Scofield, Jr., and filed Mch. 1, 1823, page 267.

STAMFORD PROBATE RECORDS.
Volume 12, 1819.

Weed, Seth, continued :
Apl. 21, 1819, antenuptial agreement with Abigail Webb dated, page 264.

Weed, William F., June 5, 1820, Mary Weed appointed his guardian, page 72.

Weeks, Joseph, of Stamford, Oct. 23, 1821, made choice of Theodore Davenport to be his guardian, page 182.

Welch, Mary, late of Stamford, will dated ---, probated Oct. 12, 1819, all to Jacob Scofield and his wife Hannah Scofield formerly of Stamford, but now of Philipstown in the State of New York, except a gold ring and gold nubs bequeathed to Abigail, daughter of John Hoyt, Jr., of Stamford. Executor Joseph Silliman of New Canaan. Witnesses John Hoyt, Jr., Henry Marshall, and Mary Stevens, page 35.
Inventory taken Oct. 8th, 1819, by John Hoyt, Jr., and Nathan Seely, and filed Oct. 12, 1819, page 36.

Whelpley, Ann, late of Greenwich, widow of Daniel Whelpley, will dated Apl. 14, 1820, probated May 16, 1820, mentions her son Henry Whelpley, granddaughter Phebe Marshall, granddaughter Loisa Whelpley daughter of her son Henry Whelpley; daughters Phebe Murphy, Ann Hyatt, Lucretia Worden, Mary Knapp, and Charlotte Merritt; grandson Daniel Whelpley. Executor her son Henry. Witnesses Jeduthan Ferris, Lemuel Ferris, and Jabez Mead, page 95.
May 16, 1820, order to advertise for claims, page 96.
Inventory taken May 16, 1820, by Lemuel Ferris and Benjamin Page, and filed Nov. 6, 1820, page 96.

Whiting, Samuel F., late of the City of New York, June 18, 1821, letters of administration on his estate granted to Joshua Ferris of Greenwich, who was ordered to advertise for claims, page 200.
Inventory of his property in Greenwich taken by Jeduthan Ferris and Jabez Mead, and filed Aug. 18, 1821, page 192.
May 6, 1822, commissioners appointed to adjust claims of creditors, page 216.
May 2, 1823, report of commissioners to adjust claims filed, and proceedings of commissioners reviewed, page 287.

STAMFORD PROBATE RECORDS.
Volume 12, 1819.

Wilmot, David W., of Stamford, Feb. 9, 1822, William Wilmot appointed his guardian, page 189.

Wilmot, Hannah, late of Stamford, will dated Apl. 22, 1819, probated July 2, 1819, all to her husband Joseph Wilmot No Executor. Witnesses Susannah Bell, Abigail Wilmot, and Abigail Stevens, page 3.
Inventory taken July 3, 1819, by Joseph Gray and John Leeds, and filed July 3, 1819, page 4.

Wilson, Burrage, of Greenwich, Feb. 7, 1820, made choice of James Green, Jr., to be his guardian, page 74.

Youngs, Hanhah, late of Stamford, will dated Jan. 20, 1820, probated Jan. 31, 1820, mentions her nephews Jonathan Youngs, deceased, Lewis Youngs, Jeremiah Youngs, and Samuel Youngs, now of Philadelphia; nieces Ruth Davis, Keziah Bonnons, daughters of her brother Jeremiah; nephew Frederic Youngs son of Samuel Youngs; sister Elisabeth Youngs; Phebe Carter daughter of her sister; Sally Capers, and Julia Wallace daughter of said Phebe Carter. Executor Dr. Warren Percival. Witnesses Joseph Wood, Greenleaf S. Webb, and Catharine Selleck, page 59.
Jan. 31, 1820, order to advertise for claims, page 60.
Inventory taken Mch. 16, 1820, by John Bell and Jeremiah Andreas, and filed Mch. 22, 1820, page 60.

STAMFORD PROBATE RECORDS.
Volume 13, 1824.

Adams, John, late of Greenwich, Nov. 6, 1826, letters of administration on his estate granted to his widow Mary Adams, who was ordered to advertise for claims, page 244. Inventory taken Nov. 21, 1826, by Ebenezer Mead and Asahel Palmer, and filed Dec. 13, 1826, page 244. Nov. 24, 1828, his administratrix now deceased, and Nathaniel E. Adams appointed administrator de bonus non, page 329.

Augur, John, late of Stamford, will dated Apl. 4, 1827, probated Apl. 26, 1827, all to his wife, Nancy for life, and remainder to the male heirs of William Hoyt, Jr., the brother of his said wife, and to his brother Jared Augur. Executors his wife and Jotham Hoyt. Witnesses James Young, John Young, and Leander Hoyt, page 276. Apl. 30, 1827, order to advertise for claims, page 277. Inventory taken May 4, 1827, by Jacob Stevens, Jr., and Leander Hoyt, and filed Aug. 26, 1828, page 277.

Bates, Gershom, late of Stamford, Dec. 29, 1823, estate ordered distributed to his widow, Hannah Bates, and children Hannah E. Bates, Mary J. Bates, William H. Bates, Martha S. Bates, Lewis H. Bates, and Samuel G. Bates, page 17.
Mch. 16, 1824, estate distributed accordingly, page 1.

Belcher, Elisha, Dr., late of Greenwich, will dated Apl. 12, 1825, probated Jan. 1826, mentions his wife Lydia, and children Elisha R., William N., Clarissa Sackett, Mary White, Sarah Palmer, Elizabeth U. Strang, Ann or Augusta White, and Lydia Mead. Executors his son Elisha R. and sons-in-law Dr. Darius Mead and Bartow F. White. Witnesses Gilbert Close, Nathaniel Knapp, and Zalmon Minor, page 223.
June 21, 1825, codicil dated, additional bequests to

STAMFORD PROBATE RECORDS.
Volume 13, 1824.

Belcher, Elisha, Dr., continued:
    his wife, page 224.
    Jan. 1826, Bartow F. White declined to qualify, and letters to the other two, who were ordered to advertise for claims, page 225.
    Inventory taken Jan. 22, 1826, by Gilbert Close and Stephen Waring, and filed Mch. 6, 1826, page 225.
    May 1, 1826, estate ordered distributed according to his will, page 226.
    Dec. 25, 1826, time for final settlement extended page 227.

Brown, Elizabeth, late of Greenwich, May 4, 1824, letters of administration on her estate granted to Robert Brown of New York City, who was ordered to advertise for claims, page 22.

Brown, Henry, of Cincinnati, Mch. 25, 1828, the court appointed James Graham of Cincinnati to be his guardian, page 245.
    Sept. 8, 1828, his 1/2 interest in real estate in Darien, ordered sold, pages 313 and 314.
    Sept. 8, 1828, real estate sold to Henry Bates of Darien, and report of sale filed, page 314.

Brown, Martha, late of Stamford, Jan. 30, 1826, letters of administration on her estate granted to Benjamin Waring and Stephen B. Provost, both of Stamford, who were ordered to advertise for claims, page 256.
    Inventory taken by Peter Smith and Jotham Hoyt, and filed Mch. 29, 1826, pages 256 and 257.

Brown, Peter, deaf and dumb, late of Stamford, Feb. 13, 1826, his former administrator being now deceased, letters de bonus non were granted to Charles T. Leeds, page 192.

Brown, Peter, late of Stamford, Feb. 13, 1826, his widow, Polly Brown, having refused to qualify, letters of administration on his estate granted to Charles T. Leeds, who was ordered to advertise for claims, page 192.
    Inventory taken Apl. 19, 1826, by Isaac Holly and Silas Scofield, and filed May 1, 1826, page 193.
    Apl. 27, 1827, account filed, and necessaries allowed his widow, page 195.

Bunnell, or Bunhill, Lockwood, late of Stamford, Aug. 14, 1825, his widow having refused to qualify, letters of

STAMFORD PROBATE RECORDS.
Volume 13, 1824.

Bunnell, Lockwood, continued:
    administration on his estate granted to Charles Knapp of Stamford, and commissioners appointed to adjust claims of creditors, page 144.
    Inventory taken Oct. 24, 1825, by Daniel Lockwood and William Waterbury, Jr., and filed Nov. 7, 1825, page 145.
    Oct. 29, 1825, personal property ordered sold, and report of sale filed, page 146.
    Apl. 24, 1826, report of commissioners to adjust claims filed, page 146.
    Aug. 15, 1826, necessaries allowed his widow, page 147.

Burtis, Elizabeth, late of Stamford, will dated Dec. 26, 1818, probated May 17, 1824, all to her sisters Hannah Leeds and Rhoda Leeds. Executor Cary Leeds. Witnesses John Leeds, Peter Brown, and John W. Leeds, page 20.
    May 17, 1824, order to advertise for claims, page 21.
    Inventory taken June 4, 1824, by Erastus H. Weed and Isaac Quintard, and filed June 12, 1824, page 21.
    Nov. 1824, commissioners appointed to adjust claims of creditors, page 190.
    May 9, 1825, report of commissioners filed, and an appeal taken by Gideon Leeds, and his claim adjudicated, page 191.
    Apl. 8, 1825, time for final settlement extended page 190.
    Oct. 19, 1825, account filed, and real estate ordered sold to pay debts, page 190.
    Aug. 8, 1826, account filed, and creditors ordered paid eighty two cents on the dollar, page 192.

Bush, David, late of Greenwich, Dec. 21, 1807, estate ordered distributed to his widow, Sarah Bush, and children Mary, Sally, Elizabeth, Fanny, Charlotte, Grace, Justus L., and Ralph I., page 61.
    Feb. 7, 1814, estate distributed to his widow Sarah Bush, and children Justus L., Ralph I., Mary Davis, Sarah Rogers, Elizabeth Grigg, Fanny Bush, Charlotte Bush, and Grace Bush, page 61.
    Dec. 6, 1824, his widow, Sarah Bush, being now deceased, the real estate set off to her as her dower, ordered distributed to Mary Davis, Sarah Rogers, Elizabeth Grigg, Fanny Bush, Charlotte St. John, Grace Bush, and Justus L. Bush, he having purchased the interest of Ralph I., children of decedent, page 93.
    Dec. 31, 1824, estate distributed accordingly, page 93.

STAMFORD PROBATE RECORDS.
Volume 13, 1824.

Bush, Samuel, late of Greenwich, will dated Nov. 11, 1825, probated Jan. 15, 1827, mentions his wife Ann, and children Maria, Nelson, William, David, Henry, and Leveret. Executors his wife and sons David, and Henry, Nelson and William. Witnesses Sarah Rogers, Charlotte A. Hicks, and Charles Hawley, page 330.
Jan. 15, 1827, David, William, and Nelson refused to qualify, and letters granted to Ann and Henry, who were ordered to advertise for claims, page 330.
Inventory taken Feb. 15, 1827, by Zophar Mead and Thomas A. Mead, and filed Mch. 2, 1827, page 331.

Bush, Sarah, late of Greenwich, will dated Sept. 9, 1820, probated Sept. 18, 1824, mentions her children Isaac S. Isaacs, Benjamin Isaacs, Sarah wife of Joseph Rogers, Esther wife of William Knapp, Elizabeth Belden, Charlotte wife of Stephen St. John, Fanny Bush, Grace Bush, Dr. Ralph I. Bush, and Justus L. Bush, grandchildren George Isaacs, William H. Isaacs, Emily Isaacs, and Charles Isaacs, children of her deceased son William Isaacs. Executor her son Justus L. Bush. Witnesses Elizabeth Rogers, Maria Bush, and James B. Fairchild, page 42.
Sept. 18, 1824, order to advertise for claims, page 42.
Inventory taken Oct. 23, 1824, by Jabez Mead and Stephen Waring, and filed Nov. 6, 1824, page 43.

Butler, Joseph, colored, of Stamford, Aug. 23, 1828, appointed guardian of his son William Butler, page 296.

Clapp, Thomas, late of Greenwich, will dated 22nd day of 5th month, 1827, probated Mch. 19, 1828, mentions his nephew Thomas Carpenter, niece Deborah Pugsley; Thomas and Allen sons of his nephew William Sutton; nephew and niece John and Mary Sands; tract of land for the Friends School in Purchase; sister Mary Carpenter and her children John, William, Charles, Joseph, Martha, Sarah, and Dorcas; Phebe wife of James Field and her son Thomas C.; the children of his nephew William Sutton, viz: John, Phebe, Mary, Alice, and Elizabeth; the five children of Benjamin Cornell by his former wife Alice; to Silas' son Thomas C.; James Nash; Sarah wife of Jonah Brundage; the children of William Cornell; the two children of John Squariman; Deborah Pugsley; Richard, Sarah, and William Pugsley; niece Mary Sands; the children of Thomas Veal; the children of his nephew John Carpenter; the children of his three nephews, viz: William, Joseph, and Charles Carpenter; the children of his nephew Jesse Sutton; the two daughters of his

STAMFORD PROBATE RECORDS.
Volume 13, 1824.

Clapp, Thomas, continued :
uncle Thomas Clapp, viz : the wives of Skidmore and Ally, and unto the children of their brother James Clapp; the children and grandchildren of his uncle Silas Clapp late of Rhode Island; the children and grandchildren of his uncle Edward Hallock, viz : Clement Sands, et al; the wife and children of Nathaniel Higby; the children of James and Anne Brush; Elizabeth Underhill and her son Mott; Mary Fowler; Hannah wife of Caleb Paulding; legacies to various Friends Meetings; the children of Mary Pugsley; the children of sister Dorcas; James son of Patrick McKay; John son of William Sutton; the children and grandchildren of his two sisters Dorcas and Mary. Executors nephews William Sutton, William Carpenter, Thomas Carpenter, and James Field. Witnesses Samuel Millis, James T. Carpenter, and Job Carpenter, page 266.
Mch. 19, 1828, order to advertise for claims, page 269.
Inventory taken by Thomas Green and Daniel Matthews, and filed Feb. 7, 1828, page 269.
Mch. 9, 1829, time for final settlement extended, page 270.

Clock, Martin, late of Darien, Mch. 10, 1824, distribution of that part of his estate set off to his widow as her dower made to Hetty wife of Jared Bell, Harriet Sammis, Samuel Clock, Nelly Clock, Hiram Clock, Oliver Clock, Rebecca wife of David Bell, Sally Clock, and Betsy Clock, his heirs at law, page 70.

Clock, Martin, late of Darien, May 18, 1824, John Weed, executor, estate ordered distributed to his widow, Patty Clock, and children Hetty Bell, Rebecca Bell, Hiram Clock, Samuel Clock, Oliver Clock, Nelly Clock, Harriet Clock, Sally Clock, and Betsy Clock, page 23.
June 5, 1824, estate distributed accordingly, page 24.

Close, Gideon, late of Greenwich, Feb. 2, 1824, dower of his widow, Bethia Close, ordered set out, page 12.
Feb. 2, 1824, dower set out, page 12.

Close, Jonathan, late of Greenwich, Apl. 4, 1825, petition of Job Lyon of Greenwich, guardian of Mary Rebecca Close a daughter of decedent, for leave to sell the real estate of said minor in Greenwich, and sale ordered page 201.

STAMFORD PROBATE RECORDS.
Volume 13, 1824.

Crennell, Abigail Jane, late of Stamford, Feb. 6, 1827, Cary Leeds, administrator, filed a new bond, page 203.

Curtis, Jeremiah, late of Stamford, will dated Feb. 23, 1813, probated Nov. 23, 1824, mentions his wife Debory, and children Phebe Stevens, Abigail, Jeremiah, HHenry, Edmond, and John. Executors sons John and Jeremiah. Witnesses Reuben Scofield, John Seely, and Enoch Stevens, page 80.
Nov. 23, 1824, order to advertise for claims, page 80.
Inventory taken Mch. 5, 1825, by Thaddeus Hanford and Jotham Hoyt, and filed Mch. 5, 1825, page 80.

Dayton, Gilbert, late of Greenwich, Jan. 26, 1826, his widow refused to qualify, and letters of administration on hisestate granted to Thomas Carpenter, who was ordered to advertise for claims, page 149.
Inventory taken Jan. 19, 1826, by John Carpenter and Aaron Field, and filed Feb. 6, 1824, page 149.
Sept. 10, 1826, account filed, and necessaries allowed to widow, page 150.

Denton, Daniel, late of Greenwich, Oct. 1824, necessaries allowed his widow, Abigail Denton, page 34.

Dixon, Eliza, wife of Thomas P. Dixon, late of Stamford, will dated Sept. 24, 1824, probated Oct. 24, 1824, mentions her husband Thomas P. Dixon, and mother Sally Hoyt. Executor her husband. Witnesses Richard Fox, Margaret Dixon, and Joseph Wood, page 72.
Oct. 24, 1824, order to advertise for claims, page 72.
Inventory taken Nov. 1, 1824, by David Hoyt, and RichardFox, and filed Nov. 11, 1824, page 73.

Dixon, Sarah Ann, and Catherine Dixon, Jan. 12, 1825, petition of their guardian, Isaac Wardwell, for leave to sell the real estate of said minors in Stanford formerly of Joseph S. Hoyt, and saleordered, page 75.
Apl. 7, 1825, part of their real estate sold to Jotham Hoyt, page 74.

Ferris, Ebenezer, late of Stamford, will dated Aug. 5, 1822, probated Jan. 16, 1824, mentions his wife Abigail, now deceased, Melliscent Lewis, Charlotte Ferris of New

York City, daughter of "my brother Ebenezer Ferris, deceased"; Rev. Mr. Flandereau, preacher at New Rochelle; Selleck Jones of Darien, Rev. Enoch Ferris, "son of

STAMFORD PROBATE RECORDS.
Volume 13, 1824.

Ferris, Ebenezer, continued :
    my brother John Ferris, deceased" Executor said Selleck Jones, and if he be deceased Joseph Wood of Stamford. Witnesses Joseph Wood, John Lewis, and Harvey Pencyer, page 26.
    Jan. 16, 1824, order to advertise for claims, page 27.
    Inventory taken Jan. 17, 1824, by Isaac Holly and Erastus H. Weed, and filed Feb. 7, 1825, page 46.

Ferris, Lemuel, late of Greenwich, will dated May 1, 1825, probated June 25, 1825, mentions his wife Susan, and children Susan, Sarah, Jane, Ann, Juliet, Esther, Alexander, Jabez, Lemuel, Sabrina Bunnell, and John. Executors daughter Susan, and either of sons Alexander, Jabez, or Lemuel. Witnesses Walter Swan, James Swan, and Samuel Webb, page 338.
    June 25, 1825, letters to Susan and Lemuel, who were ordered to advertise for claims, page 339.
    Inventory taken Aug. 15, 1825, by Isaac Holly and Benjamin Page, and filed Aug. 15, 1825, page 340.

Ferris, Nathaniel, sometimes called Jr., late of Greenwich,
    Apl. 19, 1824, letters of administration on his estate granted to Jonathan Finch and Charles Smith of Greenwich, who were ordered to advertise for claims, pages 22 and 31.
    Inventory taken Apl. 21, 1824, by David Wood, Jared Smith, and Charles Smith, and filed July 1, 1824, page 31.
    May 1, 1824, dower of his widow, Permelia Ferris, set out, page 32.
    Oct. 20, 1824, necessaries allowed his widow, page 33.
    Dec. 22, 1824, account filed, and real estate ordered sold to pay debts, page 45.
    Jan. 1, 1825, real estate sold to Arza Marshall, and report of sale filed, page 45.
    Mch. 11, 1825, his widow, Permelia Ferris, appointed guardian of Harry, Lydia Ann, Rebecca, and Lockwood, children of decedent, page 58.
    Mch. 11, 1825, estate ordered distributed to James, Riley, Marilda Mead, Catherine, Clara, Nathaniel, William, Edwin or Edmond, Harry, Lydia Ann, Rebecca, and Lockwood, children of decedent, page 64.
    Mch. 23, 1825, estate distributed accordingly, page 64.

Ferris, Peter, absent from the state and unheard of for many years, Nov. 19, 1825, Margaret Ferris and Mary Ferris, his daughters, made choice of Harvey Lounsbury to be

STAMFORD PROBATE RECORDS.
Volume 13, 1824.

Ferris, Peter, continued :
    their guardian, who was also appointed guardian of Martha Ferris, alias Patty Ferris, another daughter of about 11 years of age, page 92.
    Dec. 12, 1825, his daughter Julia Anne Ferris, over 12 years of age, made choice of Harvey Lounsbury of Kent in the State of New York to be her guardian, page 129.
    Mch. 7, 1826, petition for leave to sell the interest of said minors in the real estate left by Gideon Lounsbury, late of Stamford, deceased, and sale ordered, pages 129 and 130.

Ferris, Ransford A., late of Stamford, Feb. 7, 1824, letters of administration on his estate granted to Nehemiah Hoyt, Jr., who was ordered to advertise for claims, page 17.
    Inventory taken Mch. 6, 1824, by Ebenezer Smith and Thomas June, and filed Mch. 16, 1824, page 17.
    Aug. 26, 1824, necessaries allowed his widow, Elizabeth Ferris, page 34.
    Nov. 23, 1824, account filed, and real estate ordered sold to pay debts, page 34.
    Feb. 1, 1825, real estate sold to Allan S. Mead, and report of sale filed, page 44.

Ferris, Stephen, late of Greenwich, June 28, 1824, letters of administration on his estate granted to Jaduthan Ferris who was ordered to advertise for claims, page 49.
    Inventory taken July 6, 1824, by Enos Lockwood and Ashbel Palmer, and filed Aug. 28, 1824, page 49.

Fowler, David, June 18, 1828, the court appointed Hezekiah Hobby of Greenwich guardian of David N. Fowler of Newburgh, N. Y., a son of said David Fowler, about 5 years of age, having property in Greenwich, page 295.

Gray, Phebe, of Darien, June 18, 1824, appointed guardian of her children Catherine Gray, and Julia A. Gray, and Almira Gray, page 28.

Green, James, late of Greenwich, will dated Mch. 10, 1813, probated Jan. 30, 1828, mentions his wife Susannah, and children James, Thomas, Reuben, Joseph, Benjamin, Sarah Wilson, and Nancy Husted. Executors sons Benjamin and Joseph. Witnesses Nancy Seaman, James Banks, Jr., and Obadiah Banks, page 281.
    Jan. 30, 1828, order to advertise for claims, page 282.
    Inventory taken Feb. 1, 1828, by David Brown and Platt Mead, and filed Mch. 1, 1828, page 282.

STAMFORD PROBATE RECORDS.
Volume 13, 1824.

Haight, Daniel, of Greenwich, Dec. 5, 1825, Eunice Haight, over 12 years of age, his minor daughter, made choice of said Daniel Haight to be her guardian, who was also appointed guardian of Sarah, Nehemiah W., Phebe, and Epenetus, his other minor children, page 103.

Hobby, Jabez M., late of Greenwich, will dated Nov. 10, 1823, probated Jan. 13, 1824, mentions his wife Abigail, heirs of his daughter Nancy Peck, daughter Mary wife of Nehemiah Mead, and grandson Jabez Hobby Mead. Executors brother Hezekiah Hobby, and Hezekiah Tracy. Witnesses Eunice Kneeland, Huldah Tracy, and Zabed Finch, page 15.
Jan. 13, 1824, order to advertise for claims, page 16.
Inventory taken Jan. 1824, by Samuel Bush and Isaac Mead, Jr., and filed Feb. 4, 1824, page 16.
Oct. 1824, account filed, and estate ordered distributed to his widow Abigail, and children Mary wife of Nehemiah Mead, and Nancy Peck, now deceased, and Jabez Hobby Mead, page 39.
Jan. 3, 1825, estate distributed accordingly, page 39.

Hobby, John, late of Greenwich, will dated May 18, 1826, probated Sept. 2, 1826, mentions his wife Mary, and child George Adams Hobby. Executor John Adams, Jr. Witnesses Ard Reynolds, Charles Smith, and John Adams, Jr. page 212.
Sept. 2, 1826, order to advertise for claims, page 213.
Sept. 14, 1826, letters of administration with the will annexed granted to Jared Smith of Greenwich, who was ordered to advertise for claims, page 213.
Inventory taken Sept. 20, 1826, by Charles Smith and Amos Mead, and filed Apl. 3, 1827, page 213.

Hobby, Ruth, late of Greenwich, Mch. 10, 1825, letters of administration on her estate granted to Aaron Husted, who was ordered to advertise for claims, page 73.

Holmes, John, late of Darien, Apl. 14, 1824, Nancy Slauson, only executrix, discharged, and her husband Lewis Slauson, appointed administrator with the will annexed in her place, page 4.

Howe, David, late of Darien, Jan. 22, 1825, his widow, Sally Howe, refused to qualify, and letters of administration on his estate granted to Jeremiah Andreas of Darien, who was ordered to advertise for claims, page 82.
Inventory taken Mch. 7, 1825, by Cary Bell and Azariah Waterbury, and filed Mch. 7, 1825, page 82.

STAMFORD PROBATE RECORDS.
Volume 13, 1824.

Howe, Isaac, late of Greenwich, will dated Apl. 19, 1823, probated Jan. 23, 1824, mentions his children Sally wife of Gilbert Close, Betsy wife of Rufus Knapp, Kezia Howe, Rachel Howe, Esther Howe, Laura Howe, Lucy Howe, Cornelia Howe, Jonas Howe, Nehemiah Howe, and Samuel Howe. Executors Gilbert Close, Jonas Howe, and Nehemiah Howe. Witnesses Hezekiah Tracy, Amos Hobby, and David Mead, page 14.
Jan. 23, 1824, order to advertise for claims, page 15.
Inventory taken Jan. 27, 1824, by Samuel Close and Daniel Peck, and filed Mch. 18, 1824, page 15.

Howe, James, late of Darien, Sept. 3, 1825, letters of administration on his estate granted to Jesse Selleck of Darien, who was ordered to advertise for claims, page 108.
Inventory taken by Samuel Whiting and Isaac Pencyer, and filed Sept. 21, 1825, page 108.

Hoyt, Bates, late of Warwick, N. Y., Oct. 22, 1827, Charles and James Harvey, sons of decedent, made choice of Jeremiah Andreas of Darien to be their guardian, who was also appointed guardian of Thaddeus and Bates, other sons of decedent, under 14 years of age, page 197.
Oct. 22, 1827, petition for leave to sell the real estate of said minors, and sale ordered, page 247.

Hoyt, Benjamin, late of Stamford, Feb. 29, 1828, letters of administration on his estate granted to Joseph S. Hoyt, who was ordered to advertise for claims, page 317.
Inventory taken Mch. 5, 1828, by Thaddeus Hanford and Jotham Hoyt, and filed Apl. 7, 1828, page 318.

Hoyt, Billy, late of Stamford, Oct. 7, 1825, his widow having refused to qualify, letters of administration on his estate granted to William Hoyt, 3rd, son of deceased, who was ordered to advertise for claims, page 242.
Inventory taken Dec. 24, 1825, by Peter Smith, Jr., and Silas Hoyt, and filed Apl. 3, 1826, page 243.
Apl. 3, 1827, William Hoyt, a son of deceased, of Stamford, appointed guardian of his brothers George Hoyt about 13 years of age, and James H. Hoyt, about 18 years of age, pages 198 and 199.

Hoyt, Darius, late of Darien, Oct. 9, 1824, his widow, Harriet refused to qualify, and letters of administration on his estate granted to John Brown, of Stamford, who was ordered to advertise for claims, page 86.

STAMFORD PROBATE RECORDS.
Volume 13, 1824.

Hoyt, Darius, continued :
    Inventory taken Oct. 13, 1824, by Daty Weed and Jeremiah Andreas, and filed Apl. 28, 1825, page 87.
    Dec. 5, 1825, account filed, and real estate ordered sold to pay debts, page 88.

Hoyt, Darius, late of Darien, Jan. 29, 1827, Jerome Bates Hoyt, William Augustus Hoyt, and George Allen Hoyt, sons of decedent, made choice of John Brown of Stamford to be their guardian, who was also appointed guardian of Charles Henry Hoyt, Mary Hoyt, Eliza Hoyt, Elizabeth Hoyt, and Hannah Audelia Hoyt, other children of decedent, page 198.

Hoyt, Elihu, late of Stamford, May 22, 1828, his widow having refused to qualify, letters of administration on his estate granted to Jotham Hoyt, who was ordered to advertise for claims, page 279.
    Inventory taken May 23, 1828, by Thaddeus Hanford and Asahel Young, and filed Mch. 20, 1829, page 279.
    Mch. 28, 1828, account filed, and necessaries allowed his widow, page 281.

Hoyt, Enoch, late of Stamford, July 11, 1827, letters of administration on his estate granted to his widow, Sally Ann Hoyt, and commissioners appointed to adjust claims of creditors, page 296.
    Inventory taken July 21, 1827, by Richard Fox and Amzi Scofield, and filed July 30, 1827, page 296.
    Feb. 25, 1828, report of commissioners to adjust claims filed, page 298.
    Mch. 19, 1829, account filed, and necessaries allowed his widow, page 299.

Hoyt, Isaac, late of Stamford, will dated June 6, 1828, probated June 17, 1828, mentions his wife Elizabeth, and daughter Betsy wife of David Barnum. Executor Samuel Lockwood. Witnesses Samuel Brash, Mercy Hoyt, and Theodosia Bates, page 307.
    June 17, 1828, order to advertise for claims, page 307.
    Inventory taken by William Waterbury and Peter Smith, Jr., and filed Aug. 7, 1828, page 308.

Hoyt, John, late of Stamford, Mch. 7, 1825, his widow refused to qualify, and letters of administration on his estate granted to William Hoyt and Leander Hoyt, who were ordered to advertise for claims, page 115.
    Inventory taken Mch. 14, 1825, by Thaddeus Hanford and Jotham Hoyt, and filed Apl. 5, 1825, page 116.

STAMFORD PROBATE RECORDS.
Volume 13, 1824.

Hoyt, John, continued:
    Additional inventory filed Dec. 16, 1825, page 118.
    Mch. 28, 1826, account filed, and estate ordered distributed to his widow, Rebecca Hoyt, and his heirs-at-law, viz: William Hoyt, Samuel Hoyt, heirs of Elizabeth Larkin, Mary wife of Nathan H. Reed, heirs of Benjamin Hoyt, Melancthon Hoyt, heirs of John Hoyt, Abigail Harden, Joseph Warren Hoyt, and Leander Hoyt, page 159.
    Apl. 27, 1826, estate distributed accordingly, page 160.

Hoyt, Shadrach, late of Stamford, Aug. 29, 1823, letters of administration on his estate granted to Stephen Bishop and James R. Hoyt, who were ordered to advertise for claims, page 11.
    Inventory taken Sept. 2, 1823, by Isaac Quintard and Erastus H. Weed, and filed Oct. 27, 1823, page 11.

Hoyt, William C., of Stamford, about 15 years of age, Dec. 12, 1828, made choice of his mother, Hannah Hoyt, of Stamford to be his guardian, page 307.

Hubbard, Gabriel, late of Stamford, Oct. 26, 1827, his widow, refused to qualify, and letters of administration on his estate granted to John Raymond of New Canaan and Stephen B. Provost of Stamford, page 320.
    Inventory taken Nov. 27, 1827, by Davis Lockwood and John W. Leeds, and filed Dec. 24, 1827, page 321.
    Oct. 27, 1827, commissioners appointed to adjust claims of creditors, pages 327 and 328.
    June 25, 1828, report of commissioners to adjust claims filed, page 328.

Hubbard, Henry, late of Greenwich, will dated Jan. 22, 1822, probated Sept. 3, 1825, mentions his wife Hannah, and sons Nathaniel, Andrew and Gabriel, devised real estate in the Town of Chester, N. Y., and daughters Hannah Todd, Sally wife of Levi Ingersoll, Lydia wife of William Palmer, and Mary Hubbard; four youngest sons Henry S., Abraham, Harvey, and William; grandsons Holly Hubbard and John Hubbard, sons of his deceased son John Hubbard. Executors his sons Nathaniel, Henry S., and Abraham. Witnesses Stephen Waring, Burwell Betts, and Henry Davis, page 95.
    Sept. 3, 1825, order to advertise for claims, page 97.
    Inventory taken by Conklin Husted and Jared Smith, and filed, Oct. 22, 1825, page 97.
    Mch. 2, 1826, time for final settlement extended, page 189.

STAMFORD PROBATE RECORDS.
Volume 13, 1824.

Husted, Elnathan, late of Greenwich, Feb. 24, 1825, letters of administration on his estate granted to Nancy Husted, his widow, and William A. Husted, who were ordered to advertise for claims, page 75.
Inventory taken Mch. 14, 1825, by William Husted and Jonas Howe, and filed Mch. 23, 1825, page 75.
Additional inventory filed Apl. 8, 1825, page 76.
Mch. 9, 1827, dower ordered set out, page 270.
Apl. 5, 1827, dower set out to his widow, Nancy Husted, page 270.

Husted, Nathaniel, late of Greenwich, will dated Jan. 14, 1826 probated Feb. 13, 1826, mentions his wife Ruth, and children Benjamin, Jonathan, James, Nathaniel, Samuel, and Polly. Executors his sons Nathaniel and Samuel. Witnesses Nehemiah Brown, John Knapp, and Ard Reynolds, page 152.
Feb. 13, 1826, order to advertise for claims, page 153.
Inventory taken Mch. 8, 1826, by Nehemiah Brown and William Husted, and filed Mch. 11, 1826, page 153.

Husted, Sarah, formerly of Greenwich, Apl. 14, 1826, a niece and devisee for life of Sarah Ferris, late of Greenwich, deceased, is now deceased, and her sons Joseph and Jared Husted, both died before her; that Sarah wife of Daniel Reynolds, Mary wife of Converse Bacon, Jane wife of Frederick Smith, Henry Husted, Samuel Husted, George Husted, and Deborah widow of Isaac Reynolds are the only children of said Sarah Husted, who were living at the time of her death. The estate of said Sarah Ferris devised to said Sarah Husted for life, ordered distributed to her children living at the time of her decease, page 151.
Aug. 5, 1826, estate distributed accordingly, page 151.

Ingersoll, Simeon, late of Greenwich, will dated Dec. 11, 1827, probated Jan. 21, 1828, mentions his wife Sarah, and children Alexander S., John Jarvis, Alton, and Sarah Ingersoll, grandsons Platt C. Ingersoll and Simeon Ingersoll, sons of Alexander Ingersoll. Executors son John Jarvis Ingersoll of New York City and David Wood of Greenwich. Witnesses Israel K. Wood, William P. Reynolds, and Benjamin Johnson, page 249.
Jan. 21, 1828, order to advertise for claims, page 250.

Jessup, Ann, late of Greenwich, will dated Feb. 11, 1824, probated May 9, 1825, mentions her daughters Ann Rundle, Mary Jessup and Sarah Lockwood, sons Ebenezer Jessup,

STAMFORD PROBATE RECORDS.
Volume 13, 1824.

Jessup, Ann, continued :
and Edward Jessup, children of her son Jonathan Jessup, children of her son James Jessup, children of her son Peter Jessup, children of her daughter Hannah Lockwood, children of her son Gershom Jessup, children of her son Timothy Jessup, and grandson Samuel Jessup a son of said Mary Jessup. Executors son Edward Jessup and son-in-law Peter Lockwood. Witnesses Charles Hendrie, Samuel Ferris, Jr., and Joshua Ferris, page 142
May 9, 1825, order to advertise for claims, page 143.
Inventory taken May 10, 1825, by Enos Lockwood and Drake Lockwood, and filed May 11, 1825, page 144.

Jessup, Jonathan, late of Greenwich, June 20, 1825, on the Application of Frederick Lockwood, of Greenwich, husband of MaryAnn, a daughter of Gershom Jessup, deceased, the said Gershom Jessup being a son and heir and devisee of said Jonathan Jessup, deceased, that part of the estate of said Jonathan Jessup set off to his widow as her dower, she being now deceased, ordered distributed to James Jonathan Jessup, Edward Jessup, Ebenezer Jessup, Ann wife of Jeremiah Rundle, Mary wife of William Peacock, Sarah wife of Daniel Lockwood, the heirs at law of Hannah deceased wife of Peter Lockwood, heirs at law of Peter Jessup, deceased, heirs at law of Gershom Jessup, deceased, heirs at law of James Jessup, deceased, and heirs at law of Timothy Jessup, deceased, being the children and devisees of said Jonathan Jessup, deceased, page 203.
July 13, 1825, estate distributed accordingly, page 204.

Jessup, Jonathan, late of Greenwich, Apl. 14, 1827, his widow, Kezia Jessup, refused to qualify, and letters of administration on his estate granted to Daniel Lockwood of Stamford, who was ordered to advertise for claims, page 286.
Inventory taken Apl. 19, 1827, by Drake Lockwood and Samuel Ferris, Jr., and filed June 23, 1827, page 286.
July 10, 1828, petition of Kezia Jessup, widow of deceased, for the removal of the administrator, page 287.
Feb. 10, 1828, administrator removed, and Kezia Jessup appointed in his place, page 287.
Aug. 6, 1828, account filed, and commissioners appointed to adjust claims of creditors, page 288.
Mch. 30, 1829, report of commissioners filed, page 288.
Aug. 23, 1828, personal property ordered sold, and report of sale filed, page 289.
Apl. 18, 1829, necessaries allowed his widow, page 289.
Dec. 13, 1827, Joshua Beal Jessup and Jonathan Jessup,

STAMFORD PROBATE RECORDS
Volume 13, 1824.

152.

Jessup, Jonathan, continued :
sons of decedent, made choice of their mother Kezia Jessup of Greenwich, to be their guardian, who was also appointed guardian of John Anson Jessup, Julius Augustus Jessup, Cornelius James Jessup, Charles Edward Jessup, Sarah Jeannette Jessup, and Ann Eliza Jessup, other children of decedent, page 242.

June, Nathaniel, late of Stamford, will dated Feb. 14, 1816, probated Nov. 7, 1825, all to his wife Hannah. Executors his son-in-law Eber Smith, and son Isaac June. Witnesses Daniel Nichols, Jabez Smith, and Jonathan Smith, page 107.
Nov. 9, 1825, the executors named in the will having refused to qualify, letters of administration with the will annexed granted to Isaac Lockwood, 3rd, who was ordered to advertise for claims, page 107.
Inventory taken Nov. 14, 1825, by Solomon Clason and Abel Reynolds, and filed Jan. 2, 1826, page 107.

Keeler, Mary, late of Greenwich, widow of William Keeler, Sept. 7, 1826, letters of administration on her estate granted to Asahel Palmer of Greenwich, who was ordered to advertise for claims, page 239.

Knapp, Charles, late of Greenwich, Aug. 31, 1826, letters of administration on his estate granted to his son Charles Knapp of Greenwich, who was ordered to advertise for claims, page 235.

Knapp, Edmund, late of Greenwich, May 8, 1824, real estate sold to Henry S. Knapp, and report of sale filed, page 58.

Knapp, Eliza, late of Stamford, Mch.24, 1827, letters of administration on her estate granted to Abel Reynolds of Stamford, who was ordered to advertise for claims, page 263.
Inventory taken Apl. 28, 1827, by Isaac Lockwood, Jr., and Jonathan Scofield, and filed June 6, 1827, page 264.

Knapp, Enos, late of Greenwich, will dated June 10, 1812, probated Nov. 24, 1824, mentions his wife Mary, and children Isaac, Enos, and Rhoda wife of Benjamin Page, grandchildren David Peck, Charles Peck, Enos Peck, Sally Peck, and Rhoda Peck, children of his daughter Mary, deceased wife of Whitfield Peck. Executors

STAMFORD PROBATE RECORDS.
Volume 13, 1824.

Knapp, Enos, continued :
sons Isaac and Enos. Witnesses Mary Davenport, Jerusha Davenport, and Ebenezer Davenport, page 51.
Codicil dated June 11, 1812, page 52.
Nov. 24, 1824, order to advertise for claims, page 53.
Inventory taken by Drake Lockwood and Asahel Palmer, and filed Dec. 3, 1824, page 53.
Dec. 15, 1824, his widow accepts the provisions in his will, and her portion order set out, page 54.
Jan. 15, 1825, widow's portion set out, page 55.

Knapp, Joshua, late of Stamford, Mch. 1, 1827, on the application of Ruth Knapp, a daughter of deceased, estate ordered distributed to his heirs at law, viz: to the heirs at law of Walter Knapp, deceased, Israel Knapp, Rebecca Wyx, Sally Kainworthy, Ruth Knapp, and the heirs of Eliza Knapp, deceased, page 172.
Mch, 22, 1827, estate distributed accordingly, page 172.

Knapp, Ruth, late of Stamford, Mch. 24, 1827, letters of administration on her estate granted to Abel Reynolds of Stamford, who was ordered to advertise for claims, page 255.
Inventory taken Apl. 28, 1827, by Isaac Lockwood and Jonathan Scofield, and filed June 6, 1827, page 255.
Sept. 24, 1827, commissioners appointed to adjust claims of creditors, page 255.
June 21, 1828, report of commissioners filed page 256.
Sept. 5, 1827, account filed, and personal property ordered sold, page 256.

Knapp, William, late of Greenwich, will dated July 2, 1818, probated Dec. 1, 1825, mentions his wife Esther, and children William B., Henry I., Benjamin I., Albert, Frederic, William, Elisabeth Titus, Sarah W. Mead, Esther R. Belcher, Susan I. Knapp, and Julia Ann Knapp. His blackman Charles to be given his freedom. Executors his wife, brother-in-law Benjamin Isaacs of Bedford, Jabez Mead and Justus L. Bush of Greenwich. Witnesses Leverett Bush, Fanny Bush, and Grace Bush, page 174.
Dec. 1, 1825, order to advertise for claims, page 175.
Inventory taken Jan. 25, 1826, by Isaac Holly and Joseph Brush, and filed Mch. 7, 1826.

Leeds, Gideon, late of Stamford, will dated Feb. 15, 1816, probated Mch. 24, 1827, personal property bequeathed to his wife Rhoda, whom he appointed executrix. Witness-

STAMFORD PROBATE RECORDS.
Volume 13, 1824.

Leeds, Gideon, continued :
es Reuben Scofield, William Crissy, and Joseph Wood, page 215.
Mch. 24, 1827, order to advertise for claims, page 215.
Inventory taken by Richard Fox and James Webb, and filed July 27, 1827, page 215.

Leeds, Harry, late of Stamford, will dated Mch. 14, 1825, probated Oct. 6, 1825, mentions his brother John W. Leeds, Theodore Leeds a son of Jacob W. Leeds, deceased, mother Honor Leeds, Prudence Hunt, and her sister, Permillia Holly and sister, father John Leeds. Executor brother John W. Leeds. Witnesses Hannah Leeds, and Eliza Husted, page 109.
Oct. 9, 1825, order to advertise for claims, page 110.
Inventory taken Dec. 7, 1825, by Joseph Gray and William Wilmot, and filed Dec. 7, 1825, page 110.

Leeds, Jacob W., late of Stamford, will dated July 2, 1824, probated Oct. 21, 1824, mentions his wife Sarah W., and son Theodore. Executor brother John W. Leeds. Witnesses Joseph Gray and Cary Leeds, page 56.
Oct. 21, 1824, order to advertise for claims, page 57.
Inventory taken Oct. 23, 1824, by Joseph Gray and William Wilmot, and filed Oct. 23, 1824, page 57.
Oct. 21, 1824, John W. Leeds appointed guardian of Theodore Leeds, a son of decedent, about eighteen months of age, page 41.

Lewis, Huldah, late of Stamford, will dated Dec. 20, 1819, probated Nov. 29, 1824, mentions her children Elias L. Waring, John H. Waring, Thomas Waring, Ephraim Waring, and Huldah wife of Epenetus Sniffen. Executor her brother Seth Hickcock. Witnesses William Holly, Sally E. Hoyt, and John Augur, page 77.
Nov. 29, 1824, order to advertise for claims, page 77.
Inventory taken Nov. 29, 1824, by Isaac Holly and Jonathan Brown, and filed Nov. 29, 1824, page 78.
Additional inventory filed June 20, 1825, page 78.
June 20, 1825, account filed, and distribution ordered to Elias L. Warren, John H. Warren, Thomas Warren, Ephraim Warren, and Huldah Sniffen, children of deceased, page 78.
June 27, 1825, estate distributed accordingly, page 79.

Lockwood, Caleb, late of Greenwich, will dated Sept. 10, 1823, probated Jan. 29, 1824, all to his wife Sarah, who was appointed executrix. Witnesses Thomas Peck, Joshua Ferris, and Mary Peck, page 23.

STAMFORD PROBATE RECORDS.
Volume 13, 1824.

155.

Lockwood, Caleb, continued :
>Jan. 29, 1824, order to advertise for claims, page 23.
Inventory taken Feb. 6, 1824, by Drake Lockwood and Rufus Peck, and filed Oct. 16, 1824, page 37.

Lockwood, Daniel, Jr., late of Stamford, Oct. 11, 1827, his widow refused to qualify, and letters of administration on his estate granted to Abel Reynolds of Stamford, who was ordered to advertise for claims, page 259.
Inventory taken by Isaac Ayres and William White, Jr., and filed Oct. 27, 1828, page 259.
Nov. 10, 1828, account filed, and necessaries allowed his widow, page 260.
Nov. 10, 1828, real estate ordered sold to pay debts, page 260.
Dec. 6, 1828, real estate sold to Stephen Lockwood and Cephas Lockwood, and report of sale filed, page 260.

Lockwood, Fanny, late of Greenwich, will dated Feb. 7, 1825, probated Dec. 14, 1825, mentions her mother Deborah Lockwood, brother Uriah Lockwood, sisters Deborah and Sarah, and father Frederic Lockwood. Executrix her Mother and Joshua Ferris. Witnesses Deborah Selleck, Ann Peck, and Joshua Ferris, page 167.
Dec. 14, 1825, order to advertise for claims, page 168.
Inventory taken by Joshua Ferris and Jabez Mead, and filed Feb. 4, 1826, page 169.

Lockwood, Hannah, widow, late of Stamford, Sept. 10, 1824, letters of administration on her estate granted to Shadrach Lockwood and Abel Reynolds, who were ordered to advertise for claims, page 50.
Inventory taken Sept. 16, 1824, by Henry Waring and Oliver Lockwood, and filed Mch. 17, 1825, page 50.
Mch. 22, 1825, account filed, and real estate ordered sold to pay debts, page 51.
Mch. 28, 1825, real estate sold to Peter Lockwood, Hannah Scofield, and Lucretia Scofield, and report of sale filed, page 74.
Mch. 29, 1825, estate ordered distributed to Hannah Scofield and Abigail Lockwood, Shadrach Lockwood, and to the heirs of Josiah Lockwood, children of deceased, page 68.
Apl. 5, 1825, estate distributed accordingly, page 68.

Lockwood, Isaac, late of Greenwich, Oct. 29, 1827, letters of administration on his estate granted to William Waterbury, Jr., of Stamford, who was ordered to advertise for claims, page 289.

STAMFORD PROBATE RECORDS.
Volume 13, 1824.

Lockwood, Isaac, continued :
    Inventory taken Dec. 5, 1827, by George Ferris, Jr., and Samuel Husted, and filed Jan. 30, 1828, page 290.

Lockwood, John, late of Stamford, (died in 1786), Oct. 27, 1824, on the application of Shadrach Lockwood of Stamford, one of the heirs at law of deceased, that part of his estate set off to his widow, Hannah, now deceased as her dower, ordered distributed to his heirs at law, viz: the legal representatives of Josiah Lockwood, Shadrach Lockwood, Hannah Scofield, and Abigail Lockwood, children of deceased, page 58.
Estate distributed accordingly, page 59.

Lockwood, Lewis, late of New York City, Dec. 28, 1824, letters of administration on his estate granted to Priscilla Lockwood, his widow, and Davis Lockwood of Stamford, who were ordered to advertise for claims, page 81.
Inventory taken by Stephen B. Provost and Augustus Lockwood, and filed Mch. 12, 1825, page 81.

Lockwood, Luther, late of Stamford, Nov. 27, 1827, his widow refused to qualify, and letters of administration on his estate granted to Nehemiah Hait, Jr., who was ordered to advertise for claims, page 251.
Inventory taken Dec. 3, 1827, by Calvin Hoyt and Alfred Smith, and filed Dec. 10, 1827, page 251.
Feb. 12, 1828, dower of his widow, Polly Lockwood, ordered set out, page 252.
Mch. 10, 1828, dower set out, page 252.
Oct. 16, 1828, account filed, and necessaries set out to his widow, page 252.
Oct. 16, 1828, account filed, and real estate ordered sold to pay debts, page 329.
Real estate sold in three parcels to Thaddeus Lockwood, Calvin Hoyt, and Alfred Smith, and report of sale filed, page 329.

Lockwood, Reuben, late of Greenwich, Apl. 12, 1828, account filed by the administrator, and estate ordered distributed to his heirs at law, viz: Enos Lockwood, Messenger Lockwood, Elizabeth Lockwood, Abigail Ferris, Martha Ferris, and the heirs of Sarah Lamb, page 233.
May 5, 1828, estate distributed accordingly, page 233.

Lockwood, Samuel, late of Stamford, June 10, 1826, letters of administration on his estate granted to his widow Sally Lockwood, and his son Ezra Lockwood, who were ordered

STAMFORD PROBATE RECORDS.
Volume 13, 1824.

Lockwood, Samuel, continued :
 to advertise for claims, page 176.
 Inventory taken July 1, 1826, by Jeremiah Andreas and John Bell, Jr., and filed Aug. 4, 1826, page 177.
 Mch. 7, 1827, account filed, and estate ordered distributed to his widow, and children Ezra and Horace, page 177.
 Mch. 26, 1827, estate distributed accordingly, page 177.

Lockwood, Smith, late of Stamford, Nov. 10, 1828, his widow refused to qualify, and letters of administration on his estate granted to Isaac Ferris of Greenwich, who was ordered to advertise for claims, page 316.
 Inventory taken by Abel Reynolds and Aaron Davis, and filed Mch. 2, 1829, page 316.
 Jan. 12, 1829, commissioners appointed to adjust claims of creditors, page 317.

Lounsbury, Enos, late of Stamford, Dec. 23, 1826, Charles Lounsbury, a son of decedent, about 14 years of age, made choice of Ezekiel Scofield of Stamford to be his guardian, page 196.

Lounsbury, Gideon, late of Stamford, will dated Oct. 27, 1823, probated Apl. 13, 1825, mentions his wife Abigail, and ante-nuptial agreement, and children James, John, Zabud, Gideon, Harvey, Hannah Ferris, Deborah Ketcham, and Maria Hercy(?). Executors his son Harvey and John Weed, Jr. Witnesses William Webb, Sylvanus B. Thompson and Noah Webb, page 88.
 Apl. 13, 1825, order to advertise for claims, page 89.
 Inventory taken Apl. 15, 1825, by William Webb and Isaac Holly, and filed Aug. 5, 1825, page 90.

Lounsbury, Hardy, of New York City, parent and natural guardian of Samuel Lounsbury, Aug. 7, 1826, petitioned the court for leave to sell the real estate in Greenwich of said minor, and sale ordered, page 200.

Lounsbury, Nathan, of Stamford, about 18 years of age, Apl. 27, 1825, made choice of Watts Comstock of New Canaan to be his guardian, page 73.

Lyon, Benjamin W., late of Greenwich, June 26, 1826, his widow refused to qualify, and letters of administration on his estate granted to William Husted and James Lyon of Greenwich, and commissioners appointed to adjust claims of creditors, page 156.

STAMFORD PROBATE RECORDS.
Volume 13, 1824.

Lyon, Benjamin W., continued:
    Mch. 7, 1827, report of commissioners filed, page 155.
    Inventory taken July 1, 1826, by Augustus Lyon, William Husted, and David Brown, and filed July 5, 1826, page 156.
    July 5, 1826, personal property ordered sold, page 156.
    Mch. 25, 1827, necessaries allowed his widow, page 157.
    Sept. 4, 1826, time for final settlement extended, pages 189, and 334.
    Mch. 23, 1827, dower of his widow, Deborah Lyon, ordered set out, page 189.
    Apl. 7, 1827, dower set out, page 189.

Lyon, Benjamin W., (the elder), late of Greenwich, Aug. 9, 1826, estate ordered distributed to the heirs of Benjamin W. Lyon, the younger, now deceased, James Lyon, Daniel Lyon, and Thomas Lyon, according to his will, his youngest son Thomas being now of age, page 156.
    Nov. 8, 1826, estate distributed accordingly, page 157.

Lyon, Daniel, late of Greenwich, will dated Mch. 9, 1824, probated June 5, 1824, mentions his wife Betty L., and children Joseph, Charles, Daniel, Betsy wife of Elliot Palmer, Fanny wife of Morris Mead, Mary wife of George Derby, Jerusha Lyon, and Rebecca Lyon. Executor his son Daniel. Witnesses J. Rogers, Sarah Rogers, and Elizabeth Rogers, page 18.
    June 6, 1824, order to advertise for claims, page 19.
    Inventory taken June 20, 1824, by Ebenezer Mead and Ephraim Marshall, and filed July 24, 1824, page 38.
    Jan. 1825, real estate ordered sold to pay debts, page 38.
    Mch. 28, 1824, real estate sold to Isaac Holly, Jr., and report of sale filed, page 60.
    Feb. 28, 1825, his widow, Betty L. Lyon, declined to accept the provisions in his will, and her dower ordered set out, page 71.
    Mch. 16, 1825, dower set out, page 71.

Marshall, Amy, late of Greenwich, May 22, 1824, letters of administration on her estate granted to Nathaniel Palmer, who was ordered to advertise for claims, page 21.
    Inventory taken June 2, 1824, by Isaac Holly and Ebenezer Mead, and filed June 16, 1824, page 22.
    Apl. 26, 1825, time for final settlement extended to May 22, next, page 73.
    Nov. 4, 1825, account filed, and real estate ordered sold to pay debts, page 216.

STAMFORD PROBATE RECORDS.
Volume 13, 1824.

Marshall, Amy, continued:
    Jan. 16, 1826, her administrator, Nathaniel Palmer, now deceased, and Hannah Marshall was appointed in his place, page 216.
    Jan. 16, 1826, account filed, and real estate ordered sold to pay debts, page 216.
    Jan. 17, 1826, real estate sold to Orpha Marshall and Benjamin Page, and report of sale filed, page 217.

Mead, Abraham, late of Greenwich, will dated Jan. 11, 1816, probated Jan. 17, 1828, mentions his wife Keziah, and children Deborah, Zophar, and Isaac. Executors sons Zophar and Isaac. Witnesses Ephraim Mead, Noah Mead, and Jonas Mead, page 258.
    Jan. 17, 1828, order to advertise for claims, page 258.
    Inventory taken Feb. 28, 1828, by Thomas A. Mead and Nelson Bush, and filed Mch. 13, 1828, page 259.

Mead, David, late of Greenwich, will dated July 5, 1824, probated Sept. 17, 1828, mentions his wife Cloe, and children Leonard, John Wallace, Gilbert, Theodore Barnum, David Wood, Robert, Clarissa, and Rachel Maria. Executors brother Darius Mead, Jr., and Jabez Mead. Witnesses Shadrach Mead, Samuel B. Mead, and Rachel Mead, page 310.
    Sept. 17, 1828, order to advertise for claims, page 310.
    Inventory taken by Amos Mead and Isaac Holly, and filed Dec. 8, 1828, page 311.

Mead, Jonah, late of Greenwich, will dated Dec. 8, 1818, probated Mch. 5, 1827, mentions his wife Mary, and children Drake, Lot, Rachel wife of Daniel Close, Polly, wife of Andrew Hubbard, Electa wife of Manoah Mead, Azuba wife of Ephraim Mead, and Hannah Mead, and his wife's brother Abner Mead. Executors sons Lot and Drake. Witnesses Sally W. Wood, Silas Wood, and Francis Wood, page 247.
    Mch. 5, 1827, order to advertise for claims, page 248.
    Inventory taken by Isaac Mead, Jr., and Zophar Mead, and filed Sept. 15, 1825, page 248.

Mead, Jonathan, late of Greenwich, Apl. 23, 1825, his widow refused to qualify, and letters of administration on his estate granted to Simeon H. Minor, who was ordered to advertise for claims, page 111.
    Inventory taken by Isaac Holly and Jared Reynolds, and filed July 18, 1825, page 111.

STAMFORD PROBATE RECORDS.
Volume 13, 1824.

Mead, Nehemiah, Jr., late of Greenwich, will dated May 3,
1819, probated Mch. 29, 1826, mentions his wife Ruth,
and children Sarah Mead, Ruth Caroline Mead, Laura
Mead, William Henry Mead, James Richard Mead, and Samuel H. Mead, brother-in-law Stephen Davis, and sister
Bethia wife of said Stephen Davis. Executor Isaac
Mead, Jr. Witnesses Elias Harroway, John Horton,
and Jabez Mead, page 179.
Mch. 29, 1826, order to advertise for claims, page 180.
Inventory taken by Isaac Holly and Stephen Waring, and
filed June 6, 1826, page 180.
Dec. 4, 1826, account filed, and estate ordered distributed to his widow and children, according to his
will, page 181.
Mch. 28, 1827, estate distributed accordingly, page 182.
Mch. 28, 1827, agreement between his heirs dated,
page 188.
Nov. 30, 1826, James Richard Mead, a son of decedent,
made choice of Charles Knapp of Stamford to be his
guardian, page 199.

Mead, Theodosia, late of Greenwich, will dated May 27, 1818,
probated Nov. 15, 1827, mentions her children Polly
Mead, and Sally wife of Benjamin Mead. Executor her
son Obadiah Mead. Witnesses Sally Close, James Lowden, and Gilbert Close, page 243.
Nov. 15, 1827, order to advertise for claims, page 244.
Inventory taken Dec. 5, 1827, by Silas H. Mead and
Darius Mead, and filed Jan. 10, 1828, page 244.

Merritt, Gilbert, late of Rye, will dated Oct. 24, 1823, probated Mch. 1, 1824, mentions his wife Abigail, and
children Delilah wife of Sylvanus Merritt of New Rochelle, Penelope wife of William Slater, Jr., of the
Town of Rye, and Hannah wife of Benjamin Merritt of the
Town of Rye. Executors Sylvanus Merritt of New Rochelle, William T. Provost and William Slater, Jr., of
Rye. Witnesses Robert Merritt, Nathaniel Hyatt and
George Francis, page 3.
Mch. 1, 1824, order to advertise for claims, page 4.
Inventory taken Mch. 4, 1824, by Jonas Mead and Daniel
Lyon, and filed Mch. 17, 1824, page 4.
July 5, 1824, his widow, Abigail Merritt, declined to
accept the provisions in his will, and her dower was
ordered set out, pages 35 and 59.
Aug. 21, 1824, dower set out, page 60.

STAMFORD PROBATE RECORDS.
Volume 13, 1824.

Miller, Eliza A., late of Stamford, Mch. 6, 1824, letters of administration on her estate granted to Daniel Youngs, who was ordered to advertise for claims, page 22.

Miller, James, formerly of Stamford, deceased, Mch. 7, 1825, Elbert Alonzo and Maria Emeline, children of decedent, made choice of Nathan White of Stamford to be their guardian, page 73.

Morehouse, Catharine, widow, late of Darien, Jan. 26, 1825, letters of administration on her estate granted to Henry Morehouse of Darien, who was ordered to advertise for claims, page 83.
Inventory taken Jan. 31, 1825, by Gershom Scofield and Jeremiah Andreas, and filed Mch. 21, 1825, page 83.
Mch. 29, 1825, Lavina Nichols and Paulina Nichols, both about 15 years of age, children of decedent, made choice of Aaron Davis to be their guardian, page 84.

Newman, Sarah, late of Stamford, will dated Aug. 21, 1821, probated Nov. 9, 1826, all to her children Sally Newman and Catharine Lapham. Executor Samuel Lockwood of Stamford. Witnesses Ezekiel Archer, Levinia Bishop, and Susannah H. Bishop, page 207.
Nov. 9, 1826, order to advertise for claims, page 208.
Inventory taken by David Hoyt, and Samuel Smith, and filed Dec. 23, 1826, page 208.

Newman, Stephen, late of Stamford, Feb. 17, 1827, his widow, Sarah Newman, being now deceased, that part of his estate set off to her as her dower, ordered distributed to Rufus Newman, the heirs of Ralph Newman, deceased, the heirs of Maltbie Newman, deceased, Stephen Newman, Catharine Lapham, Andrew Newman, Rebecca wife of John K. Bishop, and Sally Newman, being the heirs at law of deceased, page 206.
Mch. 16, 1827, estate distributed accordingly, page 206.

Palmer, Jeremiah, late of Stamford, will dated Apl. 10, 1824, probated Oct. 6, 1825, mentions his wife Mary and children Mary F. Keeler, Sally Palmer, James Ferris Palmer, Bethel Palmer, Walter Palmer, and Sarah Palmer. Executors sons James F. and Walter. Witnesses Daniel Lockwood, Rhua Ann Lockwood, and Rufus A. Lockwood, page 334.
Oct. 6, 1825, order to advertise for claims, page 336.
Inventory taken Oct. 12, 1825, by Eber Smith and Solomon Clason, and filed Jan. 16, 1826, page 336.

STAMFORD PROBATE RECORDS.
Volume 13, 1824.

Palmer, Jeremiah, continued:
Apl. 20, 1827, time for final settlement extended, page 338.

Palmer, Nathaniel, late of Greenwich, Feb. 13, 1826, his widow refused to qualify, and letters of administration on his estate granted to Stephen Palmer and Ezekiel Close of Greenwich, who were ordered to advertise for claims, page 271.
Inventory taken Feb. 27, 1826, by Samuel Peck and Benjamin Husted, and filed Apl. 5, 1826, page 271.
Mch. 25, 1827, commissioners appointed to adjust claims of creditors, page 273.
Mch. 26, 1827, necessaries allowed his widow, and dower ordered set out, page 273.
Mch. 31, 1827, dower set out to his widow, Rachel Palmer, page 274.
Feb. 9, 1827, time for final settlement extended, page 275.
Apl. 1828, personal property ordered sold and report of sale filed, page 275.

Peck, Alexander, late of Greenwich, Nov. 13, 1826, letters of administration on his estate granted to Asahel Palmer of Greenwich, who was ordered to advertise for claims, page 214.
Inventory taken Nov. 27, 1826, by Joshua Ferris and Frederick Lockwood, and filed Dec. 16, 1826, page 214.

Peck, Benjamin, late of Greenwich, Mch. 31, 1827, Hannah Reed Peck, a daughter of decedent, about 16 years of age, made choice of David Brown of Greenwich to be her guardian, page 199.

Peck, Charles, of Flushing, Oct. 1824, his children Thomas H. Peck and Mehitabel Peck, both over 14 years of age, made choice of Hezekiah Hobby of Greenwich to be their guardian, who was also appointed guardian of Charles Edgar Peck, about 12 years of age, another son of said Charles Peck, page 41.

Peck, Elias, Jr., of Greenwich, Apl. 1, 1826, the court appointed William Husted of Greenwich guardian of Wilson Peck, Elias Read Peck, and Jonathan Peck, children of said Elias Peck, Jr., page 129.

Peck, Isaac, late of Greenwich, will dated Mch. 24, 1821, probated Nov. 3, 1827, mentions his wife Betsy, and children Sands Furman Peck, Isaac Peck, grandchildren, viz:

STAMFORD PROBATE RECORDS.
Volume 13, 1824.

Peck, Isaac, continued :
Charles Henry Peck, John Walter Peck, and Stephen Sands Peck. Executrix his wife. Witnesses Susan Caroline Ferris, Joshua Ferris, and Deborah Selleck, page 236. Nov. 3, 1827, order to advertise for claims, page 237. Inventory taken Nov. 26, 1827, by Asahel Palmer and Frederic Lockwood, and filed Nov. 28, 1827, page 237.

Peck, Joseph, late of Greenwich, Nov. 13, 1826, his widow being incapable of administering his estate, letters of administration on his estate granted to Asahel Palmer, who was ordered to advertise for claims, page 217. Inventory taken Nov. 27, 1826, by Joshua Ferris and Frederick Lockwood, and filed Dec. 16, 1826, page 218. Oct. 18, 1827, account filed, and necessaries set off to his widow, pages 218 and 219.

Peck, Robert, late of Greenwich, will dated Jan. 11, 1812, probated Nov. 19, 1827, mentions his wife Ann, and children Molly wife of Samuel Whiting of Darien, Ann wife of Abraham Peck of Warwick, Orange County, N. Y., and Elias Peck, Jr., daughter-in-law Levina Peck widow of his son Robert Peck, deceased, grandson Robert Peck a son of said Robert Peck, deceased, and Ann Peck a daughter of said Robert Peck, deceased. Executor son Elias. Witnesses Lewis Peck, Alvin Palmer, and Jabez Mead, page 315.
Dec. 14, 1827, Elias Peck, Jr., refused to qualify, and letters of administration with the will annexed granted to Samuel Whiting of Darien, who was ordered to advertise for claims, page 315.
Inventory taken Dec. 21, 1827, by Drake Lockwood and Isaac Knapp, and filed Jan. 12, 1828, page 315.

Peck, Whitfield, late of Greenwihh, May 1, 1826, distribution ordered to his children David, Sally wife of George Ferris, Charles, Rhoda, and Enos, of all the property left to them by the will of Enos Knapp, late of Greenwich, deceased, page 164.
May 11, 1826, estate distributed accordingly, page 164.

Pencyer, Henry, late of -------, Oct. 17, 1823, on the application of Isaac Pencyer and Hannah Pencyer, administrators, the court discharged said Hannah as administratrix, page 5.
Nov. 25, 1822, real estate in New Canaan sold, and report of sale filed, page 5.

STAMFORD PROBATE RECORDS.
Volume 13, 1824.

Raymond, Ira, late of ----, May 3, 1828, Samuel L. Raymond, a son of decedent, about 15 years of age, made choice of Joseph White of Stamford to be his guardian, page 245

Raymond, Stephen, late of Darien, Jan. 15, 1829, testate, time for final settlement extended, page 313.

Robbins, John, late of Greenwich, Feb. 26, 1828, letters of administration on his estate granted to Platt Mead of Greenwich, who was ordered to advertise for claims, page 283.
Inventory taken Feb. 28, 1828, by Daniel Peck and Joseph Green, and filed Mch. 1, 1829, page 283.
Feb. 2, 1829, Hannah Maria Robbins, a daughter of decedent, about 12 years of age, made choice of Platt Mead to be her guardian, who was also appointed guardian of Sackett, Julia Ann, William, and Cornelius, other children of decedent, page 284.
Apl. 20, 1829, real estate of said minors ordered sold, page 285.
Apl. 24, 1829, real estate sold to John Smith Husted of Greenwich, and report of sale filed, page 285.

Rundle, Charles, late of Greenwich, will dated Sept. 26, 1825, probated Nov. 21, 1825, mentions his wife Cynthia, and children Charles, William, James, Deborah, Hannah, Benoni, and Alfred. Executors his sons Benoni and Alfred. Witnesses Benjamin I. Knapp, Adaline Hitchcock, and Julia A. Knapp, page 169.
Nov. 21, 1825, order to advertise for claims, page 170.
Inventory taken by Reuben Finch and Charles Smith, and filed Dec. 13, 1825, page 170.

Rundle, Reuben, late of Greenwich, inventory taken Jan. 6, 1824, by Abraham Close and Gilbert Close, and filed Jan. 9, 1824, pages 5 and 47.
Dec. 1824, account filed, and real estate ordered sold to pay debts, pages 47 and 56.
Jan. 13, 1825, real estate sold to Abraham Close, and report of sale filed, page 48.

St. John, Ezra, late of Stamford, Sept. 26, 1825, letters of administration on his estate granted to his widow, Ruamah St. John, and Abel Reynolds, both of Stamford, who were ordered to advertise for claims, page 122.
Inventory taken Nov. 1, 1825, by Theodore Davenport and Samuel Smith, and filed Nov. 1, 1825, page 122.

STAMFORD PROBATE RECORDS.
Volume 13, 1824.

St. John, Ezra, continued :
    Additional inventory filed Apl. 5, 1826, page 124.
    Mch. 27, 1826, necessaries allowed his widow, page 124.
    Apl. 5, 1826, account filed, and real estate ordered sold to pay debts, page 125.
    Jan. 30, 1828, William B. St. John, a son of decedent, about 14 years of age, made choice of Richard Fox of Stamford to be his guardian, page 238.
    Apl. 21, 1828, guardian authorized to sell the real estate of said minor, page 238.
    Apl. 28, 1828, real estate in Stamford sold to Simeon H. Minor and Daniel Barnum, and report of sale filed, page 238.

Scofield, Gershom, late of Darien, will dated Mch. 8, 1825, probated Apl. 15, 1825, mentions his wife Lydia, and children Darius H., Ezra, Ira, Lydia Waring, Sally B. Palmer, granddaughter Mary Elizabeth Richards a daughter of Phebe, a deceased daughter, grandson Alvah Scofield, and the children of his deceased son Rufus. Executors sons Ezra and Darius. Witnesses David Richmond, Polly Waring and Charles Hawley, page 99.
    Apl. 15, 1825, order to advertise for claims, page 101.
    Inventory taken May 27, 1825, by Henry Bates and Samuel B. Warren, and filed June 14, 1825, page 101.
    Additional inventory filed June 19, 1825, page 103.
    Aug. 16, 1826, that part of his estate not specifically devised ordered distributed to his widow, Lydia Scofield, and sons Ezra, Darius H., and Ira, grandson Alvah, and the children of Rufus, according to his will, page 138.
    Dec. 15, 1826, estate distributed to his widow, Lydia Scofield, and sons Ezra and Darius H., grandson Alvah, and the children of Rufus, page 140.

Scofield, Isaac, Jr., late of Stamford, Dec. 3, 1827, letters of administration on his estate granted to William White, Jr., of Stamford, who was ordered to advertise for claims, page 263.
    Inventory taken Dec. 21, 1827, by Selleck Scofield and John Husted, and filed Dec. 22, 1827, page 263.

Scofield, Israel, late of ----, Dec. 16, 1825, account filed by the administrator, and estate ordered distributed to Ezra Scofield, Amos Scofield, Gideon Scofield, Hannah Weed, Mercy Scofield, and the heirs of Jacob Scofield, the heirs at law of deceased, page 84.

STAMFORD PROBATE RECORDS.
Volume 13, 1824.

Scofield, Obadiah, late of Stamford, Jan. 5, 1824, report of commissioners to adjust claims filed, page 28.
Jan. 31, 1824, necessaries allowed his widow, Polly, Scofield, page 29.
Feb. 4, 1824, account filed, and real estate ordered sold to pay debts, page 29.
Mch. 6, 1824, real estate sold to David Hoyt, Oliver Lockwood, and Stephen Lockwood, and report of sale filed, page 29.
June 14, account filed by E. H. Weed, administrator, a and creditors ordered paid forty two and 1/2 cents on the dollar, page 29.
Jan. 26, 1825, additional inventory filed, page 27.
Mch. 23, 1825, real estate sold to Oliver Sherwood, and report of sale filed, page 44.
Dec. 16, 1825, account filed, and creditors ordered paid seven cents on the dollar, page 84.
Aug. 24, 1826, Seth W. Scofield, a son of decedent, about 16 years of age, made choice of Samuel Webb to be his guardian, page 198.

Scofield, Samuel C., late of Stamford, Sept. 5, 1825, letters of administration on his estate granted to his widow, Polly Scofield, who was ordered to advertise for claims page 130.
Inventory taken by John Weed, 2nd, and Jotham Hoyt, and filed Jan. 26, 1826, page 130.

Seely, Selleck, late of Darien, will dated June 23, 1826, probated July 3, 1826, all to his wife Mary for life, and remainder to his heirs at law. Executors Abram Clock and Joseph Weed. Witnesses Abram Clock, Samuel Benedict, and Stephen Fowler, page 229.
July 3, 1826, Abram Clock declined to qualify, and letters were granted to Joseph Weed, who was ordered to advertise for claims, page 229.
Inventory taken by Richard Bell and Holly Bell, and filed Sept. 2, 1826, page 230.

Selleck, Benjamin, late of Greenwich, June 9, 1826, Sands Edwin Selleck, about 14 years of age, a son of decedent, made choice of his mother, Deborah Selleck, of Greenwich to be his guardian, who was also appointed guardian of Stephen Peck Selleck, another son of decedent, about 12 years of age, page 129.

Selleck, Darling, late of Stamford, will dated July 10, 1821, probated June 2, 1824, mentions his children Harvey,

STAMFORD PROBATE RECORDS.
Volume 13, 1824.

Selleck, Darling, continued :
Anson, Milden, Sally, Sabra, and her daughter Jane, his housekeeper, Olive a daughter of John Waters, deceased, formerly the wife of George Deal. Executors Isaac Ayres and Selleck Scofield. Witnesses Seymour Jarvis, Maria E. Leeds, and S. H. Minor, page 19.
June 2, 1824, order to advertise for claims, page 20.
Inventory taken June 3, 1824, by James Lockwood and Jeremiah Curtis, and filed June 16, 1824, page 27.
Mch. 7, 1825, account filed, and estate ordered distributed according to his will, and estate distributed accordingly, page 66.

Selleck, Wray, late of Stamford, Oct. 9, 1823, estate ordered distributed to the legal representatives of Henry Selleck, late of Darien, Wray Selleck of Norwalk, Hinman Selleck, the legal representatives of Uriah Selleck, Gould Selleck, Sarah wife of Smith Place, Lydia Bell, and Jane wife of Jedediah Fareweather, according to deceased's will, page 6.
Aug. 31, 1823, estate distributed accordingly, page 6.

Sherwood, Jabez, late of Greenwich, Mch. 31, 1827, William B. Sherwood, a son of decedent, about 16 years of age, made choice of James Green, Jr., of Greenwich to be his guardian, page 199.
Aug. 23, 1827, David Brown of Greenwich appointed guardian of Hannah Sherwood, a daughter of decedent, about seven years of age, page 197.

Sherwood, Nathan, late of Stamford, June 16, 1824, necessaries allowed his widow, Abigail Sherwood, page 30.
June 16, 1824, estate ordered distributed to his widow Abigail, and children Samuel, Levi, and Emeline Sherwood, page 30.
June 19, 1824, estate distributed accordingly, page 30.

Slason, Daniel, late of Darien, will dated May 3, 1825, probated Aug. 1, 1825, mentions his wife Betsy, and children John, Rebecka, Elizabeth, Mary, Jacob, and provided for an unborn child. Executor John Waterbury. Witnesses Thaddeus Bell, Azariah Waterbury and Nancy Little, page 125.
Aug. 1, 1825, order to advertise for claims, page 125.
Inventory taken Aug. 9, 1825 by Isaac Bishop and Holly Bell, and filed Aug. 11, 1825, page 126.
June 15, 1826, account filed, and real estate ordered sold to pay debts, page 128.

STAMFORD PROBATE RECORDS.
Volume 13, 1824.

Slason, Daniel, continued :
Mch. 12, 1827, John, Rebecca, and Elizabeth, children of decedent, made choice of their mother Betsy Slason of Darien, to be their guardian, page 197.
Sept. 16, 1828, real estate sold in three parcels to Betsy Slason, Charles I. Leeds, and Isaac Bishop, and report of sale filed, page 295.

Slauson, Hannah, late of Stamford, will dated Sept. 15, 1823, probated Mch. 5, 1827, estate to her husband Thomas Slauson, for life, and remainder to her late brothers and sisters children, all her brothers and sisters now deceased, except Ann wife of Jacob Hoyt and Abigail wife of Gideon Lounsbury, who may share. Executor John Hoyt. Witnesses Reuben Hoyt, Jonathan N. Husted, and Stephen Bishop, page 210.
Mch. 5, 1827, order to advertise for claims, page 211.
Inventory taken by Peter Husted and Gilbert Scofield, and filed Apl. 2, 1827, page 211.
Sept. 17, 1827, account filed, and real estate ordered sold to pay debts, page 211.
Oct. 18, 1827, real estate sold to Jacob Bishop of Stamford, and report of sale filed, page 212.

Smith, Amos, late of Stamford, Jan. 16, 1827, that part of his estate set off to his widow as her dower, she being now deceased, ordered distributed to Hannah wife of Nathaniel Mills, Sarah wife of Joseph Smith, Polly wife of Epenetus Marvin, and Abigail wife of Messenger Palmer, daughters and devisees of deceased, page 158.
Jan. 27, 1827, estate distributed accordingly, page 158

Smith, Ephraim, of Stamford, about 14 years of age, Mch. 6, 1825, made choice of Alva June of Stamford to be his guardian, page 198.

Smith, George A., of New York City, Sept. 24, 1827, appointed guardian of his daughter Mary R. Smith of the age of eight years, page 199.

Smith, Isaiah, late of Stamford, Dec. 31, 1812, account filed by Bethiah Smith, administratrix, and real estate ordered sold to pay debts, page 275.
Jan. 21, 1829, real estate not sold, and a new order of sale granted, and real estate sold to Benjamin Matthews, and report of sale filed, pages 275 and 276.

STAMFORD PROBATE RECORDS.
Volume 13, 1824.

Smith, Israel, late of Stamford, Apl. 25, 1825, letters of administration on his estate granted to Anna Smith, his widow, and Jonathan Husted of Stamford, who were ordered to advertise for claims, page 85.
Inventory taken July 23, 1825, by Ralph Hoyt and Sands Adams, and filed July 23, 1825, page 85.
Apl. 25, 1825, Anna Smith appointed guardian of Emeline Smith, about three years of age, a daughter of decedent, page 73.

Smith, John, late of Stamford, Apl. 15, 1826, William Smith, a son of decedent, about 16 years of age, made choice of Calvin Hoyt of Stamford to be his guardian, page 198.

Smith, Samuel, late of Stamford, Apl. 5, 1827, on the application of the wife of Elijah Scofield, who claims to be the owner of all the right of Simeon Smith, deceased in that part of the estate of said Samuel Smith, deceased, which was set off to his widow as her dower, she being now deceased, said dower interest was ordered distributed to Simeon Smith, heirs of Isaiah Smith, deceased, heirs of Azetta Smith, deceased, heirs of Azuba Smith, deceased, heirs of Elijah Smith, deceased, children of said Samuel Smith, deceased, page 264.
Estate distributed accordingly, page 264.
Apl. 14, 1827, on the application of the wife of Elijah Scofield, who claims to be the owner of all the right of Simeon Smith, deceased, in that part of the estate of said Samuel Smith, deceased, which belonged to Elijah Smith, deceased, son of said Samuel Smith, deceased, in that part of the estate of said Samuel Smith, deceased, set off to his widow as her dower, she being now deceased, said estate ordered distributed to the heirs of Simeon Smith, heirs of Isaiah Smith, heirs of Azetta Smith, and heirs of Azuba Smith, the brothers and sisters of said Elijah Smith, deceased, page 309.
Apl. 23, 1827, estate distributed accordingly, page 309.

Smith, Solomon, late of Stamford, May 5, 1828, his widow refused to qualify, and letters of administration on his estate granted to Solomon Smith, Jr., who was ordered to advertise for claims, page 318.
Inventory taken June 30, 1828, by Solomon Clason and Benjamin Smith, and filed June 30, 1828, page 318.

Stevens, Abigail, late of Darien, will dated Apl. 9, 1823, probated July 3, 1824, mentions her children Darius Stevens, Sophia Stevens, Harriet Stevens, Charles G.

STAMFORD PROBATE RECORDS.
Volume 13, 1824.

Stevens, Abigail, continued :
    Smith, and Leonidas Stevens. Executor Ashbel Scofield
    Witnesses Martha Holly, Seth Scofield, and Lewis Richards, page 35.
    July 3, 1824, order to advertise for claims, page 36.
    Inventory taken July 3, 1824, by Nathaniel Waterbury
    and John Hoyt, Jr., and filed Aug. 25, 1824, page 36.
    Dec. 4, 1824, additional inventory filed, page 60.
    Mch. 21, 1825, real estate sold to Joseph Smith of New
    Canaan, and report of sale filed, page 115. -

Stevens, Lavinia, late of Darien, Aug. 1824, Abigail Stevens,
    administratrix, now deceased, and Ashbel Scofield, appointed administrator de bonus non, page 35.

Stevens, Obadiah, late of Darien, July 3, 1824, Ashbel Scofield
    appointed guardian of Leonidas Stevens, a son of decedent, about five years of age, page 35.
    Apl. 29, 1824, petition of said guardian for leave to
    sell the interest of said minor in the real estate of
    the decedent, page 6.
    July 8, 1824, account filed, page 41.
    Jan. 21, 1825, Harriet and Sophia, daughters of
    decedent, made choice of Ashbel Scofield to be their
    guardian, page 41.
    Apl. 27, 1829, Ashbel Scofield, as guardian of Sophia
    Stevens, discharged, and Darius Stevens of Darien appointed in his place, page 283.

Studwell, Anthony, late of Greenwich, will dated July 25,
    1823, probated Dec. 8, 1824, mentions his wife ----,
    and children Enoch, Anthony, James, Drake, Hannah wife
    of Elijah Scofield, and Betsy wife of David Tucker.
    Executor Elijah Scofield of Stamford. Witnesses Lockwood Reynolds, Catherine Reynolds, and Daniel Nichols,
    pages 148 and 222.
    Dec. 8, 1824, order to advertise for claims, page 148.
    Jan. 8, 1825, appeal taken from probate, page 222.
    Inventory taken Dec. 10, 1824, by Abel Reynolds and
    Henry Hait, and filed Feb. 7, 1825, page 148.
    Nov. 23, 1825, time for final settlement extended,
    page 149.

Swan, Walter, late of Greenwich, June 26, 1826, his widow refused to qualify, and letters of administration on his
    estate granted to Jabez Mead and Benjamin Page, who
    were ordered to advertise for claims, page 290.
    Inventory taken Aug. 18, 1826, by Isaac Holly and Henry
    Ritah, and filed Aug. 18, 1826, page 291.

STAMFORD PROBATE RECORDS.
Volume 13, 1824.

171.

Swan, Walter, continued :
Aug. 1, 1828, time for final settlement extended, page 293.
Dec. 10, 1828, petition of Margaret Swan, widow of deceased, for the removal of Jabez Mead on account of infirmities, page 294.
Dec. 22, 1828, Jabez Mead removed as administrator, and Asahel Palmer appointed in his place, page 295.
Mch. 29, 1829, account filed, and necessaries allowed his widow, page 294.

Taylor, Joseph, Jr., late of Greenwich, June 5, 1826, letters of administration on his estate granted to his widow, Polly Taylor and Thomas Green, who were ordered to advertise for claims, page 261.
Inventory taken June 6, 1826, by Jared Strang and David Brown, and filed July 7, 1826, page 261.
Apl. 5, 1827, time for final settlement extended, page 262.
Mch. 2, 1827, necessaries allowed his widow, page 262.

Taylor, Nathaniel, late of Greenwich, Mch. 21, 1825, estate ordered distributed to his widow, Mary Taylor, and children Joseph, Daniel, and Jotham, page 105.
June 28, 1825, estate distributed accordingly, page 105

Titus, John H., late of Greenwich, Oct. 19, 1827, Mary U. Titus and Susan K. Titus, children of decedent, made choice of Jabez Mead of Greenwich, to be their guardian, page 197.

Todd, Hannah, late of Stamford, will dated Sept. 11, 1827, probated Oct. 4, 1827, mentions her children Harvey Todd, Gabriel H. Todd, Henry Todd, and grandson John Todd Mills. Executor son Harvey. Witnesses Smith R. Libby, William Todd and William Crabb, page 299.
Oct. 10, 1827, order to advertise for claims, page 300.
Inventory taken Dec. 6, 1827, by John Husted and Isaac Ayres, and filed Dec. 10, 1827, page 300.

Todd, John, Jr., late of Stamford, Feb. 1, 1828, that part of his estate set off to his widow as her dower, she being now deceased, ordered distributed to his children, viz: Henry, heirs of Lydia Mills, Harvey, and Gabriel, page 301.
Feb. 6, 1828, estate distributed accordingly, pages 301 and 302.

STAMFORD PROBATE RECORDS.
Volume 13, 1824.

Todd, Washington, late of Stamford, July 31, 1827, George W. Todd, a son of decedent, about 15 years of age, made choice of his brother William Todd to be his guardian, page 196.

Walmsley, William, late of Stamford, (Darien), will dated Mch. 6, 1808, probated Aug. 15, 1827, mentions his wife Prudence, and children Sarah Walmsley, Elizabeth E., wife of William Young, Epenetus V., Mary, George, Abigail, Nancy, and William. Executor Charles Knapp. Witnesses Warren Percival, John Weed, and Samuel Webb, page 241.
Aug. 24, 1827, Charles Knapp refused to qualify, and letters of administration with the will annexed granted to William Walmsley, who was ordered to advertise for claims, page 241.
Inventory taken by John Bell and Joseph Hoyt, and filed Oct. 31, 1827, page 242.

Wardwell, Jacob, late of Darien, Mch. 9, 1826, his widow, Esther S. Wardwell, refused to qualify, and letters of administration on his estate granted to Ashbel Scofield, who was ordered to advertise for claims, page 165.
Inventory taken Mch. 15, 1826, by Thaddeus Bell and Josiah Lockwood, and filed Apl. 3, 1826, page 165.
Dec. 1, 1826, necessaries allowed his widow, page 167.
Dec. 1, 1826, account filed, and real estate ordered sold to pay debts, page 166.
Dec. 25, 1826, real estate sold to James Wardwell and Esther S. Wardwell, and report of sale filed, page 167.

Waring, Noah, late of Stamford, Nov. 29, 1824, letters of administration on his estate granted to Stephen Bishop, and commissioners appointed to adjust claims of creditors, page 103.
Inventory taken Dec. 25, 1824, by Solomon Clason and Abel Reynolds, and filed Jan. 19, 1825, page 103.
Dec. 18, 1824, personal property ordered sold, and report of sale filed, page 104.
Jan. 18, 1826, report of commissioners to adjust claims filed, page 104.

Waring, Samuel, late of Stamford, Oct. 3, 1825, his widow, Sarah Waring, refused to qualify, and letters of administration on his estate granted to Jeremiah Andreas, who was ordered to advertise for claims, page 94.
Inventory taken Oct. 1, 1825, by Joshua Scofield and Samuel Whiting, and filed Oct. 11, 1825, page 94.

STAMFORD PROBATE RECORDS.
Volume 13, 1824.

Waring, Samuel, continued :
    June 23, 1826, account filed, and necessaries allowed his widow, page 133.
    Mch. 5, 1827, his widow, Sarah Waring, appointed guardian of Mary, Elizabeth, and James, children of decedent, page 199.
    Mch. 5, 1827, estate ordered distributed to his children Sands, Henry, Phebe Sherwood, Hannah Ellison, Catherine, Deborah, Martha, Mary, Elizabeth, and James, page 131.
    Mch. 15, 1827, estate distributed accordingly, page 131.

Waring, Samuel, formerly of Stamford, Mch. 5, 1827, on the application of John Waring, son of Samuel Waring, formerly of Stamford, deceased, distribution ordered of that part of his realestate set off to his widow, Mary Waring, as her dower, she being now deceased, to John Waring, Betsy Clock, Hannah Lyon, Mary Washburn, Nancy Washburn, James Waring, the legal representatives of Samuel Waring, a deceased son of said Samuel first mentioned, the legal representatives of Sarah, a deceased daughter of said Samuel first mentioned, and the legal representatives of Sylvanus Waring, deceased, page 133.
    Mch. 14, 1827, estate distributed accordingly, page 134.

Waring, Thaddeus, late of Darien, Jan. 13, 1826, letters of administration on his estate granted to his widow, Deborah Waring, who was ordered to advertise for claims page 209.
    Inventory taken Aug. 19, 1826, by Joseph Hoyt and John Weed, Jr., and filed Oct. 13, 1826, page 209.
    Mch. 26, 1827, necessaries allowed his widow, page 210.
    Mch. 26, 1827, account filed, and estate ordered distributed to his widow, and children William, Jacob, Jesse, Henry F., Elizabeth Sybell, Mary Chadayne, and Hannah Clock, page 219.
    June 4, 1827, estate distributed accordingly, page 220.

Waring, Thankful, late of Stamford, Nov. 5, 1827, letters of administration on her estate granted to William White, Jr., of Stamford, who was ordered to advertise for claims, page 265.
    Inventory taken Nov. 9, 1827, by Selleck Scofield and Joel Waring, and filed Dec. 22, 1827, page 265.

Waterbury, Benjamin, late of Stamford, June 2, 1823, estate ordered distributed to Epenetus Waterbury, Sarah wife of

STAMFORD PROBATE RECORDS.
Volume 13, 1824.

Waterbury, Benjamin, continued :
of John Little, Deodate Waterbury, Polly Waterbury, Bethiah Waterbury, Samuel Waterbury, and to the legal representatives of Nathaniel Waterbury, his only heirs at law, page 48.
June 3, 1823, estate distributed accordingly, page 48.

Waterbury, James, late of Darien, will dated Jan. 26, 1827, probated Nov. 5, 1827, all to his wife Sally conditionally, and appointed her executrix. Witnesses Sally Weed, Mary E. Weed, and John Weed, Jr., page 246.
Nov. 5, 1827, order to advertise for claims, page 246.
Inventory taken Jan. 11, 1828, by John Bell and Cary Bell, and filed Feb. 4, 1828, page 246.

Waterbury, Jonathan, late of Stamford, June 6, 1825, Sylvester E., and Chs. E., both over 14 years of age, children of decedent, made choice of their mother, Sally Waterbury, to be their guardian, page 79.
Mch. 13, 1826, petition of Sally Waterbury, guardian of Appollus W. and Sylvester E., sons of decedent, for leave to sell the real estate in Stamford of said minors, and sale ordered, page 202.
Mch. 22, 1826, real estate sold to Smith Weed of Stamford, and report of sale filed, page 202.

Webb, Nathaniel, late of Stamford, will dated Feb. 24, 1826, probated Jan. 4, 1828, mentions his wife Esther, and children Henry W., Lawson or Lanson, and Polly wife of Bethel Palmer. Executrix his wife. Witnesses Caty Lounsbury, Robert R. Barlow, and Samuel Webb, page 253.
Jan. 14, 1828, order to advertise for claims, page 253.
Inventory taken Jan. 22, 1828, by Selleck Scofield and Isaac Ayres, and filed Mch. 10, 1828, page 254.

Webb, Samuel, late of ----, May 1, 1828, account filed by his administrators, and estate ordered distributed to his widow, and children, viz: heirs at law of Henry, Mary, Cornelia, William S., Caroline wife of William H. Holly, Catharine, Angeline, James A., Lucy P., Frances, and Elizabeth, page 311.
Oct. 15, 1828, estate distributed accordingly, page 312.

Webb, William A., late of Stamford, will dated June 10, 1827, probated Aug. 3, 1827, mentions his sister Mary Webb, and brother David Webb. Executors sister Mary and Epenetus W. Nichols. Witnesses Thankful Webb, Hephsibah Scofield, and Elizabeth Lockwood, page 239.
Aug. 3, 1827, order to advertise for claims, page 239.

STAMFORD PROBATE RECORDS.
Volume 13, 1824.

175.

Webb, William A., continued:
Inventory taken by Isaac Lockwood and Solomon Guernsey, and filed Aug. 30, 1827, page 240.

Weed, Aaron, late of Stamford, will dated Mch. 5, 1824, probated Sept. 10, 1825, mentions his wife Hannah. Executor William Webb. Witnesses Mary Webb, Caroline Webb, and Samuel Webb, page 118.
The executor named in the will refused to qualify, and the widow being incapacitated, letters of administration with the will annexed granted to Cary Leeds, page 118.
Sept. 10, 1825, order to advertise for claims, page 118.
Inventory taken Sept. 12, 1825, by Joseph Gray and John Thompson, and filed Sept. 12, 1825, page 119.
Sept. 12, 1825, commissioners appointed to adjust claims of creditors, and personal property ordered sold, page 120.
Mch. 27, 1826, report of commissioners to adjust claims filed, page 120.
Apl. 5, 1826, necessaries allowed his widow, page 121.
Apl. 5, 1826, account filed, and real estate ordered sold to pay debts, page 121.
Apl. 17, 1826, real estate sold to Henry Webb, and report of sale filed, page 122.

Weed, Asahel, late of Stamford, will dated Nov. 14, 1825, probated Dec. 16, 1825, mentions his children John, Asahel, Polly Weed, Betsy wife of Elijah Scofield, and Anna wife of Walsey Burtis. Executors his sons John and Asahel. Witnesses Josiah W. Scofield, Ezra Scofield, Jr., and John L. Scofield, page 113.
Dec. 16, 1825, order to advertise for claims, page 114.
Inventory taken Dec. 21, 1825, by Peter Scofield, Jr., and Isaac Scofield, and filed Mch. 1, 1826, page 114.
Mch. 30, 1827, estate ordered distributed according to his will, page 227.
Apl. 6, 1827, estate distributed to John Weed, Jr., Asahel Weed, Polly Weed, Anna Burtis, and Betsy Scofield, page 227.

Weed, Henry, Jr., late of Darien, Aug. 29, 1825, his widow, refused to qualify, and letters of administration on his estate granted to William H. Weed, who was ordered to advertise for claims, page 112.
Inventory taken Oct. 22, 1825, by Peter Husted and Lewis Clauson, and filed Oct. 24, 1825, page 112.

STAMFORD PROBATE RECORDS.
Volume 13, 1824.

Weed, James H., late of Darien, Mch. 1, 1824, necessaries allowed his widow, Nancy Weed, page 5.
Mch. 4, 1825, Isaac Weed, Jr., of Darien, appointed guardian of James Jarvis Weed and William Hervey Weed, sons of decedent, page 58.
Mch. 18, 1825, estate ordered distributed to his widow, Nancy Weed, and children James Jarvis Weed and William Hervey Weed, page 69.
Estate distributed accordingly, page 69.

Weed, John, 3rd, late of Stamford, Mch. 1, 1808, account filed by Samuel Webb, administrator, and real estate ordered sold to pay debts, page 5.
Mch. 17, 1808, real estate sold to William Webb, and report of sale filed, page 5.

Weed, Jonas, late of Darien, Dec. 1, 1823, dower of his widow, Rebekah Weed, ordered set out, page 7.
Jan. 5, 1824, dower set out, page 7.
Dec. 1, 1823, account filed, and real estate ordered sold to pay debts, page 8.
Feb. 26, 1824, part of his real estate sold to John Waterbury, and Anna Weed, and report of sale filed, page 9.
Mch. 27, 1824, estate ordered distributed to Jonas Weed, Jr., Paul Weed, Mary Weed, Anna Weed, and Sarah wife of Alfred Webb, page 9.
Apl. 6, 1824, estate distributed accordingly, page 9.

Weed, Martha, late of Stamford, will dated Mch. 28, 1817, probated Mch. 21, 1825, mentions her children Maria Hoyt, and granddaughter Abigail Weed Williams of New York City. Executor Joseph B. Hoyt. Witnesses Elizabeth Wooster, Sarah H. Waterbury, and Samuel Webb, page 91.
Mch. 21, 1825, order to advertise for claims, page 91.
Inventory taken Mch. 28, 1825, by Cary Leeds and Erastus H. Weed, and filed Mch. 16, 1824, page 92.

Weed, William F., of Darien, about 14 years of age, Aug. 30, 1825, made choice of his mother, Mary Weed, to be his guardian, page 129.

Wheaton, Samuel, late of Stamford, will dated Apl. 2, 1827, probated July 26, 1828, all to his wife Mary, and appointed her executrix. Witnesses Davis Lockwood, Abel Reynolds, and Charles Hawley, page 305.
July 26, 1828, Mary Wheaton refused to qualify; also refusal of administration by Calvin Clason and Eliza

STAMFORD PROBATE RECORDS.
Volume 13, 1824.

Wheaton, Samuel, continued:
    Ann Clason "on the estate of our deceased father Samuel Wheaton", and letters of administration with the will annexed granted to Solomon Clason of Stamford, who was ordered to advertise for claims, page 305.
    Inventory taken by Seth Smith and Isaac Lockwood, 3rd, and filed Oct. 11, 1828, page 306.

Whiting, Charles, late of Darien, will dated May 10, 1823, probated Mch. 27, 1829, mentions his wife Hannah, and children Deborah Raymond, Mary Raymond, Samuel and grandchild William Burr Whiting. Executors his wife and son Samuel. Witnesses Thaddeus Bell, Holly Bell, and Betsy Bell, page 332.
    Mch. 27, 1829, order to advertise for claims, page 332.
    Inventory taken by Holly Bell and Joel Hurlbutt, and filed Apl. 6, 1829, page 333.

Whitney, Isaac, late of Stamford, Feb. 13, 1826, letters of administration on his estate granted to James Waring of Greenwich, who was ordered to advertise for claims, page 128.
    Inventory taken by Royal L. Gay and Frederic Lockwood, and filed Apl. 11, 1826, page 128.

Wilmot, Joseph, late of Stamford, will dated June 15, 1826, probated Dec. 17, 1827, mentions his children John, William, Eben, Joseph, Hannah wife of Abijah Scofield, and Sarah wife of Elihu Scofield. Executor his son William. Witnesses Henry B. Seely, Joseph A. Gray, and Samuel Webb, page 235.
    Dec. 17, 1827, order to advertise for claims, page 236.
    Inventory taken Feb. 4, 1828, by John R. Leeds of New Canaan and Charles L. Leeds of Stamford, and filed Mch. 20, 1828, page 236.I.

Wilson, Sarah, late of Greenwich, widow of Nehemiah Wilson, will dated Apl. 4, 1825, probated Apl. 15, 1825, mentions the children of her deceased daughter Eunice Peck, viz: Wilson Peck, Elias Reed Peck, and Jonathan Peck, who are to receive 1/2, and the other 1/2 to the children of her daughter Desire Haight, viz: Eunice Haight, Sally Haight, Nehemiah Wilson Haight, Phebe Haight, and Epenetus Haight. Executor Jared Strang. Witnesses John Brown, Jesse Slawson, and Susannah W. Slawson, page 135.
    Apl. 15, 1825, order to advertise for claims, page 136.

STAMFORD PROBATE RECORDS.
Volume 13, 1824.

Wilson, Sarah, continued :
    Inventory taken Apl. 21, 1825, by James Green, Jr., and Platt Mead, and filed Apl. 25, 1825, page 136.

Wilson, Thomas M., late of Rye, Feb. 1825, letters of administration on his estate granted to his widow Betsy Wilson and Richard Mead, who were ordered to advertise for claims, page 112.
    Inventory taken May 24, 1825, by Alvan Mead and Platt Mead, and filed May 24, 1825.

STAMFORD PROBATE RECORDS.
Volume 14, 1828.

Adams, Abraham, late of Stamford, Nov. 22, 1830, his widow refused to qualify, and letters of administration on his estate granted to William H. Holly of Stamford, who was ordered to advertise for claims, page 288.
Nov. 1830, inventory taken by George Brown and Davis Lockwood, and filed Mch. 1, 1832, page 396.
Mch. 26, 1833, Sarah E., Frances, and Jno. W., over 14 years of age, children of decedent, made choice of their mother Sarah Adams of Stamford to be their guardian, who was also appointed guardian of George W., Mary E., Emily A., and Charles E., other children of decedent, page 453.

Adams, John, late of Greenwich, Mch. 13, 1830, account filed, and estate ordered distributed to his children, viz: Mary E. Adams, Nathaniel E. Adams, Marilda H. Adams, Susan C. Adams, Sarah K. Adams, John Augustus Adams, and Joseph H. Adams, page 210.
Mch. 1830, estate distributed accordingly, page 211.
Mch. 3, 1830, John Augustus, about 15 years of age, a son of decedent, made choice of Nathaniel Adams of Greenwich to be his guardian, page 174.

Adams, John, a minor of Stamford, owner of 1/4 interest of land in Stamford, Aug. 20, 1828, on the application of Samuel Lockwood of Greenwich, his guardian, real estate of said minor ordered sold, page 10.
Dec. 19, 1829, real estate sold to Charles Knapp, and report of sale filed, page 164.

Adams, Morehouse, of Stamford, May 15, 1830, assignment for the benefit of creditors to William H. Holly of Stamford, page 212.
June 14, 1830, commissioners appointed to adjust claims of creditors, page 214.
May 1830, inventory taken by Davis Lockwood and Samuel

STAMFORD PROBATE RECORDS.
Volume 14, 1828.

Adams, Morehouse, continued:
Lockwood, and filed Mch. 16, 1831, page 244.
Dec. 15, 1830, report of commissioners to adjust claims filed, page 244.
June 10, 1830, personal property ordered sold, page 245.
Mch. 16, 1831, personal property sold, and report of sale filed, page 245.
Mch. 16, 1831, account filed, and real estate ordered sold to pay debts, page 363.
Real estate sold, and report of sale filed, Mch. 16, 1831, page 364.

Adams, Reuben, late of Stamford, Apl. 5, 1828, his son John Adams of Stamford, about 18 years of age, made choice of Samuel Lockwood of Stamford to be his guardian, page 84.

Addington, John, late of Greenwich, will dated Nov. 5, 1829, probated Jan. 22, 1831, mentions his wife Elizabeth and son John. Executor Silas Davis of Greenwich. Witnesses Huldah Tracy, Elizabeth Grigg, and Darius Mead, Jr., page 252.
Jan. 22, 1831, order to advertise for claims, page 253.
Inventory taken by Thomas A. Mead and Nelson Bush, and filed Feb. 7, 1831, page 253.

Anderson, William, late of Greenwich, will dated Mch. 26, 1821 probated Dec. 18, 1829, mentions his children Jeremiah, Mary, Hannah, Eliph, Stephen, Dorothy Merritt, Anna Brown, granddaughters Sarah Matthews, Susannah Anderson, the five lawful children of his son Mather Anderson. Executors son Jeremiah, and Aaron Field. Witnesses Hachaliah Carhart, Nehemiah Sherwood, and Nehemiah Purdy, page 158.
Dec. 18, 1829, order to advertise for claims, page 159.
Inventory taken Dec. 31, 1829, by Jared Strang and Nehemiah Sherwood, and filed Jan. 23, 1830, page 160.
Dec. 19, 1829, realestate ordered sold as authorized in his will, page 292.
Real estate sold to Mary Anderson and Hannah Anderson, and report of sale filed Oct. 25, 1830, page 293.

Avery, Peter, late of Greenwich, Nov. 6, 1827, letters of administration on his estate granted to his widow, Elizabeth Avery, and commissioners appointed to adjust claims of creditors, page 41.
Inventory taken by William Husted and Thomas A. Mead, and filed July 2, 1828, page 41.

STAMFORD PROBATE RECORDS.
Volume 14, 1828.

Avery, Peter, continued:
July 2, 1828, report of commissioners to adjust claims filed, page 42.

Avery, Peter, late of Greenwich, Mch. 25, 1833, his widow being now deceased, the court on the application of Esben Husted of Greenwich, assignee as he claims of Israel K. Avery and other children and devisees of deceased, estate ordered distributed to testator's children, or their assignee, according to his will, viz: to Israel K. Avery, Ira Avery, Peter Knapp, Arna Wilson, Walter Avery, Elizabeth Denton, John Avery, Hannah Denton, Catharine Collory, Reuben Avery, and Abraham Avery, page 448.
Apl. 3, 1833, estate distributed accordingly, to Reuben Avery, Arna Willson, Walter Avery, heirs of Catharine Collory, heirs of Peter Avery, Israel K. Avery, heirs of Ira Avery, and heirs of John Avery, page 449.

Ayres, Bradley, late of Stamford, will dated Mch. 10, 1825, probated June 7, 1825, mentions his wife Sarah, and Polly wife of Samuel Scofield. Executor Abishai Scofield. Witnesses Reuben Scofield, John L. Scofield, and Betsy Lockwood, page 29.
June 7, 1825, order to advertise for claims, page 30.
Inventory taken June 10, 1825, by Isaac Scofield and Luther Weed, and filed Aug. 6, 1825, page 30.
Apl. 4, 1826, time for settlement extended, page 31.
Apl. 13, 1831, account filed, and real estate ordered sold to pay debts, page 246.
Apl. 26, 1831, real estate sold to David Waterbury of Stamford, and report of sale filed, page 247.

Ayres, Sarah, late of Stamford, will dated Sept. 2, 1830, probated Nov. 26, 1830, mentions Cornelia daughter of John Ingersoll of Stamford, niece Polly wife of Epenetus Scofield of New Jersey, nephew John Ingersoll of Stamford, and Polly wife of David Waterbury of Stamford. Executor Abishai Scofield of Stamford. Witnesses Nathaniel Scofield, John L. Scofield, and Jotham Hoyt, page 383.
Nov. 26, 1830, order to advertise for claims, page 383.

Bates, Jonathan, late of Stamford, Apl. 28, 1817, on the application of his executor, Henry Bates, estate ordered distributed to said Henry,&Hannah wife of Benjamin Brown, according to his will, page 100.
Apl. 24, 1827, estate distributed accordingly, page 100.

STAMFORD PROBATE RECORDS.
Volume 14, 1828.

Bates, Gershom, late of Stamford, Aug. 28, 1829, necessaries allowed his widow, page 405.

Bates, Seely, late of Darien, Oct. 9, 1829, letters of administration on his estate granted to Nehemiah S. Bates of Bedford and Jeremiah Andreas of Darien, who were ordered to advertise for claims, page 149.
Inventory taken by Henry Bates and John Bell, and filed Jan. 7, 1830, page 169.
Nov. 1, 1830, account filed, and real estate ordered sold to pay debts, page 338.
Real estate sold to Henry Weed, Henry Scribner, Welsey Burtit, and David Hoyt, and report of sale filed, Apl. 11, 1832, page 339.

Bell, Noah, late of Stamford, May 7, 1831, account filed by his executor, his widow now deceased, and distribution ordered to his children Ezekiel, Francis, Prudence, and Rebecca, page 347.
Sept. 13, 1831, estate distributed accordingly, page 347

Bishop, Isaac, late of Darien, will dated Oct. 1, 1828, probated Oct. 22, 1828, mentions his children Catherine wife of Darius Stevens, and Andrew. Executor Clark Bissell of Norwalk. Witnesses ——, page 66.
Oct. 22, 1828, order to advertise for claims, page 66.
Inventory taken by John Bell and Henry Bates, and filed Dec. 9, 1828, page 67.
Dec. 26, 1828, his widow, Charlotte Bishop, appealed from the probate of said will, pages 69 and 70.
Sept. 17, 1829, time for settlement extended, page 149.

Bishop, John Knowles, late of Stamford, Aug. 28, 1829, letters of administration on his estate granted to Alexander N. Holly of Stamford, who was ordered to advertise for claims, page 137.
Inventory taken Sept. 2, 1829, by Cary H. Leeds and Samuel Smith, and filed Oct. 21, 1829, page 137.
Aug. 28, 1829, Alexander N. Holly appointed guardian of John Henry Bishop and Sarah C. R. Bishop, children of decedent, page 138.
Petition of Alexander N. Holly guardian of John Henry and Sarah C. R., children of decedent, for leave to sell the real estate of said minors in Stamford, and on July 26, 1831, sale ordered, pages 276 and 277.
Aug. 11, 1831, real estate sold to Cary H. Leeds, and report of sale filed Aug. 24, 1831, page 277.

STAMFORD PROBATE RECORDS.
Volume 14, 1828.

Bishop, John Knowles, continued:
 Dec. 11, 1829, commissioners appointed to adjust claims of creditors, page 177.
 Oct. 15, 1830, report of commissioners filed, page 329.

Bishop, Rebecca, late of Stamford, late wife of John K. Bishop now deceased, Oct. 17, 1829, letters of administration on her estate granted to her sister Sally Newman, who was ordered to advertise for claims, page 149.
 Inventory taken by Jonathan Brown and Samuel Smith and filed Mch. 7, 1831, page 286.
 Mch. 16, 1831, account filed, and real estate ordered sold to pay debts, page 249.
 Real estate sold to Stephen B. Provost and Cary H. Leeds, Apl. 7, 1831, and report of sale filed, page 249.

Blackman, Elizabeth, late of Stamford, Aug. 1, 1833, letters of administration on her estate granted to Nathaniel D. Haight, who was ordered to advertise for claims, page 506.

Blanchard, Isaac, late of Stamford, will dated Sept. 21, 1831, probated Dec. 7, 1832, mentions his mother Elizabeth Blanchard, nephew and niece Ira and Sally Maria Blanchard children of Daniel Blanchard, deceased, and John Blanchard. Executor Horace Scofield. Witnesses Elijah Knapp, Augustus Scofield, and Albert Cloak, page 493.
 Dec. 7, 1832, order to advertise for claims, page 493.
 Inventory taken Dec. 10, 1832, by Henry Waring and Oliver Lockwood, and filed June 18, 1833, page 494.

Blanchard, Jacob, late of Stamford, Apl. 2, 1831, his widow refused to qualify, and letters of administration on his estate granted to Abel Reynolds of Stamford, who was ordered to advertise for claims, page 264.
 Inventory taken Apl. 14, 1831, by Joseph Smith and Silas Hoyt, and filed Apl. 14, 1831, page 264.
 Nov. 5, 1831, account filed, and necessaries allowed his widow, page 264.
 Nov. 5, 1831, account filed, and real estate ordered sold to pay debts, page 464.
 Real estate sold to Isaac Blanchard of Stamford, and report of sale filed Mch. 7, 1833, page 464.

Bouton, Mahala, late of Greenwich, will dated Apl. 24, 1829, probated June 10, 1829, all to her husband Daniel Bouton. Executors Stephen Waring and Henry Ritch, both of Greenwich. Witnesses Ephraim Lane, George H. Lane,

STAMFORD PROBATE RECORDS.
Volume 14, 1828.

Bouton, Mahala, continued :
    and William H. Mead, page 61.
    June 10, 1829, order to advertise for claims, page 62.
    Sept. 25, 1829, inventory taken by Benjamin Page and
    William H. Mead, and filed Feb. 8, 1830, page 180.

Bragg, Isaac F., of Stamford, Nov. 5, 1829, assignment for
    the benefit of creditors to Simeon H. Minor and Smith
    Scott, page 161.
    Nov. 9, 1829, commissioners appointed to adjust claims
    of creditors, page 162.
    Inventory taken by William Waterbury, Jr., and George
    Brown, and filed Nov. 14, 1829, page 163.
    July 27, 1830, report of commissioners filed, page 231.
    Aug. 7, 1830, report of assignees filed, page 233.
    Sept. 13, 1830, review of proceedings of commissioners
    to adjust claims ordered, page 233.
    Sept. 13, 1830, report of assignees approved, pages 348
    and 349.
    Feb. 1, 1831, property sold, and report of sale filed,
    page 246.
    Feb. 1, 1831, account filed, and creditors ordered
    paid 36 cents on the dollar, page 246.

Briggs, John, of Stamford, over 14 years of age, Aug. 6, 1831,
    made choice of Alva Briggs of Stamford to be his guar-
    dian, page 273.

Briggs, Nathaniel, late of Greenwich, will dated May 6, 1833,
    probated July 3, 1833, mentions his wife Mary, and
    children Isaac, Lockwood, Marvey, Nathaniel, Lydia
    Buckout, and Amy Ferris. Executor Ira Lockwood.
    Witnesses Ezekiel Reynolds, Jr., Augustus L. Reynolds,
    and Ard Reynolds, page 486.
    July 3, 1833, order to advertise for claims, page 487.
    Inventory taken July 12, 1833, by Jared Smith and
    Ephraim Marshall, and filed July 20, 1833, page 487.

Brown, George, Jr., late of Stamford, Jan. 21, 1831, his fa-
    ther, John Brown of Stamford, refused to qualify, and
    letters of administration on his estate granted to Char-
    les Brown of Stamford, who was ordered to advertise
    for claims, page 292.

Brown, Peter, late of Stamford, Apl. 27, 1827, account filed,
    by his administrator, and real estate ordered sold to
    pay debts, page 99.

STAMFORD PROBATE RECORDS.
Volume 14, 1828.

Brown, Peter, continued:
    Nov. 5, 1827, real estate sold to Polly Brown of Stamford, and report of sale filed, page 99.
    Nov. 5, 1827, his widow, Polly Brown, appointed guardian of William Peter Brown, Mary Elizabeth Brown, and Eliza Catharine Brown, children of decedent, page 83.
    Jan. 21, 1828, on the petition of said guardian, real estate of said minors at North Stamford, ordered sold, pages 83. and 84.
    Jan. 21, 1828, real estate sold to Stephen B. Provost of Stamford, and report of sale filed, page 84.

Brundage, Jonah, of Rye, June 18, 1832, Sally J. Brundage and Jonah C. Brundage, children of said Jonah Brundage, over 14 years of age, made choice of their father to be their guardian, page 344.

Brush, Benjamin, 3rd, late of Greenwich, Oct. 26, 1830, his widow refused to qualify, and letters of administration on his estate granted to Joseph Brush and Stephen Warring of Greenwich, who were ordered to advertise for claims, page 252.
    Inventory taken of store at the Lower Landing of J. and B. Brush & Co., by Benjamin I. Knapp and Amos Finch, and filed Feb. 7, 1831, page 252.

Brush, Edmund Burke, late of Greenwich, inventory taken by Amos Finch and William Smith, and filed Oct. 27, 1832, page 507.

Brush, Joseph, of Greenwich, June 11, 1832, appointed guardian of his children Amos Mead, Richard Edward, Theodore and Elizabeth Sarah, page 344.

Cargill, Betsy, late of Stamford, Oct. 30, 1829, letters of administration on her estate granted to Abel Reynolds of Stamford, who was ordered to advertise for claims, page 150.
    June 14, 1830, account filed, and real estate ordered sold to pay debts, page 215.
    Real estate sold to Alva Briggs and Samuel Provost, page 215.
    Dec. 12, 1829, inventory taken by Eben Smith and Solomon Clason, and copied on page 214.

Clapp, Thomas, late of Greenwich, Sept. 17, 1829, time for settlement exetended, page 134.
    Apl. 19, 1830, Sarah Brundage, a daughter of Dorcas Brundage, late of Westchester County, deceased, sister

STAMFORD PROBATE RECORDS.
Volume 14, 1828.

Clapp, Thomas, continued:
of said Thomas Clapp, deceased, appealed from the probate of his will, page 175.

Clason, Ard, late of Stamford, Feb. 20, 1830, letters of administration on his estate granted to Solomon Clason, who was ordered to advertise for claims, page 174.
Feb. 23, 1830, inventory taken by Drake Studwell and Isaac Lockwood, 3rd, and filed Apl. 3, 1830, page 199.
July 4, 1831, account filed, andestate ordered distributed to his heirs at law, viz: Solomon Clason, Benjamin Clason, Abigail Jessup, heirs of Isaac Clason, deceased, and the heirs of Stephen Clason, deceased, page 335.
Sept. 15, 1831, estate distributed accordingly, page 335.

Clock, Nathaniel, late of Darien, will dated July 19, 1828, probated Nov. 21, 1831, mentions his wife Sarah and children Albert, James, deceased, Henry, Catherine Richards, Elizabeth Scofield, Mary Seely, and Deborah Clock. Executor his son-in-law Lewis Richards. Witnesses Abram Clock, David Clock, and Phebe Clock, page 317.
Nov. 21, 1831, order to advertise for claims, page 317.
Inventory taken Nov. 22, 1831, by Abram Clock and John Weed, Jr., and filed Nov. 23, 1831, page 318.
Additional inventory on page 320.
Real estate sold to Henry Clock of Darien, son of decedent, Usual Weed of Darien, and Abram Clock of Darien, and report of sale filed, Nov. 15, 1832, page 509.

Close, Bethiah, widow of Gideon Close, late of Greenwich, will dated Mch. 2, 1829, probated June 8, 1829, mentions her sister Frances Hobby, sister Charlotte H. Close, late brother Abraham Hobby's children, and niece Elizabeth C. Mead. Executor Edward Close. Witnesses Darius Mead, Jr., Lucy P. Close, and Shadrach Mead, page 155.
June 8, 1829, order to advertise for claims, page 155.
Inventory taken June 9, 1829, by Samuel Peck and Elias Peck, and filed June 11, 1829, page 156.

Close, Shadrach, late of Greenwich, Feb. 4, 1829, letters of administration on his estate granted to his widow, Pininnah Close and Samuel Ferris of Greenwich, who were ordered to advertise for claims, page 4.
Inventory taken Feb. 10, 1829, by Benjamin Page and Charles Smith, and filed Mch. 4, 1829, page 4.

STAMFORD PROBATE RECORDS.
Volume 14, 1828.

Close, Shadrach, continued :
  Nov. 13, 1829, account filed, and necessaries allowed his widow, page 196.
  Dec. 22, 1829, account filed, and realestate ordered sold to pay debts, page 339.
  Real estate sold to Samuel Ferris of Greenwich, and report of sale filed June 13, 1832, page 339.

Corning, Edward, guardian of James B. Stebbins and of his children Jasper Corning and James Corning, the real estate of said minors sold to Isaac Selleck and Enos B. Lockwood, and report of sale filed May 29, 1833, page 464.

Cox, Sally, late of Stamford, Dec. 10, 1832, letters of administration on her estate granted to her husband Robert Cox of Stamford, page 445.

Dan, Sylvanus, late of Stamford, Apl. 27, 1831, his widow refused to qualify, and letters of administration on his estate granted to Jonathan Dan and Nehemiah Hait, Jr., of Stamford, who were ordered to advertise for claims, page 345.
  Inventory taken Apl. 29, 1831, by Isaac Ayres and Alfred Smith, and filed May 3, 1831, page 345.
  June 2, 1832, account filed, and real estate ordered sold to pay debts, page 346.
  Real estate sold to Allen S. Mead of Stamford and William Smith, Jr., and report of sale filed July 14, 1832, page 346.

Davenport, John, late of Stamford, will dated Oct. 19, 1830, probated Dec. 18, 1830, mentions his wife Mary Sylvester, and children John A., Theodore, Elizabeth Huntington wife of Peter W. Radcliffe, Mary Wells wife of James Boorman, and Matilda wife of Peter Lockwood, granddaughter Julia Matilda daughter of John A. Davenport, and grandson James Radcliffe Davenport. Executors sons John Alfred, Theodore, and son-in-law Peter W. Radcliffe. Witnesses George Hanford Knapp, Julia M. Davenport, and Rufus Hoyt, page 260.
  Dec. 22, 1830, order to advertise for claims, page 262.
  Inventory taken by Davis Lockwood and Ezra Knapp, and filed Nov. 25, 1831.

Dayton, Gilbert, late of Greenwich, Sept. 18, 1826, dower of his widow, Ann Dayton, ordered set out, page 39.
  Mch. 20, 1827, dower set out, page 39.

STAMFORD PROBATE RECORDS.
Volume 14, 1828.

Dayton, James, late of Greenwich, Nov. 26, 1830, letters of administration on his estate granted to Samuel Close, who was ordered to advertise for claims, page 272.
Inventory taken Dec. 24, 1830, by Aaron Field and John Carpenter, and filed Dec. 27, 1830, page 272.
Nov. 7, 1831, account filed, and real estate ordered sold to pay debts, page 360.
Real estate sold to Nathaniel Dayton of Greenwich, and report of sale filed Mch. 15, 1832, page 360.

Denton, Joseph, late of Greenwich, Nov. 3, 1829, letters of administration on his estate granted to Humphrey Denton of Greenwich, who was ordered to advertise for claims, page 139.
Nov. 24, 1829, inventory taken by Aaron Husted and Drake Husted, and filed Nov. 24, 1829, page 170.

Dibble, Emeline, late of Greenwich, will dated Dec. 11, 1832, probated Feb. 4, 1832, mentions Aunt Rebecca wife of Uncle Seymour Hobby, Laura wife of Allen Hobby, cousin Caroline Hobby daughter of Uncle Seymour Hobby of Greenwich, and brother Alexander Dibble. Executor Uncle Seymour Hobby. Witnesses Hannah Mead, Seymour Hobby, and Samuel Close, page 470.
Feb. 4, 1832, order to advertise for claims, page 471.
Inventory taken by Gideon Holmes and Isaac Peck, and filed Apl. 29, 1833, page 471.

Dixon, Philemon, late of Greenwich, Jan. 25, 1827, letters of administration on his estate granted to Asahel Palmer, who was ordered to advertise for claims, page 105.
Inventory taken by John H. Reynolds and Abel Palmer, and filed Feb. 3, 1827, page 105.

Dodgshan, Enoch, late of New York City, Dec. 10, 1830, letters of administration on his estate granted to his widow Hannah, who was ordered to advertise for claims, page 405.

Downs, Seth, of Greenwich, about 15 years of age, Nov. 10, 1832, made choice of Benjamin Brush, Jr., to be his guardian, page 456.

Dunn, Joseph, late of Greenwich, Sept. 19, 1828, his widow, Jerusha Dunn, refused to qualify, and his children being minors, letters of administration on his estate granted to Benjamin Tripp of North Castle, who was ordered to advertise for claims, page 62.

STAMFORD PROBATE RECORDS.
Volume 14, 1828.

Dunn, Joseph, continued :
    Inventory taken Sept. 20, 1828, by Lewis Mead and Obadiah Mead, and filed Dec. 11, 1828, page 62.

Escott, Rhoda, late of Darien, will dated Apl. 14, 1829, probated Oct. 13, 1829, mentions her nephew Samuel Ferris son of her sister Sary Ferris of Norwalk, brother Zeriah Whitney, nieces Sary Ferris, Lavina Ferris, Emelia A. Ferris, and Mary Ferris, daughters of her sister Sary Ferris; Sophire Hoyt, Julia Hoyt, Betsy A. Morehouse, and Cornelia Weed, daughters of her sister Hannah Slason. Executor Warren Percival of Darien. Witnesses Abram Clock, Samuel Mather, and Sally A. Holly, page 150.
    Oct. 13, 1829, order to advertise for claims, page 151.
    Oct. 27, 1829, inventory taken by Jonathan Bates and Warren Percival, and filed Jan. 4, 1830, page 182.

Felmette, Jeffery, late of Greenwich, will dated Sept. 21, 1830, probated Oct. 13, 1832, all to his wife Dinah. Executor Samuel Close. Witnesses Lydia K. Mead, Huldah Tracy, and John Jay Tracy, page 447.
    Oct. 13, 1832, order to advertise for claims, page 447.
    Inventory taken Oct. 15, 1832, by Augustus Lyon and William Husted, and filed Nov. 9, 1832, page 448.

Ferris, Ethan, late of Greenwich, Jan. 14, 1833, his widow refused to qualify, and letters of administration on his estate granted to Asahel Palmer, who was ordered to advertise for claims, page 467.
    Inventory taken Jan. 18, 1833, by Frederick Lockwood and Henry Ritch, and filed June 24, 1833, page 467.

Ferris, Jeduthan, late of Greenwich, will dated Mch. 25, 1831, probated Apl. 25, 1831, mentions his wife Mary Lockwood, and children Isaac, Joseph, and Mary. Executors his sons Isaac and Samuel Ferris, Jr. Witnesses Ethan Ferris, Peter Ferris, and Jabez Mead, page 298.
    Apl. 25, 1831, order to advertise for claims, page 299.
    Inventory taken June 13, 1831, by Asahel Palmer and Peter Ferris, and filed June 13, 1831, page 299.

Ferris, Lemuel, late of Greenwich, Apl. 2, 1831, estate ordered distributed, page 273.
    Apl. 1831, estate distributed to his widow, ----, and children Susan, Esther, Julia, Jane Ann, and Sarah, page 333.

STAMFORD PROBATE RECORDS.
Volume 14, 1828.

Ferris, Permelia, of Greenwich, guardian of Lockwood Ferris of
    Greenwich, Oct. 17, 1832, petition for leave to sell
    the real estate of said minor in Stamford, and sale
    ordered, pages 439 and 440.
    Feb. 8, 1833, real estate sold to Stephen B. Provost
    and Ebenezer Smith, both of Stamford, guardian is the
    mother of minor, and report of sale filed Apl. 11,
    1833, page 510.

Field, Mary, late of Greenwich, widow of Uriah Field, will
    dated 9th day, 12th month, 1826, probated Apl. 29,
    1831, mentions her children James Field, Abigail Mott,
    Elizabeth Carpenter, Hannah Field, Sarah Griffen,
    Mary Griffen, and Anna F. Haviland; granddaughters
    Mary Mathews a daughter of Robert Field, Maria M.
    Field a daughter of Josiah Field, Mary Haviland a
    daughter of John Haviland, Mary Field a daughter of
    James Field, Sarah Field a daughter of Aaron Field,
    Esther Quimby a daughter of Josiah Field, and Mary
    Quimby a daughter of Daniel Quimby, grandchildren the
    children of Mary widow of Daniel Griffen, viz: Hannah,
    Anna, David, and Daniel; the children of her daughter
    Anna F. wife of John Haviland, viz: Mary, Jane, James,
    Maria, and Elizabeth; and the sons of Rebecca. Ex-
    ecutors sons Robert Field and James Field. Witnesses
    Daniel Mathews, Uriah Field, and Thomas C. Field,
    page 256.
    Apl. 29, 1831, Robert Field refused to qualify, and
    letters granted to James Field, who was ordered to ad-
    vertise for claims, page 257.
    Inventory taken Apl. 4, 1831, by Thomas Carpenter and
    Daniel Mathews, and filed Apl. 29, 1831, page 258.

Finch, Nathaniel, late of Greenwich, will dated July 9, 1829,
    probated Aug. 11, 1829, all to his wife Abigail. Ex-
    ecutors his wife and James Green. Witnesses James P.
    Anderson, Elizabeth Anderson, and Ann Wilson, page 139.
    Aug. 11, 1829, order to advertise for claims, page 140.
    Inventory taken Aug. 19, 1829, by Platt Mead and Jo-
    seph Green, and filed Aug. 20, 1829, page 140.

Finney, Phebe, late of Stamford, will dated July 15, 1825,
    probated June 7, 1830, mentions her daughter Caroline
    wife of Harvey Ferris and their children, viz: Caro-
    line Elizabeth Ferris, Frances Emeline Ferris, Susan
    Ann Ferris, and William Isaac Ferris. Executor Henry
    Little. Witnesses E. W. Walmsley, Joseph Gorham, and
    Maria Seely, page 224.
    June 7, 1830, order to advertise for claims, page 225.

STAMFORD PROBATE RECORDS.
Volume 14, 1828.

Finney, Phebe, continued :
    Inventory taken Nov. 23, 1830, by Royal S. Gay and Horace Waterbury, and filed May 4, 1831, page 272.

Fowler, David H., of Newburgh, N. Y., Oct. 29, 1829, his guardian Hezekiah Hobby discharged, and David Fowler of said Newburgh appointed in his place, page 149.

Gray, Hannah, late of Stamford, wife of Joseph Gray, will dated July 4, 1828, probated Oct. 6, 1832, mentions her daughters Hannah, Molly, Elizabeth, Julia Ann, and sons Cary H., and Joseph A.; granddaughters Rebecca C. Mather, Catherine S. Gray, and Hannah E. Gray. Executor her son Cary H. Witnesses Samuel Beach, John Leeds, and Charles T. Leeds, page 417.
    Oct. 8, 1832, order to advertise for claims, page 418.
    Inventory taken Oct. 15, 1832, by John Brown and William H. Holly, and filed Oct. 15, 1832, page 419.

Gray, Joseph, late of Stamford, will dated Aug. 2, 1831, probated Oct. 6, 1832, mentions his children Hannah, Molly, Elizabeth, Joseph Alfred, Julia Ann, and Cary Holly, and Elizabeth Gray widow of his deceased son William Leeds Gray; granddaughters Catherine Sands Gray and Hannah Elizabeth Gray, and Rebecca Catherine Mather; uncle of his children Henry R. Selleck of Darien; deceased brother Daniel Gray. Executor his son Cary Holly Gray. Witnesses David Hoyt, John Brown, and George C. Hoyt, page 419.
    Oct. 8, 1832, order to advertise for claims, page 422.
    Inventory taken by John Brown and William H. Holly, and filed Oct. 15, 1832, page 422.

Hobby, Clemence, late of Greenwich, widow of Thomas Hobby, will dated Jan. 13, 1821, probated Oct. 29, 1829, mentions her children Jabez M. Hobby, Jr., Joseph Hobby, Walter Hobby, Caleb Hobby, Molly Adams, Clemence Marshall, and the children of her deceased daughters Sally Avery and Betsy Mead; sister Sarah Knapp, and granddaughter Mary Jerusha Hobby a daughter of her son Jabez M. Hobby, Jr. Executor her son Jabez M. Hobby, Jr. Witnesses Eben Knapp, Sanford R. Knapp, and Samuel M. Fitch, page 142.
    Oct. 29, 1829, order to advertise for claims, page 143.
    Inventory taken by Alvan Mead and John Jay Tracy, and filed Nov. 24, 1829, page 193.

STAMFORD PROBATE RECORDS.
Volume 14, 1828.

Hobby, Jabez M., late of Greenwich, June 18, 1828, commissioners appointed to partition his estate among the children of Nancy Peck, a deceased daughter, viz: Thomas H. Peck, Mehitabel wife of Thomas M. Lyon, Charles Edgar Peck, and David a son of Abigail Jane H. Fowler, a deceased daughter of said Nancy deceased, devised to them by said Jabez M. Hobby. The said Mehitabel, Charles E., and David being minors with guardians, page 8.
June 21, 1828, partition made accordingly, page 8.

Holly, Abraham, late of Darien, Jan. 30, 1828, his widow refused to qualify, and letters of administration on his estate granted to Henry Bates of Darien, who was ordered to advertise for claims, page 23.

Holly, Isaac, late of Stamford, Feb. 6, 1827, his widow refused to qualify, and letters of administration on his estate granted to his sons William Henry Holly and Edwin S. Holly, who were ordered to advertise for claims, page 75.
Inventory taken Feb. 17, 1827, by David Hoyt and Silas Scofield, and filed Mch. 5, 1827, page 85.
Mch. 3, 1828, Eleanor Holly of Stamford appointed guardian of Catherine E., Julia A., George F., and Charles F., children of decedent, page 91.
Mch. 3, 1828, account filed, and necessaries allowed his family; estate ordered distributed to his widow Eleanor, and children William H., Edwin S., Alexander N., David F., Mary S., Nancy E., Hannah M., Catherine E., Charles F., George F., and Julia A., page 90.
Mch. 5, 1828, estate distributed accordingly, page 91.

Holly, Stephen, late of Stamford, Apl. 4, 1833, his widow being incapacitated to act, letters of administration on his estate granted to Silas Holly, who was ordered to advertise for claims, page 484.
Inventory taken by Selleck Scofield and Isaac Ayres, and filed Apl. 11, 1833, page 484.

Holmes, Caleb, of Greenwich, about 17 years of age, Mch. 19, 1829, made choice of Jonas Howe of Greenwich to be his guardian, page 5.

Holmes, Hannah, late of Greenwich, Feb. 24, 1831, letters of administration on her estate granted to her son Luke Holmes, who was ordered to advertise for claims, page 501.

STAMFORD PROBATE RECORDS.
Volume 14, 1828.

Holmes, Reuben H., of Darien, as guardian and husband of Caty Holmes, Apl. 10, 1830, petition for leave to sell the realestate of said minor, and sale ordered, page 228.

Horton, Charles, of Stamford, about 19 years of age, Mch. 19, 1831, made choice of Simeon H. Minor to be his guardian, page 260.

Howe, Bowers, late of Stamford, will dated Sept. 2, 1817, probated June 10, 1829, mentions his wife Ruth, and children Reuama wife of Silvanus Weed of Lenox, N. Y., heirs of Polly deceased wife of Azariah Waterbury, William, and Isaac. Executor son Isaac. Witnesses Mary Weed, Mary Weed, 2nd, and Nathan Weed, page 72. June 10, 1829, order to advertise for claims, page 73. Inventory taken June 27, 1829, by Cary Bell and Holly Bell, and filed July 2, 1829, page 73.

Howe, Isaac, of Darien, Apl. 14, 1830, his daughters Betsy Howe and Sarah Howe of Darien, made choice of their father, said Isaac Howe, to be theirguardian, page 193. Apl. 14, 1830, petition of Isaac Howe, guardian for his children Betsy, Sarah, and Smith, for leave to sell the real estate of said minors, and sale ordered, page 227.

Hoyt, Billy, late of Stamford, Mch. 13, 1828, on the application of William Hoyt of Stamford, guardian of James H. and George, children of decedent, the real estate left by Thaddeus Hoyt, deceased, in Stamford, ordered sold, page 96.

Hoyt, Cary, late of Darien, will dated July 27, 1831, probated Mch. 30, 1832, mentions his brother Ebenezer Hoyt, and sisters Rhoda and Millicent Hoyt. Executor Abram Clock of Darien. Witnesses Sherman Husted, William H. Bishop, and Abigail Weed, page 394. Mch. 30, 1832, order to advertise for claims, page 395. Inventory taken by Ashbel Scofield and William H. Lockwood, and filed June 14, 1832, page 395.

Hoyt, Charles H., and Eliza Hoyt, of Darien, over 14 years of age, Mch. 11, 1833, made choice of their brother George A. Hoyt of New York City to be their guardian, who was also appointed guardian of Elizabeth Hoyt and Hannah Hoyt of Darien, and their former guardian, discharged, page 448.

STAMFORD PROBATE RECORDS.
Volume 14, 1828.

194.

Hoyt, Darius, late of Darien, Aug. 11, 1826, pursuant to order of Dec. 5, 1826, real estate sold to pay debts to Thaddeus Hoyt, & Ezekiel Curtis, and report of sale filed, page 21.

Hoyt, Darius, late of Darien, June 9, 1828, on the petition of John Brown of Stamford guardian of Jerome Bates Hoyt, William Augustus Hoyt, George Allen Hoyt, Charles Henry Hoyt, Mary Hoyt, Eliza Hoyt, Elizabeth Hoyt, and Hannah Amelia Hoyt, minor children of decedent, owners of 1/10 of the real estate in Stamford and Darien left by Thaddeus Hoyt, late of Stamford, deceased, said real estate ordered sold, page 21.
Mch. 9, 1830, petition of Jerome B. Hoyt, a son of decedent, for the removal of John Brown, administrator, said administrator removed, and Jerome Bates Hoyt of Darien appointed in his place, pages 166 and 167.

Hoyt, Enoch, late of Stamford, Sept. 9, 1830, dower of his widow ordered set out, page 255.
Oct. 5, 1830, dower set out to his widow, Sally Ann Hoyt, page 255.
Aug. 24, 1830, Calvin G. Hoyt about 18 years of age, a son of decedent, made choice of Jotham Hoyt of Stamford to be his guardian, page 240.
Mch. 18, 1831, James Nelson Hoyt of Stamford, about 16 years of age, a son of decedent, made choice of Simeon H. Minor to be his guardian, page 243.
Dec. 15, 1832, Sarah Mehetabel Hoyt, about 12 years of age, a daughter of decedent, made choice of Royal L. Gay to be her guardian, who was also appointed guardian of Samuel Willard, Harriet, Sally Ann, John Smith, and Clarissa Augusta, other children of decedent, all under 12 years of age, page 417.
Dec. 15, 1832, his administratrix, Sally Ann Hoyt, discharged, and letters de bonus non granted to Daniel Lockwood, page 472.
Mch. 23, 1833, account filed, and real estate ordered sold to pay debts, page 461.
Real estate sold to Sally Ann Hoyt, widow of deceased, and report of sale filed July 18, 1833, page 461.

Hoyt, Epenetus, late of Stamford, will dated Feb. 18, 1831, probated Dec. 5, 1831, mentions his son Jotham, daughter Mary Weed Betts, and grandchildren William Morgan Hoyt, and Betsy Maria Hoyt. Executors his son Jotham, and son-in-law Andrew Betts. Witnesses Samuel Young, Joseph Davenport, and Amanda Scofield, page 389.

STAMFORD PROBATE RECORDS.
Volume 14, 1828.

Hoyt, Epenetus, continued :
Dec. 5, 1831, order to advertise for claims, page 390.
Inventory taken Dec. 7, 1831, by Luther Weed and John Young, and filed July 25, 1832, page 390.

Hoyt, James Edward, of Stamford, Oct. 20, 1830, made choice of his mother, Abigail Hoyt, to be his guardian, page 240.

Hoyt, John Peter, of Stamford, about 15 years of age, Nov. 9, 1831, made choice of his mother, Hannah Hoyt, of Stamford, to be his guardian, page 344.

Hoyt, Joseph S., late of Stamford, June 16, 1832, letters of administration on his estate granted to John Seely of Stamford, who was ordered to advertise for claims, his mother having refused to qualify, page 383.
Inventory taken by Jotham Hoyt and Luther Weed, and filed Nov. 14, 1832, page 484.

Hoyt, Mary, formerly of Darien, now of New York City, over 14 years of age, Aug. 3, 1833, made choice of George A. Hoyt of New York City to be her guardian, page 458.

Hoyt, Sally, late of Darien, widow of Nathaniel Hoyt, Jan. 16, 1832, her son Ralph Hoyt and daughter Sally Hoyt refused to qualify, and letters of administration on her estate granted to Thomas Reed of Norwalk, who was ordered to advertise for claims, page 356.

Hoyt, Samuel, late of Darien, will dated Oct. 19, 1832, probated July 10, 1833, mentions his wife Betsy, and children Rufus, Samuel S. S., and Ann S. Tillman, granddaughters Mary Catherine and Elizabeth Tillman; and John R. P. a son of said Samuel S. S. Executor his son Rufus. Witness Samuel Beach, page 454.
July 10, 1833, order to advertise for claims, page 455.
Inventory taken Jan. 10, 1833, by Ezra Knapp and J. B. Waterbury, and filed July 27, 1833, page 455.

Hoyt, Shadrach, late of Stamford, June 8, 1833, letters of administration on his estate granted to his widow, Hannah Hoyt and son James S. Hoyt, who were ordered to advertise for claims, page 501.
Inventory taken July 19, 1833, by David Holly and Davis Lockwood, and filed Aug. 13, 1833, page 501.

Hoyt, Thaddeus, late of Stamford, Oct. 13, 1826, his widow refused to qualify, and letters of administration on his estate granted to Thaddeus Hoyt and Joshua Scofield,

STAMFORD PROBATE RECORDS.
Volume 14, 1828.

Hoyt, Thaddeus, continued :
    both of Darien, and Daniel Lockwood of Stamford, who
    were ordered to advertise for claims, page 109.
    Inventory taken Oct. 18, 1826, by William Waterbury, Jr
    and Peter Smith, Jr., and filed Nov. 2, 1826, pages 110
    and 113.
    Feb. 8, 1828, account filed, and real estate ordered
    sold to pay debts, page 113.
    Mch. 27, 1828, real estate sold to the children of
    Darius Hoyt, late of Darien, deceased, viz: Jerome
    Bates Hoyt, William A. Hoyt, George A. Hoyt, Charles H.
    Hoyt, Mary Hoyt, Elisa Hoyt, Elizabeth Hoyt, and Han-
    nah A. Hoyt, and another parcel to Theodore Davenport,
    and report of sale filed, page 114.

Hoyt, William, late of Stamford, Sept. 18, 1828, his widow,
    refused to qualify, and letters of administration
    on his estate granted to John W. Hoyt, who was ordered
    to advertise for claims, page 66.
    Oct. 1828, inventory taken by James Davenport and
    Jotham Hoyt, and filed Nov. 2, 1829, page 152.
    Apl. 27, 1830, account filed, and real estate ordered
    sold to pay debts, page 184.

Hubbard, Gabriel, late of Stamford, May 2, 1829, account filed
    and real estate ordered sold to pay debts, page 247.
    Mch. 15, 1830, real estate sold to David Holly, Rob-
    ert Cox, and Edmond Lockwood, and report of sale fil-
    ed, page 248.
    Mch. 1, 1830, dower of his widow ordered set out, and
    set out Mch. 13, 1830, page 167.

Hubbard, Hannah P., of Stamford, mother and guardian of Ellen
    Hubbard, George D. Hubbard, Samuel Hubbard, Mary H.
    Hubbard, Hannah P. Hubbard, David H. Hubbard, and Har-
    riet E. Hubbard, Jan. 31, 1831, petition for the sale
    of the real estate of said minors, in Stamford, and
    sale ordered, page 254.
    Real estate sold to Edmund Lockwood and Daniel G. Scott
    and report of sale filed Aug. 13, 1831, page 276.

Hubbard, Henry, late of -----, June 4, 1827, testate, time for
    settlement extended, page 22.

Hunt, Thomas, late of Darien, Dec. 12, 1828, his widow being
    incapable of qualifying, letters of administration on
    his estate granted to Henry Bates, page 10.

STAMFORD PROBATE RECORDS.
Volume 14, 1828.

Husted, Roswell, late of Greenwich, Jan. 24, 1833, his widow refused to qualify, and letters of administration on his estate granted to David D. Husted of North Castle, N. Y., who was ordered to advertise for claims, page 443.
Inventory taken by Benjamin Brush and Jacob Dayton, Jr., and filed Mch. 5, 1833, page 443.

Ingersoll, Simon, late of Greenwich, inventory taken Jan. 26, 1828, by Benjamin Brush and Joseph Ingersoll, and filed Mch. 26, 1832, page 407.
Mch. 28, 1829, time for executors to account extended, page 409.
Feb. 3, 1832, executors now deceased, and Daniel Lockwood appointed administrator with the will annexed, and trustee of the trusts created by said will, page 469

Jessup, Jonathan, late of Greenwich, Jan. 28, 1828, additional inventory filed, page 74.
Mch. 27, 1828, time for settlement extended, page 3.
Apl. 18, 1829, account filed, and realestate ordered sold to pay debts, page 75.
June 13, 1829, real estate sold to Edwin Buxton of Stamford, and report of sale filed, page 75.

Jones, George, of Darien, over 14 years of age, Mch. 22, 1833, made choice of John Bell, Jr., of Darien, to be continued as his guardian, page 489.

Jones, Horace H., of Darien, about 18 years of age, Jan. 16, 1832, made choice of Holly Hanford of New Canaan to be his guardian, page 382.

Jones, James, of Darien, about 20 years of age, Jan. 16, 1832, made choice of John Bell of Darien to be his guardian, page 376.

Jones, Josiah, late of Stamford, Jan. 13, 1832, that part of his estate set out to his widow, as her dower, ordered distributed to his children Amos, Smith, Isaac, Sarah Allen, Hannah Lockwood, and Abigail Thompson, page 365.
Feb. 22, 1832, estate distributed to Hannah wife of Lewis S. Lockwood, heirs of Smith Jones, deceased, heirs of Amos Jones, deceased, and Isaac Jones, who purchased the interests of Sarah Allen and Abigail Thompson, page 365.

STAMFORD PROBATE RECORDS.
Volume 14, 1828.

Jones, Sarah, late of Stamford, Feb. 25, 1831, letters of administration on her estate granted to her son Isaac Jones, who was ordered to advertise for claims, page 254.
Inventory taken Feb. 28, 1831, by Enoch Stevens and Gould Raymond, and filed Apl. 26, 1831, page 254.
Jan. 28, 1832, estate ordered distributed to her daughter Hannah Lockwood, son Isaac Jones, heirs of Amos Jones, deceased son, daughter Abigail Thompson, and daughter Sally Allen, page 358.
Feb. 22, 1832, estate distributed to Hannah Lockwood, and Isaac Jones, who purchased the interests of the heirs of Amos Jones, deceased, and also of Abigail Thopmson and Sally Allen, page 359.

Jones, Selleck, late of Darien, Dec. 9, 1831, letters of administration on his estate granted to Jeremiah Andreas and Epenetus W. Walmsley of Darien, who were ordered to advertise for claims, page 278.
Inventory taken Dec. 10, 1831, by Henry Bates and Thomas Reed, and filed Jan. 21, 1832, page 278.
Dec. 20, 1831, Nancy Olivia Jones, a daughter of decedent, about 15 years of age, made choice of Samuel Raymond of New Canaan to be her guardian, page 382.
Apl. 7, 1832, John Bell, Jr., of Darien, appointed guardian of George, William, and Samuel, sons of decedent, page 378.

Jones, Smith, late of Stamford, Feb. 13, 1832, that part of his estate set off to his mother, Sarah Jones, now deceased, as her dower in the estate of Josiah Jones, deceased, ordered distributed to the brothers and sisters of deceased, viz: Isaac Jones, heirs of Amos Jones deceased, Hannah wife of Lewis S. Lockwood, Sally Allen, and Abigail Thompson, page 361.
Feb. 23, 1832, estate distributed to Hannah wife of Lewis S. Lockwood, heirs of Amos Jones, deceased, and Isaac Jones, who purchased the interests of Abigail Thompson and Sally Allen, page 361.

Jones, Thomas, late of Stamford, June 12, 1832, his widow refused to qualify, and letters of administration on his estate granted to Jotham Hoyt, who was ordered to advertise for claims, page 398.
Inventory taken by Stephen Chichester and Elijah Scofield, and filed Sept. 10, 1832, page 489.

June, Nathaniel, late of Stamford, Sept. 4, 1826, account filed and real estate ordered sold, page 24.

STAMFORD PROBATE RECORDS.
Volume 14, 1828.

June, Nathaniel, continued :
  Sept. 4, 1826, necessaries allowed his widow, page 25.

Knapp, Abigail, late of Stamford, will dated Dec. 2, 1824, probated Sept. 4, 1830, mentions her son Charles, Elizabeth wife of said Charles, and their children, viz: Mary E. Taylor, John William Knapp, Charles Sylvanus Knapp, and Lorenzo E. Knapp; her daughter Sarah wife of Eliphalet St. John, and granddaughter Abigail Delia Silliman, and son Lorenzo C. St. John. Executor son Charles. Witnesses Enoch Scofield, Ann Scofield, and Charles Hawley, page 238.
  Sept. 4, 1830, order to advertise for claims, page 239.

Knapp, Abigail, late of Greenwich, will dated Apl. 13, 1832, probated May 1, 1832, mentions her children George James, Susan wife of Israel June, Nancy wife of Isaac Booker, David Burrage Knapp, and William Reynolds, grandson William son of George James. Executor her son William Reynolds. Witnesses John W. Reynolds, Daniel S. Betts, and Jabez Mead, page 386.
  June 9, 1832, order to advertise for claims, page 386.
  Inventory taken by Asahel Palmer and Henry Ritch, and filed July 10, 1832, page 387.

Knapp, Isaac, late of Stamford, July 27, 1829, letters of administration on his estate granted to his father, Rufus Knapp, who was ordered to advertise for claims, page 70.
  Inventory taken by Augustus Lockwood and Henry Burley, and filed Aug. 14, 1829, page 198.
  July 12, 1830, account filed, and estate ordered distributed to his brothers and sisters of the whole blood, five in number, page 223.

Knapp, Isaac, late of Stamford, Dec. 22, 1832, his widow refused to qualify, and letters of administration on his estate granted to Daniel Lockwood of Stamford, who was ordered to advertise for claims, page 445.
  Inventory taken Dec. 31, 1832, by Eben Smith and Walter Palmer, and filed Jan. 25, 1833, page 445.

Knapp, Joshua, late of North Castle, Westchester County, N. Y. will dated Sept. 14, 1826, probated Aug. 29, 1831, mentions his wife Charity, and children Jasper, Joshua, Samuel, Nathaniel, Rachel wife of Abraham Brown, Charity Knapp, and Sarah Knapp. Executors his sons Joshua and Samuel. Witnesses Benjamin Isaacs, Reuben Knapp, and William A. Oliver, page 274.

STAMFORD PROBATE RECORDS.
Volume 14, 1828.

Knapp, Joshua, continued :
Probated in Westchester County, Apl. 11, 1831.
Aug. 29, 1831, order to advertise for claims, page 275.
Inventory taken by Samuel Close and Daniel Peck, and filed Nov. 4, 1831, page 276.

Knapp, Mary, late of Greenwich, widow of Enos Knapp, will dated July 3, 1827, probated Aug. 2, 1832, all personal property to her daughter Rhoda wife of Benjamin Page Executor her son-in-law Benjamin Page. Witnesses Mary Ann Lockwood, Rhoda Peck, and Jabez Mead, page 434.
Aug. 20, 1832, order to advertise for claims, page 435.
Inventory taken Sept. 19, 1832, by Peter Ferris and Henry Dayton, and filed Sept. 22, 1832, page 435.

Knapp, Samuel, late of Stamford, June 14, 1828, his widow, Susannah Knapp, being now deceased, that part of his estate set off to her as her dower, ordered distributed to Jacob Knapp, Isaac Knapp, Stephen Knapp, and the heirs of Joshua Knapp, deceased, according to his will, page 59.
June 18, 1828, estate distributed accordingly, page 60.

LeCraft, Daniel Tucker, of Stamford, formerly of New York City, over 14 years of age, Sept. 6, 1831, xxxxxxxxx made choice of Dr. Nathaniel D. Haight of Stamford to be his guardian, page 343.

Leeds, John, late of Stamford, will dated Jan. 6, 1830, probated Dec. 8, 1831, mentions his wife Honor, son John W., and grandson Charles H., a son of John W. Leeds. Executor his son John W. Witnesses Cary Leeds, William P. Lockwood, and John R. Leeds, page 393.
Dec. 10, 1831, order to advertise for claims, page 393.
Inventory taken Jan. 26, 1832, by Joseph Gray and George Brown, and filed Jan. 26, 1832, page 394.

Leeds, Theodore, late of Stamford, Dec. 9, 1828, letters of administration on his estate granted to his mother, Sarah W. Leeds, page 53.

Lockwood, Charles, late of Greenwich, will dated Oct. 1, 1828, probated Oct. 10, 1832, mentions his wife Mary, and children Charles, Israel, Thankful Webb, Sally Morris, and John, grandson Charles Alfred the eldest son of his son Charles. Executor Justus L. Bush,. Witnesses Peter Ferris, Benjamin Page, and Joseph Wilmot, page 435.

STAMFORD PROBATE RECORDS.
Volume 14, 1828.

Lockwood, Charles, continued:
    Oct. 10, 1832, the executor refused to qualify and letters with the will annexed granted to Charles Lockwood son of testator, who was ordered to advertise for claims, page 436.
    Inventory taken by Asahel Palmer and Alexander Hendrie, and filed Oct. 27, 1832, page 437.
    Dec. 12, 1832, appeal taken from probate, page 438.

Lockwood, Ebenezer, of Stamford, Nov. 13, 1832, the father and natural guardian of Maria, Hannah, Charles and William H. Lockwood, petitioned for leave to sell the real estate of said minors in Stamford, and sale ordered, pages 438 and 439.
    Real estate sold to Oliver Lockwood of Stamford, and report of sale filed, Mch. 9, 1833, page 439.

Lockwood, Elizabeth, late of Stamford, will dated Sept. 16, 1826, probated Nov. 2, 1831, mentions her deceased husband Stephen Lockwood, and children Oliver Lockwood, Henry Lockwood, Stephen Lockwood, and Elizabeth wife of Enos Knapp. Executor her son Oliver. Witnesses Peter Knapp, Gabriel Hubbard, and Charles Hawley, pages 377 and 430.
    Nov. 2, 1831, order to advertise for claims, page 378.
    Inventory taken Nov. 5, 1831, by Solomon Clason and Caleb Knapp, and filed Jan. 30, 1833, and Mch 13, 1833, pages 432 and 433.
    Mch. 9, 1833, estate ordered distributed to Stephen Lockwood, Oliver Lockwood, and Henry Lockwood, sons of deceased, page 434.

Lockwood, Gilbert, late of Greenwich, Apl. 1, 1830, testate, mention made of Tamer wife of Adam Clark and William a son of Ruth, sister of said testator, both now living, and Richard Lockwood, now deceased; Dr. Nathaniel B. Haight of Stamford appointed trustee of said estate, page 184.

Lockwood, Hanford, of New York City, July 16, 1832, appointed guardian of his wife Susan Lockwood, page 347.

Lockwood, Lewis, late of Stamford, June 28, 1830, letters of administration on his estate granted to Abel Reynolds, who was ordered to advertise for claims, pages 225 and 313.
    Inventory taken by Jared Holly and Robert R. Barlow, and filed Aug. 11, 1830, page 226.

STAMFORD PROBATE RECORDS.
Volume 14, 1828.

Lockwood, Lewis, continued :
    Feb. 7, 1831, account filed, and necessaries allowed his widow, page 313.
    Apl. 2, 1831, commissioners appointed to adjust claims of creditors, page 314.
    Oct. 12, 1831, report of commissioners filed, page 315.
    Feb. 7, 1831, account filed, and real estate ordered sold to pay debts, page 316.
    Nov. 23, 1831, widow's dower ordered set out, page 316.
    Dec. 28, 1831, dower set out, page 316.
    Mch. 9, 1833, report of commissioners to adjust claims filed, page 503.
    Apl. 29, 1833, report of commissioners to adjust claims filed, page 479.
    Real estate sold to John Robinson of Stamford, and report of sale filed, page 479.

Lockwood, Philip, late of Greenwich, will dated Aug. 7, 1827, probated Nov. 26, 1831, mentions his wife Hannah and children Sally Waterbury, Hannah Hoyt, and Eliza Weed, grandson Philip Lockwood. Executors his sons-in-law William Waterbury and Erastus H. Weed. Witnesses Ann Gilbert, Seymour Jarvis, and S. H. Minor, page 388.
    Codicil dated Mch. 26, 1831, page 388.
    Nov. 26, 1831, order to advertise for claims, page 389.

Lockwood, Reuben, late of Stamford, June 14, 1827, letters of administration on his estate granted to Enos Lockwood of Greenwich, who was ordered to advertise for claims, page 104.
    Inventory taken Aug. 2, 1827, by Joshua Ferris and Samuel Ferris, Jr., and filed Aug. 8, 1827, page 104.

Lockwood, Richard, late of Stamford, Mch. 27, 1829, letters of administration on his estate granted to his widow, Hannah Lockwood, and Abel Reynolds, of Stamford, who were ordered to advertise for claims, page 28.
    Inventory taken June 15, 1829, by John Brown and James Webb, and filed July 1, 1829, page 28.

Lockwood, Rufus, late of Stamford, Mch. 2, 1829, letters of administration on his estate granted to Samuel Lockwood, and commissioners appointed to adjust claims of creditors, page 40.

Lockwood, Sarah, late of Greenwich, will dated June 14, 1824, probated Feb. 6, 1827, mentions her children George Lockwood, Jr., Betsy Lockwood, Jerusha, Amy, David,

STAMFORD PROBATE RECORDS.
Volume 14, 1828.

Lockwood, Sarah, continued:
and Webster; grandson Benjamin a son of Caleb Lockwood, and grandchildren the children of her daughter Sarah, deceased. Executor son George. Witnesses Joshua Ferris, John H. Lockwood, and Ann Peck, page 97.
Feb. 6, 1827, order to advertise for claims, page 98.
Inventory taken Feb. 21, 1827, by Drake Lockwood and Rufus Peck, and filed Mch. 7, 1827, page 98.
Jan. 21, 1828, real estate sold by her executor to George Peck of Greenwich, and report of sale filed, page 99.

Lockwood, Smith, late of   Aug. 7, 1829, report of commissioners to adjust claims filed, page 174.
Aug. 31, 1829, necessaries set off to his widow, page 175.
Aug. 30, 1829, account filed, and real estate ordered sold to pay debts, page 175.
Dec. 14, 1829, real estate sold to Benjamin Matthews and to the widow of decedent, and report of sale filed, page 176.

Lockwood, William, late of Greenwich, Mch. 26, 1828, letters of administration on his estate granted to Mills Lockwood, who was ordered to advertise for claims, page 71.
Inventory taken by Charles Smith and Amos Mead, mentions his widow, Sarah Lockwood, and filed Apl. 11, 1828, page 71.
Mch. 27, 1829, time for settlement extended, page 72.

Lounsbury, Abigail, widow, late of Darien, Mch. 11, 1830, letters of administration on her estate granted to John Weed, Jr., who was ordered to advertise for claims, page 178.
Inventory taken Mch. 1830, by Phineas Waterbury and Joseph Weed, and filed Apl. 14, 1830, page 178.

Lounsbury, Elizabeth, late of Stamford, Apl. 17, 1830, letters of administration on her estate granted to Amos L. Lounsbury and Samuel Lounsbury, both of New York City, who were ordered to advertise for claims, page 183.
Inventory taken June 28, 1830, by Cary Leeds and Samuel Smith, and filed June 28, 1830, page 223.

Lounsbury, Jane, late of Stamford, Oct. 13, 1831, letters of administration on her estate granted to Nathaniel Adams of Greenwich, xwho was ordered to advertise for claims, page 286. xhusband of one of the daughters of deceased.

STAMFORD PROBATE RECORDS.
Volume 14, 1828.

Lounsbury, Jane, continued:
    Inventory taken by R. R. Barlow and Stephen Lockwood, and filed Oct. 17, 1832, page 410.
    Jan. 14, 1833, account filed, and estate ordered distributed to her children Justus Lounsbury, heirs of Amasa Lounsbury, deceased, Sally Haight, Polly Adams, John Lounsbury, and Abigail Lounsbury, page 440.
    Feb. 23, 1833, estate distributed accordingly, page 440.

Lounsbury, John, Captain, late of Stamford, will dated May 28, 1828, probated Aug. 7, 1828, all to his wife Jerusha. Executors his wife and son Stephen. Witnesses Ann Gilbert, J. H. Minor, and S. H. Minor, page 15.
    Aug. 7, 1828, order to advertise for claims, page 16.
    Inventory taken Aug. 16, 1828, by Warren Scofield and Abishai Scofield, and filed Oct. 24, 1828, page 16.
    Aug. 7, 1829, time for settlement extended, page 17.

Lyon, Mary, late of Greenwich, will dated June 26, 1832, probated Aug. 24, 1832, mentions Deborah wife of Gilbert Lyon, Abigail Jane wife of Henry Davis, Hannah Lyon a daughter of Abram Lyon, and Emeline Lyon a daughter of Abram Lyon. Executor Seth Lyon. Witnesses Gershom Buckley, Abby Merritt, and Lydia Grigg, page 424.
    Aug. 24, 1832, order to advertise for claims, page 424.
    Inventory taken Aug. 28, 1832, by Jonas Mead and John Olmstead, and filed Aug. 28, 1832, page 425.

McIntyre, John, late of Darien, May 1, 1826, estate ordered distributed to James McIntyre, Henry McIntyre, and the heirs of John McIntyre, the younger, page 508.

Mead, Daniel S., late of Greenwich, will dated Dec. 18, 1831, probated Jan. 16, 1832, mentions his wife Rachel, and children Zette, Rachel Elizabeth, Silas Mervin, Daniel Smith, Jared, and Edwin, owned land in Greenwich, Ohio. Executor his son Daniel Smith Mead. Witnesses Jabez Mead, Jonas Mead, and Alvan Mead, page 349.
    Jan. 16, 1832, order to advertise for claims, page 350.
    Inventory taken Feb. 14, 1832, by Thomas A. Mead and Nelson Bush, and filed Mch. 16, 1832, page 350.

Mead, Jared, late of Greenwich, will dated May 20, 1824, probated Aug. 24, 1832, mentions his children Daniel Smith, Jared, Alvan, Lydia Lockwood, Alma, Hannah wife of Jonas Mead, grandchildren Hannah, Almira, Ebenezer, and Emeline Zette children of Zette, deceased, wife of Colonel Ebenezer Mead, owned land in Greenwich, Ohio. Executors his sons Daniel S. and Alvan. Witnesses

STAMFORD PROBATE RECORDS.
Volume 14, 1828.

Mead, Jared, continued :
Benjamin Page, Jabez Mead, and Samuel Peck, Jr., page 498.
Aug. 24, 1832, letters to Alvan Mead, Daniel S. Mead being now deceased, who was ordered to advertise for claims, page 500.

Mead, Jonathan, late of Greenwich, July 3, 1826, account filed and commissioners appointed to adjust claims of creditors, page 124.
Mch. 7, 1827, report of commissioners filed, page 125.
Mch. 14, 1827, necessaries allowed his widow, page 125.
Feb. 7, 1828, creditors ordered paid, page 126.

Mead, Nehemiah, late of Greenwich, will dated Oct. 15, 1829, probated Dec. 27, 1830, mentions his wife Esther, and children Nehemiah, Huldah Tracy, Mehetabel wife of Royal Dunton, Polly wife of Willet Sherwood, and Andrew, grandson Jeremiah Fog a son of Zachariah Mead, deceased. Executor Samuel Close. Witnesses Isaac Holly, Conklin Husted, and John Jay Tracy, page 265.
Dec. 27, 1830, order to advertise for claims, page 266.
Inventory taken Dec. 30, 1830, by Joseph Brush and Benjamin I. Knapp, and filed Jan. 25, 1831, page 266.
Feb. 8, 1831, additional inventory filed, page 328.
Mch. 13, 1832, account filed, and necessaries allowed his widow, page 327.
Mch. 15, 1832, account filed, and real estate ordered sold to pay debts, page 472.
Real estate sold to Willett Sherwood, and report of sale filed, Nov. 9, 1832, page 472.

Mead, Rachel, late of Greenwich, widow of Richard Mead, will dated Sept. 19, 1831, probated Oct. 21, 1831, mentions her sons Whitman Mead and Zophar Mead; Araminta, Mary Elizabeth and Sarah Amelia children of said Zophar Mead; grandchildren Grace and Henrietta children of said Whitman Mead; grandchildren Amos Mead, Richard Edward, Theodore, and Sarah Elizabeth children of Joseph Brush; grandson William Henry Sackett a son of John Sackett, and also Rachel Elizabeth, Abigail Sarah, and Mary Ann granddaughters and daughters of said John Sackett; grandchildren and children of said John Sackett, viz: Henry L., Rachel Elisabeth, Whitman Mead, Abigail Sarah, Mary Ann, and Thomas Mead. Executor Jonas Howe. Witnesses Sarah Mead and Jabez Mead, page 403.
Oct. 21, 1831, order to advertise for claims, page 404.

STAMFORD PROBATE RECORDS.
Volume 14, 1828.

Mead, Rachel, continued :
Inventory taken by Isaac Mead, Jr., and Alvan Mead, and filed Dec. 10, 1831, page 404.

Mead, Reuben, late of Greenwich, Jan. 23, 1833, his son Nathan Mead refused to qualify, and letters of administration on his estate granted to Simeon H. Minor of Stamford, who was ordered to advertise for claims, page 444. Inventory taken by Earle Smith and Rufus Knapp and filed Jan. 25, 1833, page 445.

Mead, Richard, late of Greenwich, May 14, 1826, his widow, Rachel Mead, refused to qualify, and letters of administration on his estate granted to his son Thomas A. Mead, who was ordered to advertise for claims, page 31. Inventory taken May 25, 1826, by Isaac Mead, Jr., and Samuel Bush, and filed Aug. 16, 1826, page 31.

Mead, Rogers, late of Greenwich, Mch. 22, 1830, letters of administration on his estate granted to John Jay Tracy of Greenwich, and commissioners appointed to adjust claims of creditors, page 192 195.
Inventory taken Apl. 29, 1830, by Justus Sackett and Thomas A. Mead, and filed Apl. 30, 1830, page 196.
Nov. 27, 1830, account filed, and real estate ordered sold to pay debts, page 248.
Jan. 21, 1831, real estate sold to Augustus Lyon of Greenwich, and report of sale filed, page 248.
Oct. 28, 1830, report of commissioners filed, page 364.

Mead, Seth, late of Greenwich, will dated Nov. 21, 1825, probated Dec. 5, 1825, mentions his children Sarah Elizabeth, Walter Hobby, and John Hanford. Executors Hezekiah Hobby of Stamford and brother Walter Mead of Montgomery, Orange County, N. Y. Witnesses John Jay Tracy, Samuel D. Hobby, and Lemuel Addington, page 102.
Jan. 13, 1826, order to advertise for claims, page 103.
Inventory taken Jan. 1826, by Isaac Mead, Jr., and Daniel S. Mead, and filed Feb. 27, 1827, page 103.
Aug. 28, 1827, real estate sold by the executors to Zophar Mead, and report of sale filed, page 104.

Mead, Whitman, of Greenwich, Aug. 20, 1832, the court appointed Ephraim Mead of Greenwich guardian of Grace W. Mead and Henrietta Mead of Brooklyn, N. Y., children of said Whitman Mead, page 417.

Mead, Zophar, of New York City, Aug. 1 1832, on his request Thomas A. Mead of Greenwich, was appointed guardian of

STAMFORD PROBATE RECORDS.
Volume 14, 1828.

Mead, Zophar, continued :
 Araminta Mead, Mary Elizabeth Mead, and Sarah Amelia Mead, daughters of said Zophar Mead, page 382.

Merritt, Adam, late of Greenwich, Apl. 26, 1832, letters of administration on his estate granted to his son William A. Merritt, xwho was ordered to advertise for claims, page 389. xof New York City.

Mills, Amos, of   Apl. 14, 1828, the court appointed William White, Jr., of Stamford, guardian of his son John Todd Mills of Bedford, about 10 years of age, page 82.
 Dec. 21, 1832, petition for leave to sell the real estate of said minor in the estate of John Todd, Jr., late of Stamford, and sale ordered, pages 478 and 479. Real estate sold to William L. Holly of Stamford, and report of sale filed, Mch. 12, 1833, page 479.

Mills, Samuel, Jr., late of Greenwich, Oct. 11, 1824, letters of administration on his estate granted to his widow, Martha Mills and Benjamin Husted, Jr., of Greenwich, who were ordered to advertise for claims, page 26.
 Inventory taken Dec. 8, 1824, by Nathaniel Palmer and Samuel Peck, and filed Oct. 10, 1825, page 26.
 Oct. 10, 1825, time for settlement extended, page 27.

Morehouse, Alexander, late of New York City, will dated Apl. 12, 1827, probated Sept. 4, 1827, mentions his wife Betsy Ann, and children Alexander and Sarah Elizabeth Morehouse. Executors Maurice Hoyt of New York City, and John Weed, Jr., of Darien. Witnesses George Mather, Samuel Husted, and Mary Ann Mather, and William Eginy, page 11.
 Sept. 4, 1827, John Weed, Jr., refused to qualify, and letters granted to Maurice Hoyt, page 13.
 Inventory taken Oct. 6, 1827, by Joshua Scofield and Thaddeus Hoyt, and filed Jan. 10, 1828, page 13.

Nash, James, of Greenwich, July 16, 1832, appointed guardian of his daughter Anna Nash, page 339.

Newman, Anna, late of Stamford, will dated June 3, 1830, probated Sept. 6, 1830, all to her mother Thankful Newman. Executor her brother Edwin Newman. Witnesses Benjamin Matthews, Sarah Matthews, and Samuel Lockwood, page 234.
 Sept. 6, 1830, order to advertise for claims, page 234.

STAMFORD PROBATE RECORDS.
Volume 14, 1828.

Newman, Anna, continued:
   Inventory taken by Solomon Clason and N. Hubbard, and filed Mch. 2, 1831, page 251.

Newman, Harvey, late of Greenwich, June 25, 1832, his widow refused to qualify, and letters of administration on his estate granted to Ard Reynolds of Greenwich, who was ordered to advertise for claims, page 384.
   Inventory taken by Amos Finch and Ezekiel Reynolds, and filed July 10, 1832, page 384.

Newman, Maltbie, late of Stamford, Oct. 17, 1831, Royal L. Gay appointed guardian of Drake Newman a son of decedent, over 14 years of age, pages 482 and 483.

Newman, Nathaniel, late of   Mch. 20, 1826, account filed, and real estate ordered sold to pay debts, page 120.
   Mch. 27, 1826, real estate sold to Andrew June, and report of sale filed, page 120.
   Mch. 28, 1826, estate ordered distributed to his children Henry, Rosetta widow of Jared Reynolds, Polly wife of Luther Lockwood, John, Elizabeth wife of Elvin Ferris, Edwin, Patty Newman, and Ann Newman, and Electa wife of Andrew June, page 121.
   May 20, 1826, estate distributed accordingly, page 121.

Palmer, Denham, late of Greenwich, June 19, 1830, his executor being now deceased, letters of administration with the will annexed granted to George A. Palmer of Greenwich, page 292.
   May 16, 1831, account filed, and real estate ordered sold to pay debts, page 293.
   Real estate sold to Henry Palmer, and report of sale filed, June 15, 1831, page 293.

Palmer, John, late of Greenwich, Jan. 28, 1831, his widow, refused to qualify, and letters of administration on his estate granted to Asahel Palmer of Greenwich, and commissioners appointed to adjust claims of creditors, page 289.
   Inventory taken Jan. 29, 1831, by Henry Ritch and Daniel S. Betts, and filed Jan. 29, 1831, page 289.
   Aug. 13, 1831, report of commissioners filed, page 290.
   Sept. 1, 1831, account filed, necessaries allowed his widow, and real estate ordered sold to pay debts, page 291.
   Sept. 20, 1831, real estate sold to John H. Reynolds and Jonathan Bonnell, and report of sale filed, page 291

STAMFORD PROBATE RECORDS.
Volume 14, 1828.

Palmer, John, continued:
    Aug. 22, 1831, dower of his widow ordered set out, and on Aug. 29, 1831, same set out to Phebe Palmer, widow of deceased, page 362.

Palmer, John Albert, of Greenwich, over 14 years of age, Feb. 5, 1833, made choice of Royal L. Gay of Stamford to be his guardian, page 458.

Palmer, Nathaniel, late of Greenwich, Oct. 10, 1827, report of commissioners to adjust claims filed, page 57.
    Mch. 20, 1829, account filed, and real estate ordered sold to pay debts, pages 190 and 191.
    Mch. 19, 1830, real estate sold to Abram Mead, Major Lockwood, Nancy Lockwood, Josephus Palmer, Lot Mead, Drake Mead, Charlotte Moe, Edmund Mead, and John Adams, Caleb Husted, Justus Sackett, and Rachel Palmer, and report of sale filed, page 191.
    Mch. 19, 1830, creditors ordered paid, page 193.

Palmer, Seth, late of Greenwich, will dated July 14, 1824, probated Feb. 1, 1831, mentions his wife Deborah, grandsons Seth P. Quintard, Peter D. Quintard, Robert P. Quintard, Isaac Quintard, Jr., son-in-law Isaac Quintard, the elder, and great grandson Seth the son of Robert P. Quintard, great grand daughter, the daughter of Peter Smith, Jr., of Stamford, "by my granddaughter Hannah, deceased", devised an acre of land to the First Society. Executors his wife and grandsons Peter D. and Isaac. Witnesses Joseph Gray, Henry Close, and Charles Hawley, page 308.
    Feb. 1, 1831, his widow refused to qualify, and letters granted to said Isaac and Peter D., who were ordered to advertise for claims, page 311.
    Inventory taken Feb. 24, 1831, by Benjamin Page and Frederick Lockwood, and filed Mch. 10, 1831, page 311.
    Jan. 24, 1832, additional inventory filed, page 292.

Patterson, Stephen, of Darien, over 14 years of age, Apl. 1, 1833, made choice of Rufus Hoyt of Darien to be his guardian, page 461.

Peck, Aaron, late of Greenwich, will dated Apl. 25, 1833, probated Aug. 7, 1833, mentions his wife Hannah, daughters Deborah and Hannah, grandchildren George P. Ferris, and his sister Mary P. Peck, granddaughter Margaret Smith and her brother Luther Hennings, grandchildren Elizabeth Peck, David Peck, Henry Peck, Hannah Peck, Harriet

STAMFORD PROBATE RECORDS.
Volume 14, 1828.

Peck, Aaron, continued :
Peck, and Mary Peck. Executor his grandson George P. Ferris. Witnesses William Finch, William Peck, and Ezekiel Finch, page 490.
Aug. 7, 1833, order to advertise for claims, page 491.
Inventory taken Aug. 13, 1833, by Edward Close and James Smith, and filed Aug. 24, 1833, page 491.

Peck, Abigail, of Greenwich, about 19 years of age, Apl. 25, 1832, made choice of Israel Peck of Greenwich to be her guardian, page 372.
Apl. 25, 1832, petition for leave to sell the real estate of said minor in Greenwich, and sale ordered, page 357.
Real estate sold to Eliphalet Peck of Greenwich, and report of sale filed July 10, 1832, page 358.

Peck, Charles Edgar, son of Charles Peck, of Newburgh, N. Y., July 3, 1829, made choice of David H. Fowler of said Newburgh to be his guardian, page 70.
Mch. 8, 1830, petition for leave to sell the real estate of said minor in Greenwich, and sale ordered, page 173.
Mch. 11, 1830, real estate sold to Henry Bush, Nelson Bush, and William Bush of Greenwich, and report of sale filed, page 173.

Peck, Gilbert, late of Greenwich, will dated Jan. 8, 1823, probated Mch. 14, 1833, mentions his wife Deborah, and nephew Gilbert Peck Finch, and niece Deborah Peck. Executor "my brother Eliphalet Peck." Witnesses Huldah Tracy, Phebe E. Knapp, and Hezekiah Tracy, page 459
Mch. 14, 1833, the executor refused to qualify, and letters with the will annexed granted to Gilbert P. Finch, who was ordered to advertise for claims, page 460.
Inventory taken Aug. 24, 1832, by Jonas Howe and Thomas A. Mead, and filed Aug. 28, 1832, page 460.

Peck, Gilbert, late of Greenwich, inventory taken Mch. 20, 1833, by Solomon Peck and Benjamin W. Husted, and filed Mch. 26, 1833, page 483.

Peck, Hannah, late of Greenwich, wife of Ebenezer Peck, will dated May 21, 1827, probated July 13, 1830, mentions her children Ebenezer Peck, father Edmond Lockwood, deceased, daughter-in-law Elizabeth wife of her son Ebenezer Peck, granddaughters Nancy and Julia, daugh-

STAMFORD PROBATE RECORDS.
Volume 14, 1828.

Peck, Hannah, continued:
ters of her son Ebenezer Peck. Executor Edwin Lounsbury of Stamford, the husband of said Nancy. Witnesses Ann Peck, Mary Knapp and Jabez Mead, page 207. July 13, 1830, order to advertise for claims, page 208. Inventory taken Aug. 13, 1830, by Frederick Lockwood and Horace Waterbury, and filed Aug. 13, 1830, page 208.

Peck, Israel, late of Greenwich, Apl. 13, 1830, provisions of his will not complied with, and Samuel Close, Thomas A. Mead, and William H. Holly appointed to distribute part of the estate, page 236.
Apl. 27, 1830, part of his estate distributed to his children Israel Peck, Livina Brown, Nehemiah Peck, and Rachel Peck, page 237.

Peck, Jabez, late of Greenwich, Oct. 25, 1831, letters of administration on his estate granted to Israel Peck, husband of a daughter of deceased, who was ordered to advertise for claims, page 399.
Inventory taken Nov. 30, 1831, by Samuel Close and Thomas A. Mead, and copied on page 399.

Peck, Moses, late of Greenwich, Mch. 11, 1829, letters of administration on his estate granted to Samuel Peck, Jr., of Greenwich, who was ordered to advertise for claims, page 27.
Inventory taken by Asahel Palmer and Nathaniel Adams, and filed Aug. 28, 1829, page 153.

Peck, Samuel, late of North Castle, Apl. 8, 1831, letters of administration on his estate granted to Joshua Smith of North Castle, page 399.

Penoyer, James H., about 15 years of age, and Richard Smith Penoyer, under 14 years of age, of Darien, Oct. 8, 1829, their guardian Isaac Penoyer of Darien discharged, and Noah Weed of New Canaan appointed in his place, page 138.

Pine, Samuel, late of Rye, N. Y., will dated Mch. 4, 1828, probated Oct. 27, 1832, mentions his daughters Sarah wife of Underhill Purdy, and Hannah, son James, and mother Sarah Pine. Executors Merritt Brown, Jesse Slauson, and son James. Witnesses Minott Mitchell, William H. Thorne, and Charles T. Cromwell, page 425. Oct. 31, 1832, order to advertise for claims, page 426. Inventory taken Nov. 3, 1832, by Thomas Green and

STAMFORD PROBATE RECORDS.
Volume 14, 1828.

Pine, Samuel, continued :
    Platt Mead, and filed Dec. 4, 1832, page 428.

Purdy, Elias, late of Greenwich, Dec. 16, 1828, letters of administration on his estate granted to his widow, Clara Purdy, who was ordered to advertise for claims, page 33.
    Inventory taken Dec. 19, 1828, by Gilbert Close and Isaac Peck, Jr., and filed Feb. 2, 1829, page 33.

Raymond, Munson G., late of Darien, Nov. 13, 1826, letters of administration on his estate granted to his widow, Sally Raymond, who was ordered to advertise for claims, page 94.
    Inventory taken Nov. 29, 1826, by Henry Bates and Samuel Whiting, and filed Dec. 4, 1826, page 94.
    Mch. 3, 1828, account filed, and necessaries allowed his widow, page 95.
    Mch. 29, 1833, account filed, and estate ordered distributed to his widow, and children, viz: Charles F., Ann Elizabeth Jelliff, Julia A., Sally S., William A., Samuel M., and Mary J., page 476.
    Estate distributed to his widow Sally Raymond, and his children as aforesaid, page 476.

Raymond, Sally Ann, of Stamford, over 14 years of age, Sept. 17, 1833, made choice of Joseph White of Stamford to be her guardian, page 445.

Raymond, Stephen, late of Darien, will dated Dec. 12, 1827, probated Jan. 14, 1828, mentions his wife Mary and children Sylvanus S., Stephen, Sally Selleck, Betsy Bell, Susan Carr, Delia Raymond, Fanny Lockwood, and grandson James Raymond a son of James a deceased son. Executors son Sylvanus S., and son-in-law Jacob Lockwood. Witnesses William H. Weed, Charles B. Weed, and John V. Green, page 18.
    Jan. 14, 1828, order to advertise for claims, page 19.
    Inventory taken Jan. 26, 1828, by Samuel Whiting and John Bell, and filed Feb. 29, 1828, page 19.

Reynolds, Ambrose, late of Greenwich, will dated Apl. 8, 1825, probated Jan. 22, 1831, mentions his wife Mary, and children Sally Husted, Polly Reynolds, Bethia Reynolds, Eunice Reynolds, Jared, and Benjamin, other children previously provided for. Executors sons Jared and Benjamin. Witnesses David Holly, Jr., Charles D. Hoyt, and Charles Hawley, page 258.

STAMFORD PROBATE RECORDS.
Volume 14, 1828.

Reynolds, Ambrose, continued :
    Jan. 22, 1831, order to advertise for claims, page 260.
    Inventory taken Mch. 21, 1831, by Samuel Peck and
    Jonathan A. Close, and filed Mch. 21, 1831, page 260.

Reynolds, Deborah, late of North Castle, Westchester County,
    N. Y., widow of Sylvanus Reynolds, late of Bedford,
    will dated May 2, 1820, probated July 12, 1832, estate to her brother Nathan Merritt, to the children of
    brother Joseph Merritt, deceased, to the children of
    brother Jotham Merritt, deceased, sister Molly wife of
    Gabriel Manning, sister Amy wife of Jesse Baker, and
    sister Ruth widow of Thomas Wilson, deceased. Executor her brother Nathan Merritt. Witnesses Caleb Merritt, Jr., Elizabeth Merritt, and Charity B. Merritt,
    page 401.
    Codicil dated Sept. 30, 1823, page 402.
    July 12, 1832, order to advertise for claims, page 403.

Reynolds, Debory, late of Greenwich, July 23, 1832, inventory
    taken by Thomas Green and Platt Mead, and filed Sept.
    3, 1832, by Benjamin Isaacs, executor, page 497.

Reynolds, James H., late of Greenwich, Mch. 29, 1833, his
    widow refused to qualify, and letters of administration
    on his estate granted to William H. Mead, and commissioners appointed to adjust claims of creditors, pages
    502 and 503.
    Inventory taken May 6, 1833, by Zenas Mead and William
    H. Mead, and filed Aug. 23, 1833, page 503.

Reynolds, Lockwood, late of Greenwich, will dated Jan. 11,
    1827, probated June 21, 1827, mentions his wife Catherine, and children Augustus L. and Julia, owned land
    in Chester, Warren County, N. Y. Executor son Augustus L. Witnesses Ezekiel Reynolds, Jr., Nathaniel
    Briggs, Jr., and Ard Reynolds, page 126.
    Codicil dated Mch. 8, 1827, page 128.
    June 21, 1827, order to advertise for claims, page 129.
    Inventory taken June 27, 1827, by Jared Smith and
    Ephraim Marshall, and filed Aug. 7, 1827, page 130.
    Apl. 21, 1828, necessaries allowed for the support of
    his family, page 132.

Rich, Lemuel, late of Greenwich, Jan. 22, 1827, his widow refused to qualify, and letters of administration on his
    estate granted to Asahel Palmer of Greenwich, who was
    ordered to advertise for claims, page 115.

STAMFORD PROBATE RECORDS.
Volume 14, 1828.

Rich, Lemuel, continued :
    Inventory taken by Henry Whelpley and Frederick Lockwood, and filed Feb. 3, 1827, page 115.
    Jan. 26, 1828, time for settlement extended, page 116.
    Mch. 27, 1828, necessaries allowed for the support of his family, page 116.
    Mch. 27, 1828, account filed, and estate ordered distributed to his widow Susan, and children Maria wife of Thomas Wilson, Sophia wife of Jacob Morrell, Polly Hughes, Abraham Rich, and the heirs at law of Sarah, deceased wife of George A. Smith, page 116.
    Apl. 1828, estate distributed accordingly, page 117.

Rogers, Fitch, late of Stamford, will dated Nov. 20, 1826, and redated Apl. 7, 1828, probated July 5, 1828, mentions his wife Hannah, and children Catherine Sherwood, Harriet, Fitch, and Emily S. Rogers, and son-in-law John S. Winthrop. Executors his wife, John W. Holly, and Seymour Jarvis. Witnesses Ann Gilbert and John W. Leeds, page 76.
    Codicil dated Dec. 18, 1826, page 77.
    July 5, 1828, order to advertise for claims, page 77.

Rowell, William, late of Greenwich, will dated Mch. 9, 1831, probated Aug. 2, 1831, mentions his children Permelia Brett, Stratton, Abraham, Daniel, Elizabeth Brett, and Mary Brundage, granddaughter Harriet Adams. Executor son-in-law Gilbert Brett. Witnesses Thomas Purdy, Bartow F. White, and John Purdy, page 336.
    Aug. 2, 1831, order to advertise for claims, page 337.
    Inventory taken Aug. 3, 1831, by Obadiah Mead and Benoni Peck, and filed Aug. 4, 1831, page 337.

Rundle, Charles, late of   Nov. 10, 1826, necessaries allowed for the support of his family, page 115.

Sackett, Justus, late of Greenwich, will dated June 23, 1813, probated June 30, 1828, mentions his wife Ann, and children Mary Brown, Sally Secor, Betsy Wilson, Justus, William Henry, and John. Executors sons Justus, William and John. Witnesses Richard Mead, Jerusha Davenport and Ebenezer Davenport, page 79.
    June 30, 1828, order to advertise for claims, page 81.
    Inventory taken by Alvan Mead and Thomas A. Mead, and filed Aug. 8, 1828, page 81.
    May 5, 1831, additional inventory, page 328.
    June 16, 1830, dower of his widow ordered set out, and on June 29, 1830, set out, page 206.

STAMFORD PROBATE RECORDS.
Volume 14, 1828.

Sackett, Justus, continued:
    Sale of real estate by his executors, Calves Island to Joseph Brush, and other parcels to Augustus Lyon, and Elisha B. Sackett, David Mead, Jr., and report of sale filed June 6, 1831, page 328.

St. John, Ezra, late of   Sept. 5, 1827, real estate sold to David Barnum of Stamford and William Webb of Stamford, and report of sale filed, page 82.

Sands, John, of Greenwich, July 9, 1832, appointed guardian of his daughter Mary Elizabeth Sands about 5 years of age, page 372.

Scofield, Darius K., late of Darien, Mch. 31, 1828, his widow refused to qualify, and letters of administration on his estate granted to Lewis Weed of Norwalk, who was ordered to advertise for claims, page 1.
    Inventory taken Apl. 12, 1828, by John Bell and Henry Bates, and filed Apl. 22, 1828, page 1.
    Apl. 6, 1828, time for settlement extended, page 3.
    Mch. 22, 1830, his widow, Sally Scofield, of Darien, appointed guardian of her son George Warren Scofield, page 190.
    Mch. 22, 1830, account filed, and estate ordered distributed to his widow, Sally Scofield, and to his only child George W. Scofield, page 180.
    Mch. 25, 1830, estate distributed accordinly, page 181.

Scofield, Ezra, Jr., late of Stamford, Aug. 13, 1831, letters of administration on his estate granted to Abisha Scofield of Stamford, who was ordered to advertise for claims, page 342.
    Inventory taken by Seth Buxton and Isaac Scofield, and filed Jan. 26, 1832, page 342.

Scofield, Ezra, late of Darien, July 27, 1832, Rheua Elizabeth, Catherine, Charles N., Sidney, and Esther A., children of decedent, made choice of their brother William R. Scofield of Darien to be their guardian, who was also appointed guardian of Mary and Henry other children of decedent, page 396.
    Sept. 10, 1832, petition for leave to sell the real estate of said minors given to them by the will of Nathaniel Clock, deceased, and sale ordered, page 412.
    Real estate sold to Lewis Richards of Troy, N. Y., and report of sale filed Nov. 27, 1832, page 413.

STAMFORD PROBATE RECORDS.
Volume 14, 1828.

Scofield, Gideon, late of Stamford, will dated -----, probated
Oct. 11, 1828, all to his wife Eliza. Executor Jotham Hoyt. Witnesses Hezekiah Bishop, Henry Knapp, and Betsy Knapp, page 22.
Oct. 11, 1828, order to advertise for claims, page 22.
Inventory taken Oct. 18, 1828, by Peter Lockwood and Hezekiah Bishop, and filed Mch. 18, 1829, page 23.

Scofield, Hannah, wife of Elijah Scofield of New Canaan, Mary wife of James Studwell of Stamford, Catherine Scofield of Stamford, and Emmeline Smith of Stamford, a minor, owners in equal shares in common of real estate in Stamford, and desire a partition thereof, Feb. 9, 1833, Anna Seely, mother of said Emmeline, petitioned the court for assistance in making such partition, and commissioners were appointed to make partition, and partition made accordingly, page 480.

Scofield, John, late of Stamford, will dated Aug. 3, 1826, probated Apl. 27, 1833, mentions his wife Martha, and children James, John, Silas, Robert, deceased, Elisabeth deceased wife of Rufus Knapp, Susannah Bishop, and her children Leander, Alfred, and Morris. Executors his sons John and Silas. Witnesses Abigail Scofield, Martha Lounsbury, and Charles Hawley, page 504.
Apl. 27, 1833, order to advertise for claims, page 505.

Scofield, Julia, of Stamford, over 12 years of age, Jan. 28, 1833, made choice of Fitch Rogers to be her guardian, page 417.

Scofield, Nathan H., late of Stamford, Aug. 23, 1832, his widow refused to qualify, and letters of administration on his estate granted to William Scofield, Jr., of Stamford, and commissioners appointed to adjust claims of creditors, pages 450 and 451.
Inventory taken Aug. 29, 1832, by Augustus Scofield and Ezra Dibble, and filed Aug. 29, 1832, page 450.
Mch. 22, 1833, report of commissioners to adjust claims filed, page 451.
Mch. 2, 1833, personal property ordered sold to pay debts, page 452.
Mch. 22, 1833, necessaries allowed his widow, page 453.
Mch. 22, 1833, account filed, and real estate ordered sold to pay debts, page 452.
Real estate sold to George Rosborough, Augustus Scofield, and Horace Scofield, and report of sale filed Apl. 6, 1833, page 452.

STAMFORD PROBATE RECORDS.
Volume 14, 1828.

Scofield, Peter, late of Stamford, will dated July 24, 1806, probated June 14, 1830, mentions his wife Hannah, and children Warren, Walter, Peter, Jr., Clara wife of Richard Fox, and Sarah wife of Thomas June. Executor his son Warren. Witnesses Ebenezer Davenport, Jerusha Davenport, and Mary Davenport, page 216.
1st codicil dated Aug. 25, 1806, page 217.
2nd codicil dated Aug. 17, 1807, page 218.
3rd codicil dated Mch. 20, 1811, page 218.
4th codicil dated Aug. 20, 1827, wife now deceased, page 219.
June 14, 1830, order to advertise for claims, page 220.
Inventory taken June 15, 1830, by James Davenport and Isaac Scofield, and filed June 18, 1830, page 221.

Scofield, Robert, late of Stamford, Mch. 19, 1828, estate ordered distributed to his devisees according to his will, viz: to his widow Hannah, and his surviving children George, James Bell, Holly, Oliver, Robert, Eliza wife of Ezra Lockwood, Sally wife of Israel Lockwood, Emily Scofield, and Hannah Scofield, Darius Scofield being now deceased, page 306.
Mch. 18, 1828, estate distributed accordingly, page 306.

Scofield, Samuel, late of Stamford, will dated Aug. 24, 1822, probated Jan. 28, 1832, mentions his wife Barbara. Executor his son Elijah Scofield of New Canaan. Witnesses William Davenport, Isaac W. Jones, and Chauncey S. Stevens, page 399.
Jan. 28, 1832, order to advertise for claims, page 400.
Apl. 28, 1832, commissioners appointed to adjust claims of creditors, page 401.
Feb. 7, 1832, inventory taken by James Davenport and Abishai Scofield, and filed Aug. 21, 1832, page 411.
Jan. 24, 1833, report of commissioners to adjust claims filed, page 412.

Seely, John, late of Stamford, Mch. 13, 1832, letters of administration on his estate granted to his son John Seely, who was ordered to advertise for claims, page 398.
Inventory taken by Gould Raymond and Enoch Stevens, and filed Apl. 2, 1832, page 398.
July 6, 1833, account filed, and necessaries allowed his widow, page 494.

Seely, Selleck, late of Darien, June 18, 1832, account filed by his executor, and real estate ordered sold to pay debts, page 462.

STAMFORD PROBATE RECORDS.
Volume 14, 1828.

Seely, Selleck, continued :
Real estate sold to Mary Seely, and report of sale
filed Dec. 21, 1832, page 462.

Seely, Wyx, late of Darien, will dated 26th day 9th month,
1829, probated Oct. 6, 1829, mentions his wife Phebe,
and children Elisha, the children of Selleck, deceased,
Elizabeth Reed, Phebe Riblet, Catherine, and Mary.
Executors Abram Clock and Albert Seely. Witnesses
Stephen Ferris, Epenetus W. Walmsley, and John Ferris,
page 144.
Oct. 6, 1829, order to advertise for claims, page 145.
Inventory taken by John Bell and Joseph Weed, and filed Nov. 13, 1829, page 164.

Selleck, Raymond, late of Darien, Sept. 26, 1831, Stephen R.
Selleck 14 years of age, a son of decedent, made choice
of John Ferris of Darien to be his guardian, who was
also appointed guardian of Mary Selleck eight years if
age, page 344.

Selleck, Stephen, late of Darien, Sept. 8, 1829, his widow
refused to qualify, and letters of administration
on his estate granted to Epenetus W. Walmsley of Darien
who was ordered to advertise for claims, page 145.
Inventory taken Oct. 1, 1829, by Henry Bates and Thomas Reed, and filed Oct. 26, 1829, page 146.
Mch. 31, 1831, account filed, and estate ordered distributed to his widow, and his heirs at law, viz: Ann
Selleck, Polly wife of Epenetus W. Walmsley, Hannah
wife of Stephen Hoyt, daughters of deceased, and to
Stephen R. Selleck and Mary Selleck, children of Raymond Selleck, deceased, and grandchildren of said
deceased, page 352.
Aug. 13, 1831, estate distributed accordingly, page 352.
Feb. 27, 1830, dower of his widow, Letitia Selleck,
ordered set out, page 182.
Mch. 30, 1830, dower set out, page 183.

Seymour, Drake, late of Greenwich, Dec. 2, 1830, his heirs at
the time of his death were Mary Seymour, Susan Seymour,
Delia wife of James Tillot, Sabrina B. wife of Peter
Tillot, and Sarah H. wife of Samuel Annan, and said
Mary having died since the decease of said Drake, distribution ordered of the estate of said Drake and said
Mary to the aforesaid Susan, Delia, Sabrina, and Sarah,
page 286.
Dec. 23, 1830, estate distributed accordingly, page 287.

STAMFORD PROBATE RECORDS.
Volume 14, 1828.

Seymour, Mary, late of Greenwich, Mch. 24, 1830, letters of administration on her estate granted to Samuel Arman, the husband of a sister of deceased, who was ordered to advertise for claims, page 184.
May 19, 1830, inventory taken by Thomas A. Mead, and Alvan Mead, and filed Apl. 6, 1830, page 238.

Shaw, Andrew, late of Darien, Mch. 30, 1832, his widow refused to qualify, and letters of administration on his estate granted to Cary Bell of Darien, who was ordered to advertise for claims, page 378.
Inventory taken by Holly Bell and George Walmsley, and filed Apl. 7, 1832, page 379.
Dec. 13, 1832, account filed, and real estate ordered sold to pay debts, page 462.
Real estate sold to Lucy Walmsley and Sylvanus B. Thompson, and report of sale filed, Feb. 9, 1833, page 463.
Dec. 13, 1832, necessaries allowed his widow, page 463.

Shaw, Hannah, late of Darien, Feb. 4, 1833, letters of administration on her estate granted to Shadrach Hoyt, husband of Hannah the only surviving child of decedent, who was ordered to advertise for claims, page 442.
Inventory taken Feb. 5, 1833, by Joseph Hoyt and George Walmsley, and filed Feb. 7, 1833, page 442.
July 4, 1833, Shadrach Hoyt now deceased, and letters de bonus non granted to George Walmsley of Darien, page 492.

Shaw, James, late of Darien, Dec. 17, 1828, his widow refused to qualify, and letters of administration on his estate granted to John Bell of Darien, who was ordered to advertise for claims, page 56.
Inventory taken Dec. 19, 1828, by Abram Clock and Joseph Hoyt, and filed copied on page 56.
Mch. 8, 1830, account filed, and necessaries allowed his widow, and on Apl. 10, 1830, dower set out, page 168.
Apl. 8, 1830, account filed, and real estate ordered sold to pay debts, page 229.
Sept. 13, 1830, real estate sold to Andrew Shaw and Shadrach Hoyt, page 229.

Shaw, Mary C., of Darien, over 14 years of age, Feb. 8, 1833, made choice of her mother Louisa W. Shaw of Darien to be her guardian, who was also appointed guardian of her other children James A. Shaw, William F. Shaw, and Frederick L. Shaw, under 14 years of age, page 439.

STAMFORD PROBATE RECORDS.
Volume 14, 1826.

Sherwood, Daniel, late of Greenwich, will dated May 14, 1826, probated June 8, 1826, mentions his children Hungerford, Daniel, Willet, Hannah Anderson, Mary Miller, Ann Sherwood, Sally Parrott, and Fanny Kirk, grandson William B. Sherwood; Hannah Sherwood a daughter of Jabez Sherwood; granddaughter Hannah Reed Peck a daughter of Benjamin Peck. Executors Platt Mead and Jared Strang. Witnesses Joseph Taylor, Read Peck, and Thomas A. Nash, page 34.
June 8, 1826, order to advertise for claims, page 35.
Inventory taken June 12, 1826, by Thomas Green and William Husted, and filed June 16, 1826, pages 35 and 36.
Mch. 19, 1827, account filed, and real estate ordered sold to pay debts, page 36.
Apl. 2, 1827, real estate sold to David Brown, page 37.
Apl. 4, 1827, reappraisal of real estate ordered, page 37.
Apl. 14, 1827, reappraisal filed, page 38.
Apl. 14, 1827, his sons consent to take the real estate at the reappraisement value, page 38.

Slason, Betsy, late of Darien, Nov. 1, 1830, letters of administration on her estate granted to William Andreas of Darien, who was ordered to advertise for claims, page 330.
Inventory taken Nov. 4, 1830, by John Bell and Jeremiah Andreas, and filed Dec. 23, 1830, page 330.
May 16, 1831, commissioners appointed to adjust claims of creditors, page 331.
Nov. 21, 1831, report of commissioners filed, page 331.
Dec. 10, 1831, account filed, and real estate ordered sold to pay debts, page 332.
Jan. 14, 1832, report of sale filed, page 332.

Slawson, Daniel, late of   Apl. 24, 1826, his widow, Betsy Slawson, accepted the provisions of his will, page 13.

Smith, Hanford M., late of Stamford, Aug. 30, 1827, his widow refused to qualify, and letters of administration on his estate granted to Augustus Lockwood of Stamford, and Alexander Hendrie of Greenwich, and commissioners appointed to adjust claims of creditors, page 42.
Inventory taken Sept. 1, 1827, by Isaac Lockwood and Daniel Lockwood, and filed Sept. 13, 1827, page 43.
Sept. 3, 1827, order to sell said estate, and report of sale filed, page 45.
Oct. 15, 1828, report of commissioners to adjust claims

STAMFORD PROBATE RECORDS.
Volume 14, 1828.

Smith, Hanford M., continued:
    filed, page 45.
    Oct. 7, 1828, necessaries allowed his widow, page 47.

Smith, Henry, late of Greenwich, Mch. 19, 1829, letters of administration on his estate granted to Solomon Studwell, who was ordered to advertise for claims, page 26.
    Inventory taken by Stephen Waring and Ephraim Marshall, and filed May 2, 1829, page 25.
    Mch. 19, 1830, account filed by his administrator, and estate ordered distributed to his heirs at law, viz: Isaac Smith, a brother, Hannah Smith, Fanny Studwell, and Betsy Denton, sisters, and to the heirs of John Smith, a deceased brother, page 185.
    Apl. 18, 1830, estate distributed accordingly, page 186.

Smith, Isaac, late of Stamford, Dec. 4, 1827, his widow refused to qualify, and letters of administration on his estate granted to Epenetus W. Nichols and Isaac M. Smith of Stamford, who were ordered to advertise for claims, page 26.
    Inventory taken by Isaac Lockwood and Royal L. Gay, and filed Sept. 18, 1830, page 234.

Smith, Isaac, late of Stamford, July 14, 1831, on the application of Peter Smith, 3rd, husband of Rheua, a daughter of deceased, estate ordered distributed to his widow, ------, and children viz: Isaac M., William H., Charles E., Rheua, and Mary Smith, page 366.
    July 30, 1831, estate distributed accordingly, page 367.

Smith, John, late of Stamford, Mch. 19, 1830, Betsy Ann Smith, about 12 years of age, a daughter of decedent, made choice of Abel Reynolds to be her guardian, page 193.
    Abigail Smith, about 12 years of age, a daughter of decedent, made choice of Solomon Clason of Stamford to be her guardian, page 190.

Smith, John, late of Greenwich, Apl. 30, 1832, his widow refused to qualify, and letters of administration on his estate granted to Isaac Holly of Greenwich, who was ordered to advertise for claims, page 357.
    Inventory taken June 30, 1832, by Daniel Lyon, Jr., and Ephraim Marshall, and filed July 3, 1832, page 357.
    Jan. 14, 1833, account filed, and real estate ordered sold to pay debts, page 506.
    Real estate sold to Isaac Holly, Jr., and report of sale filed, Feb. 27, 1833, page 507.

STAMFORD PROBATE RECORDS.
Volume 14, 1828.

Smith, Josiah, late of Stamford, will dated Apl. 8, 1826, probated Dec. 16, 1830, mentions his wife Sarah, and children Earle, Josiah, Electa Hawley, Arney wife of Benjamin Hoyt, and Abigail wife of Samuel Nichols. Mentioned a parcel of land in Illinois in the tract approproated for military bounties. Executors his sons Earle and Josiah. Witnesses Isaac Lockwood, Smith Scott, and Charles Hawley, page 320.
Dec. 16, 1830, Order to advertise for claims, page 322.
Inventory taken Dec. 18, 1830, by Ebn. Smith and Isaac Lockwood, and filed Feb. 28, 1832, page 322.
Mch. 25, 1831 widow's dower ordered set out, page 325.
Apl. 9, 1831, dower set out, page 326.

Smith, Martha, late of Stamford, will dated Oct. 3, 1814, probated Dec. 29, 1832, mentions granddaughter Martha Smith, daughter of Eben Smith, grandson John Smith Studwell, deceased daughter Martha Newman, and other daughters not named. Executors Solomon Smith and Drake Studwell. Witnesses Daniel Nichols, Robert Nichols, and Benjamin~~Clawson~~, page 496. xClawson.
Dec. 29, 1832, Solomon Smith now deceased, Drake Studwell refused to quakify, and letters of administration with the will annexed granted to Solomon Clawson, who was ordered to advertise for claims, page 496.

Smith, Mary Esther, about 18 years of age, of Stamford, Apl. 13, 1830, her mother, Lydia Smith of Stamford, appointed her guardian, page 187.

Smith, Phebe Eleanor, pf Stamford, over 12 years of age, June 11, 1833, made choice of her mother, Lydia Smith, of Stamford to be her guardian, page 464.

Smith, William Harvey, late of Stamford, Sept. 22, 1831, letters of administration on his estate granted to Epenetus W. Nichols of Stamford, who was ordered to advertise for claims, page 369.
Inventory taken Sept. 22, 1831, by Royal L. Gay and Horace Waterbury, and filed Sept. 22, 1831, and Mch. 21, 1832, page 369.
June 8, 1832, estate ordered distributed to his brothers and sisters, viz: Isaac M. Smith, Mary Smith, Rheua wife of Peter Smith, 3rd, and Charles E. Smith, page 370.
June 15, 1832, estate distributed accordingly, page 370.
Mch. 30, 1832, account filed, and realestate ordered

STAMFORD PROBATE RECORDS.
Volume 14, 1828.

Smith, William Harvey, continued:
    sold to pay debts, page 510.
    Real estate sold to Isaac M. Smith, and report of sale filed Mch. 23, 1833, page 510.

Stebbins, David, late of New York City, Mch. 22, 1832, petition of Edward Corning of New York City, father and natural guardian of Jasper Corning and James Corning, sons of Elizabeth C., a daughter of decedent, for leave to sell the real estate of said minors in Stamford, and sale ordered, page 414.
    Also as guardian of Jane B. Stebbins, a daughter of decedent, and sale ordered, page 415.

Stevens, Jacob, late of Stamford, Nov. 14, 1829, letters of administration on his estate granted to Selleck Scofield and Gould Raymond of Stamford, who were ordered to advertise for claims, page 172.
    Feb. 7, 1830, commissioners appointed to adjust claims of creditors, page 172.
    Inventory taken Feb. 28, 1828, by Isaac Ayres and John Seely, Jr., and filed Jan. 27, 1830, page 302.
    Dec. 23, 1830, report of commissioners to adjust claims filed, page 304.
    Feb. 23, 1831, account filed, and necessaries allowed his widow, page 305.
    Mch. 2, 1831, account filed, and real estate ordered sold to pay debts, page 305.
    Real estate sold to Jonathan Dan, Edmond Scofield, Richard M. Raymond, and Jacob Stevens, and report of sale filed, Apl. 29, 1831, page 305.

Stivers, James, late of Greenwich, Nov. 19, 1832, his widow refused to qualify, and letters of administration on his estate granted to his son James Edward Stivers of North Castle, who was ordered to advertise for claims, page 429.
    Inventory taken Dec. 6, 1832, by Thomas Carpenter and Oliver Mathews, and filed June 10, 1833, page 429.

Swan, Walter, late of Greenwich, July 5, 1827, time for settlement extended, page 4.
    Mch. 28, 1829, account filed, and real estate ordered sold to pay debts, page 197.
    Real estate sold to Robert Cox of Stamford and Eliza Swan, and report of sale filed, page 197.
    June 13, 1829, dower of his widow ordered set out, and dower set out, page 171.

STAMFORD PROBATE RECORDS.
Volume 14, 1828.

Taylor, Joseph, late of Greenwich, June 29, 1832, Sally M. Taylor, Cynthia G. Taylor, and George Taylor, children of decedent, over 14 years of age, made choice of James Wilson of Greenwich to be their guardian, who was also appointed guardian of Merritt G. Taylor another child of decedent, page 344.
June 29, 1832, petition for leave to sell the real estate of said minors in Greenwich, and sale ordered, page 416.
Real estate sold to William Mosier of Greenwich, and report of sale filed Oct. 8, 1832, page 416.

Tillman, John, late of Stamford, Apl. 27, 1832, Ann S. Tillman, parent and guardian of Mary C., Elizabeth Ann, and John H. Tillman, children of decedent, asked for leave to sell the real estate of said minors in Stamford, and sale ordered, page 301.
Real estate sold to Solomon Guernsey, and report of sale filed July 18, 1832, page 302.

Titus, Mary H., about 16 years of age, and Susan K. Titus, about 14 years of age, of Greenwich, Apl. 13, 1829, made choice of Benjamin Isaacs of Bedford, N. Y., to be their guardian in place of Jabez Mead, discharged, page 59.

Tracy, Hezekiah, late of Greenwich, Aug. 10, 1827, his widow refused to qualify, and letters of administration on his estate granted to his son John Jay Tracy of Greenwich, who was ordered to advertise for claims, pages 135 and 141.
Inventory taken Aug. 21, 1827, by Stephen Waring and Alvan Mead, and filed Sept. 8, 1827, page 135.
Mch. 15, 1830, Horatio Nelson Tracy, over 14 years of age, a son of decedent, made choice of his mother Huldah Tracy to be his guardian, page 187.
Mch. 15, 1830, account filed, and estate ordered distributed to his widow, Huldah Tracy, and children John Jay Tracy, and Horatio Nelson Tracy, page 187.
Estate distributed accordingly, page 188.

Wardwell, James, late of Darien, will dated Sept. 29, 1829, probated Dec. 23, 1830, all to his wife Hannah for life, remainder to his children Sally wife of Isaac Northrup, and Abigail wife of Joseph Judson. Executrix his wife. Witnesses Abram Cleek, Charles Lockwood, and Cary H. Gray, page 263.
Dec. 23, 1830, his widow refused to qualify, and let-

STAMFORD PROBATE RECORDS.
Volume 14, 1828.

Wardwell, James, continued :
    ters granted to Thaddeus Hoyt of Darien, who was ordered to advertise for claims, page 263.
    Inventory taken Dec. 25, 1830, by Henry Weed and William Andreas, and filed Feb. 24, 1831, page 263.

Waring, Henry, late of Greenwich, June 14, 1831, letters of administration on his estate granted to his son Stephen Waring of Greenwich, who was ordered to advertise for claims, page 288.

Waring, Samuel, late of Darien, June 17, 1826, dower of his widow set out, page 406.
    June 23, 1826, account filed, and real estate ordered sold to pay debts, page 119.
    Real estate sold to Jacob Lockwood of Darien, and report of sale filed, page 119.

Waring, Scudder, late of Stamford, will dated Sept. 27, 1827, probated Nov. 1, 1830, all to his wife Abigail. Executor Isaac Ayres. Witnesses Smith R. Sibley, Charlotte Brown, and Jemima H. Miller, page 267.
    Nov. 1, 1830, the executor refused to qualify, and letters granted to Isaac Ayres and Smith R. Sibley, and commissioners appointed to adjust claims of creditors, pages 267 and 268.
    Inventory taken Nov. 4, 1830, by John Husted and Selleck Scofield, and filed Dec. 23, 1830, page 268.
    July 21, 1831, report of commissioners filed, page 270.
    July 21, 1831, necessaries allowed his widow, page 271.
    July 21, 1831, account filed, and real estate ordered sold to pay debts, page 271.
    Aug. 24, 1831, real estate sold to Nathan White, Abigail Brown, and James Searles, page 271.
    Aug. 24, 1831, report of sale filed, page 272.

Waterbury, Amos H., of Stamford, Jan. 27, 1829, general assignment to William H. Holly of Stamford for the benefir of creditors, page 5.
    Inventory taken Jan. 29, 1829, by Joseph Hoyt and Aaron R. Bartram, and filed Feb. 26, 1829, page 7.
    Mch. 16, 1829, commissioners appointed to adjust claims of creditors, page 7.
    Oct. 24, 1829, report of commissioners filed, page 132.
    Mch. 20, 1829, personal property ordered sold, page 134.
    Nov. 7, 1829, personal property sold, page 134.
    Nov. 7, 1829, account filed, page 208.
    June 16, 1830, real estate sold to Harvey Nash, and Samuel Braden of Stamford, and report of sale filed,

STAMFORD PROBATE RECORDS.
Volume 14, 1828.

Waterbury, Amos H., continued :
    page 209.
    June 16, 1830, creditors ordered paid 2 8/10 cents on the dollar, page 209.

Waterbury, John, late of Darien, Apl. 12, 1830, his widow refused to qualify, and letters of administration on his estate granted to William H. Holly of Stamford, who was ordered to advertise for claims, page 196.
    May 1, 1830, inventory taken by John Leeds and Josiah Lockwood, and filed July 28, 1830, page 223.
    Apl. 29, 1830, account filed and commissioners appointed to adjust claims of creditors, page 224.
    Dec. 14, 1830, time for commissioners to report extended, page 373.
    July 25, 1831, report of commissioners filed, page 373.
    Apl. 29, 1831, review of said report asked for by Daniel Bostwick of New Canaan, page 374.
    July 29, 1831, claim of said Daniel Bostwick confirmed, page 374.
    Sept. 2, 1831, real estate ordered sold to pay debts, page 375.
    Sept. 20, 1831, real estate sold to Peter Waterbury of Darien, Holly Bell of Darien, George Weed of Darien, and on Oct. 5, 1831, to Ebenezer Hoyt, and report of sale filed Mch. 20, 1832, page 375.
    Sept. 2, 1831, account approved, page 376.

Waterbury, William, late of Stamford, will dated Sept. 10, 1829, probated Sept. 23, 1830, mentions his wife Mary, and children Ebenezer, Rufus, Henry, William, deceased, Samuel deceased, Mary Scofield, Sarah Adams, Betsy Weeks, and Nancy Kirby. Executor son-in-law Stephen Kirby. Witnesses Seymour Jarvis, Jerusha E. Gilbert, and Simson H. Minor, page 240.
    Sept. 23, 1830, the executor refused to qualify, and letters of administration with the will annexed granted to Testator's widow Mary, and John Brown of Stamford, who were ordered to advertise for claims, page 240
    Inventory taken by Cary H. Leeds and Isaac Vardwell, and filed Nov. 29, 1830, page 340.
    Aug. 18, 1831, account filed, and necessaries allowed his widow, page 341.
    May 7, 1831, his widow, Mary Waterbury, refused the provisions in his will in lieu of dower, and commissioners appointed to set out dower, page 341.
    Mch. 1832, dower set out, page 342.

STAMFORD PROBATE RECORDS.
Volume 14, 1828.

Webb, Mary, late of Stamford, Aug. 2, 1833, letters of administration on her estate granted to Henry Waterbury of Darien, who was ordered to advertise for claims, page 497.
Inventory filed Aug. 3, 1833, page 497.

Webb, Samuel, Dr., late of Stamford, Jan. 19, 1827, his widow refused to qualify, and letters of administration on his estate granted to Seymour Jarvis and William H. Holly of Stamford, who were ordered to advertise for claims, page 106.
Inventory taken Jan. 26, 1827, by David Hoyt and Peter Smith, Jr., and filed Feb. 10, 1827, pages 106 and 109.
May 1, 1828, necessaries allowed for the support of his family, page 109.
Mch. 10, 1828, James., &Lucy P., children of decedent, made choice of William Henry Webb to be their guardian, who was also appointed guardian of Frances W. and Elizabeth, other children of decedent, page 109.

Webb, Wilse, late of Darien, will dated Feb. 25, 1829, probated Apl. 12, 1831, mentions his wife Hannah, and children Philander, Isaac, and Mary Sheffield. Executor Hezekiah Scofield. Witnesses John Weed, Jr., William Webb, and Samuel Beach, page 296.
Apl. 12, 1831, order to advertise for claims, page 297.
Inventory taken Apl. 16, 1831, by Joseph Hoyt and Alfred Webb, and filed Apl. 29, 1831, page 297.

Weed, Abigail, late of Stamford, will dated July 4, 1828, probated Aug. 28, 1828, mentions her niece Lavinia wife of Caleb Knapp of Stamford, nephews Thomas Marshall and Gilbert Marshall, niece Sally Howe of Darien the daughter of Jacob Howe. Executor Jotham Hoyt of Stamford Witnesses Ralph Hoyt, Leander Hoyt, and Nathaniel D. Haight, page 78.
Sept. 4, 1828, order to advertise for claims, page 79.

Weed, Asahel, late of   Mch. 12, 1827, account filed by his executors, and real estate ordered sold to pay debts, page 24.
Mch. 26, 1827, real estate sold to Seth Miller and John Dean, and report of sale filed, page 24.

Weed, Enos, late of Stamford, Oct. 21, 1828, letters of administration on his estate granted to his son Daniel H. Weed, and commissioners appointed to adjust claims of creditors, page 14.
Inventory taken Oct. 21, 1828, by Richard Fox and Sam-

STAMFORD PROBATE RECORDS.
Volume 14, 1828.

Weed, Enos, continued:
uel Weed, and filed Nov. 15, 1828, page 14.
July 4, 1829, report of commissioners filed, page 15.
Nov. 5, 1828, account filed, and personal property ordered sold, page 243.
Nov. 24, 1829, personal property sold, and report of sale filed, page 243.
Dec. 17, 1829, account filed, and real estate ordered sold to pay debts, page 185.
Mch. 10, 1830, real estate sold to Lydia Smith, page 185.

Weed, Gideon, late of Darien, Feb. 28, 1826, that part of his estate set off to his widow as her dower, she being now deceased, distributed to his children viz: Daty, Selleck, Abraham, Jacob, Gideon, Isaac, Martha wife of Epenetus Lounsbury, Hannah wife of James Wardell, and Abigail Waterbury, page 63.

Weed, Hannah, widow, late of Stamford, will dated Oct. 13, 1822, probated Apl. 29, 1828, devised to her brother Amos Scofield house and lot, and rest, residue and remainder to all her heirs at law. Executor brother Amos Scofield. Witnesses John Weed, Sally Weed, and Reuben Scofield, page 48.
Apl. 29, 1828, order to advertise for claims, page 49.
Inventory taken May 12, 1828, by Warren Scofield and Isaac Scofield, and filed June 13, 1829, page 49.

Weed, Hannah, late of   June 13, 1829, account filed by her administrator C. T. A., and real estate ordered sold to pay debts, page 507.

Weed, Henry, late of Darien, June 21, 1831, Frederick A. Weed of New York City, a son of decedent, about 17 years of age, made choice of John J. Leeds to be his guardian, page 273.
June 13, 1831, Charles E. Weed of New York City appointed guardian of James Albert, and Theodore Eugene, other children of decedent, both under 14 years of age, page 273.

Weed, John, late of Stamford, Jan. 18, 1830, David Weed about 17 years of age, a son of decedent, made choice of John Scofield, 3rd, of Stamford to be his guardian, page 157.

Weed, Jonathan, late of Stamford, will dated Nov. 7, 1825, probated Dec. 1, 1826, mentions his children Erastus H.

STAMFORD PROBATE RECORDS.
Volume 14, 1828.

Weed, Jonathan, continued :
    Weed, Sarah E. Weed, Thirza Hoyt, and Lydia Secfield.
    Executors sons Erastus H. and Daniel A. Witnesses
    Gould Raymond, William H. Hawley, and S. H. Minor,
    page 53.
    Dec. 19, 1826, Erastus H. Weed and Daniel A. Weed re-
    fused to qualify, and letters granted to Erastus H.
    Weed and John Augur, who were ordered to advertise for
    claims, page 54.
    Inventory taken Dec. 19, 1826, by Abishai Scofield and
    Luther Weed, and filed Nov. 7, 1827, page 54.

Weed, Sarah, late of Darien, will dated Mch. 23, 1833, pro-
    bated Apl. 1, 1833, mentions her daughter Julia M.
    Weed, sons Frederick A. Weed, James A. Weed, and Theo-
    dore E. Weed. No executor. Witnesses S. H. Minor,
    William Leeds, and Eliza A. Leeds, page 469.
    Apl. 1, 1833, letters with the will annexed granted to
    Cary H. Gray of Stamford, who was ordered to advertise
    for claims, page 469.
    Inventory taken Apl. 9, 1833, by Joseph Hoyt and Daniel
    David B. Burr, and filed June 13, 1833, page 469.

Weed, Selleck, late of Darien, will dated Aug. 17, 1832, pro-
    bated Oct. 8, 1832, mentions his wife Mary, and Steph-
    en I. Patterson. Executor Henry C. Scribner of New
    Canaan. Witnesses Holly Bell, William Andreas, and
    Henry Weed, page 457.
    Oct. 8, 1832, order to advertise for claims, page 457.
    Inventory taken Oct. 15, 1832, by William Andreas and
    Holly Bell, and filed Nov. 3, 1832, page 457.
    Apl. 13, 1833, account filed, and real estate ordered
    sold to pay debts, page 495.
    Real estate sold to Mary Weed of Darien, widow of de-
    cedent, and report of sale filed June 27, 1833,
    page 495.

Weeks, Joseph H., of Stamford, Nov. 9, 1829, assignment for
    the benefit of creditors to William H. Holly, page 203.
    Inventory taken Nov. 14, 1829, by Davis Lockwood and
    Seely Miller, and filed Dec. 9, 1829, page 205.
    Nov. 27, 1829, commissioners appointed to adjust claims
    of creditors, page 205.
    Nov. 27, 1829, estate ordered sold, page 363.
    Estate sold, and report of sale filed, page 363.
    June 16, 1830, commissioners to adjust claims to con-
    tinue with their duties, page 210.
    Oct. 15, 1830, report of commissioners filed, page 230.

STAMFORD PROBATE RECORDS.
Volume 14, 1828.

Weeks, Joseph H., continued:
Nov. 29, 1830, account filed, and creditors ordered paid 30 cents and 9 mills on the dollar, page 245.

White, William, late of Stamford, will dated Nov. 19, 1819, probated Oct. 3, 1831, mentions his wife Susannah, and children William, Daniel, Nathaniel, Smith, Anson, Joseph, Benjamin, Betsy Wood, and Abigail Webb. Executor his son William. Witnesses Smith R. Sibley, Hetty Raymond, and John Scofield, page 285.
Oct. 3, 1831, order to advertise for claims, page 286.
Inventory taken by Selleck Scofield and Harvey Todd, and filed Dec. 5, 1831, page 294.

Whiting, Molly, late of Darien, Mch. 6, 1832, letters of administration on her estate granted to her son Jesse Whiting of Darien, who was ordered to advertise for claims, page 371.
Inventory taken by Abram Clock and Holly Bell, and filed Apl. 30, 1832, page 371.

Whiting, Samuel, late of Darien, will dated June 11, 1831, probated Mch. 6, 1832, mentions his children Hannah, Alice, Phebe, Mary, Maria, Elizabeth, Anne Carpenter, Harvey, and Jesse. Executors his sons Jesse and daughter Hannah. Witnesses Alvah Waterbury, Anson Waterbury, and Joseph Weed, page 371.
Mch. 6, 1832, order to advertise for claims, page 372.
Inventory taken by Abram Clock and Holly Bell, and filed Apl. 30, 1832, page 397.

Wilcox, William L., late of Greenwich, Nov. 1, 1832, letters of administration on his estate granted to James Green of Greenwich, who was ordered to advertise for claims, page 473.
Inventory taken Nov. 7, 1832, by Augustus Lyon and Odle Close, and filed Nov. 12, 1832, page 473.

Wilson, Thomas M., late of Rye, July 19, 1830, commissioners appointed to adjust claims of creditors, page 222.
Feb. 10, 1831, report of commissioners filed, page 406.

Wood, David, late of Greenwich, will dated Dec. 18, 1831, probated Jan. 14, 1832, mentions his wife Sally W., and children George, Silas, Frances Dodge, Julius L., Henry M., and David. Executors his wife and son Julius L. Witnesses Hugh Mackay, William Peck, and George Austin, page 379.

STAMFORD PROBATE RECORDS.
Volume 14, 1828.

Wood, David, continued:
    Jan. 30, 1832, order to advertise for claims, page 380.
    Inventory taken Feb. 13, 1832, by Edward Brush and
    Alfred Rundle, and filed Feb. 18, 1832, page 381.
    Dec. 10, 1832, his widow, Sally W. Wood, renounced
    the provisions in his will and applied for her dower,
    which was ordered set out, page 506.
    Jan. 9, 1833, dower set out, page 492.
    Jan. 26, 1833, account filed, and commissioners ap-
    pointed to adjust claims of creditors, pages 508 and
    509.

Wooden, Isaac, late of Stamford, will dated Nov. 7, 1830,
    probated Jan. 3, 1831, mentions his children Mary and
    her children, and Patrick Laurie the husband of said
    Mary. Executors brother Solomon Wooden, and nephews
    Daniel Fleet and James Fleet of Oyster Bay, and John
    Wood of Huntington. Witnesses Thomas Smith, Stephen
    Bayles, and Isaac Smith, Jr., page 241.
    Jan. 3, 1831, no record of any letters, page 242.
    May 9, 1831, John Wood of Huntington, L. I., and James
    Fleet of Oyster Bay, L. I., declined to qualify as ex-
    ecutors, page 295.
    Inventory taken Jan. 3, 1831, by Augustus Lockwood and
    Peter Smith, Jr., and filed May 27, 1831, page 295.

Wooden, Sarah, late of Stamford, will dated Nov. 15, 1827,
    probated May 1, 1829, mentions her daughter Mary Lau-
    rie, and son in law Patrick Laurie, and their chil-
    dren. Executors and trustees Simeon H. Minor and
    Thomas Hurtell. Witnesses Daniel Smith, Catharine
    Smith, and Mary Fox, page 250.
    Dec. 11, 1830, said Thomas Hurtell refused to qualify,
    and letters granted to Simeon H. Minor, who was or-
    dered to advertise for claims, page 251.
    Inventory taken Dec. 13, 1830, by Peter Smith, Jr.,
    and William H. Holly, and filed Jan. 22, 1831, page 251.

Youngs, Elizabeth, late of Darien, will dated Aug. 16, 1821,
    probated Apl. 22, 1833, all to her daughter Phebe
    Carter for life, and remainder to Sally wife of Will-
    iam Caper and Julia wife of George H. Wallace, dau-
    ghters of said Phebe Carter. Executor William Caper.
    Witnesses Sally Weed, Alva Waring, and Sarah Weed,
    page 465.
    Apl. 22, 1833, order to advertise for claims, page 465.
    Inventory taken by Isaac Gray and George I. Barlow,
    and filed Aug. 5, 1833, page 466.

STAMFORD PROBATE RECORDS.
Volume 14, 1828.

232.

Youngs, James, late of Stamford, Apl. 10, 1829, letters of administration on his estate granted to Leander Hoyt of Stamford, and commissioners appointed to adjust claims of creditors, page 50.
Inventory taken Apl. 11, 1829, by Jacob Stevens, Jr., and Ebenezer Dean, and filed May 2, 1829, page 50.
May 2, 1829, personal property ordered sold, page 52.
Nov. 9, 1829, account filed, and necessaries allowed his widow, page 201.
Dec. 1829, report of commissioners filed, page 200.
Feb. 1, 1830, real estate ordered sold to pay debts, page 202.
Mch. 21, 1830, real estate sold, and report of sale filed, page 202.
Mch. 24, 1830, creditors ordered paid 3 1/2 cents on the dollar, page 203.
Feb. 1, 1830, personal property sold, and report of sale filed, page 243.

Youngs, Richard, late of Darien, June 8, 1829, his widow being incapable, and his children to qualify, letters of administration on his estate granted to John Weed, Jr, of Darien, who was ordered to advertise for claims, page 59. x refused
Inventory taken June, 1829, by Abram Clock and Joseph Weed, and filed Oct. 6, 1829, page 154.

STAMFORD PROBATE RECORDS.
Volume 15, 1834.

Adams, Phebe, late of Greenwich, will dated Feb. 3, 1837, probated July 6, 1837, all to her husband, John Adams, and appointed him executor. Witnesses Elihu Lounsbury, Alton J. Palmer, and Charles J. Palmer, page 247. Inventory taken Sept. 4, 1837, by Ezekiel Close and Abram Mead, and filed Sept. 12, 1837, page 248.

Addington, Elizabeth, late of Greenwich, will dated Dec. 5, 1835, probated Mch. 21, 1836, mentions her children Betsy widow of Abraham Knapp, deceased, and Delilah wife of Nehemiah Daniels, granddaughter Emeline Knapp, a daughter of Abraham Knapp, deceased. Executor Samuel Close. Witnesses Burtis Banks, John E. Knapp, and Edward A. Knapp, page 186.
Mch. 21, 1836, order to advertise for claims, page 187. Inventory taken by Nelson Bush and Thomas A. Mead, and filed May 8, 1836, page 188.

Addington, Samuel, late of Greenwich, Sept. 29, 1835, his mother and sister refused to qualify, and letters of administration on his estate granted to Samuel Close of Greenwich, who was ordered to advertise for claims page 181.
Inventory taken Oct. 1, 1835, by Nelson Bush and Albert Knapp, and filed Jan. 1, 1836, page 181.

Anderson, Israel, late of Rye, N. Y., will dated 24th day, 3rd month, 1832, probated Oct. 15, 1833, mentions his children Rachel M. Anderson, Phebe A. wife of Aaron Haight, Rebecca C., wife of Artemas M. Carpenter, grandchildren Rachel M. Cromwell and Israel A. Cromwell, children of Charles Cromwell. Executors sons-in-law Aaron Haight and Artemas M. Carpenter and Rachel M. Anderson. Witnesses Moses Haight, Abijah Haviland, and Patience Haviland, page 230.

STAMFORD PROBATE RECORDS.
Volume 15, 1834.

Anderson, Israel, continued :
    Inventory taken Nov. 26, 1833, by John C. Sherwood and
    William A. Merritt, and filed Nov. 26, 1833, page 263.

Anderson, Joseph, late of Greenwich, will dated Mch. 11, 1837,
    probated Nov. 22, 1837, mentions his wife Anna, and
    children Edmund, William, Phebe LaCount, Matthew, Henry,
    and Joseph, granddaughter Hannah Ann Anderson. Ex-
    ecutors brother Jeremiah Anderson and son William.
    Witnesses William A. Merritt, Richard H. Arthur, and
    Hacaliah Carhart, Jr., page 275.
    Nov. 22, 1837, Jeremiah Anderson refused to qualify,
    and letters granted to testator's son William, who was
    ordered to advertise for claims, page 276.
    Inventory taken Nov. 24, 1837, by Nehemiah Sherwood
    and John C. Sherwood, and filed June 30, 1838, page 326.

Augur, John, late of Stamford, Apl. 6, 1829, account filed,
    by his executor, and real estate ordered sold to pay
    debts, page 362.
    Real estate sold to Dr. Nathaniel D. Haight, and report
    of sale filed July 21, 1838, page 362.

Ayres, Bradley, late of Stamford, June 18, 1838, distribution
    approved, and estate distributed to Polly Waterbury,
    heirs of Reuben Ayres, heirs of Lydia Scofield, heirs
    of Polly Waring, heirs of Jonathan Ayres, heirs of Sal-
    ly Bates, and heirs of Elizabeth Scofield, page 300.

Ayres, Sarah, widow, late of Stamford, inventory taken Nov.
    30, 1830, by John Weed, Jr., and Isaac Scofield, and
    filed June 18, 1838, page 305.

Barnum, David, late of Stamford, will dated Mch. 10, 1838,
    probated Apl. 14, 1838, all to his wife Betsy. Execu-
    tor Silas H. Ferris. Witnesses William Raymond, Da-
    rius Walton, and William H. Holly, page 302.
    Apl. 14, 1838, order to advertise for claims, page 302.
    Inventory taken Apl. 17, 1838, by Royal L. Gay and
    Peter Smith, and filed Apl. 28, 1838, pages 358 and 359

Bates, Gershom, late of   May 11, 1836, William Henry
    Bates, a son of decedent, 18 years of age, made choice
    of James L. Weed of Darien to be his guardian, page 139.

Bates, Henry, late of Darien, June 17, 1840, letters of ad-
    ministration on his estate granted to Edward Scofield
    of Darien, who was ordered to advertise for claims,
    page 433.

STAMFORD PROBATE RECORDS.
Volume 15, 1834.

Bates, Henry, continued :
    Inventory taken by Thomas Reed and John Bell, and filed Aug. 29, 1840, page 434.

Bates, Jerome, late of Darien, will dated Jan. 2, 1836, probated Sept. 26, 1839, mentions his wife Hannah, daughter Harriet, the five children of his deceased daughter Eliza Reynolds, daughter Mary Elizabeth, and son George Seaman. Executor son George Seaman Bates. Witnesses Thaddeus Betts, Gershom Bradley, and Frederick Belden, page 401.
    Sept. 26, 1839, order to advertise for claims, page 402
    Inventory taken by Joseph Mather, Jr., and Daty Weed, and filed Nov. 18, 1839, page 402.

Bates, William H., late of Stamford, Feb. 7, 1838, letters of administration on his estate granted to James L. Weed of Darien, the husband of a sister of decedent, who was ordered to advertise for claims, page 296.
    Inventory taken Mch. 30, 1838, by Ashbel Scofield and William Scofield, and filed Apl. 24, 1838, page 296.
    Aug. 13, 1838, account filed, and real estate ordered sold to pay debts, page 340.
    Real estate sold to Hait Scofield of Stamford, and report of sale filed, page 340.

Bennett, Elizabeth, late of Stamford, Mch. 10, 1841, letters of administration on her estate granted to Mary Smith of Stamford, who was ordered to advertise for claims, page 512.
    Inventory taken Apl. 1, 1841, by William H. Holly, and filed Apl. 1, 1841.

Bell, Isaac, late of Stamford, will dated Apl. 16, 1834, probated Sept. 28, 1840, mentions his first wife Anna, and present wife Charity, two sons Abraham and John Isaac, both now deceased, son Abraham by his present wife, Alfred Knapp and Noah Knapp sons of his present wife. Executors wife and Noah Knapp. Witnesses John R. Leeds John J. Leeds and Adaline Fairchild, page 488.
    Sept. 28, 1840, order to advertise for claims, page 489.
    Inventory taken Sept. 30, 1840, by William Scofield and John R. Leeds, and filed Oct. 5, 1840, page 489.

Bishop, Andrew, late of Darien, Aug. 14, 1834, letters of administration on his estate granted to William Andreas of Darien, who was ordered to advertise for claims, page 77.

STAMFORD PROBATE RECORDS.
Volume 15, 1834.

Bishop, Andrew, continued :
    Inventory taken by Joel Hurlbutt and Holly Bell, and filed Oct. 14, 1834, page 77.

Bishop, Delia M., of Chatham, Morris County, N. J., over 12 years of age, no date, (Apl. 1835), made choice of her brother Edwin Bishop of Stamford to be her guardian, page 87.

Bishop, Edwin, of Stamford, guardian of his sisters Delia M. Bishop of Chatham, N. J., and Julia Bishop, May 2, 1835 and July 6, 1835, asked leave to sell the real estate of said minors in Stamford, and sale ordered, pages 113 and 114.
    Real estate sold to William Scofield and Isaac Scofield, sons of Solomon Scofield, and report of sale filed Feb. 29, 1836, page 113.

Bishop, Hezekiah, late of Stamford, Mch. 15, 1839, his widow being unable to act, letters of administration on his estate granted to his son Erastus H. Bishop, who was ordered to advertise for claims, page 399.
    Inventory taken Mch. 22, 1839, by Samuel Weed and Peter Lockwood, and filed Mch. 25, 1839, page 400.
    Feb. 17, 1840, account filed, and allowance to his widow, page 400.
    Feb. 17, 1840, account filed, and real estate ordered sold to pay debts, page 400.
    Feb. 29, 1840, real estate sold to Peter Lockwood of Stamford, and John Wilmot of Stamford, and report of sale filed, page 401.
    Mch. 10, 1840, estate ordered distributed to his widow, and children, viz: Erastus C., Eliza H. wife of Edwin Scofield, and Polly Ann wife of John Wilmot, page 475.
    Mch. 11, 1840, estate distributed accordingly, page 476.

Bishop, John K., late of   Nov. 23, 1837, Sarah Catherine Rebecca, of Stamford, a daughter of decedent, over 12 years of age, made choice of William Newman to be her guardian, page 299.

Bishop, Julia, of Stamford, over 12 years of age, July 6, 1835, made choice of her brother Edwin Bishop, to be her guardian, page 111.

Blackman, Alfred, of Stamford, over 14 years of age, Oct. 19, 1834, made choice of Dr. Nathaniel D. Haight of Stamford to be his guardian, page 63.

STAMFORD PROBATE RECORDS.
Volume 15, 1834.

Blackman, Alfred, continued :
July 7, 1837, his guardian asked leave to sell the real estate of said minor in Stamford, and sale ordered page 277.
Real estate sold to Augustus Scofield and Horace Scofield, and report of sale filed Dec. 2, 1837, page 277.

Blackman, Elizabeth, late of Stamford, Sept. 16, 1834, letters of administration on her estate granted to Henry Waring of Stamford, who was ordered to advertise for claims, page 13.

Blanchard, Elizabeth, widow, late of Stamford, June 21, 1833, inventory taken by Abel Reynolds and Augustus Scofield, and filed by N. D. Haight, administrator, page 97.
Mch. 31, 1834, account filed, and real estate ordered sold to pay debts, page 98.
Real estate sold to William Scofield and his brother Isaac Scofield, sons of Solomon Scofield, and report of sale filed Apl. 1, 1834, page 98.

Blanchard, Elizabeth, widow, late of Stamford, inventory taken Sept. 23, 1834, by Abel Reynolds and Joseph Smith and filed Apl. 30, 1835, by H. Waring, administrator, page 95.

Blanchard, Ira, and Sally Maria Blanchard, both of Stamford, over 14 years of age, Mch. 13, 1834, made choice of Abel Reynolds of Stamford to be their guardian, page 17.
Said minors are owners, as tenants in common, with Oliver Lockwood and Silas Hoyt of Stamford of real estate in Stamford, subject to the life estate of the widow of Jacob Blanchard. Mch. 20, 1834, commissioners appointed to make partition thereof, page 195.
July 28, 1835, partition made accordingly to said Silas, Ira, Sally Ann, and Oliver, page 196.

Blanchard, Isaac, late of   Aug. 24, 1833, account filed by his executor, and real estate ordered sold to pay debts, page 7.
Real estate sold to Oliver Lockwood and Asa Ferris, and report of sale filed June 21, 1834, page 7.

Briggs, Shadrach, late of Stamford, Nov. 27, 1840, his widow refused to qualify, and letters of administration on his estate granted to Abel Reynolds of Stamford, who was ordered to advertise for claims, page 455.
Inventory taken Dec. 28, 1840, by Stephen June and

STAMFORD PROBATE RECORDS.
Volume 15, 1834.

Briggs, Shadrach, continued :
    Russell R. Barlow, and filed Dec. 28, 1840, page 455.
    June 10, 1842, account filed, allowance to widow, and
    real estate ordered sold to pay debts, page 456.
    Real estate sold to Samuel Briggs of Stamford, and re-
    port of sale filed Mch. 24, 1842, page 456.

Brown, Allen, of Greenwich, over 14 years of age, Mch. 3,
    1834, made choice of his brother Nehemiah Brown, Jr.,
    of Greenwich, to be his guardian, page 11.

Brown, John, of Stamford, parent and guardian of Henry Brown
    of Stamford, Mch. 14, 1834, asked leave to sell the
    real estate of said minor in Stamford, being 1/30th
    interest in the estate of Thaddeus Hoyt, deceased, and
    sale ordered, page 306.

Brown, Jonathan, late of Stamford, will dated Nov. 12, 1839,
    probated Feb. 10, 1840, mentions his wife Hannah, and
    children Edmund, Nancy widow of Zalmon Knapp, and
    Martha Jane wife of Henry Cogger. Executor Sands Adam
    Adams. Witnesses James H. Trowbridge, Seely Miller,
    and William H. Holly, page 420.
    Feb. 10, 1840, order to advertise for claims, page 421.
    Inventory taken Mch. 19, 1840, by Cary H. Leeds and
    Samuel Smith, and filed Mch. 19, 1840, page 422.

Brown, Josiah, formerly of Greenwich, late of New York City,
    will dated Oct. 1, 1823, probated Apl. 25, 1834, all
    to his wife Mary Brown, whom he appointed executrix.
    Witnesses Zeno Carpenter, James H. Reynolds, and Rich-
    ard L. Mott, page 98.
    Apl. 25, 1834, order to advertise for claims, page 99.
    Inventory taken Aug. 21, 1834, by Jared Smith and Amos
    Smith, and filed Nov. 4, 1834, page 100.

Brown, Nehemiah, late of Greenwich, will dated June 8, 1839,
    probated Aug. 22, 1840, mentions his wife Elizabeth,
    and children Julia Kirk, Sarah Ford, and Eliza Snyder.
    Executor Bartow F. White. Witnesses Isaac Peck, Major
    Brown, Jr., and Benjamin Husted, Jr., page 509.
    Aug. 22, 1840, order to advertise for claims, page 509.
    Inventory taken Sept. 12, 1840, by Samuel Brown and
    Nathaniel Husted, and filed Oct. 22, 1840, page 510.

Brown, Polly, of Stamford, guardian of her children William P.
    Brown, Mary E. Brown, and Eliza C. Brown of Stamford,
    Dec. 14, 1834, asked leave to sell the real estate of

STAMFORD PROBATE RECORDS.
Volume 15, 1834.

Brown, Polly, continued :
    said minors in Stamford, and sale ordered, page 140.
    Real estate sold to Benjamin Scofield and Alfred Scofield of Stamford, and report of sale filed Apl. 1, 1835, page 141.
    Apl. 1, 1835, Polly Brown, discharged as guardian of her children William P. Mary E., and Eliza C., and John W. Leeds appointed in her place, page 87.
    Apl. 1, 1835, the aforesaid minors by their guardian, John W. Leeds, asked leave to sell their real estate in Stamford, and sale ordered, page 107.
    Real estate sold to Benjamin Scofield and Alfred Scofield of Stamford, and report of sale filed June 19, 1835, page 107.

Brundage, Jonah, late of Rye, N. Y., will dated July 5, 1828, probated Dec. 27, 1839, mentions his wife Sarah, and children Silas, Samuel, Jonah, Lydia, Betsy Ann, and Sally. Executors his wife and sons Silas and Samuel. Witnesses John H. Smith, William Strang, and Allen Strang, page 431.
    Dec. 27, 1839, Samuel Brundage refused to qualify and letters granted to Silas Brundage and Sarah Brundage, who were ordered to advertise for claims, page 432. Inventory taken by Hacaliah Carhart and William A. Merritt, and filed Feb. 25, 1840, page 433.

Brush, Benjamin, 3rd, late of Greenwich, Jan. 23, 1836, time to settle account extended, page 233.

Brush, Edmund Burke, late of Greenwich, Aug. 20, 1833, letters of administration on his estate granted to his brother Platt Brush, who was ordered to advertise for claims, page 232.
    Sept. 25, 1837, Platt Brush, now deceased, and letters de bonus non granted to Joseph Brush of Greenwich, page 260.

Brush, Edwin, Jr., Jan. 6, 1840, made choice of Josephus Brush of Stamford to be his guardian, page 386.

Brush, Martha, late of Greenwich, widow of James Brush, will dated Nov. 19, 1832, probated Oct. 18, 1838, mentions her children James Brush, David Brush, Edward Brush, Edmond Brush, and Rachel Rundle, granddaughters children of her son Edward Brush, grandsons Henry, Stephen, and Edward, Jr., children of her son Edward Brush, granddaughter Mary daughter of said Edward Brush,

STAMFORD PROBATE RECORDS.
Volume 15, 1834.

Brush, Martha, continued ;
granddaughter Theresia Van Kleek, grandchildren the children of her daughter Sally Van Kleek. Executor son David Brush. Witnesses Harriet Reynolds, Elizabeth P. Reynolds, and Ard Reynolds, page 367.
Oct. 18, 1838, order to advertise for claims, page 369.
Inventory taken Nov. 22, 1838, by William Finch and Joseph Brush, and filed Dec. 17, 1838, page 370.

Brush, Platt, late of Greenwich, Sept. 25, 1837, his widow refused to qualify, and letters of administration on his estate granted to Joseph Brush and Gilbert Close, Jr., who were ordered to advertise for claims, page 259.
Inventory taken Sept. 22, 1837, by Benjamin Brush and Alfred Rundle, and filed June 1, 1838, page 303.

Burley, Silas, late of Greenwich, will dated Nov. 23, 1811, probated Sept. 3, 1833, mentions his wife Deborah, and children Henry, Charlotte Husted, Polly Keeler, Cynthia Burley, Deborah Burley, Amy Burley, Emeline Burley, Isaac, Silas, Walter, and Samuel. Executrix his wife. Witnesses Lot Palmer, Warren Palmer, and Jabez Mead, page 57.
Codicil dated Mch. 12, 1812, Cynthia now the wife of Lot Palmer, page 57.
Sept. 13, 1833, the widow refused to qualify, and letters of administration with the will annexed granted to Seth P. Quintard of Greenwich, who was ordered to advertise for claims, page 58.
Inventory taken by Henry Ritch and Edwin Lounsbury, and filed Mch. 17, 1834, page 58.
Apl. 28, 1834, account filed, and necessaries allowed his widow, page 59.

Burtis, Betsy M., late of Greenwich, will dated June 21, 1838, probated   owned land in Michigan and Ohio, mentions her brother-in-law David Burtis, sister Sally wife of Daniel Merritt of Greenwich, and her two youngest daughters Sarah and Cynthia Merritt, nephew Daniel B. son of said Sally Merritt, sister Nancy wife of Drake Husted, brothers Lewis Lyon and Augustus Lyon. Executor said Daniel Merritt. Witnesses Sarah Hubbard, Sarah A. Hubbard, and Samuel Close, page 291.
Order to advertise for claims, page 292.
Inventory taken by Henry Bush and Nelson Bush, and filed Sept. 4, 1838, page 370.

STAMFORD PROBATE RECORDS.
Volume 15, 1834.

Bush, Ann, late of Greenwich, will dated May 28, 1835, probated Nov. 25, 1836, mentions her children Henry Bush, Nelson Bush, Maria Bush, Leveret Bush, William Bush, and Julia Hicks. Executors her sons Henry and Nelson. Witnesses James Mosher, Augustus Mead and Samuel Close, page 238.
Nov. 25, 1836, order to advertise for claims, page 239.
Inventory taken by Samuel Close and Thomas A. Mead, and filed June 15, 1837, page 304.

Bush, David W., late of Greenwich, Oct. 31, 1835, letters of administration on his estate granted to his brother Henry Bush of Greenwich, who was ordered to advertise for claims, page 203.
Inventory taken by Augustus Mead and Thomas A. Mead, and filed Feb. 6, 1836, page 203.

Bush, Elsor, colored, late of Greenwich, will dated Apl. 1, 1835, probated Apl. 20, 1835, mentions his wife Dinah, father York, and brother Ralph. Executor Thomas A. Mead. Witnesses Handford Mead, Samuel Close, and Abraham Prime, page 240.
Apl. 20, 1835, order to advertise for claims, page 240.

Caldwell, Samuel, late of ~~Greenwich~~ Stamford, will dated Apl. 25, 1839, probated May 4, 1839, mentions his wife Sarah, and son Joseph. Owned land in Bedford and North Castle. Executor Jared M. Benedict. Witnesses Elizabeth Hoyt, John W. Lockwood, and Charles H. Lockwood, page 487.
May 4, 1839, order to advertise for claims, page 487.
Inventory taken May 7, 1839, by Joseph Smith, and filed July 7, 1839, page 488.

Carhart, Hacaliah, late of Greenwich, will dated Mch. 17, 1837, probated June 7, 1838, mentions his wife ---- and children Isaac A., Hannah Lyon, Margaret Newman, Elizabeth Adams, Hacaliah, Joshua and Alfred. Executors his sons Hacaliah and Alfred, and son-in-law Barnabas S. Adams. Witnesses John Purdy, Jotham Sherwood and Israel A. Dusenbury, page 281.
June 7, 1838, order to advertise for claims, page 282.
Inventory taken June 8, 1838, by Purdy Anderson and John C. Sherwood, and filed June 19, 1838, page 282.

Clason, Benjamin, late of Stamford, Mch. 9, 1838, his widow refused to qualify, and letters of administration on his estate granted to his son Stephen Clason, who was ordered to advertise for claims, page 313.

STAMFORD PROBATE RECORDS.
Volume 15, 1834.

Clason, Benjamin, continued :
Inventory taken Mch. 16, 1838, by Solomon Clason and Daniel Lockwood, and filed June 7, 1838, page 313.
Feb. 18, 1839, account filed, and allowance to his widow, page 378.

Clock, John, late of Darien, will dated July 3, 1821, probated Apl. 27, 1838, mentions his wife Sarah, and children Abraham, David, Hannah, and Phebe. Executor his son Abraham. Witnesses John Weed, Jr., Warren Percival and Isaac Gray, page 293.
Apl. 27, 1838, order to advertise for claims, page 294.
Inventory taken June 11, 1838, by John Weed, Jr., and Joseph Hoyt, and filed June 12, 1838, page 294.
Apl. 29, 1839, account filed, and allowance to his widow, page 341.

Close, David, of Greenwich, over 14 years of age, Aug. 5, 1837, made choice of his brother Aaron Close of Rye to be his guardian, page 258.

Close, Henry, late of Greenwich, June 22, 1837, his widow refused to qualify, and letters of administration on his estate granted to Abraham H. Close, page 260.

Close, Joseph, late of Greenwich, will dated Mch. 31, 1840, probated Sept. 2, 1840, mentions his wife Charlotte, nephew Joseph Close, Jr., son of his brother Solomon Close, and Charlotte Peck a niece of his wife. Executor Jacob Dayton, Jr. Witnesses Tompkins Close, Tompkins Close, Jr., and Zachariah Close, page 490.
Sept. 2, 1840, Jacob Dayton, Jr., refused to qualify, and letters granted to Joseph Close, who was ordered to advertise for claims, page 491.

Close, Odle, late of Greenwich, will dated Oct. 7, 1834, probated Oct. 13, 1834, mentions his wife Rachel E., and brother Shadrach Close, now deceased. Executors Joseph Brush and his brother Edward Close. Witnesses Samuel Close, Albert Knapp, and George H. Lane, page 89.
Oct. 13, 1834, order to advertise for claims, page 90.
Inventory taken Oct. 14, 1834, by William Smith and Amos Finch, and filed Apl. 20, 1835, page 90.
Feb. 29, 1836, commissioners appointed to adjust claims of creditors, page 100.
Aug. 13, 1836, new commissioners to adjust claims of creditors appointed, pages 183 and 184.
Sept. 22, 1836, report of commissioners filed, page 184

STAMFORD PROBATE RECORDS.
Volume 15, 1834.

Close, Odle, continued :
    Oct. 8, 1836, account filed, and creditors ordered paid 61 48/100 cents on the dollar, page 185.

Close, Shadrach J., of Greenwich, over 14 years of age, Feb. 16, 1837, made choice of Samuel Ferris of Greenwich to be his guardian, page 209.

Curtis, John, late of Stamford, will dated Jan. 28, 1837, probated Feb. 24, 1837, all to his wife Polly. Executors his wife and son-in-law Isaac Jones. Witnesses N. D. Haight, Henry Curtis and Seth Seely, page 213.
    Inventory taken by Heth Stevens and Seth Seely, and filed Mch. 6, 1837, page 215.
    Mch. 1837, commissioners appointed to adjust claims of creditors, page 214.
    June 13, 1837, list of creditors, and report of commissioners filed, Jan. 25, 1838, pages 287 and 288.
    Feb. 21, 1838, account filed, and real estate ordered sold to pay debts, page 289.
    Real estate sold to Nathan or Nathan'l Lockwood, and report of sale filed June 8, 1838, page 289.

Dan, Charles, late of Stamford, son of Sylvanus Dan, deceased, Feb. 26, 1836, letters of administration on his estate granted to Nehemiah Hait, Jr., who was ordered to advertise for claims, page 175.
    Inventory taken by Alfred Smith and Allen S. Mead, and filed June 13, 1836, page 175.

Dan, Charles, late of Stamford, Sept. 24, 1836, account filed and real estate ordered sold to pay debts, page 233.
    Real estate sold to Rev. Nehemiah Sherwood, George M. Hubbard and Stephen Lockwood, Jr., and report of sale filed Apl. 26, 1837, page 234.

Dan, Eliza, late of New York City, Dec. 14, 1839, letters of administration on her estate granted to Alexander S. Ingersoll of Stamford, who was ordered to advertise for claims, page 416.
    Inventory taken, stated that decedent was a daughter of Silvanus Dan, late of Stamford, who was a son of Squire Dan, and filed Feb. 17, 1840, page 416.
    Nov. 23, 1840, account filed, and real estate ordered sold to pay debts, page 417.
    Nov. 23, 1840, real estate sold to Jonathan Dan, and report of sale filed, page 417.

STAMFORD PROBATE RECORDS.
Volume 15, 1834.

244.

Dan, Squire, late of Stamford, will dated Apl. 21, 1836, probated Apl. 1, 1839, mentions his wife Rhoda, and children Polly, Nancy, Hannah, Lydia, Sally, and the children of his wife by her first husband, not named. Executor son Jonathan. Witnesses Samuel Lockwood, Charles Hawley, and Betsy Tucker, page 398.
Apl. 1, 1839, order to advertise for claims, page 398.
Inventory taken July 5, 1839, by William Young and Harvey Scofield, and filed July 15, 1839, page 399.

Dan, Sylvanus, late of Stamford, Mch. 5, 1836, Eliza Dan, a daughter of decedent, under 14 years of age, now of Mamaroneck, the court appointed Nehemiah Hait, Jr., of Stamford to be her guardian, page 110.
Mch. 5, 1836, her guardian asked leave to sell the real estate of said minor in Stamford, and sale ordered, page 182.
Real estate sold to Rev. Nehemiah Sherwood, and report of sale filed June 13, 1836, page 183.

Dayton, James, late of Greenwich, Aug. 27, 1833, account filed, and real estate ordered sold to pay debts, page 62.
Real estate sold to Nathaniel Dayton of Greenwich, and report of sale filed Nov. 16, 1833, page 62.

Downs, George L., of Greenwich, over 14 years of age, Sept. 8, 1836, made choice of Arba Smith of Greenwich to be his guardian, page 182.

Fancher, David, late of Darien, will dated Oct. 10, 1827, probated Sept. 10, 1834, mentions his children Charles, Henry, Sally wife of Henry Foster, Martha, and Darius, grandson William Denton. Executors Elias Fancher and Henry Fancher. Witnesses Abram Clock, Samuel Gorum, and Abigail Gorum, page 161.
Sept. 10, 1834, order to advertise for claims, page 162.
Inventory taken Sept. 11, 1834, by Leander Hoyt and Isaac Whiting, and filed Oct. 10, 1834, page 162.

Ferris, Asa M., late of Stamford, Nov. 12, 1840, letters of administration on his estate granted to his widow Susan Ferris and Luke Smith of Stamford, who were ordered to advertise for claims, page 482.
Inventory taken by Solomon Smith and Isaac Lockwood, and filed Dec. 16, 1841, page 482.
July 12, 1841, account filed, and allowance to his widow, page 482.

STAMFORD PROBATE RECORDS.
Volume 15, 1834.

Ferris, Ethan, late of Greenwich, Jan. 13, 1834, account filed by his administrator, and allowance to his widow, page 22.

Ferris, Mary, late of Greenwich, Sept. 9, 1833, letters of administration on her estate granted to her son, Joshua Ferris, of Greenwich, who was ordered to advertise for claims, page 242.

Ferris, Polly, late of Stamford, widow of Asa Ferris, will dated Apl. 20, 1840, probated Nov. 15, 1841, all to her daughters Sarah Ferris, Mary A. Ferris, and Polly A. wife of Nathaniel Scofield. No executor. Witnesses James W. Weeks, William Scofield, and N. D. Haight, page 483.

Ferris, Sylvanus, of Stamford, over 14 years of age, Sept. 4, 1835, made choice of Royal L. Gay to be his guardian, page 110.

Field, Robert, late of North Castle, Westchester County, N.Y., will dated 30th day, 8th month, 1834, probated July 2, 1838, mentions his children Fanny, Henry C., Gulydina, Elizabeth C., Mary Mathews, Abigail Griffin, Uriah, Jacob W., and Willett, grandsons Robert Mathews, Charles Robert Field, and Robert Field,.. Executors sons Uriah and Henry C. Witnesses Edmund Field, Hannah Field, and James Field, page 495.
July 2, 1838, order to advertise for claims, page 496.
Inventory taken July 2, 1838, by Thomas Carpenter and Richard B. Carpenter, and filed July 2, 1838, page 497.

Finch, Jonathan, Farmer, late of Greenwich, will dated July 3, 1832, probated May 9, 1836, mentions his 2nd wife Rhoda and son Reuben. Executors brother-in-law Edmond Mead, and grandson Amos Finch, both of Greenwich. Witnesses Jeremiah Slater, Elizabeth Newman and Ard Reynolds, page 192.
May 9, 1836, order to advertise for claims, page 194.
Inventory taken May 16, 1836, by Benjamin Brush, Jr., and Joseph Ingersoll, and filed May 20, 1836, page 194.
Mch. 14, 1837, account filed, and allowance to his widow, page 202. 204.

Gray, Cary H., late of Stamford, Feb. 24, 1836, letters of administration on his estate granted to his widow, Sally J. Gray and James H. Hoyt of Stamford, who were ordered to advertise for claims, page 234. 235.

STAMFORD PROBATE RECORDS.
Volume 15, 1834.

Gray, Cary H., continued :
    Sept. 19, 1836, account filed, and commissioners appointed to adjust claims of creditors, page 235.
    Inventory taken Mch. 28, 1836, by Ebenezer Smith, Jr., and Ezra Lockwood, and filed Mch. 29, 1836, page 235.
    May 13, 1836, additional inventory filed, page 236.
    Aug. 1, 1837, report of commissioners filed, page 265.
    May 1, 1837, review asked for by the administrators and some creditors, pages 267 and 268.
    July, 1837, review heard, and report filed, page 268.
    Mch. 18, 1839, account filed, and allowance to his widow, page 358.

Gray, Catherine Sands, of Darien, over 12 years of age, Sept. 3, 1833, made choice of her mother, Elizabeth Gray, to be her guardian, who was also appointed guardian of Hannah E. Gray, another of her daughters, under 12 years of age, page 32.

Gray, Joseph, late of Stamford, Mch. 9, 1836, his executor, Cary H. Gray, now deceased, and letters with the will annexed granted to Sally J. Gray, the widow and administratrix of said Cary H. Gray, page 155.

Green, Anthony, late of Greenwich, colored, Aug. 22, 1836, letters of administration on his estate granted to James Wilson of Greenwich, who was ordered to advertise for claims, page 204.
    Inventory taken Sept. 6, 1836, by John S. Heustis and Platt Mead, and filed Nov. 4, 1836, page 205.

Green, Benjamin, late of Greenwich, will dated Apl. 29, 1840, probated Aug. 17, 1840, mentions his wife Eunice, and children Thomas, Dewitt C., Deborah L., Abram L., Benjamin, Jr., George W., William H., and Charles E., brother Thomas Green, deceased. Executor his wife and son Abram L. Witnesses Mary Green, Jotham Merritt and Samuel Close, page 471.
    Aug. 17, 1840, order to advertise for claims, page 473.
    Inventory taken Aug. 20, 1840, by James Willson and Nathan S. Mead, and filed Aug. 31, 1840, page 473.
    Nov. 1, 1841, Charles E., and Thomas, children of decedent, over 14 years of age, made choice of their brother Abraham L. Green to be their guardian, who was also appointed guardian of Dewitt C. and Deborah L., other children of decedent, page 465.
    Aug. 31, 1840, Benjamin, a son of decedent, about 20 years of age, made choice of James Willson of Greenwich to be his guardian, page 423.

STAMFORD PROBATE RECORDS.
Volume 15, 1834.

Green, Benjamin, continued:
    Aug. 31, 1840, James Willson, guardian of Benjamin, a son of decedent, asked leave to sell the real estate of said minor in Greenwich, and sale ordered, page 463. Real estate sold to Abram L. Green, and report of sale filed Nov. 16, 1840, page 463.

Green, Joseph, late of Greenwich, will dated Sept. 14, 1835, probated Jan. 23, 1836, mentions his wife Elizabeth, and children Mary widow of Joseph Taylor, Jr., Sarah wife of James Wilson, Cynthia Green, Rebecca Green, and Nancy Green. Executers his wife and Isaac Peck, Jr. Witnesses Eliza Close, Sarah A. Lyon, and Samuel Close, page 228.
    Jan. 23, 1836, order to advertise for claims, page 229. Inventory taken Jan. 26, 1836, by Platt Mead and Daniel Sherwood, and copied on page 230.

Green, Mercy, late of Stamford, will dated Mch. 12, 1829, probated Mch. 19, 1838, all to her niece Sarah Green Waring, now of New York City. Executor John Hoyt of Stamford. Witnesses Thaddeus Bell, David Waterbury, and Elizabeth Waterbury, page 292.
    Mch. 19, 1838, order to advertise for claims, page 293. Inventory taken by Peter Husted and Henry Hoyt, and filed Apl. 2, 1838, page 293.

Green, Susannah, late of Greenwich, Jan. 30, 1836, letters of administration on her estate granted to her son-in-law Daniel Merritt of Greenwich, page 233.

Green, Thomas, late of Greenwich, will dated June 1, 1833, probated Aug. 23, 1834, mentions his wife Mary, nephew James Wilson and Sarah his wife of Greenwich, John Green late of Greenwich the father of his wife, and she was an only child, brother Reuben Green; Samuel and John B. sons of Jotham Wilson, deceased; brothers Benjamin Green and Joseph Green; bequest for the use of Delia Palmer, her grandchild Hester Purdy, or William Purdy; Nancy Wilson, Thomas Wilson, Polly Wilson, Ann wife of Caleb Husted, and Sarah Wilson, children of Jotham Wilson; Mary Taylor, Cynthia Green, Rebecca Green, and Nancy Green, daughters of his brother Joseph Green; Sally wife of James Wilson, Jeremiah, Thomas, and Nancy wife of James Merritt, children of his brother Reuben Green; sister Nancy wife of Peter Husted, and Sally widow of Jotham Wilson. Executors his wife, nephew James Wilson, William Bush of Rye, and Isaac Peck, 3rd, of Round Hill. Witnesses Joseph Stedwell,

STAMFORD PROBATE RECORDS.
Volume 15, 1834.

Green, Thomas, continued :
of Rye, Jotham Merritt of Greenwich, and I. W. Tompkins of White Plains, page 65.
Apl. 23, 1834, letters to Mary Green and James Wilson, who were ordered to advertise for claims, page 69.
Sept. 1, 1834, William Bush refused to qualify, and Letters to Isaac Peck, 3rd, page 70.
Inventory taken Sept. 2, 1834, by Platt Mead and James Field, and filed Oct. 20, 1834, page 70.
Sept. 7, 1835, account filed, no issue, and distribution ordered to his widow, Mary Green, and his brothers and sisters, viz: James, Joseph, Reuben, Benjamin, Sally Wilson of Greenwich, and Nancy wife of Peter Husted of New York City, page 156.
Appeal taken by James Green, page 157.
May 4, 1836, estate settled, and receipts from all the heirs at law above named, page 158.

Guernsey, Solomon, late of Stamford, Mch. 12, 1841, his widow refused to qualify, and letters of administration on his estate granted to Samuel Lockwood and Jacob S. Guernsey, both of Stamford, who were ordered to advertise for claims, page 457.
Inventory taken May 3, 1841, by Frederick Lockwood and William H. Holly, and filed May 3, 1841, page 457.
Mch. 7, 1842, account filed, allowance to widow, and real estate ordered sold to pay debts, page 459.

Hait, David N., late of Pound Ridge, Jan. 23, 1838, his widow refused to qualify, and letters of administration on his estate granted to Charles H. Sarles of Pound Ridge, who was ordered to advertise for claims, page 309.

Hait, David N., late of Stamford, Feb. 18, 1839, account filed, and an allowance to his widow, page 343.
Aug. 1, 1838, commissioners appointed to adjust claims of creditors, page 343.
Feb. 18, 1839, report of commissioners filed, page 344.

Hait, J W., of New York City, and Mary A. P. Hait of Peekskill, about 19 and 12 years of age respectively Dec. 3, 1840, made choice of their mother, Mary A. Hait to be their guardian, page 423.
Dec. 3, 1840, their guardian asked leave to sell the real estate of said minors in Stamford, and sale ordered, page 500. Real estate sold to Nehemiah Hait, Jr., and report of sale filed, page 501.

STAMFORD PROBATE RECORDS.
Volume 15, 1834.

Hait, Martha Jane, seven years of age, and Sarah Matilda Hait,
four years of age, both of Pound Ridge, Oct. 7, 1839,
the court appointed Charles H. Sarles of Pound Ridge
to be their guardian, page 362.
Oct. 7, and 15, 1839, their guardian asked leave to
sell the realestate of said minors in Stamford, and
Sale ordered, pages 423 and 462.
Real estate sold to Walter Sarles and Greenleaf Youngs
and report of sale filed, page 462.

Hall, David, late of Greenwich, Feb. 26, 1839, letters of administration on his estate granted to his son George
Hall of New York City, who was ordered to advertise
for claims, page 411.
Inventory taken Apl. 27, 1839, by John Sands and
Daniel M. Griffin, and filed May 5, 1839, page 412.

Hedden, Zadoc, late of Stamford, June 20, 1840, letters of
administration on his estate granted to Isaac Quintard,
Jr., of Stamford, who was ordered to advertise for
claims, page 442.
Inventory taken June 20, 1840, by Davis Lockwood and
William H. Holly, page 442.
Feb. 1, 1841, account filed, and commissioners appointed to adjust claims of creditors, page 442.
Aug. 30, 1841, report of commissioners filed, page 443.
Aug. 30, 1841, account filed, and real estate ordered
sold to pay debts, page 443.
Real estate sold to James H. Minor of Stamford on
Sept. 20, 1841, and report of sale filed, page 444.
Aug. 30, 1841, account filed, and creditors ordered paid
50 9/10 cents on the dollar, page 444.

Henderson, Hugh, late of Greenwich, will dated June 22, 1834,
probated July 14, 1834, all to his daughter Sally
wife of William Funston. Executor Thomas A. Mead.
Witnesses Samuel Close, Jacob Weed, and Odle Close,
page 178.
July 14, 1834, order to advertise for claims, page 179.
Inventory taken by Alvan Mead and I. S. Weed, and filed
Jan. 31, 1835, page 179.

Hendrie, Hannah, widow, late of Greenwich, Sept. 4, 1837, letters of administration on her estate granted to Royal L
Gay of Stamford, who was ordered to advertise for
claims, page 259.
Oct. 4, 1837, inventory taken by Charles Knapp and
Davis Lockwood, and filed Oct. 19, 1837, page 283.

STAMFORD PROBATE RECORDS.
Volume 15, 1834.

Hobby, Amos, late of Greenwich, May 4, 1836, his widow refused to qualify, and letters of administration on his estate granted to John Smith of Greenwich, who was ordered to advertise for claims, page 163.
Inventory taken May 6, 1836, by Alfred Rundle and Titus Mead, and filed May 31, 1836, page 163.
Mch. 18, 1837, additional inventory filed, page 217.

Hobby, Amos, of Greenwich, Apl. 27, 1840, his guardian, Beal B. Lockwood, asked leave to sell the real estate of said minor in Greenwich, subject to the dower of the widow of Amos Hobby, deceased, and sale ordered, page 425.
Real estate sold to Isaac Holly, Jr., of Greenwich, and report of sale filed, page 425.

Hobby, Harry, colored, late of Greenwich, Jan. 16, 1834, letters of administration on his estate granted to Samuel Lockwood of Stamford, who was ordered to advertise for claims, page 233.

Hobby, Jabez M., late of Greenwich, Dec. 22, 1834, letters of administration on his estate granted to Jabez Mead, 3rd of Greenwich, husband of the only child of deceased, who was ordered to advertise for claims, page 127.
Inventory taken by Stephen Waring and William H. Mead, and filed June 29, 1835, page 127.

Holly, Isaac, late of Stamford, Apl. 23, 1836, Elenor Holly of Stamford as the guardian and parent of Catherine E., Charles Frederick, George T., and Julia Ann, children of decedent, asked leave to sell the real estate of said minors in Stamford, and sale ordered, page 201.

Holly, Sarah, late of Stamford, June 12, 1834, her husband, Newman Holly, now deceased, her daughter Hannah, and her granddaughter Abigail being long since married, and Abigail now deceased leaving children, and her sons John and Joseph being long since deceased, both childless, estate ordered distributed to Josiah, Hannah, heirs of David, and heirs of Abigail, according to her will, page 15.
Sept. 8, 1834, estate distributed to Josiah Holly, Hannah wife of Michael Harms, heirs of David Holly, and heirs of Abigail wife of Israel Knapp, deceased, page 16.

Holly, Stephen, late of Stamford, Jan. 14, 1834, account filed by his administrator, and allowance to his widow, page 39.

STAMFORD PROBATE RECORDS.
Volume 15, 1834.

Holly, Stephen, Stephen, continued:
Jan. 18, 1834, estate ordered distributed to his widow ----, and children Silas, Sally wife of William Scofield, Phebe wife of Hezron Scofield, Clarissa wife of Philander Smith, Huldah wife of Robert R. Barlow, and Sabrina wife of Levi Sherwood, page 40.
Mch. 6, 1834, estate distributed accordingly, page 40.

Hoyt, Charles H., Mary Hoyt, Elizabeth Hoyt, Hannah A. Hoyt, and Eliza Hoyt, formerly of Darien, but now of New York City, Aug. 3, 1833, by their guardian, George A. Hoyt, of New York City, asked leave to sell the real estate of said minors in Darien, and sale ordered, page 27.
Real estate sold to Thaddeus Hoyt and Rufus Hoyt, subject to the life interest of Harriet Hoyt the mother of said minors, and report of sale filed Apl. 2, 1834, page 27.
Mch. 6, 1834, also petition for leave to sell the real estate of said minors in Stamford, late of Thaddeus Hoyt, deceased, and sale ordered, page 28.
Real estate sold to Silas H. Ferris, and Asa M. Ferris of Stamford, and report of sale filed July 21, 1834, page 28.

Hoyt, David, late of Stamford, July 13, 1838, his widow, refused to qualify, and letters of administration on his estate granted to his son George C. Hoyt and Royal L. Gay, both of Stamford, who were ordered to advertise for claims, page 385.
Inventory taken Aug. 3, 1838, by Henry Waring and Davis Lockwood, and filed Sept. 18, 1838, page 385.
Feb. 5, 1839, account filed, and allowance to his widow, page 386.
July 1, 1839, account resettled, and real estate ordered sold by Davis Lockwood to pay debts, page 465.
Real estate sold to George C. Hoyt of Stamford, and report of sale filed, page 466.

Hoyt, Elizabeth, widow, late of Stamford, Dec. 28, 1835, letof administration on her estate granted to Samuel Lockwood, who was ordered to advertise for claims, page 163.
Inventory taken by Isaac Quintard, Jr., and Fitch Rogers, and filed Jan. 21, 1836, page 163.

Hoyt, Enoch, late of Stamford, Mch. 20, 1829, account filed by his administrators, and real estate ordered sold to pay debts, page 244.
Dec. 2, 1833, estate distributed to his children

STAMFORD PROBATE RECORDS.
Volume 15, 1834.

Hoyt, Enoch, continued:
  Maria L. Weed, Nancy E. Hoyt, James N., Samuel W.,
  John S., Sally Ann Hoyt, Clarissa Hoyt, Sarah M. Hoyt,
  Harriet Hoyt, Susan M. Hoyt, and Royal L. Gay, assignee
  of Calvin G. Hoyt, a son, page 244.
  Jan. 17, 1834, petition of Simeon H. Minor and Royal L.
  Gay, guardians of James N., Samuel W., John S., Sally A.
  Caroline, Sarah M., Harriet, and Susan M., all of
  Stamford, children of decedent, for leave to sell the
  real estate of said minors in Stamford, and sale ordered, pages 38 and 39.
  Real estate sold to John Seely, and report of sale
  filed, page 39.
  Mch. 9, 1835, Royal L. Gay, guardian of Samuel W.,
  James, Susan M., Sally Ann, Sarah M., Harriet, and
  Clarissa A., children of decedent, removed, and John
  Seely of Stamford appointed in his place, page 62.

Hoyt, Hannah, of Stamford, guardian of her children George E.
  Hoyt, Frances Hoyt, and Emily Hoyt of Stamford, Mch.
  14, 1834, asked leave to sell the real estate of said
  minors in Darien, and sale ordered, page 137.
  Real estate sold to Henry Weed of Darien, and report
  of sale filed, May 17, 1836, page 137.

Hoyt, Hannah, late of New Canaan, formerly of Stamford, will
  dated Aug. 30, 1828, probated Apl. 21, 1837, mentions
  her niece Sarah Tuttle, children of Agar Tuttle and
  said Sarah E. Tuttle, viz: Henry, Harriet E., and
  Sarah H., brother Shadrach Hoyt, and sister Mary wife
  of Ebenezer Smith. Executor brother Shadrach Hoyt.
  Witnesses Charles A. Hanford and Harvey Bouton, page 236
  Apl. 21, 1837, Shadrach Hoyt, now deceased, and letters
  granted to Ebenezer Smith, who was ordered to advertise
  for claims, page 237.
  Apl. 18, 1837, inventory taken by Peter Husted and
  John Brown, and filed Feb. 14, 1838, page 315.

Hoyt, James S., late of Stamford, Feb. 4, 1836, his widow refused to qualify, and letters of administration on her
  estate granted to James William Spencer of New York
  City, who was ordered to advertise for claims, page 173.
  Inventory taken by Samuel Lockwood and John W. Leeds,
  and filed Nov. 29, 1836, page 173.
  Dec. 3, 1836, the court appointed James William Spencer of New York City to be the guardian of William S.
  Hoyt of Stamford, a son of decedent, under 14 years of
  age, page 209.
  Jan. 25, 1836, personal property distributed to his

STAMFORD PROBATE RECORDS.
Volume 15, 1834.

Hoyt, James S., continued :
widow, Mary Hoyt, and William S. Hoyt, son and only
heir at law of decedent, page 203.

Hoyt, Jesse, late of Stamford, will dated Nov. 27, 1833, probated Aug. 12, 1834, mentions his wife, and son Ezra.
Executor Nathaniel D. Haight. Witnesses Isaac Scofield, John A. Scofield, and Nathaniel D. Haight,
page 78.
Aug. 12, 1834, executor refused to qualify, page 78.
Aug. 15, 1834, letters granted to Nathaniel D. Haight,
who was ordered to advertise for claims, page 78.
Inventory taken Sept. 19, 1834, by Abishai Scofield
and Ezekiel Scofield, and filed Mch. 31, 1835, page 79.
Apl. 29, 1835, account filed, and personal property
allowed his widow, page 79.
Apl. 29, 1835, account filed, and real estate ordered
sold to pay debts, page 182.

Hoyt, John, late of Stamford, June 23, 1834, on motion of
James B. Scofield, assignee as he claims of several
of the heirs of decedent, distribution ordered of
that part of decedent's estate which was set off to
his widow as her dower to his heirs at law, or their
assigns, page 149.
July 18, 1834, distribution made to the heirs of Benjamin Hoyt, deceased, Abigail Harden, heirs of Elisabeth Larkin, deceased, heirs of John Hoyt, deceased,
Samuel Hoyt, Melancthon Hoyt, heirs of William Hoyt,
deceased, Mary Reed, Joseph H. Hoyt, and Leander Hoyt,
page 150.

Hoyt, Joseph D., of Buffalo, N. Y., about 14 years of age,
Dec. 26, 1838, made choice of Daniel Lockwood of Buffalo to be his guardian, page 492.
Aug. 12, 1839, petition for leave to sell the real estate of said minor in Stamford, and sale ordered by
Polly Hoyt, guardian, in place of Daniel Lockwood,
pages 493 and 494.

Hoyt, Joseph D., late of Stamford, Jan. 19, 1839, his widow
refused to qualify, and letters of administration on
his estate granted to Francis S. Ellis of Stamford, who
was ordered to advertise for claims, page 407.
Inventory taken Jan. 30, 1839, by Augustus Lockwood
and George E. Waring, and filed Mch. 25, 1839, page 407.
Jan. 4, 1840, Surrogate's Court, Erie County, N. Y.,
Daniel Lockwood, guardian of Joseph D. Hoyt, son

STAMFORD PROBATE RECORDS.
Volume 15, 1834.

Hoyt, Joseph D., continued :
of decedent, resigned, with the consent of said minor, Polly Hoyt, widow of decedent, David Chamberlin, Francis S. Ellis husband of Harriet, and Sarah E., heirs of dededent, and Polly Hoyt appointed in his place, page 407.

Hoyt, Ralph, late of Darien, June 8, 1835, his widow refused to qualify, and letters of administration on his estate granted to Henry Bates, who was ordered to advertise for claims, page 168.
Inventory taken June 17, 1835, by William H. Bates and Edward Scofield, and filed July 11, 1835, page 168.
Apl. 2, 1836, dower of his widow set out, page 169.
June 15, 1836, account filed, and commissioners appointed to adjust claims of creditors, pages 169 and 170.
Mch. 23, 1839, report of commissioners filed, page 345.
Mch. 23, 1839, account filed, and allowance to his widow, page 344.
Mch. 23, 1839, account filed, and real estate ordered sold to pay debts, page 349.
Real estate sold to Molly Raymond of Darien and John Reed, and report of sale filed Apl. 6, 1839, page 349.

Hoyt, Ralph, late of Stamford, Nov. 2, 1839, his widow refused to qualify, and letters of administration on his estate granted to Ezra Scofield and Joseph W. Hoyt, who were ordered to advertise for claims, page 477.
Inventory taken Dec. 2, 1839, by Selleck Scofield and Benjamin M. Weed, and filed Jan. 27, 1840, page 478.
June 9, 1840, allowance to his widow, page 478.
Apl. 30, 1840, account filed, and commissioners appointed to adjust claims of creditors, page 480.
Mch. 8, 1841, report of commissioners filed, page 480.

Hoyt, Sally Ann, of Stamford, about 16 years of age, July 29, 1840, made choice of Smith Scott of Stamford to be her guardian, page 423.

Hoyt, Shadrach, late of Stamford, Mch. 14, 1834, George E. Hoyt and Frances Hoyt, children of decedent, over 14 years of age, made choice of their mother Hannah Hoyt to be their guardian, who was also appointed guardian of Emily, another child of decedent, under 12 years of age, page 25.

STAMFORD PROBATE RECORDS.
Volume 15, 1834.

255.

Hoyt, Susan M., of Stamford, over 12 years of age, Jan. 12, 1833, made choice of Royal L. Gay to be her guardian, page 62.

Hoyt, William S., of Stamford, Jan. 25, 1837, his guardian William Spencer of New York City, asked leave to sell the real estate of said minor in Stamford, and sale ordered, page 234.

Hubbard, Gabriel, late of Stamford, Apl. 4, 1839, personal property sold, page 307.

Hubbard, Hannah P., of Stamford, Jan. 14, 1837, guardian of her children George D. Hubbard, Samuel Hubbard, Mary H. Hubbard, Hannah P. Hubbard, David H. Hubbard, and Harriet E. Hubbard, asked leave to sell the real estate of said minors in Stamford, and sale ordered, page 306.

Hubbard, John, of Greenwich, over 14 years of age, Nov. 28, 1834, made choice of his mother Sarah Hubbard to be his guardian, page 77.

Husted, Amos, late of Greenwich, Sept. 12, 1834, his widow refused to qualify, and letters of administration on his estate granted to Esbon Husted, who was ordered to advertise for claims, page 104.
Inventory taken Sept. 15, 1834, by Jonas Howe and Elias Peck, and filed Oct. 16, 1834, page 105.
Oct. 23, 1834, account filed, and allowance to his widow, page 105.
Oct. 23, 1834, dower of his widow ordered set out, page 105.
Dec. 22, 1834, dower set out to his widow, Sarah Husted page 106.

Husted, Drake, late of Greenwich, will dated Feb. 22, 1838, probated Sept. 11, 1838, mentions his wife Nancy, and children Joseph B., Sarah M. wife of Augustus Mead, and William A. Husted. Executors his wife and Augustus Mead. Witnesses Betsy M. Burtis, David Husted and Samuel Close, page 349.
Sept. 11, 1838, order to advertise for claims, page 350.
Inventory taken Sept. 26, 1838, by Thomas A. Mead and Zaccheus Mead, and filed Oct. 16, 1838, page 351.

Husted, Hannah, late of Greenwich, dead over seven years, July 21, 1837, Drake Husted, a son of deceased being incapable of acting, and another son, William Husted, owing the estate, letters of administration on her es-

STAMFORD PROBATE RECORDS.
Volume 15, 1834.

Husted, Hannah, continued:
    tate granted to her daughter, Sarah Husted, page 252.

Husted, Roswell, late of Greenwich, Dec. 13, 1833, account filed by his administrator, and allowance to his widow, page 22.
July 4, 1823, dower of his widow ordered set out, page 23.
Aug. 13, 1834, dower set out, page 23.
July 4, 1834, account filed, and real estate ordered sold to pay debts, page 24.
Real estate sold to Conklin Husted, and report of sale filed Sept. 2, 1834, page 25.
Dec. 21, 1833, the court appointed Conklin Husted guardian of Roswell Albert Husted, a son of decedent under one year of age, page 55.
Dec. 21, 1833, Conklin Husted, guardian of Roswell Mead Husted, asked leave to sell the real estate of said minor in Greenwich, subject to the dower of his mother, and sale ordered, pages 32 and 33.
Mch. 4, 1839, Roswell M. Husted, six years of age, his guardian Conklin Husted, discharged, and David A. Husted of North Castle appointed in his place, page 364.
Apl. 11, 1842, David A. Husted removed, and Titus Mead of Greenwich appointed in his place, page 507.

Husted, William, late of Greenwich, will dated Sept. 16, 1837, probated Nov. 6, 1837, mentions his wife Mary, and children Hannah, Phebe Ann, David and Benjamin, and brother Drake Husted. Executors his wife and son Benjamin. Witnesses Zabed Finch, Esbin Husted, and Charles Hawley, page 326.
Nov. 6, 1837, order to advertise for claims, page 328.
Inventory taken by Platt Mead and David Brown, and filed Nov. 30, 1837, page 329.

Ingersoll, Nathaniel, late of Greenwich, will dated Jan. 5, 1831, probated Dec. 3, 1834, mentions his wife Abigail, and children Abigail Mead, Rebecca Ingersoll, Hannah Ingersoll, Joseph, and Ann Brush; granddaughters Abigail I. Reynolds, and Emeline Holly, and grandson David Ingersoll. Executor his son Joseph. Witnesses Ann Eliza Reynolds, Elizabeth P. Reynolds, and Ard Reynolds, page 132.
1st codicil dated June 23, 1831, page 133.
2nd codicil, dated Apl. 6, 1832, granddaughter Abigail I. Reynolds now the wife of William H. Mead, page 134.
Dec. 3, 1834, order to advertise for claims, page 135.
Inventory taken Jan. 15, 1835, by Jared Smith and Amos

STAMFORD PROBATE RECORDS.
Volume 15, 1834.

Ingersoll, Nathaniel, continued:
    Finch, and filed Mch. 25, 1835, page 135.
    Mch. 26, 1835, William H. Mead of Greenwich and his wife Abigail I., a granddaughter and legatee of testator, Stephen Holly of Greenwich and Emeline A., his wife, a granddaughter and legatee of testator, and Ann Brush, a daughter of testator, appealed from the probate of said will, page 136.

Isaacs, Isaacs S., late of Norwalk, Mch. 3, 1835, letters of administration on his estate granted to his sons Benjamin Isaacs and Charles Isaacs, who were ordered to advertise for claims, page 233.

Jones, Ephraim, late of Stamford, Nov. 13, 1837, letters of administration on his estate granted to his son Isaac W. Jones, who was ordered to advertise for claims, the widow refused to qualify, page 273.
    Inventory taken by James Davenport and Edwin Scofield, and filed Dec. 23, 1837, page 273.
    June 18, 1838, account filed, and allowance to his widow, page 356.
    June 18, 1838, account filed, and real estate ordered sold to pay debts, page 357.
    Real estate sold to Nelson Scofield of Stamford, and report of sale filed Sept. 22, 1838, page 357.

Jones, Enos, late of Stamford, will dated Mch. 5, 1836, probated Aug. 20, 1836, mentions his children Henry, Watson, Polly wife of Elihu Dan, Tammy Jones, Emeline wife of Joseph Ballac, and Ezra. Executor son Henry. Witnesses N. D. Haight, Jared Stevens, and Samuel Avery, page 177.
    Aug. 20, 1836, order to advertise for claims, page 178.
    Inventory taken by Jacob Stevens and John Seely, and filed Oct. 20, 1836, page 178.

Jones, George H., of Darien, John Bell, Jr., of Darien his guardian, the real estate of said minor sold to Jeremiah Andreas and Jarvis Weed, and report of sale filed Mch. 9, 1837, page 243.

Jones, Henry, of Darien, Sept. 6, 1839, made choice of his mother, Sarah Jones of Darien, to be his guardian, page 387.

Jones, Nehemiah, formerly of Stamford, having abandoned his wife, and for a long time has been a lunatic, the interest of his wife in his real estate in Stamford or-

STAMFORD PROBATE RECORDS.
Volume 15, 1834.

Jones, Nehemiah, continued :
dered sold by a Resolution of the General Assembly,
passed May 30, 1837, by Royal L. Gay, page 313.
Interest sold to Selleck Scofield, and report of sale
filed Apl. 28, 1838, page 314.

Jones, Samuel A., of Darien, John Bell, Jr., of Darien, his
guardian, the real estate of said minor sold to William
Smith, Jr., of New York City, and report of sale filed
Feb. 10, 1837, page 244.

Jones, Selleck, late of Darien, Mch. 11, 1834, account filed
by his administrator, and estate ordered distributed
to his children Isaac S., James, Horace F., Nancy O.,
George, William, and Samuel, page 47.
Mch. 19, 1834, estate distributed to James Jones, assignee of Isaac S. Jones, James Jones, Horace F. Jones,
Nancy O. Jones, William Jones, Samuel Jones, and George
Jones, page 47.
June 12, 1836, William Jones of Darien, a son of decedent over 14 years of age, made choice of John Bell, Jr.
of Darien to be his guardian, page 127.
Mch. 25, 1834, George, William, and Samuel, by their
guardian John Bell, Jr., asked leave to sell their
real estate in Norwalk, Darien, and Stamford, and sale
ordered, pages 20 and 21.

Jones, Thomas, late of Stamford, Mch. 23, 1835, account filed
and allowance to his widow, page 155.

Jones, William, of Darien, John Bell, Jr., of Darien, his
guardian, the real estate of said minor sold to Noah
Knapp of Darien, and report of sale filed Mch. 9,
1837, page 243.

Jordon, William, late of Greenwich, will dated Apl. 16, 1822,
probated Oct. 17, 1838, mentions his wife Hannah, and
children Marcy Ferris, Betsy Ferris, Phebe Adams, Alla
Ennis and her son William Jordon Ennis. Executors his
wife and John Adams. Witnesses Abraham Close,
Hanford Reynolds, and Major Lockwood, page 359.
Oct. 17, 1838, both executors refused to qualify, and
letters granted to Ira Lockwood of Greenwich, who was
ordered to advertise for claims, page 359.
Inventory taken Oct. 18, 1838, by William Smith and
Amos Mead, and filed Oct. 25, 1838, page 360.
Feb. 11, 1839, commissioners appointed to adjust claims
of creditors, pages 360 and 361.
Sept. 2, 1839, report of commissioners filed, page 361.

STAMFORD PROBATE RECORDS.
Volume 15, 1834.

Jordon, William, continued :
> Sept. 18, 1839, account filed, and allowance to his widow, page 361.
> Sept. 18, 1839, account filed, and real estate ordered sold to pay debts, page 380.
> Real estate sold to John Adams of Greenwich, and report of sale filed, page 380.

Judson, Joseph, late of Darien, Aug. 9, 1841, letters of administration on his estate granted to William Andreas of Darien, who was ordered to advertise for claims, page 449.
> Inventory taken Oct. 18, 1841, by Jacob Lockwood and Charles Weed, Jr., and filed Oct. 18, 1841, page 449.
> Mch. 17, 1842, account filed, and allowance to his widow, page 450.

June, Hannah, late of Stamford, Sept. 8, 1834, letters of administration on her estate granted to Abel Reynolds of Stamford, who was ordered to advertise for claims, page 154.
> Inventory taken by Edwin Newman and William Hobby, and filed Mch. 15, 1834, page 154.
> Oct. 5, 1835, account filed, and real estate ordered sold to pay debts, page 154.
> Real estate sold to Arza Marshall of Stamford, and report of sale filed Dec. 11, 1835, page 154.

June, Hannah, late of Stamford, Dec. 11, 1835, estate ordered distributed to her children Nancy Clark, Zabed June, Isaac June, Prudence Dixon, heirs of Betsy deceased wife of Eber Smith, and the heirs of Hannah deceased wife of James Smith, page 264.
> Apl. 28, 1836, estate distributed accordingly, page 264.

June, Reuben, late of Stamford, Mch. 11, 1839, his widow refused to qualify, and letters of administration on his estate granted to Nehemiah Hait, Jr., who was ordered to advertise for claims, page 454.
> Inventory taken Apl. 1, 1839, by Ransford A. Ferris and Alfred Smith, and filed Apl. 1, 1839, page 454.
> Mch. 21, 1842, account filed, and allowance to his widow, and real estate ordered sold to pay debts, pages 454 and 455.

Knapp, Caroline, Elizabeth Knapp, and Esther Knapp, all of Stamford, over 12 years of age, July 13, 1840, made choice of their brother, Joshua Knapp, to be their guardian, who was also appointed guardian of Edmund Knapp,

STAMFORD PROBATE RECORDS.
Volume 15, 1834.

Knapp, Caroline, continued :
under the age of years, page 433.
July 13, 1840, their guardian, asked leave to sell the real estate of said minors in Stamford, and sale ordered, pages 468, and 469.
Real estate sold to Edgar Studwell of Stamford, and report of sale filed Nov. 11, 1840, page 469.

Knapp, Hannah C., about 18 years of age, and Eunice C. Knapp, about 15 years of age, both of Greenwich, Jan. 25, 1842 made choice of Joshua Knapp of Greenwich to be their guardian, who was also appointed guardian of Sarah M. Knapp, about 9 years of age, page 505.
Jan. 25, 1842, petition for leave to sell the real estate of said minors in Greenwich, and sale ordered, page 506.
Real estate sold to Odel C. Knapp, and report of sale filed Apl. 25, 1842, page 506.

Knapp, Enos, late of Greenwich, June 15, 1833, his widow now deceased, and personal property ordered distributed to his children Isaac, Enos, and Rhoda Page, page 59.
June 22, 1833, estate distributed accordingly, page 59.

Knapp, Ezra, of Stamford, Mch. 29, 1834, general assignment to Stephen B. Provost and Joshua B. Ferris of Stamford for the benefit of creditors, page 50.
Inventory taken Mch. 31, 1834, by Davis Lockwood and Isaac Quintard, and filed Apl. 7, 1834, page 51.
Apl. 14, 1834, commissioners appointed to adjust claims of creditors, page 51.
Nov. 11, 1834, report of commissioners filed, page 52.
Apl. 7, 1834, personal property ordered sold, page 52.
Aug. 16, 1834, real estate ordered sold, page 53.
Jan. 5, 1835, real estate sold to Theodore Davenport, and report of sale filed, page 53.

Knapp, Isaac, late of Stamford, Mch. 2, 1835, account filed by his administrator, and allowance to his widow, page 86.
Mch. 14, 1835, account filed, and real estate ordered sold to pay debts, page 86.
Real estate sold to Joshua Knapp, and report of sale filed Apl. 4, 1835, by Daniel Lockwood, administrator, page 87.

Knapp, Isaac, late of Stamford, Mch. 14, 1835, his widow refused to qualify, and letters of administration on his

STAMFORD PROBATE RECORDS.
Volume 15, 1834.

Knapp, Isaac, continued:
  estate granted to Harvey Lockwood and Horace Scofield, who were ordered to advertise for claims, page 147.
  Inventory taken Mch. 23, 1835, by Peter Lockwood and Joshua Smith, and filed Mch. 23, 1835, page 147.
  Sept. 10, 1835, account filed, and commissioners appointed to adjust claims of creditors, pages 147 and 148.
  July 15, 1837, report of commissioners filed, page 329.
  June 4, 1838, dower of his widow set out, page 329.
  Apl. 28, 1838, account filed, and real estate ordered sold to pay debts, 337.
  Real estate sold to Erastus C. Bishop, N. D. Haight, and William H. Knapp, all of Stamford, and report of sale filed Aug. 8, 1838, page 338.
  Aug. 9, 1838, creditors ordered paid 76 02/100 cents on the dollar, page 338.

Knapp, Israel, late of Stamford, Feb. 7, 1835, Sarah B. Knapp of New York City, a daughter of decedent, over 12 years of age, made choice of Ezra Lockwood to be her guardian, page 55.

Knapp, Jacob, late of Stamford, Jan. 15, 1834, his widow refused to qualify, and letters of administration on his estate granted to his sons Isaac Knapp and William H. Knapp of Stamford, who were ordered to advertise for claims, page 63.
  Inventory taken by Jonathan Scofield and Horace Scofield, and filed Jan. 23, 1834, page 63.

Knapp, James, of Stamford, May 4, 1837, no father, or mother, made choice of Edwin Bishop of Stamford to be his guardian, page 210.

Knapp, Joshua, late of North Castle, June 29, 1839, dower ordered set out to his widow, Charity Knapp, page 387.
  Oct. 12, 1839, dower set out, page 388.

Knapp, Nathaniel, Colonel, late of Greenwich, Jan. 22, 1836, letters of administration on his estate granted to his widow, Elizabeth C. Knapp and Bartow F. White, who were ordered to advertise for claims, page 160.
  Inventory taken Jan. 27, 1836, by Joseph Brush and Amos Finnh, and filed Mch. 9, 1836, page 160.

Knapp, Reuben E., of Greenwich, over 14 years of age, Sept. 14, 1838, made choice of Allen R. Knapp of Greenwith to be his guardian, page 363.

STAMFORD PROBATE RECORDS.
Volume 18, 1834.

Knapp, Walter Newman, and David Holly Knapp, of Stamford, both under 14 years of age, June 16, 1834, the court appointed Ezra Lockwood of Stamford to be their guardian, page 17.

Knapp, Walter N., David H. Knapp, of Stamford, and Sarah B. Knapp, of New York City, Feb. 20, 1835, by their guardian Ezra Lockwood, asked leave to sell their real estate in Stamford, and sale ordered, page 108.
Real estate sold to Cary H. Gray and Michael Harms, and report of sale filed Dec. 26, 1835, page 108.

Leeds, Abraham, late of Stamford, Nov. 11, 1839, his widow being unable to act, letters of administration on his estate granted to John R. Leeds of Darien, who was ordered to advertise for claims, page 426.
Inventory taken Jan. 11, 1840, by William Scofield, Jr. and Nelson D. Scofield, and filed Feb. 1, 1840, page 426.

Leeds, Cary H., late of Stamford, Mch. 7, 1841, letters of administration on his estate granted to Samuel Leeds and Alexander N. Holly, who were ordered to advertise for claims, page 456.
Inventory taken Mch. 13, 1841, by Ezra Lockwood and Stephen B. Provost, and filed Apl. 23, 1841, page 457.
Feb. 12, 1842, estate ordered distributed to his children viz: Emily wife of Alexander N. Holly, Lorenzo, Sylvester, Samuel, Angeline wife of David Knapp, Cornelia wife of Selleck Waterbury, Smith, Sarah, James T., and Marian, page 466.
Feb. 24, 1842, estate distributed to Sylvester Leeds, two shares, one in his own right and one as assignee of Lorenzo Leeds, to James Leeds, Samuel Leeds seven shares, one in his own right and one each as assignee of the aforesaid Emily, Angeline, Cornelia, Sarah(Smith), Marian, and Sarah,(Smith not mentioned), page 467.

Leeds, Elisha, late of Stamford, May 30, 1842, former administrator now deceased, and letters de bonus non granted to John W. Leeds of Stamford, page 516.

Leeds, Rhoda, late of Stamford, will dated July 27, 1827, probated Dec. 14, 1838, mentions her nephew Captain John Brown, and his daughters Abigail, Mary and Elizabeth. Executor said Captain John Brown. Witnesses Solomon Clason, William H. Holly, and Charles Hawley, page 429.
Dec. 14, 1838, order to advertise for claims, page 430.

STAMFORD PROBATE RECORDS.
Volume 15, 1834.

Leeds, Sarah, late of Darien, will dated Nov. 13, 1834, probated Mch. 21, 1836, 1/2 to her son William E. Leeds, and the other 1/2 to the executor for the benefit of the children of Charles T. Leeds, daughters Sally Weed, Polly Brown, Eliza Leeds and Catherine Dixon. Executor her son William E. Leeds. Witnesses Honor Leeds, Mary E. Brown, and Ann E. Holly, page 174.
Mch. 21, 1836, order to advertise for claims, page 174.
Inventory taken by Josiah Lockwood and John Holmes, and filed May 4, 1836, page 175.

Leeds, William E., late of Darien, will dated Jan. 28, 1837, probated Feb. 25, 1837, mentions his brother Charles T. Leeds, sister Catherine Dixon, and her son William E. Dixon. Executor brother Charles T. Leeds. Witnesses Joshua B. Ferris, Eliza A. Leeds, and David B. Burr, page 216.
Feb. 25, 1837, order to advertise for claims, page 216.
Inventory taken by Josiah Lockwood and John Holmes, and filed Apl. 24, 1837, page 217.

Leeker, Morris, and Charles Leeker, of New York City, Apl. 30, 1840, their guardian, William Andreas of Darien, asked leave to sell the real estate of said minors in Darien, being their interest in the estate of Lydia Weed, late of Darien, deceased, and sale ordered, page 502.
Real estate sold to Ebenezer Weed of Darien, and report of sale filed, July 25, 1840, pages 502 and 505.

Lockwood, Andrew, late of Greenwich, Sept. 29, 1834, his widow refused to qualify, and letters of administration on his estate granted to Joshua B. Ferris of Stamford, who was ordered to advertise for claims, page 85.
Inventory taken by Alexander Hendrie and Cornelius Ford and filed Apl. 29, 1835, page 85.
Apl. 27, 1835, account filed, and allowance to his widow, page 86.

Lockwood, Charles, late of Greenwich, Feb. 6, 1834, the share of his widow, Mary Lockwood, ordered set out, page 125.
Mch. 18, 1834, share accordingly set out, page 125.

Lockwood, Drake, late of Greenwich, will dated Jan. 12, 1832, probated Mch. 28, 1839, mentions his wife Mary, and children Mary, Charlotte, Angeline, Eliza, Frederick A. John, and Leaticia M. Peck. Executors his sons John and Frederick A. Witnesses Stephen Lockwood, Jr., Angeline Knapp, and Joshua Ferris, page 404.
Mch. 28, 1839, order to advertise for claims, page 404.

STAMFORD PROBATE RECORDS.
Volume 15, 1834.

Lockwood, Drake, continued :
    Inventory taken by Charles Hendrie and Asahel Palmer, and filed Apl. 6, 1839, page 405.

Lockwood, Enos, late of Greenwich, will dated Oct. 19, 1831, probated Sept. 8, 1837, mentions his wife Sarah, and sons Beal B. and Enos B., grandson William Maurice Lockwood a son of Maurice Lockwood a deceased son. Executor his son Beal B. Witnesses Messenger Lockwood, John Lockwood, and Charles Hxxx Hawley, page 254.
Sept. 8, 1837, order to advertise for claims, page 256.
Inventory taken Oct. 21, 1837, by George Ferris, Jr., and David Lockwood, and Solomon Clason, and filed Mch. 10, 1838, page 297.

Lockwood, Hannah, late of Greenwich, will dated Aug. 16, 1836, probated Aug. 23, 1836, mentions Jonathan Scofield, Phebe Weeks, and nieces Polly Scofield and Nancy Smith. Executor Isaac H. Smith. Witnesses Cornelius Ford, Hannah Ford, and Lucy D. Quintard, page 215.
Aug. 23, 1836, order to advertise for claims, page 215.
Inventory taken by George Ferris and Alexander Hendrie, and filed Feb. 20, 1837, page 216.

Lockwood, Isaac, late of Stamford, will dated Mch. 21, 1833, probated Aug. 22, 1836, mentions his brothers Augustus Lockwood, Peter Lockwood, and Frederick Lockwood, sisters Mary Selleck, Abigail Hoyt, Betsy Sturges, and Rebecca Hoyt. Executor brother Frederick. Witnesses Hervey Hobby, Ann Weed, and Charles Hawley, page 198. Codicil dated Oct. 19, 1833, and appointed as executor his brother Augustus.
Aug. 22, 1836, order to advertise for claims, page 199.
Inventory taken by Royal L. Say and Isaac Lockwood, and filed Aug. 31, 1836, page 200.

Lockwood, Jacob, late of Darien, June 25, 1835, his sister, Susan Lockwood, refused to qualify, and letters of administration on his estate granted to Abram Clock of Darien, who was ordered to advertise for claims, page XX 180.
Inventory taken June 26, 1835, by John Bell, Jr., and Jacob Penoyer, and filed July 1, 1835, page 181.

Lockwood, Lewis, late of Stamford, Mch. 13, 1837, account filed, and real estate ordered sold to pay debts, page 261 Real estate sold to Isaac L. Lockwood and John Robertson, and report of sale filed June 14, 1837, page 261.

STAMFORD PROBATE RECORDS.
Volume 15, 1834.

Lockwood, Mills, late of Greenwich, Nov. 4, 1839, his widow refused to qualify, and letters of administration on his estate granted to Abel Reynolds of Stamford, who was ordered to advertise for claims, page 436.
Inventory taken Nov. 7, 1839, by Conklin Husted and Alfred Rundle, and filed Nov. 11, 1839, page 346.
Nov. 18, 1839, commissioners appointed to adjust claims of creditors, page 437.
Mch. 1, 1842, report of commissioners filed, page 437.
July 8, 1840, exceptions to report filed, page 438.
Mch. 21, 1842, account filed, allowance to his widow, and real estate ordered sold to pay debts, page 439.

Lockwood, Philip, late of   inventory taken Jan. 13, 1832, by George Ferris, Jr., and Alexander Hendrie, and filed by William Waterbury, executor, page 96.

Lockwood, Sarah, late of Stamford, Mch. 17, 1838, her husband, Daniel Lockwood, refused to qualify, and letters of administration on her estate granted to Earl Smith of Stamford, who was ordered to advertise for claims, page 304.

Lockwood, Sarah, wife of Joseph Lockwood, formerly of New York City, now being in Stamford, will dated Oct. 5, 1830, probated ------, mentions her son Andrew Lockwood. Executor John Weed, Jr., of Stamford. Witnesses David Waterbury, Ezra Scofield, Jr., and John L. Scofield, page 450.
Inventory taken by Aaron Dean and John Dean, and filed Mch. 20, 1841, page 450.

Lockwood, William Maurice, of Greenwich, over 14 years of age, Sept. 8, 1837, made choice of Beal B. Lockwood of Greenwich to be his guardian, page 253.

Luker, Morris, and Charles Luker, of New York City, Apl. 30, 1840, the court appointed William Andreas of Darien to be their guardian, page 422.

Marshall, Henry, late of Greenwich, Nov. 21, 1837, letters of administration on his estate granted to his brother William S. Marshall, who was ordered to advertise for claims, page 296.
Inventory taken Dec. 28, 1837, by Benjamin Page and Henry Ritch, and filed Jan. 23, 1838, page 296.
Jan. 23, 1838, account filed, and commissioners appointed to adjust claims of creditors, page 303.

STAMFORD PROBATE RECORDS.
Volume 15, 1834.

Marshall, Orpah, late of Greenwich, will dated Oct. 10, 1833, probated Jan. 30, 1839, mentions her sister Hannah Marshall, Isaac Mosher a son of her sister Deborah Whelpley, niece Orpah Peck a daughter of Nehemiah Peck, and Isaac Mosher, Jr., a son of my said nephew Isaac Mosher. Executor Asahel Palmer. Witnesses Henry Whelpley, Deborah Whelpley, and Jabez Mead, page 413.
Jan. 30, 1839, order to advertise for claims, page 413.
Inventory taken by Lot Palmer and Henry Ritch, and filed Feb. 5, 1839, page 414.

Marshall, Sarah, late of Darien, will dated Aug. 2, 1836, probated Jan. 2, 1842, mentions her friends Henry Clock, Jr and Debby Clock, and the children of Mary Fisher by her first husband, Selleck Seely, deceased. Executor Albert Seely. Witnesses Abram Clock, Sarah Clock, and Elisha Seely, page 513.
Jan. 2, 1842, order to advertise for claims, page 513.
Inventory taken Jan. 24, 1842, by Abram Clock and George J. Bowler, and filed Jan. 24, 1842, page 514.

Mather, Joseph, late of Darien, will dated Dec. 16, 1831, probated Mch. 11, 1840, mentions his wife Sarah, and children Moses, Joseph, David S., Rana or Raua, Phebe, Betsy Lockwood, Hannah Selleck, Sarah Richards, Clara Street, and Nancy Bell. Executor his son Joseph. Witnesses Lewis Weed, Charles Weed, and Daty Weed, page 497.
Mch. 11, 1840, order to advertise for claims, page 498.
Inventory taken Apl. 20, 1840, by Daty Weed and Edward Scofield, and filed Apl. 25, 1840, page 499.

Mead, Daniel S., late of Greenwich, July 10, 1835, Jared Mead, a son of decedent, over 14 years of age, made choice of Thomas A. Mead to be his guardian, page 111, and the court appointed Joseph Brush guardian of Edwin, a son of decedent, page 109.
Aug. 4, 1835, the court appointed Rachel Mead to be guardian of her son Silas Merwin, another son of decedent, page 110.
Aug. 4, 1835, petition for leave to sell the real estate of said minors in Greenwich, page 308.
June 23, 1840, Darius Mead, Jr., guardian of Silas Merwin Mead, asked leave to sell the real estate of said minor in Greenwich, and sale ordered, page 499.
Real estate sold to Edwin Mead of Greenwich, and report of sale filed Dec. 23, 1840, pages 500 and 505.

STAMFORD PROBATE RECORDS.
Volume 15, 1834.

Mead, Elizabeth, late of Greenwich, June 18, 1839, letters of administration on her estate granted to Bartow F. White of Greenwich, who was ordered to advertise for claims, page 406.
Inventory taken June 18, 1839, and filed June 18, 1839, page 407.

Mead, Louisiana Cordelia, Sept. 20, 1841, her guardian Isaac Dean of Stamford asked leave to sell the real estate of said minor in Norwalk, and sale ordered, pages 469 and 470.
Real estate sold to Legrand W. Craw and Richard Bates, the one of Darien and the other of Norwalk, and report of sale filed Mch. 16, 1842, page 470.

Mead, Luther, of Greenwich, Sept. 4, 1834, has been absent for more than seven years unheard of, and is considered dead intestate; and letters of administration on his estate granted to Rev. Zachariah Mead, who was ordered to advertise for claims, page 126.

Mead, Manoah, late of Greenwich, Feb. 1, 1839, his widow refused to qualify, and letters of administration on his estate granted to Drake Mead of Greenwich, who was ordered to advertise for claims, page 381.
Inventory taken by Elias Peck and Isaac Lyon, and filed Mch. 9, 1839, page 381.
Aug. 19, 1839, allowance to his widow, page 382.
Aug. 19, 1839, account filed, and real estate ordered sold to pay debts, page 382.
Real estate sold to Elias Peck of Greenwich, and report of sale filed, page 383.

Mead, Mary, late of Greenwich, widow of Jonah Mead, will dated Aug. 13, 1835, probated Apl. 3, 1837, mentions her children Drake Mead and Hannah Mead. Executor her son Drake. Witnesses Sarah W. Mead and Jabez Mead, page 239.
Apl. 3, 1837, order to advertise for claims, page 240.
Inventory taken May 20, 1837, by Amos Mead and Isaac Lyon, and filed June 16, 1837, page 261.

Mead, Nehemiah, late of Greenwich, Mch. 12, 1834, account filed, and estate ordered distributed according to his will, page 6.
Mch. 21, 1834, estate distributed to Mehitabel wife of Royal Dunton, a daughter, Andrew Mead for life, a son, Polly wife of Willet Sherwood, a daughter, Jeremiah Fog son of Zachariah Mead, a grandson, and Huldah

STAMFORD PROBATE RECORDS.
Volume 15, 1834.

Mead, Nehemiah, continued,
    Tracy, a daughter, page 6.

Mead, Rachel, of Somers, N. Y., Jan. 5, 1835, appointed guardian of her son Jeremiah F. Mead, under 14 years of age, page 63.

Mead, Reuben, late of Stamford, Jan. 25, 1834, account filed, and commissioners appointed to adjust claims of creditors, pages 148 and 149.
Dec. 30, 1834, report of commissioners filed, page 149.
Mch. 23, 1835, account filed, and real estate ordered sold to pay debts, page 149.

Mead, Sarah W., of Greenwich, Feb. 1, 1841, appointed guardian of her children William K. Mead, about 16 years of age, and Mary E. Mead, about 18 years of age, page 424.
Feb. 1, 1841, petition for leave to sell the real estate of said minors in Greenwich, and sale ordered, subject to the dower right of their mother, page 474.
Real estate sold to Samuel Jessup of Greenwich, and report of sale filed Apl. 12, 1841, page 475.

Merritt, Caroline, late of Greenwich, will dated June 29, 1839, probated Nov. 18, 1839, mentions her mother Mary W. Merritt, and brother Jotham Merritt. Executors Merritt Brown and James W. Brown, both of Rye. Witnesses George Whitcomb, Lawrence Brown, and William Strang, page 414.
Nov. 18, 1839, Merritt Brown refused to qualify, and letters granted to James W. Brown, who was ordered to advertise for claims, page 415.
Inventory taken Nov. 20, 1839, by Samuel G. Cornell and William Strang, and filed Dec. 10, 1839, page 416.

Merritt, Elijah, late of Greenwich, July 1, 1837, his widow refused to qualify, and letters of administration on his estate granted to Colonel Thomas A. Mead of Greenwich, who was ordered to advertise for claims, page 260.
Inventory taken by David Brown and William B. Sherwood, and filed Apl. 7, 1838, page 295.

Merritt, Elizabeth, late of Greenwich, Mch. 6, 1838, letters of administration on her estate granted to Samuel Close, who was ordered to advertise for claims, page 295.
Inventory taken Mch. 28, 1838, by Seth Lyon and Fitch Lyon, and filed Apl. 23, 1838, pages 295 and 355.

STAMFORD PROBATE RECORDS.
Volume 15, 1834.

269.

Merritt, Jeremiah A., late of Greenwich, June 15, 1835, Anderson Merritt of North Castle, guardian of Mary Elizabeth Merritt and William C. Merritt of North Castle, children of decedent, asked leave to sell the real estate of said minors in Greenwich, and sale ordered, subject to the dower rights of their mother, Maria Merritt, page 185.
Maria Merritt, of Greenwich, Mch. 4, 1839, appointed guardian of her children Theodore Merritt, Elizabeth Merritt, James Harvey Merritt, and Phinehas Merritt, all under 12 years of age, page 363.
Mch. 4, 1839, petition for leave to sell the real estate of the latter minors in Greenwich, page 365.
Real estate of the latter minors sold to John A. Merritt, and report of sale filed Mch. 3, 1840, page 491.

Miller, Jonathan, late of Stamford, Sept. 10, 1834, his widow refused to qualify, and letters of administration on his estate granted to his son Seth Miller, who was ordered to advertise for claims, page 122.
Inventory taken Nov. 3, 1834, by John Dean and John Weed, Jr., and filed Nov. 8, 1834, page 122.
Dec. 10, 1835, account filed, and real estate ordered sold to pay debts, page 123.
Real estate sold to Seely Miller, and report of sale filed Feb. 20, 1836, p. 123.
Dec. 10, 1836, dower of his widow ordered set out, and set out, page 299.

Mills, Samuel, late of Greenwich, will dated July 9, 1824, probated Feb. 12, 1841, mentions his children Charlotte Todd, and Olla Husted, grandsons Samuel Mills and Roswell Mills, sons of his son Samuel Mills, late deceased. Executors Conklin Husted and son-in-law Benjamin Husted, Jr. Witnesses Stephen Waring, James Waring, and Benjamin I. Knapp, page 504.
Feb. 12, 1841, order to advertise for claims, page 504.
Inventory taken Feb. 12, 1841, by Ezekiel Close and David Dayton, and filed Feb. 20, 1841, page 505.

Moe, Charlotte, late of Greenwich, Nov. 18, 1839, letters of administration on her estate granted to Elizabeth Moe, who was ordered to advertise for claims, page 426.
Inventory taken by Jonas Howe and Jonathan A. Close, and filed Jan. 18, 1840, page 427.

STAMFORD PROBATE RECORDS.
Volume 15, 1834.

Morehouse, Sarah Elizabeth, of New York City, over 12 years of age, June 23, 1836, made choice of Maurice Hoyt of Warwick, N. Y., to be her guardian, page 170.
June 23, 1836, petition for leave to sell the real estate of said minor in Darien, and sale ordered, page 176.

Morehouse, Silas, late of Stamford, Nov. 27, 1839, his widow refused to qualify, and letters of administration on his estate granted to Solomon Clason, and commissioners appointed to adjust claims of creditors, page 417.
Inventory taken Dec. 10, 1839, by William Hobby and Daniel Lockwood, and filed Mch. 9, 1840, page 418.
June 10, 1840, report of commissioners to adjust claims filed, page 418.
Oct. 19, 1840, account filed, and creditors ordered paid 55 3/10 cents on the dollar, page 418.

Nash, Mary Ann, of Stamford, Apl. 21, 1838, appointed guardian of her daughter Georgiana Nash, page 298.

Newman, Harvey, late of   Apl. 24, 1834, account filed and an allowance to his widow, page 12.

Newman, James M., late of Stamford, Dec. 29, 1836, letters of administration on his estate granted to Ezra H. Bishop of Darien, who was ordered to advertise for claims, page 243.
July 1, 1837, account filed, and commissioners appointed to adjust claims of creditors, page 253.
Inventory taken by Solomon Guernsey and James H. Hoyt, and filed Jan. 29, 1838, page 283.
Feb. 23, 1838, report of commissioners to adjust claims of creditors filed, page 283.
Mch. 19, 1838, account filed, and creditors ordered paid 78 61/100 cents on the dollar, page 285.

Palmer, Abigail, late of   will dated   probated Nov. 27, 1833, all to her daughter Catharine Shepperd, except certain bquests to her daughters Ann Scofield, and Hetty Platt, and sons David L. Palmer, and Lounsbury Palmer. No executor. Witnesses Mary Palmer, Hannah Palmer, and Nathaniel D. Haight, page 82.
Nov. 27, 1833, letters of administration with the will annexed granted to Catharine Shepperd, who was ordered to advertise for claims, page 82.
Inventory taken Nov. 29, 1833, by Joseph Smith and Oliver Lockwood, and filed Apl. 21, 1835, page 83.

STAMFORD PROBATE RECORDS.
Volume 15, 1834.

Palmer, Abigail, late of Stamford, Jan. 7, 1839, letters of administration on her estate granted to Hannah Palmer and James P. Palmer, who were ordered to advertise for claims, page 357.
Inventory taken by Joseph Smith and Ebenezer Smith, and filed Mch. 25, 1839, page 357.

Palmer, Deborah, late of Greenwich, July 29, 1837, letters of administration on her estate granted to her grandson Seth P. Quintard, who was ordered to advertise for claims, page 258.

Palmer, John A., of Stamford, 19 years of age, June 13, 1836, his guardian Royal L. Gay of Stamford discharged, page 182.

Palmer, Seth, late of Greenwich, the personal property retained by his widow sold Aug. 12, 1837, page 312.

Peck, Aaron, late of Greenwich, Mch. 11, 1834, account filed, by his executor, and real estate ordered sold to pay debts, page 12.
Real estate sold to John Chappel, and report of sale filed June 10, 1834, page 12.

Peck, Ebenezer, late of Greenwich, will dated Aug. 28, 1829, probated Oct. 7, 1833, mentions his wife Hannah and children Anna, Rufus, Hannah widow of Ezra Lockwood, Elizabeth wife of Augustus Lockwood, Deborah wife of Elias Raymond, and Polly wife of Pearson Peck. Executor son-in-law Augustus Lockwood. Witnesses Mary S. Hawley, Peter Jessup and Charles Hawley, page 90.
1st Codicil dated Sept. 1, 1829, page 92.
2nd codicil dated Oct. 26, 1829, page 92.
Oct. 7, 1833, Order to advertise for claims, page 93.
Inventory taken by Henry Ritch and Asahel Palmer, and filed Oct. 30, 1835, page 93.

Peck, Ebenezer, late of Stamford, Nov. 14, 1837, his widow refused to qualify, and letters of administration on his estate granted to Royal L. Gay of Stamford, who was ordered to advertise for claims, page 272.
Inventory taken by Frederic Lockwood and Henry Waring and filed Nov. 15, 1837, page 272.

Peck, Elias, formerly of Greenwich, Mch. 15, 1838, having been long absent from the state, and being in the opinion of the court not a proper person to be guardian of his son

STAMFORD PROBATE RECORDS.
Volume 15, 1834.

Peck, Elias, continued :
    Jonathan Peck of Greenwich, over 14 years of age, and Joseph Brush of Greenwich, was appointed in his place, page 299.

Peck, Gilbert, late of Greenwich, Aug. 30, 1832, his widow refused to qualify, and letters of administration on his estate granted to Gilbert P. Finch of Greenwich, who was ordered to advertise for claims, page 9.
    Mch. 7, 1833, account filed, and allowance to his widow, page 9.

Peck, Hannah, late of Greenwich, will dated Oct. 13, 1837, probated Aug. 26, 1839, all to her daughter Deborah Ferris, and appointed her executrix. Witnesses Maria Brown, Hannah Peck, and Charles Hawley, page 405.
    Aug. 26, 1839, order to advertise for claims, page 406.
    Inventory taken Sept. 9, 1839, by Conklin Husted and William Finch, and filed Sept. 14, 1839, page 406.

Peck, Harriet, of Greenwich, over 12 years of age, Nov. 11, 1839, made choice of David Peck of Greenwich to be her Guardian, page 387.

Peck, Henry, about 18 years of age, Hannah Peck, about 15 years of age, and Mary Peck, about 12 years of age, Oct. 21, 1839, made choice of William Finch of Greenwich to be their guardian, page 387.
    Dec. 2, 1839, petition for leave to sell the real estate of said minors in Greenwich, and sale ordered, page 428.
    Real estate sold to Ebenezer Mead of Bedford, N. Y., and report of sale filed, page 429.
    Mch. 15, 1841, petition for leave to sell the real estate of said minors in Greenwich, and sale ordered, page 503.
    Real estate sold for $37.98, it being their right in their portion of the estate of their deceased sister, Harriett Peck, and report of sale filed June 14, 1841, page 503.

Peck, Isaac, Jr., late of Greenwich, will dated May 19, 1820, probated Oct. 8, 1838, mentions his wife Hannah, and nephew Isaac Peck, 3rd, niece Huldah wife of Benoni Peck, father Theophilus Peck, deceased, Isaac Peck, 5th, son of Samuel Peck, Israel Peck, and Whitman youngest son of the aforesaid Samuel Peck. Executors his wife and Isaac Peck, 3rd. Witnesses Elisha Belcher, Gilbert Close, and Samuel Close, page 351.

STAMFORD PROBATE RECORDS.
Volume 15, 1834.

Peck, Isaac, Jr., continued :
    Inventory taken Nov. 1838, by Nehemiah Howe and Jonas Howe, and filed Nov. 5, 1838, page 354.

Peck, Jared, late of Greenwich, Aug. 14, 1837, letters of administration on his estate granted to his brother Benoni Peck and Gilbert P. Finch the husband of a sister of deceased, who were ordered to advertise for claims, page 258.
    Inventory taken Aug. 18, 1837, by Platt Mead and James Wilson, and filed Aug. 21, 1837, page 258.

Peck, John Walter, of Freehold, N. J., and Charles Henry Peck of New York City, both over 14 years of age, June 17, 1837, made choice of Deborah Selleck of Greenwich to be their guardian, page 263.
    June 21, 1837, petition for leave to sell the real estate of said minors in Greenwich, and sale ordered, page 300.
    Real estate sold to Stephen P. Selleck and Lot Palmer, and report of sale filed Nov. 16, 1837, page 301.

Peck, Ruth Maria, of Greenwich, over 12 years of age, Dec. 29, 1838, made choice of Jabez Mead, 3rd, of Greenwich to her guardian, page 367.

Peck, Samuel, late of Greenwich, will dated Feb. 12, 1841, probated Aug. 30, 1841, mentions his wife Mary, and children Anna M., Jane, Sophia, Obadiah, Samuel, Whitman, and Isaac. Executors sons Obadiah and Isaac. Witnesses Darius Mead, Jr., Lydia K. Mead, and Julia Ann Mead, page 484.

Pencyer, Isaac, late of Darien, will dated Sept. 22, 1829, probated Oct. 23, 1833, his wife now deceased, surviving children Jesse, Henry, Jacob, John, Samuel, Alanson and Hannah Husted. Executor his son Samuel. Witnesses Jesse Selleck, Morris Tuthill, and Elizabeth Gray, page 41.
    Oct. 23, 1833, order to advertise for claims, page 42.
    Inventory taken Oct. 25, 1833, by Jeremiah Andreas and Abram Clock, and filed Dec. 20, 1833, page 42.
    July 21, 1834, account filed, and estate ordered distributed to said Jesse, Henry, Jacob, John, Samuel, Alanson, and Hannah, page 43.
    Sept. 29, 1834, estate distributed accordingly, page 44.

STAMFORD PROBATE RECORDS.
Volume 15, 1834.

Penoyer, Jacob, late of Darien, will dated Feb. 23, 1837, probated Apl. 25, 1837, mentions his wife Elizabeth, daughter Loiza Bagley, and grandson Morris E. Penoyer. Executors his wife and Abram Clock. Witnesses George H. Wallace, Samuel Gorum and Albert Seely, page 237.
Apl. 25, 1837, order to advertise for claims, page 238.
Inventory taken May 3, 1837, by Enos Tuttle and George I. Bowler, and filed June 16, 1837, page 262.
Mch. 24, 1838, rights of his widow, Elizabeth Penoyer, ordered set out, page 279.
May 4, 1838, rights set out, page 280.
June 16, 1842, account filed, and personal property ordered distributed to his widow, Elizabeth Penoyer, grandson Morris E. Penoyer, and daughter Louisa Bagley, according to his will, page 427.
June 17, 1840, estate distributed accordingly, page 428.
Morris E. Penoyer, over 15 years of age, Apl. 30, 1838, made choice of Abram Clock to be his guardian, page 298

Penoyer, Samuel, late of Darien, will dated Aug. 12, 1830, probated Nov. 2, 1839, all to his niece Anna Tuttle of Darien, and appointed her his executrix. Witnesses Abram Clock, Elisha Seely, and George I. Bowler, page 410.
Nov. 2, 1839, order to advertise for claims, page 410.
Inventory taken Nov. 22, 1839, by Abram Clock and George I. Bowler, and filed Nov. 25, 1839, page 411.

Platt, Frederick, late of Poundridge, Westchester County, N.Y. will dated Aug. 7, 1840, probated Nov. 13, 1841, mentions his wife and children, no names. Executors William Weed, and son John B. Platt. Witnesses Ezra Lockwood, Samuel Provost, and Willis Hoyt, page 514.
Nov. 13, 1841, order to advertise for claims, page 515.
Inventory taken Apl. 25, 1842, by Selleck Scofield and Alfred Ayres, and filed May 16, 1842, page 515.
May 17, 1842, account filed, and real estate ordered sold to pay debts, page 516.
Real estate sold to Hetty Platt of Poundridge, and report of sale filed May 19, 1842, page 516.

Potts, Isaac, late of Stamford, Oct. 10, 1833, his widow refused to qualify, and letters of administration on his estate granted to Dr. Nathaniel D. Hait of Stamford, who was ordered to advertise for claims, page 119.
Inventory taken Oct. 28, 1834, by Gould Raymond and John Curtis, and filed Mch. 31, 1835, page 119.
Apl. 4, 1835, account filed, and commissioners appointed to adjust claims of creditors, pages 119 and 120.

STAMFORD PROBATE RECORDS.
Volume 15, 1834.

Potts, Isaac, continued :
  Nov. 14, 1835, report of commissioners filed, page 120.
  Nov. 21, 1835, account filed, and real estate ordered
  sold to pay debts, page 120.
  Real estate sold to George Austin, and report of sale
  filed Apl. 18, 1836, page 121.

Purdy, Elias, late of Greenwich, Nov. 2, 1833, account filed
  by his administrator, and estate ordered distributed
  to his widow, ----, and children Caleb, Mary E., Sally
  A., and Harriet M., and Elias, page 75.
  Nov. 5, 1833, estate distributed to his widow, ----, and
  children Caleb, Elias, Hannah, and Sally A., and
  Mary E., page 76.

Purdy, Thomas, late of Greenwich, will dated Dec. 23, 1826,
  probated Nov. 9, 1836, all to his wife Tamson for life,
  and remainder to his children Calvin, Deborah Dayton,
  Mary, Phebe, Sally, Ann, John, and William. Executors Benjamin Green and David Brown. Witnesses John
  Robbins, Can. Robbins, and Jared Strang, page 189.
  Nov. 9, 1836, executors refused to qualify, and letters
  with the will annexed granted to Tamson Purdy and
  Calvin Purdy, who were ordered to advertise for claims,
  page 190.
  Inventory taken Nov. 18, 1836, by Benoni Peck and Bartow F. White, and filed Dec. 15, 1836, page 190.

Raynor, Adelaid Louisa, of Greenwich, Sept. 14, 1838, the Court
  appointed her uncle, Allen R. Knapp of Greenwich, to
  be her guardian, page 362.

Redfield, Bradley, late of Greenwich, Oct. 27, 1837, his widow refused to qualify, and letters of administration
  on his estate granted to his brother Isaac B. Redfield
  of Greenwich and Nathan S. Mead of Greenwich a brother
  in law, who were ordered to advertise for claims,
  page 275.
  Inventory taken Nov. 3, 1837, by Benoni Peck and James
  Willson, and filed Dec. 20, 1837, page 275.
  Nov. 26, 1838, dower of his widow ordered set out,
  page 346.
  Dec. 7, 1838, dower set out to his widow, Harriet Redfield, page 346.
  Nov. 28, 1838, account filed, and allowance to his
  widow, page 347.
  Mch. 25, 1839, account filed, and real estate ordered
  sold to pay debts, page 347.
  Real estate sold to Platt Mead of Greenwich, page 347.

STAMFORD PROBATE RECORDS.
Volume 15, 1834.

Redfield, Bradley, continued :
    Dec. 20, 1837, James Redfield over 14 years of age, made choice of Isaac B. Redfield to be his guardian, page 275.
    Platt M. Redfield, Edwin Redfield, Sally Redfield, Mary Redfield, and Bradley Redfield, all under 14 years of age, except Platt M., Dec. 27, 1838, the court appointed Platt Mead of Greenwich to be their guardian, page 348.
    Dec. 27, 1838, petition for leave to sell the real estate of said minors in Greenwich, and sale ordered, page 348.

Reynolds, Ard, of Greenwich, Mch. 19, 1838, appointed guardian of his children Ann Eliza, John G., Harriet E., over 14 years of age, and Julia H., under 12 years of age, page 298.

Reynolds, Deborah, late of Greenwich, Dec. 22, 1837, her sons refused to qualify, and letters of administration on her estate granted to Peter Boulanger, also called Peter Baker, husband of Abigail, a daughter of deceased who was ordered to advertise for claims, page 273.
    Inventory taken by Charles Hendrie and Beal B. Lockwood, and filed July 24, 1838, page 334.
    Sept. 14, 1838, account filed, and real estate ordered sold to pay debts, page 334.
    Dec. 14, 1838, real estate sold to Hannah Hoyt, page 335.

Reynolds, James H., late of Greenwich, Oct. 4, 1833, inventory taken by Zenas Mead and William Timpany, and filed Oct. 8, 1833, page 101.
    Sept. 21, 1838, account filed, and real estate ordered sold to pay debts, page 367.
    Real estate sold to Isaac Holly, Jr., of Greenwich, page 367.
    Oct. 17, 1833, report of commissioners to adjust claims of creditors filed, page 8.
    May 1, 1834, account filed, and an allowance to his widow, page 8.

Reynolds, Jared, late of Greenwich, Jan. 17, 1834, Susan Reynolds, Elmerretta Reynolds, Althea Reynolds, of Stamford, children of decedent, over 14 years of age, made choice of Edwin Newman to be their guardian, who was also appointed guardian of Amy Jane Reynolds, another child of decedent under 12 years of age, page 3.

STAMFORD PROBATE RECORDS.
Volume 15, 1834.

Reynolds, Jared, continued :
    Feb. 7, 1834, petition for leave to sell the real estate of said minors in Greenwich, and sale ordered, page 9.
    Feb. 7, 1834, petition by George Scofield of Stamford, husband and therefore guardian of Mary Elisabeth Scofield, a daughter of decedent, for leave to sell the real estate of said minor in Greenwich, and sale ordered, pages 64 and 65.

Reynolds, William, late of Greenwich, May 5, 1834, letters of administration on his estate granted to Joshua B. Ferris of Stamford, who was ordered to advertise for claims, page 53.
    Inventory taken Nov. 12, 1834, by Benjamin Page and Frederic Lockwood, real estate subject to the life estate of the widow, Mary Lockwood, and filed Feb. 17, 1835, page 53.

Reynolds, William P., late of Rye, Dec. 26, 1839, inventory taken and recorded on page 389.

Richards, Isaac, late of Darien, Mch. 21, 1838, his widow refused to qualify, and letters of administration on his estate granted to Ebenezer Weed, the husband of a sister of deceased of Darien, who was ordered to advertise for claims, page 304.

Robbins, Parris, late of Greenwich, will dated July 13, 1835, probated Aug. 28, 1838, mentions his wife Mary, and children Elisa wife of Samuel Peck of New York City, Catherine Robbins, and Alonzo F. Robbins. Executor Asahel Palmer of Greenwich. Witnesses Peter Ferris, Samuel Jessup, Jr., and Jabez Mead, page 383.
    Aug. 28, 1838, order to advertise for claims, page 383.
    Inventory taken by Henry Ritch and Lot Palmer, and filed Sept. 11, 1838, page 384.
    June 10, 1839, account filed, and an allowance to his widow, page 384.

Roberts, Amos, late of Darien, will dated Jan. 16, 1832, probated Oct. 21, 1838, mentions his wife Deborah, and children Catherine wife of Ezra Mills, and David. Executor son David. Witnesses Isaac Hoyt, Nane Hoyt, and Kilbourn F. Hoyt, page 378.
    Nov. 13, 1838, letters of administration with the will annexed granted to Henry Bates of Darien, who was ordered to advertise for claims, page 379.

STAMFORD PROBATE RECORDS.
Volume 15, 1834.

Roberts, Amos, continued :
> Inventory taken by William H. Bates and Thomas Reed, and filed May 5, 1839, page 379.
> Oct. 1839, account filed, and estate ordered distributed according to his will, viz: to his heirs David Roberts, Catherine Mills, Mary Crane, Sarah Roberts, Amos S. Roberts, children of Justus Roberts, deceased, Nathan Roberts, Phebe Roberts, and to the heirs of Deborah S. Roberts, who died since the testator without issue, each 1/9, page 389.
> Oct. 23, 1839, estate distributed accordingly, page 390.

Rogers, Fitch, late of Stamford, Inventory taken by Samuel Lockwood and George Brown, and filed Feb. 5, 1834, page 161.

Rogers, Hannah, late of Stamford, Dec. 26, 1835, letters of administration on her estate granted to her son Fitch Rogers of Stamford, page 242.

Rosco, Abraham, late of Greenwich Oct. 7, 1833, his widow refused to qualify, and letters of administration on his estate granted to Conklin Husted of Greenwich, who was ordered to advertise for claims, page 71.
> Inventory taken Oct. 10, 1833, by David Dayton and Samuel W. Todd, and filed Nov. 8, 1833, page 72.
> Mch. 26, 1834, account filed, and commissioners appointed to adjust claims of creditors, page 72.
> Oct. 27, 1834, report of commissioners filed, page 72.
> Oct. 29, 1834, allowance to his widow, page 73.
> Oct. 29, 1834, dower ordered set out, page 74.
> July 26, 1835, dower set out, page 74.
> Mch. 11, 1835, account filed, and real estate ordered sold to pay debts, page 74.
> Real estate sold to Rev. Farnum Knowlton of Greenwich, and report of sale filed Mch. 28, 1835, page 75.

Sackett, Ann, late of Rye, N. Y., widow of Justus Sackett, will dated July 22, 1829, probated July 12, 1837, mentions her daughters Sally Secor and Betsy Wilson, granddaughters Sarah Isaacs Sackett, Catherine Ann Sackett, Maria Holly Sackett, and Rebecca Augusta Sackett, daughters of her son William Henry Sackett, and Rachel E. Sackett a daughter of her son John Sackett. Executrices her daughters Sally Secor and Betsy Wilson. Witnesses David Lyon, Henry Lyon, and John Brown, page 248.
July 12, 1837, order to advertise for claims, page 249.

STAMFORD PROBATE RECORDS.
Volume 15, 1834.

Sackett, Joseph, late of Greenwich, June 30, 1840, letters of administration on his estate granted to Selleck Scofield of Stamford, who was ordered to advertise for claims, page 439.
Inventory taken July 3, 1840, by Charles Hendrie and Henry Ritch, and filed July 7, 1840, page 440.
Jan. 7, 1841, account filed, and commissioners appointed to adjust claims of creditors, page 440.
Nov. 22, 1842, report of commissioners filed, page 441.

Sackett, Whitman M., late of Greenwich, Oct. 31, 1835, letters of administration on his estate granted to Thomas A. Mead of Greenwich, who was ordered to advertise for claims, page 180.
Inventory taken Dec. 3, 1835, by Abraham H. Close and Hanford Mead, and filed Jan. 1, 1836, page 180.

Scofield, Abigail, late of Stamford, Apl. 23, 1823, estate ordered distributed to Ezra Scofield, Jr., Sarah wife of Stephen Hoyt, legal representatives of Esther deceased wife of Isaac Lounsbury, and the legal representatives of Phinehas Scofield, page 4.
May 5, 1823, estate distributed accordingly, page 4.

Scofield, Anna, widow, late of Stamford, Oct. 24, 1836, letters of administration on her estate granted to Selleck Scofield, who was ordered to advertise for claims, page 242.
Feb. 3, 1837, inventory taken by John Weed, Jr., and David Waterbury, and filed July 4, 1837, page 264.
Real estate sold to John L. Scofield, and report of sale filed Dec. 5, 1837, page 270.

Scofield, Clarissa, late of Stamford, will dated Aug. 31, 1829, probated Dec. 1, 1834, mentions her husband Warren Scofield, nieces Pometia Rockwell, Sally A. Rockwell, and Clarissa Ann Rockwell, nephew John Webster Rockwell, sisters Sarah Morgan, Cynthia Hunt, Ruth Townsend, Caty Ambler, and Fanny Olmsted, brother Harvey Rockwell. Executors brother Harvey Rockwell, friends Thomas Mead, and Josiah Gilbert. Witnesses Peter Scofield, Jr., Alonzo Scofield, and Joseph Scofield, page 190.
Dec. 1, 1834, Thomas Mead and Josiah Gilbert refused to qualify, and letters granted to Harvey Rockwell, who was ordered to advertise for claims, page 191.
Inventory taken Dec. 2, 1834, by Peter Scofield and Isaac Scofield, and filed Feb. 20, 1835, page 192.

STAMFORD PROBATE RECORDS.
Volume 15, 1834.

Scofield, Edwin, late of   Aug. 25, 1836, Samuel W.
    Scofield of New York City, a brother of deceased appointed guardian of Rufus, Samuel, and Edwin Lewis of Walden, N. Y., sons of decedent, all under 12 years of age, page 164.

Scofield, Ezra, Jr., late of Stamford, Mch. 12, 1832, account filed and real estate ordered sold to pay debts, page 305.
    Real estate sold to Nathaniel Scofield, and report of sale filed June 18, 1836, page 305.

Scofield, Hait, late of Stamford, will dated June 11, 1840, probated Oct. 1, 1840, mentions his sons Sylvanus, Harris, and Abijah, and daughter Abigail; sons of his son Abijah, viz: William Harris Scofield and Henry Lewis Scofield, Hannah wife of said Abijah, daughters of said Abijah, viz: Maria and Louisa, and two other daughters of said Abijah. Executor son Harris.
    Witnesses Stephen Clason, Lorenzo Leeds, and Martha C. Hawley, page 459.

Scofield, James E., of Darien, 15 years of age, Dec. 7, 1838, made choice of Maria E. Leeds of Darien to be his guardian, page 363.

Scofield, John, late of Stamford, inventory taken by Silas Hoyt and John Brown, and filed Feb. 4, 1834, page 79.

Scofield, John, late of Stamford, Apl. 28, 1834, account filed by his executor, and real estate ordered sold to pay debts, page 170.
    Real estate sold to David Wilmot and Royal L. Gay, and report of sale filed June 2, 1836, page 171.

Scofield, John, late of Stamford, Jan. 29, 1835, estate ordered distributed according to his will, page 80.
    Mch. 11, 1835, estate distributed to his children Silas, John, to the children of Robert, deceased; Leander, Alfred, and Morris Bishop children of Susannah Bishop a daughter, to the children of Elizabeth xdeceased wife of Rufus Knapp, page 80.

Scofield, Levi, late of Stamford, Oct. 16, 1837, his widow refused to qualify, and letters of administration on hos estate granted to Harvey Lockwood, and commissioners appointed to adjust claims of creditors, page 270.
    Inventory taken Nov. 22, 1837, by Silas Hoyt and George Scofield, and filed Dec. 21, 1837, page 272.

STAMFORD PROBATE RECORDS.
Volume 15, 1834.

Knapp, Isaac, continued:
    estate granted to Harvey Lockwood and Horace Scofield, who were ordered to advertise for claims, page 147.
    Inventory taken Mch. 23, 1835, by Peter Lockwood and Joshua Smith, and filed Mch. 23, 1835, page 147.
    Sept. 10, 1835, account filed, and commissioners appointed to adjust claims of creditors, pages 147 and 148.
    July 15, 1837, report of commissioners filed, page 329.
    June 4, 1838, dower of his widow set out, page 329.
    Apl. 28, 1838, account filed, and real estate ordered sold to pay debts, 337.
    Real estate sold to Erastus C. Bishop, N. D. Haight, and William H. Knapp, all of Stamford, and report of sale filed Aug. 8, 1838, page 338.
    Aug. 9, 1838, creditors ordered paid 76 02/100 cents on the dollar, page 338.

Knapp, Israel, late of Stamford, Feb. 7, 1835, Sarah B. Knapp of New York City, a daughter of decedent, over 12 years of age, made choice of Ezra Lockwood to be her guardian, page 55.

Knapp, Jacob, late of Stamford, Jan. 15, 1834, his widow refused to qualify, and letters of administration on his estate granted to his sons Isaac Knapp and William H. Knapp of Stamford, who were ordered to advertise for claims, page 63.
    Inventory taken by Jonathan Scofield and Horace Scofield, and filed Jan. 23, 1834, page 63.

Knapp, James, of Stamford, May 4, 1837, no father, or mother, made choice of Edwin Bishop of Stamford to be his guardian, page 210.

Knapp, Joshua, late of North Castle, June 29, 1839, dower ordered set out to his widow, Charity Knapp, page 387.
    Oct. 12, 1839, dower set out, page 388.

Knapp, Nathaniel, Colonel, late of Greenwich, Jan. 22, 1836, letters of administration on his estate granted to his widow, Elizabeth C. Knapp and Bartow F. White, who were ordered to advertise for claims, page 160.
    Inventory taken Jan. 27, 1836, by Joseph Brush and Amos Finnh, and filed Mch. 9, 1836, page 160.

Knapp, Reuben E., of Greenwich, over 14 years of age, Sept. 14, 1838, made choice of Allen R. Knapp of Greenwith to be his guardian, page 363.

STAMFORD PROBATE RECORDS.
Volume 15, 1834.

Scofield, Richard, late of Stamford, Dec. 20, 1839, letters
of administration on his estate granted to Seely Miller
and James H. Scofield, who were ordered to advertise
for claims, page 422.
Inventory taken Dec. 30, 1839, by Seely Miller and
James H. Scofield, and filed Dec. 30, 1839, page 422.

Seely, John, late of Stamford, July 6, 1833, account filed,
and real estate ordered sold to pay debts, page 126.
Real estate sold to Seth Seely of Stamford, and report
of sale filed Oct. 26, 1833, page 127.

Seely, Sarah Ann, of Stamford, about 10 years of age, Oct. 22,
1839, the court appointed Royal L. Gay of Stamford to
be her guardian, page 387.
Apl. 11, 1840, her guardian, Royal L. Gay, resigned,
and John R. Leeds appointed in his place, page 475.

Seely, Sarah Jane, of Darien, over 12 years of age, Aug. 7,
1835, made choice of her brother Sands Seely to be her
guardian, who was also appointed guardian of his brother Elisha Seely of Darien, page 111.

Seely, William H., John A. Seely, Henry L. Seely, and Sarah
Ann Seely, all of Stamford, Apl. 11, 1840, made choice
of John R. Leeds of Stamford to be their guardian,
page 424.

Selleck, Ann, late of Darien, will dated Oct. 17, 1837, probated Oct. 24, 1837, all to her sister Betsy Selleck.
Executor Isaac Brown. Witnesses Abram Clock, Elisabeth Gray, and Julia B. Gorham, page 273.
Oct. 24, 1837, order to advertise for claims, page 274.
Inventory taken Oct. 31, 1837, by Henry Gorham and
Joseph Gorham, and filed Nov. 15, 1837, page 274.

Selleck, Mary, of Darien, over 14 years of age, Apl. 7, 1838,
made choice of Stephen Raymond of Darien to be her guardian, page 298.

Selleck, Samuel, late of Darien, will dated Aug. 5, 1834, probated Jan. 21, 1836, mentions his wife Hannah, and
children Phebe Selleck, Theodosia Selleck, Angeline Selleck, Caroline Selleck, George Selleck, and Nancy Bell,
grandchildren Isaac Jones, James Jones, Horace A.
Jones, Nancy O. Jones, George Jones, William Jones, and
Samuel Jones. Executor John Bell, Jr. Witnesses
Joseph A. Gray, Benjamin Jones, and George Hill,
page 158.

STAMFORD PROBATE RECORDS.
Volume 15, 1834.

Selleck, Samuel, continued:
June 28, 1836, order to advertise for claims, page 159.
Inventory taken Mch. 10, 1836, by Jacob Lockwood and
Jesse Whiting, and filed Mch. 18, 1836, page 160.
Apl. 17, 1837, estate distributed to his children Nancy
Bell, Angelina Selleck, Phebe Selleck, Theodosia Selleck, Caroline Selleck, and Hannah Selleck, widow of
deceased, page 315.

Shaw, Andrew, late of Darien, Feb. 28, 1834, Nancy Shaw and
Hannah Shaw of Darien, children of decedent, over 14
years of age, made choice of Cary Bell of Darien to
be their guardian, who was also appointed guardian of
Phebe and Frederick B., other children of decedent,
page 25.
Mch. 14, 1834, petition for leave to sell the real estate of said minors in Darien, and sale ordered,
page 21.
Real estate sold to Henry Weed, Jr., and George Walmsley, and report of sale filed June 9, 1834, page 21.
Mch. 14, 1834, Isaac Quintard, Jr., of Stamford,
guardian of Caroline, Eliza, and Maria Shaw, children
of decedent, asked leave to sell the real estate of
said minors in Darien, and sale ordered, page 26.
Real estate sold to Henry Weed, Jr., and George Walmsley, and report of sale filed, page 26.

Shaw, Hannah, late of Darien, inventory taken Feb. 12, 1833,
by Joseph Hoyt and filed Oct. 24, 1833, page 32.
Mch. 4, 1834, account filed by her administrator, and
estate ordered distributed to her children, viz: Hannah Hoyt, the children of William Shaw, deceased,
children of Frederick Shaw, deceased, and the children
of Andrew Shaw, deceased, page 13.
Mch. 15, 1834, estate distributed accordingly, page 14.

Shaw, James, late of Darien, Mch. 4, 1834, on the application
of Cary Bell, guardian of the children of Andrew Shaw,
who are heirs at law of said deceased, estate ordered
distributed to the heirs at law of said deceased, viz:
Hannah Hoyt, a daughter, the children of William Shaw,
a deceased son, the children of Frederick Shaw, a deceased son, and the children of Andrew Shaw, a deceased
son, page 54.
Mch. 17, 1834, estate distributed accordingly, page 54.

Sherwood, Willet, late of Greenwich, will dated Dec. 17, 1835,
probated Mch. 3, 1836, all to his wife Mary for life,
and remainder to his children. Executors his wife and

STAMFORD PROBATE RECORDS.
Volume 15, 1834.

Sherwood, Willet, continued :
    Daniel Sherwood. Witnesses Samuel Close, Frederick Sherwood, and Gilbert H. Taylor, page 205.
    Mch. 3, 1836, order to advertise for claims, page 206.
    Inventory taken Mch. 28, 1836, by Platt Mead and David Brown, and filed Apl. 2, 1836, page 206.
    Aug. 29, 1837, executor ordered to account, page 256.
    Real estate in Horseneck sold to Gilbert P. Finch of Greenwich, and report of sale filed Sept. 4, 1837, page 256.

Sherwood, William C., of Greenwich, about 16 years of age, Mch. 12, 1842, the court appointed D. Jerome Sands of Greenwich to be his guardian, page 491.

Sibell, John F., late of Darien, Oct. 12, 1837, his widow refused to qualify, and letters of administration on his estate granted to Ezra H. Bishop of Darien, and commissioners appointed to adjust claims of creditors, page 271.
    Inventory taken Oct. 24, 1837, by John Weed, Jr., and George Walmsley, and filed Oct. 26, 1837, page 271.
    Oct. 26, 1837, personal property ordered sold, page 272.
    Oct. 16, 1838, an allowance to his widow, page 335.
    Aug. 1, 1838, report of commissioners filed, page 335.
    July 24, 1838, account filed, and real estate ordered sold to pay debts, page 337.
    Real estate sold to Catherine S. wife of Elias Hatfield of New York City, and report of sale filed Oct. 16, 1838, page 337.
    Oct. 16, 1838, creditors ordered paid 94 5/10 cents on the dollar, page 337.

Skelding, James, late of Stamford, Apl. 28, 1834, letters of administration on his estate granted to his widow, Letitia Skelding of Stamford, and Henry K. Skelding of New York City, who were ordered to advertise for claims, page 88.
    Inventory taken May 6, 1834, by Samuel Lockwood and John V. Leeds, and filed July 4, 1834, page 88.

Slason, Nathaniel, late of Stamford, will dated Mch. 13, 1810, probated June 9, 1835, mentions his wife Hannah, and his seventeen children, viz: Lydia wife of James Weed, Hannah wife of Jonathan Slason, Silvanus, Nathaniel, James, Mary wife of Robert Pelton, Joseph, Sarah wife of William Egry, Smith, Francis, Sophia, Julia, Isaac, Betsy Ann, Cornelia, William Platt, and George Nelson. Executrix his wife. Witnesses Gershom Scofield,

STAMFORD PROBATE RECORDS.
Volume 15, 1834.

Slason, Nathaniel, continued:
Sands Seely, and Sally Scofield, page 151.
June 9, 1835, order to advertise for claims, page 152.
Inventory taken June 12, 1835, by Joshua Scofield and Abram Clock, and filed June 16, 1835, page 152.

Smith, Abigail W., of Stamford, Mch. 14, 1835, her guardian, Solomon Clason, asked leave to sell the real estate of said minor in Stamford, and sale ordered, page 115.

Smith, Alvah, late of Greenwich, Apl. 19, 1836, letters of administration on his estate granted to his widow, Hannah Smith, William Smith of Greenwich, and Samuel Rundle of Somerstown, N. Y., who were ordered to advertise for claims, page 179.
Inventory taken Apl. 27, 1836, by Joseph Brush and Alfred Rundle, and filed June 1, 1836, page 180.
Dec. 18, 1838, Alfred Rundle and Alvah Mead of Greenwich, guardians of Sally B., Charles B., and Rachel A Smith, children of decedent, asked leave to sell the real estate of said minors in Greenwich, and sale ordered, page 364.

Smith, Ann, late of Stamford, Nov. 15, 1838, letters of administration on her estate granted to her son, Charles E. Smith, of Stamford, who was ordered to advertise for claims, page 381.
Inventory taken by Selleck Scofield and George Lounsbury, and filed Apl. 1, 1838, page 381.

Smith, Benjamin, late of Stamford, will dated Aug. 28, 1833, probated Nov. 4, 1834, mentions his wife Sally, Arba Smith a son of his brother Jared Smith, brothers Charles Smith and Jared Smith, cousin Alva Smith, brother-in-law Amos Mead. Executor cousin Alva Smith. Witnesses George S. Wood, Sarah Ferris, and Joshua B Ferris, page 138.
Nov. 6, 1834, order to advertise for claims, page 139.
Inventory taken Nov. 13, 1834, by Abel Reynolds and Amos Finch, and filed Dec. 31, 1834, page 139.
May 18, 1836, Alva Smith now deceased, and letters with the will annexed granted to Arba Smith of Greenwich, page 139.

Smith, Ebenezer, late of Stamford, Mch. 11, 1837, letters of administration on his estate granted to his son, Ebenezer Smith, who was ordered to advertise for claims, page 242.

STAMFORD PROBATE RECORDS.
Volume 15, 1834.

Smith, Ebenezer, Sr., late of   inventory taken by George Hubbard and George Lounsbury, and filed Feb. 8, 1838, page 330.

Smith, Ebenezer, late of Stamford, Feb. 1, 1838, Henry H. Smith, a minor, is the owner as tenant in common with Ebenezer Smith, Alfred Smith, Mary wife of Arza Marshall, and Sarah wife of Joseph Smith of real estate in Stamford, subject to the dower of his mother Julia A. Smith, his guardian, said Julia A. Smith, desires partition of said real estate, and commissioners appointed to make partition thereof. Said Ebenezer, Alfred, Mary, and Sarah claiming as heirs of their deceased father Ebenezer Smith and their mother Mary Smith, and said Henry claiming under his deceased father Lyman H. Smith, a son of said Ebenezer Smith, deceased, and Mary Smith, deceased, page 331.
Mch. 13, 1838, partition made accordingly, page 331.
Henry Hubbard Smith of Stamford, under 14 years of age, Feb. 1, 1838, the court appointed Julia A. Smith of Stamford to be his guardian, page 304.

Smith, Edwin, of Rye, Dec. 13, 1841, says he is the son of Abigail Finch of Greenwich, who is old and infirm, receives a pension, and is unable to manage her affairs, asked for a conservator, page 510.
Jan. 29, 1842, Henry Waring of Stamford appointed conservator, page 511.
Inventory taken Feb. 12, 1842, and filed Feb. 19, 1842, page 512.

Smith, Eliza Ann, of Stamford, over 14 years of age, Apl. 20, 1835, made choice of Nathan White of Stamford to be her guardian, page 110.

Smith, Gould, late of Stamford, Apl. 1, 1835, letters of administration on his estate granted to his brother Joshua Smith, who was ordered to advertise for claims, page 101
Inventory taken Nov. 7, 1835, by Josiah Smith and Henry Waring, and filed Feb. 29, 1836, page 101.

Smith, John, late of Stamford, Mch. 3, 1836, Abigail W. Smith, a daughter of decedent, over 12 years of age, residing in New York City, made choice of her brother William M. Smith of Greenwich to be her guardian, page 111.
Apl. 30, 1835, Betsy Ann Smith, formerly of Stamford, now of New York City, over 12 years of age, made choice of her brother William M. Smith of Greenwich to be her Guardian, page 111.

STAMFORD PROBATE RECORDS.
Volume 15, 1834.

Smith, John, continued:
    Mch. 5, 1836, petition for leave to sell the real estate of said minors in Stamford, and sale ordered page 171.
    Real estate sold to Rev. Nehemiah Sherwood, and report of sale filed June 13, 1836, page 172.
    Mch. 14, 1835, petition of Abel Reynolds of Stamford, guardian of said Betsy Ann Smith, for leave to sell the real estate of said minor in Stamford, and sale ordered, page 172.
    Real estate sold to Rev. Nehemiah Sherwood, and report of sale filed June 13, 1836, page 173.

Smith, John Cotton, late of Stamford, Feb. 20, 1837, letters of administration on his estate granted to his father, Rev. Daniel Smith, who was ordered to advertise for claims, page 242.

Smith, Lyman H., late of Stamford, will dated June 29, 1837, probated July 17, 1837, mentions his wife Julia A., and son Henry. Executors his wife and brother in law George M. Hubbard. Witnesses Nehemiah Hait, Jr., and Hugh Mackay, page 257.
    July 17, 1837, order to advertise for claims, page 257.
    July 29, 1837, inventory taken by Edwin Newman and William Hobby, and recorded on page 315.

Smith, Martha, late of Stamford, inventory taken Jan. 15, 1833 by Calvin Clason and Harvey Lockwood, and filed Mch. 13 1834, page 56.
    Mch. 13, 1834, account filed, and estate ordered distributed to her children, viz: to the heirs of Martha Newman, Hannah Hubbard, Prudence Reed, Elizabeth Studwell, Susannah Smith, and to the children of Mary Whiting, deceased, page 83.
    Estate distributed accordingly, page 84.

Smith, Rachel Augusta, of Greenwich, over 12 years of age, Sept. 18, 1837, made choice of Alvah Mead of Greenwich to be her guardian, page 259.

Smith, Rebecca Elizabeth, of New York City, over 12 years of age, Apl. 14, 1836, made choice of John Husted of Stamford to be her guardian, page 181.
    Sept. 14, 1836, petition for leave to sell the real estate of said minor in Stamford, and sale ordered, subject to the dower of her mother, Rebecca Ann Rowland, page 208.
    Real estate sold to Joseph Smith, and report of sale filed Apl. 22, 1837, page 209.

STAMFORD PROBATE RECORDS.
Volume 15, 1834.

Smith, Sally, of Stamford, over 12 years of age, Sept. 18, 1837, made choice of Alfred Rundle of Greenwich to be her guardian, and who was also appointed guardian of Charles Benjamin Smith of Greenwich, under 12 years of age, page 259.

Smith, Seth, late of Stamford, Apl. 20, 1835, Hetty wife of Henry Cook of Stamford, Nancy wife of Samuel H. Reynolds of Stamford, and Eliza Ann Smith, a minor, are owners as tenants in common of real estate in Stamford, the late homestead of Seth Smith, deceased, said Henry Cook and Nathan White, as guardians of said Eliza Ann, petitioned for the appointment of commissioners to partition said real estate, and commissioners appointed page 116.
July 24, 1835, said real estate partitioned among said Nancy, Eliza Ann, and Hetty, and agreement filed, page 117.

Smith, William M., late of Stamford, will dated Jan. 20, 1834, probated Mch. 3, 1834, mentions his wife Ann, and children William, Ellen, Charles E., James and George. Executors his wife, George E. Waring, and Smith R. Sibley. Witnesses Jonathan D. Weeks, David Rider, and Hugh Mackay, page 29.
Mch. 7, 1834, order to advertise for claims, page 30.
Inventory taken by Selleck Scofield and John Husted, and filed Apl. 5, 1834, page 30.
Oct. 29, 1834, account filed, and an allowance to his widow, page 31.
Dec. 27, 1834, account filed, and real estate ordered sold to pay debts, page 103.
Real estate sold to Charles E. Smith, and report of sale filed July 20, 1835, page 103.

Sniffen, William, of Greenwich, over 14 years of age, Mch. 2, 1837, made choice of Samuel Close of Greenwich to be his guardian, page 209.

Stevens, James, late of Greenwich, Mch. 12, 1834, account filed, and estate ordered distributed to his widow and children, viz: Maria Searles, Eliza Scofield, James E. Stevens, William Stevens, and Rufus S. Stevens, p page 311.
Estate distributed accordingly, page 312.
(This family should be Stivers)

STAMFORD PROBATE RECORDS.
Volume 15, 1834.

Stevens, James, late of Stamford, May 1, 1835, his widow, xxx
Mary Stevens, refused to qualify, and letters of administration on his estate granted to Jesse Whiting of Darien, who was ordered to advertise for claims, page 123.
Inventory taken by John Brown and William Waterbury, and filed June 15, 1835, page 124.
Feb. 3, 1836, account filed, and an allowance to his widow page 124.

Stevens, Mary, May 1, 1835, appointed guardian of her children Mary H. Stevens and Ann C. Stevens of Stamford, over 12 years of age, page 109.
Feb. 3, 1836, petition for leave to sell the real estate of said minors in Stamford, and sale ordered, page 207.
Real estate sold to John A. Finney, and report of sale filed Apl. 26, 1837, page 208.
July 30, 1836, petition for leave to sell the real estate of said minors in Stamford, and sale ordered, page 307.
Real estate sold to Edward Lambden of New Rochelle, and report of sale filed Nov. 25, 1836, page 308.

Stevens, Mary, of Darien, Feb. 3, 1841, by her guardian and husband, Leonidas Stevens of Darien, asked for leave to sell her real estate in Darien, and sale ordered page 464.
Real estate sold to the widow Mary Raymond and Epenetus W. Walmsley, both of Darien, and report of sale filed Apl. 17, 1841, page 465.

Stivers, James, late of Greenwich, Mch. 12, 1834, account filed, and estate ordered distributed to his widow, and children, viz: Maria Searles, Eliza Scofield, James E. Stivers, William Stivers, and Rufus M. Stivers page 311.
Estate distributed accordingly, page 312.
Rufus M. Stivers of Greenwich, under 14 years of age, Mch. 15, 1834, the court appointed his brother James E. Stivers of North Castle, N. Y., to be his guardian, page 11.
Dec. 24, 1836, petition for leave to sell the real estate of said minor in Greenwich, and sale ordered, page 210.
Real estate sold to Nathaniel Miller and Richard P. Carpenter, subject to the dower of Sarah Stivers, and report of sale filed Apl. 21, 1837, page 211.

STAMFORD PROBATE RECORDS.
Volume 15, 1834.

Strang, Jared, late of Greenwich, will dated Apl. 18, 1837, probated July 27, 1837, mentions his children William, Margaret R. Vail, and her son Henry Allen Vail, children Mary, Catherine, Allen, and his daughter Sarah Hunt Strang, son John and his son James Henry Strang; and Ann Eliza Strang a daughter of Daniel Strang. Executors son William, Samuel Close, and Seth Lyon. Witnesses Joseph Stedwell, Jonah C. Brundage, and John W. Sherwood, page 249.
July 17, 1837, Samuel Close and Seth Lyon refused to qualify, and letters granted to William Strang, who was ordered to advertise for claims, page 252.
Inventory taken by James Willson and Samuel Close, and filed Sept. 16, 1837, page 260.

Strang, William, late of Greenwich, will dated May 22, 1840, probated Aug. 31, 1840, mentions his brother John Strang, James Henry Strang a son of said John Strang, father Jared Strang, sisters Mary Strang and Catherine Strang. Executor James Wilson of Greenwich. Witnesses Silas Brundage, William A. Merritt, and William H. Carhart, page 434.
Aug. 31, 1840, order to advertise for claims, page 435.
Inventory taken Sept. 2, 1840, by Jotham Merritt and Nathan S. Mead, and filed Sept. 7, 1840, page 435.

Stogdill, Amy, late of Greenwich, July 12, 1835, letters of administration on her estate granted to her brother Henry Stogdill of Harlem, N. Y., who was ordered to advertise for claims, page 104.
Inventory taken July 23, 1834, by J. T. Mead and Thomas A. Mead, and filed Mch. 28, 1836, page 104.

Street, George, late of Darien, Oct. 3, 1834, his widow refused to qualify, and letters of administration on his estate granted to Henry Bates of Darien, who was ordered to advertise for claims, page 140.
Inventory taken by Thomas Reed and William H. Bates, and filed Nov. 26, 1834, page 140.

Studwell, Anthony, late of Greenwich, Apl. 26, 1838, his widow now deceased, and the remainder of his estate ordered distributed to his children Drake, heirs of Anthony, deceased, and the heirs of James, deceased, according to his will, page 285.
May 10, 1838, estate distributed accordingly, page 286.

Studwell, Drake, late of Stamford, will dated Feb. 27, 1837, probated July 3, 1838, mentions his wife Elisabeth, and children John S., Luther H., Edgar, William Allen,

STAMFORD PROBATE RECORDS.
Volume 15, 1834.

Studwell, Drake, continued :
    Polly Ann, Eliza Ann, and Alanson. Executors his wife
    and Solomon Smith. Witnesses Lorenzo Leeds, Dixon D.
    Ufford, and Charles Hawley, page 372.
    Codicil dated Sept. 13, 1837, page 373.
    July 3, 1838, order to advertise for claims, page 373.
    Inventory taken Aug. 16, 1838, by Alfred Smith and
    Earl Smith, and filed Sept. 15, 1838, page 374.
    Feb. 22, 1839, account filed, and estate ordered dis-
    tributed to his widow, Elizabeth Studwell, and children
    John S., Luther H., Edgar, William Allen, Polly Ann,
    Eliza Ann, and Alanson, page 374.
    Mch. 15, 1839, estate distributed accordingly, page 376.

Studwell, Enoch, late of Greenwich, will dated May 23, 1840,
    probated Dec. 14, 1840, mentions his brother Anthony
    Studwell's widow, James Studwell's widow, Drake Stud-
    well's widow, sister Betsy Tucker, nephew Alanson
    Studwell, and sister Hannah Scofield. Executor Augus-
    tus Reynolds. Witnesses William Ferris, Catharine Rey-
    nolds, and N. D. Haight, page 444.
    Dec. 14, 1840, order to advertise for claims, page 445.
    Inventory taken Jan. 2, 1841, by Ard Reynolds and
    Ephraim Marshall, and filed June 2, 1841, page 445.

Studwell, James, late of Stamford, Feb. 2, 1835, letters of
    administration on his estate granted to his widow Mary
    Studwell, who was ordered to advertise for claims,
    page 197.
    Inventory taken Feb. 9, 1835, by David Smith and Alfred
    Smith, and filed Mch. 25, 1835, page 197.

Taylor, George, and Merritt G. Taylor, of Greenwich, Dec. 24,
    1838, their guardian, James Willson of Greenwich, ask-
    ed for leave to sell the real estate of said minors in
    Greenwich, and sale ordered, page 355.

Tillman, John, late of Stamford, June 17, 1836, account filed
    by Anne Tillman, as guardian of her children Mary C.,
    Elizabeth A., and John H. Tillman, shows real estate
    sold to Alfred Bishop, Horace Barnum, Solomon Garnsey,
    and John Brown, subject to her dower; the Hutton Farm
    sold to Josiah Smith, and the Tannery sold to Stephen
    B. Provost; also shows that William Tillman was a bro-
    ther of deceased; and Samuel Hoyt, deceased, was the
    father of said guardian, page, 219.
    Aug. 31, 1833, petition for leave to sell the real es-
    tate of said minors in Stamford, and sale ordered,
    pages 10 and 11.

STAMFORD PROBATE RECORDS.
Volume 15, 1834.

Tillman, John, continued:
    Real estate sold to Alfred Bishop of Chatham, N. Y., and report of sale filed, Dec. 31, 1833, page
    Mch. 7, 1835, asked for leave to sell the real estate of said minors in Stamford, and sale ordered pages 111 and 112.
    Real estate sold to Horace Barnum, and report of sale filed June 27, 1835, page 112.

Tillott, Sabrina B., late of Greenwich, will dated July 18, 1832, probated Sept. 6, 1836, all to her husband Peter I. Tillott, and appointed him executor. Witnesses J. Cotton Smith, John Bissell, and Charles Hawley, page 217.
    Sept. 6, 1836, appeal taken by testatrix's sister Sarah wife of Samuel Annan of Fishkill, N. Y., and Susan Seymour of Fishkill, another sister, to be notified of the hearing, page 218.
    Inventory taken by Alan Mead and Thomas A. Mead, and filed Sept. 7, 1836, page 219.

Tompkins, Abram D., of Stamford, Aug. 5, 1834, general assignment to Jonathan M. Hall of Stamford and Nehemiah S. Bates of Bedford, for the benefit of creditors, page 142
    Inventory taken Sept. 16, 1834, by Cephas Lockwood and Joseph W. Heusted, and filed Sept. 17, 1834, page 144.
    Sept. 15, 1834, commissioners appointed to adjust claims of creditors, page 143.
    Apl. 16, 1835, report of commissioners filed, page 144.
    Sept. 17, 1834, personal property ordered sold, page 145
    Report of sale filed Sept. 14, 1835, page 146.
    Report of commissioners to adjust claims reviewed and corrected Sept. 14, 1835, page 146.

Tracy, Huldah, late of Greenwich, will dated Feb. 21, 1837, probated Mch. 15, 1837, mentions her stepson John Jay Tracy, son Horatio Nelson Tracy, deceased, Caroline A. William L., and Hezekiah T., children of James and Caroline Sivals of New York; sisters Polly widow of Willet Sherwood, and Mehitable wife of Royal Dunton, and brother Andrew Mead. Executor stepson John Jay Tracy. Witnesses Gilbert H. Taylor, William Briggs, and Samuel Close, page 211.
    Mch. 15, 1837, order to advertise for claims, page 212.
    Inventory taken by Alvan Mead and Thomas A. Mead, and filed Mch. 25, 1837, page 213.

Waring, Charles E., of Stamford, 19 years of age, July 27, 1839, made choice of Stephen B. Provost of Stamford to be his guardian, page 363.

STAMFORD PROBATE RECORDS.
Volume 15, 1834.

Waring, Jacob, formerly of Darien, late of Savannah, Ga.,
will dated Aug. 14, 1833, probated Oct. 5, 1833, mentions his nephew Robert Thaddeus Waring, and brother
Henry F. Waring. Executors said Henry F. Waring,
Henry D. Weed, and William W. Foster. Witnesses Nehemiah Perry, Abijah Ressegine, and Thomas Morris,
page 93.
Oct. 5, 1833, letters to said Henry F. Waring, others
refused, who was ordered to advertise for claims,
page 94.
Inventory taken Oct. 5, 1833, by Silvanus B. Thompson
and Ezra H. Bishop, and filed Oct. 8, 1833, page 95.

Warring, Jesse, late of Darien, Mch. 2, 1839, his widow refused to qualify, and letters of administration on his
estate granted to Ezra H. Bishop of Darien, who was
ordered to advertise for claims, page 412.
Inventory taken Mch. 14, 1839, by John Weed, Jr., and
N. A. Bouton, and filed June 10, 1839, page 412.

Waring, John, late of Darien, will dated Dec. 12, 1833, probated Dec. 20, 1833, all to his friend Jacob Bell of
New York City, who is to maintain testator's
sister Betty Clock. Executor John Bell of Darien.
Witnesses Abram Clock, Morris Tuthill, and Sally Capes,
page 152.
Dec. 20, 1833, order to advertise for claims, page 153.
Inventory taken Dec. 26, 1833, by Jeremiah Andreas and
Henry Bates, and filed Jan. 18, 1834, page 153.

Waring, Robert F., of New York City, over 14 years of age,
June 24, 1839, made choice of his father Henry F.
Waring to be his guardian, page 365.
June 24, 1839, petition for leave to sell the real estate of said minor in Darien, and sale ordered,
page 366.
Real estate sold to George Walmsley, and report of sale
filed, page 367.

Waterbury, Azariah, late of Darien, June 4, 1838, letters of
administration on his estate granted to his widow,
Sarah Waterbury, who was ordered to advertise for
claims, page 300.
Inventory taken by Holly Bell and Joseph Hoyt, and
filed Aug. 7, 1838, page 370.

Waterbury, David, late of Stamford, will dated Dec. 30, 1833,
probated Oct. 14, 1834, mentions his wife Elizabeth,
and children Mary wife of Seth Buxton, Sally Howe,

STAMFORD PROBATE RECORDS.
Volume 15, 1834.

Waterbury, David, continued:
 Betsy wife of Peter Lockwood, Abigail H. Seely, and John H. Waterbury. Executor son-in-law Peter Lockwood Witnesses S. H. Minor, Ezra Lockwood, and Henry Webb, page 164.
 Oct. 14, 1834, order to advertise for claims, page 165.
 Inventory taken by Harvey Lockwood and Shadrach Lockwood, and filed Oct. 20, 1834, page 165.

Waterbury, Esther Conway, of Darien, about 16 years of age, Jan. 22, 1841, made choice of Phebe Weed of Darien to be her guardian, page 423.

Waterbury, George, late of Whitesboro, Montgomery County, N.Y. July 7, 1838, his widow refused to qualify, and letters of administration on his estate granted to Royal L. Gay, who was ordered to advertise for claims, page 435.
 Inventory taken July 31, 1838, by Charles T. Leeds and David B. Burr, and filed Aug. 4, 1838, page 436.

Waterbury, Isaac, late of Darien, Aug. 19, 1839, letters of administration on his estate granted to Leander Hoyt of Darien, page 403.
 Inventory taken Aug. 30, 1839, by Jacob Lockwood and Holly Bell, and filed Sept. 2, 1839, page 403.
 May 4, 1840, account filed, and an allowance to his widow, page 403.

Waterbury, Julius Henry, of   about 15 years of age, Aug. 30, 1841, made choice of John Waterbury of Darien to be his guardian, who was also appointed guardian of Nathaniel Waterbury, Mary Louisa Waterbury, Charlotte Waterbury, John Clark Waterbury, and Lucretia Waterbury, page 492.

Waterbury, Nathaniel, late of Darien, will dated Mch. 4, 1833, probated Dec. 6, 1838, mentions his children John, Polly wife of Rev. Lemuel B. Hull, Jerry, and Henry. Executors son John, and Rev. Lemuel B. Hull. Witnesses John Bell, Jr., Ezra Lockwood, and Isaac Weed, Jr., page 394.
 Dec. 5, 1838, Rev. Lemuel B. Hull refused to qualify, and letters granted to John Waterbury, who was ordered to advertise for claims, page 397.
 Inventory taken Dec. 1838, by John Bell, Jr., and Abram Clock, and filed Feb. 22, 1839, page 397.
 May 15, 1841, estate ordered distributed according to his will, viz: 1/4 to his son John; 1/4 to said John Waterbury as trustee for son Jerry; 1/4 to said John

STAMFORD PROBATE RECORDS.
Volume 15, 1834.

Waterbury, Nathaniel, continued :
    Waterbury, as trustee for the heirs of son Henry; and 1/4 to daughter Polly wife of Lemuel B. Hull, page 447. May 15, 1841, estate distributed accordingly, page 448.

Waterbury, Polly, late of Darien, will dated Mch. 21, 1834, probated Apl. 22, 1834, all to her son Gilbert G. Waterbury, except certain bequests to the Darien Congregational Church, to Abigail Waterbury of Darien, to nieces Nancy Waterbury and Polly Little, and to sister Bethia Waterbury. Executor her son Gilbert G. Witnesses Holly Bell, A. B. Bradley, and Charles Richards, page 60.
    Apl. 22, 1834, order to advertise for claims, page 60.
    Inventory taken Apl. 30, 1834, by William Andreas and Holly Bell, and filed June 9, 1834, page 61.

Waterbury, Rebecca, late of Darien, will dated Sept. 22, 1834, probated Feb. 21, 1835, mentions the children of her brother Isaac Waterbury, deceased, viz: George, Polly, David, John, Fanny, Nancy, Peter L., Isaac N., Julia A. and Isaac W. Bacon a grandson of said Isaac Waterbury, deceased. Executor said George Waterbury. Witnesses Mary Scofield, John Slason, and Betsy Hoyt, page 241.

Waterbury, Sarah, late of Darien, will dated Oct. 17, 1832, probated Dec. 19, 1832, mentions her sisters Lydia wife of Joseph Richards and Hannah wife of John Henderson, Alfred son of Joseph and Lydia Richards, and Harriet Tubbs. Executors Edward Scofield of Darien and Joseph Richards of Norwalk. Witnesses Alice Whiting, Rusmah Waterbury, and Jesse Whiting, page 17.
    Dec. 19, 1832, Joseph Richards refused to qualify, and letters granted to Edward Scofield, who was ordered to advertise for claims, page 18.
    Inventory taken Dec. 22, 1832, by Jeremiah Andreas and Holly Bell, and filed Feb. 4, 1832, page 18.
    Sept. 2, 1833, account filed, and real estate ordered sold to pay debts, page 19.
    Real estate sold to George Buxton of Stamford, and report of sale filed Dec. 7, 1833, page 19.

Webb, Augustus, late of Stamford, Mch. 23, 1836, letters of administration on his estate granted to his widow, Naomi Webb, who was ordered to advertise for claims, page 188.
    Inventory taken by Peter Smith, Jr., and George Brown, and filed Apl. 23, 1836, page 188.

STAMFORD PROBATE RECORDS.
Volume 15, 1834.

Webb, Ebenezer, late of Stamford, will dated Aug. 26, 1833, probated Sept. 8, 1834, mentions his wife Phebe, and children Rufus, deceased, James, Ebenezer, Darius, George, Elnathan T., Washington, Hannah, Rebecca Knapp, Harriet, and Phebe Selleck. Executors his sons Darius and Elnathan Todd Webb. Witnesses Daniel Smith, D. W. Smith, and Charles Hawley, page 96.
Sept. 8, 1834, order to advertise for claims, page 97.
Inventory taken Sept. 18, 1834, by Davis Lockwood and Royal L. Gay, and filed Nov. 6, 1834, page 97.

Webb, Elisa, of New York City, parent of Mary V. Webb of said City, July 3, 1833, asked for leave to sell the real estate of said minor in Stamford, and sale ordered, page 175.

Webb, Epenetus, late of Stamford, July 20, 1835, account filed by John Scarret, administrator, page 141.

Webb, Polly, late of Darien, will dated May 30, 1835, probated July 1, 1835, all to her daughter Adeline A. Little. Executor son-in-law Henry Little. Witnesses Abram Clock, Benjamin Little, and Warren Little, page 155.
July 1, 1835, order to advertise for claims, page 156.
Inventory taken Aug. 18, 1835, by John Weed, Jr., and George J. Bowler, and filed May 28, 1836, page 156.

Webb, William, late of Stamford, Dec. 15, 1840, his widow refused to qualify, and letters of administration on his estate granted to Ezra Bishop of Darien, who was ordered to advertise for claims, page 446.
Inventory taken Dec. 17, 1840, by Nathaniel A. Bouton and William Weed, and filed Jan. 22, 1841, page 446.
Jan. 28, 1842, account filed, and an allowance to his widow, page 446.

Weed, Abigail, late of   inventory taken Sept. 5, 1828, by Abel Reynolds, and Daniel L. Palmer, and filed Mch. 23, 1835, by Jotham Hoyt, executor, page 201.

Weed, Ann, late of Stamford, Mch. 20, 1837, her only son refused to qualify, and letters of administration on her estate granted to Alfred Webb of Stamford, who was ordered to advertise for claims, page 243.
Inventory taken Mch. 21, 1837, by Horace Waterbury and Edwin Lounsbury, and filed Aug. 19, 1837, page 263.

STAMFORD PROBATE RECORDS.
Volume 15, 1834.

Weed, Elbert, of Darien, over 14 years of age, Feb. 8, 1834, made choice of John R. Leeds to be his guardian, page 11.

Weed, Elizabeth, late of Stamford, will dated Feb. 6, 1840, probated June 14, 1841, all to her daughters Sarah Scofield and Mary E. Wilmot, mentions deceased son Nathan, and late husband Samuel Weed. Executor ------ Witnesses S. H. Minor, Lydia Smith, and Mary Esther Smith, page 494.

Weed, Frances Marian, of New York City, about 17 years of age, Feb. 7, 1842, made choice of Isaac Weed, Jr., of Darien to be her guardian, page 474.

Weed, Frederick, late of Darien, will dated Nov. 13, 1840, probated Nov. 26, 1840, mentions his wife Phebe, and Esther Conrey Waterbury, Frederick Weed Waterbury, half brother Jacob Weed, half sister Kesiah Waterbury, William Waterbury, 3rd, and Alexander Studwell of New York City. Executors William Waterbury, 3rd, and Alexander Studwell. Witnesses Alexander Studwell, Henry Little, and Charles H. Waterbury, page 507.
Nov. 26, 1840, order to advertise for claims, page 508.
Inventory taken Dec. 24, 1840, by Abram Clock and Elisha Seely, and filed Dec. 28, 1840, page 509.

Weed, Frederick A., formerly of Darien, but now of New York City, Mch. 8, 1834, his guardian John Leeds of Darien, asked for leave to sell the real estate of said minor in Stamford, and sale ordered, pages 88 and 89.
Real estate sold to John James Leeds of Stamford, and report of sale filed Aug. 8, 1834, page 89.

Weed, Hannah, late of Greenwich, Feb. 15, 1838, letters of administration on her estate granted to Jacob T. Weed of Greenwich, who was ordered to advertise for claims, page 305.
Inventory taken July 25, 1838, by Alvan Mead and Thomas A. Mead, and filed Aug. 7, 1838, page 334.

Weed, Henry, late of   Mch. 8, 1834, John R. Leeds of Stamford guardian of James Elbert Weed of Darien, a son of decedent, asked for leave to sell the real estate of said minor in Stamford, and sale ordered, pages 115 and 116.
Real estate sold to John James Leeds of Stamford, and report of sale filed Aug 1, 1834, page 116.

STAMFORD PROBATE RECORDS.
Volume 15, 1834.

Weed, Holly B., late of Darien, Nov. 26, 1838, his heir at law, Deborah Weed, refused to qualify, and letters of administration on his estate granted to Leander Hoyt of Darien, who was ordered to advertise for claims, page 355.
Inventory taken Dec. 5, 1838, by Jacob Lockwood and William Andreas, and filed June 19, 1839, page 355.

Weed, James J., and William H. Weed, of New York City, Apl. 13, 1839, their guardian Isaac Weed, Jr., of Darien, asked for leave to sell the real estate of said minors in Darien, and sale ordered, page 371.x and Stamford. Real estate sold to Nathaniel A. Bouton of Darien, and report of sale filed, page 371.

Weed, Jarvis, of Darien, Mch. 30, 1840, general assignment to Edward Scofield of Darien, for the benefit of creditors, page 451.
Inventory taken Mch. 30, 1840, by Holly Bell and Ira Scofield, and filed June 8, 1840, page 452.
Apl. 6, 1840, commissioners appointed to adjust claims of creditors, page 452.
Mch. 1, 1841, report of commissioners to adjust claims filed, page 453.
Mch. 22, 1841, account filed, and creditors ordered paid 7 1/10 mills on the dollar, page 453.

Weed, John, late of Stamford, will dated Dec. 2, 1835, probated Aug. 11, 1838, all to his wife for life, and remainder to his grandchildren Sally Ann and Charles Sylvester Weed. Executor N. D. Haight. Witnesses N. D. Haight, Munson Buxton, and Alvah Scofield, page 341.
Aug. 11, 1838, N. D. Haight refused to qualify, and letters granted to John Brown of Stamford, who was ordered to advertise for claims, page 342.
Inventory taken by Peter Lockwood and Samuel Weed, and filed Jan. 31, 1839, page 342.
Mch. 19, 1839, account filed, and an allowance to his widow, page 343.

Weed, John, 3rd, late of Stamford, Feb. 3, 1837, on motion of William Webb, as assignee of Henry Weed, son of decedent, and as assignee of Polly, deceased daughter of decedent, estate ordered distributed to his widow, and his heirs at law, or their assigns, viz: 1/3 to the assignee of said Henry, 1/3 to the assignee of said Polly, and 1/3 to William M. Weed a son of deceased, page 310.
Feb. 4, 1837, estate distributed accordingly, page 310.

STAMFORD PROBATE RECORDS.
Volume 15, 1834.

Weed, Julia M., of Darien, Feb. 8, 1834, appointed guardian of her orphan brother, Theodore E. Weed of Darien, under 14 years of age, page 17.

Weed, Nelson, late of Stamford, Dec. 6, 1838, objections to his widow as administratrix filed, and letters of administration on his estate granted to his sister Elizabeth Weed, who was ordered to advertise for claims, page 392.
Inventory taken Dec. 7, 1838, by Sands Adams and James B. Scofield, and filed Dec. 7, 1838, page 392.
Dec. 23, 1838, commissioners appointed to adjust claims of creditors, pages 392 and 393.
Jan. 20, 1840, report of commissioners filed, page 393.
Jan. 20, 1840, account filed, and creditors ordered paid 55 3/10 cents on the dollar, page 394.

Weed, Samuel, and his wife Elizabeth Weed, late of Stamford, wills dated Aug. 9, 1839, probated June 14, 1841, mentions their grandchildren, the children of Nathan Weed, deceased, viz: William H., Alexander, Theodore, Sarah E., and Mary A., and the widow of said Nathan Weed. Executor ----. Witnesses Harvey Knapp, Mary Esther Smith, and N. D. Haight, page 485.
June 14, 1841, admitted to probate as the will of Samuel Weed, deceased, and not as the will of Elizabeth Weed, she having made another will and this day admitted to probate, page 485.

Weed, Sarah, late of Darien, Nov. 1, 1833, account filed, and real estate ordered sold to pay debts, page 121.
Real estate sold to John W. Bates, Ezra Lounsbury, Alfred Bishop, and John Scofield, and report of sale filed Mch. 11, 1835, page 121.

Weed, Theodore E., of Darien, Mch. 8, 1834, his sister and guardian, Julia M. Weed of Darien, asked for leave to sell the real estate of said minor in Stamford, and sale ordered, page 194.
Real estate sold to John James Leeds of Stamford, and report of sale filed Aug. 5, 1834, page 195.

Wheaton, Mary, late of Stamford, will dated Aug. 5, 1829, probated Apl. 11, 1834, mentions her daughter Eliza Ann wife of Calvin Clason, son John S. Wheaton, and the children of a deceased daughter Mary late wife of Rufus Scofield, deceased. Executor Solomon Clason of Stamford. Witnesses Samuel Heusted, William Provost, and Charles Hawley, page 102.

STAMFORD PROBATE RECORDS.
Volume 15, 1834.

Wheaton, Mary, continued :
    Apl. 11, 1834, order to advertise for claims, page 102.
    Inventory taken Apl. 20, 1834, by Jonathan Hoyt and
    Edwin Newman, and filed Apl. 25, 1835, page 103.

White, Jacob, Jr., late of Stamford, Apl. 20, 1837, that part
    of his estate which was set off to his widow as her
    dower, ordered distributed to his children, viz: Anna
    Young, Sarah Bostwick, Esther Smith, Nathan White,
    Henry White, to the heirs of Hannah Young, deceased,
    to the heirs of Maria Howe, deceased, and to Jacob
    White, page 278.
    Dec. 23, 1837, estate distributed as above ordered,
    except that Nathan White purchased the rights of Jacob
    White, and the heirs of Maria Howe, deceased, and re-
    ceived their share, page 278.

White, Richard H., of Darien, May 10, 1837, general assignment
    to James H. Hoyt of Stamford, for the benefit of credi-
    tors, page 265.
    Inventory taken by Abram Clock and John Weed, Jr
    and filed June 19, 1838, page 325.
    July 3, 1837, commissioners appointed to adjust claims
    of creditors, page 265.
    Mch. 5, 1838, report of commissioners filed, page 325.

Whiting, Samuel, late of Darien, Mch. 15, 1838, proceedings to
    remove Jesse Whiting, one of his executors, pages 289
    and 290.

Wilcox, William L., late of Greenwich, Dec. 4, 1832, commis-
    sioners appointed to adjust claims of creditors, page 1.
    Dec. 4, 1832, personal property ordered sold to pay
    debts, page 1.
    Sept. 7, 1833, report of commissioners filed, page 2.
    Oct. 7, 1833, account filed, and creditors ordered
    paid 18 1/2 cents on the dollar, page 3.

Wilmot, James, late of Stamford, Nov. 3, 1834, letters of ad-
    ministration on his estate granted to his widow, Abi-
    gail Wilmot, who was ordered to advertise for claims,
    page 200.
    Inventory taken by John Brown and Ezra Dibble, and
    filed Dec. 19, 1834, page 200.
    June 22, 1835, commissioners appointed to adjust claims
    of creditors, page 201.

Winthrop, John S., of Stamford, Sept. 30, 1835, his children
    Charles E. R., Catherine R., Cornelia, Harriet, and

STAMFORD PROBATE RECORDS.
Volume 15, 1834.

Winthrop, John S., continued :
    Emily R., made choice of their brothers Henry R. Winthrop and John S. Winthrop, Jr., of New York City to be their guardians, who were also appointed guardians of Francis B. and Susan R., of Stamford, other children of said John S. Winthrop of Stamford, page 109.

Wood, David, late of Greenwich, Sept. 20, 1833, report of commissioners to adjust claims of creditors filed, page 33.
    Mch. 22, 1833, account filed, and real estate ordered sold to pay debts, page 37.
    Dec. 21, 1833, creditors ordered paid 87 71/100 cents on the dollar, page 37.

Wood, Frances Amanda, of Darien, over 12 years of age, Sept/14, 1835, made choice of Dr. Warren Percival of Darien to be her guardian, page 110.

Wooster, William N., of Stamford, over 14 years of age, Aug. 15, 1835, made choice of William H. Webb of Stamford to be his guardian, page 110.

STAMFORD PROBATE RECORDS,
Volume 16, 1841.

Adams, Polly, late of Stamford, Jan. 31, 1843, letters of administration on her estate granted to Maltby Jelliff, of Wilton, who was ordered to advertise for claims, page 352.
Inventory taken by Thaddeus Hanford and Harvey Lockwood, and filed Apl. 22, 1843, page 352.

Avery, John, late of Greenwich, Jan. 30, 1843, account filed, and real estate ordered sold to pay debts, page 348. Real estate sold to Henry Merritt of Greenwich, and report of sale filed Apl. 22, 1843, page 348.

Avery, John, late of Greenwich, Jan. 17, 1842, on the application of Rachel Banks and Betsy Townsend, daughters of decedent, Zophar Avery removed as administrator, and Samuel Close of Greenwich appointed in his place, page 91.
Inventory taken Feb. 24, 1842, by Thomas A. Mead and Nelson Bush, and filed Mch. 5, 1842, page 92.

Avery, Walter, late of Greenwich, will dated Mch. 15, 1836, probated Dec. 28, 1842, all to his wife Clarissa, and appointed her his executrix. Witnesses William B. Sherwood, William E. Ferris, and Cornelia J. Graham, page 196.
Dec. 28, 1842, order to advertise for claims, page 196.
Inventory taken by Feb. 1843, by William B. Sherwood and Alvan Mead, and filed Feb. 27, 1843, page 210.

Banks, James, late of Greenwich, will dated Mch. 13, 1837, probated June 20, 1844, mentions his children Elizabeth Reynolds, and Catherine Reynolds, grandchildren James Pine, Sarah Purdy, and Hannah Pine. Executors his grandson James Pine, and daughters Elizabeth Reynolds and Catherine Reynolds, Witnesses William E. Reynolds, Margarette Miller, and Ard Reynolds, page 391.

STAMFORD PROBATE RECORDS.
Volume 16, 1841.

Banks, James, continued :
June 20, 1844, letters to James Pine, others declined, who was ordered to advertise for claims, page 392. Inventory taken by Augustus L. Reynolds and Ephraim Marshall, and filed Aug. 14, 1844, page 403.

Banks, Mary, late of New York City, Dec. 22, 1842, letters of administration on her estate granted to Augustus Lyon, of Greenwich, who was ordered to advertise for claims, page 344.
Inventory taken by Samuel Close and William Newman, and filed Mch. 4, 1844, page 344.

Bartow, Daniel, late of Stamford, Apl. 12, 1843, letters of administration on his estate granted to Rufus Ayres of Poundridge and Robert R. Bartow of Stamford, who were ordered to advertise for claims, page 321.

Bates, Mary, an alleged lunatic, of Darien, Nov. 24, 1843, her brother in law Darius Waterbury, and her nephew Samuel Waterbury, asked for the appointment of a conservator, page 279.
Dec. 9, 1843, William Andreas of Darien appointed such conservator, page 280.
Dec. 26, 1843, the conservator asked leave to sell the real estate of said incompetent in Darien, and sale ordered, page 281.
Real estate sold to Charles Weed, Jr., of Darien, and report of sale filed Jan. 25, 1844, page 283.

Bates, Sarah, of Darien, an alleged lunatic, Nov. 24, 1843 her brother in law Darius Waterbury, and her nephew Samuel Waterbury, asked for the appointment of a conservator, page 280.
Dec. 8, 1843, William Andreas of Darien appointed such conservator, page 281.
Dec. 26, 1843, the conservator asked leave to sell the real estate of said incompetent in Darien, and sale ordered, page 281.
Real estate sold to Charles Weed, Jr., of Darien, and report of sale filed Jan. 25, 1844, page 283.

Bell, Abraham, late of Stamford, will dated Mch. 30, 1835, probated Apl. 3, 1843, all to my two sisters Susannah and Mercy. No executor. Witnesses Henry Waterbury, John Dibble, Jr., and Epenetus Webb, page 217.

STAMFORD PROBATE RECORDS.
Volume 16, 1841.

Bell, Mersy, late of Stamford, will dated July 23, 1841, probated Nov. 2, 1842, mentions Sally Wilmot, widow of John Wilmot of Stamford, Maria Dibble a daughter of John Dibble, deceased, and Noah Knapp of Darien. Executor Joseph Hoyt. Witnesses John Dibble, James Hull, and Samuel Lockwood, Jr., page 183.
Nov. 2, 1842, order to advertise for claims, page 184.
Inventory taken by Sylvanus B. Thompson of Stamford and Ezra H. Bishop of Darien, and filed Mch. 7, 1843, page 184.

Bell, Prudence, late of Stamford, Aug. 12, 1844, letters of administration on her estate granted to Charles Brown, who was ordered to advertise for claims, page 403.

Bell, Susannah, late of Stamford, will dated Mch. 30, 1835, probated Apl. 3, 1843, all to my brother Abraham and my sister Mercy. No executor. Witnesses Henry Waterbury, John Dibble, Jr., and Epenetus Webb, page 216.

Bouton, William H., late of Stamford, Jan. 17, 1842, his widow refused to qualify, and letters of administration on his estate granted to Nathaniel D. Hait, who was ordered to advertise for claims, page 104.
Inventory taken by Benjamin M. Weed and Ebenezer Smith, and filed Jan. 21, 1842, page 105.
July 20, 1842, commissioners appointed to adjust claims of creditors, pages 157 and 264.
Feb. 20, 1843, report of commissioners filed, page 264.
Mch. 10, 1843, account filed, allowance to his widow, and real estate ordered sold to pay debts, page 265.
Real estate sold to Ami Waters of Stamford, and report of sale filed Apl. 24, 1843, page 265.
Aug. 22, 1843, account filed, and creditors ordered paid twenty one cents and one mill on the dollar, page 266.

Brown, George, of Stamford, Dec. 4, 1842, on the application of Royal L. Gay, Selleck Scofield, and Ebenezer Lockwood selectmen of Stamford, George L. Brown was appointed his conservator, page 179.
Inventory taken by the conservator, and filed Dec. 26, 1842, page 180.

Brown, Henry, late of Stamford, Mch. 14, 1842, inventory taken by Davis Lockwood and filed Mch. 16, 1842, page 126.
Feb. 10, 1843, account filed, and an allowance to his widow, page 276.

STAMFORD PROBATE RECORDS.
Volume 16, 1841.

Brown, John, late of Stamford, Sept. 25, 1841, letters of administration on his estate granted to Charles Brown of Stamford, who was ordered to advertise for claims, page 25.
Inventory taken Oct. 11, 1841, by Bates Fox and Ami Scofield, and filed Oct. 30, 1841, page 25.
Apl. 7, 1842, account filed, and real estate ordered sold to pay debts, page 25.

Brown, Lucy, of Stamford, Mch. 1, 1843, the application of her brother Gideon Leeds of Wilton for the appointment of a conservator, page 350.
Mch. 14, 1843, John R. Leeds of Stamford appointed her conservator, page 351.

Brush, Edward, late of Stamford, will dated Aug. 26, 1843, probated Apl. 22, 1844, mentions his sons Josephus and Edward, and granddaughter Sarah Husted the child of my daughter Cornelia. Executors son Josephus, and friend Shubel Brush. Witnesses William Brush, Benjamin S. Downes, and Shubel Brush, page 353.
Apl. 22, 1844, order to advertise for claims, page 353.
Inventory taken by Ard Reynolds and Alfred Rundle, and filed June 4, 1844, page 354.

Brush, Edward L., about 18 years of age, of Stamford, Aug. 8, 1844, made choice of Shubal Brush of Greenwich to be his guardian, page 399.

Brush, Josephus, late of Stamford, will dated Apl. 22, 1844, probated Aug. 8, 1844, mentions his brother Edward L. Brush, niece Sarah Cornelia Husted, and aunt Sarah Van Kleek. Executor Shubal Brush of Greenwich. Witnesses James Brush, Benjamin S. Downs, and Shubal Brush, page 398.
Aug. 8, 1844, order to advertise for claims, page 399.

Bunnell, Jonathan, late of Greenwich, Oct. 30, 1843, letters of administration on his estate granted to his widow, Sabina Bunnell of Greenwich and Royal L. Gay of Stamford, who were ordered to advertise for claims, page 366
Inventory taken by Stephen B. Provost and Davis Lockwood, and filed Dec. 18, 1843, page 366.

Bunnell, Polly, late of Stamford, Apl. 8, 1842, letters of administration on her estate granted to Samuel Lockwood of Stamford, who was ordered to advertise for claims, page 89.

STAMFORD PROBATE RECORDS.
Volume 16, 1841.

Bunnell, Polly, continued :
> Inventory taken by Isaac M. Smith and Frederick A. Smith, and filed Apl. 27, 1842, page 89.
> Apl. 15, 1843, account filed, and real estate ordered sold to pay debts, page 368.
> Real estate sold to Mary E. Taylor and Charles S. Knapp of Stamford, and John W. Knapp and Lorenzo E. Knapp of New Orleans, La., and report of sale filed June 1, 1844, page 368.

Burley, Henry, of Greenwich, Nov. 24, 1842, on the application of Amy Burley of Greenwich, Frederick Lockwood of Greenwich was appointed his conservator, page 190.
> Mch. 15, 1844, now capable of managing his affairs, his conservator was discharged, page 285.

Classon, Benjamin, late of Stamford, Feb. 25, 1839, account filed, and real estate ordered sold by Earl Smith to pay debts, page 124.

Clock, Abram, of Darien, parent and guardian of Edward A. Clock of New York City, Jan. 11, 1843, asked leave to sell the real estate of said minor in Darien, and sale ordered, page 252.
> Apl. 7, 1843, Edward A. Clock, over 14 years of age, formerly of Darien, but now of New York City, made choice of Abram Clock to be his guardian, page 285.
> Dec. 30, 1843, said Edward A. Clock, being the owner in common with Edward Scofield, Abigail wife of Holly Bell, Hannah E. wife of William R. Scofield, and Julia wife of Abram Clock, all of Darien, and George Scofield of New York City, of a tract of land in Darien, the court appointed Isaac Weed, Jr., of Darien to assist Abraham Clock of Darien, guardian of said minor, to partition said lands, page 380.
> Jan. 19, 1844, partition made, and agreement duly executed, page 381.

Close, Edward, late of Greenwich, June 24, 1839, letters of administration on his estate granted to his sons Gideon Close and Edwin T. Close, who were ordered to advertise for claims, page 95.
> Inventory taken Sept. 23, 1839, by Conklin Husted and Gilbert Close, and filed Oct. 4, 1839, page 95.

Close, Edwin, of Greenwich, a minor, his real estate sold to Gideon Close, Odel Close, George C. Close, and Shadrach M. Close, and report of sale filed June 17, 1844, page 380.

STAMFORD PROBATE RECORDS.
Volume 16, 1841.

Close, Edwin T., late of Greenwich, Mch. 10, 1843, his widow
   refused to qualify, and letters of administration on
   his estate granted to Alfred Bundle of Greenwich, who
   was ordered to advertise for claims, page 323.
   Inventory taken by Conklin Husted and Benjamin Brush,
   and filed May 9, 1843, page 323.
   June 29, 1843, the court appointed Guy B. Hobby of
   North Castle guardian of Edwin Close of Greenwich, (a
   son of decedent), page 324.
   June 29, 1843, petition for leave to sell the real estate of said minor in Greenwich, viz: the right of his
   father in and to 1/5 of the estate of Edward Close,
   deceased, and sale ordered, page 325.

Cock, Eleanor, of Darien, Dec. 6, 1842, the court appointed
   William Scofield to be her guardian, page 185.

Cox, Robert, late of Greenwich, June 10, 1839, his widow refused to qualify, and letters of administration on his
   estate granted to Peter Ferris of Greenwich, who was
   ordered to advertise for claims, page 130.
   Inventory taken by Henry Ritch and Jonathan D. Weeks,
   and filed June 22, 1839, page 131.
   July 1, 1839, commissioners appointed to adjust claims
   of creditors, page 130.
   June 17, 1842, report of commissioners filed, page 131.
   June 17, 1842, account filed, and allowance to his
   widow, page 132.
   Nov. 18, 1842, account filed, and creditors ordered
   paid one cent and three mills and eight tenths of a
   mill on the dollar, page 197.

Curtis, Ezekiel, late of Stamford, will dated Sept. 30, 1840,
   probated Jan. 18, 1843, all to his wife Sarah. Executor Isaac Scofield of Stamford. Witnesses Richard
   Cox, Elizabeth Cox, and Abishai Scofield, page 302.
   Jan. 18, 1843, order to advertise for claims, page 304.
   xxxxxxxxxxxxxxxxxxxxxxxxxxxxxx
   Inventory taken by Amzi Scofield and Richard Fox, and
   filed Mch. 18, 1843, page 270.
   Aug. 5, 1843, account filed, and real estate ordered
   sold to pay debts, page 271.
   Real estate sold to Richard Cox of Stamford, and report
   of sale filed Jan. 1, 1844, page 271.

Dan, John, late of Stamford, will dated Feb. 19, 1844, probated Apl. 4, 1844, mentions his wife Elizabeth F.,
   and children Elizabeth, Maria Slater, Angelina Ophelia,
   Louisa Augusta Bruce, Rachel Lockwood Van Patten,

STAMFORD PROBATE RECORDS.
Volume 16, 1841.

Dan, John, continued :
 Alfred Theodore, Walter Smith, Elvin Lorenzo, and Frances Helena. Executors his wife and Walter S. Clawson. Witnesses Harvey Scofield, Nehemiah Bates, and Walter W. Clawson, page 364.
 Apl. 4, 1844, order to advertise for claims, page 365.
 Inventory taken by Nathan White and Harvey Scofield, and filed June 8, 1844, page 365.

Dayton, Jacob, late of Greenwich, Apl. 7, 1843, letters of administration on his estate granted to Samuel B. Dayton of Greenwich, who was ordered to advertise for claims, page 240.
 Inventory taken by Joseph Close and Conklin Husted, and filed Aug. 7, 1843, page 241.

Dibble, Maria, over 12 years of age, of Stamford, Aug. 31, 1843, made choice of Ezra H. Bishop of Darien to be her guardian, page 286.

Dixon, Isaac, of Stamford, Aug. 23, 1841, Stephen Ferris of Darien appointed his conservator, page 145.
 Inventory filed Aug. 30, 1841, page 145.

Dodgeshun, Enoch, late of New York City, June 6, 1842, on the application of John R. Palmer of Greenwich, Hannah Dodgeshun, administratrix, removed, and Royal L. Gay appointed in her place, page 50.
 Aug. 13, 1842, account filed, and real estate ordered sold to pay debts, page 163.
 Real estate sold to Beal B. Lockwood of Greenwich, and report of sale filed Sept. 3, 1842, page 164.
 Sept. 13, 1843, dower of his widow, Hannah Dodgeshun, ordered set out, and set out Sept. 14, 1843, page 260.

Ferris, Ann, late of Greenwich, will dated Aug. 30, 1839, probated Aug. 31, 1842, mentions her son Joseph Ferris, all to her daughter Ruth Davis widow of Walter Davis, and appointed her and Peter Ferris executors. Witnesses Samuel Close, Benjamin Page, and Augustus R. Newman, page 202.
 Sept. 7, 1842, order to advertise for claims, page 202.
 Inventory taken by Benjamin Page and Augustus R. Newman, and filed Oct. 31, 1842, page 203.

Ferris, Mary L., late of Greenwich, will dated Apl. 25, 1842, probated May 25, 1842, all to her grandchildren, the heirs of William H. and Mary Keeler, viz: Phebe Ann

STAMFORD PROBATE RECORDS.
Volume 16, 1841.

Ferris, Mary L., continued :
Keeler, Josephine Keeler, and Mariana Keeler, and all the children that said William H. and Mary Keeler may hereafter have. Executor said William H. Keeler. Witnesses Chauncey Ayres, Hannah Brown, and Hannah Scofield, page 79.
May 28, 1842, order to advertise for claims, page 80.
July 18, 1842, inventory taken by Peter Ferris and Chauncey Smith, and filed Mch. 4, 1843, page 215.

Ferris, Samuel, Jr., late of Greenwich, will dated May 14, 1842 probated June 13, 1842, mentions his wife Esther, and children Caroline, Susan, Henrietta, Ann, Sarah, Mary, Hannah, Stephen R., Nathaniel H., and Samuel H. Executrix his wife. Witnesses Joshua B. Ferris, Beal B. Lockwood, and Josephus Peck, page 137.
June 13, 1842, order to advertise for claims, page 138.
July 27, 1842, inventory taken by Charles Hendrie and Beal B. Lockwood, and filed Aug. 20, 1842, page 160.
Jan. 13, 1842, Nathaniel H., about 18 years of age, Samuel H., about 14 years of age, and Mary W., children of decedent, made choice of their mother Esther Ferris to be their guardian, who was also appointed guardian of Hannah H., another child of decedent, page 140.

Field, Aaron, late of Greenwich, will dated 10th day of 5th month, 1838, probated Apl. 22, 1844, mentions his wife Jane, and children Sarah E. Field, Ann Field, Eliza Field, and Hannah Field. Executors his sons Charles and Richard. Witnesses James Field, Edmund Field, and William C. Field, page 296.
Apl. 22, 1844, letters to Richard Field, who was ordered to advertise for claims, page 296.
Inventory taken by Edmund Field and William C. Field, and filed Apl. 29, 1844, page 299.

Finch, Abigail, late of Greenwich, will dated Dec. 28, 1840, probated Sept. 9, 1842, mentions her daughter Elizabeth Anderson, widow of James P. Anderson, son Edwin Smith, daughter Parmelia Ferris, widow of Nathaniel Ferris; granddaughter Lucinda Palmer, a daughter of my daughter Ruth Palmer, daughter Polly wife of Sylvanus Marshall of Stamford, and granddaughter Amanda Anderson. Executor Samuel Close of Greenwich. Witnesses John S. Husted, D. Jerome Sands, and James Peck, page 169.
Probate contested, page 169.
Sept. 17, 1842, order to advertise for claims, page 171
Appeal taken from probate by Sylvanus Marshall and

STAMFORD PROBATE RECORDS.
Volume 16, 1841.

Finch, Abigail, continued:
    Polly Marshall, his wife, a daughter of testatrix, pages 171 and 215.
    Feb. 13, 1843, Samuel Close of Greenwich, executor, resigned, and Arza Marshall of Stamford appointed in his place, page 275.
    Feb. 9, 1844, inventory filed, page 275.

Finch, Reuben, late of Stamwich in Greenwich, will dated Apl. 7, 1837, probated June 13, 1839, mentions his wife Abigail, and children, no names. Executors his wife and son Amos. Witnesses Hugh Mackay, Caroline Knapp and George Knapp, page 83.
    June 13, 1839, order to advertise for claims, page 84.
    Inventory taken by Benjamin Brush, Jr., and Alfred Rundle, and filed Aug. 1, 1839, page 85.

Finch, William, of Greenwich, July 20, 1842, general assignment for the benefit of creditors to Ard Reynolds of Greenwich, page 151.
    Inventory taken by Alfred Rundle and Major Brown, Jr., and filed Aug. 13, 1842, page 153.
    Aug. 13, 1842, commissioners appointed to adjust claims of creditors, page 156.

Ford, Eliakim, late of Greenwich, will dated July 12, 1837, probated June 2, 1841, mentions his wife Hannah, and children Cornelius, Sarah, Letitia Hendrie, Benjamin, and Lucy Quintard. Executors daughter Sarah and son in law Alexander Hendrie. Witnesses S. B. Provost, Smith Scott, and Charles Hawley, page 135.
    June 2, 1841, letters to Sarah Ford, who was ordered to advertise for claims, page 136.

Gray, Cary H., late of Stamford, Apl. 15, 1839, account filed by his administrators, and real estate ordered sold to pay debts, page 224.
    Land in Darien sold to Royal L. Gay of Stamford, and land in Stamford sold to Hezekiah Weed, William Talmage, and William Hoyt, Jr., all of Stamford, and report of sale filed May 8, 1843, page 225.

Green, James, late of Greenwich, will dated June 28, 1841, probated July 20, 1842, mentions Charity W. wife of Josiah Purdy of Rye, Josiah Purdy, Jr., and his sister Mary W. Purdy children of said Josiah Purdy, nephews James Wilson, John Benjamin Wilson, and Samuel Wilson, nieces Ann Heustis, Polly Haight, Nancy sister of said Polly, Sally Finny, and nephew Thomas Wilson all children of my sister Sally Wilson; Jeremiah Green,

STAMFORD PROBATE RECORDS.
Volume 16, 1841.

Green, James, continued:
    Nancy, Patty, Elizabeth, Susan, and Mary, children of my deceased brother Reuben Green; Samuel Dann, William Tenby and William Van Benthuysen; Polly, Rebecca, Cynthia, and Nancy children of my deceased brother Joseph Green. Executors James Wilson, Josiah Purdy, and John Benjamin Wilson. Witnesses Mary S. Hawley, Charles A. Hawley, and Charles Hawley, page 147.
    Codicil dated June 17, 1842, revoked legacy to Nancy wife of James Merritt described in said will as one of the children of my brother Reuben Green, who by mistake was described therein as my deceased brother, page 148.
    July 20, 1842, letters to James Wilson and John B. Wilson, who were ordered to advertise for claims, page 149.
    Inventory taken July 21, 1842, by Nathan S. Mead and Jotham Merritt, and filed Aug. 13, 1842, pages 149 and 155.
    July 20, 1843, time for final settlement extended, page 351.

Grigg, Elizabeth, late of Greenwich, will dated July 3, 1844, probated July 25, 1844, mentions Aaron a son of Caleb Husted, Mary Jane a daughter of said Caleb Husted, Cynthia E., wife of Sanford Mead, and Mary wife of said Caleb Husted. Executor Sanford Mead. Witnesses Samuel Close, John R. Grigg, and Julia Ann Horton, page 397.
    July 25, 1844, order to advertise for claims, page 397.

Hanford, Augustus, late of Stamford, Sept. 21, 1841, letters of administration on his estate granted to Thaddeus Hanford of Stratford, who was ordered to advertise for claims, page 105.
    Inventory taken by Gideon W. Lockwood and Luther Weed, and filed Dec. 13, 1841, page 105.
    Dec. 20, 1841, account filed, and commissioners appointed to adjust claims of creditors, page 122.
    Apl. 11, 1842, report of commissioners filed, page 166.

Harvey, Thomas M., formerly of New York City, late of Stamford will dated Mch. 22, 1839, probated Nov. 5, 1841, mentions his wife Elinor, and children Juliet and Thomas M. Executors his wife, Rev. William H. Bangs, and Abel T. Anderson of New York City. Witnesses David Grew, William Harvey Low, and Samuel Denny, page 51.
    Nov. 5, 1841, letters granted to Elinor Harvey and William H. Bangs, who were ordered to advertise for claims, page 52.

STAMFORD PROBATE RECORDS.
Volume 16, 1841.

Harvey, Thomas M., continued :
    Inventory taken Dec. 23, 1841, by Stephen B. Provost and Richard Stanton, and filed Dec. 23, 1841, page 53.

Hobby, Amos, late of Greenwich, Dec. 14, 1839, Beal B. Lockwood appointed guardian of Amos M., about 12 years of age, a son of decedent, page 78.
    July 30, 1842, Beal B. Lockwood resigned, and Jacob T. Weed appointed guardian in his place, page 158.

Hobby, Hezekiah, late of Greenwich, Jan. 21, 1843, letters of administration on his estate granted to his son Samuel D. Hobby of Greenwich, who was ordered to advertise for claims, page 347.
    Inventory taken by Thomas A. Mead and Zaccheus Mead and filed Apl. 3, 1843, page 348.

Holly, Elena, pf Stamford, Dec. 29, 1841, guardian of her children George F. Holly and Julia Ann Holly, asked leave to sell the real estate of said minors in Stamford, and sale ordered, page 143.
    Real estate sold to Alexander N. Holly of Stamford, and report of sale filed Mch. 11, 1842, page 144.

Holly, Isaac, late of Stamford, Mch. 17, 1842, that part of his estate set offf to his widow Elena Holly, as her dower, ordered distributed to Alexander N. Holly 10/11 and to Edwin S. Holly 1/11, page 144.
    May 12, 1842, estate distributed accordingly, page 156.

Holly, John William, late of Stamford, will dated Feb. 13, 1835, probated Dec. 3, 1838, mentions his son in law William H. McKinney, sister Mary, devised land to St. John's Church to be used as a cemetery for his descendants. Executors his sons John M., William W., Alfred A., and son in law Henry Hudson. Witnesses Samuel Lockwood, Hannah Weed, and Mary Doty, page 69.
    Dec. 3, 1838, John M. Holly and Henry Hudson refused to qualify, and letters granted to William W. Holly and Alfred A. Holly, who were ordered to advertise for claims, page 70.
    Inventory taken by William Weed of Stamford and Ezra H. Bishop of Darien, and filed Jan. 29, 1839, page 70.

Holly, Sarah, late of Stamford, Apl. 12, 1843, letters of administration on her estate granted to Reuben Hoyt of Stamford, who was ordered to advertise for claims, page 342.
    Inventory taken by Hezekiah Scofield and Charles Brown,

STAMFORD PROBATE RECORDS.
Volume 16, 1841.

Holly, Sarah, continued :
and filed May 1, 1843, page 342.
Oct. 30, 1843, account filed, and real estate ordered
sold to pay debts, page 342.
Real estate sold to Stephen Bishop of Stamford, and
report of sale filed Oct. 30, 1843, page 343.

Holmes, John, late of Greenwich, will dated Mch. 13, 1839,
probated June 12, 1841, all to his son John Augustus.
Executor Major Brown, Jr. Witnesses Henry S. Hubbard,
and William H. Holly, page 53.
June 12, 1841, order to advertise for claims, page 54.
Inventory taken June 16, 1841, by Nathaniel Husted and
Samuel Brown, and filed Sept. 6, 1841, page 54.

Holmes, Mary, late of Greenwich, Nov. 15, 1841, letters of administration on her estate granted to Ebenezer Mead of
Greenwich, who was ordered to advertise for claims,
page 11.
Inventory taken Jan. 3/1842, by Jabez Mead, Jr., and
Jonas Mead, Jr., and filed Jan. 24, 1842, page 11.

Hoyt, Abigail, of Stamford, Aug. 19, 1841, appointed guardian
of her children Mary Elizabeth Hoyt, 18 years of age,
Harriet Atwood Hoyt, and Henry M. Hoyt, page 20.
Aug. 9, 1841, petition for leave to sell the real estate of said minors in Stamford, and sale ordered,
pages 20 and 21.
Real estate sold to Royal L. Gay and George C. Hoyt,
and report of sale filed Nov. 1, 1841, page 21.

Hoyt, David, late of Stamford, Mch. 8, 1841, dower of his
widow, Abigail Hoyt, ordered set out, page 107.
Mch. 8, 1841, dower set out, page 107.

Hoyt, Ebenezer, late of Darien, will dated July 4, 1837, probated Mch. 6, 1843, mentions his sisters Rhoda and
Melicent Hoyt, nephew Harren or Harris Seely's son
Mason Griffin Seely, niece Martha Reed, nephews Henry
Weed, Cary Weed, Noah Weed, Joseph Seely, and Cary H.
Seely, nieces Hannah Reed, Betsy Seely, Sally Jennings,
and Isabella Jennings, nephews Rufus Weed's two sons
Ebenezer Selleck Weed and John Rufus Weed. Executor
Ashbel Scofield of Stamford. Witnesses Abram Clock,
Julia Clock, and Charles Finnigan, page 356.
Mch. 6, 1843, order to advertise for claims, page 356.
Inventory taken by Hezekiah Scofield and Harris Scofield
and filed Apl. 18, 1843, page 357.

STAMFORD PROBATE RECORDS.
Volume 16, 1841.

Hoyt, George, late of Stamford, Nov. 10, 1838, letters of administration on his estate granted to his brother James H. Hoyt, who was ordered to advertise for claims, page 77.

Hoyt, John S., of Stamford, Nov. 19, 1842, his present guardian, John Seely, resigned, and Royal L. Gay was chosen in his place, page 185.

Hoyt, Julia, late of Darien, Feb. 13, 1843, letters of administration on her estate granted to John R. Leeds of Stamford, who was ordered to advertise for claims, page 343.
Inventory taken by John Holmes and Seth Stevens, both of Darien, and filed Apl. 3, 1843, page 343.

Hoyt, Milicent, late of Darien, will dated Feb. 17, 1843, probated May 2, 1844, mentions her nephew Noah Weed, the children of a deceased nephew Cary Weed, nephews Joseph Seely and Cary Seely, nieces Hannah Reed, Betsy Seely, Sally Jennings, and Isabel Jennings, nephew Henry Weed, Abigail Weed the widow of a deceased nephew Rufus Weed, and niece Martha Reed. Executor Ashbel Scofield. Witnesses Abram Clock, Sherman Husted, and Gilbert G. Waterbury, page 385.
Codicil dated Sept 8, 1843, legacy to my sister Rhoda Hoyt, page 385.

Hoyt, Ralph, late of Stamford, Apl. 19, 1841, dower of his widow ordered set out, page 68.
Apl. 19, 1841, dower set out, page 68.

Hoyt, Rebecca, widow, late of Stamford, Mch. 7, 1842, letters of administration on her estate granted to William Scofield, Jr., who was ordered to advertise for claims, page 90.
Inventory taken by John R. Leeds of Stamford and Hiram Crissy of New Canaan, and filed Mch. 14, 1842, page 90.

Hoyt, Samuel H., late of Stamford, Apl. 25, 1842, his widow refused to qualify, and letters of administration on his estate granted to his son Augustus Hoyt of North Castle, who was ordered to advertise for claims, page 90.
Inventory taken Apl. 26, 1842, by Ebenezer Dean and Aaron Dean, and filed May 2, 1842, page 92.
Oct. 24, 1842, account filed, and commissioners appointed to adjust claims of creditors, pages 181 and 275.
May 8, 1843, report of commissioners filed, page 276.

STAMFORD PROBATE RECORDS.
Volume 15, 1841.

Hubbard, Gabriel, late of Stamford, Feb. 18, 1843, Hannah,
 Elizabeth, and David, all of New York City, and over 12
 years of age, children of decedent, made choice of
 George C. Waring to be their guardian, page 278.
 Feb. 18, 1843, petition for leave to sell the real estate of said minors in Stamford, subject to the dower
 of Hannah Hubbard, widow of decedent, and sale ordered,
 page 258.
 Real estate sold to Deborah Crabb and William Kenworthy
 and report of sale filed June 10, 1843, page 259.

Husted, Amos, late of Greenwich, Oct. 14, 1843, Esbon Husted
 of Greenwich administrator, neglected his duties, and
 desired to be discharged, and the court discharged said
 Esbon Husted, and appointed Abraham Mead of Greenwich
 in his place, page 261.

Husted, Jonathan, of Greenwich, Nov. 7, 1842, general assignment for the benefit of creditors to Nathaniel Husted
 and Samuel Rundle, page 172.
 Inventory taken by Alfred Rundle and Samuel Brown, and
 filed Dec. 9, 1842, page 173.
 Dec. 19, 1842, commissioners appointed to adjust claims
 of creditors, pages 174 and 192.
 June 17, 1843, report of commissioners filed, page 262.
 Jan. 31, 1843, assignee ordered to sell the real estate, page 351.

Husted, Nathan, late of Darien, Oct. 27, 1842, letters of administration on his estate granted to Hannah Husted and
 Stephen Husted, both of Darien, who were ordered to advertise for claims, page 198.
 Inventory taken Nov. 4, 1842, by Abram Clock and William Wilmot, and filed Nov. 14, 1842, page 174.
 June 3, 1843, account filed, allowance to his widow,
 and real estate ordered sold to pay debts, page 268.
 Real estate sold to Benjamin Little and his wife Dorcas
 Little, both of Darien, and report of sale filed July
 11, 1843, page 270.

Jarvis, Seymour, late of Stamford, will dated Aug. 1, 1843,
 probated Nov. 11, 1843, mentions his wife Isabella, and
 children Martha Margaret, Mary Hannah, Harriet Elizabeth, Lavinia Todd, Albertina Seymour, Sarah Peters, and
 Samuel Odell Jarvis. Executor Charles Hawley of Stamford. Witnesses Joshua B. Ferris, Ambrose S. Todd,
 and William T. Minor, page 311.
 Nov. 11, 1843, executor refused to qualify, and letters
 granted to Martha M. Jarvis and Mary H. Jarvis, who
 were ordered to advertise for claims, page 312.

STAMFORD PROBATE RECORDS,
Volume 16, 1841.

Jarvis, Seymour, continued:
    Inventory taken by James H. Minor and William T. Minor, and filed Mch. 8, 1844, page 313.

Jessup, Samuel, late of Greenwich, June 22, 1843, his widow refused to qualify, and letters of administration on his estate granted to Peter Ferris of Greenwich, who was ordered to advertise for claims, page 371.
    Inventory taken by Charles Hendrie of Stamford and Joseph D. Ferris of Greenwich, and filed July 4, 1843, page 372.
    Nov. 28, 1843, commissioners appointed to adjust claims of creditors, page 372.
    June 13, 1844, report of commissioners filed, page 373.
    June 19, 1844, account filed, allowance to his widow, and real estate ordered sold to pay debts, page 387.
    June 19, 1844, dower of his widow, ordered set out, page 387.
    July 1, 1844, new commissioners appointed to set out the dower of his widow, page 390.
    July 9, 1844, dower set out, page 396.

Judson, Joseph, late of Darien, Mch. 17, 1842, account filed, and real estate ordered sold to pay debts, page 125.

June, Joseph, late of Fitsville, Ohio, Mch. 21, 1842, letters of administration on his estate granted to his brother Alva June of Stamford, who was ordered to advertise for claims, page 123.

June, Joseph, late of Hartland, Ohio, Sept. 12, 1842, Sally June the guardian of Reuben A., Joseph H., Charles E., and Linus P., all of said Hartland, children of decedent, asked leave to sell the real estate of said minors in Stamford, belonging to the estate of Reuben June, late of Stamford, subject to the dower of Mary June, and also the dower of Sally June in 1/4 thereof, and sale ordered to be made by Nehemiah Hait, Jr., page 186.
    Real estate sold to Alva June, and report of sale filed Dec. 17, 1842, page 186.

King, James J., late of New York City, Jan. 6, 1840, letters of administration on his estate granted to John A. Davenport of New York City, who was ordered to advertise for claims, page 77.

Knapp, Allen R., late of Greenwich, will dated Dec. 7, 1837, probated Jan. 3, 1842, all to his mother Sophia Knapp for life, and remainder to his sisters Frances S. Knapp

STAMFORD PROBATE RECORDS.
Volume 16, 1841.

317.

Knapp, Allen R., continued:
and Phebe C. Knapp. Executor his brother Charles W. Knapp. Witnesses Eliza Close, W. R. Close, and Samuel Close, page 114.
Jan. 3, 1842, the executor refused to qualify, and letters granted to William H. Mead of Greenwich, who was ordered to advertise for claims, page 114.
Inventory taken by Titus Mead and Solomon Mead, and filed Apl. 28, 1842, page 115.

Knapp, Charles, late of Stamford, will dated Dec. 5, 1840, probated Jan. 11, 1841, mentions his wife Elizabeth, and children John W., Mary E. Taylor, Charles S., and Lorenzo E., niece Amanda M. Lockwood, and grandson Charles K. Taylor a son of Mary E. Taylor. Executors his brother in law Dr. Samuel Lockwood and daughter Mary E. Taylor. Witnesses Lyman Lockwood, Henry Waring, and Charles Hawley, page 99.
Jan. 11, 1841, order to advertise for claims, page 101.
Inventory taken by Henry Waring and Royal L. Gay, and filed Feb. 15, 1841, page 102.

Knapp, Elizabeth, late of Stamford, will dated Aug. 7, 1841, probated Nov. 18, 1841, mentions her daughter Mary E. Taylor, sons John W. Knapp, Charles S. Knapp, and Lorenzo E. Knapp, and sister Polly Bunnell. Executrix her daughter Mary E. Taylor. Witnesses Samuel Lockwood, Ann M. Lockwood, and Amanda M. Lockwood, page 92.

Knapp, Elizabeth C., about 16 years of age, and Charles W. Knapp, about 14 years of age, both of Stamford, Aug. 7, 1844, made choice of Lewis Legrand Whitney to be their guardian, page 398.

Knapp, Esther, late of Greenwich, Mch. 6, 1843, letters of administration on her estate granted to Benjamin I. Knapp of Greenwich, who was ordered to advertise for claims, page 226.
Inventory taken by Henry Ritch and Joseph D. Ferris, and filed May 6, 1843, page 227.

Knapp, Hannah B., of Greenwich, over 12 years of age, Aug. 31, 1842, made choice of Jared O. Knapp of Greenwich to be her guardian, page 169.

Knapp, Hezekiah, late of Stamford, will dated Jan. 13, 1832, probated Jan. 21, 1841, mentions his wife Mary, and children Rufus, Luther, Bethia wife of Charles Gaylor, Polly wife of Rufus Newman, Hannah wife of Isaac Wardwell, and Sally wife of John Scofield, Executors

STAMFORD PROBATE RECORDS.
Volume 16, 1841.

Knapp, Hezekiah, continued:
his wife, and Isaac Wardwell. Witnesses Samuel Lockwood, Deborah Knapp, and Bethia Knapp, page 15.
Codicil dated Apl. 24, 1834, devise to his daughter Bethia Gaylor revoked, and same devised to Isaac Wardwell and William Wardwell, son of Isaac Wardwell, both of Stamford, to hold same so long as said Bethia remainded the wife of Charles Gaylor, page 15.
Jan. 21, 1841, letters to Samuel Lockwood, who was ordered to advertise for claims, the widow having refused to qualify, page 16.
Inventory taken Feb. 15, 1841, by Frederick Lockwood and Henry Waring, and filed Feb. 15, 1841, pages 17, 18, and 178.
Jan. 10, 1842, account filed, allowance to his widow, and real estate ordered sold to pay debts, page 18.
Real estate sold to Joseph Selleck, Jr., of Stamford, Enos B. Lockwood, Beal B. Lockwood, and Rufus Knapp, and report of sale filed June 18, 1842, page 139.
Oct. 1, 1842, account filed, and shows that his widow, Mary Knapp and Isaac Wardwell are now deceased, and estate ordered distributed to his children Polly widow of Rufus Newman, Hannah S., widow of Isaac Wardwell, Rufus, Sally widow of John Scofield, Luther, and to William Wardwell, as trustee, page 230.
June 16, 1843, estate distributed accordingly, except the share of Luther was assigned to Joseph Selleck, Jr. page 231.

Knapp, Jared, late of Greenwich, June 8, 1839, letters of administration on his estate granted to his widow Mary Knapp, who was ordered to advertise for claims, page 19.
Inventory taken July 7, 1839, by Isaac Peck and Nathaniel Husted, and filed Aug. 13, 1839, page 19.
May 4, 1840, account filed, and allowance to his widow, page 19.
May 4, 1840, real estate ordered sold to pay debts, page 168.
Real estate sold to Benjamin Knapp and Joseph Knapp, and report of sale filed Sept. 12, 1842, page 168.
Mch. 7, 1842, dower of his widow, Mary Knapp, set out, page 124.

Knapp, Lodema, late of Stamford, Apl. 24, 1843, letters of administration on her estate granted to Royal L. Gay, who was ordered to advertise for claims, page 241.
Inventory taken by Jonathan D. Weeks and Edwin Lounsbury, and filed Aug. 26, 1843, page 241.

STAMFORD PROBATE RECORDS.
Volume 16, 1841.

Knapp, Mary, late of Stamford, will dated July 1, 1835, probated Mch: 1, 1844, mentions her children Eliza A. Knapp, Betsy wife of Harvey Knapp, and heirs of Selleck Hoyt. Executor N. D. Haight. Witnesses N. D. Haight Hezekiah Bishop, and Polly Bishop, page 368.
Mch. 1, 1844, order to advertise for claims, page 369.

Knapp, Mary, late of Stamford, Sept. 21, 1842, letters of administration on her estate granted to Royal L. Gay, who was ordered to advertise for claims, page 175.
June 6, 1843, account filed, and estate ordered distributed to Polly widow of Rufus Newman, Hannah E. widow of Isaac Wardwell, Rufus Knapp, Sally widow of John Scofield, Luther Knapp, and Bethia wife of Charles Gaylor, page 233.
June 16, 1843, estate distributed accordingly, except the share of Luther Knapp was assigned to Joseph Selleck, Jr., page 234.

Knapp, Philena, of Greenwich, over 14 years of age, Sept. 12, 1842, made choice of Mary Knapp of Greenwich to be her guardian, page 169.

Knapp, Titus, late of Greenwich, will dated Mch. 10, 1837, probated Oct. 29, 1838, mentions his grandsons Henry K. Skelding of New York City, and William K. Quintard, and granddaughter Sarah K. Marshall. Executors Joshua B. Ferris and grandson William K. Quintard. Witnesses Peter Lockwood, Cornelius Ford, and Ann Ferris, page 26.
Oct. 29, 1838, executors refused to qualify, and letters granted to Samuel Lockwood of Stamford, who was ordered to advertise for claims, page 27.

Lapham, Catherine, late of Stamford, Feb. 6, 1844, letters of adminsitration on her estate granted to William Newman, who was ordered to advertise for claims, page 318.
Inventory taken by William Hoyt, Jr., and Joseph D. Warren, and filed Apl. 3, 1844, page 318.

Larkin, Mary J., Ann E. Larkin, and Charles E. Larkin, all over 12 years of age and of Stamford, Feb. 4, 1843, made choice of their mother, Mary Ann Larkin, of Stamford to be their guardian, who was also appointed guardian of her other children John, George F., Franklin, and Harriet N., page 198.

Leeds, Anna, late of Darien, May 3, 1842, on the application of Rebecca Leeds, a daughter of decedent, estate or-

STAMFORD PROBATE RECORDS.
Volume 16, 1841.

Leeds, Anna, continued :
 dered distributed to Joseph H. Leeds a son of decedent
 five shares, his own and the shares of Lucy Brown, Mary
 A. Austin, Gideon Leeds, and Lavinia Brown, who sold
 their share to said Joseph; and to said Rebecca Leeds
 one share, page 31.
 May 3, 1842, estate distributed accordingly, page 31.

Leeds, Hannah, late of Stamford, wife of Cary Leeds, will
 dated Dec. 4, 1830, probated Mch. 26, 1842, all to her
 daughter Hannah. Executor John V. Leeds. Witnesses
 Joseph Gray, Honor Leeds, and John R. Leeds, page 119.
 Mch. 26, 1842, order to advertise for claims, page 119.

Leeds, Lorenzo, late of Stamford, Apl. 9, 1842, his widow refused to qualify, and letters of administration on his
 estate granted to Stephen B. Provost, who was ordered
 to advertise for claims, page 89.
 Inventory taken by Smith Scott and David Lockwood, and
 filed May 10, 1842, page 89.
 Additional inventory filed Dec. 9, 1842, pages 193
 and 194.
 Sept. 23, 1842, account filed, page 193.
 Oct. 17, 1842, account filed, and commissioners appointed to adjust claims of creditors, pages 195 and
 196.
 June 24, 1843, report of commissioners filed, page 376.
 July 8, 1843, exceptions to the above report filed, and
 an appeal taken, page 376.
 June 15, 1844, appeal discontinued, and report accepted, page 378.

Lewis, Isaac, late of Greenwich, will dated Aug. 18, 1824,
 probated Sept. 7, 1840, mentions his wife Hannah, and
 children Mary Elisabeth Mason, Sarah Lewis, Zachariah,
 Isaac, Jr., Hannah Buffett, and Roswell V. Executors
 sons Zachariah and Isaac, Jr., and son in law Platt
 Buffett. Witnesses Charles V. Davenport, Augustus
 Lyon, and Jabez Mead, page 27.
 Codicil dated Sept. 6, 1837, Roswell V. now deceased
 and his share to the children of said Roswell V., and
 reserves a family burying ground in the rear of his
 house and lot, page 28.
 Sept. 7, 1840, order to advertise for claims, page 30.
 Inventory taken Sept. 8, 1840, by Darius Mead and
 Zaccheus Mead, Jr., and filed Sept. 14, 1840, page 31.

Lockwood, Davis, late of Stamford, May 7, 1844, letters of
 administration on his estate granted to Samuel Lockwood
 Jr., and Royal L. Gay, both of Stamford, who were or-

STAMFORD PROBATE RECORDS.
Volume 16, 1841.

Lockwood, Davis, continued :
dered to advertise for claims, page 367.
Inventory taken by Stephen B. Provost and Richard
Stanton, and filed May 25, 1844, page 367.

Lockwood, Deborah, late of Greenwich, will dated Sept. 25, 1835
probated Aug. 30, 1841, mentions her nieces Abigail
Jane and Deborah Ann. Executor her brother Ira Lockwood. Witnesses Harvey Briggs, Ann Elisa Reynolds,
and Ard Reynolds, page 87.
Aug. 30, 1841, order to advertise for claims, page 88.
No property, except a note for $200., page 88.

Lockwood, Drake, late of Greenwich, Sept. 6, 1841, estate ordered distributed according to his will to his children, viz: Letitia wife of Rufus Peck, John, Frederic A
Eliza, Angeline, and Charlotte, Mary Lockwood another
daughter died after testator without issue, page 35.
Sept. 9, 1841, estate distributed accordingly, page 36.

Lockwood, Henry, late of Greenwich, will dated Aug. 12, 1843,
probated June 22, 1844, mentions his second wife
Fanny, Henry and Mason Jones sons of David Jones,
Mary E. Mead a daughter of his second wife, Delia wife
of Charles Timpany, Jane St. John a daughter of David
Jones, Elizabeth Jones a daughter of David Jones,
Henry Rich, nephew Joseph Bush, Lockwood Davis, David
Jones and Delia A. Rowell's two children. Executor
Nathaniel D. Haight. Witnesses Emma Purdy, Ann E.
Stewart, and Joanna Studwell, page 393.
Codicil dated Sept. 16, 1843, page 395.
June 22, 1844, order to advertise for claims, page 395.
Note. The name "Jones" referred to in the foregoing
will is undoubtedly "Johns"

Lockwood, Jonathan, late of Greenwich, Sept. 28, 1843, account
filed, and estate ordered distributed to his children
Edmund, Jr., heirs at law of Mills, deceased, and the
heirs at law of William, page 245.
Nov. 4, 1843, estate distributed to the aforesaid Edmund Lockwood, heirs at law of the aforesaid William
Lockwood, and Alton Ingersoll of Greenwich, who purchased all the right, title and interest of the aforesaid
Mills Lockwood, deceased, page 245.

Lockwood, Luther, late of Stamford, Feb. 8, 1844, estate ordered distributed to his children Eliakim, Lydia Ann
wife of Hanford Briggs, Henry B., and Nathaniel N.,
page 244.

STAMFORD PROBATE RECORDS.
Volume 16, 1841.

Lockwood, Luther, continued:
    Apl. 1, 1844, estate distributed to Nathaniel Lockwood, Eliakim Lockwood, Hanford Briggs, Henry B. Lockwood having assigned his share to Nathaniel Lockwood and Hanford Briggs, page 244.

Lockwood, Maria, late of Stamford, Nov. 28, 1843, letters of administration on her estate granted to John O'Brien of Brooklyn, N. Y., her nearest relative, who was ordered to advertise for claims, page 260.
    Inventory taken by James H. Hoyt and Joseph D. Warren, and filed Nov. 28, 1843, page 261.

Lockwood, Mary, late of Greenwich, will dated Jan. 27, 1840, probated June 21, 1841, mentions her daughters Letitia wife of Rufus Peck, Charlotte Lockwood, Angeline Lockwood, and Eliza Lockwood. Executor her son Frederic A Lockwood. Witnesses Joshua Ferris, Letitia Ferris, and Charles Hendrie, page 136.
    June 21, 1841, order to advertise for claims, page 137.

Lockwood, Mills, late of Greenwich, Feb. 28, 1843, order for the publication of notice of sale, page 336.
    Mch. 25, 1843, the authority of the commissioners to adjust claims of creditors continued, page 389.
    Sept. 19, 1843, an appeal taken by the administrator, page 390.

Lockwood, William, late of Greenwich, Sept. 28, 1843, estate ordered distributed to his brothers and sisters, viz: Edmund Lockwood, Jr., Mary Ferris, Elizabeth Brundage, Sarah Judson, Hannah Reynolds, Deborah Lounsbury, Alla Ferris, Lydia Keeler, heirs of Mills Lockwood, deceased, and the heirs of Clarissa Ferris, page 248.
    Oct. 10, 1843, estate distributed to William H. Reynolds assignee of Mary Ferris and Edmund Lockwood; and to Alton Ingersoll who purchased all the right, title and interest of all the other heirs at law, page 248

Lounsbury, Ezra, of Stamford, May 21, 1844, his daughters Mary Emily and Betsy Maria, both over 12 years of age, made choice of their father to be their guardian, who was also appointed guardian of his other children Nri Willard, and Leonard Franklin, page 334.

Lyon, Job, late of Greenwich, will dated July 11, 1832, probated Oct. 19, 1841, mentions his children Abigail B. wife of Isaac Holly, Jr., and Isaac. Executor son Isaac. Witnesses Sarah W. Mead, Julia B. Mead, and

STAMFORD PROBATE RECORDS.
Volume 16, 1841.

Lyon, Job, continued:
   Jabez Mead, page 116.
   Oct. 19, 1841, order to advertise for claims, page 117.
   Inventory taken Nov. 20, 1841, by Drake Mead and Elias Peck, and filed Jan. 27, 1842, page 117.

Lyon, Joshua, late of Greenwich, will dated July 11, 1837, probated Nov. 18, 1841, mentions his children Gilbert, Samuel, Joshua, John, Hannah Knapp, Betsy Mosier, Phebe Sands, and Sarah Lyon a deceased daughter. Executors his sons Joshua and John. Witnesses William Merritt, John Petrie, and Charles Hawley, page 80.
   Codicil dated July 26, 1837, devised drift way to his sons and other privileges, page 82.
   Nov. 18, 1841, order to advertise for claims, page 82.
   Inventory taken Nov. 24, 1841, by Lockwood K. Merritt and Samuel Close, and filed Nov. 26, 1841, page 83.
   Apl. 23, 1844, estate ordered distributed according to his will, viz: to his son Gilbert, and to the heirs of his son Joshua, page 338.
   Apl. 26, 1844, estate distributed accordingly, page 339.

Lyon, Joshua, late of Rye, June 21, 1843, letters of administration on his estate granted to his brother Gilbert Lyon of Rye, who was ordered to advertise for claims, page 337.
   Inventory taken by Samuel Close and Lockwood K. Merritt and filed Aug. 24, 1843, page 337.
   Additional inventory filed Apl. 22, 1844, page 337.
   Apl. 23, 1844, account filed, and estate ordered distributed to his heirs at law, viz: Betsy wife of William Mosier of Greenwich, Hannah Knapp of Greenwich, heirs of Sarah Lyon late of Greenwich, Samuel Lyon of Greenwich, Gilbert Lyon of Rye, Phebe wife of David Sands of Greenwich, and John Lyon of Greenwich, page 340
   Apl. 26, 1844, estate distributed accordingly, page 340.

McQuean, Robert, late of St. Louis, Mo., Nov. 5, 1838, letters of administration on his estate granted to John A. Davenport of New York City, page 106.

Marshall, Mary, of Greenwich, Oct. 28, 1843, application of Stephen W. Marshall for the appointment of a conservator, page 388.
   Nov. 13, 1843, Peter Ferris of Greenwich appointed such conservator, page 388.

Marvin, Epenetus, late of Stamford, Apl. 6, 1842, his widow refused to qualify, and letters of administration on

STAMFORD PROBATE RECORDS.
Volume 16, 1841.

Marvin, Epenetus, continued :
> his estate granted to Joseph Smith of Stamford, page 55.
> Inventory taken by Josiah Smith and Amos Smith, and filed May 14, 1842, page 56.
> Oct. 8, 1842, account ordered filed, page 197.
> Oct. 24, 1842, account filed, and real estate ordered sold to pay debts, page 273.
> Real estate sold to Mary Marvin of Stamford, and report of sale filed, page 273.
> Aug. 1, 1843, additional real estate ordered sold to pay debts, page 274.
> Real estate sold to Mary Marvin of Stamford, and report of sale filed Aug. 1, 1843, page 274.
> Oct. 24, 1842, dower of his widow, Mary Marvin, ordered set out, page 188.
> Oct. 24, 1842, dower set out, page 188.
> Oct. 24, 1842, account filed, and an allowance to his widow, page 189.
> Apl. 6, 1843, time for final settlement extended, page 218.

Matthews, Charity, late of Greenwich, will dated July 3, 1839, probated June 12, 1841, legacies to her son Daniel, grandson Daniel Carhart, granddaughter Samantha Carhart, grandson Abel S. Fisher, grandson William a son of her son Abijah Matthews, grandson Jacob Matthews, granddaughter Abigail Jane Matthews, granddaughter Adelia Sarles a daughter of Dorinda Sarles/ and remainder to her surviving children and the grandchildren of her deceased daughter Deborah Fisher and Elizabeth Carhart. Executor son Oliver Matthews. Witnesses Abel Smith and Abel Smith, Jr., page 62.
> June 12, 1841, order to advertise for claims, page 62.
> Inventory taken June 29, 1841, by James Field and Nathaniel Miller, and filed July 12, 1841, page 63.

Mead, Darius, late of Greenwich, will dated Apl. 18, 1831, probated Sept. 6, 1841, mentions his wife Hannah, and his daughters Anna, Alla, Huldah, and Adelia, and his son Alva. Executors wife and son Alva. Witnesses Isaac Peck, Jr., Isaac Peck, 3rd, and Gilbert Close, page 56.
> Sept. 6, 1841, letters to Alva Mead, who was ordered to advertise for claims, page 57.
> Inventory taken by Isaac Peck and James Field, and filed Nov. 15, 1841, page 58.

Mead, Deborah, late of Greenwich, will dated July 3, 1841, probated Apl. 15, 1844, mentions Esther Mead, Sarah Mead, brother Isaac Mead, Mark Mead, and Oliver Mead.

STAMFORD PROBATE RECORDS.
Volume 16, 1841.

Mead, Deborah, continued :
    Executor Oliver Mead. Witnesses Jonas Stafford and
    Sarah Mead, page 362.
    Apl. 15, 1844, order to advertise for claims, page 362.
    Inventory taken by Daniel S. Mead and Jared Mead, and
    filed May 28, 1844, page 363.

Mead, Isaac, late of Greenwich, will dated Feb. 22, 1839, pro-
    bated Jan. 4, 1840, all to his wife Mary. Executor
    Elias Peck. Witnesses Samuel Jessup, Jr., Joseph E.
    Brush, and Jabez Mead, page 63.
    Jan. 4, 1840, executor refused to qualify, and letters
    of administration with the will annexed granted to
    Mary Mead, widow of testator, who was ordered to ad-
    vertise for claims, page 64.

Mead, Jabez, late of Greenwich, will dated Sept. 12, 1839,
    probated Dec. 20, 1839, mentions his wife Sarah W. and
    children Julia B., Mary E., and William K. Executor
    Thomas A. Mead. Witnesses Joseph Brush, Drake Mead,
    and Benjamin I. Knapp, page 60.
    Dec. 20, 1839, order to advertise for claims, page 61.
    Inventory taken Dec. 28, 1839, by Joseph Brush and
    Albert Knapp, and filed Feb. 11, 1840, page 61.

Mead, Job, late of Greenwich, will dated Aug. 27, 1838, pro-
    bated Mch. 11, 1839, mentions his wife Elsy, and chil-
    dren Abram, Amanda L., Eliza V., and Zaccheus, Jr.
    Executors sons Zaccheus and Abram. Witnesses Lydia
    Sutherland, Josephus Palmer, and Samuel Close, page 58.
    Mch. 11, 1839, order to advertise for claims, page 59.
    Inventory taken by Charles Smith and Jonas Howe, and
    filed Apl. 12, 1839, page 60.

Mead, Louisiana Cordelia, of Stamford, Sept. 23, 1841, 7 years
    of age, Isaac Dean of Stamford appointed her guardian,
    page 64.

Mead, Selah, late of Greenwich, June 13, 1842, his widow re-
    fused to qualify, and letters of administration on his
    estate granted to Solomon Gansey of Greenwich, who was
    ordered to advertise for claims, page 106.
    Inventory taken by Zaccheus Mead and Nelson Bush, and
    filed June 15, 1842, page 107.
    June 13, 1842, account filed, and commissioners ap-
    pointed to adjust claims of creditors, page 122.
    June 27, 1842, report of commissioners filed, page 167.
    Dec. 19, 1842, dower of his widow, Sarah Mead, ordered
    set out, pages 181 and 182.
    Dec. 19, 1842, dower set out, page 182.

STAMFORD PROBATE RECORDS.
Volume 16, 1841.

Mead, Selah, continued :
  Dec. 19, 1842, account filed, and real estate ordered sold to pay debts, pages 181 and 205.
  Real estate sold to Isaac Van Voorhis of New York City, and report of sale filed Dec. 31, 1842, page 205.

Mead, Zophar, late of Greenwich, will dated Sept. 25, 1838, probated Jan. 9, 1844, mentions his wife Huldah, and children Oliver, Abraham, Esther, and Sarah. Executor his brother Isaac Mead, Jr. Witnesses Sarah V. Mead, Julia B. Mead, and Jabez Mead, page 301.
  Jan. 9, 1844, executor refused to qualify and letters granted to Augustus Mead, who was ordered to advertise for claims, page 302.
  Inventory taken by Zaccheus Mead, Jr. and Nelson Bush and filed Feb. 3, 1844, page 303.

Merritt, John, late of Greenwich, Oct. 2, 1841, letters of administration on his estate granted to Curtiss Merritt of Rye and John A. Merritt of Greenwich, who were ordered to advertise for claims, page 104.
  Inventory taken by David Brown and Thomas A. Mead, and filed Nov. 26, 1841, page 104.

Merritt, John, late of Greenwich, June 6, 1843, Maria Merritt of Greenwich, guardian of Theodore Merritt, Elizabeth Merritt, James H. Merritt, and Phineas Merritt, all of Greenwich, asked for leave to sell the interest of said minors in the real estate of decedent in Greenwich, and sale ordered, page 256.
  Real estate sold to John A. Merritt, and report of sale filed Mch. 26, 1844, page 257.

Merritt, Sarah, late of Greenwich, June 13, 1840, letters of administration on her estate granted to Nehemiah Merritt of New York City, who was ordered to advertise for claims, page 14.
  Inventory taken Dec. 19, 1840, by Augustus Mead and Oliver Mead, and filed Dec. 19, 1840, page 14.

Minor, Simeon H. late of Stamford, will dated Aug. 31, 1827, probated Aug. 15, 1840, mentions his three children, no names, and niece Maria wife of John J. Leeds. No executor. Witnesses Samuel Beach, Charles Hawley, and John W. Leeds, page 126.
  Aug. 15, 1840, letters to James H. Minor and William T. Minor, sons of testator, who were ordered to advertise for claims, page 126.

STAMFORD PROBATE RECORDS.
Volume 16, 1841.

Minor, Simeon H., continued :
Inventory taken by Stephen B. Provost and Davis Lockwood, and filed May 9, 1842, page 127.

Morrell, John, late of Greenwich, Mch. 6, 1843, his widow refused to qualify, and letters of administration on his estate granted to Robert Clark of Greenwich, who was ordered to advertise for claims, page 327.
Inventory taken by Ephraim Golden and Benjamin Page, and filed Mch. 18, 1843, page 327.
Mch. 18, 1843, commissioners appointed to adjust claims of creditors, page 329.
Sept. 30, 1843, report of commissioners filed, page 330
Mch. 26, 1844, account filed, and an allowance to his widow, page 330.
Mch. 26, 1844, real estate ordered sold to pay debts, page 384.
Real estate sold to William Morrell of Greenwich, and report of sale filed June 17, 1844, page 384.
July 13, 1844, account filed, and creditors ordered paid 17 cents on the dollar, page 397.

Nestele, Emily, Joanna Nestele, and Sophia Nestele, all of Stamford, June 18, 1842, made choice of Heth Stevens to be their guardian, page 140.

Newman, Lucy J., of Stamford, Aug. 1, 1843, appointed guardian of her children Edward T. Newman, over 14 years of age, and John E. Newman, page 284.

Newman, Rufus, late of Stamford, Mch. 7, 1842, his widow refused to qualify, and letters of administration on his estate granted to his son in law William H. H. Hallock, who was ordered to advertise for claims, page 145.
Inventory taken Mch. 30, 1842, by Edwin S. Holly and William Weed, and filed Apl. 11, 1842, page 204.
Nov. 14, 1842, account filed, and allowance to his widow, page 205.
Nov. 22, 1842, dower of his widow, Polly Newman, ordered set out, page 205.
Nov. 14, 1842, account filed, and real estate ordered sold to pay debts, page 212.
Real estate sold to William Newman of Stamford, and report of sale filed Mch. 29, 1843, page 212.
Mch. 29, 1843, estate ordered distributed to his widow, Polly Newman, and children John, heirs of Hezekiah, Mary wife of Seely Daniels, Hannah wife of Asa Davis, Sally wife of Morris Bishop, Rufus, Luther, and Elisabeth wife of William H. H. Hallock, page 213.
Mch. 30, 1843, estate distributed accordingly, page 214.

STAMFORD PROBATE RECORDS.
Volume 16, 1841.

Newman, Stephen, late of Stamford, will dated Mch. 11, 1841, probated Sept. 18, 1843, mentions his wife Amy, and children Mary C., Jane A., William and Sally L. Brown. Executors his son William and son in law William L. Smith. Witnesses Fitch Rogers, Joshua B. Ferris, and Samuel Leeds, page 360.
Sept. 18, 1843, order to advertise for claims, page 361. Inventory taken by Silas Scofield, and John R. Scofield and filed Nov. 18, 1843, page 361.

Newman, Zadoc, late of Stamford, will dated -----, probated Aug. 23, 1843, mentions his wife Catherine, great nephew Zadoc Harden, now or late of Mount Hope, N. Y., the three daughters of his deceased sister Clarissa Scofield, the late wife of David Scofield. Executrix his wife. Witnesses Chauncey Ayres, Charles A. Hawley, and Charles Hawley, page 299.
Aug. 23, 1843, order to advertise for claims, page 300. Inventory taken by Henry Waring and Frederick Lockwood, and filed Sept. 12, 1843, page 300.

Palmer, Abigail, late of Stamford, Apl. 24, 1842, estate ordered distributed to her heirs at law, viz: Mary Palmer, who is the legal representative by purchase of Sally M. wife of James Dusenbury, and Roswell G. Palmer three shares, to Hannah Palmer, one share, to James P. Palmer, one share, to Joseph F. Palmer, one share, and to Finetta wife of Amariah E. Baker of Texas, one share, page 38.
Apl. 24, 1840, estate distributed accordingly, page 38.

Palmer, Asahel, late of Greenwich, will dated May 12, 1840, probated June 13, 1840, mentions his wife Jemima, Rexene wife of John Richards, niece Semantha Waterbury, widow of Ebenezer Waterbury, and her son Asahel Augustus Waterbury, and nephew Asahel P. Bailey. Executors his wife and Asahel P. Bailey. Witnesses Jonathan Bunnell, Deborah Fairchild, and Joshua Ferris, page 10.
June 13, 1840, order to advertise for claims, page 10. Inventory taken June 24, 1840, by Peter Ferris and Henry Ritch, and filed June 24, 1840, page 10.

Palmer, James F., late of Stamford, will dated Apl. 14, 1842, probated May 14, 1842, mentions his wife Sally B., and son James D. Executors his wife and Royal L. Gay. Witnesses Daniel Lockwood, Stephen Clason, and William H. Holly, page 97.

STAMFORD PROBATE RECORDS.
Volume 16, 1841.

Palmer, James F., continued :
    May 14, 1842, order to advertise for claims, page 98.
    Inventory taken by Eber Smith and Solomon Classon, and filed June 6, 1842, page 116.

Peacock, Mary, late of Greenwich, widow of William Peacock, will dated Apl. 24, 1835, probated May 29, 1842, mentions her daughters Sally wife of Stephen Underhill of Oyster Bay, Julia Ann Peacock, and granddaughter Mary Peacock. Executors Benjamin Page and Parris Robbins. Witnesses Peter Ferris, Benjamin Page, and Jabez Mead, page 112.
Codicil dated Mch. 18, 1842, page 113.
May 29, 1842, letters to Benjamin Page, who was ordered to advertise for claims, page 113.
Inventory taken June 11, 1842, by Frederick Lockwood and Daniel Lyon, and filed July 14, 1842, page 165.

Peacock, William, late of Greenwich, will dated Nov. 25, 1840, probated May 29, 1842, mentions his sisters Sarah Underhill, Julia Ann Peacock, niece Mary Peacock, nephews William Holmes, William Underhill, and Dodsworth Highly Peacock; Eliza Ann Peacock; legal heirs of his brother Ralph Peacock, and mother Mary Peacock. Executor his brother in law Stephen Underhill of Oyster Bay, Witnesses Horace B. Smith, William Horton, and Seaman H. Sniffin, page 96.
May 29, 1842, order to advertise for claims, page 97.
June 11, 1842, inventory taken by Frederick Lockwood and Daniel Lyon, and filed July 14, 1842, page 165.

Peck, Alathea, of Greenwich, widow of Rev. David Peck, Feb. 17 1844, David Banks the husband of her daughter Marilda, asked for the appointment of a conservator, page 277.
Mch. 19, 1844, Josiah Wilcox of Greenwich appointed conservator for said Alathea Peck, but refused to qualify, and David Peck was appointed in his place, page 278.

Peck, Jared, late of Greenwich, Apl. 20, 1840, estate ordered distributed to his brothers and sisters, viz: Eliphalet Peck, Jr., of Greenwich, David Peck of Greenwich, Phebe wife of John Bretel of Rye, Marilda wife of David Banks of Greenwich, Cillah Peck of Greenwich, Ruth wife of William Johnson of New York City, Alathea wife of Gilbert P. Finch of Greenwich, and Delilah Peck of Greenwich, page 33.
Apl. 22, 1840, estate distributed accordingly, page 34.

STAMFORD PROBATE RECORDS.
Volume 16, 1841.

Pendell, Elizabeth, late of Stamford, will dated Oct. 26, 1841, probated Jan. 28, 1842, all to her husband William Pendell, and appointed him executor. Witnesses Timothy Reynolds, Charles A. Hawley and Charles Hawley, page 98.
Jan. 28, 1842, order to advertise for claims, page 99.

Penoyer, Charles E., late of Darien, June 16, 1843, letters of administration on his estate granted to John Hoyt of Stamford, who was ordered to advertise for claims, page 239.
Inventory taken by John Holmes and George R. Stevens, and filed Aug. 7, 1843, page 239.
Feb. 12, 1844, account filed, and real estate ordered sold to pay debts, page 240.
Real estate sold to Henry F. Waring of Stamford, and report of sale filed Mch. 1, 1844, page 240.

Pettit, Hannah, late of Darien, Mch. 21, 1842, letters of administration on her estate granted to Gilbert G. Waterbury of Darien, who was ordered to advertise for claims, page 90.
Inventory taken by Holly Bell and William Andreas, and filed Mch. 24, 1842, page 91.
Nov. 18, 1842, account filed and estate ordered distributed to her brothers and sisters, vis: William Wardwell, Mary Waterbury, Betsy Wardwell, legal heirs of Isaac Wardwell, deceased, legal heirs of James Wardwell, deceased, legal heirs of Sarah Batterson, deceased and to the legal heirs of Abigail Scoffield, deceased, page 211.
Mch. 21, 1843, estate distributed accordingly, page 211.

Provost, Samuel, late of Stamford, will dated Aug. 1, 1831, probated Dec. 27, 1843, mentions his wife Anna, and children Harry, Jerry, William, James, Rufus, Mary, and John. Executrix his wife. Witnesses Anna Scofield, Frances E. Scofield, and Smith R. Sibley, page 319.
Dec. 27, 1843, executrix refused to qualify, and letters granted to John Provost, 3rd, of Stamford, who was ordered to advertise for claims, page 320.
Inventory taken by Stephen June and Henry Raynolds, and filed Feb. 3, 1844, page 359.

Quintard, Abraham, late of Stamford, will dated Sept. 28, 1843, probated Jan. 31, 1844, mentions his children Mary Quintard, Ann Beach, Elizabeth Quintard, and Daniel D. Quintard. Appointed his son Charles trustee for said

STAMFORD PROBATE RECORDS.
Volume 16, 1841.

Quintard, Abraham, continued :
Ann. No executor. Witnesses Edmund Lockwood, Patrick Laurie, and Charles Hawley, page 283.

Reynolds, Ambrose, late of Greenwich, Feb. 7, 1844, letters of administration on his estate granted to his widow, Amy M. Reynolds, who was ordered to advertise for claims, page 294.
Inventory taken by Jonathan A. Close and Titus Mead, and filed Mch. 5, 1844, page 294.

Reynolds, Stephen, late of New York City, Aug. 12, 1843, letters of administration on his estate granted to Ezekiel Reynolds of Greenwich, who was ordered to advertise for claims, page 242.
Inventory taken by David Banks and Alfred Rundle, and filed Sept. 27, 1843, page 242.
Aug. 12, 1843, commissioners appointed to adjust claims of creditors, page 242.
Mch. 2, 1844, report of commissioners filed, page 243.

Reynolds, William P., late of Port Chester, N. Y., June 1, 1839, letters of administration on his estate granted to Abraham Reynolds of Stamford, who was ordered to advertise for claims, page 78.

Robbins, Mary, late of Greenwich, Sept. 3, 1839, letters of administration on her estate granted to Peter Ferris of Greenwich, who was ordered to advertise for claims, page 78.

Roberts, Deborah, late of Darien, will dated July 17, 1835, probated Oct. 21, 1838, mentions her children Catherine wife of Ezra Mills, Phebe Roberts, Deborah S. Roberts, Nathan Roberts, David Roberts, Mary Crane, Sarah Roberts, Amos S. Roberts, to the heirs of Justus Roberts, Susan widow of Justus Roberts, Lorayanna and Elizabeth the daughters of Amos S. Roberts. Executor her son David. Witnesses John Reed, Sarah Reed, and Phebe Comstock, page 40.
Nov. 13, 1838, executor refused to qualify, and letters granted to Henry Bates of Darien, who was ordered to advertise for claims, page 41.
Nov. 29, 1839, account filed, and real estate ordered sold to pay debts, page 41.

Rogers, Fitch, late of Stamford, will dated Aug. 30, 1837, probated July 11, 1843, all to his wife Mary Elizabeth for life, if she shall have issue living at the time of

STAMFORD PROBATE RECORDS.
Volume 16, 1841.

Rogers, Fitch, continued :
   testator's death, if no issue, then absolutely. Executrix his wife. Witnesses Sands Seely, Ann Gilbert, and S. H. Minor, page 298.
   July 13, 1843, order to advertise for claims, page 298.
   Inventory taken by Stephen B. Provost, and Richard Stanton, and filed Oct. 20, 1843, page 299.

Rogers, Mary, of Darien, June 28, 1841, appointed guardian of her son Henry B. Rogers, page 78.

Rogers, Sarah, late of Greenwich, will dated July 28, 1841, probated Aug. 10, 1844, mentions her children Elisa Rogers, Sarah Rogers, Charlotte Rogers, and Maria wife of Southy Grinnalds. Executor Richard D. Davis of Poughkeepsie, N. Y. Witnesses Catherine A. Benson, Mary Ann McIntire, and Charles Hawley, page 400.
   Aug. 10, 1844, executor refused to qualify, and letters agranted to Henry Bush of Greenwich, who was ordered to advertise for claims, page 401.
   Aug. 10, 1844, Richard D. Davis, trustee for Maria Grinnalds refused to act, and Henry Bush appointed in his place, page 402.

Rose, Ann, late of Greenwich, will dated Dec. 24, 1841, probated Jan. 10, 1842, all to her husband William A. Rose for life, and remainder to his son Calvin A. Rose, except legacies of her friend Mary Ann Patten of New York City, Mrs Ann Mayo of New York City, Catherine the niece of her brother Samuel Thornton and the wife of a Frenchman residing in Beaver Street, New York City, and Mrs. Mary Ann Brower of New York City, and to the Baptist Society in Stamford. Executor her husband. Witnesses Deborah Fairchild, Samantha Bailey, and Charles Hawley, page 93.
   Jan. 10, 1842, order to advertise for claims, page 94.
   Inventory taken by Seth P. Quintard and Abel Palmer, and filed Jan. 22, 1842, page 95.
   July 16, 1842, additional inventory filed, page 158.

Rundle, Phineas, late of Greenwich, Feb. 13, 1843, letters of administration on his estate granted to Samuel Rundle and Alvah Mead, both of Greenwich, who were ordered to advertise for claims, page 347.
   Inventory taken by Isaac Peck and Alfred Rundle, and filed Mch. 30, 1843, page 347.

Sackett, Joseph, late of Greenwich, June 18, 1842, estate ordered distributed to the legal representatives of Richard Sackett, a deceased brother, the legal repre-

STAMFORD PROBATE RECORDS.
Volume 16, 1841.

Sackett, Joseph, continued:
sentatives of Nathaniel Sackett, a deceased brother, and the legal representatives of Hannah Betts, a deceased sister, page 146.
June 23, 1843, estate distributed accordingly, page 378.
Sept. 21, 1843, an appeal taken from the foregoing distribution by Hannah Betts of Greenwich, page 379.

Sarles, James, late of Stamford, Oct. 18, 1841, his widow refused to qualify, and letters of administration on his estate granted to William Todd, who was ordered to advertise for claims, page 54.
Inventory taken Nov. 1, 1841, by George Lounsbury and Charles Miller, and filed Nov. 1, 1841, page 55.

Scofield, Abigail, late of Stamford, Apl. 28, 1841, letters of administration on her estate granted to James W. Weeks of Stamford, who was ordered to advertise for claims, page 12.

Scofield, Alfred, late of Stamford, Oct. 15, 1841, his widow refused to qualify, and letters of administration on his estate granted to Harvey Lockwood of Stamford, who was ordered to advertise for claims, page 105.
May 29, 1842, account filed, and commissioners appointed to adjust claims of creditors, page 122.
Dec. 13, 1842, report of commissioners filed, allowance to his widow, and her dower ordered set out, page 176.
Jan. 14, 1843, dower set out, page 177.
Dec. 13, 1842, real estate ordered sold to pay debts, and sold to Alanson Studwell of Stamford, and report of sale filed Jan. 14, 1843, page 177.
Jan. 14, 1843, account filed, and creditors ordered paid 61 cents on the dollar, page 178.

Scofield, Alpheus, late of Stamford, will dated Mch. 24, 1828, probated Feb. 5, 1844, mentions his wife Elizabeth, and children Hezekiah, Darius S., and Phebe Lounsbury, and grandson Charles William Lockwood. Executor his son Hezekiah. Witnesses Daniel Lockwood, Joshua Scofield, and Charles Hawley, page 288.
Codicil dated July 30, 1833, legacy to Phebe revoked, page 290.
Codicil dated Aug. 31, 1842, legacy to Phebe and her husband Ezra Lounsbury, page 290.
Codicil dated June 22, 1843, Phebe now deceased, and her legacy to her four children, page 291.
Feb. 6, 1844, order to advertise for claims, page 292.

STAMFORD PROBATE RECORDS.
Volume 16, 1841.

Scofield, Alpheus, continued :
Inventory taken by Charles Brown and Amzi Scofield, and filed Apl. 29, 1844, page 292.

Scofield, Ezra, late of Stamford, will dated Mch. 24, 1837, probated July 30, 1840, mentions his wife Amelia, and children Hannah Elizabeth, Mary S. wife of George A. Weed, and Nancy Scofield. No executor. Witnesses S. H. Minor, Augustus Scofield, and Betsy A. Lounsbury, page 118.
July 30, 1840, his widow refused to qualify, and letters granted to Henry Waring of Stamford, who was ordered to advertise for claims, page 118.
Inventory taken by Augustus Scofield and Horace Scofield, and filed Aug. 15, 1840, page 119.

Scofield, Ezra, late of New York City, will dated Nov. 17, 1834, probated Feb. 6, 1844, mentions his wife Sarah, sister Rebecca Bostwick, brothers Isaac, Frederick, brother Selleck, deceased brother Benjamin, and Henry or Harry a son of said Benjamin Scofield, deceased. Executors brother Isaac Scofield, nephew Seth W. White, and friend Odell Lockwood. Witnesses Thomas R. Lee, John P. Rolfe, and John H. Lee, page 305.
Feb. 6, 1844, order to advertise for claims, page 308.
Inventory taken by Royal L. Gay and John W. Leeds, and filed Apl. 6, 1844, page 309.

Scofield, Jared, late of Stamford, will dated June 25, 1843, probated Aug. 12, 1843, all to his son Alvah and daughter Caroline. Executor sons Harvey and Amos. Witnesses Aaron Dean, John Weed, and Ralph Palmer, page 345.
Aug. 12, 1843, order to advertise for claims, page 345.
Inventory taken by John Dean and Gould Davis, and filed Nov. 25, 1843, page 346.

Scofield, Jonas, late of Stamford, will dated Oct. 3, 1835, probated June 16, 1842, mentions his children William, Mary, and Edwin. Executor his son William. Witnesses Benjamin Tryon, Mary Tryon, and Charles Hawley, page 129.
June 16, 1842, order to advertise for claims, page 129.
Inventory taken June 23, 1842, by Ashbel Scofield and John J. Leeds, and filed Aug. 4, 1842, page 199.

Scofield, Sarah, late of Stamford, will dated Oct. 17, 1835, probated June 16, 1842, mentions her children William, Mary and Edwin, and granddaughter Sally Maria Scofield. No executor. Witnesses John R. Leeds, James H. Hoyt,

STAMFORD PROBATE RECORDS.
Volume 16, 1841.

Scofield, Sarah, continued :
and Julia Hoyt, page 127.
Codicil dated Oct. 3, 1835, page 128.
June 16, 1842, letters to William Scofield, Jr., a son of testatrix, who was ordered to advertise for claims, page 128.
Inventory taken June 23, 1842, by Ashbel Scofield and John J. Leeds, and filed Aug. 4, 1842, page 199.

Scofield, Warren, late of Stamford, June 22, 1844, letters of administration on his estate granted to Amzi Scofield of Stamford, who was ordered to advertise for claims, page 393.

Scofield, William, late of Stamford, Oct. 31, 1842, his widow refused to qualify, and letters of administration on her estate granted to Charles W. Scofield and William W. Youngs, both of Stamford, who were ordered to advertise for claims, page 201.
Inventory taken by Selleck Scofield and Floyd T. Palmer, and filed Jan. 3, 1843, page 201.

Scofield, William Harris, late of Stamford, June 6, 1842, his widow refused to qualify, and letters of administration on his estate granted to Chauncey Ayres of Stamford, who was ordered to advertise for claims, page 123.
Inventory taken by Ashbel Scofield and Peter Husted, and filed June 15, 1842, page 123.
Additional inventory filed July 29, 1842, page 164.
June 23, 1842, account filed, and commissioners appointed to adjust claims of creditors, pages 146 and 158.
Feb. 10, 1843, account filed, allowance to his widow, and dower ordered set out, page 267.
Feb. 10, 1843, real estate ordered sold to pay debts, page 267.
Real estate sold to Richard Fox of Stamford, subject to the encumbrances contained in the will of Hait Scofield, deceased recorded in Volume 15 of wills, page 459, and also to the dower rights of the widow of deceased, and report of said filed June 3, 1843, page 268.

Selleck, Jesse, late of Darien, Dec. 18, 1841, letters of administration on his estate granted to Elisha Seely and Elizabeth Gray, both of Darien, who were ordered to advertise for claims, page 64.
Inventory taken by William Andreas and Enos Tuttle, and filed Mch. 16, 1842, page 65.
Apl. 11, 1842, account filed, and estate ordered distributed to his children Catherine wife of Morris Tut-

STAMFORD PROBATE RECORDS.
Volume 16, 1841.

Selleck, Jesse, continued:
    hill, Elisabeth Gray widow of William L. Gray, Sands Selleck, Henry R. Selleck, and the legal representatives of James Selleck, deceased, page 65.
    Apl. 23, 1842, estate distributed accordingly, but to James B., a son of said James Selleck, deceased, page 66.

Selleck, Letitia, widow, late of Darien, Sept. 14, 1841, letters of administration on her estate granted to Edward Scofield of Darien, who was ordered to advertise for claims, page 78.
    Inventory taken by Thomas Reed and Stephen Ferris, and filed Feb. 7, 1842, page 103.

Selleck, Stephen, late of Darien, Oct. 10, 1841, that part of his estate set off to his widow as her dower ordered distributed to his children Ann, heirs of Raymond, deceased, Hannah wife of Stephen Hoyt, and Polly wife of Epenetus W. Walmsley, page 110.
    Oct. 1841, estate distributed accordingly, page 111.

Selleck, Sylvanus, late of Greenwich, will dated Apl. 15, 1844 probated June 5, 1844, mentions his children Sylvanus, Ralph, Gold, Sands, Ally Dayton, who was the wife to Nathaniel Dayton, Marilda Selleck, Maria Merritt, widow of Jeremiah Merritt, Caroline wife of Solomon Peck, Ann Brown, widow of David Brown, and Clara wife of William Kinch. Executor Bartow F. White of Greenwich. Witnesses Silas Husted, Benjamin Knapp, Jr., and Bartow F. White, page 370.
    June 5, 1844, order to advertise for claims, page 371.
    Inventory taken Aug. 3, 1844, by Ezekiel Close and Samuel Mills, and copied on page 402 1/2.

Sherwood, Daniel, late of Greenwich, July 6, 1842, his sons Frederick A., Nelson, James, and William H. refused to qualify, and letters of administration on his estate granted to Dr. Bartow F. White, who was ordered to advertise for claims, page 159.
    Inventory taken by Alfred Rundle and Nathaniel Husted, and filed Aug. 23, 1842, page 159.
    Sept. 6, 1842, Mary E., and Jane Ann, children of decedent, made choice of Bartow F. White of Greenwich to be their guardian, who was also appointed guardian of George E., Sarah H., Charles T., Samuel E., Maria C., and Augustus other children of decedent, pages 167 and 169.

STAMFORD PROBATE RECORDS.
Volume 16, 1841.

Sherwood, Daniel, continued :
    Sept. 24, 1842, petition for leave to sell the real estate of said minors in Greenwich, and sale ordered page 206.
    Jan. 20, 1843, real estate sold to Silas Husted, and report of sale filed Jan. 23, 1843, page 207.
    Mch. 28, 1844, Bartow F. White removed as guardian, page 287.
    Mch. 28, 1844, James Sherwood appointed guardian of his brother and sister Charles T. Sherwood and Sarah H. Sherwood; and Nelson Sherwood appointed guardian of his brothers and sister George B. Sherwood, Samuel B. Sherwood, Augustus Sherwood, and Maria C. Sherwood, page 287 and 288.

Smith, Arba, late of Greenwich, July 11, 1838, his widow refused to qualify, and letters of administration on his estate granted to Augustus L. Reynolds, who was ordered to advertise for claims, page 44.
    Inventory taken by Joseph Brush and Floyd T. Palmer, and filed Sept. 7, 1838, page 44.
    June 7, 1842, account filed, and allowance to his widow, page 45.
    Mch. 15, 1844, account filed, and real estate ordered sold to pay debts, page 349.
    Real estate sold to Jared Smith of Greenwich, subject to widow's dower, and report of sale filed May 4, 1844, page 349.

Smith, Charles W., late of Greenwich, Oct. 29, 1842, on the Application of their grandfather, Samuel Brundage, the court appointed William Brundage guardian of Samuel Smith, 11 years of age, and Sarah Smith, 8 years of age, children of decedent, page 191.

Smith, David, late of Stamford, will dated May 23, 1840, probated July 8, 1840, mentions his daughters Lavinia White, Sally Smith, and Mary Smith. No executor. Witnesses John Banks, Shadrach Briggs, and N. D. Haight page 21.
    July 8, 1840, letters granted to Joseph Smith, Jr., of Stamford, who was ordered to advertise for claims page 22.
    Inventory taken by Alfred Ayres and Alva June, and filed Aug. 15, 1840, page 22.

Smith, Ebenezer, late of Stamford, May 12, 1838, the petition of Julia A. Smith of Stamford, guardian of Henry H. Smith, for leave to sell the real estate of said minor

STAMFORD PROBATE RECORDS.
Volume 16, 1841.

Smith, Ebenezer, continued :
 in Stamford, subject to the dower of said Julia A.
 Smith, and sale ordered, page 120.
 Real estate sold to Alfred Smith and Joseph Smith, both
 of Stamford, being said minor's share in the estate
 of Ebenezer Smith, deceased, and to Ard Reynolds of
 Greenwich, and Benjamin Mathews of Stamford, and report
 of sale filed Oct. 21, 1838, page 121.

Smith, Eloy, late of Stamford, will dated Mch. 17, 1838, pro-
 bated June 18, 1842, mentions his daughters Mary Phil-
 ips, Sally Cooper, and Susan. Executors Seymour
 Jarvis and Charles Hawley. Witnesses A. M. Burton,
 Uriah Turner, and Samuel Lockwood, page 140.
 June 18, 1842, order to advertise for claims, page 142.
 Inventory taken by Davis Lockwood and S. B. Provost,
 and filed July 27, 1842, page 162.

Smith, James, A., late of Stamford, will dated Oct. 21, 1841,
 probated Nov. 1, 1841, estate to his father and mother
 during their lives, and remainder to his brothers
 David W. Smith and sister Mary E. Rogers. No executor. Witnesses George S. Smith and Margaret Henderson, page 86.
 Nov. 1, 1841, letters of administration with the will
 annexed granted to testator's father Rev. Daniel Smith,
 who was ordered to advertise for claims, page 86.
 Inventory taken by Stephen B. Provost and Smith Scott,
 and filed Sept. 6, 1841, page 87.

Smith, Mary, widow of Joseph Smith, late of New Canaan, now
 93 years of age and resides in Stamford, Sept. 3, 1842,
 the application of her son, Joseph Smith of New Canaan,
 for the appointment of a conservator denied, and an appeal taken, pages 191 and 197.

Smith, Sarah, late of Greenwich, widow of Gould Smith, late
 of Stamford, will dated Jan. 10, 1839, probated Mch. 12,
 1841, mentions her daughters Sarah wife of Abraham
 Rowell of Greenwich, and Hannah wife of Josiah Lane of
 Greenwich. Executor Asahel Palmer. Witnesses Samuel Jessup, Jr., Robert Morrell, Jr., and Jabez Mead,
 page 85.
 Mch. 12, 1841, Asahel Palmer now deceased, and letters
 to Josiah Lane, who was ordered to advertise for claims
 page 85.

Stevens, Mary, late of Stamford, Mch. 15, 1842, letters of administration on her estate granted to James H. Hoyt of

STAMFORD PROBATE RECORDS.
Volume 16, 1841.

Stevens, Mary, continued :
    Stamford, who was ordered to advertise for claims, page 55.
    Inventory taken May 4, 1842, by Joseph D. Warren and Horace Waterbury, and filed May 4, 1842, page 55.

Stevens, Mary, over 12 years of age, of Darien, Feb. 4, 1843, made choice of Stephen R. Selleck of New York City to be her guardian, page 228.

Strang, Sarah H., of Greenwich, over 12 years of age, Mch. 12, 1844, made choice of James Wilson of Greenwich to be her guardian, page 279.

Taylor, Charles R., of Stamford, over 14 years of age, Apl. 13 1843, made choice of his mother Mary E. Taylor to be his guardian, page 217.

Treadwell, Francis, of Greenwich, May 18, 1844, application of Edmund Thompson of Greenwich for the appointment of a conservator, page 388.
    June 7, 1844, Ard Reynolds of Greenwich appointed conservator for said Francis Treadwell, page 388.

Wallace, George H., late of Darien, Mch. 20, 1843, letters of administration on his estate granted to Henry B. Wallace of Darien, page 218.
    Apl. 1, 1843, commissioners appointed to adjust claims of creditors, page 218.
    Inventory taken by Abram Clock and George J. Bowler, and filed Apl. 1, 1843, page 219.
    Report of commissioners filed, page 272, Nov. 3, 1843.
    Nov. 11, 1843, account filed, and an allowance to his widow, page 272.

Wardwell, Isaac, late of Stamford, will dated June 27, 1834, probated Mch. 18, 1841, mentions his wife Hannah, and children Polly Daniels, Sally Adams, Hannah Scofield, William, Rufus, Isaac, James, Abigail, and Betsy. Executor son William. Witnesses S. B. Provost, Seely Miller, and Charles Hawley, page 41.
    Codicil dated June 13, 1836, daughter Betsy now married and legacies changed, page 42.
    Inventory taken May 1, 1841, by Silas Scofield and William Weed, and filed May 1, 1841, page 44.
    Mch. 13, 1843, account filed, and estate ordered distributed to his widow Hannah, and children William, Rufus, Isaac, James, Abigail, Polly wife of Pliny Daniels, Sally wife of William Henry Adams, Hannah wife

STAMFORD PROBATE RECORDS.
Volume 15, 1841.

Wardwell, Isaac, continued :
    of Seth W. Scofield, and Betsy wife of William C. Hoyt, page 220.
    Apl. 1843, estate distributed accordingly, page 222.

Waring, Stephen, late of Greenwich, will dated July 1, 1837, probated May 1, 1840, mentions his wife Mary, and his niece Ann Waring, nephew Stephen Waring a son of his brother Henry Waring, sister Betsy wife of Jonathan Ferris, and brother James Waring. Executor brother James Waring. Witnesses Darius Mead, Jr., Alexander Green, and Charles Hawley, page 1.
    May 1, 1840, order to advertise for claims, page 3.
    Inventory taken by Isaac Holly and Joseph Brush, and filed May 16, 1840, page 3.
    July 19, 1841, commissioners appointed to adjust claims of creditors, page 4.
    Mch: 7, 1842, report of commissioners filed, page 4.
    Mch. 14, 1842, account filed, allowance to his widow, and real estate ordered sold to pay debts, pages 6 and 8.
    Mch. 10, 1842, dower of his widow ordered set out, page 7.
    Mch. 12, 1842, dower set out, page 7.
    May 4, 1842, account filed, and creditors ordered paid 95 cents on the dollar, page 6.

Waterbury, Azariah, late of Darien, Apl. 2, 1840, account filed by his administratrix, and estate ordered distributed to his widow and children, viz: Rheuame, Catherine wife of Ezra H. Bishop, Selleck, Phebe, Mary, Ann, Samuel C., and Edwin, page 12.
    Apl. 3, 1840, estate distributed accordingly, page 12.

Waterbury, George, late of Darien, Apl. 10, 1843, the court appointed David Waterbury of Darien guardian of George W., Charles L., and Sarah Ann, children of decedent, page 228.
    Apl. 10, 1843, petition for leave to sell the real estate of said minors in Darien, and sale by Royal L. Gay ordered, page 254.
    Report of sale filed Aug. 31, 1843, sold to David Waterbury of Darien, page 346.

Waterbury, Mary, late of Darien, will dated Oct. 31, 1838, probated Aug. 23, 1842, all to the children of my deceased brother Isaac Waterbury, viz: David, John W., Peter L., Isaac N., Fanny, Julia A., Nancy Stevens, and Mary. Executrix her niece said Mary Waterbury.

STAMFORD PROBATE RECORDS.
Volume 16, 1841.

Waterbury, Mary, continued :
    Witnesses Abram Clock, James H. Talmage, and Mary Scofield, page 189.
    Inventory taken by Abram Clock and Edwin Scofield, and filed Oct. 17, 1842, page 190.
    Mch. 20, 1843, account filed, and real estate ordered sold to pay debts, page 229.
    Real estate sold to Isaac Waterbury of Darien, and Mary Waterbury, mother of said executrix, and report of sale filed Apl. 29, 1843, page 229.

Waterbury, Mary, widow, late of Darien, will dated May 3, 1843, probated Apl. 19, 1844, mentions her children David Waterbury, Peter L. Waterbury, Isaac Waterbury, John V. Waterbury, Polly Waterbury, Fanny Waterbury, and Julia Ann Waterbury. Executor her son David Waterbury. Witnesses James H. Gorham, Mary E. Scofield, and Betsy Hoyt, page 358.
    Apl. 19, 1844, order to advertise for claims, page 358.
    Inventory taken by Abram Clock and Edmund Scofield, and filed May 25, 1844, page 359.

Waterbury, William L., late of Darien, Mch. 23, 1840, his widow refused to qualify, and letters of administration on his estate granted to Abram Clock, who was ordered to advertise for claims, page 45.
    Inventory taken Mch. 26, 1840, by John Bell and Jeremiah Andreas, and filed Apl. 4, 1840, page 45.
    Jan. 25, 1841, account filed, allowance to his widow, and real estate ordered sold to pay debts, pages 45 and 46.
    Feb. 15, 1841, real estate sold to Jeremiah Andreas of Darien, and report of sale filed, page 46.

Waters, Aaron, late of Stamford, will dated Oct. 25, 1827, probated Aug. 30, 1841, mentions his wife Zilpah, and children John, Selleck, Alla Stokeum, Hannah Clawson, Rachel Waters, and Mary Hawley. Executors his wife and Selleck Scofield. Witnesses William Shepard, Deborah Curtis, and Elisa C. Campbell, page 47.
    Aug. 30, 1841, his widow refused to qualify, and letters granted to Selleck Scofield, who was ordered to advertise for claims, page 48.
    Inventory taken by Gould Raymond and George Lounsbury, and filed Nov. 1, 1841, page 48.
    Apl. 11, 1842, estate ordered distributed according to his will, page 48.
    Apl. 11, 1842, estate distributed to his widow, Zilpah and sons John and Selleck, page 49.

STAMFORD PROBATE RECORDS.
Volume 16, 1841.

342.

Waters, Elisha, late of Stamford, Dec. 20, 1842, his widow refused to qualify, and letters of administration on his estate granted to his eldest son Jared Waters, who was ordered to advertise for claims, page 199.
Inventory taken by Luther Weed and Jeremiah Curtiss, and filed Jan. 24, 1843, page 200.
July 1, 1843, account filed, and commissioners appointed to adjust claims of creditors, page 335.
Jan. 25, 1844, report of commissioners filed, page 335.
Feb. 3, 1844, account filed, and an allowance to his widow, page 336.

Waters, Sarah, of Stamford, Jan. 9, 1843, on the application of her son Jared Waters, the court appointed Selleck Scofield her conservator, page 206.

Webb, Elizabeth A., of Norfolk, Va., Mch. 11, 1842, made choice of John B. Webb of New York City to be her guardian, page 140.

Weed, Abishai, late of Stamford, Feb. 15, 1840, letters of administration on his estate granted to his sons Luther and Abishai, who were ordered to advertise for claims, page 79.
Inventory taken by John Young and Jacob Stevens, and filed Apl. 6, 1840, page 79.
Oct. 14, 1841, partition of his estate between Luther Weed, Abishia Weed, and Ebenezer Weed by agreement, page 125.

Weed, Ebenezer, late of Stamford, July 16, 1843, letters of administration on his estate granted to his widow, Maria E. Weed, who was ordered to advertise for claims, page 235.
Inventory taken by Benjamin M. Weed and Jacob Stevens, and filed Aug. 7, 1843, page 235.
Feb. 12, 1844, dower of his widow, Maria E. Weed, ordered set out, page 236.
Mch. 11, 1844, dower set out, page 236.
Feb. 12, 1844, account filed, and an allowance to his widow, and real estate ordered sold to pay debts, page 237.
Real estate sold to Isaac Selleck and Abishai Scofield, both of Stamford, and report of sale filed June 8, 1844, page 238.

Weed, Frances M., of New York City, Feb. 26, 1842, her guardian, Isaac Weed, Jr., of Darien, asked leave to sell the real estate of said minor in Darien, and sale or-

STAMFORD PROBATE RECORDS.
Volume 16, 1841.

Weed, Frances M., continued :
dered, pages 32 and 33.
Real estate sold to Elias Johnson of Darien, and report of sale filed June 4, 1842, page 33.

Weed, Frederick, late of Darien, Dec. 9, 1843, account filed, and estate ordered distributed to his widow, Phebe Weed, and Esther C. wife of Thaddeus R. Waring, formerly Esther Conrey Waterbury, page 249.
Dec. 28, 1843, estate distributed accordingly, page 250.

Weed, Henry, 3rd, late of Darien, Aug. 25, 1843, his widow refused to qualify, and letters of administration on his estate granted to William Andreas, who was ordered to advertise for claims, page 331.
Inventory taken by Holly Bell and Ebenezer Weed, and filed Sept. 23, 1843, page 331.
Apl. 15, 1844, account filed, and an allowance to his widow, page 332.
Apl. 15, 1844, dower of his widow, Matilda Weed, ordered set out, page 332.
Apl. 17, 1844, dower set out, page 333.
Apl. 15, 1844, real estate ordered sold to pay debts, page 333.
Real estate sold to Matilda Weed, and report of sale filed May 21, 1844, page 333.

Weed, Hezekiah, late of Darien, will dated June 28, 1827, probated Apl. 10, 1840, mentions his wife Rebecca, and children Catharine W., Alanson, Hezekiah, Nathaniel, James, Harvey, Maltbie, children of his son Charles, and children of his son Alfred. Executors his sons Nathaniel and Harvey. Witnesses John Weed, Jr., Mary E. Weed, and Sally Weed, page 133.
Apl. 10, 1840, order to advertise for claims, page 134.
Inventory taken by Seth Crissey and John Weed, Jr., and filed July 4, 1840, page 134.

Weed, Jacob, late of Stamford, June 8, 1842, letters of administration on his estate granted to Smith Weed of New York City, who was ordered to advertise for claims, page 106.

Weed, James, late of Darien, Jan. 3, 1840, that part of his estate set off to his widow, Lydia Weed, ordered distributed to James B. Weed, legal representatives of Mary Andreas, deceased, legal representative of Clarissa, daughter of deceased, Hezekiah Weed, Ebenezer Weed,

STAMFORD PROBATE RECORDS.
Volume 16, 1841.

Weed, James, continued :
and Catherine Weed, each 1/6, page 75..
Apl. 25, 1840, estate distributed to Catherine McDonald as her own share and as the legal representative of James B. Weed and Hezekiah Weed, whose rights she purchased, Ebenezer Weed, the legal representatives of Clarissa Holmes, and the legal representatives of Mary Andreas, page 76.

Weed, Jarvis, of Darien, Mch. 17, 1842, account filed by his assignee, and real estate ordered sold to pay debts, page 120.
Real estate sold to Lewis Tallmadge of New Canaan, and report of sale filed June 16, 1842, page 120.

Weed, Jonathan, late of Stamford, June 14, 1841, letters of administration on his estate granted to Johathan J. Weed of Stamford, who was ordered to advertise for claims, page 72.
Inventory taken June 14, 1841, by Benjamin M. Weed and Caleb Knapp, and filed Aug. 14, 1841, page 72.

Weed, Lydia, late of Darien, Jan. 3, 1840, letters of administration on her estate granted to Ebenezer Weed of Darien, who was ordered to advertise for claims, page 75
Inventory taken by Jacob Lockwood and Holly Bell, and filed Apl. 30, 1840, page 75.

Weed, Maria E., of Stamford, Aug. 7, 1843, appointed guardian of her children Charles A. Weed, Miles H. Weed, Caroline E. Weed, Martin E. Weed, and Cornelia M. Weed, page 236.

Weed, Mary, late of Stamford, Mch. 28, 1839, letters of administration on her estate granted to Ezra Lockwood of Poundridge, who was ordered to advertise for claims, page 72.

Weed, Samuel, late of Stamford, June 14, 1841, letters of administration on his estate granted to William H. Weed of Stamford, who was ordered to advertise for claims, page 115.
Inventory taken by Erastus C. Bishop and Peter Lockwood and filed Aug. 9, 1841, page 116.

Weed, Sarah, late of Darien, will dated Mch. 5, 1844, probated Mch. 11, 1844, mentions the daughters of my brother John Weed, viz. Mary E. Weed, Sarah A. Weed, and Amelia F. Weed, and said John Weed. Executor her nephew

STAMFORD PROBATE RECORDS.
Volume 16, 1841.

Weed, Sarah, continued :
    Nathaniel B. Weed. Witnesses Abram Clock, Hezekiah
    Weed, and Jane Conley, page 314.
    Mch. 11, 1844 order to advertise for claims, page 314.
    Inventory taken by Ezra H. Bishop and George Walmsley,
    and filed Apl. 8, 1844, page 315.

Weed, Selleck, late of Darien, will dated May 24, 1841, probated Oct. 30, 1841, mentions his children George Selleck and Elizabeth Deal, and grandchildren Edson W.
    Deal and Mary Deal. Executor Abram Clock. Witnesses
    Elisha Seely, Thomas Fancher, and George H. Wallace,
    page 73.
    Oct. 30, 1841, order to advertise for claims, page 74.
    Inventory taken Dec. 9, 1841, by Jacob Lockwood and
    William Andreas, and filed Dec. 31, 1841, page 74.

Weed, Usual, late of Darien, will dated Nov. 18, 1839, probated Feb. 20, 1840, mentions his wife Ann, and children John Arthur, Raymond Knapp, Edward Augustus, and
    James Alexander. Executor Seth Crissy of Darien.
    Witnesses Joshua B. Ferris, William H. Holly and Smith
    Scott, page 23.
    Feb. 20, 1840, order to advertise for claims, page 24.
    Inventory taken Apl. 10, 1840, by Joseph Hoyt and
    Holly Bell, and filed Apl. 15, 1840, page 24.
    Aug. 3, 1840, his widow refused to accept the provisions in his will, page 24.
    Apl. 25, 1842, dower of his widow, Ann Weed, ordered
    set out, and estate ordered distributed to his children John A., Raymond K., Edward A., and James A.,
    page 108.
    Dower set out, and estate distributed accordingly,
    page 108.

Weeks, James W., of Stamford, Mch. 27, 1844, parent and natural guardian of Hannah Maria, asked leave to sell the
    real estate of said minor in Stamford, and sale ordered, page 374.
    Real estate sold to Isaac Selleck, William H. Adams,
    and Ebenezer T. Webb, all of Stamford, as committee of
    the Methodist Society in the Borough of Stamford, and
    report of sale filed June 12, 1844, page 375.

Whiting, Samuel, late of Darien, June 12, 1838, account filed,
    and real estate ordered sold to pay debts, page 71.
    Real estate sold to Usual Weed of Darien, and report
    of sale filed July 30, 1838, page 71.

STAMFORD PROBATE RECORDS.
Volume 16, 1841.

Wilmot, Abigail, late of Stamford, will dated Sept. 11, 1843, probated Nov. 18, 1843, all to her daughter Anna Maria wife of William Buxton. No executor. Witnesses Isaac Bell, Mary A. Larkin, and Mary Bell, page 316.
Nov. 18, 1843, letters of administration with the will annexed granted to William Buxton, who was ordered to advertise for claims, page 316.
Inventory taken by Charles Brown and Orman Broadway, and filed Dec. 16, 1843, page 317.
Feb. 8, 1844, William Buxton resigned, and Charles Brown appointed in his place, page 317.

Wilmot, John, late of Stamford, will dated Jan. 31, 1840, probated Mch. 21, 1840, all to his wife Sally. No executor. Witnesses John R. Leeds, John J. Leeds, and Charles W. Slawson, page 102.
Mch. 21, 1840, letters granted to John J. Leeds, who was ordered to advertise for claims, page 103.
Inventory taken by John J. Leeds and William Scofield, and filed June 29, 1840, page 103.

Wilmot, Samuel, late of Darien, will dated Aug. 16, 1841, probated Oct. 29, 1842, all to his wife Belinda, and appointed her his executrix. Witnesses Nathaniel Slawson, Ira Scofield, and George S. Bell, page 187.

Winthrop, Emily R., Francis B. Winthrop, and Susan R. Winthrop, formerly of Stamford, but now of New York City, Sept. 10, 1842, their guardians Henry R. Winthrop and John S. Winthrop, Jr., asked leave to sell the real estate of said minors in Stamford, and sale ordered, page 208.

Wood, Isaac, late of Stamford, Jan. 3, 1842, letters of administration on his estate granted to Joseph Brush of Greenwich, page 72.

STAMFORD PROBATE RECORDS.
Volume 17, 1844.

Adams, William, late of Stamford, Apl. 30, 1846, letters of
administration on his estate granted to his widow,
Polly Adams, who was ordered to advertise for claims,
page 138.
Inventory taken by Thaddeus Hanford and Benjamin W.
Weed, and filed May 22, 1846, page 138.
Dec. 29, 1846, administratrix ordered to file her account, page 238.

Anderson, Hannah, late of Greenwich, will dated Dec. 16,
1844, probated Apl. 20, 1846, mentions Anna wife of
Nehemiah Brown of King Street, Hannah Brown daughter
of said Anna Brown, nephews Edmund Anderson and William Anderson of New York, Elizabeth Anderson daughter
of my brother Jeremiah Anderson, Sarah wife of Ananias
Mathews of New York, and Mary Merritt daughter of Adam
Merritt, deceased. Executors James Field and Edmund
Field. Witnesses Daniel Taylor, Elizabeth Brundage,
and James Field, page 79.
Apl. 20, 1846, order to advertise for claims, page 80.
Inventory taken by Nehemiah Purdy and John C. Sherwood,
and filed Apl. 20, 1846, page 81.
June 14, 1847, account ordered filed, page 307.

Andreas, Elizabeth L., of New York City, Dec. 2, 1847, appointed guardian of her children Julia Ann Andreas, 19
years of age, Samuel Andreas, 17 years of age, Jeremiah Andreas, 15 years of age, and Cordelia Andreas,
12 years of age, all of the City of New York, and owning real estate in Darien, page 366.

Andreas, Jeremiah, late of Darien, will dated Aug. 13, 1833,
probated Jan. 19, 1847, mentions his wife Sarah, and
children Dordas, John, Samuel, Betsy, and Rebecca.
Executors sons John and Samuel. Witnesses Charles Knapp,
Burr Scott, and Charles Hawley, page 271.

STAMFORD PROBATE RECORDS.
Volume 17, 1844.

Andreas, Jeremiah, continued :
> Jan. 19, 1847, order to advertise for claims, page 272.
> Inventory taken by Holly Bell and Edwin Scofield, and filed Feb. 23, 1847, page 273.
> Nov. 26, 1847, his widow now deceased, and daughter Dorcas married, account filed, and estate ordered distributed to his children John, children of Samuel, deceased, Betsy widow of Bates Hoyt, deceased, Rebecca widow of Alvah Scofield, deceased, and Dorcas wife of Benjamin Little, page 370, and distributed, page 371.
> Nov. 10, 1847, account ordered filed, page 360.

Augur, John, late of Stamford, Nov. 3, 1845, on the application of his administratrix, Nancy Augur, the court appointed Nathaniel D. Haight to sell the real estate to pay debts, page 183.
> Real estate sold to Nancy Augur, and report of sale filed Apl. 3, 1846, page 184.

Banks, Mary, late of New York City, Mch. 9, 1844, her estate in Greenwich ordered distributed to the legal representatives of David Lyon, deceased, legal representatives of James Lyon, deceased, legal representatives of Benjamin Lyon, deceased, legal representatives of Elizabeth Merritt, deceased, legal representatives of Sarah Banks, deceased, and the legal representatives of Daniel Lyon, deceased, page 61.
> Mch. 17, 1844, estate distributed accordingly, page 61.

Barnum, Horace, late of Stamford, will dated Oct. 18, 1843, probated May 1, 1847, mentions his wife Cynthia, and children Sarah Ann Ritch and Samuel V. Barnum. Executors Wells R. Ritch and Samuel V. Barnum. Witnesses --------, page 297.
> May 1, 1847, order to advertise for claims, page 298.
> Inventory taken by Darius Weed and Ebenezer T. Webb, and filed June 28, 1847, page 310.
> Nov. 2, 1847, account ordered filed, page 355.

Bates, John, late of Darien, will dated Jan. 6, 1848, probated Jan. 31, 1848, mentions an agreement with his wife, Esther, as to dower, and children Martha A., Samuel, John W., Ebenezer S., and George R., grandsons George Husted and Ebenezer Husted, granddaughters Sarah E. Husted and Mary E. Husted. Executors his son Ebenezer S., of New York, and Abram Cloek of Darien. Witnesses Richard Beers, Charlotte Weed, and Jane A. Beers, page 386.

STAMFORD PROBATE RECORDS.
Volume 17, 1844.

349.

Bates, John, continued:
Jan. 31, 1848, Ebenezer S. Bates refused to qualify, and letters granted to Abram Clock, who was ordered to advertise for claims, page 388.

Bates, William H., of Darien, Nov. 13, 1847, petition by the selectmen of the Town of Darien for the appointment of a conservator for said alleged incompetent, page 367.
Dec. 6, 1847, George J. Bowler appointed conservator, page 368.

Bell, Prudence, late of Stamford, inventory taken by Ezra Dibble and Orman Broadway, and filed Aug. 26, 1844, by Charles Brown, administrator, page 26.
Mch. 3, 1845, account filed, and real estate ordered sold to pay debts, page 34.
Real estate sold to Rebecca Bell, and report of sale filed May 24, 1845, page 35.
May 26, 1845, estate ordered distributed to her brothers and sisters, viz: Ezekiel Bell, Noah Bell, Jared Bell, John Bell, Francis Bell, Rebecca Bell, Sarah wife of James Sniffin, and Mary wife of Henry Webb, page 35.
May 30, 1845, estate distributed accordingly, page 36.

Bell, Rebecca, late of Stamford, June 19, 1846, letters of administration on her estate granted to John R. Leeds, who was ordered to advertise for claims, page 198.
Inventory taken June 23, 1846, by Richard Fox and Samuel Smith, and filed Jan. 18, 1847, page 207.
Feb. 15, 1847, account filed, and commissioners appointed to adjust claims of creditors, pages 208, and 279.
Dec. 31, 1847, report of commissioners filed, page 374.
Dec. 31, 1847, account ordered filed, page 374.
Jan. 15, 1848, account filed, and real estate ordered sold to pay debts, page 393.
Real estate sold to Richard Fox, and report of sale filed Mch. 1, 1848, page 392.
Mch. 10, 1848, estate ordered distributed to her heirs at law, viz: Mary wife of Henry Webb, Sarah, or Sally wife of James Sniffen, Ezekiel Bell, Noah Bell, Jared Bell, Francis Bell, and to Richard Fox he having purchased the share of John Bell, page 402.
Apl. 5, 1848, estate distributed accordingly, page 403.

Blau, Cornelia, late of New York City, will dated Nov. 7, 1847, probated Dec. 18, 1847, mentions her nephew Edwin Bates, and his daughter Frances, Mrs. James DeWolf,

STAMFORD PROBATE RECORDS.
Volume 17, 1844.

Blau, Cornelia, continued :
    Sally wife of William H. Bates, and Hannah wife of
    Richard Bates. Executor nephew Edwin Bates. Wit-
    nesses Holly Bell, Rachel Raymond, and Clarissa R. Wood
    page 368.
    Dec. 18, 1847, order to advertise for claims, page 369.
    Inventory taken by Holly Bell and Edward Scofield,
    and filed Dec. 18, 1847, page 370.
    Additional inventory filed Jan. 6, 1848, page 377.
    June 6, 1848, account ordered filed, page 435.

Briggs, Philip, late of Greenwich, Sept. 15, 1846, letters
    of administration on his estate granted to Odle C.
    Knapp of Greenwich, who was ordered to advertise for
    claims, page 214.
    Inventory taken by Seely Mead and Silas Husted, and
    filed Oct. 5, 1846, page 215.
    Jan. 9, 1847, account filed, and commissioners appoint-
    ed to adjust claims of creditors, page 216.
    Sept. 18, 1847, report of commissioners filed, page 330
    Sept. 18, 1847, account filed, and real estate ordered
    sold to pay debts, page 331.
    Sept. 18, 1847, necessaries set off to his widow, and
    also an allowance for the sppport of the family,
    page 449.
    May 6, 1848, account ordered filed, page 413.

Brown, Ann, late of Brooklyn, N. Y., Aug. 26, 1847, letters
    of administration on her estate granted to Matthew
    Antonides of Brooklyn, N. Y., who was ordered to ad-
    vertise for claims, page 336.
    Inventory taken by Jonas Howe and Zaccheus Mead, and
    filed Sept. 10, 1847, page 320.
    Mch. 28, 1848, account ordered filed, page 396.
    Mch. 31, 1848, real estate ordered sold to pay debts,
    page 447.
    Real estate sold to Zaccheus Mead of Greenwich, and
    report of sale filed June 13, 1848, page 448.

Brown, George P., of Stamford, Jan. 27, 1846, general assign-
    ment for the benefit of creditors to Sands Seely of
    Stamford, page 125.
    Inventory taken by Isaac Quintard, Jr., and John W.
    Harris, and filed Jan. 29, 1846, page 126.
    Feb. 9, 1846, commissioners appointed to adjust claims
    of creditors, page 127.
    Aug. 12, 1846, report of commissioners filed, page 218.
    Oct. 31, 1846, account ordered filed, page 219.

STAMFORD PROBATE RECORDS.
Volume 17, 1844.

Brown, Lucy, of Stamford, Feb. 10, 1845, her conservator, John R. Leeds of Stamford, asked leave to sell the real estate of said incompetent in Stamford, and sale ordered, page 176.
Real estate sold to Philip H. Brown of Stamford, and report of sale filed May 8, 1845, page 177.

Brown, Major, late of Greenwich, will dated Nov. 9, 1837, probated Sept. 27, 1847, all to his daughters Ruth, Sarah, and Electa. Executrix his daughter Ruth Brown. Witnesses William A. Husted, Jr., Rebecca R. Close, and Samuel Close, page 346.
Sept. 27, 1847, order to advertise for claims, page 347.
Inventory taken by Isaac Peck and Ard Knapp, and filed Oct. 30, 1847, page 353.
Oct. 30, 1847, personal property ordered sold, page 353.
Apl. 10, 1848, account ordered filed, page 397.

Brown, Rebecca, late of Darien, will dated June 15, 1845, probated Nov. 1, 1845, all to her niece Rebecca Weed, daughter of Benjamin Weed of Darien. Executor her nephew Isaac Weed of Darien. Witnesses Abram Clock, Nathaniel B. Weed, and Benjamin Weed, Jr., page 91.
Nov. 1, 1845, order to advertise for claims, page 91.
Inventory taken by John Bell, Jr. and Abram Clock, and filed Dec. 8, 1845, page 92.

Brundage, Samuel, late of Greenwich, will dated Sept. 24, 1846 probated July 12, 1847, mentions his wife Mary, and children Rebecca wife of James Britt, Permela wife of William Bittis, Sally wife of William Hubbard, William, Hiram, and Thomas C. Executors his wife and sons William and Thomas C. Witnesses Ezra Keeler, Abraham Rowell, and Bartow F. White, page 314.
July 12, 1847, order to advertise for claims, page 315.
Inventory taken by Ezra Keeler and Josiah Wilcox, and filed Aug. 23, 1847, page 329.
Jan. 31, 1848, account ordered filed, page 385.

Brush, Benjamin, late of Greenwich, will dated Apl. 27, 1839, probated Aug. 26, 1847, mentions his wife Semantha, and children Fanny F. Rundle, Deborah B. Finch, Sarah, and Joseph; children of my son Edward, viz: Emma C., Shadrach M., Rebecca Ann, Mary A., and Semantha B.; children of my daughter Semantha, viz: Amarantha, (Hobby) Ann Louisa, Julia Augusta, and David Augustus, and daughter in law Maria. Executor son Joseph. Witnesses Hugh Mackay, Jeremiah Platt, and Gilbert Close, Jr., 340.

STAMFORD PROBATE RECORDS.
Volume 17, 1844.

Brush, Benjamin, continued:
    Aug. 26, 1847, order to advertise for claims, page 341.
    Inventory taken by Gilbert Close and Alfred Rundle,
    and filed Apl. 10, 1848, page 399.

Brush, Edward, late of Stamford, Nov. 5, 1844, account filed,
    and real estate ordered sold to pay debts, page 102.
    Real estate sold to Charles Brush of Stamford and Lock-
    wood Ferris of Greenwich, and report of sale filed,
    Mch. 12, 1845, page 102.

Brush, Edward L., of Greenwich, about 19 years of age, May 12,
    1845, his guardian Shubal Brush removed, and Alfred
    Rundle appointed in his place, page 113.

Brush, Josephus, late of Greenwich, inventory taken by Ard
    Reynolds and Alfred Rundle, and filed Sept. 3,
    1844, page 29.
    Mch. 12, 1844, account filed, and real estate ordered
    sold to pay debts, page 30.
    Real estate sold to Charles Brush of Stamford, and re-
    port of sale filed Apl. 14, 1845, page 31.

Brush, Maria C., late of Greenwich, will dated Feb. 1, 1848,
    probated Apl. 6, 1848, mentions her father in law Ben-
    jamin Brush, sisters Louisa Close, Abigail Close,
    Nancy Close, and Mary A. Palmer. Executor her bro-
    ther Ezekiel Close of Greenwich. Witnesses Joseph
    Close, Sarah Banks, and Bartow F. White, page 400.
    Apl. 6, 1848, order to advertise for claims, page 402.

Bunnell, Jonathan, late of Greenwich, Aug. 24, 1845, adminis-
    trator ordered to file his account, page 19.
    Sept. 8, 1845, account filed, and real estate ordered
    sold to pay debts, page 181.
    Real estate sold to George Bunnell of Greenwich, and
    report of sale filed Sept. 29, 1845, page 182.

Bonnell(Bunnell), Sabrina, of Greenwich, Nov. 5, 1846, ap-
    pointed guardian of her children John H. Bonnell,
    about 20 years of age, Pierre U. Bonnell, about 18 years
    of age, Govenier M. Bonnell, about 14 years of age,
    and William Astor Bonnell, about 11 years of age,
    page 206.

Burley, Deborah, late of Greenwich, Oct. 16, 1845, letters of
    administration on her estate granted to Seth P. Quintard
    of Greenwich, who was ordered to advertise for claims,
    page 116.

STAMFORD PROBATE RECORDS.
Volume 17, 1844.

Burley, Deborah, continued :
    Inventory taken by Seth P. Quintard and Daniel M. Ritch, and filed Nov. 1, 1845, page 263.
    May 20, 1846, account filed, and commissioners appointed to adjust claims of creditors, page 174.
    Report of commissioners filed, Dec. 28, 1846, page 263.
    Oct. 26, 1848, account ordered filed, page 474.

Burley, Henry, late of Greenwich, Feb. 9, 1847, letters of administration on his estate granted to Selleck Scofield of Stamford, who was ordered to advertise for claims, page 283.
    Inventory taken by Henry Ritch and Henry Dayton, and filed Apl. 8, 1847, page 283.

Burley, Samuel, late of Greenwich, Oct. 13, 1845, letters of administration on his estate granted to Selleck Scofield of Stamford, who was ordered to advertise for claims, page 115.
    Inventory taken by Henry Ritch and Seth P. Quintard, and filed Dec. 17, 1845, page 181.
    Jan. 29, 1847, Joshua B. Ferris of Stamford appointed guardian of Emily Burley of Greenwich, a daughter of decedent, page 207.

Burley, Silas, late of Greenwich, May 4, 1846, personal property not sufficient to pay the legacies bequeathed to his children, Cynthia now the wife of Lot Palmer, Deborah now the wife of John H. Reynolds, Amy Burley, and Emeline now the wife of George Marshall, and Deborah the widow of testator being now deceased, the real estate was ordered sold to pay said legacies, page 171.
    Real estate sold to the aforesaid Cynthia Palmer, Deborah Reynolds, Amy Burley, and Emeline Marshall, and report of sale filed June 1, 1846, page 171.
    June 1, 1846, his son Silas having predeceased the testator, estate ordered distributed to his children Henry, Isaac, Walter, and the heirs at law of Samuel, page 172.
    June 3, 1846, Isaac Burley, conveyed his interest to Henry Burley, and the estate was distributed to testator's children Henry, and Walter, and the heirs at law of Samuel, page 172.

Burton, Augustus, of Darien, about 16 years of age, Oliver B. Burton, Julia E. Burton, Mary A. Burton, and Charles H. Burton, Nov. 4, 1846, the court appointed Joel Hurlburt of Darien to be their guardian, page 206.

STAMFORD PROBATE RECORDS.
Volume 17, 1844.

Bush, Justus Luke, late of Greenwich, Aug. 29, 1844, letters
of administration on his estate granted to his widow,
Sally Bush, who was ordered to advertise for claims,
page 154.
Inventory taken by Nelson Bush and Benjamin I. Knapp,
and filed Dec. 20, 1844, page 154.
Jan. 13, 1845, administratrix removed, and Ard Reynolds
appointed in her place, page 155.
Aug. 4, 1845, commissioners appointed to adjust claims
of creditors, page 155.
Mch. 11, 1847, report of commissioners filed, page 287.
Mch. 25, 1847, Samuel G. Cornell, administrator of the
estate of William Knapp, deceased, appealed from the
report of said commissioners, page 289.
July 26, 1847, appeal abandoned, page 322.
July 6, 1847, time for final settlement extended,
page 311.
July 29, 1847, personal property ordered sold,
page 359.
Sept. 27, 1847, account ordered filed, page 346.
Nov. 1, 1847, necessaries allowed the widow and family
of deceased, page 360.
Nov. 1, 1847, account filed, and creditors ordered
paid 50 cents on the dollar, page 360.
Mch. 28, 1848, account ordered filed, page 397.

Clark, Cyrus, late of Greenwich, Feb. 20, 1847, letters of
administration on his estate granted to George A.
Palmer of Greenwich, who was ordered to advertise for
claims, page 284.
Inventory taken by Henry Ritch and Lot Palmer, and
filed May 21, 1847, page 285.
Feb. 21, 1848, account ordered filed, page 389.

Clark, Elizabeth, late of Greenwich, Oct. 18, 1845, letters
of administration on her estate granted to Joseph Brush
who was ordered to advertise for claims, page 115.

Clason, Solomon, late of Stamford, will dated Feb. 10, 1845,
probated Apl. 15, 1848, mentions his children Martha
Clason, Seth, Lewis, Ruth Smith, and four children of
son Smith, deceased, and son in law Earle Smith, set
apart from his real estate a plot four rods square for
a burial ground for himself and his family and his descendants, own property in Peekskill, N. Y. Executor son Seth. Witnesses Marianna C. Hawley, Mary S.
Hawley, and Charles Hawley, page 432.
June 3, 1848, order to advertise for claims, page 435.

STAMFORD PROBATE RECORDS.
Volume 17, 1844.

Clason, Solomon, continued:
    Inventory taken by Daniel Lockwood and Josiah Smith, and filed Sept. 2, 1848, page 477.

Close, Charlotte, late of Rye, May 20, 1848, letters of administration on her estate granted to Joseph Close of Greenwich, who was ordered to advertise for claims, page 426.

Close, Gilbert, late of Greenwich, Jan. 10, 1846, his widow refused to qualify, and letters of administration on his estate granted to his son Isaac O. Close, who was ordered to advertise for claims, page 133.
    Inventory taken by Daniel Peck and William Peck, and filed Feb. 2, 1846, page 133.
    Mch. 29, 1847, account ordered filed, page 217.
    Apl. 12, 1847, account filed, and real estate ordered sold to pay debts, page 353.
    Real estate sold to Odle C. Knapp of Greenwich, and report of sale filed Oct. 30, 1847, page 354.
    Nov. 1, 1847, account filed, and estate ordered distributed to his children Isaac O., Sarah E., and Charlotte C. Dole, page 355.
    Nov. 3, 1847, estate distributed accordingly, page 356.

Cook, Hannah, late of Stamford, widow of Joseph P. Cook, late of Danbury, will dated Feb. 7, 1845, probated Mch. 20, 1845, all to Ann Eliza wife of Andrew Bishop of Stamford. Executor Andrew Bishop. Witnesses George V. Youngs, Sarah A. Gray, and William H. Holly, page 47.
    Mch. 20, 1845, order to advertise for claims, page 48.
    Inventory taken by William H. Holly and Stephen B. Provost, and filed Mch. 20, 1845, page 48.

Curtis, Hester Ann, of Stamford, about 16 years of age, June 11, 1845, made choice of Alexander Provost to be her guardian, page 114.

Dan, Elizabeth F., late of Stamford, Mch. 30, 1847, letters of administration on her estate granted to Walter S. Clawson of Stamford, who was ordered to advertise for claims, page 295.
    Inventory taken by Charles W. Scofield and Harvey Lockwood, and filed Apl. 29, 1847, page 296.
    Apl. 15, 1847, commissioners appointed to adjust claims of creditors, page 295.
    Jan. 5, 1848, report of commissioners filed, page 377.

STAMFORD PROBATE RECORDS.
Volume 17, 1844.

Dan, John, late of Stamford, Apl. 27, 1845, account filed, and real estate ordered sold to pay debts, page 55.
Apl. 15, 1848, his widow now deceased, and real estate ordered sold to pay legacies and debts, page 420.
Real estate sold to Charles Slater of Stamford, and report of sale filed May 1, 1848, page 421.
May 2, 1848, estate ordered distributed to his children according to his will, viz: Elizabeth M. wife of Charles Slater, Angelina O. wife of Abel O. French, Louisa A. wife of George W. Bruce, Rachel L. wife of Harry A. Van Patten, Alfred T. Dan, Walter S. Dan, Elvin L. Dan, and Francis H. Dan, page 426.
May 9, 1848, estate distributed accordingly, page 427.
July 3, 1847, Walter S. Dan of Oberlin, Ohio, over 14 years of age, and Elvin L. Dan of New York City, over 14 years of age, made choice of Walter S. Clason of Stamford to be their guardian, who was also appointed guardian of Francis H. Dan of New York City, under 12 years of age, page 312.

Davenport, James, late of Stamford, will dated June 30, 1845, probated Feb. 2, 1846, mentions his wife Martha, and children John H., George, Isaac L., Sylvester, and the children of my son James A. Executors George Davenport and Isaac L. Davenport. Witnesses Andrew G. Carpenter Joseph Remington, and William Weed, page 136.
Feb. 2, 1846, order to advertise for claims, page 137.
Inventory taken by Isaac Scofield and William Davenport, and filed Mch. 23, 1846, page 137.

Davenport, James A., of New York City, July 17, 1847, appointed guardian of his children Charles F., Ralsey, and Emma, all under 12 years of age, page 313.
July 17, 1847, petition for leave to sell the real estate of said minors in North Stamford, page 313.
Sept. 25, 1847, real estate ordered sold, page 351.
Real estate sold to Isaac L. Davenport of Stamford, and report of sale filed Dec. 27, 1847, page 351.

Dayton, Jacob, late of Greenwich, Feb. 17, 1845, his widow refused to qualify, and letters of administration on his estate granted to his son Samuel B. Dayton, who was ordered to advertise for claims, page 55.
Inventory taken by Alfred Rundle and Conklin Husted, and filed Mch. 13, 1845, page 56.
Sept. 15, 1845, commissioners appointed to adjust claims of creditors, page 57.
Mch. 23, 1846, report of commissioners filed, page 57.

STAMFORD PROBATE RECORDS.
Volume 17, 1844.

Dayton, Jacob, continued :
    Mch. 23, 1846, account filed, and real estate ordered sold to pay debts, page 58.
    Real estate sold to Leonard Mead of Greenwich, and report of sale filed Mch. 23, 1846, page 58.
    Mch. 23, 1846, account filed, and creditors ordered paid 72 9/10 cents on the dollar, page 59.

Downing, George, late of New York City, will dated 31st day, 5th month, 1841, probated May 5, 1848, mentions his daughters Ann Augusta wife of Joseph Sackett, Angelina Downing, and son Augustus C., granddaughters Georgianna Sackett, Emma Augusta Sackett, Josephine Sackett, and Sarah Levina Sackett. Executors son Augustus C., Peter S. Titus, and Charles Hicks, all of New York City. Witnesses Samuel Willets, Daniel T. Willets, and Amos Willets, page 408.
    Codicil dated Apl. 6, 1842, page 411.

Emmerson, Mary E., 19 years of age, John Chadwick, 18 years of age, and Ann E. Chadwick, 16 years of age, all of New York, but owning real estate in Greenwich, Apl. 4, 1848, made choice of Matthew Antonides of Brooklyn to be their guardian, page 422.
    Apl. 4, 1848, petition for leave to sell the real estate of said minors in Greenwich, and sale ordered, pages 422 and 423.
    Real estate sold to Sanford Mead of Greenwich, and report of sale filed June 13, 1848, page 424.

Ferris, Asa M., late of Stamford, Sept. 6, 1841, account filed and real estate ordered sold to pay debts, page 78.
    Real estate sold to Isaac Lockwood of Stamford, and report of sale filed Mch. 17, 1846, page 79.
    Note. Susan one of the administratives became the wife of James Disbrow since Sept. 6, 1841, and before Mch. 17, 1846.

Ferris, Jonathan, late of Greenwich, will dated June 22, 1842, probated May 11, 1846, mentions his wife ----, and children James, Samuel, Hannah, Ann, and Susan. Executor Peter Ferris of Greenwich. Witnesses Peter Ferris, Augustus R. Newman, and Solomon Peck, Jr., page 122.
    May. 11, 1846, order to advertise for claims, page 123.
    Inventory taken June 17, 1846, by Henry Ritch and Lot Palmer, and filed June 18, 1846, page 191.
    Dec. 19, 1846, account ordered filed, page 217.

STAMFORD PROBATE RECORDS.
Volume 17, 1844.

Ferris, Lemuel, late of Greenwich, will probated June 25, 1825, and on Oct. 23, 1847, his estate was ordered distributed to his children Alexander, now deceased, ~~Index~~ Jabez, and Lemuel, page 363.
Nov. 16, 1847, estate distributed accordingly, page 363.

Field, Hannah, late of Greenwich, will dated Nov. 20, 1845, probated Jan. 26, 1846, mentions Hannah Field a daughter of my brother Aaron Field, deceased, Hannah F. Griffin a daughter of my sister Mary Griffin, Hannah L. Field a daughter of Edmund Field, Hannah Field a daughter of Thomas C. Field, Elias Hicks Field, and James Field, Jr., sons of James Field, Aaron Quimby a son of Moses I. Quimby, deceased, and Anner F. Havaland. Executors my brother James Field, and his son William C Field. Witnesses Abel Smith, Daniel E. Tripp, and Jasper W. Carpenter, page 111.
Jan. 26, 1846, order to advertise for claims, page 112.
Inventory taken Jan. 24, 1846, by Richard B. Carpenter & ~~Inde~~ Edmund Field, and filed Jan. 27, 1846, page 132.
June 14, 1847, account ordered filed, page 307.

Finch, Christina, late of Greenwich, will dated Nov. 7, 1831, probated May 3, 1845, mentions her children Edward Brush, Anna wife of John Hobby, Mary wife of Asa Hobby, Christina wife of Daniel Banks, and Elizabeth wife of David Dayton, Jr. Executor Daniel Banks of Greenwich. Witnesses David Banks, Jr., Hanford Briggs, and Samuel Close, page 14 1/2.
May 3, 1845, the executor refused to qualify, and letters granted to Conklin Husted of Greenwich, who was ordered to advertise for claims, page 15.
Inventory taken by Alfred Rundle and Gilbert Close, and filed May 23, 1845, page 16.
Dec. 22, 1845, account ordered filed, page 17.

Green, Rauben, late of Greenwich, will dated Jan. 27, 1847, probated Mch. 26, 1847, mentions his wife Gleanar, and children Nancy Merritt, Elizabeth Green, Susan Green, Thomas Green, James Green, and Reuben Green, grandsons Sniffin Merritt a son of Nancy Merritt, and James Henry a son of James Green. Executor James Willson of Greenwich. Witnesses Jonathan S. Heustis, Charles Willson and Nathaniel Willson, page 285.
Mch. 26, 1847, order to advertise for claims, page 286.
Inventory taken by John B. Wilson and Nathan S. Mead, and filed May 17, 1847, page 287.
Nov. 11, 1847, real estate ordered sold, page 361.
Mch. 17, 1848, account ordered filed, page 394.

STAMFORD PROBATE RECORDS.
Volume 17, 1844.

Griffen, Hannah, late of Greenwich, will dated 30th day, 6th month, 1846, probated Aug. 24, 1846, mentions her daughter Sarah G. wife of William M. Cromwell, and son Daniel M. Griffen, and daughter Esther G. Schureman; granddaughter Mary Jane Cromwell, and grandson John D. Griffen. Executors son Daniel M. Griffen, and son in law Joseph Schureman. Witnesses Benjamin F. Burling, and Hannah Burling, page 203.
Aug. 24, 1846, order to advertise for claims, page 204.
Inventory taken by John Sands and Edmund Field, and filed Aug. 24, 1846, page 204.
July 6, 1847, account ordered filed, page 312.

Grigg, Elizabeth, late of Greenwich, inventory taken by John Henderson and Zaccheus Mead, Jr., and filed Sept. 16, 1844, page 17.
Jan. 21, 1844, executor ordered to file his account, page 18.

Grigg, Elizabeth, late of Greenwich, Aug. 4, 1847, letters of administration on her estate granted to John R. Grigg of Greenwich, who was ordered to advertise for claims, page 325.
Inventory taken by Augustus Mead and Nelson Bush, and filed Oct. 2, 1847, page 348.
Mch. 16, 1848, account ordered filed, page 394.

Grigg, Henry, late of Greenwich, Sept. 7, 1846, letters of administration on his estate granted to Ebenezer W. Kingsley of Summerstown, Westchester County, N. Y., who was ordered to advertise for claims, page 261.
Inventory taken by Augustus Mead and Nelson Bush, and filed Sept. 30, 1846, page 261.
Mch. 27, 1847, account ordered filed, page 262.

Grigg, John, late of the West India Islands, formerly of Greenwich, July 14, 1847, letters of administration on his estate granted to Sanford Mead of Greenwich, who was ordered to advertise for claims, page 312.
Inventory taken by Jonas Howe and Zaccheus Mead, and filed Sept. 10, 1847, page 320.
Mch. 20, 1848, account ordered filed, page 396.
Mch. 31, 1848, real estate ordered sold to pay debts, page 446.
Real estate sold to Zaccheus Mead of Greenwich, and report of sale filed June 13, 1848, page 446.
Apl. 6, 1848, estate ordered distributed to his brothers and sisters, viz: Mary wife of Caleb Husted,

STAMFORD PROBATE RECORDS.
Volume 17, 1844.

Grigg, John, continued.
and the heirs of Ann Brown, deceased, page 406.
Apl. 14, 1848, estate distributed accordingly, page 406.

Grigg, William C., of Greenwich, about 19 years of age, Mch. 25, 1848, made choice of Thomas A. Mead to be his guardian, page 453.
Mch. 25, 1848, petition for leave to sell the real estate of said minor in Greenwich, and sale ordered, pages 453 and 454.

Halligan, John, late of Greenwich, Apl. 28, 1848, letters of administration on his estate granted to Augustus Mead of Greenwich, who was ordered to advertise for claims, page 414.
Inventory taken by Zaccheus Mead and Joseph E. Russell, and filed Aug. 14, 1848, page 458.
Aug. 15, 1848, necessaries set off to his widow, and personal property ordered sold, pages 458 and 459.
Oct. 21, 1848, commissioners appointed to adjust claims of creditors, pages 476 and 477.

Hanford, Ebenezer, late of Darien, Oct. 19, 1844, letters of administration on his estate granted to Abram Clock of Darien, who was ordered to advertise for claims, page 177.

Harvey, Thomas M. late of Stamford, Mch. 24, 1845, letters of(M) administration on his estate granted to Isaac Quintard of Stamford, who was ordered to advertise for claims, page 187.
Inventory filed May 24, 1845, page 187.
Nov. 3, 1845, commissioners appointed to adjust claims of creditors, page 188.
May 2, 1846, report of commissioners filed, page 188.
June 8, 1846, account filed, and creditors ordered paid 6 23/100 cents on the dollar, page 189.

Hicks, Charles, of New York City, the parent and natural guardian of Henry R. Hicks of New York City, May 2, 1848, petition for leave to sell the real estate of said minor in Greenwich, and sale ordered, pages 455 and 456.
Real estate sold to Seth Miller of Stamford, and report of sale filed July 12, 1848, page 457.

Hobby, Abigail, widow of Jabez M. Hobby, of Greenwich, Feb. 17 1846, the application of her grandson in law, Thomas M. Lyon of New York City for the appointment of a conser-

STAMFORD PROBATE RECORDS.
Volume 17, 1844.

Hobby, Abigail, continued:
vator for said alleged incompetent, page 84.
Mch. 9, 1846, Samuel Close of Greenwich appointed such conservator, page 85.

Hobby, Abigail, late of Greenwich, Sept. 4, 1847, letters of administration on her estate granted to Augustus Mead of Greenwich, who was ordered to advertise for claims, page 338.
Inventory taken by Thomas A. Mead and Nelson Bush, and filed Sept. 24, 1847, page 345.
May 26, 1848, account ordered filed, page 431.

Hobby, William, late of Stamford, Aug. 4, 1845, his widow refused to qualify, and letters of administration on his estate granted to George M. Hubbard of Stamford, who was ordered to advertise for claims, page 53.
Inventory taken by Elkanah Mead and Jonathan Hoyt, and filed Aug. 29, 1845, page 54.

Holly, John M., of Stamford, Jan. 12, 1847, general assignment for the benefit of creditors to William Hoyt of Stamford, page 235.
Inventory taken by Smith Weed and James H. Hoyt, and filed Jan. 25, 1847, page 237.
Jan. 25, 1847, commissioners appointed to adjust claims of creditors, page 236.

Holly, Oscar L., of Stamford, Apl. 3, 1846, general assignment for the benefit of creditors to Jared Holly of Stamford, page 134.
Inventory taken by Smith R. Sibley and George Lounsbury, and filed May 14, 1846, page 136.
Apl. 13, 1846, commissioners appointed to adjust claims of creditors, page 135.
Nov. 16, 1846, report of commissioners filed, page 212.
Nov. 23, 1846, account filed, and real estate ordered sold, page 213.
Real estate sold to Charles H. Sarles of Poundridge,

and report of sale filed, Feb. 18, 1847, page 213.
Feb. 18, 1847, account filed, and creditors ordered paid one cent and eight mills on the dollar, page 214.

Houschell, John, of Stamford, about 17 years of age, May 3, 1848, made choice of Stephen Haight to be his guardian, page 113.

STAMFORD PROBATE RECORDS.
Volume 17, 1844.

Howe, William, late of Darien, Nov. 24, 1845, letters of administration on his estate granted to Ezra H. Bishop of Darien, who was ordered to advertise for claims, Page 129.
Inventory taken by Joseph Hoyt of Stamford and Nathaniel A. Bouton of Darien, and filed Feb. 9, 1846, page 129.
June 8, 1846, account filed, and commissioners appointed to adjust claims of creditors, page 186.
Mch. 11, 1847, report of commissioners filed, page 267.
Apl. 17, 1847, account filed and necessaries set off to his widow, and dower ordered set out, page 268.
Apl. 29, 1847, dower set out, page 268.
Apl. 17, 1847, real estate ordered sold to pay debts, page 269.
Real estate sold to Andrew Richards of Darien, George Richards, Smith Howe, and Abigail Howe, widow of deceased, and report of sale filed May 14, 1847, page 269.
Mch. 29, 1847, account ordered filed, page 270.
May 14, 1847, account filed, and creditors ordered paid 97 cents on the dollar, page 270.

Hoyt, Betsy, late of Stamford, will dated May 3, 1841, probated Jan. 1, 1845, all to Royal L. Gay of Stamford in trust for the benefit of her niece Abigail wife of Jesse Whiting, remainder contingent. Witnesses James H. Weed, Emma Eliza Tucker, and Robert Tucker, page 199.
Jan. 1, 1845, letters of administration with the will annexed granted to Royal L. Gay, who was ordered to advertise for claims, page 200.
Inventory taken by Frederick Lockwood and Stephen B. Provost, and filed Feb. 5, 1845, page 129.

Hoyt, Betsy, late of Darien, will dated Aug. 13, 1834, probated Mch. 1, 1845, all to her niece Mary Elizabeth wife of Joseph H. Scofield for life, and remainder to her issue. Witnesses Stephen B. Provost, B. S. Mead, and Charles Hawley, page 150.
Mch. 1, 1845, letters of administration with the will annexed granted to Abram Clock of Darien, who was ordered to advertise for claims, page 150.
Inventory taken by William Andreas and Edward Scofield, and filed Mch. 22, 1845, page 151.
Dec. 15, 1845, commissioners appointed to adjust claims of creditors, page 151.
Report of commissioners filed, page 210, Aug. 29, 1846.
Aug. 27, 1846, account ordered filed, page 211.

STAMFORD PROBATE RECORDS.
Volume 17, 1844.

Hoyt, David, late of Stamford, Feb. 5, 1839, account filed by his administrator, and real estate ordered sold to pay debts, page, 33.
Real estate sold to Shadrach Smith of New York City, and report of sale filed Apl. 2, 1839, page 33.

Hoyt, Hannah, widow, late of Stamford, will dated Sept. 26, 1844, probated Jan. 25, 1847, mentions her children, George E. Hoyt, Mary E., Frances, and Emily. Executrix her daughter Mary E. Hoyt. Witnesses Nathaniel Adams, David Holly, and Charles Hawley, page 250.
Jan. 25, 1847, order to advertise for claims, page 251.
Inventory taken by Richard Stanton and Roswell Hoyt, and filed Mch. 2, 1847, page 251.

Hoyt, Ralph, late of Stamford, May 12, 1845, Adolphus D., and Theodosia, children of decedent, made choice of William Davenport to be their guardian, page 178.
May 12, 1845, petition for leave to sell the real estate of said minors in Stamford, and sale ordered, page 178.
Real estate sold to Edwin Bishop of Stamford, and report of sale filed, June 16, 1846, page 179.
Mch. 3, 1845, his administrator, Ezra Scofield, now deceased, and Isaac Scofield appointed in his place, and real estate ordered sold to pay debts, page 179.
Real estate sold to Harrison Teller and Henry Raymond, both of Stamford, and report of sale filed May 24, 1845, page 180.

Hoyt, Rhoda, late of Darien, will dated Feb. 11, 1843, probated June 12, 1845, mentions her nephews Noah Weed, Cary Weed, deceased, Joseph Seely, Cary Seely, and Henry Weed, nieces Hannah Reed, Betsy Seely, Sally Jennings, Isabel Jennings, and Martha Reed, and Abigail Weed widow of my deceased nephew Rufus Weed. Executor Ashbel Scofield of Stamford. Witnesses Abram Clock Sherman Husted, and Gilbert G. Waterbury, page 106.
Codicil dated Apl. 14, 1845, bequests to Sarah M. Jennings, Delia C. Seely and Cary H. Seely, page 107.
June 12, 1845, order to advertise for claims, page 108.
Inventory taken by Hezekiah Scofield, Jr., and Richard Fox, and filed Aug. 6, 1845, page 109.

Hoyt, Shadrach, late of Stamford, Apl. 2, 1847, letters of administration on his estate granted to Mary E. Haff of Brooklyn, N. Y., who was ordered to advertise for claims, the former administrators Hannah Hoyt and James S. Hoyt, now deceased, page 252.

STAMFORD PROBATE RECORDS.
Volume 17, 1844.

Hoyt, Thaddeus, late of Darien, will dated Mch. 14, 1846, probated Apl. 28, 1846, all to his wife Rebecca for life, and remainder to his heirs at law. Executors sons Rufus Hoyt and Isaac L. Hoyt. Witnesses Gilbert G. Waterbury, Joel Hurlbutt, and Hugh Patterson, page 100.
Apl. 28, 1846, order to advertise for claims, page 100.
Inventory taken by Holly Bell and Edward Scofield, and filed June 19, 1846, page 198.

Hoyt, William S., Captain, late of Stamford, Feb. 16, 1847, letters of administration on his estate granted to John W. Hoyt of New York City, who was ordered to advertise for claims, page 275.
Inventory taken by James H. Hoyt and Joseph D. Warren, and filed Apl. 3, 1847, page 276.
Aug. 28, 1847, commissioners apppointed to adjust claims of creditors, page 333.
Mch. 13, 1848, report of commissioners filed, page 393.

Husted, Amos, late of Greenwich, Nov. 1, 1846, account filed, and real estate ordered sold to pay debts, page 182.

Isaacs, Isaac, late of Norwalk, inventory taken by James Seymour and E. B. Bennett, and filed Oct. 5, 1846, by Charles Isaac surviving administrator, page 220.
Oct. 8, 1846, account ordered filed, page 221.

Jessup, Ebenezer, late of Greenwich, will dated Sept. 22, 1843 probated June 27, 1845, mentions his wife Rebecca, and children William, Elizabeth Powelson of Troy, N. Y., Ebenezer, Rhuea S. Marsh of New York City, and grandson William I. Jessup. Executor his son in law Charles Marsh. Witnesses S. B. S. Bissell, Beal B. Lockwood, and Susan Lockwood, page 27.
June 27, 1845, the executor refused to qualify, and letters granted to Charles Hendrie of Stamford, who was ordered to advertise for claims, page 28.
Inventory taken by Beal B. Lockwood and Kimberly Ferris and filed Mch. 12, 1845, page 28.

Jessup, Samuel, late of Greenwich, Oct. 18, 1844, account filed, and creditors ordered paid 80 4/10 cents on the dollar, page 133.

Johns, David, of Greenwich, Sept. 24, 1845, appointed guardian of his children Mason T., about 18 years of age, and Elizabeth R., about 14 years of age, page 114.

STAMFORD PROBATE RECORDS.
Volume 17, 1844.

June, Sarah, late of Stamford, Jan. 5, 1848, letters of administration on her estate granted to Richard Fox of Stamford, who was ordered to advertise for claims, page 376.
Inventory taken by Joseph Smith, Jr., and Jonathan Hoyt, and filed Feb. 26, 1848, page 391.
Oct. 2, 1848, account ordered filed, page 469.

June, Thomas, late of Stamford, Jan. 5, 1848, letters of administration on his estate granted to Richard Fox of Stamford, who was ordered to advertise for claims, page 375.
Inventory taken by Joseph Smith, Jr., and Jonathan Hoyt and filed Feb. 26, 1848, page 390.
Mch. 10, 1848, personal property ordered sold, page 391.
Oct. 2, 1848, account ordered filed, page 468.

June, William S., late of Stamford, Aug. 12, 1846, letters of administration on his estate granted to Mary A. June of Stamford, who was ordered to advertise for claims, page 277.
Inventory taken by Edwin Lounsbury and Harvey Hobby, and filed Sept. 26, 1846, page 277.
June 12, 1847, account ordered filed, page 307.

Knapp, Charity, late of North Castle, Westchester County, N. Y. will dated Feb. 1, 1837, probated Apl. 14, 1848, mentions her children Charity B. Knapp, Joshua Knapp of New York City, Samuel Knapp of North Castle, Rachel Brown of New York City, and the heirs of my son Nathaniel Knapp, late of Greenwich, deceased. Executor son Samuel. Witnesses G. B. Hobby, Jonathan Hobby, and Leander M. Palmer, page 416.
May 6, 1848, executor refused to qualify, and letters granted to Bartow F. White of Greenwich, who was ordered to advertise for claims, page 417.
Inventory taken by Israel Peck and Daniel Peck, and filed June 17, 1848, page 452.

Knapp, Esther, late of Greenwich, Mch. 21, 1846, Benjamin I. Knapp, administrator, removed, and Samuel G. Cornell of Greenwich appointed in his place, page 153.

Knapp, Henry E., Julia A. Knapp, and Catherine E. Knapp, Dec. 1, 1845, the court appointed Samuel G. Cornell of Greenwich to be their guardian, page 159.

STAMFORD PROBATE RECORDS.
Volume 17, 1844.

Knapp, Martha, late of Stamford, will dated Oct. 16, 1846, probated Jan. 28, 1847, mentions her sisters Ann Hait and Abigail Waring, nieces Elizabeth Hait, Louisa Brush and Sarah Waring, sister in law Polly Knapp, niece Mary Barret and her daughter Antionette, nieces Elizabeth Slater, Deborah Barnum, Mary Jane Brown, and Jeremiah Knapp. Executor Smith R. Sibley. Witnesses Elnathan Todd, Frederick B. Scofield, and Hugh Mackay, page 228.
Jan. 28, 1847, order to advertise for claims, page 229.
Inventory taken by Selleck Scofield and Isaac Ayres, and filed Apl. 6, 1847, page 230.
July 30, 1847, account ordered filed, page 317.

Knapp, Mary, late of Stamford, Mch. 15, 1845, inventory taken by Ebenezer Lockwood, and Peter Lockwood, and filed Mch. 15, 1845, page 59.
Apl. 18, 1845, account filed, and real estate ordered sold to pay debts, page 60.
Real estate sold to Harvey Knapp of Stamford, and report of sale filed May 4, 1846, page 60.

Knapp, William, late of Greenwich, Dec. 26, 1844, executor now deceased, and letters of administration with the will annexed granted to Samuel G. Cornell of Greenwich, page 153.

Little, Henry, of Stamford, Mch. 28, 1846, general assignment for the benefit of creditors to Henry Raymond of Stamford, page 69.
Inventory taken by Stephen Haight and Smith Teller, and filed Apl. 6, 1846, page 71.
Apl. 6, 1846, commissioners appointed to adjust claims of creditors, page 71.
Oct. 29, 1846, report of commissioners filed, page 282.
Sept. 29, 1847, account ordered filed, page 348.
Oct. 9, 1847, account filed, and creditors ordered paid 46 cents and eight mills on the dollar, page 350.
Oct. 17, 1848, account ordered filed, page 475.
Oct. 28, 1848, account filed, and creditors ordered paid one cent and three mills on the dollar, page 475.

Lockwood, Davis, late of Stamford, Sept. 30, 1844, account filed, and commissioners appointed to adjust claims of creditors, page 19.
Apl. 11, 1845, report of commissioners filed, page 20.
May 1, 1845, account filed, and real estate ordered sold to pay debts, page 21.

STAMFORD PROBATE RECORDS.
Volume 17, 1844.

Lockwood, Davis, continued :
    Real estate sold to Rebecca Lockwood and William V.
    Lockwood, both of Stamford, and report of sale filed
    copied on page 21.
    Apl. 21, 1845, administrator ordered to file his ac-
    count, page 22.
    May 1, 1845, allowance to the widow and children,
    page 22.
    May 1, 1845, account filed, and creditors ordered paid
    14 cents on the dollar, page 23.

Lockwood, Hannah, late of Greenwich, will dated July 28, 1845,
    probated Aug. 4, 1845, all to her brother Timothy L.
    Lockwood of New York City, and sister Sally Lockwood
    of Greenwich. Executor Captain Charles Hendrie. Wit-
    nesses Chauncey Ayres, Enos B. Lockwood, and S. Lewis
    Clason, page 52.
    Aug. 4, 1845, order to advertise for claims, page 52.
    Inventory taken by John Brampton and Beal B.
    Lockwood, and filed Sept. 29, 1845, page 53.

Lockwood, Henry, late of Greenwich, inventory taken by Ard
    Reynolds and Ephraim Marshall, and filed Sept. 3, 1844,
    page 6.
    May 6, 1845, account ordered filed, page 17.

Lockwood, Ira, late of Greenwich, will dated Feb. 9, 1832,
    probated May 25, 1846, mentions his wife Clementine, and
    children Ralph, Hanford, and Lydia Ostrander, and
    grandson Ira Lockwood Ostrander son of Isaac and Lydia
    Ostrander. Executor son Hanford. Witnesses Ann Eliza
    Reynolds, Elizabeth P. Reynolds, and Ard Reynolds,
    page 160.
    May 25, 1846, order to advertise for claims, page 162.
    Inventory taken by Ard Reynolds and Ephraim Marshall,
    and filed June 16, 1846, page 186.

Lockwood, Josiah, late of Darien, will dated Mch. 17, 1846,
    probated Sept. 22, 1846, mentions his children Celia E.
    Charlotte B., Martha Jane, Mary Ann, Sarah E., Frances
    L., Abigail S., Harriet N., William H., the children
    of my daughter Hannah Mariah, deceased, and the chil-
    dren of my son Samuel L., reserved a burial plot. Ex-
    ecutor Ashbel Scofield of Stamford. Witnesses George
    R. Stevens, Daniel Scofield, and David B. Burr,
    page 223.
    Codicil dated Aug. 29, 1846, page 224.
    Sept. 22, 1846, order to advertise for claims, page 225.
    Inventory taken by Richard Fox and Luther S. Scofield,

STAMFORD PROBATE RECORDS.
Volume 17, 1844.

Lockwood, Josiah, continued :
    and filed Nov. 28, 1846, page 225.
    Dec. 3, 1847, account ordered filed, page 366.
    Dec. 18, 1847, account filed, and real estate ordered
    sold to pay debts, page 418.
    Real estate sold to Cecilia E. Lockwood of Darien, and
    report of sale filed Mch. 25, 1848, page 418.

Lockwood, Julia A., of Stamford, Apl. 9, 1845, appointed guardian of her children William R. Lockwood, about 13 years of age, and Henry W. Lockwood, about 11 years of age, page 115.

Lockwood, Mills, late of Greenwich, Mch. 21, 1842, account filed, and real estate ordered sold to pay debts, page 49.
    Real estate sold to Alton Ingersoll of Greenwich, and report of sale filed Mch. 17, 1845, page 49.
    Mch. 17, 1845, account filed, and creditors ordered paid 87 5/10 cents on the dollar, page 101.

Lockwood, Noah, late of Greenwich, July 7, 1845, his widow refused to qualify, and letters of administration on his estate granted to George Ferris, Jr., of Greenwich, who was ordered to advertise for claims, page 63.
    Inventory taken by Beal B. Lockwood and Cornelius Ford, and filed Sept 1., 1845, page 63.
    Feb. 28, 1846, dower of his widow ordered set out, and set out Mch. 20, 1846, to Ruth Lockwood, page 65.
    June 22, 1846, account filed, and real estate ordered sold to pay debts, page 63.
    Real estate sold to John Brampton of Greenwich, and report of sale filed Mch. 4, 1846, page 64.

Lockwood, Priscilla, late of Stamford, Nov. 8, 1847, letters of administration on her estate granted to Royal L. Gay who was ordered to advertise for claims, page 358.
    Inventory filed Nov. 17, 1847, page 362.
    May 15, 1848, account ordered filed, page 425.

Lockwood, Shadrach, late of Stamford, Dec. 4, 1844, letters of administration on his estate granted to John W. Lockwood, who was ordered to advertise for claims, page 43.
    Inventory taken by Ebenezer Lockwood and Selleck Scofield, and filed Feb. 3, 1845, page 44.

STAMFORD PROBATE RECORDS.
Volume 17, 1844.

Lockwood, William, late of Stamford, Aug. 17, 1844, letters of administration on his estate granted to Julia A. Lockwood and Henry Waring, both of Stamford, who were ordered to advertise for claims, page 23.
Inventory taken by Alfred Hoyt and Samuel Lockwood, and filed Sept. 24, 1844, page 24.

Lounsbury, Isaac, late of Stamford, will dated May 5, 1841, probated Mch. 30, 1846, mentions his wife Nancy, and children Sarah Rosborough, and James Isaac, grandchildren Sarah Elizabeth Rosborough and Mary Catherine Lounsbury. Executor Selleck Scofield of Stamford. Witnesses Smith R. Sibley, Walter S. Clason, and Charles E. Husted, page 98.
Mch. 30, 1846, order to advertise for claims, page 99.
Inventory taken by Smith R. Sibley and George Lounsbury, and filed Apl. 8, 1847, page 278.
Apl. 8, 1847, account ordered filed, page 279.
Apl. 19, 1847, account filed, and real estate ordered sold to pay debts, page 357.
Real estate sold to Nancy Lounsbury, and report of sale filed Nov. 5, 1847, page 358.

Lounsbury, Mary Catherine, of New Canaan, about 11 years of age, May 3, 1847, the court appointed Hezekiah Scofield of Stamford to be her guardian, page 262.
June 2, 1847, petition for leave to sell the real estate of said minor in Stamford, page 304.
Aug. 14, 1847, sale ordered, page 325.
Real estate sold to Nancy Lounsbury, and report of sale filed Nov. 5, 1847, page 326.

Lyon, Joshua, late of Greenwich, Nov. 18, 1846, estate ordered distributed according to his will to his children Samuel Lyon and John Lyon, page 209.
Jan. 20, 1847, estate distributed accordingly, page 209.

McDonald, Timothy, late of Stamford, Mch. 21, 1848, letters of administration on his estate granted to William W. Lounsbury of Stamford, who was ordered to advertise for claims, page 400.
Inventory taken by Jeremiah N. Ayres and Miles Riley, and filed May 29, 1848, page 431.
Nov. 27, 1848, account ordered filed, page 476.

McGown, Francis, of Greenwich, Mch. 21, 1846, general assignment for the benefit of creditors to Joseph Brush of Greenwich, page 130.

STAMFORD PROBATE RECORDS.
Volume 17, 1844.

McGown, Francis, Continued :
>   Inventory taken by Stephen B. Provost and Gilbert Marshall, Jr., and filed June 4, 1846, page 132.
>   Mch. 30, 1846, commissioners appointed to adjust claims of creditors, page 131.
>   June 4, 1847, report of commissioners filed, page 300.

Mathews, Benjamin, of Stamford, May 10, 1847, was appointed guardian of his children Benjamin S., about 19 years of age, James L., about 15 years of age, William H., and Sarah Jane, page 298.

Mathews, Mary L., of Stamford, about 18 years of age, July 27, 1846, made choice of Benjamin Mathews of Stamford to be her guardian, page 205.

Mead, Abraham D., late of Greenwich, will dated Dec. 31, 1844, probated Oct. 27, 1845, mentions Jonas Stafford, Daniel Smith Mead, Isaac Howe Mead, Lyman Mead, Edward Mead, and Augustus Mead. Executor Augustus Mead. Witnesses Jared Mead, and William Allen, page 89.
>   Inventory taken by Henry Bush and Nelson Bush, and filed Dec. 3, 1845, page 132.

Mead, Calvin, late of Greenwich, will dated Jan. 11, 1845, probated July 13, 1847, mentions his children Mary Jane, Lucinda, Thirsa, and Lizetta. Executors sons Leander, Marcus, and Rufus. Witnesses Silas H. Mead, Silas D. Mead, and James L. Palmer, page 318.
>   July 13, 1847, order to advertise for claims, page 319.
>   Inventory taken by Silas H. Mead and Henry Mead, and filed Sept. 9, 1847, page 319.

Mead, Drake, of Greenwich, Mch. 7, 1845, his sons Cornelius, about 16 years of age, and William J., about 12 years of age, made choice of their father said Drake Mead to be their guardian, page 109.

Mead, Ebenezer, late of Greenwich, will dated Aug. 10, 1844, probated Nov. 20, 1844, all to his wife Fanny for life, and remainder to his daughter Deborah Ann. Executors his wife and George Hobby. Witnesses Hugh McKay, Mary Briggs, and Isaac Briggs, page 74.
>   Nov. 20, 1844, order to advertise for claims, page 74.
>   Inventory filed Nov. 30, 1844, page 90.

Mead, Ebenezer, Colonel, late of Greenwich, will dated Nov. 3, 1842, probated Oct. 13, 1845, mentions his wife Eliza-

STAMFORD PROBATE RECORDS.
Volume 17, 1844.

Mead, Ebenezer, Colonel, continued.
 beth, and children Hannah wife of Seely Mead, Almira Mead, Emeline wife of Daniel Krutzer, Zetta wife of Irad C. Day, Rev. Ebenezer Mead, Rev. Enoch Mead, and Theodore H. Mead. Executor son Theodore H. Witnesses James Waring, Robert Clark, and Joseph Ferris, page 75.
 Oct. 15, 1845, order to advertise for claims, page 76.
 Inventory taken by Titus Mead and Jabez Mead, and filed Dec. 6, 1845, page 77.
 Jan. 2, 1847, account ordered filed, page 279.

Mead, Jehiel, late of Greenwich, will dated Jan 19, 1842, probated Nov. 24, 1845, mentions his wife Phebe, and children Harriet wife of Silas H. Mead, and Caleb Hanford Mead. Executor Bartow F. White. Witnesses Isaac Peck, Richard L. Rudd, and Bartow F. White, page 92.
 Nov. 24, 1845, order to advertise for claims, page 93.
 Inventory taken by Isaac Peck and Ard Knapp, and filed Feb. 19, 1846, page 103.
 Feb. 4, 1847, account ordered filed, page 209.

Mead, Mary, late of Greenwich, Apl. 6, 1848, refers to a former distribution of July 20, 1816, recorded in Book XI, page 219, to the heirs of Mary Grigg, deceased, which has never been distributed, that the heirs of Ann Brown, deceased, one of the heirs of said Mary Grigg, applied for a distribution of said tract among the heirs of said Mary Grigg, deceased, viz: Walter Grigg, John Grigg, Elizabeth Grigg, Mary wife of Caleb Husted, Ann Brown, and Lilly Ann Blair, and it was ordered that said tract be distributed among the aforesaid heirs or their assigns, page 407.
 Apl. 14, 1848, 1/3 distributed to the legal representatives of said John Grigg and Ann Brown, now merged in one person, and 2/3 to the legal representatives of Walter Grigg, Elizabeth Grigg, Lilly Ann Blair, and Mary Husted, now merged in one person, page 407.

Mead, Platt, late of Greenwich, will dated July 1, 1837, probated Sept. 20, 1847, mentions his wife Deborah, and children Nathan S., Gideon, Hannah wife of Daniel Peck, and Harriet wife of Bradley Redfield, grandchildren, the children of John Robbins, deceased, viz. Maria M. Robbins, Julia Ann Robbins, Sackett Robbins, William Robbins, and Cornelius Robbins. Executor son Nathan S Witnesses James Willson, Charles A. Hawley, and Charles Hawley, page 342.

STAMFORD PROBATE RECORDS.
Volume 17, 1844.

Mead, Platt, continued :
    Sept. 20, 1847, the executor refused to qualify, and letters granted to Thomas A. Mead of Greenwich, who was ordered to advertise for claims, page 344.
    Inventory taken by Augustus Mead and Nelson Bush, and filed Oct. 4, 1847, page 349.
    Mch. 25, 1848, commissioners appointed to adjust claims of creditors, page 398.
    Sept. 30, 1848, report of commissioners filed, page 469.
    Jan. 20, 1848, personal property ordered sold, page 384.

Mead, Shadrach, late of Greenwich, will dated Jan. 5, 1844, probated Oct. 26, 1844, all to his wife Abigail. Executor William H. Mead of Greenwich. Witnesses Rebecca Ingersoll, Leonard Mead, and Joseph Brush, page 88.
    Oct. 26, 1844, order to advertise for claims, page 88.
    Appeal from probate taken by testator's nephew, Titus Mead of Greenwich, page 89.

Mead, Zaccheus, late of Greenwich, will dated Apl. 15, 1833, probated Jan. 13, 1847, mentions his wife Deborah, and children Elsey wife of Job Mead, Hannah wife of Rev. Mark Mead, grandsons Zaccheus Mead, Jr., and Jonas, and Sylvester sons of Rev. Mark Mead. Executor grandson Zaccheus Mead, Jr. Witnesses Eliza Close, Caroline H. Smith and Abraham H. Close, page 264.
    Jan. 13, 1847, order to advertise for claims, page 266.
    Inventory taken by Augustus Mead and Nelson Bush, and filed Feb. 24, 1847, page 266.

Meeker, Aaron, late of Stamford, Sept. 4, 1847, letters of administration on his estate granted to Lorenzo Meeker of Stamford, who was ordered to advertise for claims, page 337.
    Inventory taken by Samuel Lockwood, Jr., and Sands Seely, and filed Nov. 2, 1847, page 355.

Merritt, John A., of Greenwich, Mch. 31, 1846, the application of his relative Solomon Gurnsey of Greenwich for the appointment of a conservator, page 87.
    Apl. 1846, Thomas A. Mead appointed conservator for said incompetent, page 88.
    Petition for leave to sell the real estate of said incompetent, and sale ordered, page 301.

Merritt, Jotham, late of Rye, Mch. 19, 1848, letters of administration on his estate granted to John A. Merritt of Rye, page 425.

STAMFORD PROBATE RECORDS.
Volume 17, 1844.

Miller, David, late of Stamford, Oct. 28, 1844, letters of
administration on his estate granted to his widow Anna
(Weed) Miller and William B. Weed of Stratford, who were ordered to advertise for claims, page 103.
Inventory taken by Samuel Dean, Jr., and David Waterbury, and copied on page 103.
June 17, 1846, account filed, and estate ordered distributed to his widow and heirs at law, page 193.
June 18, 1846, estate distributed to his widow Anna
Miller, and children Louisa A. Palmer, Edgar G. Miller,
and Harriet A., wife of William B. Weed, page 193.
June 18, 1846, Edgar G. Miller, about 18 years of age,
made choice of William B. Weed of Stratford to be his
guardian, page 197.
July 30, 1846, petition for leave to sell the real estate of said minor in Stamford, page 303.

Mills, Nathaniel, late of Stamford, Nov. 11, 1847, his widow
refused to qualify, and letters of administration on
his estate granted to George J. Smith of Stamford, who
was ordered to advertise for claims, page 361.
Inventory taken by Joseph Smith and Josiah Smith, and
filed Jan. 8, 1848, page 383.
Jan. 17, 1848, necessaries set off to his widow, and
personal property ordered sold, page 384.
Jan. 17, 1848, dower of his widow ordered set out, and
set out Feb. 8, 1848, to Hannah Mills, page 395.
May 12, 1848, account ordered filed, page 425.
May 20, 1848, account filed, and real estate ordered
sold to pay debts, page 436.
Real estate sold to Oliver Lockwood of Stamford, and
report of sale filed June 8, 1848, page 436.

Newman, Catherine, late of Stamford, widow of Zadoc Newman,
will dated Mch. 14, 1844, probated Feb. 9, 1846, mentions her sister Hetty Platt, Ellen Ann Platt and
Catherine Weed daughters of said Hetty Platt, Julia
Ann Palmer and Phebe Palmer daughters of my brother
Lounsbury Palmer, Harriet Emily Scofield daughter of
William Scofield, deceased; Abigail Palmer and Emma
Catherine Palmer daughters of my brother Daniel L. Palmer; Henry Waring and his daughter Clarissa E. Waring;
Clark Sanford Brown, Sally wife of Lyman Lockwood,
Betsy wife of Stephen Lockwood, Gabriel Platt son of
said Hetty Platt, and Dr. Nathaniel D. Haight. Executor Clark Sanford Brown. Witnesses Frederic Lockwood, D. W. Smith, and Charles Hawley, page 93.
Codicil dated Oct. 31, 1845, revoked legacy to Henry
Waring, and bequeathed same to his daughter Clarissa E.

STAMFORD PROBATE RECORDS.
Volume 17, 1844.

Newman, Catherine, continued :
    Waring; revoked legacy to Harriet E. Scofield; Catherine Weed, now deceased, and her share to Ellen Ann Platt, Julia Ann Palmer, and Phebe Palmer, page 95.
    Feb. 9, 1846, order to advertise for claims, page 97.
    Inventory taken by Seth Miller and Joseph Selleck, and filed Apl. 18, 1846, page 98.
    Dec. 12, 1846, account ordered filed, page 210.
    Sept. 23, 1847, account ordered filed, page 345.
    Note. Testatrix was a daughter of Abigail Palmer, and a devisee under her will probated Nov. 27, 1833, at which time she was known as Catherine Shepperd. The said Abigail Palmer was a daughter of Monmouth Lounsbury, who died in 1759.
    Proceedings continued until 1873.

Newman, Edward T., Lucretia T. Newman, and John E. Newman,
    Feb. 3, 1846, their guardian Lucy J. Newman, of New York City, asked leave to sell the real estate of said minors in Stamford, and sale ordered, page 139.
    Real estate sold to John Newman of New York City, and Report of sale filed May 14, 1846, page 139.

Newton Alvin P., late of Stamford, Sept. 10, 1846, letters of administration on his estate granted to Joseph Newton of Stamford, who was ordered to advertise for claims, page 208.
    Inventory taken by J. M. Hall and Isaac Wardwell, and filed Sept. 12, 1846, page 208.

Page, Benjamin, late of Greenwich, will dated May 25, 1843, probated Aug. 15, 1844, mentions his wife Rhoda, and children Benjamin, Aphelia wife of George J. Smith of Stamford, Elizabeth wife of Jotham Merritt of Greenwich, and to his son Joseph E. testator devised a tract of land given him by his father Joseph Page in the Province of Upper Canada. Executor son Benjamin. Witnesses E. Sniffin, Eliza Close, and Samuel Close, page 1.
    Codicil dated Jan. 1, 1844, legacy to his son Joseph, and appointed Samuel Close executor in conjunction with his son Benjamin Page, page 2.
    Aug. 15, 1844, order to advertise for claims, page 3.
    Inventory taken by Henry Rich and Augustus Newman, and filed Dec. 3, 1844, page 3.

Palmer, Delia, Mrs., late of Greenwich, Jan. 27, 1845, letters of administration on her estate granted to Samuel G.

STAMFORD PROBATE RECORDS.
Volume 17, 1844.

Palmer, Delia, continued :
    Cornell of Greenwich, who was ordered to advertise for claims, page 25.
    Inventory taken by Samuel G. Wilson and Elisha Lyon, and filed Feb. 26, 1845, page 26.

Peck, Elias, late of Greenwich, will dated May 4, 1839, probated May 25, 1846, mentions his wife Mary, and children Albert Nathan Peck, William Peck, John Peck, Mary Mead Peck, Harriet Hobby Peck, and Abraham Hobby Peck, and grand son Albert Mead Peck. Executor son Abraham Hobby Peck. Witnesses Peter Ferris, Samuel Jessup, Jr., and Jabez Mead, page 165.
    May 25, 1846, order to advertise for claims, page 166.
    Inventory taken by Jonas Howe and Jeremiah Howe, and filed June 8, 1846, page 174.
    May 25, 1846, testator's grandson, Albert Mead Peck, having died before arriving at the age of 21 years, in which event his legacy was to go Albert Nathan Peck, eldest son of testator, in trust for his benefit, the court thereupon appointed Abraham Hobby Peck of Greenwich to receive said legacy as trustee, page 164.
    May 25, 1847, account ordered filed, page 301.

Peck, John F., late of Greenwich, Oct. 15, 1845, letters of administration on his estate granted to Peter Ferris of Greenwich, who was ordered to advertise for claims, page 143.
    Inventory taken by Joseph D. Ferris and Henry Ritch, and filed Jan. 9, 1846, page 143.

Peck, Mary, late of Greenwich, Oct. 13, 1845, letters of administration on her estate granted to Peter Ferris of Greenwich, who was ordered to advertise for claims, page 128.
    Inventory taken by Joseph D. Ferris and Henry Ritch, and filed July 9, 1846, page 128.
    Sept. 12, 1846, account ordered filed, page 218.

Peck, Solomon, Jr., Aug. 28, 1847, petition of said Solomon Peck, Jr., of Greenwich, for the appointment of commissioners to partition the real estate owned in common by the petitioner, Jeduthan Peck of Greenwich, and Emeline W. Wells of New York City, a minor, and commissioners appointed, page 334.
    Aug. 28, 1847, partition made accordingly, page 335.

STAMFORD PROBATE RECORDS.
Volume 17, 1844.

Pendell, William, late of New York City, will dated Apl. 21, 1845, probated Oct. 21, 1846, all to his wife Elizabeth and appointed her executrix. Witnesses John Woods, John B. Hunter, and Henry U. R. Spencer, page 232.
Oct. 21, 1846, order to advertise for claims, page 233.
Inventory taken by Abel Reynolds and Isaac Lockwood, and filed Apl. 3, 1847, page 234.
May 8, 1847, account ordered filed, page 267.

Perry, Sarah B., of Fairfield, Mch. 4, 1846, her guardian, Julia B. Perry of Fairfield, asked leave to sell the real estate of said minor in Darien, and sale ordered, page 163.
Real estate sold to Peter Waterbury of Darien, and report of sale filed May 18, 1846, page 164.

Platt, Ellen Ann, of Stamford, about 16 years of age, Apl. 9, 1846, made choice of Selleck Scofield of Stamford to be her guardian, page 159.

Platt, John B., late of Stamford, Aug. 20, 1845, letters of administration on his estate granted to Henry Waring of Stamford, who was ordered to advertise for claims, page 51.
Inventory taken by Selleck Scofield and Smith R. Sibley, and filed Oct. 2, 1845, page 51.

Raymond, Daniel S., Mary E. Raymond, Thomas B. Raymond, Richard S. Raymond, and Charles M. Raymond, all of Syracuse, N. Y., July 12, 1843, petition of their guardian, Katherine T. Sackett of Syracuse, N. Y., for leave to sell the interest of said minors in real estate in Greenwich, late of Joseph Sackett, deceased, and real estate ordered sold by Royal L. Gay of Stamford, pages 471 and 472.
Real estate sold to Z. W. Cogswell of Syracuse, N. Y., and report of sale filed Oct. 25, 1848, page 474.

Raymond, Gould S., of Darien, about 16 years of age, June 29, 1846, made choice of Abram Clock of Darien to be his guardian, page 205.

Raymond, Mary, late of Darien, will dated Dec. 30, 1845, probated Mch. 26, 1846, mentions her children Betsy wife of Andrew Bell, Stephen Raymond, Susan Cook, Fanny Lockwood, Sally Selleck, and Delia McGuire, grandsons Charles L. Raymond, Gould Raymond, and James Raymond. Executor son in law Jacob Lockwood. Witnesses Joshua

STAMFORD PROBATE RECORDS.
Volume 17, 1844.

Raymond, Mary, continued:
    B. Ferris, E. W. Walmsley, and Albert Seely, pages 167 and 463.
    Mch. 26, 1846, the executor refused to qualify, and letters granted to Abram Clock of Darien, who was ordered to advertise for claims, page 169.
    Mch. 26, 1846, appeal taken from probate by Andrew Bell of Norwalk, page 169.
    Inventory taken by John Bell, Jr., and William Andreas, and William H. Holly, and filed May 29, 1846, page 170.
    Nov. 13, 1847, account ordered filed, page 362.
    Feb. 3, 1848, account filed, and real estate ordered sold to pay legacies, page 461.

Raymond, Stephen, late of Darien, Apl. 13, 1846, his widow, Mary Raymond, now deceased, and estate ordered distributed according to his will, viz: to his children Sylvanus S., now deceased, Stephen, Betsy Bell, Sally Selleck, Delia Raymond, now McGuire, Susan Carr, now Cook, and Fanny Lockwood, and grandson James K., a son of James Raymond, page 145.
    Apl. 29, 1846, estate distributed accordingly, page 146.

Redfield, Edwin F., about 20 years of age, Sally Redfield, about 18 years of age, Miriam Redfield, about 16 years of age, and Bradley Redfield, about 11 years of age, all of Greenwich, Sept. 20, 1847, Thomas A. Mead of Greenwich appointed their guardian, page 321.

Reed, John B., of Stamford, Jan. 6, 1848, general assignment for the benefit of creditors to Charles H. Leeds of Stamford, page 378.
    Jan. 15, 1848, commissioners appointed to adjust claims of creditors, page 379.
    Jan. 15, 1848, the whole estate ordered sold, page 380.
    Inventory filed Jan. 15, 1848, page 380.
    July 17, 1848, report of commissioners filed, page 466.
    Aug. 2, 1848, account filed, and creditors ordered paid 21 5/10 cents on the dollar, page 468.

Reynolds, Augustus L., late of Greenwich, will dated Dec. 30, 1845, probated Jan. 19, 1846, all to his wife Julia R., and appointed her executrix. Witnesses Nathaniel Briggs, William Ferris, and Hugh McKay, page 71.
    Jan. 19, 1846, order to advertise for claims, page 72.
    Inventory taken by Ard Reynolds and Ephraim Marshall, and filed Feb. 6, 1846, page 72.

STAMFORD PROBATE RECORDS.
Volume 17, 1844.

Ritch, Emma C., of Fremansville, Ohio, over 14 years of age, Sept. 23, 1847, made choice of Joshua B. Ferris of Stamford to be her guardian, who was also appointed guardian of Harriet A. Ritch, Ashley W. Ritch, James H. Ritch, and Henry W. Ritch, all of Fremansville, Ohio, and owning real estate in Greenwich, page 321.
Sept. 23, 1847, petition for leave to sell the real estate of said minors in Greenwich, and sale ordered, pages 381 and 382.

Robins, Mary, late of Greenwich, May 31, 1847, account ordered filed, page 301.

Rogers, Sarah, late of Greenwich, Inventory taken by Nelson Bush and Augustus Mead, and filed Sept. 28, 1844, page 8.

Rosborough, Sarah E., of Stamford, about 19 years of age, May 3, 1847, made choice of Hezekiah Scofield of Stamford to be her guardian, page 262.
June 2, 1847, petition for leave to sell the real estate of said minor in Stamford, page 304.
Aug. 14, 1847, sale ordered, page 325.
Real estate sold to Nancy Lounsbury, and report of sale filed Nov. 5, 1847, page 326.

Rundle, Elizabeth, late of Darien, Feb. 8, 1847, letters of administration on her estate granted to Jonathan Bates of Darien, who was ordered to advertise for claims, page 299.
Inventory taken by Thomas Fowler and Edwin Bates of Darien, and filed Apl. 26, 1847, page 299.
Aug. 21, 1847, commissioners appointed to adjust claims of creditors, page 332.
Feb. 21, 1848, report of commissioners filed, page 389.
Feb. 21, 1848, account ordered filed, page 390.

Rychman, Sally B., late of Stamford, Apl. 17, 1848, letters of administration on her estate granted to Harriet D. Jarvis of Stamford, who was ordered to advertise for claims, page 415.
Nov. 11, 1848, account ordered filed, page 476.

Sarles, Aner, of Stamford, Apl. 1, 1846, appointed guardian of her children James Gordon Sarles and Dewitt Clinton Sarles, page 164.

STAMFORD PROBATE RECORDS.
Volume 17, 1844.

St. John, Abraham W., of Darien, Aug. 25, 1845, appointed
    guardian of his children Mary, about 19 years of age,
    and Benjamin, page 114.

Sarles, James, late of Poundridge, Westchester County, N. Y.,
    will dated June 5, 1840, probated July 28, 1847, men-
    tions his wife 9---, and children William, Amos, heirs
    of son Isaac, deceased, James, Ann Matilda, children
    of daughter Phebe, deceased, Sally, Deborah, Charles,
    Nehemiah, Walter, and Sutton. Executors sons Nehe-
    miah, Walter, Sutton, and Charles. Witnesses Ezra
    Lockwood,&Sally Lockwood, page 323.
    July 28, 1847, letters to Walter Sarles, page 324.

Scofield, Edward H., about 16 years of age, and Juliet Sco-
    field, about 13 years of age, June 17, 1845, made choice
    of William Raymond of Stamford, to be their guardian,
    page 113.

Scofield, Edwin, Jr., of Stamford, Jan. 15, 1847, general
    assignment for the benefit of creditors to William
    Scofield of Stamford, page 239.
    Inventory taken by Sands Seely and Edward A. Quintard,
    and filed Jan. 20, 1847, page 241.
    Jan. 25, 1847, commissioners appointed to adjust claims
    of creditors, page 240.
    July 26, 1847, report of commissioners filed, page 316.
    Sept. 27, 1847, account ordered filed, page 345.
    Oct. 2, 1848, account filed, and creditors ordered
    paid 14 cents and 4 mills on the dollar, page 349.

Scofield, George Warren, of Darien, only heir at law of Dari-
    us K. Scofield, deceased, Sept. 7, 1844, his guardian,
    Sally wife of Charles Mallory of Norwalk, asked leave
    to sell the real estate of said minor in Darien, being
    part of the estate of Gershom Scofield, deceased, sub-
    ject to the dower of said Sally Mallory, formerly the
    widow of Darius K. Scofield, and sale ordered, page 140.
    Real estate sold to Sylvanus Scofield, George Mather,
    and Henry Morehouse, all of Darien, and report of sale
    filed Apl. 9, 1845, page 142.

Scofield, Gershom, late of Darien, Mch. 19, 1845, estate or-
    dered distributed according to his will recorded in
    Book 13, page 99, to George Warren Scofield, only heir
    at law of Darius K. Scofield, deceased, son of testa-
    tor 1/2, page 41.
    Apl. 2, 1845, 1/2 of said estate distributed to said
    George Warren Scofield, a minor, subject to an encum-

STAMFORD PROBATE RECORDS.
Volume 17, 1844.

Scofield, Gershom, continued :
brance in favor of the owners of the other 1/2 of said premises, who seem to be Lydia Waring, Sally B. Palmer, and Mary Elizabeth Richards, granddaughters of testator, page 42.

Scofield, Gilbert, late of Stamford, will dated Feb. 10, 1846, Probated Aug. 9, 1847, mentions his wife Abigail, and children Levi, Ashbel, John, Seth, Henry W., Betsy, Abigail, and Ebenezer C. Executor son Ashbel. Witnesses Frederic S. Klopfer, Lester Scofield, and Hannah W. Klopfer, page 327.
Codicil dated Dec. 7, 1846, page 327.
Aug. 9, 1847, order to advertise for claims, page 328.
Inventory taken by Harris Scofield and Luther S. Scofield, and filed Oct. 16, 1847, page 350.

Scofield, Hannah, late of Stamford, Oct. 29, 1846, letters of administration on her estate granted to Richard Fox of Stamford, who was ordered to advertise for claims, page 291.
Inventory taken by Peter Lockwood and Harvey Lockwood, and filed May 15, 1847, page 291.
May 15, 1847, account ordered filed, page 292.
May 22, 1847, account filed, and real estate ordered sold to pay debts, page 292.
Real estate sold to Lucretia Scofield of Stamford, and report of sale filed June 1, 1847, page 293.

Scofield, John Avery, late of Darien, Dec. 8, 1845, letters of administration on his estate granted to William Andreas of Darien, who was ordered to advertise for claims, page 101.
Inventory taken by Holly Bell and Noah B. Weed, and filed Jan. 22, 1846, page 101.

Scofield, Rufus, Samuel W. Scofield, and Edwin L. Scofield, Mch. 28, 1844, their guardian, Samuel W. Scofield of New York City, asked leave to sell the real estate of said minors in Darien, being part of the estate of Gershom Scofield, late of Darien, deceased, and sale ordered, page 125.
Real estate sold to Edwin Scofield of Darien, and report of sale filed Nov. 1844, page 125.

Scofield, Warren, late of Stamford, inventory taken by Richard Fox and Hezekiah Scofield, and filed Aug. 24, 1844, by Amzi Scofield, administrator, page 26.

STAMFORD PROBATE RECORDS.
Volume 17, 1844.

Seely, Albert, of Stamford, Mch. 4, 1846, general assignment
    for the benefit of creditors to Royal L. Gay, Seth
    Miller, and Sands Seely of Stamford, page 156.
    Inventory taken by Stephen B. Provost and Jonathan M.
    Hall, and filed Mch. 11, 1846, page 158.
    Mch. 16, 1846, commissioners appointed to adjust claims
    of creditors, page 158.
    Oct. 31, 1846, report of commissioners filed, page 259.
    Dec. 8, 1846, account ordered filed, page 260.
    July 24, 1847, account filed, and creditors ordered
    paid 50 cents on the dollar, page 322.

Selleck, Ann, of Darien, Apl. 16, 1845, the application of
    her brother, Epenetus W. Walmsley of Darien, for the
    appointment of a conservator, page 39.
    May 5, 1845, Epenetus W. Walmsley appointed her con-
    servator, page 40.
    May 10, 1845, inventory taken by Epenetus W. Walmsley,
    conversator, and filed May 24, 1845, page 73.

Selleck, Joseph, late of Stamford, will dated Sept. 15, 1837,
    probated Mch. 25, 1846, mentions his wife Phebe, and
    children John, Polly Bell, Hannah wife of Luther Knapp,
    Joseph, and Isaac, and the children of my deceased son
    Jesse. Executors sons Joseph and Isaac. Witnesses
    Jonathan Buxton, Charles A. Hawley, and Charles Haw-
    ley, page 118.
    Codicil dated Dec. 14, 1838, Isaac's share in fee,
    page 119.
    Mch. 23, 1846, order to advertise for claims, page 120.
    Inventory taken by Henry Waring and Seth Miller, and
    filed May 14, 1846, page 121.
    Feb. 20, 1847, account ordered filed, page 264.

Selleck, Kilbourn, late of Darien, will dated June 22, 1845,
    probated July 22, 1845, mentions his wife Mary, and son
    William E. Executor Albert Seely of Stamford. Wit-
    nesses Warren Percival, Albert Seely, and William H.
    Holly, page 184.
    July 22, 1845, order to advertise for claims, page 185.
    Inventory taken by E. W. Walmsley and Stephen Raymond,
    and filed Dec. 31, 1845, page 186.

Sherwood, Nehemiah, late of Greenwich, will dated June 29,
    1833, probated Aug. 19, 1844, mentions his wife Phoebe,
    and children Calvin, Jotham, James Harvey, Betsy, Ab-
    by Jane, and Phoebe, and grandson Bishop Asbury Sher-
    wood. Executors son Jotham and Thomas Carpenter.
    Witnesses Daniel G. Scott, Samuel C. Brown, and Charles

STAMFORD PROBATE RECORDS.
Volume 17, 1844.

Sherwood, Nehemiah, continued :
    Hawley, page 9.
    Aug. 19, 1844, order to advertise for claims, page 11.
    Inventory taken by Purdy Anderson and Silas Brundage, and filed Oct. 16, 1844, page 11.

Sherwood, William B., late of Greenwich, Apl. 12, 1845, letters of administration on his estate granted to John S. Sherwood of Danbury, Nathan S. Mead of Greenwich, and Lucy A. Sherwood of Greenwich, widow of deceased, who were ordered to advertise for claims, page 66.
    Inventory taken by Zaccheus Mead, Jr., and Jabez Mead, Jr., and filed June 3, 1845, page 66.
    May 7, 1845, commissioners appointed to adjust claims of creditors, page 66.
    May 4, 1846, report of commissioners filed, page 67.
    May 4, 1846, account filed, and creditors ordered paid 3 5/10 cents on the dollar, page 68.

Sibley, Richard, late of Stamford, will dated May 18, 1811, probated Oct. 6, 1845, mentions his wife Mary, and children Betsy wife of Oliver Weed, and Smith R. Executor son Smith R. Witnesses Joel Waring, William Waring, and Reuben Scofield, page 152.

Slauson, Nancy, late of Darien, will dated Jan. 16, 1843, probated May 25, 1848, mentions her daughters Sarah Waterbury, Catherine Clock, Rebecca Lockwood, Mary Scofield, Hannah Elizabeth Holmes, and Nancy Jane Slauson. Executor son John Holmes. Witnesses Abram Clock, Hannah Clock, and Ann Lockwood, page 429.
    May 25, 1848, order to advertise for claims, page 430.
    Inventory taken by George J. Bowler and Ira Scofield, and filed June 24, 1848, page 453.

Smith, Arba, late of Greenwich, Jan. 19, 1846, Augustus L. Reynolds, administrator, now deceased, and William Smith of Greenwich appointed in his place, page 153.
    July 20, 1846, ordered that the sale of his real estate to Jared Smith be confirmed, and that William Smith, administrator de bonus non, execute the deed therefore, pages 200 and 201.
    Nov. 20, 1846, report of the execution of the aforesaid deed, page 202.
    Dec. 14, 1846, account ordered filed, page 202.

Smith, Daniel, Rev., late of Stamford, will dated July 16, 1828, probated June 15, 1845, mentions his wife Catherine, and children Julia Ann North, and Thomas M.

STAMFORD PROBATE RECORDS.
Volume 17, 1844

Smith, Daniel, Rev., continued :
    Executrix his wife. Witnesses Alexander Hendrie,
    Daniel G. Scott, and Charles Hawley, page 189.
    June 15, 1845, executrix refused to qualify, and letters
    granted to David W. Smith, son of testator, who was or-
    dered to advertise for claims, page 189.
    Inventory taken by Stephen B. Provost and Smith Scott,
    and filed June 16, 1846, page 191.

Smith, David, late of Stamford, May 18, 1842, estate distribu-
    ted to his heirs, viz: Sally Smith, Joseph Smith, Elizax
    Elizabeth a daughter of Benjamin Smith, Levina wife of
    Henry White, and Mary C. Smith, page 68.

Smith, Hezekiah P., of New Rochelle, N. Y., about 16 years of
    age, May 14, 1846, made choice of John Taffy of New
    Rochelle to be his guardian, page 114.

Smith, Joseph, Jr., late of Stamford, will dated Mch. 4, 1848,
    probated Apl. 22, 1848, mentions his wife Sarah, and
    son Charles I. Executrix his wife. Witnesses Alfred
    Smith, Henry H. Roscoe, and Hugh Mackay, page 413.
    Apl. 22, 1848, order to advertise for claims, page 414.
    Inventory taken by Nelson W. Smith and George W. Hub-
    bard, and filed June 22, 1848, page 452.

Studwell, Luther H., late of Greenwich, Apl. 11, 1846, his
    widow refused to qualify, and letters of administration
    on his estate granted to Walter Sarles of Stamford, who
    was ordered to advertise for claims, page 159.
    Oct. 5, 1846, account filed, and commissioners appoint-
    ed to adjust claims of creditors, page 280.
    Apl. 19, 1847, report of commissioners filed, page 280.
    Aug. 30, 1847, account filed, and real estate ordered
    sold to pay debts, page 337.
    Aug. 26, 1847, report of commissioners, filed, page 332.
    Oct. 15, 1847, account ordered filed, page 350.
    Nov. 9, 1847, account filed, and creditors ordered
    paid 25 cents on the dollar, page 359.

Sutherland, Silas, late of North Castle, May 24, 1847, letters
    of administration on his estate granted to his son Si-
    las Sutherland, who was ordered to advertise for
    claims, page 306.
    Inventory taken by David B. Peck and John Lawrence,
    and filed June 19, 1847, page 309.

STAMFORD PROBATE RECORDS.
Volume 17, 1844.

Sutton, William, late of Greenwich, will dated 1st month, 24th day, 1845, probated Apl. 1, 1845, mentions his children Thomas C., Allen, Phebe, Mary wife of Isaac Underhill, and Elizabeth; the children of my son John Sutton, deceased, viz: John Thomas, Elizabeth C., Phila Rebecca, Cabrilla now called Mary, Janet, and William Henry Harrison Sutton; and William son of Allen Sutton. Executors Son Allen and James Field. Witnesses Thomas Sutton, Tompkins Washburn, and Joseph Field, page 104.
Apl. 1, 1845, order to advertise for claims, page 105.
Inventory taken by Edmund Field and James Wilson, and filed Apl. 7, 1845, page 105.
June 5, 1848, his estate partitioned between his children, viz: Mary wife of Isaac Q. Underhill, Thomas C. Sutton, Elizabeth P. Sutton, Phebe C. Sutton, Alice Sutton, and Allen Sutton, and legacies to the children of his son John, deceased, and William the son of Allen Sutton, page 444.

Tuthill, Morris, late of Darien, Jan. 31, 1848, letters of administration on his estate granted to his widow, Catherine Tuthill of Darien, who was ordered to advertise for claims, page 385.
Inventory taken by George J. Bowler and John J. Bell, and filed Mch. 30, 1848, page 398.
Aug. 12, 1848, commissioners appointed to adjust claims of creditors, pages 459 and 460.
Aug. 17, 1848, necessaries set off to his widow, page 460.

Walmsley, George, of Darien, Apl. 18, 1846, the application of his brother, Epenetus W. Walmsley of Darien, for the appointment of a conservator, page 110.
May 4, 1846, Ezra H. Bishop appointed such conservator, page 111.
Jan. 7, 1848, Ezra H. Bishop his conservator discharged, page 376.

Waring, George E., of Stamford, Feb. 16, 1847, general assignment for the benefit of creditors to Joseph D. Warren, page 253.
Inventory taken by William G. Baker and John V. Harms, and filed Mch. 15, 1847, page 256.
Mch. 10, 1847, commissioners appointed to adjust claims of creditors, page 256.
Sept. 17, 1847, report of commissioners filed, page 329.
Mch. 15, and 17, orders to sell the real and personal property, page 259.

STAMFORD PROBATE RECORDS.
Volume 17, 1844.

Waring, James, late of Greenwich, will dated June 1, 1844, probated June 12, 1847, mentions his wife Betsy, and children James D., Hannah Maria wife of Joseph D. Ferris, Stephen H., Henry, Susan wife of Silas Scofield, Mary W., Ann E. Selleck, Sarah E., Isaac, and Joseph F. Executors Joseph Brush and son in law Joseph D. Ferris. Witnesses Edwin Scofield, Jr., Sally H. Ferris, and Joshua B. Ferris, page 305.
June 12, 1847, Joseph Brush refused to qualify, and letters granted to Joseph D. Ferris, who was ordered to advertise for claims, page 306.
Inventory taken by Henry Ritch and Joseph Brush, and filed June 19, 1847, page 308.
Feb. 11, 1848, account ordered filed, page 388.

Waring, Joel, late of Stamford, will dated Aug. 26, 1839, probated Sept. 9, 1846, mentions his wife Mary, daughter Maria Scofield, son in law Selleck Scofield, and Mary Louisa Lounsbury a daughter of George Lounsbury. Executors son in law Selleck Scofield, and George Lounsbury. Witnesses Smith R. Sibley, Frederick B. Scofield, and Charles E. Husted, page 221.
Sept. 9, 1846, order to advertise for claims, page 222.

Waring, Stephen, late of Greenwich, Sept. 9, 1844, creditors ordered paid the further sum of two cents on the dollar, page 50.

Waterbury, Isaac, late of Darien, Nov. 26, 1840, estate distributed to his widow Mary Waterbury, and children Fanny Waterbury, Mary Waterbury, Julia Ann Waterbury, Peter L. Waterbury, Nancy wife of George R. Stevens, heirs of Sarah Bacon, deceased, Isaac N. Waterbury, John William Waterbury, heirs of George Waterbury, deceased, and David Waterbury, page 45.

Waterbury, Israel, late of Stamford, Mch. 20, 1848, letters of administration on his estate granted to Edwin S. Holly of Stamford, who was ordered to advertise for claims, page 396.
Inventory taken by Benjamin Scofield and William Newman, and filed Mch. 30, 1848, page 399.

Webb, Albert, late of Stamford, Nov. 11, 1845, letters of administration on his estate granted to Samuel C. Brown of Stamford, who was ordered to advertise for claims, page 194.
Inventory taken by Seth Miller and James H. Trowbridge, and filed Nov. 11, 1845, page 194.

STAMFORD PROBATE RECORDS.
Volume 17, 1844.

Webb, Albert, continued:
Nov. 17, 1845, commissioners appointed to adjust the claims of creditors, page 196.
June 1, 1846, account filed, and real estate ordered sold to pay debts, page 197.
Real estate sold to Catherine Leveridge, and report of sale filed June 19, 1846, page 197.

Webb, Alfred, late of Stamford, Sept. 7, 1844, his widow refused to qualify, and letters of administration on his estate granted to Ezra H. Bishop of Darien, who was ordered to advertise for claims, page 31.
Inventory taken by Joseph Hoyt and Nathaniel A. Bouton, and filed Oct. 30, 1844, page 32.
Nov. 24, 1845, account filed, and real estate ordered sold to pay debts, page 175. Stamford
Real estate sold to Sarah Webb of Stamford, and report of sale filed June 9, 1846, page 175.

Webb, Elizabeth A., of Norfolk County, Va., Mch. 17, 1842, her guardian, John B. Webb of New York City, asked leave to sell the real estate of said minor in Stamford and sale ordered, page 77.
Real estate sold to Charles H. Webb, and report of sale filed June 13, 1842, page 78.

Webb, Joseph H., of Stamford, Jan. 5, 1848, petition of his brother, David Webb of Lewisboro, Westchester County, N. Y., for the appointment of a conservator for said alleged incompetent, page 419.
Mch. 25, 1848, Samuel Lockwood of Stamford appointed such conservator, page 420.

Webb, Naomi, of Stamford, Mch. 20, 1845, appointed guardian of her children Hannah Maria Webb, about 17 years of age, Josephine Webb, about 14 years of age, Sarah Rebecca Webb, about 12 years of age, and Frances Webb, about 10 years of age, page 34.
Mch. 20, 1845, petition for leave to sell the real estate of said minors in Stamford, and sale ordered page 40.
Real estate sold to Theodore Waterbury of Stamford, and report of sale filed June 2, 1845, page 34.

Weed, Benjamin, late of Darien, will dated Mch. 8, 1844, probated Jan. 19, 1846, mentions his wife Hannah, and children Rebecca, James Harvey, deceased, Isaac, Alvah, deceased, Louisa, deceased, Rufus, Benjamin, and Sarah, and granddaughter Mary Foster. Executor son Isaac.

STAMFORD PROBATE RECORDS.
Volume 17, 1844.

Weed, Benjamin, continued :
witnesses Bernard Keogh, Julia E. Hoyt, and James A.
Shaw, page 81.
Jan. 19, 1846, order to advertise for claims, page 83.
Inventory taken by John Bell Jr., and Abram Clock, and
filed Apl. 29, 1846, page 83.
June 30, 1847, account ordered filed, page 311.
July 3, 1847, his estate ordered distributed to his
widow, Hannah Weed, and children, viz: heirs of Alvah,
deceased, heirs of Louisa, deceased, John, Isaac, Rufus, Benjamin, Sarah, and Rebecca, page 437.
June 5, 1848, estate distributed accordingly, page 437.

Weed, James Rufus, about 20 years of age, having no father or
Mother, Nov. 29, 1844, the court appointed Abigail
Weed of Darien to be his guardian, page 113.

Weed, Luther, late of Stamford, Mch. 11, 1848, his widow refused to qualify, and letters of administration on his
estate granted to George Weed and William Weed, both
of Stamford, who were ordered to advertise for claims,
page 390.
Inventory taken by John L. Tallmadge and Joseph Scofield, and filed May 6, 1848, page 417.
Sept. 11, 1848, account ordered filed, page 468.

Weed, Mary, late of Poundridge, Nov. 13, 1845, inventory taken by Peter Lockwood and Darius Stevens, and filed Mch.
27, 1847, by Ezra Lockwood, administrator, page 143.
June 1, 1846, account filed, and real estate ordered
sold to pay debts, page 144.
Real estate sold to John Dean of Stamford, and report
of sale filed June 1, 1846, page 145.

Weed, Mary, late of Darien, July 3, 1847, her estate ordered
distributed to her heirs at law, page 441.
June 5, 1848, estate distributed to the legal representatives of Alvah Weed, deceased, legal representatives of Louisa, the deceased wife of Joseph Weed, legal representatives of Harvey Weed, deceased, legal rx
representatives of Polly, the deceased wife of Selleck
Howe, Sarah wife of John Waterbury, Rebecca Weed, a
daughter of deceased, Rufus Weed, Isaac Weed, and
John Weed, to each a ninth part, page 442.

Weed, Samuel, late of Stamford, Jan. 11, 1842, account filed,
and estate ordered distributed to his heirs at law, viz
to the children of Nathan S. Weed, a deceased son,

STAMFORD PROBATE RECORDS.
Volume 17, 1844.

Weed, Samuel, continued :
 Sally wife of Samuel Scofield, a daughter, and to Mary
 Eliza wife of Cary Wilmot, a daughter, page 450.
 Estate distributed accordingly, and distribution bill
 recorded May 29, 1848, page 450.

Weed, Sarah E., late of Stamford, Apl. 30, 1845, letters of
 administration on her estate granted to Robert M.
 Weed of West Suffield, Conn., who was ordered to advertise for claims, page 115. (115)

Weed, Selleck, late of Darien, May 24, 1841, estate ordered
 distributed according to his will, viz: to Abram Clock
 in trust 1/2, and the remaining 1/2 to Elizabeth Deal,
 a daughter of testator for life, page 116.
 Mch. 1, 1845, estate distributed accordingly, page 116.

Weed, William, of Poundridge, May 25, 1846, appointed guardian
 of his children Catherine Weed, and John Platt Weed,
 page 164.

Wells, Emeline W., of New York City, Jan. 9, 1847, petition
 of her guardian, Gilbert Hopkins of New York City, for
 leave to sell the real estate of said minor in Greenwich, page 303.
 Oct. 26, 1846, the court appointed Gilbert Hopkins of
 New York City, guardian of Emeline W. Wells, a-bout
 8 years of age, of New York City, a daughter of Emeline Wells, page 206.

White, Jacob, of Stamford, July 19, 1847, the court appointed
 Abel Reynolds of Stamford guardian of Abel R. White,
 about 16 years of age, a son of said Jacob White,
 page 311.

Wilmot, William, late of Darien, will dated Nov. 6, 1841, pro-
 bated Sept. 9, 1847, all to his wife Polly, and appoin-
 ted her executrix. Witnesses Abram Clock, George J.
 Bowler, and Edwin Finch, page 339.
 Sept. 9, 1847, order to advertise for claims, page 339.
 Inventory taken by Abram Clock and George J. Bowler,
 and filed Oct. 29, 1847, page 352.
 June 2, 1848, account ordered filed, page 431.

Wilson, Rachel, late of Greenwich, Sept. 4, 1847, letters of
 administration on her estate granted to Samuel Close
 of Greenwich, who was ordered to advertise for claims,
 page 338.

STAMFORD PROBATE RECORDS.
Volume 17, 1844.

Wolcott, Alexander S., late of Stamford, Nov. 13, 1844, his
    widow refused to qualify, and letters of administration
    on his estate granted to George W. Waring of Stamford,
    and Richard E. Patterson of New York City, who were
    ordered to advertise for claims, page 13.
    Inventory taken by Joseph D. Warren and James B. Sco-
    field, and filed Dec. 30, 1844, page 13.
    Dec. 15, 1845, account ordered filed, page 14 1/2.

Wolcott, Cynthia L., of New York City, about 13 years of age,
    Aug. 2, 1847, the court appointed Humphrey Phelps of
    New York City to be her guardian, page 324.

Wyant, Sarah, of Stamford, Mch. 17, 1846, the application of
    her brother, Henry Waring of Stamford, for the appoint-
    ment of a conservator, page 85.
    Mch. 30, 1846, Floyd T. Palmer appointed such conser-
    vator, page 86.
    Nov. 24, 1846, petition for leave to sell the real
    estate of said incompetent, and sale ordered, page 294.
    Real estate sold to Isaac Lockwood, Jr., of Stamford,
    and report of sale filed Dec. 30, 1846, page 295.

STAMFORD PROBATE RECORDS.
Miscellaneous papers not copied.
Jan. 1, 1803, to Dec. 31, 1850.

All papers in the files marked "Recorded with the Book and page", are presumed to have been recorded, although some of them may not have been copied.

Anderson, Matthias, late of Greenwich, Mch. 23, 1814, real estate sold to Isaac Howe of Greenwich pursuant to order of Nov. 2, 1813.

Andreas, Jeremiah, Jan. 6, 1838, antenuptial agreement with the widow Cynthia Hawley.

Andreas, Jeremiah J., of San Francisco, about 20 years of age, and Cordelia E. Andreas of New York City, about 17 years of age, Aug. 9, 1852, bond of their guardian William E. Sibell.

Bates, John, and Hester L. Wardwell, both of Darien, Oct. 16, 1837, antenuptial agreement.

Bates, Mary, late of Darien, will dated Apl. 3, 1833, not probated, mentions her sister Sarah Bates, and Mary wife of Charles Weed. Executor Charles Weed, Jr., of Darien. Witnesses Thaddeus Bell, Abigail Bell and Holly Bell.

Bayeux, Thomas, Dr., late of Greenwich, Sept. 5, 1811, Sally Bayeux, a daughter of decedent, about 15 years of age, made choice of Epenetus Lockwood to be her guardian.

Bell, Isaac, late of Stamford, will recorded in Book 15, page 488, but see affidavit of Mary L. Bell, and Charity E., wife of Zophar W. Horton, all of Stamford, only heirs at law of the aforesaid Isaac Bell, deceased, dated Sept. 13, 1894, and recorded in Book 39, page 583.

STAMFORD PROBATE RECORDS.
Miscellaneous papers not copied.

Bell, Prudence, late of Stamford, will dated May 26, 1843, probate refused, all to her two sisters Mary wife of Harry Webb, and Sarah wife of James Sniffin, and niece Mary Miller a daughter of said James Sniffin. Executor Harry Webb. Witnesses N. D. Haight, Charles Brown, and Phebe Haight.

Bishop, Andrew, about 15 years of age, Sept. 5, 1814, bond of Joseph P. Cook, Jr., of Danbury, guardian of said Andrew Bishop, a son of Hannah Cook, wife of said Joseph P. Cook, Jr.

Bishop, Rufus, about 13 years of age, of Stamford, Dec. 26, 1803, bond of his guardian William Bishop of Stamford.

Bostwick, Samuel, late of Bedford, Feb. 19, 1807, bond of Daniel Bostwick of Greenwich, guardian of Isaac Bostwick, about 16 years of age, a son of decedent. Sept. 3, 1811, bond of Alexander Lockwood of Stamford, guardian of Caleb Bostwick, a son of decedent.

Brown, Charles, about 17 years of age, of Stamford, Feb. 6, 1805, bond of his guardian David Nash of Stamford.

Brown, Henry, late of Stamford, Mch. 9, 1842, his widow refused to qualify, and letters of administration on his estate granted to Ezra Lockwood of Stamford, who was ordered to advertise for claims.

Brown, James, late of Greenwich, will dated Mch. 22, 1813, probate refused, Apl. 17, 1813, mentions his wife Anne, and children James, Robert, David, Josiah, Mary Lockwood, Abigail Hubbard, Hannah Kinch, grandchildren Nehemiah Brown, a son of Robert Brown, and Maria Brown, a daughter of David Brown. Executor Abraham Close.

Brown, John, late of Darien, will dated Apl. 13, 1824, not probated, all to his wife Rebecca, and appointed her executrix. Witnesses John Weed, Jr., Abigail Whiting, and Mary Whiting.

Brown, Martha, an incompetent, Dec. 8, 1847, account of her conservator, Epenetus W. Nichols, settled.

Brush, Shubal, late of Greenwich, June 4, 1811, bond of Benjamin Brush, Jr., of Greenwich, guardian of Mary, Christina, and Elizabeth, children of decedent.

STAMFORD PROBATE RECORDS.
Miscellaneous papers not copied.

Bunnell, Jonathan, late of Greenwich, June 12, 1848, estate ordered distributed to his widow, Sabrina Bunnell, and children George T., Eliza J. wife of Lorenzo Tuttle, Sabrina wife of William Bowen, Susan E., John H., Pierre U., Goveneur M., William A., Jane A., and Charlotte A.

Burton, Samuel, late of Greenwich, Sept. 9, 1812, bond of William Davenport of Stamford, guardian of Hervey Burton, about 17 years of age, William Burton, about 11 years of age, and Harriet Burton, about 9 years of age, children of decedent.

Clason, David, late of Bedford, Mch. 31, 1812, bond of Reuben Clason of Bedford, guardian of Daniel Clason, about 15 years of age, a son of decedent.

Comstock, Samuel, late of ----, Nov. 8, 1803, bond of Elsey Comstock of Stamford, guardian of Stephen Comstock, about 17 years of age.

Crab, Jonathan, about 19 years of age, of Stamford, Oct. 6, 1812, bond of his guardian John C. Crab of Stamford.

Crennell, Abigail J., late of Stamford, inventory taken Nov. 22, 1803, by David Maltbie and Joseph Bishop, and filed Nov. 22, 1803.
Nov. 22, 1803, bond of Samuel Webb of Stamford, guardian of Abigail Jane, about four months of age, a daughter of decedent.

Demorest, Samuel, Jr., of Warwick, N. Y., Jan. 24, 1840, appointed guardian by the Probate Court, Orange County, N. Y., of his daughter Sarah Maria Demorest, 18 years of age, and heir at law of her great uncle Frederick Lockwood.

Denton, Aaron, Mch. 12, 1803, bond of David Mead, of Greenwich, guardian of Evert Denton, about 15 years of age, a son of decedent.

Ferriss, Isaac, late of New York City, Jan. 5, 1808, bond of Edmond Scofield of Stamford, guardian of Isaac Ferris, about 14 years of age, a son of decedent.

Ferris, Sarah, late of Stamford, will dated June 14, 1819, not probated, bequests to the children of my daughter Sibyl Finch, to Eliza Amanda a daughter of Edward and Sibyl Finch, to Sibyl Amanda a daughter of John and

STAMFORD PROBATE RECORDS.
Miscellaneous papers not copied.

Ferris, Sarah, continued :
    Sally Finch, and to daughter Sally Finch. Executor
    Abel Reynolds of Stamford. Witnesses Joseph Smith,
    3rd, Samuel W. Dean, and Samuel Webb.

Gilman, Evans, late of Stamford, July 10, 1803, bond of Hannah Gilman of Stamford, guardian of Peggy Gilman, about 11 years of age, a daughter of decedent.

Grigg, Alexander, late of Greenwich, Feb. 15, 1806, bond of Richard Mead of Greenwich, guardian of John Grigg, about 15 years of age, and Walter Grigg, about 10 years of age, children of decedent.
    June 7, 1813, bond of Caleb Husted of Greenwich, guardian of David A. Grigg, about 16 years of age, a son of decedent.

Grigg, David, late of Greenwich, Apl. 27, 1805, account filed, and real estate ordered sold to pay debts.

Hait, Jesse, late of Stamford, July 19, 1806, dower of his widow, Lucy Ann Hait, set out.

Hobby, Deborah, late of Greenwich, widow of Jonathan Hobby, deceased, will dated Oct. 6, 1802, not probated, legacies to Sarah Reynolds a daughter of Joel Reynolds, to my daughters Abigail wife of Elijah Mead, and Elizabeth widow of Stephen Mead, deceased, grandsons Alfred and Harvey sons of David Hobby, deceased. Executor Benjamin Brush of Greenwich. Witnesses Silvanus Howe, and James Brush.

Holly, Elijah, late of Stamford, Feb. 16, 1807, bond of Hanford Hoyt, administrator.

Holly, Elizabeth, late of Stamford, will dated May 2, 1811, not probated, estate to her sister Mercy Holly for life and remainder to the Town of New Canaan for the benefit of the poor. Executor Joseph Silliman of New Canaan. Witnesses Ebenezer Ferris, Abigail Ferris, and Joseph Wood.

Hopson, Samuel, about 18 years of age, of Greenwich, Feb. 4, 1812, bond of his guardian David Wood of Greenwich.

How, Jacob, late of Stamford, inventory taken Apl. 12, 1804, by Isaac Pencyer and Nathan Weed.
    Mch. 27, 1805, Elizabeth How, widow of decedent, ap-

STAMFORD PROBATE RECORDS.
Miscellaneous papers not copied.

How, Jacob, continued :
    pointed guardian of Sally How, about 17 years of age, a daughter of decedent.

Hoyt, Enoch, late of Stamford, will dated Jan. 6, 1810, probate refused, mentions his wife Sally a daughter of Daniel Smith, and children Calvin, Nelson, Mariah E. Mary Elizabeth, Sarah A., and Mehitable. Executor William White of Stamford. Witnesses Henry Curtis, Eliza Smith, and Joseph Silliman.

Hoyt, James, late of Stamford, will dated May 14, 1832, not probated, all to his wife, Sarah Hoyt, for life, and remainder to son Rufus Hoyt, Jr., and daughter Sarah W. Leeds. Executor son Rufus. Witnesses S. H. Minor, Jonathan Jessup, and William Newman.

Hoyt, Joel, late of Stamford, or Greenwich, May 5, 1807, bond of Abigail Hoyt of Greenwich or Stamford, widow of deceased, guardian of Freeman Hoyt, about 12 years of age and Mehitable Hoyt, about 16 years of age, children of decedent.

Hoyt, John, Jr., and Rebecca Jeffrey, both of Stamford, Nov. 10, 1797, antenuptial agreement.

Hoyt, Jonathan, late of Stamford, Oct. 10, 1803, estate distributed to his widow, Mary Hoyt, and to his heirs Prudence Hoyt, Phebe Whitney, and Abigail Michel.

Hoyt, Peter, of Stamford, an incompetent, Aug. 15, 1845, account of his conservator, Royal L. Gay, filed.

Hoyt, Samuel, late of Darien, will without date, and without probate, 1814, mentions his wife Betsy, and children Rufus, Samuel, Seymour, and Ann S. Tilman; grandson John R. Hoyt, and granddaughters Mary, Catherine, and Elizabeth Tilman; and John H. Tilman.

Hoyt, Uriah, late of Stamford, Apl. 20, 1811, bond of Aaron Comstock of New Canaan, guardian of Samuel Hoyt, about 14 years of age, a son of decedent.

Husted, Ruth, late of Greenwich, widow of Nathaniel Husted, deceased, will dated Jan. 29, 1835, not probated, mentions her children Polly Husted, Benjamin Husted, and Jonathan Husted. Executor son Nathaniel Husted. Witnesses Benjamin Husted, 3rd, William Kinch, and Samuel Close.

STAMFORD PROBATE RECORDS.
Miscellaneous papers not copied.

Ireland, Job, late of Greenwich, Mch. 10, 1810, estate ordered distributed to Job Ireland, a son of Abraham Ireland and to Levi Ireland, a son of Gilbert Ireland, according to his will.

Jessup, Joram, late of Stamford, Aug. 17, 1820, bond of Sarah Jessup of New York City, guardian of Samuel Jessup, about 15 years of age, a son of decedent.

Jones, Josiah, late of Stamford, Apl. 10, 1809, bond of Enoch Stevens, guardian of Isaac Jones, about 15 years of age, a son of decedent.

June, Joshua, late of Freehold, Green County, N. Y., Apl. 11, 1805, inventory filed by Solomon Clason, administrator. June 9, 1804, report of commissioners to adjust claims of creditors filed.

Knapp, Gideon, late of Stamford, appeal from decree of Sept. 3, 1806, admitting will of testator to probate, and probate of will set aside. (Book 10, page 288)
Dec. 1807, probate of will affirmed on rehearing.
Feb. 5, 1808, letters of administration granted to Hezekiah Knapp.
Inventory taken by Robert Scofield and Jeremiah Andreas and filed Apl. 19, 1807.
Apl. 28, 1807, estate ordered distributed to Silvanus, Epenetus, and Hezekiah, brothers of deceased, Hannah Lockwood, widow, and Sarah Mead, widow, sisters of deceased; to the legal representatives of Charles Knapp, a deceased brother; and to the legal representatives of Bethia Knapp, a deceased sister.
May 1, 1807, estate distributed accordingly.

Knapp, Jonathan, late of Greenwich, Sept. 1, 1812, bond of Abigail Sutherland, guardian of William, about 20 years of age, Isaac, about 18 years of age, and Susannah, about 17 years of age, children of decedent.

Knapp, Joshua, late of Stamford, June 15, 1813, bond of Peter Knapp, guardian of Israel Knapp, a son of decedent.

Knapp, Silas, late of Washington, Dutchess County, N. Y., Aug. 27, 1811, bond of Anna Knapp, widow of deceased, guardian of Silas, about 6 years of age, and Esther Maria, about 4 years of age, children of decedent, heirs of Abigail Knapp, late of Greenwich.

STAMFORD PROBATE RECORDS.
Miscellaneous papers not copied.

Lane, John, late of Greenwich, will dated Oct. 30, 1830, not probated, all to his wife, Hannah, and appointed her his executrix. Witnesses Jabez Mead, John Horton, and Joshua Ferris.
Oct. 11, 1850, bond of Benjamin Page, administrator.

Lockwood, Gilbert, Sr., late of Greenwich, Oct. 4, 1803, bond of Elnathan Lockwood of New Canaan, administrator.
Oct. 5, 1803, inventory taken by Enos Lockwood and Frederick Lockwood.
Mch. 27, 1805, account filed, and real estate ordered sold to pay debts.
Apl. 6, 1805, estate distributed to his widow, Mary Lockwood, and children Richard, Gilbert, James, Ruth, Noah, Andrew, Elnathan, Edward, and Solomon.

Lockwood, Mary, late of Greenwich, Sept. 27, 1843, estate ordered distributed according to her will to Letitia wife of Rufus Peck, Charlotte Lockwood, Angeline Lockwood, and Eliza Lockwood.
Oct. 4, 1843, estate distributed accordingly.

Lockwood, Nathan, late of Greenwich, Feb. 15, 1803, we the heirs of deceased consent to the sale of his real estate to pay debts, Stephen Lockwood, Daniel Hubbard, Nathan Lockwood, Shubal Lockwood, Isaac Lockwood, and David Lockwood.

Lockwood, Richard, late of Stamford, will dated Nov. 14, 1828, not probated, all to his wife Hannah, and appointed her his executrix. Witnesses S. H. Minor, Philander Daskam, and J. M. Minor.

Lockwood, Ruth, of Greenwich, Apl. 7, 1812, bond of Ruth Lockwood, guardian of William P. Lockwood, about 16 years of age, a son of said Ruth Lockwood.

Lounsbury, Amos, late of Stamford, will dated Mch. 10, 1807, not probated, mentions his wife Elizabeth, and children Henry, Elizabeth, Amos Lockwood, Sally, Nancy, Rufus, Samuel, and Deborah, wife of William Keeler. Executrix his wife. Witnesses Ezekiel Smith, Rufus Newman, and Samuel Webb.

Lounsbury, Gideon, late of Stamford, May 5, 1804, estate distributed to his children James, heirs of Hannah, Gideon, Elijah, Amos, John, and Sally.

STAMFORD PROBATE RECORDS.
Miscellaneous papers not copied.

Lounsbury, Gideon, formerly a resident of the County of Delaware, N. Y., and now residing in his home town of Stamford, Conn., and Abigail Bishop of said Stamford, Mch. 2, 1811, antenuptial agreement.

Lounsbury, Thomas, late of Stamford, Apl. 7, 1812, bond of Nathaniel Mills, guardian of William Lounsbury, about 14 years of age, a son of decedent.
Apl. 7, 1812, bond of Hezekiah Weed, guardian of Sally Lounsbury, about 4 years of age, a daughter of decedent
Apl. 7, 1812, bond of William Smith, Jr., guardian of Edwin Lounsbury, about 13 years of age, a son of decedent.
Feb. 20, 1813, bond of Charles Knapp, guardian of Samuel Lounsbury, about 19 years of age, a son of decedent
Feb. 20, 1813, bond of Josiah Smith, guardian of Betsy Ann, about 7 years of age, and Polly, about 2 years of age, daughters of decedent.

Lyon, James, late of Greenwich, will dated Feb. 21, 1804, probated Nov. 27, 1804, mentions the children of his son James Lyon, late of Greenwich, deceased, sons David, Daniel, and Benjamin; grandson Daniel a son of Benjamin Lyon; daughters Sally wife of James Banks, Polly wife of Daniel Banks, Jr., and Elizabeth wife of Abraham Merritt. Executors Jabez Fitch and James Banks of Greenwich. Witnesses Thomas Huggeford, Silvanus Seaman, and Daniel Lyon, 3rd.
Inventory taken Nov. 29, 1804, by Jabez Fitch and Nehemiah Willson, and filed Dec. 17, 1804.
Feb. 8, 1805, bond of Nehemiah Willson, guardian of Augustus, about 16 years of age, and Elizabeth, about 12 years of age, children of James Lyon, deceased.

Lyon, Simeon, late of Greenwich, will dated Aug. 25, 1804, probated Aug. 17, 1807, all to his wife Mary until she remarries, remainder to his brother Joshua Lyon's son, Joshua Lyon. Executor Nehemiah Willson. Witnesses Mary Sherwood, Desire Willson, and Nehemiah Willson. Inventory taken by James Banks and Gilbert Close, and filed Sept. 8, 1807.
Nov. 18, 1808, account filed.

Mather, Joseph, late of Darien, no date (in 1841), estate distributed to his widow, Sarah Mather, and children Rana, Phebe, David S., Joseph, Clara wife of Charles Street, Hannah wife of Charles Selleck, Nancy Bell, Betsy Lockwood, Moses, and Sarah wife of Noyes Richards.

STAMFORD PROBATE RECORDS.
Miscellaneous papers not copied.

Matthews, Benjamin S., of Stamford, about two weeks of age, Nov. 15, 1850, bond of his guardian Isaac H. Smith.

Mead, Abigail, late of Greenwich, will dated June 30, 1790, probated May 11, 1807, mentions her children Robert, Ephraim, Jabez, Zenas, Elizabeth, Sarah, Rachel, Hannah and Huldah. Executor her son Robert. Witnesses Jared Mead, Ebenezer Mead, and Hannah Mead.
May 11, 1807, executor refused to qualify, and letters with the will annexed granted to Zenas Mead.
June 4, 1807, receipt for their share of the personal property signed by Job Lyon, Elizabeth Lyon, Silas Mead, Jr., Sarah Mead, Richard Mead, Rachel Mead, Joshua Mead, Hannah Mead, Zophar Mead, Huldah Mead, Ephraim Mead, Jabez Mead, and Robert Mead.

Mead, Amos, late of Greenwich, Apl. 30, 1807, inventory taken by Ebenezer Mead and Joshua Mead, and filed Apl. 30, 1807.

Mead, Nathan, late of Chambersburg, Franklin County, Pa., Nov. 12, 1812, bond of Augustus Lockwood of Stamford, administrator.

Mead, Nathaniel, and Charity Mead, his wife, late of Greenwich, will dated Aug. 22, 1804, not probated, mentions "our children" Jasper, Nathaniel, 3rd, William, Charity wife of Joshua Knapp, Rebecca wife of Shubael Knapp, Elizabeth Mead, and Ann wife of Gilbert Totton. Executors son William, and son in law Joshua Knapp. Witnesses Mary Mead, Samuel Close, and Ebenezer Mead. Codicil dated Apl. 22, 1813, makes provisions for his widow for life.

Mead, Platt, late of Greenwich, real estate sold to Erastus Rundle, and report of sale filed Apl. 2, 1849.

Mead, Shadrach, late of Greenwich, inventory taken by Henry Ritch, and Thomas A. Mead, and filed Dec. 28, 1844.

Mead, William A., late of Greenwich, Sept. 27, 1849, letters of administration on his estate granted to Mary Mead, who was ordered to advertise for claims.
Inventory taken by Thomas A. Mead and Augustus Mead, and filed Oct. 3, 1849.

Merritt, Jotham, late of Greenwich, Oct. 3, 1814, bond of Thomas Green of Greenwich, guardian of Harriet Merritt, about 19 years of age, a daughter of decedent.

STAMFORD PROBATE RECORDS.
Miscellaneous papers not copied.

Mesnard, Zalmon, about 16 years of age, of Greenwich, Dec. 23, 1806, made choice of his brother Lockwood Mead, now a resident of Greenwich, to be his guardian.

Miller, Mary, or Polly, of Greenwich, Dec. 1, 1841, petition of her brother in law, Robert P. Quintard of Greenwich, for the appointment of a conservator for said alleged incompetent.

Nichols, James, Late of Stamford, will dated May 9, 1804, probated Apl. 7, 1807, mentions his wife Anne, and children Benny, Mary wife of William Thorp, Jr., and Anne wife of Seth Webb. Executor son in law William Thorp, Jr. Witnesses Jerusha Davenport, Joseph Weed, and Ebenezer Davenport.   (Wood)

Northrop, David, of Stamford, about 16 years of age, Mch. 30, 1803, bond of his guardian John Jessup of Stamford.

Olmsted, Ebenezer, late of Ridgefield, July 6, 1807, bond of Jeremiah Andreas of Stamford, guardian of Benjamin Keeler Olmsted, about 16 years of age, a son of decedent.

Palmer, John Wood, late of Greenwich, Feb. 1, 1812, petition of Messenger Palmer to sell the realestate of Hatty Palmer, now the wife of White Webb of Greenwich, a daughter of decedent.

Palmer, Samuel, Jr., late of Greenwich, July 6, 1813, bond of Tompkins Close of Greenwich, guardian of Martin Palmer, about 15 years of age, and Sela, about 14 years of age, sons of decedent.

Parketing, Abraham, about 16 years of age, of Stamford, son of Betsy Parketing of Stamford, Apl. 7, 1811, bond of his guardian Hanford Hoyt of Stamford.

Peck, Gideon, late of Greenwich, Jan. 16, 1813, bond of Platt Mead of Greenwich, guardian of Eunice, about 19 years of age, Elizabeth, about 19 years of age, and Theophilus, about 18 years of age, children of decedent.

Peck, Nancy, late of Greenwich, June 21, 1828, estate distributed to her heirs, viz: David H. Fowler a son of Abigail Jane H. Fowler, deceased, Charles E. Peck, Mehitable wife of Thomas M. Lyon, and Thomas H. Peck.

STAMFORD PROBATE RECORDS.
Miscellaneous papers not copied.

Peck, Nathaniel, late of Greenwich, Nov. 9, 1803, bond of Jeremiah Mead, Jr., of Greenwich, administrator, with the consent of Walter Peck, a son of deceased. Inventory taken Dec. 12, 1803, by Ebenezer Mead and Andrew Mead, and filed Jan. 5, 1804.
Oct. 1, 1804, report of commissioners to adjust claims of creditors filed.

Peck, Samuel, late of Greenwich, May 3, 1808, Act of the General Assembly authorizing the sale of land of Jabez Peck, an incompetent.

Pencyer, Elizabeth, late of Stamford, Jan. 4, 1804, bond of Zipporah Haws of New York City, administratrix. Inventory taken Jan. 13, 1804, by George Mills and Silvanus Knapp, and filed Jan. 26, 1804.

Perkins, Charles, late of Stamford, Feb. 7, 1807, bond of Elizabeth Waterbury of Stamford, administratrix.

Perry, Sturges, late of Stamford, May 3, 1806, bond of Sarah Perry, widow of deceased, guardian of Esther Ann, about 17 years of age, Sturges Lewis, about 14 years of age, Samuel Church, about 11 years of age, and Harriet Maria, children of decedent.

Quintard, Elizabeth, late of Stamford, widow of Peter Quintard, deceased, will dated Oct. 15, 1835, not probated, all to her daughter Mary widow of Stephen White, deceased, late of Rome, N. Y. Executor Simeon H. Minor. Witnesses Sey. Jarvis, Ann Hickson, and Abigail Buxton.

Raymond, Sally S., of Darien, Aug. 5, 1845, petition of her brother, Charles F. Raymond of New York City, for the appointment of a conservator for said alleged incompetent.

Reynolds, George, about 10 years of age, of Greenwich, Dec. 7, 1818, bond of his guardian Deborah Reynolds of Greenwich.

Reynolds, Nathaniel, about 14 years of age, of Greenwich, Dec. 7, 1818, bond of his guardian Deborah Reynolds of Greenwich.

Roberts, Sally, late of ------Sept. 6, 1808, bond of Thaddeus Bell of Stamford, guardian of Josiah Roberts, about 13 years of age, a son of decedent.

STAMFORD PROBATE RECORDS.
Miscellaneous papers not copied.

Scofield, Betsy, late of Staford, will dated Jan. 3, 1831, not probated, all of her personal property to her husband, Levi Scofield, and real estate to him for life. Executor her husband, Levi Scofield. Witnesses Isaac Bell, Jonas Scofield, and William Scofield.

Scofield, John, and Martha Lounsbury, both of Stamford, Oct. 14, 1819, antenuptial agreement. The will of said John Scofield is recorded in Book 14, page 504, and probated Apl. 27, 1833.

Scofield, Sylvanus, late of Darien : Probate Court, District of Stamford, Oct. 14, 1831, personally appeared Sarah Scofield of Darien and here produced in court Joseph A. Gray of Darien and William Henry Holly, Jr., of Stamford, who severally made oath in due form of law, that they well knew Sylvanus Scofield, deceased, late of Darien, a Revolutionary Pensioner of the United States, and that they knew said Sarah Scofield and that during the life of said Sylvanus, and at the time of his decease she was his wife, and is now his widow. And this court doth thereupon find that said Sarah Scofield in the lifetime of said Sylvanus and at the time of his decease was the lawful wife of said Sylvanus, and is now the widow of said Sylvanus Scofield, deceased. Charles Hawley, Judge.

Selleck, Joseph, late of Stamford, June 14, 1847, in accordance with his will a plot of seventeen acres was set off to his daughter, Hannah wife of Luther Knapp, in fee, if she should survive said Luther Knapp, otherwise during her lifetime. We the undersigned children of said Luther and Hannah Knapp consent to the foregoing. James Law, Ann E. Law, Mary S. Knapp, Charles H. Knapp, Samuel Pearson, Phebe S. Pearson, Grant Judd, Hannah M. Judd, and J. T. Knapp.

Selleck, Nathan, late of Stamford, Mch. 6, 1807, bond of Wyx Seely and Edward Selleck, administrators.
Inventory taken Mch. 12, 1807, by Gershom Scofield, Nathan Weed and Charles Whiting, and filed Mch. 18, 1807.
Mch. 24, 1807, estate ordered distributed to his children Edward, Deborah wife of Amos Roberts of Stamford, Phebe wife of Thomas Comstock of New Canaan, and Catherine wife of Wyx Seely, and estate distributed accordingly.

STAMFORD PROBATE RECORDS.
Miscellaneous papers not copied.

Selleck, Wray, late of Stamford, Mch. 29, 1803, bond of David
    Bates of Stamford, guardian of Hinman Selleck, about
    15 years of age, a son of decedent.

Sherwood, Elnathan, late of Greenwich, Jan. 4, 1808, Nathan
    Sherwood, about 17 years of age, a son of decedent,
    made choice of Nehemiah Willson to be his guardian.

Sherwood, Jared, late of Greenwich, Feb. 4, 1806, bond of
    Charles Smith of Greenwich, administrator.
    Inventory taken Feb. 6, 1806, by Elkanah Mead and Jared
    Smith, and filed Feb. 6, 1806.
    Mch. 1806, dower of Pamela Sherwood, widow of deceased,
    set out.
    July 7, 1806, report of commissioners to adjust claims
    of creditors filed.

Skelding, James, late of Stamford, Feb. 5, 1806, bond of James
    Skelding, administrator, Mary Skelding, widow of de-
    ceased having refused to qualify.
    Inventory taken Mch. 8, 1806, by James Bishop and
    James Lounsbury.

Slason, Gershom, late of Stamford, Sept. 21, 1804, Henry Sla-
    son, about 16 years of age, a son of decedent, made
    choice of Thomas Reed of Norwalk to be his guardian.

Slawson, Samuel, late of Darien, will dated Nov. 10, 1846, not
    probated, all to his wife Abigail for life, and re-
    mainder to his children, except Henry, who is to have
    $50. Executor son Henry. Witnesses Abram Clock,
    Abigail How, and Seth How.

Smith, Alvah, late of Greenwich, Apl. 25, 1839, estate dis-
    tributed to his widow, Hannah Smith, and children
    Hervey, Rachel Augusta, Charles Benjamin, and Sally
    Brush Smith.

Smith, Aseneth, late of Stamford, will dated Jan. 3, 1840,
    not probated, all to his niece, Mary Smith. Executor
    Edward A. Smith of Stamford. Witnesses Smith R.
    Sibley, Henry Smith, and Nathan White.

Smith, Elijah, late of Stamford, Feb. 2, 1808, bond of Solo-
    mon Clason, of Stamford, administrator.
    Inventory taken by Daniel Nichols and Daniel Lockwood,
    and filed Mch. 1, 1808.
    Apl. 22, 1809, estate distributed to his brother Isaiah
    to the devisees named in the will of Simeon Smith, and
    to the widow Azuba Smith.

STAMFORD PROBATE RECORDS.
Miscellaneous papers not copied.

Smith, Elizabeth, widow, late of Stanwich in Stamford, will dated Jan. 26, 1789, probated May 5, 1807, mentions her youngest daughter Rue, granddaughter Elizabeth Platt, and daughter Anne. No executor. Witnesses John Smith, Ebenezer Smith, and Daniel Nichols, Jr. Jonah Ferris, administrator with the will annexed. Inventory taken June 2, 1807, by Seth Hait and Seth Smith.

Smith, Rebecca, late of Stamford, Apl. 2, 1845, letters of administration on her estate granted to her son Joseph Smith, Jr., of Stamford.

Smith, Zety, late of Stamford, Feb. 2, 1808, bond of Solomon Close, administrator.
Inventory taken by Daniel Nichols and Daniel Lockwood, Jr., and filed Mch. 1, 1808.

Startin, Sarah, late of the City of New York, will dated June 13, 1821, probated Sept. 7, 1841, and letters with the will annexed granted to Dayton Hobart of the City of New York, mentions her brother Isaac Winslow Clarke of Montreal, and his son Richard, nieces the daughters of Samuel Cabot of Boston, Richard Dunn, John McFarlane, and his son Charles S., Job Silliman, Elizabeth Ganey, Alexander Fleming of Bellow's Falls, Right Rev. John Henry Hobart, Bishop of the Protestant Church in the State of New York, her sister Susanna Copley of London, widow of John Singleton Copley, deceased, niece Mary Copley, John Atkinson formerly of the City of New York, but now of Bellow's Falls, and his wife Elizabeth Atkinson, and Rebecca Seton Maitland. Executors her brother Isaac Winslow Clarke, John Jackson Jones, John Atkinson, Jr., Richard Dunn, Jr., and Thomas Ludlow Ogden.

Stevens, Darius, Sophia Stevens, and Harriet Stevens, all of Darien, Jan. 21, 1825, petition of their guardian, Ashbel Scofield of Stamford, for leave to sell the real estate of said minors in Darien.

Stevens, William H., late of Stamford, Jan. 17, 1805, bond of Hannah Stevens, widow of deceased, administratrix. Inventory taken by Cary Hoyt and Joseph Silliman, and filed Aug. 6, 1805.

Studwell, Sarah, late of Greenwich, will dated Apl. 14, 1804, not probated, all to her son Ezekiel Studwell, except five dollars to her sons Silas Palmer and Aseal Palmer.

STAMFORD PROBATE RECORDS.
Miscellaneous papers not copied.

Studwell, Sarah, continued :
    Executors her son Ezekiel Studwell and Isaac Holly.
    Witnesses Fanny Smith, Sally Holly, and Ebenezer Mead.

Sudmon, or Sudmore, ----, late of Stamford, Mch. 28, 1806,
    bond of David Bates of Stamford, guardian of Nathaniel
    Sudmon or Sudmore, about 15 years of age, a son of de-
    cedent.

Todd, John, Jr., late of Stamford, Aug. 25, 1813, estate dis-
    tributed to his widow, Hannah Todd, and children, Henry,
    Lydia Mills, Harvey, and Gabriel.

Tuley, Andrew, of New Canaan, June 23, 1804, bond of his guar-
    dian Aaron Comstock of New Canaan.

Van Buschoten, Rachel, late of Greenwich, will dated Dec. 7,
    1802, probated Mch. 30, 1803, mentions her daughter
    Jane Ann, brothers Joseph Sackett, James Sackett, and
    Richard Sackett. Executors said Joseph Sackett and
    James Sackett and Jabez Fitch. Witnesses John
    Strang, Elizabeth Marshall, and Nancy Knapp.

Wardwell, Abigail, late of Stamford, inventory taken Aug. 5,
    1805, by John Waterbury and Thaddeus Bell, Jr., and
    filed Aug. 6, 1805, by James Wardwell, executor.

Waring, Michager, late of Stamford, May 3, 1806, bond of Cath-
    erine Waring of Greenwich, guardian of her children
    Ann, about 11 years of age, Hannah, about 9 years of
    age, and Betsy, about 6 years of age, children of de-
    dedent.

Waterbury, Jacob, late of Stamford, will dated Feb. 24, 1820,
    not probated, all to his wife, Rebecca, for life, and
    remainder to his daughter Mary wife of Deodate Finch.
    Executrix his daughter Mary. Witnesses Medad Seymour,
    Harriet A. Waterbury, and Samuel Webb.

Waterbury, James, late of Stamford, July 11, 1808, bond of
    Elizabeth Waterbury of Stamford, guardian of Warren
    Waterbury, about 16 years of age, a son of decedent.

Waterbury, Jonathan, late of Stamford, Apl. 2, 1816, petition
    of Sally Waterbury, guardian of Jonathan Waterbury,
    and parent and natural guardian of Nancy, Amos H.,
    Cornelia, and Appollos W., children of decedent, for
    leave to sell the real estate of said minors.

STAMFORD PROBATE RECORDS.
Miscellaneous papers not copied.

Waterbury, Mary, late of Stamford, will dated Apl. 21, 1804, probated June 4, 1805, mentions her sister Bethia Waterbury, brothers Benjamin, Josiah, James, and Ebenezer Waterbury. Executor Nathan Weed. Witnesses Eli Benedict, Nathaniel Waterbury, and Abigail Waterbury. Inventory taken by Charles Whiting and Gideon Weed, and filed Aug. 6, 1805.

Waterbury, Phineas, late of Stamford, Nov. 4, 1806, inventory, taken by Nathan Weed and William Walmsley, and filed Nov. 4, 1806.
Jan. 22, 1807, estate distributed to his children William, Phinehas, Noah, and Nehemiah.

Waterbury, William, late of Darien, will dated May 1, 1844, not probated, mentions his wife Barsheba, and children Henry, Polly wife of David Weed, Nancy wife of Hetchent Hutty, Hannah M. wife of William A. Smith, and George, granddaughter Fanny Stevens a daughter of Samuel Stevens Executor Abram Clock, of Darien. Witnesses Lorenzo O. Stevens, H. T Joyce, and Sally Stevens.
Will dated June 26, 1844, not probated, makes some changes in the foregoing will. Executor son in law Samuel Stevens. Witnesses Raymond K. Weed, Moses R. Clock, and Mary E. Selleck.

Waters, Jacob, late of Stamford, Sept. 19, 1803, bond of Nathan Sherwood of Stamford, guardian of Stephen Waters, about 16 years of age, a son of decedent.
Apl. 9, 1804, bond of Nathan Sherwood of Stamford, guardian of James Waters, about 14 years of age, a son of decedent.

Webb, Epenetus, late of Stamford, Aug. 20, 1832, letters of administration on his estate granted to John Scarritt of of New Haven, who was ordered to advertise for claims.

Webb, Frederick, late of Stamford, June 15, 1826, account filed, and real estate ordered sold to pay debts. Real estate sold to William Augustus Webb, and report of sale filed June 6, 1826.
July 10, 1826, estate ordered distributed to his widow, Abigail Webb, Augustus Webb, Mary Webb, Nancy Webb, Sarah E. Webb, Joseph H. Webb, Frederic Webb, and David Webb.

Webb, James, of Stamford, May 31, 1833, general assignment to Richard Fox and Joseph White for the benefit of creditors.

STAMFORD PROBATE RECORDS.
Miscellaneous papers not copied.

Webb, Sarah, late of Stamford, widow, Nov. 7, 1806, bond of
Daniel Smith of Stamford, administrator.

Weed, Ebenezer P., late of Stamford, June 20, 1804, inventory
taken by Joseph Gray and Cary Leeds, and filed July 3,
1804.
Mch. 29, 1805, bond of Mary Weed of Stamford, guardian
of Susannah Weed, about 19 years of age, a daughter of
decedent.

Weed, Gilbert D., of Darien, over 14 years of age, Feb. 8,
1834, made choice of John R. Leeds to be his guardian.

Weed, Samuel, late of Stamford, Aug. 23, 1841, estate distributed according to his will to the widow of Nathan
Weed, William H. Weed, Alexander X. Weed, Theodore E.
Weed, Sarah Elizabeth Weed, and Mary Weed.

Weed, Seth, of Stamford, and Lucy Ann Hoyt of Pound Ridge,
Westchester County, N. Y., Feb. 1, 1811, antenuptial
agreement in lieu of dower.

Weed, Thaddeus, late of Stamford, will dated Dec. 22, 1802,
probated Mch. 19, 1804, mentions the heirs of Mary
Garnsey, a deceased sister of the half blood; Hannah
Abbott, a sister of the half blood; Peter Weed, a brother of the half blood; the heirs of Martha Ferris, a
sister of the half blood; Hannah Weed, a sister of the
half blood, Rachel Whiting, a sister of the half blood;
brothers Benjamin, Jr., Ananias, and Smith Weed. Executors his brothers Benjamin Weed, Jr., and Smith
Weed. Witnesses Ebenezer Ferris, John Hough, Jr.,
and Ezra Raymond.
Apl. 14, 1804, letters issued to the aforesaid executors.

Weeks, Jane, late of Stamford, Sept. 6, 1850, bond of Hezekiah
Scofield, Jr., of Stamford, administrator.

White, Esther, of Stamford, June 29, 1843, petition of her son
Nathan White of Stamford for the appointment of a conservator of said alleged incompetent.
July 29, 1843, Nathan White appointed conservator and
bond filed.

Wood, Lemuel, late of Greenwich, Nov. 3, 1812, bond of Levi
Palmer, guardian of William Wood, about 16 years of
age, a son of decedent.

STAMFORD PROBATE RECORDS.
Miscellaneous papers not copied.

Wooster, Ebenezer, late of Stamford, Aug. 29, 1803, bond of
Elizabeth Wooster of Stamford, guardian of John, about
13 years of age, James, about 11 years of age, Ebenezer, about 9 years of age, and Henry, about 7 years
of age, children of decedent.
Dec. 1810, petition for leave to sell the real estate
of said minors and bond filed.

Youngs, Elizabeth, late of Stamford, will dated May 30, 1804,
not probated, but see Book 14, page 465, all to her
daughter Phebe Brooks, widow of Henry Brooks, late of
Norwalk, deceased, and appointed her executrix. Witnesses John Clock, John Gorum, and Hannah Youngs.

Youngs, , Rebecca, late of Stamford, will dated Apl. 30, ----
probated Dec. 6, 1803, all to her two daughters Elizabeth Youngs and Hannah Youngs. Executrix her daughter Hannah Youngs.
Dec. 6, 1803, letters granted to the aforesaid executrix.
Inventory taken by Gershom Scofield and Nathan Weed,
and filed Dec. 26, 1803.

INDEX TO ESTATES.

A.

Adams, Abraham, 179.
" Eli, 101.
" John, 138, 179.
" Morehouse, 179, 180.
" Phebe, 233.
" Polly, 302.
" Reuben, 180.
" William, 347.
Addington, Elizabeth, 233.
" John, 180.
" Samuel, 233.
" Thomas, 2.
Ambler, Isaac, 44.
" Joseph, 44, 101.
Anderson, Hannah, 347.
" Isaac, 44.
" Israel, 233, 234.
" Joseph, 234.
" Matthias, 2, 44, 45, 222, 390.
" William, 180.
Andreas, Jeremiah, 347, 348.
Augur, John, 138, 234, 348.
Avery, John, 3, 45, 302.
" Peter, 180, 181.
" Walter, 302.
Ayres, Bradley, 181, 234.
" Sarah, 181, 234.

B.

Banks, Daniel, 45.
" James, 302, 303.
" James, Jr., 101.
" Mary, 303, 348.
" Samuel, 101, 102.

B.

Baremore, Walter, 102.
Barnum, David, 234.
" Horace, 348.
Bartow, Daniel, 303.
Bates, David, 3.
" Gershom, 3, 102, 138, 182, 234.
" Henry, 234, 235.
" James, 3.
" Jerome, 235.
" John, 348, 349.
" Jonathan, 45, 181.
" Lewis S., 3, 4.
" Mary, 4, 303, 390.
" Sarah, 303.
" Seely, 182.
" William H., 235, 349.
Bayeux, Priscilla, 45.
" Thomas, Dr., 4, 46, 390.
Belcher, Elisha, Dr., 138, 139.
Bell, Abraham, 303.
" Francis, 4, 5.
" Isaac, 5, 235, 390.
" Jonathan, Jr., 102, 103.
" Mercy, 304.
" Noah, 103, 182.
" Prudence, 304, 349, 391.
" Rebecca, 349.
" Susannah, 304.
" Thaddeus, 5.
Bellamy, Isaac, 5, 46.
Bennett, Elizabeth, 235.
Betts, Nathaniel W., 5.
Bishop, Abijah, 6, 46.
" Alexander, 6, 103.
" Andrew, 235, 236.

408.

INDEX TO ESTATES.

B.

Bishop, Hannah, 46.
" Hezekiah, 236.
" Isaac, 182.
" John K., 182, 183, 236.
" Jonathan, 103.
" Rebecca, 183.
" Silas, 6.
Blackman, Elizabeth, 183, 237.
Blanchard, Elizabeth, 237.
" Isaac, 183, 237.
" Jacob, 183.
Blau, Cornelia, 349, 350.
Bostwick, Samuel, 6, 391.
Bouton, Mahala, 183, 184.
" William H., 304.
Bragg, Isaac F., 184.
Briggs, Hannah, 6.
" Nathaniel, 184.
" Phillip, 350.
" Shadrach, 237, 238.
Brown, Ann, 350.
" Bezaleel, 7.
" Charles, 103.
" David, 7.
" Deborah, 46.
" Doctor, 7, 46.
" Elizabeth, 139.
" George, 304.
" George, Jr., 184.
" George F., 350.
" Henry, 304, 391.
" James, 7, 391.
" John, 305, 391.
" Jonathan, 238.
" Josiah, 238.
" Lucy, 305, 351.
" Major, 351.
" Martha, 139, 391.
" Nehemiah, 7, 8, 238.
" Peter, 47, 103, 104, 139, 184, 185.
" Rachel, 47.
" Rebecca, 8, 47, 351.
" Samuel, 3rd, 47.
Brundage, Charity, 104.
" James, 9.
" Jonah, 239.

B.

Brundage, Samuel, 351.
Brush, Benjamin, 104, 351, 352.
" Benjamin, 3rd, 185, 239.
" Edmund B., 185, 239.
" Edward, 305, 352.
" James, 47, 48.
" Josephus, 305, 352.
" Maria C., 352.
" Martha, 239, 240.
" Platt, 240.
" Shubal, 8, 391.
Bunhill, Lockwood, 139.
Bunnell, David, 8, 48.
" Jonathan, 305, 352, 392.
" Lockwood, 139, 140.
" Polly, 305, 306.
Burley, Deborah, 352, 353.
" " Henry, 306, 353.
" Samuel, 353.
" Silas, 240, 353.
Burtis, Betsy M., 240.
" Elizabeth, 140.
Burton, Samuel, 392.
Bush, Ann, 241.
" David, 140.
" David W., 241.
" Deborah, 9.
" Elzor, 241.
" Justus L., 354.
" Samuel, 141.
" Sarah, 141.
Buxton, Ezra, 9.
" Isaac, 9.
" John, 48.
" Samuel, 48.

C.

Caldwell, Samuel, 241.
Cannon, Charles O., 104.
Cargill, Betsy, 185.
Carhart, Hacaliah, 241.
" William, 104.
Carncross, George, 48.
Carringcross, George, 48.
Clapp, Thomas, 141, 142, 185, 186.
Clark, Cyrus, 354.

INDEX TO ESTATES.

C.

Clark, Elizabeth, 354.
Clason, Ard, 186.
" Benjamin, 241, 242, 308.
" David, 392.
" Martha, 105.
" Solomon, 354, 355.
" Stephen, 9, 10.
Clock, Albert, 10.
" John, 242.
" Jonas, 10.
" Martin, 105, 142.
" Nathaniel, 186.
Close, Aaron, 49.
" Bethia, 186.
" Charlotte, 355.
" Edward, 306.
" Edwin T., 307.
" Gideon, Sr., 10.
" Gideon, 105, 142.
" Gilbert, 355.
" Henry, 242.
" Jonathan, 11, 49, 142.
" Joseph, 242.
" Odle, 242, 243.
" Odle, Jr., 11, 49.
" Shadrach, 186, 187.
Comstock, Samuel, 392.
Cook, Hannah, 355.
Cornell, John, 49.
Cox, Robert, 307.
" Sally, 187.
Crennell, Abigail J., 106, 134, 392.
Crissy, John, 11.
Curtis, Ezekiel, 307.
" Jeremiah, 143.
" John, 243.

D.

Dan, Charles, 243.
" Eliza, 243.
" Elizabeth F., 355.
" John, 49, 307, 308, 356.
" Nathan, 49, 50.
" Squire, 244.
" Sylvanus, 187, 244.

D.

Davenport, Elizabeth, 11, 13.
" Hannah, 11, 50.
" James, 50, 356.
" John, 106, 187.
" Mehitable, 12.
Davis, Abraham, 50.
" Elisha, 50.
" Walter, 106.
Dayton, David, 50.
" Gilbert, 143, 187.
" Jacob, 308, 356, 357.
" James, 188, 244.
Demill, Peter, 12.
" Sarah, 12.
Denton, Daniel, 106, 143.
" Joseph, 188.
" Samuel, 51.
Dibble, Emeline, 188.
" George, 51.
Dixon, Eliza, 143.
" Isaac, 308.
" Philemon, 188.
Dodgshan, Enoch, 188, 308.
Downing, George, 357.
Dunham, John, 51.
Dunn, Joseph, 188, 189.

E.

Edwards, John, 12, 13.
Escott, Rhoda, 189.

F.

Fancher, David, 51, 244.
Felmette, Jeffery, 189.
Ferris, Ann, 308.
" Asa M., 244, 357.
" Clauson, 13.
" David, Jr., 13, 51.
" Ebenezer, 13, 52, 143, 144.
" Ethan, 189, 245.
" Isaac, 392.
" James, 52.
" James, Jr., 52.
" Jeduthan, 52, 189.
" Jeremiah, 52.

INDEX TO ESTATES.

F.

Ferris, Jonathan, 357.
" Lemuel, 144, 139, 358.
" Mary, 52, 53, 245.
" Mary L., 308, 309.
" Nathaniel, 13, 107, 144.
" Oliver, 13, 53.
" Peter, 144, 145.
" Polly, 245.
" Ransford A., 145.
" Samuel, Jr., 309.
" Sarah, 392, 393.
" Shadrach, 53.
" Solomon, 107.
" Stephen, 145.
Field, Aaron, 309.
" Hannah, 358.
" Mary, 190.
" Robert, 245.
" Uriah, 53.
Finch, Abigail, 309, 310.
" Christina, 358.
" Jonathan, 245.
" Nathaniel, 107, 190.
" Reuben, 310.
" William, 310.
Finney, Phebe, 190, 191.
Flanegan, Daniel, 53, 54.
Ford, Eliakim, 310.

G.

George, Prince, 14.
Gorum, Daniel, 107, 108.
Gown, see McGown.
Gray, Benjamin, 108.
" Cary H., 245, 246, 310.
" Hannah, 191.
" Joseph, 191, 246.
" Philip, 14, 54.
Green, Anthony, 246.
" Benjamin, 246, 247.
" Charles, Jr., 14.
" James, 145, 310, 311.
" John, Captain, 54.
" John, 108.
" Joseph, 247.
" Mercy, 54, 247.

G.

Green, Reuben, 358.
" Susannah, 247.
" Thomas, 247, 248.
Griffen, Hannah, 359.
Grigg, Alexander, 108, 393.
" David, 393.
" Elizabeth, 311, 359.
" Henry, 359.
" John, 359, 360.
" Walter, 14, 54.
Guernsey, Solomon, 248.

H.

Haggerty, John, 54, 55.
Hait, David, 14.
" David N., 248.
" Frederick, 55.
" Jesse, 393.
" John, 15.
" Jonah, 55.
" Ruth, 15.
" Sarah, 15.
" Seth, 55.
Hall, David, 249.
Halleck, George, 15.
Halligan, John, 360.
Hanford, Augustus, 311.
" Ebenezer, 360.
Harvey, Thomas M., 311, 312, 360.
Hawley, Elijah, 15, 16.
" Elisha, 109.
Haxton, Charlotte, 16.
" Dyer, 109.
" Louisa C., 109.
Hebbard, Nathaniel, 109.
Hedden, Zadée, 249.
Henderson, Hugh, 249.
Hendrie, Hannah, 249.
" William, 16.
Hitchcock, Joseph, 16.
" Thomas, 16, 55.
Hobby, Abigail, 360, 361.
" Amos, 250, 312.
" Amy, 16, 17, 55.
" Benjamin, 17.
" Clemence, 191.

INDEX TO ESTATES.

H.

Hobby, Deborah, 393.
" Ebenezer, 56.
" Harry, 250.
" Hezekiah, 312.
" Jabez M., 146, 192, 250.
" John, 146.
" Mary, 109.
" Mills, 56.
" Ruth, 146.
" Squire, 17, 56.
" William, 361.
Holly, Abraham, 109, 110, 192.
" Elijah, 393.
" Elizabeth, 111, 393.
" Increase, 56.
" Isaac, 56, 192, 250, 312.
" John M., 361.
" John W., 312.
" Mercy, 56, 57, 110.
" Nathan, 17.
" Newman, 57.
" Oscar L., 361.
" Rheuama, 57.
" Samuel, 110.
" Sarah, 17, 18, 250, 312, 313.
" Stephen, 192, 250, 251.
Holmes, Benjamin, 18.
" Hannah, 192.
" Isaac, Jr., 18.
" Jabez, 57.
" John, 110, 111, 146, 313.
" Mary, 313.
" Reuben, 18.
Hopkins, Thomas, 57.
Hose, Henry G., 18, 58.
Howe, Bowers, 193.
" David, 18, 19, 146.
" Isaac, 147.
" Jacob, 393, 394.
" James, 147.
" Rebecca, 19.
" William, 362.
Hoyt, Abraham, 111.
" Anna, 58, 111.
" Bates, 147.
" Benjamin, 19, 58, 147.

H.

Hoyt, Betsy, 111, 362.
" Bally, 147, 193.
" Cary, 193.
" Darius, 147, 148, 194.
" David, 251, 313, 363.
" Deodate, 58.
" Ebenezer, 313.
" Elihu, 148.
" Elijah, 58.
" Elizabeth, 59, 251?
" Enoch, 59, 111, 148, 194, 251, 252, 394.
" Epenetus, 194, 195.
" Ezra, 19.
" Frederick, 59.
" George, 314.
" Hanford, 59.
" Hannah, 252, 363.
" Hervey, 111, 112.
" Isaac, 148.
" James, 394.
" James S., 252, 253.
" Jared, 19.
" Jesse, 253.
" Joel, 19, 20, 394.
" John, 60, 148, 149, 253.
" Jonah, 20.
" Jonathan, 394.
" Joseph, 20, 60.
" Joseph D., 253, 254.
" Joseph S., 195.
" Josiah, 20, 112.
" Julia, 314.
" Millicent, 314.
" Nathan, 20.
" Nathaniel, 112.
" Nezer, 20.
" Peter, 21, 394.
" Ralph, 254, 314, 363.
" Rebecca, 314.
" Rhoda, 363.
" Ruth, 21.
" Sally, 195.
" Salmon, 21.
" Samuel, 21, 60, 195, 394.
" Samuel, Jr., 60.
" Samuel H., 314.

INDEX TO ESTATES.

H.

Hoyt, Seth, 60, 112.
" Shadrach, 149, 195, 254, 363.
" Sylvanus, 60.
" Thaddeus, 195, 196, 364.
" Uriah, 21, 22, 394.
" William, 196.
" William S., Captain, 364.
" Ziba, 112, 113.
Hubbard, Gabriel, 149, 196, 255, 315.
" Henry, 149, 196.
" Nathaniel, Dr., 61.
Hunt, Thomas, 196.
Husted, Abraham, 113.
" Amos, 255, 315, 364.
" Drake, 255.
" Elnathan, 150.
" Hannah, 255, 256.
" Isaac, 61.
" Jonathan, 315.
" Nathan, 315.
" Nathaniel, 150.
" Peter, 113.
" Roswell, 197, 256.
" Ruth, 394.
" Sarah, 22, 61, 150.
" William, 256.

I.

Ingersoll, Nathaniel, 256, 257.
" Simon, 150, 197.
Ireland, Job, 22, 395.
Isaacs, Isaac, 364.
Isaacs, Isaac S., 257.

J.

Jarvis, Seymour, 315, 316.
" Stephen, 113.
Jeffery, Mercy, 22, 61.
" Samuel, 22, 23, 62.
Jeffrey, see Jeffery.
Jessup, Abigail, 23.
" Ann, 150, 151.

J.

Jessup, Ebenezer, 364.
" Jonathan, 23, 151, 152, 197.
" Joram, 23, 395.
" Peter, 24.
" Samuel, 62, 316, 364.
" Timothy, 24, 114.
Jones, Enos, 257.
" Ephraim, 257.
" Isaac, 24, 62.
" Isaac, Jr., 114.
" James, 114.
" Josiah, 197, 395.
" Katharine, 114.
" Nehemiah, 257, 258.
" Sarah, 198.
" Selleck, 198, 258.
" Smith, 62, 198.
" Thomas, 198, 258.
Jordon, William, 258, 259.
Judson, John, 114.
" Joseph, 259, 316.
June, Hannah, 259.
" Joseph, 316.
" Joshua, 395.
" Nathaniel, 152, 198, 199.
" Reuben, 259.
" Sarah, 365.
" Thomas, 365.
" William S., 365.

K.

Keeler, Mary, 152.
" William, 114, 115.
King, James J., 316.
Knapp, Abel, 24, 62.
" Abigail, 24, 199.
" Allen R., 316, 317.
" Bethia, 25.
" Charity, 365.
" Charles, 152, 317.
" Daniel, 25, 63.
" David, 25, 63.
" Edmund, 115, 152.
" Edward, 63.

INDEX TO ESTATES.

K.

Knapp, Elisa, 152.
" Elizabeth, 317.
" Enos, 152, 153, 260.
" Esther, 317, 365.
" Ezra, 260.
" Gideon, 25, 26, 395.
" Hezekiah, 317, 318.
" Isaac, 199, 260, 261.
" Israel, 63, 261.
" Jacob, 261.
" James, 26.
" Jared, 318.
" Joel, 27.
" John, 63, 64.
" Jonathan, 395.
" Joshua, 27, 64, 153, 199, 200, 261, 395.
" Lodema, 318.
" Martha, 366.
" Mary, 64, 200, 319, 366.
" Mercy, 64.
" Nathan, 64.
" Nathaniel, Colo., 261.
" Peter, 27.
" Ruth, 153.
" Samuel, 27, 200.
" Silas, 395.
" Sylvanus, 27, 28.
" Titus, 319.
" William, 153, 366.

L.

Lane, Abraham, 28, 64.
" John, 396.
Lapham, Catherine, 319.
Leeds, Abraham, 262.
" Anna, 319, 320.
" Cary H., 262.
" Elisha, 28, 64, 262.
" Gideon, 153, 154.
" Hannah, 320.
" Harry, 154.
" Jacob V., 154.
" John, 200.
" Lorenzo, 320.
" Rhoda, 262.

L.

Leeds, Sarah, 263.
" Theodore, 200.
" William B., 263.
Lewis, Amzi, Rev., 64, 65, 115.
" Beal N., 65.
" Daniel, 115, 116.
" Huldah, 154.
" Isaac, 320.
" Nathaniel B., 65.
Little, Henry, 366.
Lockwood, Amos, 65.
" Andrew, 263.
" Bethia, 65.
" Caleb, 154, 155.
" Charles, 200, 201, 263.
" Daniel, 28.
" Daniel, Jr., 155.
" Davis, 320, 321, 366, 367.
" Deborah, 321.
" Drake, 263, 264, 321.
" Edward, 116.
" Edward, Jr., 116.
" Elisabeth, 201.
" Enos, 264.
" Ezra, 116, 117.
" Fanny, 155.
" Frederick, 65, 117.
" Gilbert, Sr., 66, 396.
" Gilbert, 65, 66, 201.
" Hannah, 155, 264, 367.
" Henry, 321, 367.
" Ira, 367.
" Isaac, 66, 155, 156, 264.
" Jacob, 264.
" Jeremiah, Jr., 28, 66.
" John, 156.
" Jonathan, 66, 67, 117, 321.
" Joseph, 28, 29.
" Josiah, 117, 367, 368.
" Lewis, 156, 202, 264.
" Luther, 156, 321, 322.
" Maria, 322.
" Mary, 322, 396.
" Maurice, 117.
" Mills, 265, 322, 368.
" Nathan, 396.
" Noah, 368.

INDEX TO ESTATES.

L.

Lockwood, Philip, 202, 265.
" Priscilla, 368.
" Reuben, 156, 202.
" Richard, 202, 396.
" Rufus, 202.
" Samuel, 156, 157.
" Sarah, 202, 203, 265.
" Shadrach, 368.
" Smith, 157, 203.
" Stephen, 67.
" Thaddeus, 117, 118.
" Titus, 67.
" William, 203, 322, 369.
Lounsberry, see Lounsbury.
Lounsbury, Abigail, 203.
" Amos, 396.
" Elijah, 29.
" Elisabeth, 203.
" Enos, 157.
" Enos, Jr., 67.
" Ezra, 322.
" Gideon, 157, 396.
" Isaac, 369.
" James, 29, 67.
" Jane, 203, 204.
" Jared, 29, 68.
" John, Captain, 204.
" Lemuel, 68.
" Thomas, 68, 397.
" William, 118.
Lyon, Andrew, 68.
" Benjamin W., 68, 69, 157, 158.
" Daniel, 69, 158.
" Gilbert, 69.
" Gilbert, Jr., 29.
" James, 397.
" Job, 322, 323.
" Joshua, 323, 369.
" Martha, 29, 30.
" Mary, 204.
" Simeon, 397.
" Thomas, 118.

Mc.

McDonald, Timothy, 369.

Mc.

McGown, Francis, 369, 370.
McIntire, John, 69, 204.
McQuean, Robert, 323.

M.

Madden, Amos, 69, 118.
Marshall, Amy, 158, 159.
" Ezra, 30, 70.
" Henry, 265.
" Mary, 323.
" Orpah, 266.
" Sarah, 266.
Marvin, Epenetus, 323, 324.
Mather, Joseph, 266, 397.
" Moses, Rev., 30.
" Noyes, 30, 31.
Matthews, Charity, 324.
Mead, Abigail, 398.
" Abner, 70.
" Abraham, 119, 159.
" Abraham D., 370.
" Amos, 70, 398.
" Andrew, 119.
" Benjamin, 70.
" Calvin, 370.
" Charity, 70, 71, 398.
" Daniel S., 204, 266.
" Darius, 324.
" David, 31, 159.
" Deborah, 324, 325.
" Ebenezer, Colo., 370, 371.
" Ebenezer, 71, 370.
" Eliphalet, 71.
" Elisabeth, 267.
" Elkanah, 71.
" Isaac, 325.
" Israel, 31.
" Jabez, 325.
" Jared, 204, 205.
" Jehiel, 371.
" Jeremiah, 71.
" Job, 325.
" Jonah, 159.
" Jonathan, 159, 205.
" Joshua, 31, 71, 72.
" Manoah, 267.

INDEX TO ESTATES.

M.

Mead, Martha, 31, 72.
" Mary, 31, 72, 267, 371.
" Nancy, 119.
" Nathan, 398.
" Nathaniel, 72, 119, 398.
" Nathaniel, Jr., 72, 73.
" Nathaniel, 3rd, 72.
" Nehemiah, 205, 267, 268.
" Nehemiah, Jr., 160.
" Platt, 371, 372, 398.
" Polly, 73.
" Raphel, 205, 206.
" Reuben, 206, 268.
" Richard, 206.
" Rogers, 206.
" Ruth, 119.
" Sarah, 73.
" Selah, 325, 326.
" Seth, 206.
" Shadrach, 372, 398.
" Silas, Jr., 32, 73.
" Theodosia, 160.
" Titus, 73.
" William A., 398.
" Zaccheus, 372.
" Zophar, 326.
Meeker, Aaron, 372.
Merritt, Adam, 207.
" Caroline, 268.
" Elijah, 268.
" Elizabeth, 268.
" Gilbert, 160.
" Jeremiah A., 269.
" John, 326.
" John A., 372.
" Joseph, 74.
" Jotham, 32, 74, 372, 398.
" Sarah, 326.
Miles, John, 120.
Miller, David, 373.
" Eliza A., 161.
" James, 32, 74, 161.
" Jonathan, 269.
" Mary, or Polly, 399.
" Westover, 32, 74.
Mills, Nathaniel, 373.
" Samuel, 32, 269.

M.

Mills, Samuel, Jr., 207.
Minor, Simeon H., 326, 327.
Moe, Charlotte, 269.
Moore, Charles, 120.
" George, 74, 75.
Morehouse, Alexander, 207.
" Andrew, 75.
" Catherine, 161.
" Gershom, 32.
" Joshua, 120.
" Silas, 270.
Morrell, John, 327.
Munday, Sarah, 32, 33.
Murphy, Joseph B., 33.

N.

Nash, David, 120.
Newman, Anna, 207, 208.
" Catherine, 373, 374.
" Harvey, 208, 270.
" James M., 270.
" Maltbie, 208.
" Nathaniel, 120, 121, 208.
" Rufus, 327.
" Sarah, 161.
" Stephen, 161, 328.
" Zadoc, 328.
Newton, Alvin P., 374.
Nichols, Abraham, 33.
" Elizabeth, 33, 75.
" James, 75, 399.
" Robert, 75, 121.

O.

Olmsted, Ebenezer, 399.

P.

Page, Benjamin, 374.
Palmer, Abigail, 270, 271, 328.
" Asahel, 328.
" Deborah, 271.
" Delia, 374, 375.
" Denham, 121, 208.
" Ferris, 33, 75.

INDEX TO ESTATES.

P.

Palmer, Gilbert, 76.
" James F., 328, 329.
" Jeremiah, 161, 162.
" John, 76, 208, 209.
" John W., 399.
" Justus, 33, 76.
" Messenger, 34.
" Nathaniel, 162, 209.
" Phebe, 77.
" Samuel, 77.
" Samuel, Jr., 399.
" Seth, 209, 271.
" Vinus, 77.
Park, Eunice, 121.
Peacock, Mary, 329.
" William, 329.
Peck, Aaron, 209, 210, 271.
" Alathea, 329.
" Alexander, 162.
" Benjamin, 162.
" Ebenezer, 271.
" Elias, 375.
" Gideon, 34, 399.
" Gilbert, 210, 272.
" Hannah, 78, 210, 211, 272.
" Isaac, 162, 163.
" Isaac, Jr., 272, 273.
" Israel, 78, 211.
" Jabez, 211.
" Jared, 273, 329.
" Jerusha, 78.
" John F., 375.
" Joseph, 121, 122, 163.
" Mary, 375.
" Moses, 211.
" Nancy, 399.
" Nathaniel, 400.
" Robert, 163.
" Samuel, 78, 211, 273, 400.
" Solomon, 79.
" Stephen, 122.
" Whitfield, 163.
Pendell, Elisabeth, 330.
" William, 376.
Penoyer, Charles E., 330.
" Elizabeth, 400.
" Henry, 122, 163.

P.

Penoyer, Isaac, 273.
" Jacob, 274.
" Samuel, 274.
Perkins, Charles, 400.
Perry, Sturges, 79, 400.
Peterson, Frederick, 79.
Pettit, Hannah, 330.
Pierce, Daniel, 122, 123.
Pine, Samuel, 211, 212.
Platt, Frederick, 274.
" John P., 376.
Potts, Isaac, 274, 275.
Provost, Salmon, 79.
" Samuel, 330.
Purdy, Daniel, 79, 80.
" Elias, 212, 275.
" Thomas, 275.

Q.

Quenett, Hannah, 34, 80.
Quintard, Abraham, 330, 331.
" Elizabeth, 400.
" Peter, 34, 80.
" Peter, Jr., 123.
" Peter, 3rd., 34, 80.
" Ruth, 123.

R.

Raymond, Ezra, 34, 80.
" Ira, 80, 81, 164.
" Isaac, 34, 35.
" Mary, 376, 377.
" Munson G., 212.
" Stephen, 164, 212, 377.
Redfield, Bradley, 275, 276.
Reed, John B., 377.
Reynolds, Ambrose, 212, 213, 331.
" Ard, 276.
" Augustus L., 377.
" Deborah, 212, 276.
" Debory, 213.
" Horton, 35, 81.
" Isaac P., 81.
" James H., 213, 276.
" Jared, 123, 276, 277.

INDEX TO ESTATES.

R.

Reynolds, Joseph, 81.
" Lockwood, 213.
" Lydia, 81.
" Nathaniel, 123, 124.
" Stephen, 331.
" Timothy, 81, 82.
" William, 277.
" William P., 277, 331.
Rich, see Ritch.
Richards, Isaac, 277.
Ritch, Lemuel, 213, 214.
Robbins, John, 164.
" Mary, 331, 378.
" Parris, 277.
Roberts, Amos, 277, 278.
" Deborah, 331.
" Sally, 400.
Robins, see Robbins.
Rogers, Fitch, 214, 278, 331, 332.
" Hannah, 278.
" Sarah, 332, 378.
Rosco, Abraham, 278.
Rose, Ann, 332.
Rowell, William, 214.
Rundle, Amy, 82.
" Charles, 164, 214.
" Eli, 35.
" Elizabeth, 378.
" Nathaniel, 82.
" Phineas, 332.
" Reuben, 35, 82, 164.
" Samuel, 82, 83.
" William, 83.
Rychman, Sally B., 378.

S.

Sackett, Ann, 278.
" Joseph, 83, 279, 332, 333.
" Justus, 214, 215.
" Whitman M., 279.
St. John, Ezra, 164, 165, 215.
" Hannah, 35, 83.
" Lewis, 35.
Sanford, Clark, Dr., 124.

S.

Sarles, James, 333, 379.
Scofield, Abigail, 124, 279, 333.
" Abraham, 83.
" Alfred, 333.
" Alpheus, 333, 334.
" Anna, 279.
" Benjamin, 124.
" Betsy, 124, 401.
" Clarissa, 279.
" Daniel, 84.
" Darius K., 215.
" Edwin, 280.
" Edwin, Jr., 280, 379.
" Epenetus, 35.
" Ezra, 215, 334.
" Ezra, Jr., 215, 280.
" Gershom, 165, 379, 380.
" Gideon, 216.
" Gilbert, 84, 380.
" Hait, 280.
" Hannah, 84, 380.
" Henry, 124, 125.
" Isaac, 36.
" Isaac, Jr., 165.
" Israel, 125, 165.
" Jacob, 125.
" James, 84, 85.
" Jane, 36.
" Jared, 334.
" John, 216, 280.
" John, 3rd, 125.
" John A., 380.
" Jonas, 334.
" Levi, 280, 281.
" Mary, 281.
" Nathan, 36.
" Nathan H., 216, 281.
" Obadiah, 125, 126, 166.
" Peter, 217.
" Phineas, 126.
" Reuben, 281.
" Richard, 282.
" Robert, 85, 217.
" Samuel, 217.
" Samuel C., 166.
" Sarah, 334, 335.
" Seth, 36, 85.

INDEX TO ESTATES.

S.

Scofield, Sylvanus, 401.
" Warren, 335, 380.
" William, 335.
" William H., 335.
Seely, Abijah, 85.
" Albert, 381.
" James, 85.
" John, 217, 282.
" Selleck, 166, 217, 218.
" Wyx, 218.
Selleck, Ann, 282, 381.
" Benjamin, 166.
" Daniel, 85.
" Darling, 166, 167.
" Edward, 85, 86.
" Henry, 126.
" James, 86, 127.
" Jesse, 335, 336.
" Joseph, 381, 401.
" Kilbourn, 381.
" Letitia, 336.
" Molly, 127.
" Nathan, 401.
" Raymond, 218.
" Samuel, 282, 283.
" Stephen, 218, 336.
" Sylvanus, 336.
" Uriah, 127.
" Wray, 167, 402.
Seward, Phebe, 36.
Seymour, Drake, 86, 218.
" Mary, 219.
" Samuel, 86, 87.
Shaw, Andrew, 219, 283.
" Hannah, 219, 283.
" James, 219, 283.
" William, 127.
Sherwood, Daniel, 220, 336, 337.
" Elnathan, 402.
" Jabez, 127, 128, 167.
" Jared, 402.
" Matthew, 87, 128.
" Nathan, 128, 167.
" Nehemiah, 381, 382.
" Willet, 283, 284.
" William B., 382.
Sibell, John F., 284.

S.

Sibley, Richard, 382.
Skelding, James, 284, 402.
" John, 87.
Skidmore, Henry, 87, 128.
Skilden, John, 87.
Slason, Abraham, 88.
" Betsy, 220.
" Daniel, 167, 168, 220.
" Deliverance, 87.
" Gershom, 402.
" Hannah, 168.
" Nathan, 37, 87.
" Nathaniel, 284, 285.
Slauson, Hannah, 168.
" Nancy, 382.
Slawson, Abraham, 88.
" Daniel, 220.
" Samuel, 402.
Smith, Abel, 88.
" Alvah, 285, 402.
" Amos, 88, 128, 168.
" Ann, 285.
" Arba, 337, 382.
" Aseneth, 402.
" Benjamin, 285.
" Charles W., 337.
" Daniel, Rev., 382, 383.
" David, 129, 337, 383.
" Ebenezer, Sr., 286.
" Ebenezer, 285, 286, 337, 338.
" Eley, 338.
" Elijah, 402.
" Elizabeth, 88, 403.
" Ezekiel, 37, 88.
" Gould, 286.
" Hanford M., 220, 221.
" Henry, 221.
" Isaac, Dr., 37.
" Isaac, 221.
" Isaiah, 89, 168.
" Israel, 169.
" James A., 338.
" John, 89, 169, 221, 286, 287.
" John C., 287.
" Joseph, 129.
" Joseph, Jr., 383.
" Josiah, 222.

INDEX TO ESTATES.

S.

Smith, Josiah, 222.
" Lyman H., 287.
" Martha, 222, 287.
" Mary, 89, 338.
" Nathaniel, 89.
" Rebecca, 403.
" Reuben, 130.
" Samuel, 89, 90, 130, 169.
" Sarah, 338.
" Seth, 288.
" Simeon, 37.
" Solomon, 169.
" Stephen, 37, 38, 90.
" William H., 222, 223.
" William M., 288.
" Zety, 403.
Startin, Sarah, 403.
Stebbins, David, 223.
Stevens, Abigail, 169, 170.
" Edward, 90.
" Hellenah, 90.
" Jacob, 223.
" James, 288, 289.
" Lavinia, 130, 170.
" Mary, 338, 339.
" Obadiah, 38, 130, 131, 170.
" William H., 403.
Stivers, James, 223, 289.
Stogdill, Amy, 290.
Strang, Jared, 290.
" William, 290.
Street, George, 290.
Studwell, Anthony, 170, 290.
" Drake, 290, 291.
" Enoch, 291.
" James, 291.
" Luther H., 383.
" Sarah, 403, 404.
Sudmon, or Sudmore, ----, 404.
Sutherland, Mary, 38.
" Silas, 383.
Sutton, William, 384.
Swan, Walter, 170, 171, 223.

T.

Taber, Charles, 90.
Taylor, Joseph, 224.
" Joseph, Jr., 171.
" Nathaniel, 131, 171.
Thorp, Charles, 38, 90, 91.
" Sturges P., 131.
Tillman, John, 132, 224, 291, 292.
Tillott, Sabrina, 292.
Timpany, Mary, 91.
Titus, John H., 171.
Todd, Hannah, 171.
" John, 38, 91.
" John, Jr., 91, 171, 404.
" Washington, 92, 132, 172.
Tompkins, Abram D., 292.
Tooker, Daniel, 38, 39.
Totten, Anna, 92, 132.
Tracy, Hezekiah, 224.
" Huldah, 292.
Treadwell, Francis, 339.
Tryon, Samuel, 39, 92.
Tucker, Daniel, 38, 39.
Tuthill, Morris, 384.

V.

Vail, Abigail, 92.
Van Bun Schoten, John E., 39.
Van Busschoten, Rachel, 404.

W.

Waldrum, Nicholas, 92.
Wallace, George H., 339.
Walmsley, George, 384.
" William, 172.
Wardwell, Abigail, 404.
" Isaac, 339, 340.
" Jacob, 172.
" James, 224, 225.
Waring, George E., 384.
" Henry, 225.
" Jacob, 293.
" James, 385.
" Jesse, 293.
" Joel, 385.
" John, 293.

INDEX TO ESTATES.

W.

Waring, Jonathan, 39.
" Michagar, 93, 404.
" Noah, 39, 172.
" Samuel, 93, 172, 173, 225.
" Scudder, 225.
" Stephen, 340, 385.
" Thaddeus, 175.
" Thankful, 173.
Waterbury, Amos H., 225, 226.
" Azariah, 293, 340.
" Benjamin, 39, 173, 174.
" Bethia, 93.
" David, 40, 293, 294.
" Elizabeth, 132.
" George, 294, 340.
" Isaac, 294, 385.
" Israel, 385.
" Jacob, 404.
" James, 40, 174, 404.
" John, 226.
" Jonathan, 93, 94, 174, 404.
" Mary, 340, 341, 405.
" Nathaniel, 40, 294, 295.
" Nathaniel, Jr., 94.
" Phineas, 405.
" Polly, 295.
" Rebecca, 295.
" Samuel, 94.
" Samuel, Jr., 94.
" Sarah, 295.
" William, 226, 405.
" William L., 341.
Waters, Aaron, 341.
" Elisha, 342.
" Jacob, 405.
" John, 93.
Webb, Albert, 385, 386.
" Alfred, 386.
" Augustus, 295.
" David, 40.
" Ebenezer, 296.
" Epenetus, 296, 405.
" Frederic, 133, 405.
" James, 405.

W.

Webb, Joseph H., 386.
" Mary, 133, 227.
" Nathaniel, 94, 95, 133, 174.
" Polly, 296.
" Samuel, Dr., 227.
" Samuel, 174.
" Sarah, 406.
" Seth, 95, 133.
" William, 296.
" William A., 174, 175.
" Wilse, 227.
Weed, Aaron, 175.
" Abigail, 95, 227, 296.
" Abishai, 342.
" Amos, 95.
" Ann, 296.
" Ananias, 133.
" Asahel, 175, 227.
" Benjamin, 134, 386, 387.
" David, 95, 96.
" Ebenezer, 342.
" Ebenezer P., 96, 406.
" Elizabeth, 297, 299.
" Enos, 96, 227, 228.
" Frederick, 297, 343.
" Gideon, 134, 228.
" Hannah, 96, 228, 297.
" Henry, 228, 297.
" Henry, Jr., 175.
" Henry, 3rd, 343.
" Henry R., 96, 134.
" Hezekiah, 343.
" Holly B., 298.
" Jacob, 343.
" James, 97, 343, 344.
" James H., 134, 176.
" Jarvis, 298, 344.
" Jesse, 40, 97.
" Joel, 97.
" John, 228, 298.
" John, 3rd, 40, 97, 176, 298.
" Jonas, 41, 135, 176.
" Jonas, 3rd, 97, 98.
" Jonathan, 228, 229, 344.
" Lucy A., 98.
" Luther, 387.
" Lydia, 344.

INDEX TO ESTATES.

W.

Weed, Martha, 176.
" Mary, 41, 344, 387.
" Miles, 98.
" Nathan, 135.
" Nelson, 299.
" Raymond, 135.
" Samuel, 299, 344, 387, 388, 406.
" Sarah, 229, 299, 344, 345.
" Sarah E., 388.
" Scudder, 98.
" Scudder, Jr., 98.
" Selleck, 229, 345, 388.
" Seth, 135, 136.
" Sylvanus, 98.
" Sylvanus, Jr., 41.
" Thaddeus, 406.
" Usual, 345.
Weeks, Bartholomew, 41.
" Jane, 406.
" Joseph H., 229, 230.
" William, 98, 99.
Welch, Mary, 136.
Welles, William, 41, 42.
Wells, see Welles.
Wheaton, Mary, 299, 300.
" Samuel, 176, 177.
Whelpley, Ann, 136.
White, Esther, 406.
" Jacob, 42.
" Jacob, Jr., 300.
" Richard H., 300.
" William, 230.
Whiting, Charles, 177.
" Molly, 230.
" Samuel, 230, 300, 345.
" Samuel F., 136.
Whitney, Isaac, 177.
Wilcox, William L., 230, 300.

W.

Wilmot, Abigail, 346.
" Francis, 42, 99.
" Hannah, 137.
" James, 300.
" John, 346.
" Joseph, 177.
" Samuel, 346.
" William, 388.
Wilson, Daniel, 42, 99.
" Joseph, 42.
" Jotham, 42.
" Nehemiah, 99.
" Rachel, 388.
" Sarah, 177, 178.
" Thomas M., 178, 230.
" Uriah, 99.
Wolcott, Alexander S., 389.
Wood, David, 99, 100, 230, 231, 301.
" Isaac, 346.
" Lemuel, 406.
Wooden, Isaac, 100, 231.
" Sarah, 231.
Wooster, Ebenezer, 407.
Worden, Isaac, 100.
Wyant, Sarah, 389.

Y.

Young, see Youngs.
Youngs, Abraham, 42, 43.
" Elisabeth, 231, 407.
" Hannah, 137.
" James, 232.
" Rebecca, 407.
" Richard, 232.

INDEX TO PERSONS.

A.

Abbott, Hannah, 406.
" Polly, 98.
Adams, Abraham, 101, 179.
" Barnabas S., 241.
" Charles E., 179.
" Eli, 101.
" Elizabeth, 241.
" Emily A., 179.
" Frances, 179.
" George W., 179.
" Harriet, 214.
" John, 138, 179, 180, 209, 233, 258, 259.
" John, Jr., 15, 146.
" John, 3rd, 63.
" John A., 179.
" John W., 179.
" Joseph H., 179.
" Marilda H., 179.
" Mary, 138.
" Mary E., 179.
" Molly, 191.
" Morehouse, 179, 180.
" Nathaniel, 51, 179, 203, 211, 363.
" Nathaniel E., 138, 179.
" Phebe, 233, 258.
" Polly, 284, 302, 347.
" Reuben, 180.
" Sally, 339.
" Sands, 169, 238, 299.
" Sarah, 179, 226.
" Sarah E., 179.
" Sarah K., 179.
" Susan C., 179.
" William, 347.

A.

Adams, William H., 339, 345.
Addington, Betsy, 233.
" Caroline, 2.
" Delilah, 233.
" Elizabeth, 180, 233.
" John, 2, 180.
" Lemuel, 2, 206.
" Samuel, 233.
" Thomas, 2.
Agnew, Philip, 102.
" Susan, 102.
Aikins, Harrison, 76.
Aikman, John, 87.
Allen, Joseph, 62.
" Sally, 62, 198.
" Sarah, 197.
" William, 370.
Ambler, Caty, 279.
" Elizabeth, 96, 101.
" Isaac, 44, 80.
" Joseph, 44, 101.
" Katy, 279.
Ames, Deborah, 51.
Anderson, Abel T., 311.
" Amanda, 309.
" Anna, 180, 234.
" Dolly, 44.
" Dorothy, 180.
" Edmund, 234, 347.
" Eliph, 180.
" Elizabeth, 44, 190, 309, 347.
" Hannah, 2, 44, 180, 220, 347.
" Hannah A., 234.
" Henry, 2, 234.

INDEX TO PERSONS.

A.

Anderson, Isaac, 39, 44.
" Israel, 44, 233, 234.
" James, 44.
" James P., 190, 309.
" Jeremiah, 180, 234, 347.
" John, 2, 44.
" Joseph, 234.
" Mary, 180.
" Mather, 180.
" Matthew, 234.
" Matthias, 2, 44, 45, 390.
" Phebe, 234.
" Phebe A., 233.
" Polly, 2, 44.
" Priscilla, 2, 44.
" Prue, 44.
" Purdy, 44, 241, 382.
" Rachel M., 233.
" Rebecca, 44.
" Rebecca C., 233.
" Sally A., 2, 44.
" Stephen, 180.
" Susannah, 180.
" William, 8, 101, 180, 234, 347.
" William H., 2.
Andreas, Betsy, 347, 348.
" Cordelia, 347.
" Cordelia E., 390.
" Dorcas, 347, 348.
" Elizabeth L., 347.
" Jeremiah, 4, 6, 7, 12, 19, 24, 26, 28, 30, 31, 32, 33, 35, 40, 51, 69, 79, 80, 86, 98, 113, 124, 134, 135, 137, 138, 146, 147, 148, 157, 161, 172, 182, 198, 220, 257, 273, 293, 295, 341, 347, 348, 390, 395, 399.
" Jeremiah J., 390.
" John, 12, 347, 348.
" Julia A., 347.
" Mary, 97, 343, 344.
" Rebecca, 347, 348.
" Samuel, 347, 348.
" Sarah, 19, 347.

A.

Andreas, William, 97, 125, 220, 225, 229, 235, 259, 263, 265, 295, 298, 303, 330, 335, 343, 345, 362, 377, 380.
Annan, Samuel, 218, 219, 292.
" Sarah, 218, 292.
Antonides, Matthew, 350, 357.
Archer, Ezekiel, 161.
Armstrong, Amy, 117.
" Robert, Rev., 64.
" Sally A., 64.
Arthur, Richard H., 234.
Atkinson, Elizabeth, 403.
" John, 403.
" John, Jr., 403.
Augur, Jared, 138.
" John, 20, 65, 95, 96, 97, 130, 134, 138, 154, 229, 234, 348.
" Nancy, 20, 138, 348.
Austin, George, 230, 275.
" Mary A., 320.
Avery, Abraham, 181.
" Arna, 181.
" Betsy, 302.
" Catherine, 181.
" Clarissa, 302.
" Elizabeth, 180, 181.
" Hannah, 181.
" Ira, 181.
" Israel K., 113, 181.
" John, 3, 45, 181, 302.
" Peter, 180, 181.
" Rachel, 302.
" Reuben, 181.
" Sally, 191.
" Samuel, 257.
" Walter, 181, 302.
" Zephar, 3, 45, 302.
Ayres, Alfred, 274, 337.
" Bradley, 181, 234.
" Chauncey, 309, 328, 335, 367.
" Isaac, 59, 128, 155, 167, 171, 174, 187, 192, 223, 225, 366.

INDEX TO PERSONS.

A.

Ayres, Jeremiah N., 369.
" Jonathan, 234.
" Polly, 181, 234.
" Reuben, 234.
" Rufus, 303.
" Sarah, 59, 82, 181, 234.

B.

Babcock, William S., 88.
Bacon, Converse, 150.
" Isaac W., 295.
" John, 4.
" Martha Mx 4.
" Mary, 150.
" Sarah, 385.
Bagley, Loisa, 274.
" Louisa, 274.
Bailey, Ashbel P., 328.
" Samantha, 332.
Baker, Abigail, 276.
" Amariah E., 328.
" Amy, 213.
" Barthsheba, 88.
" Daniel, 69.
" Finetta, 328.
" Jeremiah, 88.
" Jesse, 213.
" Mary, 69.
" Peter, 276.
" Smith, 88.
" William C., 384.
Baldwin, Theophilus, 116.
Ballac, Emeline, 257.
" Joseph, 257.
Bangs, William H., Rev., 311.
Banks, Anna, 101.
" Abraham, 69.
" Burtis, 233.
" Catherine, 68, 302.
" Christina, 358.
" Daniel, 29, 30, 45, 69, 358.
" Daniel, Jr., 397.
" David, 329, 331.
" David, Jr., 358.
" Deborah, 102.
" Elisabeth, 44, 69, 302.
" George, 101.

B.

Banks, Hannah, 73.
" Isaac, 131.
" James, 29, 30, 302, 303, 397
" James, Jr. 101, 102, 145.
" John, 337.
" Joseph, 69.
" Joseph, Jr., 44.
" Joshua, 74.
" Matilda, 329.
" Mary, 29, 30, 68, 69, 303, 348.
" Nelson, 101, 102.
" Obadiah, 145.
" Obadiah, Jr., 74.
" Polly, 397.
" Sally, 397.
" Rachel, 83, 101, 102, 302.
" Samuel, 83, 101, 102.
" Sarah, 29, 30, 348, 352.
" William R., 102.
Baremore, Abraham C., 102.
" Ann, 102.
" Mary, 102.
" Walter, 102.
Barham, Aaron R., 225.
Barlow, George I., 251.
" Huldah, 251.
" Robert R., 174, 201, 204, 251.
" Russell R., 238.
Barnard, Catherine, 122.
" Robert, 122.
Barnum, Betsy, 135, 148, 234.
" Cynthia, 133, 348.
" Daniel, 165.
" David, 134, 135, 148, 215, 234.
" Deborah, 366.
" Horace, 133, 291, 292, 348
" Justus, 32.
" Samuel W., 348.
" Sarah A., 348.
Barrett, Antoinett, 366.
" Mary, 366.
Bartow, Daniel, 303.
" Robert R., 303.
Bartram, Aaron R., 225.
Bates, Abraham, 106.

INDEX TO PERSONS.

B.

Bates, Betsy, 3, 4.
" David, 3, 34, 402, 404.
" Ebenezer, 3, 4, 116.
" Ebenezer S., 348, 349.
" Edwin, 349, 350, 378.
" Eliza, 235.
" Elizabeth, 3.
" Ellen, 20.
" Esther, 348.
" Fanny, 45.
" Frances, 349.
" George R., 348.
" George S., 235.
" Gershom, 3, 4, 102, 138, 182, 234.
" Hannah, 4, 45, 102, 138, 181, 235, 350.
" Hannah E., 102, 138.
" Harriet, 235.
" Henry, 45, 108, 112, 139, 165, 181, 182, 192, 196, 198, 212, 215, 218, 234, 235, 254, 277, 290, 293, 331.
" Jacob, 10.
" James, 3, 4.
" Jerome, 235.
" John, 3, 4, 102, 348, 349, 390.
" John W., 299, 348.
" Jonathan, 20, 32, 45, 98, 181, 189, 378.
" Lavina, 3.
" Lewis H., 102, 138.
" Lewis S., 3, 4.
" Martha, 3, 4.
" Martha A., 348.
" Martha S., 102, 138.
" Mary, 3, 4, 303, 390.
" Mary E., 235.
" Mary J., 102, 138.
" Nehemiah, 308.
" Nehemiah S., 182, 292.
" Phebe, 40.
" Polly, 4.
" Richard, 45, 267, 350.
" Sally, 106, 234, 350.
" Samuel, 348.

B.

Bates, Samuel G., 102, 138.
" Sarah, 3, 4, 303, 390.
" Seely, 4, 182.
" Selleck, 4.
" Theodosia, 148.
" Walter, 45.
" William, 40, 45.
" William H., 45, 102, 138, 234, 235, 254, 278, 290, 349, 350.
Batterson, Sarah, 330.
Baxter, Sarah, 118.
Bayard, Abigail, 80.
Bayeux, Elizabeth, 46.
" Elizabeth A., 4.
" Maria, 4, 46.
" Priscilla, 4, 45, 46.
" Sally, 4, 46, 390.
" Thomas, Dr., 4, 16, 46, 390
Bayles, Stephen, 231.
Beach, Ann, 330.
" Jesse, 13.
" Sally, 13.
" Samuel, 191, 195, 227, 326.
Beardsley, Sarah M., 32.
Bedient, Elizabeth, 25.
" John, 25.
Beedle, Margaret, 32.
Beers, Jane A., 348.
" Nathan, 123.
" Richard, 348.
Belcher, Alla, 81.
" Ann, 138.
" Augusta, 138.
" Clarissa, 138.
" Elisha, Dr., 138, 139.
" Elisha, 78, 79, 81, 88, 121, 272.
" Elisha R., 77, 92, 102, 138.
" Elizabeth U., 138.
" Esther R., 153.
" Lydia, 81, 138.
" Lydia K., 81.
" Mary, 138.
" Polly, 81.
" Sarah, 138.
" William N., 138.

INDEX TO PERSONS.

B.

Belden, Elizabeth, 141.
" Frederick, 235.
Bell, Abigail, 305, 390.
" Abraham, 235, 303, 304.
" Andrew, 376, 377.
" Anna, 235.
" Betsy, 19, 102, 103, 177, 212, 376, 377.
" Cary, 5, 51, 69, 135, 146, 174, 193, 219, 283.
" Catherine, 5.
" Charity, 114, 235.
" David, 142.
" Deborah, 5.
" Deby, 114, 135.
" Ezekiel, 103, 182, 349.
" Francis, 4, 5, 103, 182, 349.
" Frederick, 4, 103.
" George S., 346.
" Hannah, 4, 5.
" Hetty, 105, 142.
" Holly, 166, 167, 177, 193, 219, 226, 229, 230, 236, 293, 294, 295, 298, 306, 330, 343, 344, 345, 348, 350, 364, 380, 390.
" Isaac, 5, 62, 114, 235, 346, 390, 401.
" Jacob, 293.
" James, 5, 10.
" Jared, 103, 142, 349.
" John, 5, 69, 102, 103, 114, 120, 134, 137, 172, 174, 182, 197, 215, 218, 219, 220, 235, 293, 341, 349.
" John, Jr., 126, 127, 134, 157, 197, 198, 212, 257, 258, 264, 282, 294, 351, 377, 387.
" John I., 235.
" John J., 384.
" Jonathan, Jr., 102, 103.
" Julia, 5.
" Leah, 4.
" Lydia, 167.
" Mary, 5, 103, 346, 349, 391.
" Mary L., 390.

B.

Bell, Mercy, 303, 304.
" Nancy, 10, 266, 282, 283, 397
" Noah, 5, 103, 182, 349.
" Polly, 381.
" Prudence, 103, 182, 304, 349, 391.
" Rebecca, 51, 103, 105, 142, 182, 349.
" Richard, 86, 114, 166.
" Rufus, 120.
" Sally, 103.
" Sally A., 103.
" Sarah, 349, 391.
" Stephen, 4, 5.
" Susannah, 5, 137, 303, 304.
" Thaddeus, 5, 19, 35, 85, 97, 98, 102, 126, 127, 135, 167, 172, 177, 247, 390, 400.
" Thaddeus, Jr., 30, 404.
Bellamy, Edwin, 45.
" Isaac, 5, 46.
" John, 5.
Benedict, Deborah, 91.
" Eli, 405.
" Jared M., 241.
" Samuel, 166.
Bennett, Elizabeth, 235.
" E. B., 364.
Benson, Catherine A., 332.
" Johanna, 50.
Betts, Andrew, 194.
" Burwell, 5, 149.
" Caroline, 5.
" Daniel, 5.
" Daniel S., 199, 208.
" Eliza A., 5.
" Filo, 5.
" Frederick, 5, 63, 83.
" Hannah, 5, 83, 333.
" Henrietta, 5.
" Mary, 5.
" Mary W., 194.
" Nathaniel W., 5.
" Sally, 50.
" Thaddeus, 104, 235.
" William M., 104.
Bishop, Abigail, 98, 397.

INDEX TO PERSONS.

B.

Bishop, Abijah, 5, 6, 46, 57, 67, 90.
" Abijah, Jr., 6.
" Alexander, 5, 6, 28, 40, 42, 57, 103.
" Alfred, 216, 280, 291, 292, 299.
" Andrew, 6, 182, 235, 236, 355, 391.
" Ann E., 355.
" Catherine, 182, 340.
" Charles F., 6.
" Charlotte, 182.
" David H., 6.
" Delia M., 236.
" Ebenezer, 46.
" Edwin, 236, 261, 363.
" Elisa H., 236.
" Ellen, 6.
" Erastus C., 236, 261, 344.
" Erastus H., 236.
" Ezra, 296.
" Ezra H., 46, 270, 284, 293, 304, 308, 312, 340, 345, 362, 384, 386.
" Hannah, 6, 46, 57, 67, 84.
" Hellenah, 90.
" Hezekiah, 67, 84, 98, 216, 236, 319.
" Isaac, 167, 168, 182.
" Jacob, 168.
" James, 402.
" John H., 182.
" John K., 6, 46, 103, 161, 182, 183, 236.
" Jonathan, 37, 80, 103.
" Joseph, 6, 7, 12, 26, 39, 61, 79, 90, 392.
" Julia, 236.
" Leander, 216, 280.
" Levina, 6, 17, 90.
" Levinia, 161.
" Mary, 84.
" Morris, 216, 280, 327.
" Polly, 319.
" Polly A., 236.
" Rebecca, 161, 183.
" Rufus, 391.

B.

Bishop, Sally, 327.
" Sarah, 36.
" Sarah C. R., 182, 236.
" Silas, 6.
" Stephen, 80, 105, 123, 149, 168, 172, 313.
" Susahnah, 57, 216, 280.
" Susannah H., 6, 90, 161.
" William, 391.
" William H., 193.
Bissell, Clark, 85, 182.
" John, 292.
" S.B.S., 364.
Bittis, Permela, 351.
" William, 351.
Blackman, Alfred, 236, 237.
" Elizabeth, 183, 237.
" Hannah, 35.
" Isaac, 35.
Blair, Letty, 108.
" Lilly A., 371.
" William, 108.
Blanchard, Daniel, 183.
" Elisabeth, 183, 237.
" Ira, 183, 237.
" Isaac, 183, 237.
" Jacob, 183, 237.
" John, 85, 183.
" Sally M., 183, 237.
Blau, Cornelia, 349, 350.
Booker, Isaac, 199.
" Nancy, 199.
Bonnell, see Bunnell.
Bonnons, Kezia, 137.
Boorman, James, 187.
" Mary W., 187.
Bostwick, Caleb, 391.
" Daniel, 6, 226, 391.
" Isaac, 391.
" Rebecca, 334.
" Sally, 22.
" Samuel, 6, 391.
" Sarah, 300.
" Stephen, 6.
Boulanger, Abigail, 276.
" Peter, 276.
Bouton, Daniel, 96, 183.
" Daniel, 3rd, 96.

INDEX TO PERSONS.

B.

Bouton, Eleazer, Jr., 96.
" Harvey, 252.
" Mahala, 183, 184.
" Marilda, 71, 119.
" Mary, 91, 96.
" Nathaniel A., 293, 296, 298, 362, 386.
" Ruth, 72.
" Samuel, 71.
" William H., 304.
Bowen, Sabrina, 392.
" William, 392.
Bowler, George J., 266, 274, 296, 339, 349, 382, 384, 388.
Bowne, Elizabeth, 99.
" James, 99.
" Thomas, 99.
Bowron, Mary, 76.
" William, 76.
Brach, Samuel, 148.
Braden, Samuel, 225.
Bradley, A. B., 295.
" Gershom, 235.
Bragg, Isaac F., 184.
Brampton, John, 367, 368.
Breadsley, James, 133.
Bretel, John, 329.
" Phebe, 329.
Breet, Elizabeth, 214.
" Gilbert, 214.
" Permelia, 214.
Briggs, Alva, 184, 185.
" Amy, 184.
" Ezra, 6.
" Hanford, 321, 322, 358.
" Hannah, 6.
" Harvey, 184, 321.
" Isaac, 184, 370.
" Jemima, 6.
" John, 6, 184.
" Lockwood, 184.
" Lydia, 184, 321.
" Mary, 118, 184, 370.
" Nathaniel, 184, 377.
" Nathaniel, Jr., 213.
" Philip, 350.
" Prudence, 6.
" Reuben, 6.

B.

Briggs, Samuel, 238.
" Shadrach, 237, 238, 337.
" William, 292.
Britt, James, 351.
" Rebecca, 351.
Broadway, Orman, 346, 349.
Broadwell, Prudence, 72.
Brooks, Henry, 407.
" Henry S., 69.
" Lavinia, 69.
" Phebe, 407.
Bross, Fanny, 91.
Brower, Mary A., 332.
Brown, Abigail, 47, 225, 362, 391.
" Abraham, 199.
" Adam, 47.
" Allen, 238.
" Ann, 108, 336, 350, 360, 371.
" Anna, 7, 180, 347.
" Anne, 391.
" Benjamin, 45, 181.
" Betsy, 72.
" Bezaleel, 7, 47.
" Charity W., 115.
" Charles, 46, 103, 184, 304, 305, 312, 334, 346, 349, 391.
" Charlotte, 225.
" Clara, 7.
" Clark S., 373.
" David, 7, 145, 158, 162, 167, 171, 220, 256, 268, 275, 284, 325, 336, 391.
" Deborah, 7, 46.
" Doctor, 5, 7, 46, 47.
" Ebenezer, 115.
" Edmund, 108, 238.
" Electa, 351.
" Eliza, 238.
" Eliza C., 185, 238, 239.
" Elizabeth, 7, 46, 139, 238, 262.
" Elizabeth L., 46.
" Emeline, 46.
" Fanny, 34.
" Francis, 47.
" George, 179, 184, 200, 278,

INDEX TO PERSONS.

B.

    295,304.
Brown, George, Jr., 184.
" George F., 350.
" George L., 304.
" Hannah, 7,45,46,181,238, 309,347,391.
" Henry, 7,40,90,101,103, 132,139,238,304,391.
" Isaac, 282.
" James, 7,391.
" James W., 268.
" Jerusha, 47,104.
" John, Captain, 262.
" John, 7,8,28,47,68,95, 99,147,148,177,184, 191,194,202,226,238, 252,278,280,289,291, 298,300,305,391.
" John, Jr., 63,112.
" Jonathan 47,58,126,133, 154,183,238.
" Josiah, 7,238,391.
" Julia, 238.
" Julia A., 46.
" Lavinia, 320.
" Lawrence, 268.
" Levi, 7.
" Levina, 78,211.
" Lucy, 305,320,351.
" Major, 7,119,351.
" Major, Jr., 238,310,313.
" Margaret, 7.
" Maria, 272,391.
" Martha, 7,47,103,104, 139,391.
" Martha J., 238.
" Mary, 214,238,262,391.
" Mary E., 185,238,239,263.
" Mary J., 368.
" Merritt, 211,268.
" Nancy, 238.
" Nathan, 78.
" Nathaniel, 7.
" Nehemiah, 7,8,83,86,150, 238,347,391.
" Nehemiah, Jr., 17,24,32, 238.
" Noah, 47.

B.

Brown, Patty, 104.
" Peter, 47,103,104,139, 140,184,185.
" Polly, 46,64,86,139,185, 238,239,263.
" Phebe, 7,65.
" Philip H., 351.
" Rachel, 7,47,199,365.
" Rebecca, 8,46,47,351,391
" Robert, 7,139,391.
" Ruth, 119,351.
" Sally, 46,133.
" Sally L., 328.
" Samuel, 34,42,55,120, 238,313,315.
" Samuel, 3rd, 47.
" Samuel C., 381,385.
" Sarah, 7,238,351.
" Susannah, 115.
" William, 7.
" William H., 46.
" William P., 185,238,239.
Bruce, George W., 356.
" Louisa A., 307,356.
Brundage, Betsy A., 239.
" Charity, 104.
" Dorcas, 185.
" David, 13.
" Elizabeth, 322,347.
" Hiram, 351.
" James, 8.
" Jonah, 8,141,185,239.
" Jonah C., 185,290.
" Lydia, 239.
" Mary, 214,351.
" Permela, 351.
" Rebecca, 351.
" Sally, 239,351.
" Sally J., 185.
" Samuel, 239,337,351.
" Sarah, 8,141,185,239.
" Silas, 239,290,382.
" Thomas C., 351.
" William, 337,351.
Brush, Abigail, 104.
" Amos M., 185,205.
" Ann, 256,257.
" Anne, 8,104,142.

INDEX TO PERSONS.

B.

Brush, Ard, 104.
" Benjamin, 8, 10, 11, 20, 38, 46, 51, 71, 81, 82, 98, 101, 104, 116, 197, 240, 307, 351, 352, 393.
" Benjamin, Jr., 8, 83, 104, 188, 245, 310, 391.
" Benjamin, 3rd, 185, 239.
" Benjamin S., 51, 104.
" Betsy, 8.
" Charles, 352.
" Christina, 8, 391.
" Cornelia, 305.
" David, 47, 239, 240.
" Deborah B., 351.
" Edmund, 239.
" Edmund B., 185, 239.
" Edward, 8, 47, 61, 82, 104, 231, 239, 305, 351, 352, 358.
" Edward, Jr., 239.
" Edward L., 305, 352.
" Edwin, Jr., 239.
" Elizabeth, 8, 391.
" Elizabeth S., 185.
" Emma C., 351.
" Fanny F., 351.
" Henry, 239.
" James, 8, 47, 48, 61, 82, 83, 142, 239, 305, 393.
" John, 8, 89.
" Jonathan, 104.
" Joseph, 81, 153, 185, 305, 215, 239, 240, 242, 261, 266, 272, 285, 325, 337, 340, 346, 351, 354, 369, 372, 385.
" Joseph E., 325.
" Josephus, 239, 305, 352.
" Louisa, 366.
" Lucy A., 104.
" Maria C., 351, 352.
" Martha, 47, 48, 61, 239, 240.
" Mary, 8, 239, 391.
" Mary A., 104, 351.
" Platt, 239, 240.
" Rachel, 47, 98, 104, 239.
" Rebecca, 104.

B.

Brush, Rebecca A., 351.
" Richard E., 185, 205.
" Ruth, 83.
" Sally, 240.
" Samantha, 81, 351.
" Samantha B., 351.
" Samuel, 8, 82, 83.
" Sarah, 47, 351.
" Sarah E., 205.
" Shadrach M., 351.
" Shubal, 8, 305, 352, 391.
" Stephen, 239.
" Theodore, 185, 205.
" William, 305.
Buckley, Gershom, 204.
Buckhout, Lydia, 184.
Buffett, Elouisa, 55.
" Hannah, 55, 320.
" Platt, 55, 320.
Bulkley, Mary, 26.
Bunhill, Lockwood, 139, 140.
Bunnell, Charlotte A., 392.
" David, 8, 48.
" Eliza J., 392.
" George, 352.
" George T., 392.
" Govenier M., 352, 392.
" Jane A., 392.
" John H., 352, 392.
" Jonathan, 208, 305, 328, 352, 392.
" Lockwood, 8, 139, 140.
" Pierre U., 352, 392.
" Polly, 117, 305, 306, 317.
" Sabrina, 144, 305, 352, 392.
" Susan E., 392.
" William A., 352, 392.
Burley, Amy, 240, 306, 353.
" Charlotte, 240.
" Cynthia, 240, 353.
" Deborah, 240, 352, 353.
" Emeline, 240, 353.
" Emily, 353.
" Henry, 199, 240, 306, 353.
" Isaac, 240, 353.
" Polly, 240.

INDEX TO PERSONS.

B.

Burley, Samuel, 240, 353.
" Silas, 240, 353.
" Walter, 240, 353.
Purling, Benjamin F., 359.
" Hannah, 359.
Burr, David B., 229, 263, 294, 367.
Burr, Phebe, 42.
Burtis, Betsy M., 240, 255.
" David, 240.
" Elizabeth, 57, 110, 140.
" Peter A., 15.
" Walsey, 175.
Burtit, Welsey, 182.
Burton, A. M., 338.
" Augustus, 353.
" Charles H., 353.
" Harriet, 392.
" Hervey, 392.
" Julia E., 353.
" Mary A., 353.
" Oliver B., 353.
" Samuel, 392.
" William, 392.
Bush, Ann, 141, 241, 256, 257.
" Charlotte, 140, 141.
" David, 140, 141.
" David W., 241.
" Deborah, 9.
" Dinah, 241.
" Elizabeth, 140, 141.
" Elsor, 241.
" Fanny, 140, 141, 153.
" Grace, 140, 141, 153.
" Henry, 141, 210, 240, 241, 332, 370.
" Joseph, 321.
" Julia, 241.
" Justus L., 14, 16, 55, 140, 141, 153, 200, 354.
" Leveret, 141, 153, 241.
" Maria, 141, 241.
" Mary, 68, 140.
" Nancy, 61.
" Nelson, 141, 159, 180, 204, 210, 233, 240, 241, 302, 325, 326, 354, 359, 361, 370, 372, 378.

B.

Bush, Ralph, 241.
" Ralph I., 140, 141.
" Rebecca, 68.
" Sabrina, 86.
" Sally, 140, 354.
" Sally L., 68.
" Samuel, 14, 61, 72, 102, 141, 146, 206.
" Sarah, 140, 141.
" William, 68, 141, 210, 241, 247, 248.
" York, 241.
Butler, Joseph, 141.
" William, 141.
Buxton, Abigail, 9, 133, 400.
" Anna M., 346.
" Betsy, 9.
" Edwin, 197.
" Emmy, 48.
" Esther, 9.
" Ezra, 9.
" George, 293.
" Isaac, 9.
" James N., 9.
" John, 9, 48.
" Jonathan, 381.
" Mary, 9, 293.
" Munson, 9, 29, 298.
" Peter, 85.
" Rachel, 9.
" Sally, 9.
" Samuel, 48, 133.
" Seth, 9, 215, 293.
" Susannah, 85.
" William, 346.

C.

Cabot, Samuel, 403.
Caldwell, Joseph, 241.
" Samuel, 241.
" Sarah, 241.
Calwell, Hannah, 9.
" Robert, 9.
Camp, David N., 45, 120.
" Elizabeth, 120.
" Isaac, 120.
" Susannah R., 120.

INDEX TO PERSONS.

C.

Campbell, Eliza C., 341.
Canfield, Hannah, 38.
Cannon, Antoinette, 104.
" Charles O., 104.
" Esther M., 104.
" George, 104.
" John C., 104.
" Sally, 104.
Caper, Phebe, 137.
" Sally, 137, 231.
" William, 231.
Capes, Sally, 293.
Cargill, Betsy, 185.
Carhart, Alfred, 241.
" Daniel, 324.
" Elizabeth, 241, 324.
" Hacaliah, 180, 239, 241.
" Hacaliah, Jr., 234.
" Hannah, 241.
" Isaac A., 241.
" Joshua, 241.
" Margaret, 241.
" Samantha, 324.
" William, 104.
" William H., 290.
Carncross, George, 48.
Carpenter, Andrew G., 356.
" Anne, 230.
" Artemas M., 233.
" Charles, 141.
" Daniel, Jr., 64.
" Dorcas, 141.
" Elizabeth, 53, 190.
" James T., 142.
" Jasper W., 356.
" Job, 142.
" John, 53, 104, 141, 143, 188.
" Joseph, 74, 141.
" Martha, 141.
" Mary, 141.
" Rebecca C., 233.
" Richard B., 245, 358.
" Richard P., 289.
" Sarah, 141.
" Silas, 8.
" Thomas, 49, 53, 74, 92, 141, 142, 143, 190, 223, 245, 381.

C.

Carpenter, Uriah, 53.
" William, 141, 142.
" Zeno, 256.
Carr, Susan, 212, 377.
Carringcross, George, 48.
Carter, Julia, 137, 231.
" Phebe, 137, 231.
" Sally, 231.
Chadayne, Daniel, 105.
" Mary, 173.
Chadwick, Ann E., 357.
" John, 357.
Chamberlain, David, 254.
Chapman, Betsy, 28.
" John, 13, 52, 53.
" Joseph, 28.
" Sally, 13, 52, 53.
Chappel, John, 271.
Chichester, Stephen, 198.
Clapp, Abel S., 88.
" Deborah, 88.
" Dorcas, 142, 186.
" James, 88, 142.
" Mary, 141, 142.
" Silas, 141, 142.
" Thomas, 49, 74, 141, 142, 185, 186.
" Thomas C., 141.
Clark, Aaron, 48, 65.
" Adam, 201.
" Cyrus, 354.
" Darius, 91.
" Edward J., 91.
" Elizabeth, 91, 354.
" Isaac W., 403.
" Nancy, 259.
" Phile, 91.
" Richard, 403.
" Robert, 327, 371.
" Robert J., 91.
" Tamer, 65, 66, 201.
Clason, Abigail, 10, 105, 186.
" Adah, 105.
" Ard, 10, 105, 186.
B Benjamin, 10, 105, 186, 222, 241, 242, 306.
" Calvin, 176, 287, 299.
" Daniel, 392.
" David, 392.

INDEX TO PERSONS.

C.

Clason, Edee, 10.
" Eliza A., 176, 299.
" Isaac, 10, 105, 186.
" Lewis, 354.
" Martha, 9, 105, 354.
" Olive, 10.
"" Reuben, 392.
" Ruth, 354.
" Seth, 10, 354.
" Smith, 82, 354.
" Solomon, 6, 10, 28, 33, 37, 50, 55, 75, 89, 105, 120, 129, 152, 161, 169, 172, 177, 185, 186, 201, 208, 221, 222, 242, 262, 264, 270, 285, 299, 329, 354, 355, 395, 402.
" Stephen, 9, 10, 186, 241, 280, 328.
" S. Lewis, 367.
" Walter S., 356, 369.
Clauson, Solomon, Jr., 128.
Clawson, Benjamin, 222.
" Hannah, 341.
" Walter S., 308, 355.
" Walter W., 308.
Clock, Abraham, 10, 93, 242.
" Abram, 108, 166, 186, 189, 193, 218, 219, 224, 230, 232, 244, 264, 266, 273, 27 274, 282, 285, 293, 294, 296, 297, 300, 306, 313, 314, 315, 339, 341, 345, 348, 349, 351, 360, 362, 363, 376, 377, 382, 387, 388, 402, 405.
" Albert, 10, 183, 186.
" Betsy, 105, 142, 173.
" Betty, 293.
" Catherine, 186, 382.
" David, 186, 242.
" Deborah, 186, 266.
" Elizabeth, 93, 105, 186.
" Edward A., 306.
" Gideon, 25, 26.
" Hannah, 173, 242, 382.
" Harriet, 105, 142.

C.

Clock, Henry, 10, 186.
" Henry, Jr., 266.
" Hetty, 105, 142.
" Hiram, 105, 142.
" Jacob V., 10.
" James, 186.
" John, 36, 37, 40, 42, 51, 87, 103, 242, 407.
" Jonas, 10.
" Julia, 306, 313.
" Martha, 105.
" Martin, 36, 105, 142.
" Mary, 186.
" Moses R., 405.
" Nancy, 10.
" Nathaniel, 10, 186, 215.
" Nelly, 105, 142.
" Oliver, 105, 142.
" Patty, 105, 142.
" Phebe, 186, 242.
" Rebecca, 105, 142.
" Sally, 10, 105, 142.
" Samuel, 105, 142.
" Sarah, 51, 105, 186, 242, 266.
Close, Aaron, 49, 242.
" Abigail, 352.
" Abraham, 7, 63, 82, 104, 115, 164, 258, 391.
" Abraham H., 242, 279, 372.
" Bethia, 105, 142, 186.
" Charlotte, 242, 355.
" Charlotte H., 186.
" Daniel, 159.
" David, 242.
" Edward, 10, 11, 102, 105, 116, 186, 210, 242, 306, 307.
" Edwin, 306, 307.
" Edwin T., 306, 307.
" Eliza, 49, 247, 317, 372, 374.
" Elizabeth, 10, 11, 49.
" Elizabeth F., 49.
" Ezekiel, 162, 233, 269, 336, 352.
" George C., 306.

INDEX TO PERSONS.

C.

Close, Gideon, Sr., 10.
" Gideon, 7,11,31,65,81, 105,142,186,306.
" Gilbert, 7,49,57,64,70, 78,82,83,99,105,138, 139,147,160,164,212, 272,306,324,351,352, 355,358,397.
" Gilbert, Jr., 240.
" Hannah, 10,11.
" Henry, 25,53,58,63,127, 209,242.
" Hervey, 63.
" Horace, 49,105.
" Isaac O., 355.
" Jonathan, 11,49,106,142.
" Jonathan A., 49,105,213, 269,331.
" Joseph, 242,308,352,355.
" Joseph, Jr., 242.
" Louisa, 352.
" Lucy, 56.
" Lucy P., 186.
" Mary R., 49,106,142.
" Nancy, 352.
" Odle, 10,11,230,242,243, 249,306.
" Odle, Jr., 11.
" Oliver F., 49.
" Pininnah, 186.
" Prue, 122.
" Rachel, 159.
" Rachel E., 242.
" Rebecca, 49.
" Rebecca R., 351.
" Rhoda, 32.
" Sally, 147,160.
" Samuel, 63,64,92,147, 188,189,200,205,211,233, 240,241,242,246,247,249, 255,268,272,284,288,290, 292,302,303,308,309,310, 311,317,323,325,351,358, 361,374,388,394,398.
" Sarah, 49.
" Sarah E., 355.
" Shadrach, 10,11,116,186, 187,242.

C.

Close, Shadrach J., 243.
" Shadrach M., 306.
" Solomon, 122,242,249,403
" Thomas, 56,67.
" Tompkins, 13,77,242,399.
" Tompkins, Jr., 242.
" William, 49,105.
" W. R., 317.
" Zachariah, 242.
Cook, Elizabeth, 57.
" Thomas, 57.
Cogger, Henry, 238.
" Martha J., 238.
Coggshall, Abigail, 88.
" Charles, 12.
" Eunice, 12.
" Frances, 12.
" George, 12.
" James, 12.
" Martha, 12.
" Mehitable, 12.
" Robert, 12.
" William, 12.
Coggswell, Alice, 12, 40.
" Hannah, 14.
" Z. W., 376.
Coleman, William, 68.
Coley, Elizabeth, 110.
" Hannah, 110.
" Samuel, 110.
Collory, Catherine, 181.
Comstock, Aaron, 394,404.
" Elsey, 392.
" James B.,106,133.
" Nancy W., 133.
" Phebe, 331,401.
" Samuel, 392.
" Stephen, 392.
" Thomas, Jr.401.
" Watts, 157.
Conley, Jane, 345.
Conn, Abraham, 52.
" Deborah, 52.
Cook, Clarissa, 95.
" Eleanor, 307.
" Hannah, 355,391.
" Henry, 288.
" Hetty, 288.

INDEX TO PERSONS.

C.

Cook, Joseph B., Jr., 6.
" Joseph P., 355.
" Joseph P., Jr., 391.
" Susan, 376, 377.
Copper, Sally, 338.
Copley, John S., 403.
" Mary, 403.
" Susannah, 403.
Cornell, Alice, 141.
" Benjamin, 141.
" Daniel, 49.
" James, 49.
" John, 49.
" Joshua, 49.
" Josiah, 49.
" Mary, 49.
" Quimby, 49.
" Samuel, 49.
" Samuel G., 268, 354, 365, 366, 375.
" Sarah, 49.
" William, 49, 141.
Corning, Edward, 187, 223.
" Elizabeth C., 223.
" James, 187, 223.
" Jasper, 187, 223.
Cornwall, William, 121.
Cowdre, Sally, 14.
Cox, Elizabeth, 307.
" Richard, 187, 307.
" Robert, 187, 196, 223, 307.
" Sally, 187.
Cozine, John R., 9.
" Rebecca, 9.
Crabb, David, 49.
" Deborah, 315.
" Elisha, 49.
" Ely, 49.
" John C., 392.
" Jonathan, 392.
" William, 171.
Crane, Mary, 278, 331.
Craw, Legrand, 267.
Crennell, Abigail J., 106, 143, 392.
Crissy, Abigail, 19.
" Hiram, 314.

C.

Crissy, Jesse, 15.
" John, 11.
" Polly, 3, 11.
" Seth, 343, 345.
" William, 19, 154.
Cromwell, Charles, 233.
" Charles T., 211.
" Israel A., 233.
" Mary J., 359.
" Rachel W., 233.
" Sarah G., 359.
" William W., 359.
Curtis, Abigail, 143.
" Deborah, 341.
" Debory, 143.
" Edmund, 143.
" Ezekiel, 194, 307.
" Henry, 143, 243, 394.
" Hester A., 355.
" Jeremiah, 56, 62, 80, 95, 143, 167, 342.
" John, 143, 243, 274.
" Phebe, 143.
" Polly, 243.
" Sarah, 36, 307.

D.

Dally, Polly, 18.
" Susannah, 18.
Dan, Alfred T., 308, 356.
" Angeline O., 307, 356.
" Charles, 243.
" Charles W., 49.
" Elihu, 257.
" Eliza, 243, 244.
" Elizabeth, 307.
" Elizabeth F., 307, 355.
" Elizabeth W., 356.
" Elvin L., 308, 356.
" Frances H., 308, 356.
" Hannah, 244.
" John, 49, 307, 308, 356.
" Jonathan, 187, 223, 243, 244.
" Louisa A., 307, 356.
" Lydia, 244.
" Maria S., 307.

INDEX TO PERSONS.

D.

Dan, Nancy, 244.
Dan, Nathan, 49, 50.
" Polly, 244, 257.
" Rachel L., 307, 356.
" Rhoda, 244.
" Sally, 244.
" Samuel, 311.
" Squire, 243, 244.
" Sylvanus, 187, 243, 244.
" Walter S., 308, 356.
Daniels, Delilah, 233.
" Mary, 327.
" Nehemiah, 233.
" Pliny, 339.
" Polly, 339.
" Seely, 327.
Daskam, John, 104.
" Philander, 396.
" Samuel, 104.
Davenport, Abigail F., 12.
" Abraham, 11, 12.
" Ann R., 88.
" Catherine, 11.
" Charles F., 356.
" Charles W., 320.
" Deodate, 19.
" Dorfus, 106.
" Ebenezer, 11, 12, 16, 23, 28, 41, 45, 66, 90, 153, 214, 217, 399.
" Elizabeth, 11, 13.
" Elizabeth C., 12.
" Elizabeth H., 187.
" Emma, 356.
" Frances L., 12, 50.
" George, 356.
" Hannah, 11, 50.
" Hezekiah R., 106.
" Isaac L., 356.
" James, 12, 50, 106, 196, 217, 257, 281, 356.
" James A., 356.
" James R., 187.
" Jerusha, 11, 41, 66, 90, 153, 214, 217, 399.
" John, 11, 41, 106, 187.
" John, Jr., 4, 11, 12, 13, 19, 40, 50.

D.

Davenport, John A., 187, 316, 323.
" John H., 356.
" Joseph, 194.
" Julia A., 106.
" Julia W., 187.
" Martha, 281, 356.
" Mary, 28, 41, 66, 153, 217.
" Mary A., 12, 106.
" Mary S., 41, 88, 187.
" Mary W., 11, 187.
" Matilda, 187.
" Mehitable, 12.
" Ralsey, 356.
" Sally, 106.
" Sarah, 11, 106, 281.
" Silas, 11.
" Sylvester, 356.
" Theodora, 11.
" Theodore, 88, 136, 164, 196, 280, 187.
" Theodosia, 106.
" William, 11, 12, 65, 106, 217, 356, 363, 392.
Davis, Aaron, 50, 117, 157, 161.
" Abigail J., 204.
" Abraham, 37, 50.
" Ann, 50.
" Asa, 327.
" Bethia, 25, 73, 78, 160.
" Catherine, 50.
" Clarissa, 50.
" Elisha, 50.
" Elizabeth, 50.
" Esther, 50.
" Gould, 334.
" Hannah, 327.
" Henry, 149, 204.
" Johanna, 50.
" Levina, 50.
" Lockwood, 321.
" Mary, 50, 140.
" Mehitable, 50.
" Nancy, 50.
" Polly, 50.
" Richard D., 332.
" Ruth, 106, 137, 308.

INDEX TO PERSONS.

D.

Davis, Sally, 50.
" Silas, 50, 180.
" Stephen, 73, 160.
" Thomas, 50.
" Walter, 50, 106, 308.
Day, Ira C., 371.
" Zetta, 371.
Dayton, Ally, 336.
" Ann, 187.
" David, 50, 269, 278.
" David, Jr., 358.
" Deborah, 275.
" Elizabeth, 358.
" Gilbert, 143, 187.
" Henry, 200, 353.
" Jacob, 308, 356, 357.
" Jacob, Jr., 242, 197, 242.
" James, 188, 244.
" Martha, 99.
" Matthew, 49.
" Nathaniel, 188, 244, 336.
" Samuel B., 308, 356.
Deal, Edson W., 345.
" Elizabeth, 345, 388.
" George, 130, 167.
" Mary, 130, 345.
" Olive, 167.
Dean, Aaron, 265, 314, 334.
" Ebenezer, 232, 314.
" Isaac, 267, 325.
" John, 227, 265, 269, 334, 387.
" Samuel, 95.
" Samuel, Jr., 373.
" Samuel W., 393.
Delevan, John, 61.
" Rachel, 61.
Demill, Cornelia A., 12.
" Elizabeth S., 12.
" Frances S., 12.
" Joseph, 12.
" Mary R., 12.
" Peter, 12, 73.
" Peter E., 12.
" Richard M., 12.
" Sarah, 12.
" Sophia, 25, 73.

D.

Demill, Thomas A., 12.
" William S., 12.
Demorest, Samuel, Jr., 392.
" Sarah M., 392.
Denny, Samuel, 311.
Denton, Aaron, 392.
" Abigail, 72, 143.
" Anna, 72.
" Betsy, 221.
" Daniel, 106, 143.
" Darius, 244.
" Elizabeth, 181.
" Everé, 31, 392.
" Hannah, 181.
" Humphrey, 51, 188.
" John M., 106.
" Joseph, 188.
" Samuel, 51.
" William, 244.
Derby, George, 158.
" Mary, 158.
Dewolf, James, Mrs., 349.
Dibble, Abigail, 51.
" Alexander, 188.
" Clarissa, 134.
" Deborah, 51.
" Elizabeth, 51.
" Emeline, 188.
" Ezra, 134, 216, 300, 349.
" George, 51.
" Grace, 51.
" John, 51, 87, 104, 304.
" John, Jr., 105, 303, 304.
" Jonathan, 51.
" Josiah, 51.
" Maria, 304, 308.
" Mary, 32.
" Mary A., 51.
" Phebe, 51.
" Ruth, 134.
" Sally, 87.
" Samuel, 51.
" Sarah, 51.
" Walter, 134.
Disbrow, James, 357.
" Susan, 357.
Disco, Phebe, 76.

INDEX TO PERSONS.

438.

D.

Dixon, Catherine, 107, 143, 263.
" Eliza, 143.
" Isaac, 308.
" Margaret, 143.
" Philemon, 188.
" Prudence, 259.
" Sarah A., 107, 143.
" Thomas P., 143.
" William E., 263.
Dodge, Frances, 230.
Dodgshan, Enoch, 188, 308.
" Hannah, 188, 308.
Dole, Charlotte C., 355.
Doty, Hannah, 76.
" John, 121.
" Lue Ann, 121.
" Mary, 312.
" William, 121.
Doughty, Hannah, 76.
Downing, Angelina, 357.
" Ann Augusta, 357.
" Augustus C., 357.
" George, 357.
Downs, Benjamin S., 305.
" George L., 244.
" Lucy A., 98, 104.
" Seth, 188.
Dunham, Esther, 51, 84.
" John, 51.
Dunn, Jerusha, 188.
" Joseph, 188, 189.
" Richard, 403.
" Richard, Jr., 403.
Dunton, Mehitable, 205, 267, 292.
" Royal, 205, 267, 292.
Dusenbury, Israel A., 241.
" James, 2x328.
" Sally M., 328.
Dwight, Mary, 88.

E.

Edwards, John, 12, 13.
Eginy, William, 207.
Egry, Sarah, 284.
" William, 284.
Ellis, Francis S., 253, 254.
" Harriet, 254.

E.

Ellison, Hannah, 173.
Emmerson, Mary E., 357.
Ennis, Alla, 258.
" William, J, 258.
Escott, Rhoda, 189.

F.

Fairchild, Adaline, 235.
" Deborah, 328, 332.
" James B., xx/141.
Fancher, Charles, 244.
" Darius, 244.
" David, 19, 51, 244.
" Ellis, 244.
" Hannah, 51.
" Henry, 244.
" Martha, 51, 244.
" Mary, 19.
" Rebecca, 51.
" Sally, 244.
" Sarah, 51, 72.
" Thomas, 345.
Fareweather, Jane, 167.
" Jedediah, 167.
Feeks, Abigail, 51.
" Betsy, 226.
" Charles, 38.
" Elizabeth, 38.
" Samuel, 38.
Felmette, Dinah, 189.
" Jeffery, 189.
Ferris, Abel, 52.
" Abigail, 52, 56, 109, 143, 156, 393.
" Alexander, 144, 358.
" Alla, 322.
" Amy, 52, 107, 184.
" Andrew, 52, 107.
" Ann, 52, 107, 144, 308, 309, 319, 357.
" Anna, 107.
" Asa, 52, 65, 66, 237, 245, 357.
" Asa M., 244, 251, 281, 357.
" Benjamin, 13, 107.
" Betsy, 13, 51, 52, 258, 340

INDEX TO PERSONS.

F.

Ferris, Caroline, 190, 309.
" Caroline E., 190.
" Catherine, 121, 144.
" Charles, 52.
" Charlotte, 143.
" Clara, 144.
" Clarissa, 107, 121, 322.
" Clarry, 107.
" Clauson, 13.
" David, Jr., 13, 51.
" Deborah, 52, 107, 272.
" Ebenezer, 13, 52, 53, 56, 109, 143, 144, 393, 406.
" Edmund, 144.
" Edwin, 144.
" Eliphalet, 52.
" Elizabeth, 77, 107, 145, 208.
" Elvin, 208.
" Emelia A., 189.
" Enoch, Rev., 143.
" Esther, 107, 144, 189, 309.
" Ethan, 52, 79, 122, 189, 245.
" Frances E., 190.
" George, 107, 163, 264.
" George, Jr., 156, 264, 265, 368.
" George P., 209, 210.
" Gideon, 107.
" Hanford, 13.
" Hannah, 52, 157, 309, 357.
" Hannah H., 309.
" Hannah M., 385.
" Harry, 144.
" Harvey, 190.
" Henrietta, 309.
" Isaac, 113, 157, 189, 392.
" Jabez, 144, 358.
" James, 52, 144, 357.
" James, Jr., 52.
" Jane, 144.
" Jane A., 189.
" Jeduthan, 52, 79, 136, 145, 189.
" Jemima, 13, 52, 53.
" Jeremiah, 52.

F.

Ferris, John, 14, 52, 107, 144, 218
" John, Jr., 14.
" Jonah, 403.
" Jonathan, 79, 340, 357.
" Joseph, 52, 76, 107, 121, 189, 308, 371.
" Joseph, Jr., 52.
" Joseph D., 316, 317, 375, 385.
" Joshua, 28, 52, 65, 66, 99, 136, 151, 154, 155, 162, 163, 202, 203, 245, 263, 322, 328, 396.
" Joshua B., 260, 263, 277, 285, 309, 315, 319, 328, 345, 353, 377, 378, 385.
" Julia, 189.
" Julia A., 145.
" Juliet, 144.
" Kimberly, 364.
" Lavina, 107, 189.
" Lemuel, 13, 25, 52, 75, 76, 91, 123, 136, 144, 189, 358.
" Letitia, 322.
" Levina, 107.
" Lewis, 107, 119.
" Lockwood, 144, 190, 352.
" Lydia A., 144.
" Marcy, 258.
" Margaret, 144.
" Maria, 53, 67.
" Marilda, 121, 144.
" Martha, 145, 156, 406.
" Mary, 52, 53, 107, 144, 189, 245, 309, 322.
" Mary A., 13, 52, 53, 245.
" Mary L., 308, 309.
" Mary W., 309.
" Mercy, 258.
" Nancy, 52.
" Nathaniel, 13, 71, 107, 144, 309.
" Nathaniel, Jr., 52, 107, 144.
" Nathaniel H., 309.
" Oliver, 13, 16, 53.
" Patty, 145.

439.

INDEX TO PERSONS.

F.

Ferris, Permelia, 144, 190, 309.
" Peter, 144, 145, 189, 200, 277, 307, 308, 309, 316, 323, 328, 329, 331, 357, 375.
" Phebe, 52.
" Polly, 245.
" Polly A., 245.
" Ransford A., 145, 259.
" Rebecca, 144.
" Riley, 144.
" Ruth, 52, 107, 308.
" Sabrina, 144.
" Sally, 163.
" Sally H., 385.
" Samuel, 56, 79, 107, 186, 187, 189, 243, 357.
" Samuel, Jr., 151, 189, 202, 309.
" Samuel H., 309.
" Sarah, 13, 52, 144, 150, 189, 245, 309, 392.
" Sarah H., 285.
" Shadrach, 52, 53.
" Silas H., 234, 251.
" Solomon, 77, 107.
" Stephen, 23, 85, 145, 218, 308, 336.
" Stephen, Jr., 23, 52.
" Stephen R., 309.
" Susan, 144, 189, 244, 309, 357.
" Susan A., 190.
" Susan C., 163.
" Sybil W., 76.
" Sylvanus, 245.
" William, 107, 121, 144, 291, 377.
" William E., 302.
" William I., 190.
Field, Aaron, 22, 49, 53, 104, 143, 180, 188, 190, 309, 358.
" Abigail, 53, 190, 245.
" Ann, 309.
" Anna F., 190.
" Anne, 53.
" Charles, 49, 53, 309.
" Charles R., 245.

F.

Field, Edmund, 245, 309, 347, 358, 359, 384.
" Elias H., 358.
" Eliza, 309.
" Elizabeth, 53, 190.
" Elizabeth C., 245.
" Esther, 190.
" Fanny, 245.
" Gulydina, 245.
" Hannah, 53, 190, 245, 309, 358.
" Hannah L., 358.
" Henry C., 245.
" Jacob W., 245.
" James, 49, 53, 74, 92, 141, 142, 190, 245, 248, 309, 324, 347, 358, 384.
" James, Jr., 358.
" Jane, 309.
" Joseph, 384.
" Josiah, 22, 49, 50, 53, 190.
" Maria M., 190.
" Mary, 53, 190, 245.
" Phebe, 141.
" Richard, 309.
" Robert, 53, 190, 245.
" Sarah, 53, 190.
" Sarah E., 309.
" Thomas C., 141, 190, 358.
" Uriah, 22, 53, 190, 245.
" Willett, 245.
" William, 74.
" William C., 309, 358.
Finch, Abigail, 190, 286, 309, 310
" Alathea, 329.
" Amos, 185, 208, 242, 245, 257, 261, 285, 310.
" Anna, 107.
" Christina, 8, 358.
" Deborah B., 351.
" Deodate, 404.
" Edward, 392.
" Edwin, 358.
" Eliza A., 392.
" Ezekiel, 210.
" Gilbert P., 210, 272, 273, 284, 329.

INDEX TO PERSONS.

F.

Finch, Griffin, 50.
" Hannah, 82.
" Isaac, 82.
" John, 392.
" Jonathan, 13, 107, 144, 245.
" Mary, 404.
" Nathaniel, 107, 190.
" Nathaniel, Jr., 99.
" Rachel, 102.
" Reuben, 47, 51, 52, 164, 245, 310.
" Reuben R., 120.
" Rhoda, 245.
" Sally, 99, 393.
" Shadrach, 120.
" Sibyl, 392.
" Sibyl A., 392.
" Sophia, 107.
" William, 101, 102, 210, 240, 272, 310.
" William, Jr., 70.
" Zabed, 102, 107, 146, 256.
Finny, Caroline, 190.
" John A., 289.
" Phebe, 190, 191.
" Sally, 310.
Fisher, Abel S., 324.
" Deborah, 324.
" Mary, 266.
Fitch, Asa, 96.
" Damaras, 96.
" Elizabeth, 52, 69, 73, 118.
" Jabez, 7, 17, 18, 32, 69, 73, 397, 404.
" Samuel M., 17, 18, 118, 191.
" Sarah, 18, 52, 72, 118.
Flandereau, ---, Rev., 143.
Flanegan, Daniel, 53, 54.
Flanigan, Charles, 313.
Fleet, Daniel, 231.
" James, 231.
Fleming, Alexander, 403.
Fletcher, Jacob, 69.
Fletinborough, ---, 54.
Ford, Benjamin, 310.

F.

Ford, Cornelius, 263, 264, 310, 319, 368.
" Eliakim, 310.
" Elizabeth A., 4, 46.
" Hannah, 264, 310.
" Letitia, 310.
" Lucy, 310.
" Oliver L., 4, 45, 46.
" Sarah, 238, 310.
Forweling, Benjamin, 49.
Foster, David, 41.
" Henry, 244.
" Mary, 386.
" Sally, 244.
" Sarah, 41.
" William W., 293.
Fowler, Abigail J. H., 192, 399.
" David, 145, 191, 192.
" David H., 191, 210, 399.
" David N., 145.
" Mary, 142.
" Stephen, 166.
" Thomas, 378.
Fox, Bates, 305.
" Clara, 217.
" Mary, 231.
" Richard, 102, 143, 148, 154, 165, 217, 227, 307, 335, 349, 363, 365, 367, 380, 405.
Francis, George, 160.
French, Abel O., 356.
" Angelina O., 356.
Frost, Deborah, 28.
Funston, Sally, 249.
" William, 249.

G.

Gale, Abigail, 88.
" Anne, 118.
Ganey, Elizabeth, 403.
Garnsey, Betsy, 125.
" Mary, 406.
" Solomon, 125, 291, 325.
Gay, Sally, 85.
" Royal L., 177, 191, 194, 208, 209, 221, 222, 234, 245, 249, 251, 252, 255, 258, 264, 271,

INDEX TO PERSONS.

442.

G.

251,252,255,258,264,271,
280,282,294,296,304,305,
308,310,313,314,317,318,
319,320,328,334,340,362,
368,376,381,394.
Gaylor, Bethia, 317,318,319.
" Charles, 317,318,319.
George, Prince, 14.
Germonds, Samuel, 25.
Gilbert, Ann, 202,204,214,332.
" Jerusha E., 226.
" Josiah, 279.
Gilman, Evans, 393.
" Hannah, 393.
" Peggy, 393.
Golden, Ephraim, 327.
Gorham, Abigail, 62.
" Henry, 282.
" James H, 341.
" Joseph, 190,282.
" Julia B., 282.
" Samuel, 62.
Gorum, Abigail, 114,244.
" Alfred, 108.
" Charity, 36.
" Charlotte, 108.
" Daniel, 36,107,108.
" George, 36,108.
" Henry, 108.
" Jane, 108.
" John, 36,407.
" Joseph, 108.
" Phebe, 108.
" Polly, 108.
" Samuel, 108,114,244,274.
Gowen, Francis, see McGown.
Graham, Cornelia J., 302.
" James, 139.
Gray, Alfred, 14,54.
" Almira, 145.
" Benjamin, 108.
" Cary H., 191,224,229,245,
246,262,310.
" Catherine, 145.
" Catherine S., 191,246.
" Daniel, 191.
" Eleanor, 14,54.

G.

Gray, Elizabeth, 246,273,282,
335,336.
" Hannah, 14,191.
" Hannah E., 191,246.
" Isaac, 105,108,123,231,
242,242.
" James, 68.
" John A., 14,54.
" Joseph, 21,22,23,46,48,49
58,62,87,137,154,175,191,
200,209,246,320,406.
" Joseph A., 177,191,282,
401.
" Julia A., 145,191.
" Mary, 14,54.
" Molly, 191.
" Phebe, 108,145.
" Philip, 14,54.
" Polly, 108.
" Rachel, 96.
" Sally J., 245,246.
" Sarah A., 355.
" William L., 191,336.
Green, Abraham, 14.
" Abraham L., 246.
" Abram L., 246,247.
" Alexander, 340.
" Anthony, 246.
" Benjamin, 116,145,246,
247,248,275.
" Benjamin, Jr., 246.
" Charles, 38.
" Charles, Jr., 14.
" Charles E., 246.
" Cynthia, 247,311.
" Deborah L., 246.
" Dewitt C., 22 246.
" Elisha, 14.
" Elizabeth, 14,108,247,
311,358.
" Eunice, 246.
" George W., 246.
" Gloaner, 358.
" James, 30,99,118,145,190,
230,248,310,311,358.
" James, Jr., 53,54,115,120,
137,167,178.

INDEX TO PERSONS.

G.

Green, James H., 358.
" Jeremiah, 247, 310.
" John, Captain, 54.
" John, 108, 247.
" John V., 212.
" Joseph, 53, 54, 120, 145, 164, 190, 247, 248, 311.
" Mary, 42, 246, 247, 248, 311.
" Mercy, 54, 247.
" Nancy, 145, 247, 248, 311, 358.
" Nathan, 14.
" Oliver, 76.
" Patty, 311.
" Polly, 311.
" Rebecca, 247, 311.
" Reuben, 14, 145, 247, 248, 311, 358.
" Sally, 310.
" Sarah, 145, 247, 248.
" Susan, 311, 358.
" Susannah, 30, 145, 247.
" Thankful, 14.
" Thomas, 54, 142, 145, 171, 211, 213, 220, 246, 247, 248, 358, 398.
" William H., 246.
Grew, David, 311.
Griffin, Abigail, 245.
" Anna, 190.
" Charles, 14.
" Daniel, 53, 190.
" Daniel M., 249, 359.
" David, 190.
" Esther G., 359.
" Hannah, 190, 359.
" Hannah F., 358.
" John, 49, 88.
" John D., 359.
" John J., 53.
" Mary, 53, 190, 358.
" Sarah, 53, 190.
" Sarah G., 359.
Grigg, Alexander, 54, 108, 393.
" Ann, 54, 108.
" Betsy, 108.

G.

Grigg, David, 393.
" David A., 393.
" Elizabeth, 140, 180, 311, 359, 371.
" Henry, 50, 54, 359.
" James, 54.
" John, 54, 108, 359, 360, 371, 393.
" John R., 311, 359.
" Letty, 108.
" Lydia, 204.
" Mary, 72, 108, 359, 371.
" Walter, 14, 54, 108, 371, 393.
" William C., 360.
Grinnalds, Maria, 332.
" Southy, 332.
Guernsey, Jacob S., 248.
" Solomon, 175, 224, 248, 270, 372.

H.

Haff, Mary B., 363.
Haggerty, John, 54, 55.
Haight, Aaron, 233.
" Daniel, 78, 99, 146.
" Desire, 99, 177.
" Epenetus, 146, 177.
" Eunice, 146, 177.
" Moses, 233.
" Nancy, 310.
" Nathaniel D., 183, 200, 201, 227, 234, 236, 237, 243, 245, 253, 257, 261, 270, 274, 281, 291, 298, 299, 304, 318, 319, 321, 337, 348, 373, 391.
" Nehemiah, 177.
" Nehemiah W., 146, 177.
" Phebe, 146, 177, 391.
" Phebe A., 233.
" Polly, 310.
" Sally, 177, 204.
" Sarah, 146.
" Stephen, 361, 366.
Hait, Ann, 14, 366.
" Cary, 15.

INDEX TO PERSONS.

H.

Hait, David, 14.
" David N., 248.
" Elizabeth, 15, 366.
" Esther, 14.
" Ezra, 15.
" Frederick, 14, 55, 74, 80, 91.
" Hannah, 14.
" Henry, 14, 15, 170.
" Henry, 3rd, 55.
" Henry, 4th, 15.
" J. W., 248.
" Jemima, 15.
" Jesse, 15, 393.
" Joel, 15.
" John, 15, 55.
" John, 4th, 15.
" Jonah, 55.
" Jonathan, 15.
" Lucy A., 55, 393.
" Martha J., 249.
" Mary, 15.
" Mary A., 14, 248.
" Mary A. P., 248.
" Nathaniel D., 304.
" Nehemiah, 15, 55.
" Nehemiah, Jr., 129, 156, 187, 243, 244, 248, 259, 287, 316.
" Reuben, 15.
" Ruth, 15.
" Sally, 14.
" Sarah, 15, 55.
" Sarah M., 249.
" Seth, 15, 36, 55, 89, 403.
" Stephen, 15.
" Thankful, 15.
Hall, David, 249.
" George, 249.
" Jonathan M., 292, 374, 381.
Halleck, Amy H., 15.
" Anna, 15.
" George, 15.
Hallet, Phebe, 49.
Halligan, John, 360.
Hallock, Edward, 142.
" Elizabeth, 327.
" William H. H., 327.

H.

Halsted, Daniel, 74.
" John, 74.
" Sarah, 68.
" William, 74.
Hanford, Augustus, 311.
" Betsy, 135.
" Charles A., 252.
" Ebenezer, 360.
" Holly, 197.
" Thaddeus, 88, 133, 134, 135, 143, 147, 148, 302, 311, 347.
Harden, Abigail, 149, 253.
" Zadoc, 328.
Harms, Hannah, 250.
" John W., 384.
" Michael, 250, 262.
Harris, John W., 350.
Harroway, Elias, 160.
Harvey, Elinor, 311.
" Juliet, 311.
" Thomas M., 311, 312, 360.
Hatfield, Catherine S., 284.
" Elias, 284.
Haviland, Abijah, 233.
" Anna F., 190.
" Anne, 53.
" Anner F., 358.
" Elizabeth, 190.
" James, 190.
" Jane, 190.
" John, 28, 53, 190.
" Maria, 190.
" Mary, 190.
" Patience, 233.
" Reed, 123.
" Solomon, 14.
Hawley, Charles, 114, 132, 133, 135, 141, 165, 176, 199, 201, 209, 212, 216, 222, 244, 262, 256, 264, 271, 272, 291, 292, 296, 299, 310, 311, 315, 316, 317, 323, 326, 328, 330, 331, 332, 333, 334, 338, 339, 340, 347, 354, 361, 363, 371, 373, 381, 383, 401.
" Charles A., 311, 328, 330, 371, 381.

INDEX TO PERSONS.

445.

H.

Hawley, Cynthia 399 (handwritten)

Hawley, Charles S., 109.
" Electa, 222.
" Elector, 108, 109.
" Elijah, 15, 16.
" Elisha, 109.
" Hannah, 15.
" Marianna C., 354.
" Martha C., 280.
" Mary, 341.
" Mary S., 271, 311, 354.
" Polly, 15.
" Sarah E., 108.
" William H., 229.
Haws, Zipporah, 400.
Haxton, Charlotte, 16.
" Dyer, 16, 109.
" Louisa C., 109.
" Sarah, 109.
Hays, Josiah, 16, 35.
" Mary, 16.
Hazard, Martha, 88.
" Peggy, 88.
Hebbard, Esther, 109.
" Hannah, 109.
" Jonathan, 109.
" Nathaniel, 109.
" Polly, 109.
" Ruth, 109.
Hedden, Zadoc, 249.
Henderson, Hannah, 295.
" Hugh, 249.
" John, 295, 359.
" Margaret, 338.
" Sally, 249.
Hendrie, Alexander, 16, 52, 61, 66, 107, 121, 201, 220, 263, 264, 265, 310, 383.
" Anne, 16.
" Charles, Captain, 367.
" Charles, 16, 117, 151, 264, 276, 279, 309, 316, 322, 364.
" Hannah, 16, 249.
" Jane, 16.
" Letitia, 65, 310.
" Mary, 16.
" William, 16.
Hennesy, Fanny, 80.
Hennings, Luther, 209.

Hercy, Maria, 157.
Heusted, see Husted.
Heustis, Ann, 310.
" John S., 246.
" Jonathan S., 358.
Hickcock, Seth, 154.
Hicks, Charles, 357, 360.
" Charlotte A., 141.
" Henry H., 124.
" Henry R., 360.
" Julia, 241.
" Oliver H., 124.
Hickson, Ann, 400.
Higby, Nathaniel, 142.
Hill, George, 282.
Hillhouse, Rebecca, 88.
Hine, Lewis, 18.
" Molly, 18.
Hitchcock, Adaline, 16, 164.
" Cyrus, 16, 55, 91.
" Elizabeth, 55.
" Hannah, 16.
" John, 16, 55.
" Joseph, 16.
" Louisa, 16.
" Mary, 16.
" Rufus, 55.
" Samuel L., 16.
" Sarah, 16.
" Thomas, 16, 55, 91.
" Thomas J., 16.
" Thyrza, 16.
" William R., 16.
Hoas, John, 76.
Hobart, Dayton, 403.
" John H., 403.
Hobby, Abby J., 17.
" Abigail, 146, 360, 361, 393.
" Abraham, 9, 186.
" Alfred, 393.
" Allen, 188.
" Amarantha, 351.
" Amos, 17, 55, 100, 121, 147, 250, 312.
" Amos N., 312.
" Amy, 16, 17, 55.
" Amy N., 55, 56.
" Andrew, 56.
" Ann L., 351.
" Anna, 81, 358.
" Anne, 8.

INDEX TO PERSONS.

H.

Hobby, Annis, 72.
" Asa, 358.
" Benjamin, 17.
" Betsy, 191.
" Caleb, 191.
" Caroline, 55,56,188.
" Clemence, 191.
" Cynthia, 55,56,113.
" David, 393.
" David A., 351.
" Deborah, 393.
" Ebenezer, 17,48,56,109.
" Eliza, 56.
" Elizabeth, 393.
" Eunice R., 56.
" Frances, 186.
" George, 370.
" George A., 146.
" George E., 56.
" Guy B., 101,307,365.
" Harry, 250.
" Harvey, 365,393.
" Hervey, 264.
" Hezekiah, 145,146,162, 191,206,312.
" Husted, 56.
" Jabez M.,146,192,250, 360.
" Jabez M.,Jr.,191.
" John, 146,358.
" Jonathan, 365,393.
" Joseph, 191.
" Julia A., 351.
" Laura, 188.
" Lucy, 56.
" Lydia, 17.
" Maria, 17.
" Mary, 9,56,109,146,358.
" Mary J., 191.
" Mills, 56.
" Molly, 191.
" Nancy, 146,192.
" Nehemiah B., 17,86.
" Philander, 17.
" Rebecca, 110,188.
" Rhoda, 86.
" Ruth, 18,56,146.
" Sally, 17,55,56,191.

H.

Hobby, Samantha B., 351.
" Samuel D., 206,312.
" Samuel S., 17,86.
" Sarah, 56.
" Seymour, 8,57,86,188.
" Squire, 17,56,113.
" Thomas, 191.
" Walter, 191.
" William, 56,259,270,287, 361.
Hobson, Allen, 56.
Holly, Abigail, 250.
" Abigail E., 12,322.
" Abraham, 109,110,192.
" Alexander N., 182,192, 262,312.
" Alfred A., 12,312.
" Ann E., 263.
" Caroline, 174.
" Catherine E., 192,250.
" Charles F., 192,250.
" Chloe, 109,110.
" Clarissa, 251.
" David, 12,17,63,72,131, 195,196,250,363.
" David, Jr., 212.
" David F., 192.
" Deborah, 56.
" Edwin S., 192,313,327, 385.
" Eleanor, 192,250.
" Elena, 312.
" Elijah, 393.
" Elizabeth, 56,109,110, 393.
" Elizabeth K., 12.
" Elnathan, 109.
" Emeline, 256.
" Emeline A., 257.
" Emily, 262.
" Enoch, 56.
" George F., 192,312.
" George T., 250.
" Hannah, 17,57,250.
" Hannah M., 192.
" Huldah, 251.
" Increase, 56.
" Isaac, 31,47,56,71,73,81,

INDEX TO PERSONS.

H.

93,94,95,101,109,111,
114,115,120,125,139,144,
153,154,157,158,159,160,
170,192,205,221,250,312,
340,404.

Holly, Isaac, Jr., 5,12,16,18,
58,64,90,158,221,250,
276,322.
" Jared,109,110,128,201,
361.
" John,17,109,250.
" John M.,12,312,361.
" John W.,12,214,312.
" Joseph,Jr.,17,250.
" Josiah,17,250.
" Julia A.,192,250,312.
" Lucy,109,110.
" Martha, 12,170.
" Mary,109,110,312.
" Mary S., 12,192.
" Mercy,56,57,110,393.
" Nancy E., 192.
" Nathan, 17.
" Newman,6,12,17,57,250.
" Oscar L., 361.
" Permillia, 154.
" Phebe, 110,251.
" Rebecca,41,88,109,110.
" Rheusma, 57.
" Sabrina, 251.
" Sally,36,251,404.
" Sally A., 189.
" Samantha R., 81.
" Samuel, 57,110.
" Sarah,17,18,81,250,312,
313.
" Silas,192,251.
" Stephen,110,192,250,
251,257.
" Susannah, 57.
" William, 154.
" William H.,174,179,
191,192,211,225,226,227,
229,231,234,235,238,248,
249,262,313,328,345,355,
377,381.
" William H.,Jr.,401.

H.

Holly, William L., 207.
" William V.,12,312.
Holmes, Absalom, 18.
" Alba, 110.
" Benjamin, 18,39.
" Betsy, 57.
" Caleb, 192.
" Caty, 193.
" Clarissa,97,344.
" David, 86.
" Eldad, 102.
" Gideon,57,82,188.
" Hannah,18,192.
" Hannah E.,110,382.
" Isaac,Jr., 18.
" Israel, 18.
" Jabez, 57.
" Jemima, 18.
" John,103,110,111,146,
263,313,314,330,382.
" John,Jr., 110.
" John A., 313.
" Jotham, 18.
" Katy, 193.
" Latham, 122,122x,97.
" Luke, 192.
" Mary,57,110,313.
" Molly, 18.
" Nancy, 110.
" Rebecca, 110.
" Reuben,18,86,119.
" Reuben H.,193.
" Ruth, 18.
Holmes, Sarah, 18.
" Sarah C., 110.
" Silas, 18.
" Stephen, 18.
" Susannah, 18.
" William, 329.
Hopkins, Elisabeth, 57.
" Gilbert, 388.
" James, 57.
" John, 76.
" Mary, 57.
" Pine, 57.
" Samuel, 57.
" Sarah, 76.

INDEX TO PERSONS.

H.

Hopkins, Thomas, 57.
" Zeruiah, 57.
Hopson, Samuel, 393.
Horton, Charity E., 390.
" Charles, 193.
" Hetty, 115, 116.
" John, 160, 393.
" Joseph, 115.
" Julia A., 311.
" Peter, 63.
" William, 329.
" Zophar M., 390.
Hose, Henry G., 18, 58.
Hough, John, Jr., 406.
" Martha, 28.
" Walter, Dr., 28.
Houschell, John, 361.
Howard, Benjamin, 64.
" Clarissa, 64.
" William, 65.
Howe, Abigail, 19, 362, 402.
" Betsy, 19, 147, 193.
" Bowers, 19, 193.
" Catherine, 19.
" Cornelia, 147.
" David, 18, 19, 146.
" Elizabeth, 18, 85, 393.
" Esther, 147.
" Henry, 19.
" Isaac, 42, 44, 70, 72, 73, 78, 99, 119, 135, 147, 193, 390.
" Jacob, 18, 19, 227, 393, 394.
" Jacob, Jr., 85.
" James, 147.
" Jeremiah, 375.
" Jonas, 78, 147, 150, 192, 210, 255, 269, 273, 325, 350, 359, 375.
" Kezia, 147.
" Laura, 147.
" Lucy, 25, 73, 147.
" Maria, 300.
" Mary, 19.
" Nehemiah, 147, 273.
" Polly, 193, 387.
" Rachel, 147.
" Raymond, 19.

H.

Howe, Rebecca, 18, 19.
" Reuama, 193.
" Ruth, 193.
" Sally, 19, 146, 147, 227, 293, 394.
" Samuel, 147.
" Sarah, 19, 193.
" Selleck, 19, 387.
" Seth, 402.
" Smith, 193, 362.
" Sylvanus, 393.
" William, 193, 362.
Howell, Charity, 72.
Hoyt, Abigail, 19, 20, 21, 58, 66, 82, 83, 136, 193, 264, 343, 394
" Abraham, 27, 111.
" Adolphus D., 363.
" Alfred, 369.
" Amos, 21.
" Ann, 168.
" Ann S., 193, 394.
" Anna, 20, 58, 111.
" Anne, 58.
" Ansen, 44, 101.
" Arney, 222.
" Augustus, 314.
" Bates, 147, 348.
" Benjamin, 12, 19, 20, 58, 60, 111, 147, 149, 222, 253.
" Betsy, 12, 21, 111, 113, 148, 193, 295, 340, 341, 348, 362, 394.
" Betsy N., 194.
" Billy, 26, 147, 193.
" Calvin, 52, 155, 169, 394.
" Calvin C., 194, 252.
" Caroline, 252.
" Cary, 54, 193, 403.
" Catherine, 58.
" Charles, 147.
" Charles D., 212.
" Charles H., 148, 193, 194, 196, 251.
" Charlotte, 39.
" Clarissa, 252.
" Clarissa A., 194, 252.
" Darius, 97, 147, 148, 194, 196

448.

INDEX TO PERSONS.

H.

Hoyt, David, 127, 143, 161, 166, 182, 191, 192, 227, 251, 313, 363.
" David N., 59.
" Deborah, 135.
" Deodate, 58.
" Ebenezer, 193, 226, 313.
" Edwin, 111.
" Elihu, 58, 111, 113, 148.
" Elijah, 41, 58, 59.
" Eliza, 60, 148, 193, 194, 196, 251.
" Elizabeth, 13, 19, 20, 41, 58, 59, 148, 193, 194, 196, 241, 251.
" Emily, 252, 254, 363.
" Enoch, 21, 59, 111, 148, 194, 251, 252, 394.
" Epenetus, 16, 19, 194, 195.
" Esther, 20.
" Ezra, 19, 22, 23, 253.
" Frances, 252, 254, 363.
" Frederick, 20, 59, 66.
" Frederick, Jr., 39, 93.
" Freeman, 20, 394.
" Genet A., 98.
" George, 147, 193, 314.
" George A., 148, 193, 194, 195, 196, 251.
" George C., 191, 251, 313.
" George E., 252, 254, 363.
" Hanford, 15, 16, 21, 59, 77, 393, 399.
" Hannah, 12, 16, 21, 22, 23, 26, 58, 59, 60, 111, 149, 193, 195, 202, 218, 219, 252, 254, 276, 283, 336, 363.
" Hannah A., 148, 194, 196, 251.
" Harriet, 147, 194, 251, 252.
" Harriet A., 313.
" Harvey, 60.
" Henry, 25, 98, 247.
" Henry, Jr., 16, 17, 21.
" Henry M., 313.
" Hervey, 60, 111, 112.
" Hezekiah, 96.

H.

Hoyt, Isaac, 20, 112, 148, 277.
" Isaac, Jr., 79, 86.
" Isaac L., 364.
" Jacob, 168.
" James, 394.
" James E., 195.
" James H., 21, 147, 193, 245, 270, 300, 314, 322, 334, 338, 361, 364.
" James N., 194, 252.
" James R., 149.
" James S., 194, 195, 252, 253, 363.
" Jane, 21, 22.
" Jared, 19.
" Jerome B., 148, 194, 196.
" Jesse, 67, 253.
" Joel, 19, 20, 394.
" John, 22, 60, 92, 112, 130, 148, 149, 168, 247, 253, 330.
" John, Jr., 22, 90, 136, 170, 394.
" John, 2nd., 130.
" John P., 195.
" John R., 394.
" John R.P., 195.
" John S., 194, 252, 253, 314.
" John W., 196, 364.
" Jonah, 20, 58, 111, 113.
" Jonathan, 21, 139, 300, 361, 365, 394.
" Joseph, Colo., 58.
" Joseph, 20, 60, 172, 173, 219, 225, 227, 229, 242, 283, 293, 304, 345, 362, 386.
" Joseph B., 176.
" Joseph D., 253, 254.
" Joseph H., 253.
" Joseph S., 111, 143, 147, 195.
" Joseph W., 60, 149, 254.
" Josiah, 20, 112.
" Jotham, 106, 112, 126, 138, 139, 143, 147, 148, 166, 181, 194, 195, 196, 198, 216, 227, 296.
" Julia, 189, 314, 335.

INDEX TO PERSONS.

H.

Hoyt, Julia A., 106.
" Julia E., 387.
" Kilbourn F., 277.
" Leander, 138, 148, 149, 227, 232, 244, 253, 294, 298.
" Lucy A., 406.
" Maria, 176.
" Maria L., 252, 394.
" Martha, 112.
" Mary, 27, 148, 194, 195, 196, 251, 252, 253, 394.
" Mary A., 60, 112.
" Mary E., 313, 363, 394.
" Mary W., 194.
" Maurice, 207, 270.
" Mehitable, 20, 394.
" Melancthon, 149, 253.
" Mercy, 20, 22, 23, 148.
" Milicent, 193, 313, 314.
" Nancy, 20, 21, 138.
" Nancy E., 252.
" Nanne, 86, 277.
" Nathan, 20.
" Nathaniel, 112, 195.
" Nehemiah, 60, 112, 117.
" Nehemiah, Jr., 145.
" Nelson, 394.
" Nezer, 15, 20, 58.
" Peter, 21, 394.
" Phebe, 59.
" Philip L., 111.
" Polly, 253, 254.
" Prudence, 16, 20, 394.
" Rachel, 60, 112.
" Ralph, 112, 135, 169, 195, 227, 254, 314, 363.
" Ralph, Jr., 65.
" Rebecca, 4, 22, 60, 66, 112, 149, 264, 314, 364.
" Reuben, 168, 312.
" Rhoda, 20, 193, 313, 314, 363.
" Roswell, 363.
" Rufus, 187, 195, 209, 251, 364, 394.
" Rufus, Jr., 394.
" Ruth, 21, 60, 112.

H.

Hoyt, Sally, 13, 21, 22, 60, 143, 195, 281, 394.
" Sally A., 148, 194, 252, 254.
" Sally E., 154.
" Salmon, 21.
" Salome, 22.
" Samuel, 21, 22, 23, 47, 60, 66, 80, 83, 90, 102, 120, 149, 195, 253, 291, 394.
" Samuel, Jr., 6, 27, 60, 88.
" Samuel H., 314.
" Samuel S.S., 195.
" Samuel W., 194, 252.
" Sarah, 20, 21, 27, 42, 59, 60, 83, 94, 99, 111, 112, 279, 281, 394.
" Sarah A., 394.
" Sarah C., 98.
" Sarah E., 254.
" Sarah M., 194, 252.
" Sarah W., 394.
" Selleck, 319.
" Seth, 21, 60, 90, 112.
" Seymour, 394.
" Shadrach, 109, 149, 195, 219, 252, 254, 363.
" Shadrach, Jr., 111.
" Silas, 125, 147, 183, 237, 280.
" Silas, Jr., 19, 38, 67, 131.
" Sophire, 189.
" Stephen, 218, 279, 336.
" Susan W., 252, 255.
" Susannah, 58.
" Sylvanus, 60.
" Thaddeus, 4, 27, 35, 147, 193, 194, 195, 196, 207, 225, 238, 251, 364.
" Thaddeus, Jr., 66, 97, 125, 134.
" Theodosia, 363.
" Thirza, 44, 101, 229.
" Uriah, 21, 22, 394.
" Warren, 27, 108.
" William, 58, 80, 98, 147, 148, 149, 193, 196, 253, 361.
" William, Jr., 20, 46, 95, 96,

INDEX TO PERSONS.

H.

138,310,319.
Hoyt, William,3rd,147.
" William A.,148,194,196.
" William C.,149,340.
" William M.,194.
" William S.,Capt.,364.
" William S.,252,253,255.
" Willis, 274.
" Ziba,58,111,112,113.
Hubbard, Abigail, 391.
" Abraham, 149.
" Andrew,149,159.
" Butler, 50.
" Clarissa, 50.
" Daniel,15,396.
" David, 315.
" David H.,196,255.
" Elizabeth,61,315.
" Ellen, 196.
" Gabriel,149,196,201, 255,315.
" George, 286.
" George D.,196,255.
" George M.,243,287, 361,383.
" Hannah,149,287,315.
" Hannah P.,196,255.
" Harriet E.,196,255.
" Harvey, 149.
" Henry,89,149,196.
" Henry S.,149,313.
" Holly, 149.
" Isaac, 61.
" John,149,255.
" Lydia,15,149.
" Margaret D., 61.
" Mary,61,149.
" Mary H.,196,255.
" Nancy, 61.
" Nathaniel,Dr.,61.
" Nathaniel,61,87,117, 128,149,208.
" Polly, 159.
" Sally,149,351.
" Samuel,196,255.
" Sarah,240,255.
" Sarah A., 240.
" William,61,149,351.

H.

Hubbell, Peter, 37.
" Sarah, 37.
Hubbs, Jane, 69.
Hubby, see Hobby.
Hudson, Henry, 312.
" John, 12.
Huggeford, Thomas,68,397.
Hughes, Polly, 214.
Hull, James, 304.
" Lemuel B.,Rev.,294,295.
" Polly, 294,295.
Hunt, Cynthia, 279.
" Prudence, 154.
" Thomas, 196.
Hunter, John B., 376.
Hurlbutt, Joel,14,177,236,353, 364.
Hurtell, Thomas, 231.
Husted, Aaron,51,78,113,146, 188,311.
" Abraham,7,113.
" Amos,11,109,113,255, 315,364.
" Ann, 247.
" Azuba, 61.
" Benjamin,61,132,150, 162,256,269,394.
" Benjamin,Jr.,76,92,207 238.
" Benjamin,3rd, 394.
" Benjamin W., 210.
" Caleb,107,108,109,113, x247,311,359,371,393,x209.
" Charles E.,369,385.
" Charlotte, 240.
" Conklin,149,205,256, 265,269,272,278,306,307, 308,356,358.
" Cynthia, 113.
" David,17,113,255,256.
" David A., 256.
" David D.,24,76,88,197.
" Deborah,61,150.
" Drake,30,113,188,240, 255,256.
" Ebenezer, 348.
" Eliza, 154.
" Elnathan,11,113,150.

INDEX TO PERSONS.

452.

H.

Husted, Esbon, 109, 181, 255, 256, 315.
" Eunice, 113.
" George, 150, 348.
" Hannah, 17, 113, 255, 256, 273, 315.
" Henry, 150.
" Isaac, 61.
" James, 150.
" Jane, 150.
" Jared, 150.
" John, 59, 92, 165, 171, 225, 287, 288.
" John S., 164.
" Jonathan, 150, 169, 315, 394.
" Jonathan N., 168.
" Joseph, 150.
" Joseph B., 255.
" Joseph W., 292.
" Martha, 61.
" Mary, 61, 68, 108, 150, 256, 311, 359, 371.
" Mary E., 348.
" Mary J., 311.
" Moses, 113.
" Moses, Jr., 32.
" Nancy, 30, 145, 150, 240, 247, 248, 255.
" Nathan, 315.
" Nathaniel, 61, 70, 72, 150, 238, 313, 315, 318, 336, 394.
" Nathaniel, Jr., 369, 121
" Orla, 269.
" Peter, 56, 113, 168, 175, 247, 248, 252, 335.
" Phebe A., 256.
" Polly, 109, 150, 394.
" Rachel, 61.
" Roswell, 197, 256.
" Roswell A., 256.
" Roswell M., 256.
" Ruth, 150, 394.
" Sally, 113, 212.
" Samuel, 61, 117, 150, 156, 207, 299.

H.

Husted, Sarah, 22, 61, 150, 255, 256, 305.
" Sarah C., 305.
" Sarah E., 348.
" Sarah M., 255.
" Sherman, 193, 314, 363.
" Silas, 336, 337, 350.
" Stephen, 315.
" William, 38, 73, 75, 78, 109, 113, 150, 157, 158, 162, 180, 189, 220, 255, 256.
" William A., 150, 255.
" William A., Jr., 351.
Hustis, Ann, 310.
" John S., 246, 309.
Huter, John, 69.
" Loretta, 69.
Hutton, Abigail, 28.
Hutty, Hetchent, 405.
" Nancy, 405.
Hyatt, Ann, 156.
" Nathaniel, 160.
" Thomas, 102.

I.

Ingersoll, Abigail, 256, 257.
" Alexander, 150.
" Alexander S., 150, 243
" Alton, 150, 321, 322, 368.
" Ann, 256, 257.
" Chloe, 110.
" Cornelia, 181.
" David, 256.
" Elizabeth, 51.
" Hannah, 32, 256.
" John, 32, 181.
" John J., 150.
" Joseph, 81, 197, 245, 256.
" Levi, 149.
" Nathaniel, 13, 256, 257.
" Platt C., 150.
" Rebecca, 256, 372.
" Sally, 149.

INDEX TO PERSONS.

I.

Ingersoll, Sarah, 38, 150.
" Simon, 150, 197.
Ireland, Abraham, 22, 395.
" Gilbert, 22, 395.
" Job, 22, 395.
" Levi, 22, 395.
" Martha, 22.
" Prudence, 22.
Isaacs, Benjamin, 51, 141, 153, 199, 213, 224, 257.
" Charles, 141, 257, 364.
" Emily, 141.
" Esther, 141.
" George, 141.
" Isaac S., 144, 257, 364.
" William, 141.
" William H., 141.

J.

James, George, 199.
" Isabel, 117.
" Mary, 87.
" William, 199.
Jarman, Elizabeth, 50.
" James, 50.
" Polly, 50.
Jarvis, Albertina S., 315.
" Elizabeth, 32.
" Harriet D., 378.
" Harriet E., 315.
" Isabella, 315.
" John, 4.
" Lavinia T., 315.
" Martha M., 315.
" Mary H., 315.
" Samuel, 32.
" Samuel O., 32, 315.
" Sarah, 32.
" Sarah P., 315.
" Seymour, 5, 32, 34, 85, 88, 167, 202, 214, 226, 227, 315, 316, 338, 400.
" Stephen, 43, 113.
Jeffery, see Jeffrey.
Jeffrey, Hannah, 22.
" Martha, 22, 23.

Jeffrey, Mercy, 22, 23, 61.
" Rebecca, 22, 394.
" Samuel, 22, 23.
Jelliff, Ann E., 212.
" Maltby, 302.
Jennings, Isabella, 313, 314, 363
" Sally, 313, 314, 363.
" Sarah M., 363.
Jessup, Abigail, 10, 23, 105, 186.
" Ann, 23, 24, 150, 151.
" Ann E., 152.
" Anne, 23.
" Charles E., 152.
" Cornelius J., 152.
" Ebenezer, 23, 150, 151, 364.
" Edward, 23, 151.
" Elizabeth, 23, 62, 364.
" George, 23.
" Gershom, 23, 151.
" Hannah, 23, 151.
" Isaac, 23.
" James, 23, 151.
" James J., 151.
" John, 23, 399.
" John A., 152.
" Jonathan, 23, 24, 151, 152, 197, 394.
" Joram, 23, 395.
" Joseph, 23.
" Joshua B., 151.
" Julius A., 152.
" Kezia, 151, 152.
" Maria, 24.
" Martha, 114.
" Mary, 23, 24, 150, 151.
" Mary A., 151.
" Peter, 23, 24, 114, 151, 271.
" Rebecca, 364.
" Rhuea S., 364.
" Sally, 24, 25.
" Samuel, 23, 24, 62, 113, 151, 268, 316, 364, 394, 395.
" Samuel, Jr., 277, 325, 338, 375.
" Sarah, 23, 113, 114, 150,

INDEX TO PERSONS.

454.

J.

151,395.
Jessup, Sarah J., 152.
" Susan, 24.
" Timothy, 23,24,114,151.
" William, 364.
" William I., 364.
Johns, David, 321,364.
" Elizabeth R., 321,364.
" Henry, 321.
" Jane, 321.
" Mason T., 321,364.
Johnson, Asel, 85.
" Benjamin, 150.
" Betsy, 122.
" Elias, 343.
" John, 122.
" Ruth, 329.
" William, 329.
" Zalpha, 4.
Jones, Abigail, 62,114,197.
" Amos, 62,197,198.
" Benjamin, 62,114,282.
" David, 321.
" Ebenezer, 28.
" Elizabeth, 321.
" Emeline, 257.
" Enos, 257.
" Ephraim, 106,257.
" Ezra, 257.
" George, 197,198,258,282.
" George H., 257.
" Hannah, 62,197.
" Henry, 257,321.
" Horace A., 282.
" Horace F., 258.
" Horace H., 197.
" Isaac, 24,62,197,198,
243,282,395.
" Isaac, Jr., 114.
" Isaac S., 258.
" Isaac W., 217,257.
" James, 114,197,258,282.
" Jane, 321.
" John J., 403.
" Josiah, 197,198,395.
" Katharine, 114.
" Mason, 321.
" Nancy O., 198,258,282.

J.

Jones, Nehemiah, 257,258.
" Polly, 257.
" Sally, 62.
" Samuel, 198,258,282.
" Samuel A., 258.
" Sarah, 28,197,198,257.
" Selleck, 24,62,114,143,
144,198,258.
" Smith, 62,197,198.
" Tammy, 257.
" Thomas, 198,258.
" Watson, 257.
" William, 198,258,282.
Jordon, Alla, 258.
" Betsy, 258.
" Hannah, 258.
" Mercy, 77,258.
" Phebe, 258.
" William, 77,258,259.
Joyce, H. T., 405.
Judd, Grant, 401.
" Hannah M., 401.
Judson, Abigail, 224.
" Amos, 114.
" Charity, 114.
" James, 114.
" John, 114.
" John, Jr., 114.
" Joseph, 224,259,316.
" Lewis, 114.
" Molly, 114.
" Rebecca, 114.
" Sarah, 114,322.
June, Alva, 168,316,337.
" Andrew, 208.
" Betsy, 36,259.
" Charles E., 316.
" Electa, 208.
" Elizabeth, 36.
" Hannah, 6,152,259.
" Harrison, 70.
" Isaac, 152,259.
" Israel, 159.
" Joseph, 316.
" Joseph H., 316.
" Joshua, 395.
" Linus P., 316.
" Mary, 36,75,84,89,316.

INDEX TO PERSONS.   455.

J.

June, Mary A., 365.
" Nancy, 259.
" Nathaniel, 6,152,198,199.
" Prudence, 259.
" Reuben, 36,84,89,259,316.
" Reuben A., 316.
" Sally, 316.
" Samuel, 105.
" Sarah, 217,365.
" Silas, 36,89.
" Stephen, 237,330.
" Susan, 199.
" Thomas, 145,217,365.
" William, 50,75,105.
" William, Jr., 89.
" William S., 365.
" Zabed, 259.

K.

Kainworthy, Sally, 153.
Keeler, Debby, 114,115,123.
" Deborah, 115,396.
" Ezra, 351.
" Hannah, 39.
" Josephine, 309.
" Lydia, 322.
" Mariana, 309.
" Mary, 152,308,309.
" Mary F., 161.
" Phebe A., 308,309.
" Polly, 240.
" Walter, 39.
" William, 64,95,111, 114,115,133,152,396.
" William H., 308,309.
Kellogg, Samuel, 39.
Kelly, Richard, 84.
" Sally, 84.
Kenworthy, Sally, 153.
" William, 315.
Keogh, Bernard, 387.
Ketcham, Deborah, 157.
Kimberly, David, 107.
" Elizabeth, 107.
Kinch, Clara, 336.
" Hannah, 391.
" William, 121,336,394.

K.

King, James J., 316.
" William, 32,33.
Kingsley, Ebenezer W., 359.
Kipp, Phebe S., 88.
Kirby, Nancy, 226.
" Stephen, 226.
Kirk, Fanny, 220.
" Julia, 238.
Klopfer, Frederick S., 380.
" Hannah M., 380.
Knapp, Abby L., 63.
" Abel, 24,62,64.
" Abigail, 21,24,25,27,104, 199,250,395.
" Abraham, 233.
" Adam, 64.
" Alanson, 78.
" Albert, 153,233,242,325.
" Alfred, 235.
" Allen R., 261,275,316, 317.
" Amanda, 78.
" Angeline, 262,263.
" Anna, 62,63,78,395.
" Ard, 351,371.
" Benjamin, 14,27,318,336.
" Benjamin I., 153,164, 185,205,269,317,325,354, 365.
" Bethia, 25,26,317,318, 319,395.
" Betsy, 63,147,216,233, 319.
" Caleb, 75,118,201,227, 344.
" Caroline, 259,310.
" Katharine E., 365.
" Charity, 24,71,199,235, 261,365,398. x72,
" Charity B., 365.
" Charles, 8,25,26,27,22,90 116,117,133,140,152,160, 172,179,199,249,317,347, 395,397.
" Charles H., 401.
" Charles S., 199,306,317.
" Charles W., 317.
" Clara, 27.

INDEX TO PERSONS.

K.

Knapp, Cornelia, 63.
" Daniel, 25, 26, 63.
" David, 25, 27, 63, 262.
" David B., 63, 199.
" David H., 262.
" Deborah, 318.
" Eben, 191.
" Edmund, 33, 100, 115, 152, 212, 259.
" Edward, 63.
" Edward A., 233.
" Elijah, 183.
" Eliza, 152, 153.
" Eliza A., 319.
" Elizabeth, 25, 63, 67, 117, 153, 199, 201, 216, 259, 280, 317.
" Elizabeth C., 261, 317.
" Emeline, 233.
" Enos, 51, 52, 78, 93, 152, 153, 163, 200, 201, 260.
" Epenetus, 25, 26, 395.
" Esther, 141, 153, 259, 317, 365.
" Esther N., 62, 395.
" Esther R., 16, 153.
" Eunice C., 260.
" Ezra, 16, 24, 27, 59, 111, 187, 195, 260.
" Fanny, 27, 63.
" Frances S., 316.
" Frederick, 153.
" George, 310.
" George H., 187.
" Gideon, 25, 26, 395.
" Hannah, 25, 26, 78, 115, 317, 323, 381, 395, 401.
" Hannah A., 98.
" Hannah B., 317.
" Hannah C., 260.
" Hannah S., 318.
" Harvey, 299, 319, 366.
" Henry, 33, 73, 216.
" Henry E., 365.
" Henry I., 153.
" Henry S., 152.
" Hezekiah, 25, 26, 317, 318, 395.

K.

Knapp, Isaac, 27, 57, 152, 153, 153, 199, 200, 260, 261, 395.
" Isaac, Jr., 117.
" Israel, 63, 153, 250, 261, 395.
" Jacob, 27, 111, 124, 200, 261.
" James, 26, 261.
" Jared, 318.
" Jared O., 317.
" Jasper, 199.
" Jeremiah, 366.
" Joel, 27.
" John, 7, 26, 63, 64, 121, 150.
" John E., 233.
" John W., 199, 306, 212, 317.
" Jonah, 98.
" Jonathan, 27, 68, 78, 95, 395.
" Joseph, 318.
" Joshua, 14, 24, 27, 64, 71, 72, 75, 153, 199, 200, 259, 260, 261, 365, 395, 398.
" Julia A., 153, 164, 365.
" J. T., 401.
" Lavinia, 227.
" Levina, 78.
" Lewis, 50.
" Lodema, 318.
" Lorenzo E., 199, 306, 317.
" Luther, 317, 318, 319, 381, 401.
" Lydemia, 27.
" Martha, 7, 366.
" Mary, 27, 64, 84, 136, 152, 200, 211, 317, 318, 319, 366.
" Mary E., 199, 317.
" Mary S., 64, 401.
" Mehitable, 50.
" Mercy, 64.
" Nancy, 27, 238, 404.
" Nathan, 64.
" Nathaniel, Colo., 261.
" Nathaniel, 64, 72, 121, 138, 199, 365.
" Nehemiah, 63.
" Noah, 62, 233, 258, 304.
" Odle C., 260, 350, 355.

INDEX TO PERSONS.

K.

Knapp, Peter, 27, 181, 201, 395.
" Phebe C., 317.
" Phebe E., 210.
" Philene, 319.
" Polly, 27, 317, 318, 366.
" Prudence, 26, 27.
" Rachel, 199, 365.
" Rebecca, 71, 72, 296, 398.
" Reuben, 26, 84, 199.
" Reuben E., 261.
" Rhoda, 152, 200, 260.
" Rosannah, 63.
" Rufus, 147, 199, 206, 216, 280, 317, 318, 319.
" Ruth, 27, 75, 81, 83, 153.
" Sally, 63, 317, 318.
" Sally A., 78.
" Samuel, 27, 199, 200, 365.
" Sanford R., 191.
" Sarah, 25, 27, 121, 191, 199, 395.
" Sarah B., 261, 262.
" Sarah M., 260.
" Sarah W., 47, 121, 153.
" Shubal, 71, 72, 398.
" Silas, 62, 78, 395.
" Sophia, 316.
" Stephen, 27, 200.
" Susan I., 153.
" Susan J., 47, 121.
" Susannah, 27, 200, 395.
" Sylvanus, 16, 23, 25, 26, 27, 28, 395, 400.
" Titus, 319.
" Uzal, 16, 21, 68.
" Walter, 18, 153.
" Walter N., 262.
" William, 4, 26, 47, 50, 121, 124, 133, 141, 153, 354, 366, 395.
" William, Jr., 24, 25, 26, 42, 63, 106.
" William, 3rd, 77.
" William B., 153.
" William H., 261.
" William Y., Jr., 87.
" Zalmon, 238.

K.

Kneeland, Eunice, 146, 146.
Knowlton, Farnum, Rev., 278.
Kosborough, George, 216.
Krutzer, Daniel, 371.
" Emeline, 371.

L.

La Count, Phebe, 234.
Lamb, Sarah, 156.
Lambden, Edward, 289.
Lane, Abraham, 28, 64.
" Deborah, 28.
" Ephraim, 91, 183.
" George H., 183, 242.
" Hannah, 338, 396.
" John, 33, 76, 396.
" Josiah, 338.
Lapham, Catherine, 161, 319.
Larkin, Ann E., 319.
" Charles E., 319.
" Elizabeth, 149, 253.
" Franklin, 319.
" George F., 319.
" Harriet N., 319.
" John, 319.
" Mary A., 319, 346.
" Mary J., 319.
Laurie, Mary, 231.
" Patrick, 231, 331.
Law, Ann E., 401.
" James, 401.
Lawrence, John, 383.
Lawton, Esther, 78.
" Seth, 78.
Le Craft, Daniel T., 200.
Lee, John H., 334.
" Thomas M., 334.
Leeds, Abraham, 262.
" Abram, 62.
" Angeline, 262.
" Anna, 319, 320.
" Cary, 3, 4, 6, 11, 15, 20, 21, 22, 23, 28, 38, 39, 44, 46, 48, 54, 58, 59, 60, 61, 62, 77, 90, 92, 93, 94, 97, 99, 102, 106, 109, 112, 140, 143, 154, 175,

INDEX TO PERSONS.

L.

176, 200, 203, 320, 406.
Leeds, Cary H., 182, 183, 226, 238, 262.
" Catherine, 263.
" Caty, 28, 64.
" Charles H., 200, 377.
" Charles I., 168, 177.
" Charles S., 28.
" Charles T., 64, 139, 191, 263, 294.
" Cornelia, 262.
" Elisha, 28, 41, 64, 262.
" Eliza, 28, 64, 263.
" Eliza A., 229, 263.
" Emily, 262.
" Gideon, 57, 140, 153, 154, 305, 320.
" Hannah, 140, 154, 320.
" Harry, 154.
" Honor, 154, 200, 263, 320.
" Jacob W., 154.
" James T., 262.
" John, 21, 23, 58, 59, 60, 102, 108, 111, 137, 140, 154, 191, 200, 226, 297.
" John J., 228, 235, 297, 299, 326, 334, 335, 346.
" John R., 177, 200, 235, 262, 282, 297, 305, 314, 320, 334, 346, 349, 351, 406.
" John W., 140, 149, 154, 200, 214, 239, 252, 262, 284, 320, 326, 334.
" Joseph H., 320.
" Katy, 28, 64.
" Lorenzo, 262, 280, 291, 320.
" Maria, 326.
" Maria E., 167, 280.
" Marian, 262.
" Polly, 64, 263.
" Rebecca, Mr, 319, 320.
" Rhoda, 57, 140, 153, 262.
" Sally, 263.
" Samuel, 262, 328.
" Sarah, 28, 64, 262, 263.
" Sarah W., 154, 200, 394.

L.

Leeds, Smith, 262.
" Susannah, 96.
" Sylvester, 262.
" Theodore, 154, 200.
" William, 229.
" William E., 28, 64, 263.
Leeker, Charles, 263, 265.
" Morris, 263, 265.
Leonard, Robert, 57, 88.
Leveridge, Catherine, 386.
Lewis, Amzi, Rev., 64, 65, 115.
" Amzi, 64.
" Beal N., 65.
" Benjamin, 115.
" Calvin, 115, 116.
" Clarissa, 64.
" Daniel, 115, 116.
" David, 115, 116.
" Elizabeth, 115, 116.
" Hannah, 320.
" Hetty, 115, 116.
" Huldah, 64, 154.
" Isaac, 65, 320.
" Isaac, Jr., 320.
" John, 144.
" Martha, 115, 116.
" Mary E., 320.
" Millicent, 143.
" Nancy, 115, 116.
" Nathan W., 64.
" Nathaniel B., 65.
" Nehemiah, 115, 116.
" Rachel, 64.
" Roswell W., 65, 320.
" Sally, 115, 116.
" Sally A., 64.
" Sarah, 320.
" Sylvanus, 115, 116.
" Zachariah, 65, 320.
Libby, Smith R., 171.
Little, Adeline A., 296.
" Benjamin, 296, 345, 348.
" Dorcas, 315, 348.
" Henry, 190, 296, 297, 366.
" John, 174.
" Nancy, 167.
" Polly, 295.

INDEX TO PERSONS.

L.

Little, Sarah, 173.
" Warren, 296.
Livingston, Sarah, 42.
Lockwood, Abigail, 28, 66, 118, 155, 156, 264.
" Abigail S., 367.
" Abraham, 64.
" Alexander, 47, 104, 391.
" Alfred, 117.
" Alla, 67, 322.
" Amanda M., 317.
" Amelia, 66.
" Amos, 65, 66.
" Amy, 117, 202.
" Ananias, 66.
" Andrew, 65, 66, 263, 265, 396.
" Angeline, 263, 321, 322, 396.
" Ann, 54, 200, 382.
" Ann M., 317.
" Anne, 118.
" Augustus, 27, 35, 60, 64, 66, 73, 156, 199, 220, 231, 253, 264, 271, 398.
" Beal B., 250, 264, 265, 276, 308, 309, 312, 318, 364, 367, 368.
" Benjamin, 203.
" Bethia, 65.
" Betsy, 28, 66, 67, 181, 202, 264, 266, 294, 373, 397.
" Caleb, 154, 155, 203.
" Celia A., 367, 368.
" Cephas, 155, 292.
" Charles, 40, 200, 201, 224, 263.
" Charles A., 200.
" Charles H., 241.
" Charles W., 333.
" Charlotte, 117, 263, 321, 322, 396.
" Charlotte B., 367.
" Clara, 66.
" Clarissa, 67, 322.
" Clementine, 367.

L.

Lockwood, Daniel, 28, 67, 105, 116, 121, 140, 151, 161, 194, 196, 197, 199, 220, 242, 253, 260, 265, 270, 328, 333, 355, 402.
" Daniel, Jr., 10, 24, 75, 155, 403.
" Daniel, 3rd, 23, 28.
" Denison, 118.
" David, 66, 202, 396.
" Davis, 117, 149, 156, 176, 179, 187, 195, 229, 249, 251, 260, 264, 296, 304, 305, 22 320, 321, 327, 338, 366, 367.
" Deborah, 67, 117, 118, 155, 321, 322.
" Drake, 93, 151, 153, 155, 163, 203, 263, 264, 321.
" Ebenezer, 20, 67, 95, 201, 304, 366, 368.
" Ebenezer, Jr., 95.
" Edmund, 65, 67, 118, 196, 210, 322, 331.
" Edmund, Jr., 321, 322.
" Edward, 66, 116, 396.
" Edward, Jr., 116.
" Eliakim, 55, 69, 321, 322.
" Eliza, 202, 217, 263, 322, 396.
" Elizabeth, 28, 40, 67, 117, 156, 174, 201, 271, 322.
" Elnathan, 66, 396.
" Enos, 16, 45, 52, 61, 65, 66, 71, 107, 145, 151, 156, 202 264, 396.
" Enos B., 117, 187, 264, 318, 367.
" Epenetus, 4, 46, 390.
" Ezekiel, 117.
" Ezra, 8, 26, 27, 28, 41, 48, 66, 73, 75, 96, 116, 117, 156, 157, 217, 246, 261, 262, 271, 274, 294, 344, 379, 387, 391.
" Fanny, 117, 155, 212, 321, 376, 377.

459.

INDEX TO PERSONS.

L.

Lockwood, Frances L., 367.
" Frederick, 28, 65, 66, 71, 117, 118, 151, 155, 162, 163, 177, 189, 209, 248, 264, 271, 277, 306, 318, 328, 329, 362, 373, 392, 396, 211, 214.
" Frederick A., 263, 321, 322.
" George, 64.
" George Jr., 202.
" Gideon W., 311.
" Gilbert, Sr., 66, 396.
" Gilbert, 65, 66, 201, 396.
" Hanford, 201, 367.
" Hannah, 23, 25, 26, 62, 66, 67, 117, 151, 155, 156, 197, 198, 201, 202, 210, 264, 271, 322, 367, 395, 396.
" Hannah M., 367.
" Harriet, 65.
" Harriet N., 367.
" Harvey, 117, 261, 280, 287, 294, 302, 333, 355, 380.
" Henry, 45, 46, 57, 201, 321, 367.
" Henry B., 321, 322.
" Henry W., 368.
" Horace, 157.
" Ira, 22, 61, 67, 107, 118, 184, 258, 321, 367.
" Isaac, 27, 66, 67, 73, 75, 93, 111, 114, 117, 118, 120, 121, 126, 131, 132, 133, 153, 155, 156, 175, 220, 221, 222, 244, 264, 357, 376, 396.
" Isaac, Jr., 53, 152, 389.
" Isaac, 3rd, 152, 177, 186.
" Isaac L., 264.
" Isabel, 117.
" Israel, 200, 217.
" Jacob, 212, 225, 259, 264, 283, 294, 298, 344, 345, 376.
" Jacob, Jr., 103.
" James, 167, 396.

L.

Lockwood, Jared, 28.
" Jeremiah, Jr., 28, 66.
" Jerusha, 202.
" John, 7, 95, 156, 200, 263, 264, 321.
" John H., 203.
" John W., 221, 241, 368
" Jonathan, 66, 67, 117, 321.
" Jonathan, Jr., 32.
" Joseph, 28, 29, 36, 265.
" Josiah, 23, 117, 155, 156, 172, 226, 263, 367, 368.
" Julia A., 368, 369.
" Leaticia M., 263.
" Letitia, 321, 396, 322
" Lewis, 117, 156, 201, 202, 264.
" Lewis S., 62, 93, 197, 198.
" Lot, 117.
" Luke, 117.
" Luther, 156, 208, 321, 322.
" Lydia, 67, 116, 204, 322, 367.
" Lydia A., 321.
" Lyman, 317, 373.
" Major, 209, 258.
" Maria, 46, 2x, 201, 322.
" Martha, 28, 72.
" Martha J., 367.
" Mary, 16, 28, 66, 67, 80, 93, 118, 200, 263, 264, 277, 321, 322, 391, 396.
" Mary A., 151, 200, 367.
" Mary S., 64.
" Matilda, 187.
" Maurice, 117, 264.
" Mercy, 95.
" Messenger, 156, 264.
" Mills, 67, 203, 265, 321, 322, 368.
" Nancy, 66, 209.
" Nathan, 243, 396.
" Nathaniel, 243, 322.
" Nathaniel N., 321.
" Noah, 65, 66, 368, 396.

INDEX TO PERSONS.

L.

Lockwood, Odell, 334.
" Oliver, 67, 155, 166, 183, 201, 237, 270, 281, 373.
" Peter, 23, 66, 67, 151, 155, 187, 216, 236, 261, 264, 281, 294, 298, 319, 344, 366, 380, 387.
" Phebe, 81.
" Philip, 59, 114, 202, 265.
" Phineas, 16.
" Polly, 117, 156, 208.
" Priscilla, 4, 46, 156, 368.
" Prudence, 87.
" Ralph, 367.
" Rebecca, 66, 264, 367, 382.
" Reuben, 156, 202.
" Rhua A., 161.
" Richard, 65, 66, 201, 202, 396.
" Rufus, 117, 202.
" Rufus A., 161.
" Ruth, 65, 66, 201, 368, 396.
" Sally, 96, 117, 156, 200, 202, 217, 367, 373, 379.
" Samuel, D.D., 317.
" Samuel, 19, 116, 117, 148, 156, 157, 161, 179, 180, 202, 207, 244, 248, 250, 251, 252, 278, 284, 305, 312, 317, 318, 319, 338, 369, 386.
" Samuel, Jr., 304, 320, 372.
" Samuel L., 367.
" Sarah, 23, 25, 28, 32, 52, 67, 117, 118, 150, 154, 151, 155, 202, 203, 264, 265, 322.
" Sarah E., 367.
" Seymour, 117.
" Shadrach, 67, 155, 156, 294, 368.
" Shubal, 396.
" Smith, 117, 157, 203.

L.

Lockwood, Solomon, 66, 396.
" Stephen, 67, 100, 155, 166, 201, 204, 373, 396.
" Stephen, Jr., 243, 263.
" Susan, 201, 264, 364.
" Tamar, 65, 66.
" Thaddeus, 117, 118, 156
" Thankful, 200.
" Timothy L., 367.
" Titus, 9, 67.
" Uriah, 117, 155.
" Webster, 203.
" William, 65, 67, 117, 203, 321, 322, 369.
" William H., 193, 201, 367.
" William M., 264, 265.
" William P., 116, 200, Ex 396.
" William R., 368.
" William W., 367.
Lounsberry, see Lounsbury.
Lounsbury, Abigail, 94, 157, 168, 203, 204, 374.
" Amasa, 204.
" Amos, 393.
" Amos L., 203, 396.
" Anna, 29.
" Anne, 67.
" Benjamin, 29.
" Betsy, 67.
" Betsy A., 68, 334, 397.
" Betsy M., 322.
" Caty, 174.
" Charles, 67, 157.
" Clara, 29.
" Clarissa, 29.
" Deborah, 102, 157, 322, 396.
" Edwin, 68, 118, 211, 240, 296, 318, 365, 397.
" Elihu, 233.
" Elijah, 29, 396.
" Elizabeth, 29, 203, 396.

INDEX TO PERSONS.

L.

Lounsbury, Enos, 157.
" Enos, Jr., 67.
" Epenetus, 134, 228.
" Eri W., 322.
" Esther, 83, 279.
" Ezra, 29, 299, 322, 333.
" George, 285, 286, 333, 341, 361, 369, 385.
" Gideon, 145, 157, 168, 396, 397.
" Hannah, 29, 67, 157, 396.
" Hardy, 157.
" Harvey, 144, 145, 157.
" Henry, 396.
" Isaac, 67, 279, 369.
" James, 15, 29, 67, 157, 396, 402.
" James I., 369.
" Jane, 203, 204.
" Jared, 15, 29, 67, 68, 83.
" Jerusha, 95, 133, 204.
" John, Captain, 204.
" John, 29, 95, 133, 157, 204, 396.
" John D., 118.
" Justus, 204.
" Katy, 174.
" Lemuel, 68.
" Leonard F., 322.
" Lydia, 125.
" Lockwood, 94.
" Maria, 157.
" Martha, 29, 134, 216, 228, 401.
" Mary C., 369.
" Mary E., 322.
" Mary L., 385.
" Monmouth, 374.
" Nancy, 211, 369, 378, 396.
" Nathan, 157.
" Nehemiah, 68.
" Patty, 125.
" Phebe, 333.

L.

Lounsbury, Polly, 68, 204, 397.
" Rufus, 396.
" Sally, 67, 204, 396, 397.
" Sally A., 68.
" Samuel, 67, 68, 157, 203, 396, 397.
" Sarah, 369.
" Seely, 38.
" Sherman, 67, 118.
" Stephen, 204.
" Thomas, 41, 68, 110, 397.
" William, 68, 118, 397.
" William W., 369.
" Zabud, 157.
Low, William H., 311.
Lowden, James, 160.
Luker, Charles, 263, 265.
" Morris, 263, 265.
Lyman, Hannah, 20.
Lyon, Abigail, 69, 118.
" Abigail E., 322.
" Abigail J., 204.
" Abraham, 32, 69, 106.
" Abram, 204.
" Andrew, 30, 68, 69.
" Anne, 69.
" Armenia, 118.
" Augustus, 29, 30, 44, 102, 158, 189, 206, 215, 230, 240, 303, 320, 397.
" Benjamin, 29, 115, 348, 397.
" Benjamin W., 30, 68, 69, 157, 158.
" Betsy, 69, 158, 323.
" Betty L., 158.
" Charles, 158.
" Charles F., 118.
" Daniel, 29, 30, 68, 69, 158, 160, 329, 348, 397.
" Daniel, Jr., 221.
" Daniel, 3rd, 397.
" David, 29, 30, 93, 278, 348, 397.
" Deborah, 69, 158, 204.
" Elisha, 118, 375.

INDEX TO PERSONS.

L.

Lyon, Elizabeth, 29, 30, 69, 397, 398.
" Elizabeth J., 30.
" Emeline, 204.
" Fanny, 158.
" Fitch, 268.
" Ferris, 14.
" Gilbert, 69, 204, 323.
" Gilbert, Jr., 29.
" Hannah, 32, 69, 93, 173, 204, 241, 323.
" Harriet H., 30.
" Henry, 278.
" Isaac, 267, 322.
" James, 29, 30, 68, 157, 158, 348, 397.
" James, Jr., 29.
" Jerusha, 158.
" Job, 31, 81, 82, 106, 142, 322, 323, 398.
" John, 106, 323, 369.
" Jonathan, 69.
" Joseph, 158.
" Joshua, 69, 79, 323, 369, 397.
" Katharine, 118.
" Lavinia, 69.
" Lewis, 30, 240.
" Loretta, 69.
" Martha, 29, 30.
" Mary, 29, 30, 32, 68, 69, 158, 204, 397.
" Mary U., 30.
" Mehitable, 192, 399.
" Nancy, 30, 115, 116.
" Phebe, 68, 323.
" Polly, 118, 397.
" Rebecca, 158.
" Sally, 30, 397.
" Samuel, 30, 69, 323, 369.
" Sarah, 29, 30, 68, 69, 323.
" Sarah A., 247.
" Sarah B., 30.
" Seth, 107, 118, 204, 268, 22, 290.
" Simeon, 32, 69, 397.
" Susannah, 30.

L.

Lyon, Tamer, 68.
" Thomas, 29, 68, 69, 118, 158.
" Thomas W., 192, 360, 399.
" Underhill, 68.
" Woolsey, 68.

Mc.

McDonald, Catherine, 344.
" Timothy, 369.
McGown, Francis, 369, 370.
McGuire, Delia, 376, 377.
McFarland, Charles S., 403.
" John, 403.
McIntire, Henry, 204.
" James, 204.
" John, 69, 204.
" Mary A., 332.
McKay, see also Mackay.
" James, 142.
" Patrick, 142.
" Hugh, 370, 377.
McKinney, William E., 312.
McLaughlin, Edward, 64.
" Edward A., 64.
" Rachel, 64.
" William L., 65.
McQuean, Robert, 323.

M.

Maby, Elizabeth, 115, 116.
" Isaac, 115.
Mackay, Betsy, 63.
" Elizabeth, 63.
" Hugh, 230, 287, 288, 310, 351, 366, 370, 377, 383.
" John, 14, 38, 63, 67, 82, 92, 115.
" John, Jr., 14, 89.
" Margaret, 14, 82.
Madden, Africa, 118.
" America, 118.
" Amos, 69, 118.
" Ezekiel, 118.
" Mary A., 118.
" Michael E., 118.

INDEX TO PERSONS.

M.

Madden, Sally, 118.
" William R., 118.
Maitland, Rebecca S., 403.
Mallory, Charles, 379.
" Sally, 379.
Maltbie, Catherine, 11.
" David, 3, 11, 95, 392.
Manna, Mary, 74.
Manning, Gabriel, 213.
" Molly, 213.
Marsh, Charles, 364.
" Rhuea S., 364.
Marshall, Abigail, 95.
" Amy, 158, 159.
" Arza, 144, 259, 286, 310.
" Clemence, 191.
" Deborah, 266.
" Elihu, 7.
" Eliza, 69.
" Elizabeth, 86, 404.
" Emeline, 353.
" Ephraim, 124, 158, 184, 213, 221, 291, 303, 367, 377.
" Ezra, 30, 70.
" George, 353.
" Gilbert, 227.
" Gilbert, Jr., 370.
" Hannah, 159, 266.
" Henry, 38, 136, 265.
" Mary, 89, 286, 323.
" Orpah, 159, 266.
" Orpha, 159, 266.
" Pamela, 72.
" Phebe, 136.
" Polly, 309, 310.
" Sarah, 266.
" Sarah K., 319.
" Stephen W., 323.
" Sylvanus, 37, 82, 89, 309.
" Thomas, 227.
" William S., 265.
Marvin, Barnabas, 108, 112, 120, 127, 218.
" Epenetus, 168, 323, 324.
" Mary, 128, 281, 324.

M.

Marvin, Polly, 168.
Mason, Mary E., 320.
" Nehemiah, 22.
Mather, Betsy, 266, 397.
" Clara, 266, 397.
" David S., 266, 397.
" George, 207, 397.
" Hannah, 30, 87, 266, 397.
" Isaac, 30.
" Joseph, 30, 266, 397.
" Joseph, Jr., 235.
" Mary A., 207.
" Moses, Rev., 30.
" Moses, 87, 266, 397.
" Nancy, 266, 397.
" Noyes, 30, 31.
" Phebe, 266, 397.
" Rana, 266, 397.
" Raymond, 32.
" Raua, 266, 397.
" Rebecca C., 191.
" Samuel, 3, 30, 32, 189.
" Sarah, 266, 397.
Matthews, Abigail J., 324.
" Abijah, 324.
" Ananias, 347.
" Benjamin, 168, 203, 338, 370.
" Benjamin S., 370, 398
" Charity, 88, 324.
" Daniel, 53, 142, 190, 324.
" Dorinda, 324.
" Jacob, 324.
" James L., 370.
" Mary, 190, 345.
" Mary L., 370.
" Oliver, 53, 223, 324.
" Robert, 245.
" Sarah, 180, 207, 347.
" Sarah J., 370.
" William, 324.
" William H., 370.
Matthias, Hannah, 79.
Mayo, Ann, 332.
Mead, Aaron, 70.
" Abigail, 72, 81, 83, 256,

INDEX TO PERSONS.

M.

372,393,398.
Mead, Abigail J., 256, 257.
" Abner, 70, 159.
" Abraham, 119, 159, 315, 326.
" Abraham D., 370.
" Abram, 209, 233, 325.
" Adelia, 324.
" Alla, 324.
" Allan, 86.
" Allan S., 145.
" Allen S., 187, 243.
" Alma, 204.
" Almira, 204, 371.
" Alvah, 285, 287, 324, 332.
" Alvan, 86, 119, 178, 191, 204, 205, 206, 214, 219, 224, 249, 292, 297, 302.
" Amanda L., 325.
" Amos, 17, 70, 71, 72, 124, 146, 159, 203, 258, 267, 285, 398.
" Amy, 17, 52, 55, 119.
" Andrew, 7, 17, 48, 55, 67, 73, 78, 83, 119, 205, 267, 292, 400.
" Angelina A., 31, 70, 71, 119.
" Ann, 398.
" Anna, 31, 71, 72, 324.
" Anne, 70.
" Araminta, 205, 207.
" Augustus, 241, 255, 326, 359, 360, 361, 370, 372, 378, 398.
" Azuba, 159.
" Benjamin, 70, 160.
" Bethia, 25, 73, 160.
" Betsy, 31, 57, 67, 71, 72, 191.
" Brockhurst, 70.
" Bush, 72.
" B. S., 362.
" Caleb H., 371.
" Calvin, 50, 70, 73, 370.
" Charity, 70, 71, 72, 398.
" Charles, 109.
" Chloe, 159.

M.

Mead, Clara, 25.
" Clarinda, 73.
" Clarissa, 159.
" Cornelius, 370.
" Cynthia E., 311.
" Cyrus, 49.
" Daniel, 119.
" Daniel S., 204, 205, 206, 266, 325, 370.
" Darius, Dr., 138.
" Darius, 70, 71, 72, 320, 324, 160
" Darius, Jr., 71, 124, 159, 180, 186, 266, 273, 340.
" David, 31, 50, 65, 70, 72, 81, 147, 159, 392.
" David, Jr., 215.
" David W., 159.
" Deborah, 159, 324, 325, 371, 372.
" Deborah A., 370.
" Drake, 115, 159, 209, 267, 323, 325, 370.
" Ebenezer, Colo., 204, 370, 371.
" Ebenezer, Rev., 371.
" Ebenezer, 7, 9, 14, 16, 18, 17, 29, 30, 31, 34, 45, 47, 65, 68, 69, 70, 71, 74, 79, 99, 113, 119, 138, 158, 204, 272, 313, 370, 398, 400, 404.
" Ebenezer, Jr., 70, 113.
" Edmund, 70, 107, 121, 209, 245.
" Edward, 52, 370.
" Edwin, 204, 266.
" Electa, 159.
" Eli, 31.
" Elijah, 393.
" Eliphalet, 71.
" Eliza V., 325.
" Elizabeth, 49, 72, 119, 267, 370, 393, 398.
" Elizabeth C., 186.
" Elkanah, 17, 71, 361, 402.
" Elnathan, 106.
" Elsey, 325, 372.
" Emeline, 371.

INDEX TO PERSONS.

M.

Mead, Emeline Z?, 204.
" Enoch, Rev., 371.
" Enoch, 17.
" Enos, 119.
" Ephraim, 45, 159, 206, 398.
" Esther, 14, 205, 324, 326.
" Eunice, 119.
" Fanny, 158, 370.
" Francis, 32, 73.
" Gideon, 371.
" Gilbert, 159.
" Grace W., 205, 206.
" Hanford, 241, 279.
" Hannah, 17, 31, 71, 72, 86, 109, 159, 138, 204, 267, 324, 371, 372, 398.
" Hannah H., 109.
" Hardy, 7, 73.
" Harriet, 371.
" Harvey, 72.
" Henrietta, 205, 206.
" Henry, 370.
" Huldah, 205, 267, 324, 326, 398.
" Ira, 7, 73.
" Isaac, 119, 159, 324, 325.
" Isaac, Jr. 73, 146, 159, 160, 206, 326.
" Isaac H., 370.
" Israel, 31, 35, 52.
" Jabez, 4, 15, 24, 32, 51, 63, 69, 71, 73, 76, 91, 98, 119, 122, 124, 136, 141, 153, 155, 159, 160, 163, 170, 171, 189, 199, 200, 204, 205, 211, 224, 240, 266, 267, 277, 320, 323, 325, 326, 329, 338, 371, 375, 396, 398.
" Jabez, Jr., 313, 382.
" Jabez, 3rd, 250, 273.
" Jabez H., 146.
" James R., 160.
" Jared, 72, 204, 205, 266, 325, 370, 398.
" Jasper, 71, 72, 398.
" Jehiel, 371.
" Jehiel, Jr., 31, 70.
" Jeremiah, 37, 71.

M.

Mead, Jeremiah, Jr., 400.
" Jeremiah F., 205, 267, 268.
" Job, 119, 325, 372.
" John, 72, 101.
" John, Jr., 71.
" John H., 206.
" John W., 159.
" Jonah, 61, 70, 159, 267.
" Jonas, 45, 50, 109, 159, 160, 204, 372.
" Jonas, Jr., 313.
" Jonathan, 71, 119, 159, 205.
" Jonathan, Jr., 71.
" Joseph, 9.
" Joshua, 31, 71, 72, 398.
" Josiah, 72.
" Jotham, 119.
" Julia A., 273.
" Julia B., 322, 325, 326.
" Justus B., 18, 31, 72.
" J. T., 290.
" Kezia, 159.
" Laura, 160.
" Leander, 370.
" Leonard, 159, 357, 372.
" Levi, 13, 52, 53, 83.
" Lewis, 189.
" Lisetta, 370.
" Lockwood, 399.
" Lot, 159, 209.
" Louisianna C., 267, 325.
" Lucinda, 370.
" Luckner, 107.
" Lucy, 73.
" Luther, 267.
" Lydia, 138, 204.
" Lydia K., 124, 189, 273.
" Lyman, 370.
" Major, 31.
" Manoah, 119, 159, 267.
" Marcus, 370.
" Marilda, 71, 119, 144.
" Mark, Rev., 372.
" Mark, 324.
" Martha, 31, 70, 72.
" Mary, 9, 31, 35, 45, 52, 61, 70, 72, 146, 159, 267, 325, 371, 398.

INDEX TO PERSONS.

M.

Mead, Mary A., 13,52,53.
" Mary E., 205,207,268, 321,325.
" Mary J., 370.
" Matthew, 72.
" Mehitable, 205,267,292.
" Morris, 158.
" Nancy, 71,73,119.
" Nathan, 26,206,398.
" Nathan S., 246,275,290, 311,358,371,382.
" Nathaniel, 63,71,72,86, 119,398.
" Nathaniel, Jr., 72,73.
" Nathaniel, 3rd, 31,72, 398.
" Nehemiah, 2,29,72,73,146, 205,267,268.
" Nehemiah, Jr., 16,25,99, 160.
" Noah, 45,159.
" Obadiah, 31,70,109,160, 189,214.
" Oliver, 324,325,326
" Pamela, 72.
" Peter, 7,18,73,75,80,99, 113,119.
" Phebe, 70,371.
" Platt, 34,53,55,74,99,54 118,124,128,131,145,164, 178,190,212,213,220,246, 247,248,256,273,275,276, 284,371,372,398,399.
" Polly, 18,73,159,160, 205,267,292.
" Prudence, 71,72,73.
" Rachel, 7,25,72,73,121, 159,204,205,206,266,268, 398.
" Rachel E., 204.
" Rachel M., 159.
" Rebecca, 71,72,398.
" Reuben, 26,206,268.
" Rheuma, 71,119.
" Richard, 9,12,14,18,45, 70,113,119,178,205,206, 214,393,398.
" Riley, 73.

M.

Mead, Robert, 18,70,73,159,398.
" Rogers, 206.
" Rufus, 370.
" Ruth, 72,109,119,160.
" Ruth C., 160.
" Sally, 17,71,160.
" Samuel, 119.
" Samuel B., 159.
" Samuel H., 160.
" Sanford, 311,357,359.
" Sarah, 25,26,32,61,72,73,160, 205,324,325,326,395,398.
" Sarah A., 205,207.
" Sarah E., 206.
" Sarah M., 255.
" Sarah W., 153,267,268,1222 322,325,326.
" Seely, 350,371.
" Selah, 325,326.
" Seth, 206.
" Shadrach, 31,35,65,72,73, 81,105,159,186,372,398.
" Silas, Jr., 32,70,73,76, 398.
" Silas D., 370.
" Silas H., 32,73,160,370, 371.
" Silas M., 204,266.
" Smith, 72.
" Solomon, 31,72,317.
" Stephen, 393.
" Sylvester, 372.
" Tamise, 73.
" Theodore B., 159.
" Theodore H., 371.
" Theodosia, 70,160.
" Thirza, 370.
" Thomas, 72,73,279.
" Thomas A., 141,159,180, 204,206,210,211,214,219, 233,241,249,255,266,279,268 290,292,297,302,312,325, 326,360,361,372,377,398.
" Titus, 73,250,256,317, 331,371,372.
" Tyler, 72.
" Walter, 72,206.

INDEX TO PERSONS.

M.

Mead, Walter H., 206.
" Walter K., 119.
" William, 71,72,132,398.
" William A., 398.
" William H., 160,184,213, 250,256,257,317,372.
" William J., 370.
" William K., 268,325.
" Whitman, 205,206.
" Zaccheus, 75,255,312, 325,350,359,360,372.
" Zaccheus, Jr., 320,325, 326,359,372,382.
" Zachariah, Rev., 267.
" Zachariah, 205,267.
" Zebulon, 119.
" Zenas, 213,276,398.
" Zetta, 204,371.
" Zophar, 141,159,205,206, 207,326,398.
" Zophar, Jr., 70,73.
Meeker, Aaron, 372.
" Lorenzo, 372.
Mellis, Samuel, 57.
Merrill, see Merritt.
Merritt, Abigail, 160.
" Abby, 204.
" Abraham, 29,30,52,397.
" Adam, 207,347.
" Amy, 213.
" Anderson, 269.
" Benjamin, 160.
" Betsy, 52.
" Caleb, Jr., 213.
" Caroline, 32,74,268.
" Charity P., 213.
" Charlotte, 136.
" Curtis, 326.
" Cynthia, 240.
" Daniel, 30,69,240,247.
" Daniel B., 240.
" Deborah, 69,213.
" Delilah, 160.
" Dorothy, 180.
" Elijah, 268.
" Eliza, 32,99.
" Elizabeth, 29,30,74, 213,268,269,326,348,374, 397.

M.

Merritt, Gilbert, 160.
" Hannah, 69,160.
" Harriet, 74,398.
" Henry, 74,362.
" James, 74,88,247,311.
" James H., 269,326.
" Jeremiah, 336.
" Jeremiah A., 269.
" John, 74,326.
" John A., 269,326,372.
" Joseph, 74,213.
" Jotham, 32,39,74,99, 213,246,248,268,290,311, 372,374,398.
" Lockwood K., 323.
" Maria, 269,326,336.
" Mary, 74,347.
" Mary A., 133.
" Mary E., 269.
" Mary W., 32,74,268.
" Molly, 213.
" Nancy, 247,311,358.
" Nathan, 74,213.
" Nehemiah, 326.
" Penelope, 160.
" Phineas, 269,326.
" Robert, 160.
" Ruth, 213.
" Sally, 30,240.
" Sarah, 240,326.
" Sniffin, 358.
" Susannah, 42,74.
" Sylvanus, 160.
" Theodore, 269,326.
" William, 323.
" William A., 207,234,22 239,290.
" William C., 269.
" Wilmot, 74.
" Wilson, 28,42.
Mesnard, Zalmon, 399.
Michel, Abigail, 394.
Miles, Charlotte, 117.
" Isaac, 117.
" John, 120.
Milder, Anna, 74,373.
" Anne, 42.
" Charles, 333.
" David, 129,373.

INDEX TO PERSONS.

M.

Miller, Edgar G., 373.
" Elbert A., 74, 161.
" Eliza A., 74, 161.
" Hannah, 32, 69, 373.
" Harriet A., 373.
" James, 32, 74, 161.
" Jemima H., 225.
" Jonathan, 83, 269.
" Louisa A., 373.
" Margarette, 302.
" Maria E., 74, 161.
" Mary, 220, 391, 399.
" Nathaniel, 289, 324.
" Polly, 399.
" Samuel, 135.
" Sarah, 69.
" Seely, 229, 238, 269, 282, 339.
" Seth, 227, 269, 360, 374, 381, 385.
" Westover, 32, 74.
Willis, Samuel, 142.
Wills, Abigail, 32.
" Alexander, 25, 49.
" Amos, 207.
" Catherine, 277, 278, 331.
" Charlotte, 269.
" Clemence, 32.
" Ezra, 277, 331.
" George, 24, 26, 400.
" Hannah, 32, 128, 168, 373.
" John, 32.
" John T., 171, 207.
" Lydia, 32, 171, 404.
" Martha, 207.
" Mary, 32.
" Nathaniel, 49, 168, 373, 397.
" Olla, 269.
" Roswell, 269.
" Samuel, 5, 32, 269, 336.
" Samuel, Jr., 207.
" Sarah, 25, 32.
Minor, James H., 204, 249, 316, 326, 396.
" Simeon H., 14, 18, 19, 33, 76, 80, 85, 87, 120, 159, 165,

M.

167, 184, 193, 194, 202, 204, 206, 226, 229, 231, 252, 294, 297, 326, 327, 332, 334, 394, 396, 400.
Minor, William T., 315, 316, 326.
" Zalmon, 138.
Mitchell, Minott, 211.
Moe, Charlotte, 209, 269.
" Elizabeth, 269.
Moore, Charles, 120.
" George, 74, 75.
" Rebecca, 72.
" Sarah, 74.
Morehouse, Alexander, 207.
" Andrew, 75.
" Betsy, 32.
" Betsy A., 189, 207.
" Catherine, 161.
" Elizabeth, 32.
" Gershom, 32.
" Henry, 161, 379.
" Joshua, 32, 88, 120.
" Mary, 32, 75.
" Phebe, 32.
" Sarah E., 207, 270.
" Silas, 270.
Morgan, Sarah, 279.
Morrell, Jacob, 214.
" John, 327.
" Joseph, 73, 124.
" Rivers, 69.
" Robert, Jr., 338.
" Sarah, 107.
" Sophia, 214.
" William, 327.
Morris, Sally, 200.
" Thomas, 293.
Mosher, Isaac, 266.
" Isaac, Jr., 266.
" James, 241.
Mosier, Betsy, 323.
" William, 224, 323.
Mott, Abigail, 53, 190.
" Clarissa, 123.
" Richard, 53.
" Richard L., 238.
Moulton, S---, 128.

INDEX TO PERSONS.

M.

Munday, Sarah, 32,33.
Munson, David, 102.
Murphy, Joseph B., 32,33.
" Phebe, 136.
" Robert, 33.

N.

Nash, Anna, 207.
" David,45,120,391.
" Edward,120.
" Elizabeth, 120.
" Georgiana, 270.
" Harvey, 225.
" James, 70,76,141,207.
" Mary A., 270.
" Rachel, 120.
" Thomas A., 220.
" William, 2x,120.
Nelson, Henry, 118.
Nestele, Emily, 327.
" Joanna, 327.
" Sophia, 327.
Newman, Allen, 120.
" Amy, 328.
" Andrew,122,161.
" Ann, 208.
" Anna,207,208.
" Augustus, 374.
" Augustus R.,308,357.
" Catherine,161,328,373, 374.
" Clarissa, 328.
" Drake, 208.
" Edward T.,327,374.
" Edwin,207,208,259, 275,287,300.
" Electa, 208.
" Elizabeth,89,208,245, 327.
" Hannah, 327.
" Harvey, 208,270.
" Henry,89,208.
" Hezekiah, 327.
" James M., 270.
" Jane A., 328.
" John,89,208,327,374.

N.

Newman, John E.,327,374.
" Lucretia T., 374.
" Lucy J.,327, 374.
" Luther, 327.
" Maltbie,161,208.
" Margaret, 241.
" Martha,22,287.
" Mary, 327.
" Mary C., 328.
" Nathaniel,120,121,208.
" Patty, 208.
" Polly,89,122,208,317, 318,319,327.
" Ralph, 27,161.
" Rebecca,25,133,161.
" Rosetta, 208.
" Rufus,18,47,161,317, 318,319,327,396.
" Sally,161,183,327.
" Sally L., 328.
" Sarah, 161.
" Stephen,161,328.
" Susannah, 27.
" Thankful,121,207.
" William,236,303,319, 327,328,385,394.
" Zadoc,95,117,133,328, 373.
" Zetty, 89.
Newton, Alvin P., 374.
" Joseph, 374.
Nichols, Abigail, 222.
" Abraham, 33,75.
" Anne,129,399.
" Benny, 399.
" Catherine, 33,50.
" Daniel,6,10,33,37,50, 65,75,89,105,117,129,152, 170,222,402.
" Daniel,Jr.,89,403.
" David, 75.
" Elizabeth,33,75.
" Epenetus V.,174,221, 222,391.
" James,75,399.
" John,27,41,75.
" Joseph, 75.

INDEX TO PERSONS.

N.

Nichols, Lavina, 161.
" Mary, 75, 399.
" Paulina, 161.
" Polly, 27.
" Robert, 75, 121, 222.
" Ruth, 75.
" Samuel, 222.
North, Julia A., 282.
Northrup, David, 399.
" Isaac, 224.
" Sally, 224.

O.

O'Brien, John, 322.
Ogden, Thomas L., 403.
Olcott, Nathaniel, 63, 64, 75.
" William, 75.
Oliver, William A., 199.
Olmstead, Benjamin H., 19.
" Benjamin K., 399.
" Ebenezer, 399.
" Fanny, 279.
" John, 204.
Onderdonk, Catherine, 19.
" Justus, 19.
Ostrander, Ira L., 367.
" Isaac, 367.
" Lydia, 367.

P.

Page, Aphelia, 374.
" Benjamin, 136, 144, 152, 159, 170, 184, 186, 200, 205, 209, 265, 277, 308, 327, 329, 374, 396.
" Elisabeth, 374.
" Joseph, 374.
" Joseph E., 374.
" Rhoda, 152, 200, 260, 374.
Palmer, Abel, 188, 332.
" Abigail, 27, 128, 168, 270, 271, 328, 373, 374.
" Adeline, 63.
" Alton J., 233.
" Alva, 76, 77.
" Alvin, 163.

Palmer, Amy, 83.
" Ann, 77, 121, 270.
" Anna, 77.
" Asa, 76.
" Asahel, 53, 121, 122, 123, 138, 145, 152, 153, 162, 163, 171, 188, 189, 199, 201, 208, 211, 213, 264, 266, 271, 277, 328, 338.
" Aseal, 403.
" Ashbel, 145.
" Azuba, 61.
" Benjamin G., 77.
" Bethel, 161, 174.
" Betsy, 72, 158.
" Catherine, 88.
" Charles J., 233.
" Charlotte, 76.
" Cynthia, 240, 353.
" Daniel L., 296, 373.
" David, 77.
" David L., 115, 270.
" Deborah, 209, 271.
" Delia, 77, 247, 374, 375.
" Denham, 121, 208.
" Edmond, 121.
" Elizabeth, 76, 77.
" Elliot, 158.
" Emma C., 373.
" Esther, 34, 40.
" Fanny, 76.
" Ferris, 33, 76.
" Floyd T., 335, 337, 389.
" George A., 208, 354.
" Gilbert, 76.
" Hannah, 52, 76, 77, 270, 271, 328.
" Henry, 121, 208.
" Hetty, 52, 76, 270, 399.
" James, 13, 52, 53, 77.
" James D., 328.
" James F., 114, 161, 328, 329.
" James L., 370.
" James P., 271, 328.
" Jemima, 13, 52, 53, 328.
" Jeremiah, 26, 161, 162.
" John, 22, 76, 88, 208, 209.

INDEX TO PERSONS.

P.

Palmer, John A., 209, 271.
" John R., 308.
" John W., 52, 399.
" Jonathan, 77.
" Joseph F., 328.
" Josephus, 209, 325, 329.
" Julia A., 373, 374.
" Justus, 33, 76.
" Leander M., 365.
" Levi, 77, 82, 83, 406.
" Linus, 76, 77.
" Lockwood, 77.
" Lot, 91, 240, 266, 273, 277, 353, 354, 357.
" Louisa A., 373.
" Lounsbury, 270, 373.
" Lucinda, 309.
" Lydia, 149.
" Marcus, 77.
" Margery, 76.
" Martin, 399.
" Mary, 52, 76, 77, 161, 22, 270, 328.
" Mary A., 281, 352.
" Mary F., 161.
" Mercy, 77.
" Messenger, 34, 76, 88, 168, 399.
" Nathan, 77.
" Nathaniel, 7, 14, 77, 119, 158, 159, 162, 207, 209.
" Oliver, 76.
" Phanny, 76.
" Phebe, 76, 77, 209, 373, 374.
" Polly, 174, 281.
" Rachel, 162, 209.
" Ralph, 76, 334.
" Roswell G., 328.
" Rundle, 77.
" Ruth, 309.
" Sally, 161.
" Sally B., 165, 328, 380.
" Samuel, 76, 77.
" Samuel, Jr., 399.
" Sarah, 76, 83, 138, 161.
" Seely, 76, 77, 399.

P.

Palmer, Seth, 209, 271.
" Silas, 403.
" Stephen, 61, 162.
" Sybil W., 52, 76.
" Walter, 161, 199, 281.
" Warren, 240.
" William, 14, 77, 149.
" Vinus, 77.
Pardee, Mary, 110.
Park, Eunice, 121.
Parketing, Abraham, 77, 399.
" Betsy, 399.
Parketon, Rodney, 78.
Parkhurst, Otis, 118.
Parrott, Sally, 220.
Patten, Mary A., 332.
Patterson, Hugh, 364.
" Richard E., 389.
" Stephen, 209.
" Stephen I., 229.
Paulding, Caleb, 142.
" Hannah, 142.
Peacock, Dodsworth H., 329.
" Eliza A., 329.
" Julia A., 329.
" Mary, 23, 151, 329.
" Ralph, 329.
" Sally, 329.
" Sarah, 329.
" William, 23, 151, 329.
Pearson, Phebe S., 401.
" Samuel, 401.
Peck, Aaron, 20, 102, 209, 210, 271
" Abigail, 78, 82, 210.
" Abigail J. M., 192.
" Abraham, 78, 163.
" Abraham H., 375.
" Alathea, 329.
" Albert M., 375.
" Albert N., 375.
" Alexander, 162.
" Allen, 31.
" Amy, 82.
" Ann, 155, 163, 203, 211.
" Anna, 78, 271.
" Anna M., 273.
" Anna N., 105.

473.

INDEX TO PERSONS.

P.   P.

Peck, Benjamin, 69, 92, 162, 220.
" Beneni, 214, 272, 273, 275.
" Betsy, 122, 162.
" Blackman, 78.
" Caroline, 336.
" Catherine, 122.
" Charles, 152, 162, 163, 210.
" Charles E., 162, 192, 210, 399.
" Charles H., 163, 273.
" Charlotte, 242.
" Cillah, 329.
" Clara, 34.
" Daniel, 63, 64, 78, 92, 147, 164, 200, 355, 365, 371.
" David, Rev., 329.
" David, 152, 163, 209, 272, 329.
" David B., 383.
" Deborah, 82, 209, 210, 271.
" Delilah, 329.
" Ebenezer, 23, 26, 45, 78, 210, 211, 271.
" Elias, 7, 34, 105, 106, 186, 255, 267, 271, 272, 323, 325, 375.
" Elias, Jr., 52, 99, 162, 163.
" Elias, Ex.B., 162, 177.
" Eliphalet, 210.
" Eliphalet, Jr., 329.
" Eliza, 277.
" Elizabeth, 34, 209, 210, 271, 399.
" Emeline, 79.
" Enos, 152, 163.
" Esther, 78.
" Eunice, 34, 44, 99, 177, 399.
" Fanny, 34.
" George, 203.
" Gideon, 34, 399.
" Gilbert, 7, 82, 210, 272.
" Hannah, 78, 209, 210, 211, 271, 272, 371.
" Hannah R., 162, 220.
" Harriet, 209, 210, 272.
" Harriet H., 375, 212.
" Henry, 209, 272.
" Huldah, 272. xx

Peck, Isaac, 17, 122, 162, 163, 188, 238, 273, 318, 324, 332, 351.
" Isaac, Jr., 212, 247, 272, 273, 324.
" Isaac, 3rd, 24, 57, 77, 78, 82x 82, 247, 248, 272, 324,
" Isaac, 5th, 272.
" Israel, 31, 78, 210, 211, 272, 365.
" Jabez, 211, 400.
" James, 309.
" Jane, 273.
" Jared, 68, 273, 329.
" Jeduthan, 79, 375.
" Jerusha, 34, 78.
" Jesse, 122.
" John, 375.
" John F., 79, 375.
" John W., 163, 273.
" Jonathan, 162, 177, 272.
" Joseph, 121, 122, 163.
" Josephus, 309.
" Julia, 210.
" Leaticia W., 263.
" Letitia, 321, 322, 396.
" Levina, 78, 163, 211.
" Lewis, 163.
" Marilda, 329.
" Mary, 34, 52, 70, 79, 152, 154, 210, 272, 273, 375.
" Mary M., 375.
" Mary P., 209.
" Mehitable, 162, 192.
" Molly, 163.
" Moses, 211.
" Nancy, 148, 192, 210, 399.
" Nathan, 42.
" Nathaniel, 400.
" Nehemiah, 42, 78, 211, 266.
" Obadiah, 273.
" Orpah, 266.
" Pearson, 271.
" Phebe, 329.
" Polly, 122, 271.
" Prue, 122.
" Rachel, 78, 211.
" Ralph, 78.
" Reed, 220.

INDEX TO PERSONS.

P.

Peck, Rhoda, 152, 163, 200.
" Robert, 163.
" Robert, Jr., 78.
" Rufus, 155, 203, 271, 321, 322, 396.
" Ruth, 329.
" Ruth M., 273.
" Sally, 78, 152, 163.
" Samuel, 31, 65, 70, 73, 78, 81, 105, 162, 186, 207, 211, 213, 272, 273, 277, 400.
" Samuel, Jr., 205, 211.
" Sands F., 162.
" Sarah, 65.
" Solomon, 79, 115, 122, 210, 336.
" Solomon, Jr., 357, 375.
" Sophia, 273.
" Stephen, 122.
" Stephen S., 163.
" Theophilus, 34, 272, 399.
" Thomas, 154.
" Thomas H., 162, 192, 399.
" Walter, 400.
" Whitfield, 152, 163.
" Whitman, 272, 273.
" William, 210, 230, 355, 375.
" Wilson, 162, 177.
Pelton, Mary, 284.
" Robert, 284.
Pendell, Elizabeth, 330, 376.
" William, 330, 376.
Pencyer, Alanson, 273.
" Alfred, 122.
" Anson D., 122.
" Betsy, 32.
" Charles E., 330.
" Elanson, 273.
" Elizabeth, 274, 400.
" Hannah, 122, 163, 273.
" Harvey, 144.
" Henry, 122, 163, 273.
" Isaac, 3, 40, 62, 103, 108, 122, 147, 163, 211, 273, 393.
" Jacob, 264, 273, 274.
" James H., 122, 211.
" Jesse, 273.
" John, 273.

P.

Pencyer, Loisa, 274.
" Louisa, 274.
" Morris E., 274.
" Richard S., 211.
" Samuel, 36, 273, 274.
" Smith, 122.
Percival, Warren, Dr., 137, 301.
" Warren, 3, 4, 105, 125, 135, 172, 189, 242, 381.
Perine, Benjamin, 16, 114.
" Sarah, 16, 114.
Perkins, Charles, 400.
Perry, Esther A., 400.
" Harriet M., 400.
" Julia B., 376.
" Nehemiah, 293.
" Samuel C., 400.
" Sarah, 400.
" Sarah B., 376.
" Sturges, 400.
" Sturges L., 400.
Peterson, Frederick, 79.
Petrie, John, 323.
Pettit, Hannah, 330.
Phelps, Humphrey, 369.
" Mary, 338.
Pierce, Daniel, 122, 123.
" Phebe, 122, 123.
Pine, Hannah, 211, 302.
" James, 211, 302, 303.
" Samuel, 211, 212.
" Sarah, 211.
Place, Sarah, 167.
" Smith, 167.
Platt, Anne, 403.
" Catherine, 373.
" Charity, 81.
" Elizabeth, 403.
" Ellen A., 373, 374, 376.
" Frederick, 274.
" Gabriel, 373.
" George, 113.
" Hetty, 270, 274, 373.
" Huldah, 94.
" Jeremiah, 351.
" John B., 274, 376.
Potts, Isaac, 274, 275/
Powelson, Elizabeth, 364.
Prendergast, James, 54.

INDEX TO PERSONS.

P.

Prime, Abraham, 241.
Provost, Alexander, 355.
" Anna, 330.
" Daniel, 36, 57, 134.
" Elizabeth, 37.
" Harry, 330.
" James, 330.
" Jerry, 330.
" John, 330.
" John, 3rd, 2x 330.
" Mary, 330.
" Rufus, 330.
" Salmon, 79.
" Samuel, 79, 135, 185, 274, 330.
" Stephen B., 111, 132, 139, 149, 156, 183, 185, 190, 260, 262, 291, 292, 305, 310, 312, 320, 321, 327, 332, 338, 339, 355, 362, 370, 381, 383.
" William, 299, 330.
" William T., 160.
Pugsley, Deborah, 141.
" Mary, 142.
" Richard, 141.
" Sarah, 141.
" William, 141.
Purdy, Abigail, 69, 79.
" Ann, 275.
" Caleb, 275.
" Calvin, 275.
" Charity W., 310.
" Clara, 212.
" Daniel, 79, 80.
" Deborah, 275.
" Elias, 212, 275.
" Emma, 321.
" Hannah, 79, 275.
" Harriet M., 275.
" Hester, 247.
" John, 79, 214, 241, 275.
" Josiah, 310, 311.
" Josiah, Jr., 310.
" Mary, 275.
" Mary B., 275.
" Mary W., 310.
" Nehemiah, 79, 80, 180, 347.

P.

Purdy, Phebe, 275.
" Rebecca, 79.
" Roger, 68.
" Sally, 275.
" Sally A., 275.
" Sarah, 211, 302.
" Tamer, 68.
" Tamson, 275.
" Thomas, 214, 275.
" Underhill, 211.
" William, 79, 80, 247, 275.

Q.

Quenett, Hannah, 14, 80.
Quimby, Aaron, 358.
" Daniel, 190.
" Esther, 190.
" Mary, 190.
" Moses I., 358.
Quintard, Abraham, 80, 330, 331.
" Ann, 330.
" Charles, 330.
" Clarissa, 2x, 123.
" Daniel D., 330.
" Edward A., 379.
" Elizabeth, 80, 330, 400
" Fanny, 80.
" Isaac, 34, 80, 140, 149, 209, 260, 360.
" Isaac, Jr., 127, 209, 249, 251, 283, 350.
" Lewis Y., 123.
" Lucy, 310.
" Lucy D., 264.
" Mary, 330, 400.
" Peter, 34, 80, 400.
" Peter, Jr., 123.
" Peter, 3rd, 34, 80.
" Peter D., 209.
" Polly, 80.
" Rebecca, 123.
" Robert P., 209, 399.
" Ruth, 34, 123.
" Seth, 209.
" Seth P., 209, 240, 271, 332, 352, 353.
" William K., 319.

INDEX TO PERSONS.

R.

Radcliffe, Elizabeth H., 187.
" Peter W., 187.
Raymond, Ann E., 212.
" Betsy, 212, 376, 377.
" Charles F., 212, 400.
" Charles L., 376.
" Charles M., 376.
" Daniel S., 376.
" Deborah, 177, 271.
" Delia, 212, 376, 377.
" Elias, 271.
" Ezra, 3, 34, 80, 406.
" Ezra F., 34.
" Fanny, 212, 376, 377.
" Gould, 80, 198, 217, 223, 229, 274, 341, 376.
" Gould S., 376.
" Hannah, 30.
" Henry, 363, 366.
" Hetty, 230.
" Hiram M., 34.
" Ira, 80, 81, 164.
" Isaac, 34, 35.
" James, 212, 376, 377.
" James K., 377.
" Jane B., 34.
" Jesse, 30.
" John, 149.
" Josiah, 34.
" Julia A., 212.
" Mary, 34, 177, 212, 289, 376, 377.
" Mary E., 376.
" Mary J., 212.
" Molly, 254.
" Munson G., 212.
" Rachel, 350.
" Rebecca, 114, 123.
" Richard M., 223.
" Richard S., 376.
" Robert, 34.
" Sally, 212, 376, 377.
" Sally A., 80, 212.
" Sally S., 212, 400.
" Samuel, 198.
" Samuel L., 80, 164.
" Samuel M., 212.

R.

Raymond, Sarah, 16.
" Stephen, 164, 212, 282, 376, 377, 381.
" Susan, 212, 376, 377.
" Sylvanus S., 212, 377.
" Thirza, 80.
" Thomas B., 376.
" William, 234, 379.
" William A., 212.
Raynor, Adelaide L., 275.
Redfield, Bradley, 275, 276, 371, 377.
" Edwin, 276.
" Edwin F., 377.
" Harriet, 275, 371.
" Isaac B., 275, 276.
" James, 276.
" Mary, 276.
" Miriam, 377.
" Platt N., 276.
" Sally, 276, 377.
Reed, Cornelia, 63.
" David, 63.
" Edward, 16.
" Elizabeth, 86, 218.
" Hannah, 313, 314, 363.
" Jane, 16.
" John, 254, 331.
" John, Jr., 86, 105, 112, 127.
" John B., 377.
" Martha, 112, 313, 314, 363.
" Mary, 149, 253.
" Nathan H., 149.
" Phebe, 86.
" Prudence, 89, 287.
" Roswell, 127.
" Sarah, 331.
" Thomas, 112, 127, 195, 198, 218, 235, 278, 290, 336, 402.
Remington, Joseph, 356.
Resseguire, Abijah, 293.
Reynolds, Abel, 82, 88, 117, 123, 128, 129, 152, 153, 155, 157, 164, 170, 172, 176, 183, 185, 201, 202, 221, 222, 233, 259, 265, 285, 287, 296, 375, 388, 393.

INDEX TO PERSONS.

R.

Reynolds, Abigail, 35, 81, 82, 276.
" Abigail I., 256.
" Abigail J., 81.
" Abraham, 83, 331.
" Allen, 82, 123.
" Althea, 276.
" Ambrose, 31, 212, 213, 331.
" Amy J., 276.
" Amy M., 331.
" Anna, 77, 81, 83.
" Ann E., 256, 276, 321, 367.
" Ard, 123, 124, 146, 150, 184, 208, 213, 240, 245, 256, 276, 291, 302, 305, 310, 321, 338, 339, 352, 354, 367, 377.
" Asa, 82.
" Augustus, 291.
" Augustus L., 184, 213, 303, 337, 377, 382.
" Benjamin, 13, 212.
" Bethia, 81, 212.
" Catherine, 170, 213, 291, 302.
" Charity, 81.
" Clark, 47.
" Cornelius, 49.
" Daniel, 150.
" Deborah, 61, 81, 123, 150, 213, 276, 353, 400.
" Debory, 213.
" Elijah, 15, 24, 82.
" Eliza, 235.
" Elizabeth, 302.
" Elizabeth P., 240, 256, 367.
" Elmaretta, 276.
" Emeline, 81.
" Eunice, 212.
" Ezekiel, 208, 331.
" Ezekiel, Jr., 124, 184, 213.
" George, 81, 82, 400.
" Hanford, 258.
" Hannah, 59, 322.

R.

Reynolds, Harriet, 123, 240.
" Harriet E., 276.
" Henry, 330.
" Hobby, 15.
" Horton, 35, 81.
" Husted, 123.
" Isaac, 150.
" Isaac P., 81.
" Israel, 22.
" James H., 81, 213, 238, 276.
" Jared, 82, 123, 159, 208, 212, 276, 277.
" Joel, 393.
" John, 49.
" John G., 276.
" John H., 188, 208, 353.
" John I., 81.
" John W., 199.
" Joseph, 81.
" Julia, 213.
" Julia H., 276.
" Julia R., 377.
" Lockwood, 170, 213.
" Lydia, 81.
" Mary, 212.
" Mary E., 277.
" Nancy, 288.
" Nathaniel, 61, 81, 123, 124, 400.
" Polly, 81, 121, 212.
" Rachel, 81.
" Rebecca, 123.
" Rosetta, 208.
" Ruth, 81.
" Sally, 212.
" Samantha, 81.
" Samuel, 81, 82, 288.
" Sarah, 61, 81, 150, 393.
" Shubal, 64.
" Stephen, 331.
" Susan, 276.
" Susannah, 49.
" Sylvanus, 213.
" Timothy, 20, 32, 36, 37, 38, 74, 81, 82, 84, 87, 89, 330.
" Titus, 61.

INDEX TO PERSONS.

R.

Reynolds, William, 82, 199, 277.
" William E., 302.
" " William H., 322.
" William P., 82, 150, 277, 331.
" Zadoc, 123.
Riblet, Phebe, 218.
Rich, see Ritch.
Richards, Alfred, 295.
" Andrew, 362.
" Anne, 135.
" Catherine, 186.
" Charles, 295.
" George, 362.
" Isaac, 277.
" John, 328.
" Joseph, 295.
" Lewis, 170, 186, 215.
" Lydia, 295.
" Mary E., 165, 380.
" Noyes, 20, 79, 112, 397.
" Rexene, 328.
" Samuel, 127.
" Sarah, 266, 397.
Richmond, David, 165.
Rider, David, 288.
Riker, Esther, 50.
Riley, Miles, 369.
Ritch, Abraham, 214.
" Ashley W., 378.
" Daniel M., 353.
" Emma C., 378.
" Harriet A., 378.
" Henry, 170, 183, 189, 199, 208, 240, 265, 266, 271, 277, 279, 307, 317, 321, 328, 353, 354, 357, 374, 375, 385, 398.
" Henry W., 378.
" James H., 378.
" Jared, 74.
" Lemuel, 213, 214.
" Maria, 214.
" Polly, 214.
" Sarah, 214.
" Sarah A., 348.
" Sophia, 214.
" Susan, 214.

R.

Ritch, Thirsa, 16.
" Wells R., 348.
Robbins, Alonzo F., 277.
" Can, 275.
" Catherine, 277.
" Cornelius, 164, 371.
" Eliza, 277.
" Hannah M., 164.
" John, 164, 275, 371.
" Julia A., 164, 371.
" Margery, 76.
" Maria M., 371.
" Mary, 277, 331, 378.
" Parris, 24, 277, 329.
" Sacket, 164, 371.
" William, 164, 371.
Roberts, Amos, 79, 277, 278, 401.
" Amos S., 278, 331.
" Catherine, 277, 278, 331.
" David, 277, 278, 331.
" Deborah, 277, 331, 401.
" Deborah S., 278, 331.
" Elizabeth, 331.
" Josiah, 35, 400.
" Justus, 278, 331.
" Lorayanna, 331.
" Mary, 278, 331.
" Nathan, 278, 331.
" Phebe, 278, 331.
" Sally, 400.
" Sarah, 278, 331.
" Susan, 331.
Robertson, John, 264.
Robinson, 202. John
Rockwell, Clarissa A., 279.
" Harvey, 279.
" John W., 279.
" Pometia, 279.
" Sally A., 279.
Rogers, Annis, 12.
" Catherine, 5, 214.
" Charlotte, 332.
" Eliza, 332.
" Elizabeth, 141, 158.
" Emily S., 214.
" Fitch, 5, 214, 216, 251, 278, 328, 331, 332.

INDEX TO PERSONS.

R.

Rogers, Hannah, 5, 214, 278.
" Harriet, 214.
" Henry B., 332.
" J --, 158.
" Joseph, 141.
" Maria, 47, 332.
" Mary, 332.
" Mary E., 331, 338.
" Nehemiah, 5.
" Sarah, 140, 141, 158, 332, 378.
Rolfe, John P., 334.
Rosborough, George, 216.
" Sarah, 369.
" Sarah E., 369, 378.
Roscoe, Abraham, 278.
" Henry H., 383.
Rose, Ann, 332.
" Calvin A., 332.
" William A., 332.
Rowell, Abraham, 214, 338, 351.
" Daniel, 214.
" Delia A., 321.
" Elizabeth, 214.
" Mary, 214.
" Permila, 70, 214.
" Sarah, 338.
" Stratton, 214.
" William, 212, 214.
Rowland, Rebecca A., 287.
Rudd, Richard L., 371.
Rundle, Abigail, 83.
" Alfred, 164, 231, 240, 250, 265, 285, 288, 305, 307, 310, 315, 331, 332, 336, 352, 356, 358.
" Amy, 82, 83.
" Ann, 150, 151.
" Anna, 83.
" Anne, 23.
" Benoni, 99, 164.
" Charity, 83.
" Charles, 61, 99, 100, 164, 214.
" Charles, Jr., 100.
" Cynthia, 164.
" Deborah, 7, 82, 164.
" Eli, 7, 82, 164. 35

R.

Rundle, Elizabeth, 83, 378.
" Erastus, 398.
" Fanny F., 351.
" Hannah, 52, 82, 83, 164.
" James, 164.
" Jeremiah, 23, 151.
" Jonathan, 7, 35, 82.
" Mary, 35.
" Nathaniel, 52, 82.
" Rundle, Phebe, 7.
" Phineas, 8, 82, 83, 332.
" Rachel, 83, 239.
" Reuben, 35, 82, 164.
" Ruth, 82, 83.
" Samuel, 82, 83, 285, 315, 332.
" Sarah, 83.
" Shadrach, 7, 82.
" William, 83, 164.
Russell, Joseph E., 360.
Ryohman, Sally B., 378.

S.

Sackett, Abigail S., 205.
" Ann, 214, 278.
" Ann A., 357.
" Bethia, 81.
" Betsy, 214.
" Clarissa, 138.
" Catherine A., 278.
" Elisha B., 215.
" Emma A., 357.
" Esther, 34.
" Georgianna, 357.
" Hannah, 83, 333.
" Henry L., 205.
" James, 34, 39, 83, 404.
" John, 51, 86, 106, 205, 214, 278.
" Joseph, 83, 279, 332, 333, 357, 376, 404.
" Josephine, 357.
" Justus, 83, 206, 209, 214, 215, 278.
" Justus, Jr., 39, 73.
" Katharine T., 376.
" Maria H., 278.

INDEX TO PERSONS.

S.

Sackett, Mary, 214.
" Mary A., 2x, 205.
" Nathaniel, 333.
" Peter, 34.
" Rachel, 404.
" Rachel E., 205, 278.
" Rebecca A., 278.
" Richard, 332, 404.
" Sally, 214, 278.
" Sarah I., 278.
" Sarah L., 357.
" Thomas M., 205.
" Whitman M., 205, 279.
" William H., 205, 214, 278.
St. John, Abraham W., 379.
" Ann, 135.
" Benjamin, 379.
" Charlotte, 140, 141.
" Daniel, 35.
" Eliphalet, 13, 40, 199.
" Ezra, 35, 83, 164, 165, 215.
" Hannah, 35, 83.
" Jane, 321.
" John, 83.
" Lewis, 35.
" Lorenzo C., 199.
" Mary, 96, 379.
" Rhua, 35.
" Ruamah, 164.
" Sarah, 25, 27, 199.
" Stephen B., 141.
" William B., 165.
Sammis, Harriet, 142.
Sands, Clement, 142.
" David, 323.
" D. Jerome, 284, 309.
" John, 141, 215, 249, 359.
" Mary, 141.
" Mary E., 215.
" Phebe, 323.
Sanford, Anna, 124.
" Clark, Dr., 124.
" Clark, 71.
" Hannah, 42.
" Henry H., 124.
" John C., 124, 131.

S.

Sanford, Nancy M., 124.
" Pamela, 124.
" Rachel, 81.
" Rhoda, 124.
Sarles, Adelia, 324.
" Amos, 379.
" Aner, 378.
" Ann M., 379.
" Charles, 379.
" Charles H., 248, 249, 361
" Deborah, 379.
" Dewit C., 378.
" Dorinda, 324.
" Isaac, 379.
" James, 333, 379.
" James G., 378.
" Nehemiah, 379.
" Phebe, 379.
" Sally, 379.
" Sutton, 379.
" Walter, 249, 379, 383.
" William, 379.
Saunders, Mary, 61.
Scarret, John, 296, 405.
Schureman, Esther G., 359.
" Joseph, 359.
Scofield, Abigail, 35, 36, 83, 84, & 89, 124, 125, 216, 279, 280, 281, 330, 333, 380.
" Abijah, 177, 280.
" Abishai, 48, 65, 84, 124, 181, 204, 215, 217, 229, 253, 281, 307, 342.
" Abraham, 83.
" Alfred, 239, 333.
" Alonzo, 279.
" Alpheus, 110, 333, 334.
" Alva, 41, 165, 298, 334, 348.
" Amanda, 194.
" Amelia, 334.
" Amos, 125, 165, 228, 334.
" Amzi, 148, 281, 305, 307, 334, 335, 380.
" " Ann, 199, 270.
" Ann E., 125.
" Anna, 110, 279, 281, 330

INDEX TO PERSONS.

S.

Scofield, Ashbel, 130, 131, 170, 172, 193, 235, 313, 314, 334, 335, 363, 367, 380, 403.
" Augustus, 111, 124, 183, 216, 237, 334.
" Azariah, 12.
" Barbara, 217.
" Benjamin, 9, 19, 20, 36, 98, 124, 239, 334, 385.
" Bethia, 65.
" Betsy, 111, 113, 124, 125, 175, 281, 380, 401.
" Caroline, 334.
" Catherine, 215, 216.
" Charles N., 215.
" Charles W., 335, 355.
" Clara, 217.
" Clarissa, 279, 328.
" Daniel, 36, 84, 367.
" Darius, 85, 217.
" Darius H., 165.
" Darius K., 215, 379.
" Darius S., 333.
" David, 36, 84, 89, 281, 328.
" Deborah, 5.
" Ebenezer C., 380.
" Ebenezer E., 125.
" Edmund, 223, 341, 392.
" Edward, 234, 254, 266, 295, 298, 306, 336, 350, 362, 364.
" Edward R., 379.
" Edwin, 236, 257, 280, 334, 341, 348, 380.
" Edwin, Jr., 379, 385.
" Edwin L., 280, 380.
" Elihu, 36, 177.
" Elijah, 37, 169, 170, 175, 198, 216, 217.
" Elisha, 41.
" Eliza, 85, 216, 217, 288, 289.
" Eliza H., 236.
" Elizabeth, 36, 58, 75, 186, 216, 234, 280, 333.
" Emily, 85, 217.
" Enoch, 199.

S.

Scofield, Epenetus, 35, 181.
" Esther, 83.
" Esther A., 215.
" Ezekiel, 118, 157, 253, 281.
" Ezra, 83, 124, 125, 135, 165, 215, 254, 334, 363.
" Ezra, Jr., 175, 215, 265, 279, 280.
" Frances E., 330.
" Frederick, 33, 72, 125, 334.
" Frederick B., 366, 385.
" George, 85, 217, 277, 280, 306.
" George W., 215, 379.
" Gershom, 3, 4, 5, 14, 30, 37, 87, 135, 161, 165, 284, 379, 380, 401, 407.
" Gideon, 84, 125, 165, 216.
" Gilbert, 38, 51, 56, 84, 130, 168, 380.
" Hait, 235, 280, 335.
" Hannah, 5, 35, 37, 84, 85, 125, 136, 155, 156, 165, 170, 177, 216, 217, 228, 280, 291, 309, 339, 380.
" Hannah E., 306, 334.
" Harriet E., 373, 374.
" Harris, 44, 101, 280, 313, 380.
" Harvey, 244, 308, 334.
" Henry, 124, 125, 215, 334.
" Henry L., 280.
" Henry W., 380.
" Hepsabah, 174.
" Hezekiah, 35, 227, 312, 313, 369, 378, 380, 333.
" Hezekiah, Jr., 363, 406.
" Herson, 110, 251.
" Hiram, 126.
" Holly, 85, 217.
" Horace, 111, 113, 183, 216, 237, 261, 334.
" Hoyt, 9, 126.

INDEX TO PERSONS.

S.

Scofield, Ira, 5,165,298,346, 382.
" Isaac, 36,84,89,124, 175,181,215,217,228,234, 236,237,253,279,307,334, 356,363.
" Isaac, Jr., 165.
" Israel, 84,125,165.
" Jacob, 125,136,165.
" James, 84,85,89,125, 216.
" James, Jr., 85.
" James B., 85,217, 253,299,389.
" James E., 280.
" James H., 282.
" Jane, 36.
" Jared, 281,334.
" John, 35,36,75,84, 89,216,230,280,299,317, 318,319,380,401.
" John, Jr., 85,125.
" John, 3rd, 125,228.
" John A., 253,380.
" John B., 253.
" John D., 126.
" John L., 175,181, 265,279.
" John R., 328.
" Jonas, 20,103,112, 334,401.
" Jonathan, 65,111, 124,152,153,261,264.
" Joseph, 125,279,387.
" Joseph H., 362.
" Joshua, 14,30,51,85, 113,124,134,172,195,207, 285,333.
" Josiah W., 175.
" Julia, 216.
" Juliet, 379.
" Leander, 280.
" Lester, 380.
" Levi, 280,281,380, 401.
" Louisa, 280.
" Lucretia, 155,380.

S.

Scofield, Luther S., 367,380.
" Lydia, 126,165,229, 234,281.
" Lydia A., 44,101.
" Margaret, 125.
" Maria, 280,385.
" Martha, 216.
" Mary, 41,84,96,98, 125,126,215,226,281,295, 299,334,341,382.
" Mary A., 126.
" Mary E., 277,341,362.
" Mary S., 334.
" Mercy, 36,125,126,165
" Nancy, 125,334.
" Nathan, 36,84.
" Nathan H., 216,281.
" Nathaniel, 65,126, 181,245,280.
" Nehemiah, 35,113.
" Nelson, 257.
" Nelson D., 262.
" Obadiah, 36,125,126, 165.
" Oliver, 85,217.
" Peter, 124,217,279.
" Peter, Jr., 135,175, 217,279.
" Phebe, 165,251,333.
" Phineas, 83,126,279.
" Polly, 83,125,166, 181,264.
" Polly A., 245.
" Rebecca, 19,334,348.
" Reuben, 15,20,21,22, 29,35,36,48,56,57,65,67, 68,83,84,85,87,91,96,98, 106,110,143,154,181,228, 281,382.
" Rhoda E., 215.
" Richard, 282.
" Robert, 17,85,216, 217,280,395.
" Rua, 5, 35.
" Rufus, 7,88,165,280, 299,380.
" Sally, 22,36,84,85,

INDEX TO PERSONS.

S.

" 126,215,217,251,285,317, 318,319,379,388.
Scofield, Sally B., 165.
" Sally M., 334.
" Samuel, 5, 36, 181, 217, 280, 388.
" Samuel C., 166.
" Samuel W., 280, 380.
" Sarah, 20, 21, 22, 36, 83, 89, 110, 135, 177, 217, 297, 334, 335, 401.
" Selleck, 91, 124, 128, 165, 167, 173, 174, 192, 223, 225, 230, 254, 258, 274, 279, 285, 288, 304, 334, 335, 341, 342, 353, 366, 368, 369, 376, 385.
" Seth, 36, 85, 130, 170, 380.
" Seth W., 166, 340.
" Silas, 85, 125, 139, 192, 216, 280, 328, 339, 385.
" Sidney, 215.
" Solomon, 35, 236, 237.
" Susan, 385.
" Susannah, 35, 216, 280.
" Sylvanus, 35, 280, 379, 401.
" Thaddeus, 5.
" Walter, 217.
" Warren, 9, 36, 48, 65, 67, 68, 84, 124, 204, 217, 228, 279, 281, 335, 380.
" William, 110, 235, 236, 237, 245, 251, 307, 334, 335, 346, 373, 379, 401.
" William, Jr., 50, 216, 262, 314, 335.
" William H., 280, 335.
" William R., 215, 306.
" William W., 125.
Scott, Burr, 347.
" Daniel G., 196, 381, 383.
" Smith, 184, 222, 254, 310, 320, 338, 345, 383.
Scribner, Henry, 182.
" Henry C., 229.

S.

Seaman, Nancy, 145.
" Sylvanus, 397.
Searles, James, 225.
" Maria, 288, 289.
Secor, Jonathan, 85.
" Sally, 214, 278.
" William, 85.
Seely, Abigail, 85.
" Abigail H., 294.
" Abijah, 85.
" Albert, 218, 266, 274, 377, 381.
" Anna, 216.
" Betsy, 313, 314, 363.
" Cary, 314, 363.
" Cary H., 313, 363.
" Catherine, 218, 401.
" Delia C., 363.
" Ebenezer, 5.
" Elisha, 218, 266, 274, 282, 297, 335, 345.
" Elizabeth, 85, 218.
" Emeline, 216.
" Ezekiel, 15.
" Henry B., 177.
" Henry L., 282.
" Harren, 313.
" Harris, 313.
" James, 85.
" John, 62, 143, 195, 217, 252, 257, 282, 314.
" John, Jr., 225.
" John A., 282.
" Joseph, 313, 314, 363.
" Lydia, 85.
" Maria, 190.
" Mary, 5, 54, 166, 186, 218, 266.
" Mason G., 313.
" Mercy, 85.
" Nathan, 136.
" Phebe, 218.
" Sally, 85.
" Sands, 282, 285, 332, 350, 372, 379, 381.
" Sarah, 36.
" Sarah A., 282.

INDEX TO PERSONS.

S.

Seely, Sarah J., 282.
" Selleck, 166, 217, 218, 266.
" Seth, 243, 282.
" Simeon, 85.
" Susannah, 85.
" Thaddeus, 54.
" Thomas, 85.
" William H., 282.
" Wyx, 86, 218, 401.
Selleck, Ally, 336.
" Angeline, 282, 283.
" Ann, 218, 282, 336, 381.
" Ann M., 385.
" Anson, 167.
" Benjamin, 166.
" Betsy, 282.
" Caroline, 282, 283, 336.
" Catherine, 86, 137, 335, 401.
" Charles, 397.
" Charlotte, 86, 127.
" Clara, 336.
" Daniel, 85.
" Darling, 166, 167.
" Deborah, 155, 163, 166, 273, 401.
" Edward, 85, 86, 401.
" Elizabeth, 336.
" George, 282.
" Gold, 336.
" Gold J., 50.
" Gould, 127, 167.
" Hannah, 86, 218, 266, 282, 283, 336, 381, 397, 401.
" Harvey, 166.
" Henry, 126, 127, 167.
" Henry R., 191, 336.
" Hinman, 167, 402.
" Isaac, 85, 187, 342, 345, 381.
" James, 86, 127, 336.
" James B., 86, 127, 336.
" Jane, 167.
" Jesse, 147, 273, 335, 336, 381.

S.

Selleck, John, 381.
" Joseph, 374, 381, 401.
" Joseph, Jr., 318, 319.
" Kilbourn, 86, 381.
" Letitia, 218, 336.
" Lydia, 167.
" Maria, 336.
" Marilda, 336.
" Mary, 66, 218, 264, 282, 381.
" Mary E., 405.
" Milden, 167.
" Molly, 127.
" Nancy, 3, 282, 283.
" Nanne, 86.
" Nathan, 401.
" Peter, 66.
" Phebe, 25, 86, 282, 283, 296, 381, 401.
" Polly, 218, 336, 381.
" Ralph, 336.
" Raymond, 218, 336.
" Sabra, 167.
" Sally, 126, 167, 212, 376, 377.
" Samuel, 282, 283.
" Sands, 336.
" Sands E., 166.
" Sarah, 167.
" Stephen, 218, 336.
" Stephen P., 166, 273.
" Stephen R., 218, 339.
" Sylvanus, 336.
" Theodosia, 282, 283.
" Thomas, 85.
" Uriah, 127, 167.
" William E., 381.
" Wray, 167, 402.
Seward, Phebe, 36.
" Rebecca A., 61.
" William, 6x, 61.
Seymour, Abigail, 32, 85, 86.
" Delia, 218.
" Delia R., 86, 87.
" Drake, 42, 86, 218.
" Elisabeth, 86.

INDEX TO PERSONS.

S.

Seymour, Hannah, 86.
" James, 364.
" Jared, 85.
" Mary, 86, 87, 218, 219.
" Medad, 404.
" Polly, 86.
" Rhoda, 86.
" Sabrina, 86.
" Sabrina B., 218.
" Samuel, 86, 87.
" Sarah H., 218.
" Susan, 218, 292.
" William, 86.
Shaw, Andrew, 219, 283.
" Caroline, 127, 283.
" Eliza, 127, 283.
" Frederick, 283.
" Frederick B., 283.
" Frederick L., 219.
" Hannah, 219, 283.
" James, 219, 283.
" James A., 219, 387.
" Louisa W., 219.
" Maria, 127, 283.
" Mary C., 219.
" Nancy, 283.
" Nancy E., 127.
" Phebe, 283.
" William, 10, 127, 283.
" William F., 219.
Sheffield, Mary, 227.
Shepard, William, 341.
Shepperd, Catherine, 270, 374.
Sherwood, Aaron, 69.
" Abby J., 381.
" Abigail, 167.
" Amy, 87.
" Ann, 220.
" Augustus, 336, 337.
" Betsy, 381.
" Bishop Asbury, 381.
" Calvin, 381.
" Catherine, 214.
" Charles T., 336, 337.
" Daniel, 118, 220, 247, 284, 336, 337.
" Daniel, Jr., 127.

S.

Sherwood, Elnathan, 402.
" Emeline, 167.
" Fanny, 220.
" Frederick, 284.
" Frederick A., 336.
" George E., 336, 337.
" Gilbert, 53.
" Hannah, 87, 167, 220.
" Hungerford, 220.
" Jabez, 127, 128, 167, 220.
" James, 336, 337.
" James H., 381.
" Jane A., 336.
" Jared, 89, 402.
" John, 87.
" John C., 234, 241, 347.
" John S., 382.
" John W., 290.
" Jotham, 241, 381.
" Levi, 167, 251.
" Lucy A., 382.
" Maria C., 336, 337.
" Mary, 87, 220, 283, 397.
" Mary E., 336.
" Matthew, 87, 128.
" Nathan, 87, 128, 167, 402, 405.
" Nehemiah, Rev., 243, 244, 287.
" Nehemiah, 44, 90, 180, 234, 381, 382.
" Nelson, 336, 337.
" Oliver, 166.
" Pamela, 402.
" Permellia, 89.
" Phebe, 173, 381.
" Polly, 205, 267, 292.
" Prudence, 87.
" Rachel, 87.
" Sabrina, 251.
" Sally, 220.
" Samuel, 167.
" Samuel B., 336, 337.
" Sarah H., 336, 337.
" Thankful, 87.
" Willet, 205, 220, 267,

INDEX TO PERSONS.

S.

       283,284,292.
Sherwood, William B.,167,220,
      268,302,382.
"   William C.,284.
"   William H.,336.
Shute, Jerusha, 88.
Sibell, John F., 284.
"   William E., 390.
Sibley, Betsy, 382.
"   Mary, 382.
"   Richard, 382.
"   Smith R.,225,230,288,
   330,361,366,369,376,382,
   385,402.
Silkman, Mary, 16.
Silliman, Abigail D.,199.
"   Job, 403.
"   John, 127.
"   Joseph,4,38,56,110,
   130,136,393,394,403.
Simmons, Electa, 110.
Sivals, Caroline, 292.
"   Caroline A., 292.
"   Hezekiah T., 292.
"   James, 292.
"   William L., 292.
Skelding, George, 37,87.
"   Henry K.,284,319.
"   James,284,402.
"   John,37,87.
"   Letitia,284.
"   Mary, 402.
"   Prudence, 87.
"   Samuel,37,87.
Skidmore, Henry,87,128.
"   William,52,91.
Skildén, see Skelding.
Slason, see also Slauson,
   and Slawson.
"   Abigail, 87.
"   Abraham, 88.
"   Ames, 87.
"   Betsy,167,168,220.
"   Betsy A., 284.
"   Cornelia, 284.
"   Daniel,167,168.
"   Deliverance, 87.
"   Ebenezer, 87.

S.

Slason, Elizabeth,167,168.
"   Francis, 284.
"   George N., 284.
"   Gershom,87,402.
"   Hannah,87,168,189,284.
"   Henry, 402.
"   Isaac, 284.
"   Jacob, 167.
"   James, 284.
"   John,167,168,295.
"   Joseph, 284.
"   Jonathan,87,284.
"   Julia, 284.
"   Leander, 131.
"   Lydia, 284.
"   Mary,167,284.
"   Millicent, 87.
"   Nathan,37,87.
"   Nathaniel,3,14,35,87,
   284,285.
"   Rebecca, 167,168.
"   Sarah, 284.
"   Smith, 284.
"   Sophia, 284.
"   Sylvanus, 284.
"   William P., 284.
Slater, Charles, 356.
"   Elizabeth, 366.
"   Elizabeth M., 356.
"   Jeremiah, 245.
"   Penelope, 160.
"   William Jr., 160.
Slauson, Hannah, 168.
"   Jesse, 211.
"   Lewis,146,175.
"   Nancy,146,382.
"   Nancy J., 382.
"   Thomas, 168.
Slawson, Abigail, 402.
"   Abraham, 88.
"   Betsy, 220.
"   Charles W., 346.
"   Daniel, 220.
"   Henry, 402.
"   Jesse,79,177.
"   Nathaniel, 346.
"   Samuel,402.
"   Susannah W., 177.

INDEX TO PERSONS.

487.

S.

Smith, Abel, 88, 324, 358.
" Abel, Jr., 324.
" Abigail, 88, 89, 118, 128, 129, 130, 168, 221, 222.
" Abigail W., 285, 286.
" Abraham, 129, 130.
" Alba, 37.
" Alexander, 129, 130.
" Alfred, 156, 187, 243, 259, 286, 291, 338, 383.
" Alvah, 89, 120, 285, 402.
" Amos, 88, 128, 168, 238, 324.
" Ann, 98, 285, 288.
" Anna, 169.
" Anne, 38, 51, 104, 403.
" Aphelia, 374.
" Arba, 244, 285, 337, 382.
" Arney, 222.
" Aseneth, 402.
" Austin, 123.
" Azetta, 169.
" Azuba, 169, 402.
" Barthsheba, 88.
" Benjamin, 15, 17, 88, 128, 169, 285, 383.
" Bethia, 168.
" Betsy, 129, 221, 259.
" Betsy A., 129, 221, 286, 287.
" Caleb, 89.
" Caroline H., 372.
" Catherine, 40, 231, 382.
" Charity, 83, 88.
" Charles, 10, 11, 15, 38, 71, 81, 119, 121, 144, 146, 164, 186, 203, 285, 325, 402.
" Charles B., 285, 288, 402.
" Charles E., 221, 222, 285, 288.
" Charles G., 131, 169, 170.
" Charles I., 383.
" Charles W., 337.
" Charlotte, 38.
" Chauncey, 309.
" Clarissa, 251.
" Daniel, Rev., 40, 287, 338, 382, 383.

S.

Smith, Daniel, 12, 28, 89, 231, 296, 394, 406.
" David, 129, 291, 337, 383.
" David, 3rd, 53, 82, 84, 87, 89.
" David W., 338, 383.
" Deborah, 88, 128.
" D. W., 296, 373.
" Earl, 87, 206, 222, 265, 291, 306, 354.
" Eben, 185, 199, 222.
" Ebenezer, Sr., 286.
" Ebenezer, 89, 145, 190, 222, 252, 271, 281, 285, 286, 304, 337, 338, 403.
" Ebenezer, Jr., 246.
" Eber, 10, 37, 89, 121, 152, 161, 259, 329.
" Edward A., 402.
" Edwin, 89, 286, 309.
" Eloy, 338.
" Electa, 38, 2x, 222.
" Elihu, 98.
" Elihu P., 95.
" Elijah, 169, 402.
" Eliza, 394.
" Eliza A., 286, 288.
" Elizabeth, 11, 88, 89, 99, 129, 383, 403.
" Ellen, 288.
" Emeline, 129, 169, 216.
" Ephraim, 168.
" Esther, 98, 300.
" Ezekiel, 37, 88, 396.
" Ezra, 129.
" Fanny, 221, 404.
" Frederick, 26, 133, 150.
" Frederick A., 306.
" George, 89, 129, 130, 288.
" George A., 168, 214.
" George J., 373, 374.
" George S., 338.
" Gould, 286, 338.
" Hanford M., 220, 221.
" Hannah, 22, 36, 37, 58, 67, 83, 88, 128, 129, 168, 221, 259, 285, 338, 402.
" Hannah M., 405.
" Harriet, 38.

INDEX TO PERSONS.

S.

Smith, Henry, 221, 287, 402.
" Henry H., 286, 337.
" Hervey, 402.
" Hetty, 288.
" Hezekiah P., 383.
" Horace B., 329.
" Isaac, Dr., 37.
" Isaac, 22, 24, 37, 89, 133, 221.
" Isaac, Jr., 22, 23, 26, 231.
" Isaac H., 264, 398.
" Isaac M., 221, 222, 223, 306.
" Isaiah, 37, 89, 168, 169, 402.
" Israel, 169.
" Jabez, 152.
" James, 81, 82, 83, 88, 101, 107, 130, 210, 259, 288.
" James A., 338.
" Jane, 133, 150.
" Jared, 13, 37, 47, 50, 51, 52, 67, 90, 104, 107, 118, 120, 144, 146, 149, 184, 213, 238, 256, 285, 337, 382, 402.
" Jerusha, 80, 88.
" Jesse, 89.
" John, 57, 88, 89, 129, 169, 221, 250, 286, 287, 403.
" John, Jr., 89.
" John C., 287, 292.
" John H., 57, 102, 239.
" Jonathan, 33, 50, 118, 129, 152.
" Joseph, 35, 38, 129, 168, 170, 183, 237, 241, 270, 271, 281, 286, 287, 324, 338, 373, 383.
" Joseph, Jr., 129, 337, 365, 383, 403.
" Joseph, 3rd, 128, 393.
" Joseph, 4th, 82.
" Joseph J., 129, 130.
" Joseph N., 91.
" Joshua, 83, 211, 261, 286.

S.

Smith, Josiah, 49, 68, 88, 222, 286, 291, 324, 355, 373, 397.
" Julia A., 38, 286, 287, 337, 338, 382.
" Lavinia, 337.
" Lucy, 110.
" Luke, 244.
" Lydia, 222, 228, 297.
" Lyman H., 286, 287.
" Margaret, 209.
" Martha, 89, 222, 287.
" Mary, 28, 37, 38, 88, 89, 128, 130, 133, 221, 222, 235, 252, 286, 337, 338, 402.
" Mary C., 383.
" Mary E., 222, 297, 299, 338.
" Mary R., 168.
" Molly, 114.
" Nancy, 129, 130, 264, 288.
" Nathaniel, 89.
" Nelson W., 383.
" Noah, 89.
" Peter, 114, 139, 234.
" Peter, Jr., 37, 147, 148, 196, 209, 227, 231, 298.
" Peter, 3rd, 221, 222.
" Phebe E., 222.
" Philander, 37, 89, 251.
" Polly, 130, 168.
" Rachel A., 285, 287, 402.
" Rebecca, 99, 123, 129, 130, 403.
" Rebecca E., 287.
" Reuben, 130.
" Rheua, 221, 222, 403.
" Rhoda, 130.
" Rue, 403.
" Ruth, 82, 88, 89, 354.
" Sally, 15, 17, 133, 285, 288, 337, 338, 383, 394.
" Sally B., 285, 402.
" Samuel, 89, 90, 130, 161, 164, 169, 182, 183, 203, 238, 337, 349.
" Sarah, 88, 89, 128, 130,

488.

INDEX TO PERSONS.

S.

168,214,222,281,286,337,
338,383.
Smith, Seth,14,21,55,82,89,
90,121,129,177,288,403.
" Shadrach,38,363.
" Simeon,37,169,402.
" Solomon,114,169,222,
244,291.
" Solomon,Jr., 169.
" Stephen,37,38,90.
" Susan, 338.
" Susannah,89,287.
" Thomas, 231.
" Thomas N., 382.
" William,129,130,169,182
185,242,258,285,288,382.
" William,Jr.,187,258,
397.
" William A., 405.
" William H.,221,222,223.
" William L.,328.
" William M.,286,288.
" Zety, 403.
Sniffin, Epenetus,154,374.
" Huldah, 154.
" James,103,349,391.
" Sally,103,349.
" Sarah,349,391.
" Seaman H.,329.
" William, 288.
Snyder, Eliza, 238.
Spencer, Henry U.R., 376.
" James W., 252.
" William, 255.
Squariman,John, 141.
Squire, Susannah, 42.
Stafford, Jonas, 325,370.
Stanton, Richard,312,321,332,
363.
Startin, Sarah, 403.
Stebbins, David, 223.
" Elizabeth C., 223.
" James B., 187.
" Jane B., 223.
Stedwell, Joseph,247,290.
Stephens, Jacob,Jr.,135.
Steut, Hannah, 72.

S.

Stevens, Abigail,62,130,131,
137,169,170.
" Amy, 56.
" Ann C., 289.
" Catherine, 182.
" Charles G., 169.
" Chauncey S., 217.
" Darius,130,169,170,
182,387,403.
" David,11,90,106.
" Edward,38,90.
" Elisha, 90.
" Emmy, 405.
" Enoch,56,80,143,198,
217,395.
" George R.,330,367,385
" Hannah,22,403.
" Harriet,169,170,403.
" Hellenah, 90.
" Heth,243,327.
" Jacob,35,81,223,257,
342.
" Jacob,Jr.,56,130,138,
232.
" James,80,108,130,131,
288,289.
" James E., 288.
" Jane, 38,90.
" Jared, 257.
" Lavinia, 130,131,170.
" Leonidas,130,131,170,
289.
" Lorenzo O., 405.
" Lydia, 38,90.
" Mary,38,136,289,338,
339.
" Mary H., 289.
" Nancy,340,385.
" Obadiah,38,90,130,
131,170.
" Phebe, 143.
" Rufus S., 288.
" Sally, 405.
" Samuel,90,405.
" Sarah,38,90.
" Seth,38,62,90,314.
" Sophia,169,170,403.

INDEX TO PERSONS.

S.

Stevens, William, 38, 288.
" William H., 90, 403.
Stewart, Ann E., 321.
Stiles, Ann, 52.
Stivers, James, 223, 289.
" James E., 223, 289.
" Rufus M., 289.
" Sarah, 289.
" William, 289.
Stogdill, Amy, 290.
" Henry, 290.
Stokeum, Alla, 341.
Stone, Ezekiel, 85.
" Sally, 85.
Strang, Allen, 239, 290.
" Ann E., 290.
" Catherine, 290.
" Daniel, 290.
" Elizabeth U., 138.
" Henry, 69.
" James H., 290.
" Jared, 2, 8, 44, 45, 118, 124, 171, 177, 180, 220, 275, 290.
" John, 290, 404.
" Margaret, 290.
" Mary, 290.
" Sarah H., 290, 339.
" William, 239, 268, 290.
Stratton, Prudence, 6.
Street, Charles, 397.
" Clara, 266, 397.
" George, 290.
" Henry, 104.
Studwell, Alanson, 291, 333.
" Alexander, 297.
" Anthony, 170, 290, 291.
" Betsy, 170, 291.
" Drake, 33, 37, 121, 123, 170, 186, 222, 290, 291.
" Edgar, 260, 291.
" Eliza A., 291.
" Elizabeth, 65, 287, 290, 291.
" Enoch, 170, 291.
" Ezekiel, 403, 404.
" Fanny, 221.

S.

Studwell, Hannah, 37, 170, 291.
" James, 37, 170, 216, 290, 291.
" Joanna, 321.
" John S., 222, 290, 291.
" Joseph, 247, 290.
" Luther H., 290, 291, 383.
" Mary, 216, 291.
" Polly A., 291.
" Richard, 81.
" Sarah, 403, 404.
" Solomon, 221.
" William A., 290, 291.
Sturges, Betsy, 66, 264.
" Elisabeth, R., 90.
" George W., 90.
" Harriet, 90.
" Mary A., 90.
" Samuel, Rev., 66.
" Samuel, 16.
" Strong, 90, 96.
Sudmon, or Sudmore, ----, 404.
"   "   Nathaniel, 404.
Sutherland, Abigail, 395.
" John B., 77.
" Lydia, 38, 325.
" Mary, 38.
" Roger, 38.
" Silas, 14, 77, 383.
" Silas, Jr., 77.
Sutton, Alice, 141, 384.
" Allen, 141, 171, 384.
" Anna, 72.
" Cabrilla, 384.
" Elizabeth, 141, 384.
" Elizabeth C., 384.
" Elizabeth P., 384.
" Janet, 384.
" Jesse, 141.
" John, 141, 142, 384.
" John T., 384.
" Mary, 141, 384.
" Phebe, 141, 384.
" Phebe C., 384.
" Phila R., 384.

INDEX TO PERSONS.

S.

Sutton, Thomas, 141, 384.
" Thomas C., 384.
" William, 92, 104, 141, 142, 384.
" William H. H., 384.
Swan, Eliza, 223.
" James, 144.
" Margaret, 171.
" Walter, 144, 170, 171, 223.
Sybell, Elizabeth, 173.

T.

Taber, Charles, 90.
Taffy, John, 383.
Talmadge, James M., 341.
" John, 4.
" John L., 387.
" Lewis, 344.
" Sarah, 3, 4, 21.
" Seymour, 21.
" William, 310.
Taylor, Charles K., 317.
" Charles R., 339.
" Cynthia G., 224.
" Daniel, 171, 347.
" George, 224, 291.
" Gilbert H., 284, 292.
" Isaac, 90.
" Joseph, 171, 220, 224.
" Joseph, Jr., 131, 171, 247.
" Jotham, 171.
" Mary, 171, 247.
" Mary E., 199, 306, 317, 339.
" Merritt G., 224, 291.
" Nathaniel, 131, 171.
" Polly, 171.
" Sally M., 224.
Teller, Harrison, 363.
" Smith, 366.
Tenby, William, 311.
Thompson, Abigail, 197, 198.
" Adaline, 63.
" Amy, 63.
" Caroline, 63.

T.

Thompson, Charles K., 63.
" Cornelia, 63.
" Edmund, 339.
" Fanny, 63.
" Harriet, 63.
" James, 63.
" John, 40, 175.
" Margaret, 63.
" Sylvanus B., 157, 219, 293, 304.
" William A., 63.
Thorn, Ann, 63.
" Anna, 63.
" William, 63.
" William H., 211.
Thornton, Samuel, 332.
Thorp, Charles, 38, 90, 91.
" David B., 131.
" Mary, 399.
" Sturges P., 59, 131.
" William, Jr., 399.
Tillman, Andrew P., 132.
" Anne, 291.
" Anne S., 132, 195, 224, 394.
" Catherine, 394.
" Elizabeth, 132, 195, 394.
" Elizabeth A., 224, 291.
" John, 111, 132, 224, 291, 292.
" John H., 132, 224, 291, 394.
" Mary, 394.
" Mary C., 132, 195, 224, 291.
" William, 291.
Tillott, Delia, 218.
" James, 218.
" Peter, 218.
" Peter I., 292.
" Sabrina B., 218, 292.
Timpany, Charles, 321.
" Delia, 321.
" Elizabeth, 91.
" John, 16.
" Mary, 91.

INDEX TO PERSONS.

T.

Timpany, Michael C., 91.
" William, 276.
Titus, Elizabeth, 153.
" John H., 171.
" Mary H., 224.
" Mary U., 171.
" Peter S., 357.
" Susan K., 171, 224.
Todd, Ambrose, Rev., 32.
" Ambrose S., 315.
" Charlotte, 92, 132, 269.
" Deborah, 91.
" Elnathan, 39, 91, 366.
" Gabriel, 38, 171, 404.
" Gabriel H., 91, 171.
" George W., 172.
" Hannah, 91, 149, 171, 404.
" Harvey, 91, 171, 230, 404.
" Henry, 38, 171, 404.
" Jemima, 91.
" John, 38, 91.
" John, Jr., 91, 171, 207, 404.
" Lavinia, 32.
" Lavinia H., 32.
" Lydia, 404.
" Martha J., 32.
" Mary, 91.
" Noah, 91.
" Phebe, 91.
" Samuel W., 278.
" Washington, 91, 92, 132, 172.
" William, 132, 171, 172, 333.
Tolaton, Elizabeth, 76.
Tompkins, Abram D., 292.
" Deborah, 38.
" I. W., 248.
" Nancy, 39.
" Sarah, 39.
Tooker, Daniel, 38, 39.
Totten, Anna, 71, 72, 92, 132, 398.
" Betsy, 92.
" Charity, 92.
" Esther, 92.
" Gilbert, 71, 72, 79, 92, 132, 398.
" Moses, 92.

T.

Totten, Rebecca, 92.
" Samuel, Jr., 92.
Town, Sarah, 80.
Townsend, Betsy, 302.
" Elizabeth, 61.
" Esther N., 104.
" Rebecca, 79.
" Ruth, 279.
" Solomon, 104.
Tracy, Hezekiah, 69, 73, 86, 106, 113, 119, 124, 146, 147, 210, 224.
" Horatio N., 224, 292.
" Huldah, 146, 180, 205, 210, 224, 267, 292, x189
" John J., 189, 191, 205, 206, 224, 292.
Treadwell, Francis, 339.
Tripp, Benjamin, 188.
" Daniel, 76, 88.
" Daniel E., 358.
" John, 76.
" Mary, 76.
" Samuel, 76.
" Samuel H., 76.
Trowbridge, James H., 238, 385.
Tryon, Benjamin, 62, 92, 112, 334.
" Mary, 334.
" Rowland, 57, 59, 62, 92, 103, 113.
" Samuel, 39, 92, 92.
Tubbs, Harriet, 295.
Tucker, Betsy, 170, 244, 291.
" Daniel, 38, 39.
" David, 170.
" Emma E., 362.
" Robert, 362.
" Sarah, 38, 90.
" William, 38, 90.
Tuley, Andrew, 404.
Tupper, David, 39.
Turner, Uriah, 338.
Tuthill, see Tuttle.
Tuttle, Agar, 252.
" Anna, 274.
" Catherine, 335, 384.
" Eliza J., 392.

INDEX TO PERSONS.

T.

Tuttle, Enos, 51, 274, 335.
" Harriet E., 252.
" Henry, 252.
" Lorenzo, 392.
" Martha, 51.
" Morris, 105, 273, 293, 335, 384.
" Sarah, 252.
" Sarah E., 252.
" Sarah H., 252.

U.

Ufford, Dixon D., 291.
Underhill, Elizabeth, 142.
" Isaac Q., 384.
" Mary, 384.
" Mott, 142.
" Sally, 329.
" Sarah, 329.
" Stephen, 329.
" William, 329.

V.

Vail, Abigail, 92.
" Henry A., 290.
" Margaret R., 290.
Van Benthuysen, William, 311.
Van Bunschoten, John E., 39.
" Jane A., 404.
" Rachel, 404.
Van Cleck, Henry, 47.
" Sarah, 47.
Van Kleek, Sally, 240.
" Sarah, 305.
" Theresia, 240.
Van Patten, Harry A., 356.
" Rachel L., 307, 356.
Van Voorhis, Isaac, 326.
Veal, Thomas, 141.

W.

Waldrum, Cynthia, 92.
" Nicholas, 92.
Walker, Nancy E., 45, 119.

Walker, Rheuma, 45, 71, 107, 119.
" Timothy, 29, 45, 47, 65, 70, 71, 107, 119, 121.
Wallace, George H., 231, 274, 339, 345.
" Henry B., 339.
" Julia, 137, 231.
Walmsley, Abigail, 172.
" Elizabeth E., 172.
" Epenetus W., 172, 190, 198, 218, 289, 336, 377, 381, 384.
" George, 172, 219, 283, 284, 293, 345, 384.
" Lucy, 219.
" Mary, 172.
" Nancy, 172.
" Polly, 218, 336.
" Prudence, 172.
" Sarah, 172.
" William, 10, 19, 25, 43, 47, 172, 405.
Walton, Abigail, 130.
" Darius, 234.
" Thomas, 130.
Wardwell, Abigail, 224, 339, 404.
" Betsy, 330, 339, 340.
" Esther S., 172.
" Hannah, 134, 224, 228, 317, 330, 339.
" Hannah S., 318, 319.
" Hester L., 390.
" Isaac, 85, 103, 107, 143, 226, 317, 318, 319, 330, 339, 340, 374.
" Jacob, 172.
" James, 4, 134, 172, 224, 225, 228, 330, 339, 404.
" Mary, 330.
" Polly, 339.
" Rufus, 339.
" Sally, 224, 339.
" William, 318, 330, 339.
Waring, Abigail, 39, 225, 366.
" Abraham, 39.
" Alfred, 39.
" Alva, 231.

INDEX TO PERSONS.

W.

Waring, Ann, 340,404.
" Ann M., 385.
" Benjamin, 139.
" Betsy, 39,173,340,385, 404.
" Catherine, 93,173,404.
" Charles E., 292.
" Clarissa, 67.
" Clarissa E., 373.
" Deborah, 173.
" Elias L., 154.
" Elizabeth, 36,39,93, 173.
" Ephraim, 154.
" Esther C., 343.
" George, 253.
" George C., 315.
" George E., 255,288,384.
" George W., 389.
" Hannah, 93,173,404.
" Hannah M., 385.
" Henry, 155,173,183, 225,237,251,271,286,317, 318,328,334,340,369,373, 376,381,385,389.
" Henry F., 173,293,330.
" Hezron, 39.
" Huldah, 154.
" Isaac, 385.
" Jacob, 173,293.
" James, 39,93,173,177, 269,340,371,385.
" James D., 385.
" Jesse, 39,173,293.
" Joel, 14,39,55,74,80, 91,92,173,382,385.
" John, 93,173,293.
" John H., 154.
" Jonathan, 39.
" Joseph, 39,82,91.
" Joseph F., 385.
" Jotham, 39.
" Lydia, 165,380.
" Maria, 385.
" Marilda, 39.
" Martha, 173.

W.

Waring, Mary, 39,66,93,173, 340,385.
" Mary A., 93.
" Mary W., 385.
" Michael, 39.
" Michager, 93,404.
" Nancy, 39,173.
" Noah, 39,172.
" Phebe, 173.
" Polly, 81,165,234.
" Rebecca, 39.
" Robert F., 293.
" Robert T., 293.
" Samuel, 36,39,62,66,93, 172,225.
" Sands, 173.
" Sarah, 81,93,172,173, 366.
" Sarah E., 385.
" Sarah G., 247.
" Scudder, 225.
" Stephen, 81,139,141,149, 160,183,185,221,224,225, 250,269,340,385.
" Stephen H., 385.
" Susan, 385.
" Sylvanus, 93,173.
" Thaddeus, 40,173.
" Thaddeus R., 343.
" Thankful, 173.
" Thomas, 154.
" William, 173,382.
Warren, Elias L., 154.
" Ephraim, 154.
" Huldah, 154.
" John H., 154.
" Joseph D., 319,322,339, 364,384,389.
" Samuel B., 87,107,165.
" Thomas, 154.
Washburn, Joseph, 93.
" Marshall, 93.
" Mary, 93,173.
" Mary A., 93,173.
" Nancy, 173.
" Tompkins, 384.

INDEX TO PERSONS.

W.

Waterbury, Abigail, 4, 40, 93, 94, 134, 228, 295, 405.
" Abigail H., 294.
" Alvah, 230.
" Amos H., 94, 225, 226, 404.
" Ann, 340.
" Anson, 230.
" Appollos W., 94, 132, 174, 404.
" Asahel A., 328.
" Azariah, 135, 146, 167, 193, 293, 340.
" Barsheba, 405.
" Benjamin, 39, 93, 173, 174, 405.
" Bethiah, 93, 174, 295, 405.
" Betsy, 94, 96, 226, 294.
" Catherine, 340.
" Charles E., 94, 174.
" Charles H., 297.
" Charles L., 340.
" Charlotte, 294.
" Cornelia, 94, 262, 404.
" Darius, 303.
" David, 12, 24, 40, 45, 181, 247, 265, 279, 293, 294, 295, 340, 341, 373, 385.
" Deodate, 30, 39, 93, 174.
" Ebenezer, 93, 94, 226, 328, 405.
" Ebenezer, Jr., 27.
" Edwin, 340.
" Elizabeth, 12, 40, 132, 247, 293, 400, 404.
" Emmy, 48.
" Enos, 65, 96.
" Epenetus, 173.
" Esther C., 294, 297, 343.
" Ezra, 93.
" Fanny, 295, 340, 341, 385.

Waterbury, Frederick, 28.
" Frederick W., 297.
" George, 294, 295, 340, 385, 405.
" George W., 340.
" Gilbert G., 295, 314, 363, 364.
" Hannah, 4, 94, 113, 133
" Hannah M., 405.
" Harriet A., 404.
" Henry, 132, 226, 227, 294, 295, 303, 304, 405.
" Horace, 191, 211, 222, 296, 339.
" Huldah, 94.
" Isaac, 4, 294, 295, 340, 341, 385.
" Isaac N., 295, 340, 385
" Israel, 385.
" Jacob, 404.
" James, 40, 93, 174, 404, 405.
" Jemima, 40.
" Jerry, 294.
" John, 5, 47, 66, 167, 176, 226, 294, 295, 387, 404.
" John, Jr., 99.
" John C., 294.
" John H., 294.
" John W., 340, 341, 385.
" Jonathan, 21, 93, 94, 174, 404.
" Jonathan B., 96, 195.
" Joseph, 94.
" Josiah, 93, 405.
" Julia A., 295, 340, 314, 385.
" Julius H., 294.
" J. P., 195.
" Keziah, 297.
" Lucretia, 294.
" Mary, 3, 226, 293, 330, 340, 341, 385, 404, 405.
" Mary L., 294.
" Molly, 26.
" Moses, 40.

INDEX TO PERSONS.

496.

W.

Waterbury, Nancy, 86, 93, 94, 226, 295, 340, 385, 404, 405.
" Nathaniel, 3, 11, 15, 22, 23, 38, 40, 41, 54, 59, 60, 64, 66, 68, 91, 93, 94, 95, 97, 108, 111, 122, 133, 170, 174, 294, 295, 405.
" Nathaniel, Jr., 15, 94, 95.
" Nathaniel, 2nd, 3, 4.
" Nehemiah, 405.
" Noah, 405.
" Peter, 226, 376.
" Peter L., 295, 340, 341, 385.
" Phebe, 40, 340.
" Phineas, 103, 203, 405.
" Polly, 4, 174, 181, 193, 234, 294, 295, 341, 405.
" Prudence, 27.
" Rebecca, 295, 404.
" Reuma, 93.
" Ruamah, 295, 340.
" Rufus, 226.
" Ruth, 94.
" Sally, 21, 93, 94, 132, 174, 202, 293, 404.
" Samantha, 328.
" Samuel, 4, 94, 174, 226, 303.
" Samuel, Jr., 94.
" Samuel C., 340.
" Sarah, 40, 93, 173, 226, 293, 295, 382, 385, 387.
" Sarah A., 340.
" Sarah H., 21, 94, 176.
" Selleck, 262, 340.
" Sylvester E., 94, 174.
" Thaddeus, 94.
" Theodore, 386.
" Thomas, 113.
" Uriah, 40, 42, 62, 114.
" Warren, 404.
" William, 24, 26, 148, 202, 226, 265, 289, 405.

W.

Waterbury, William, Jr., 140, 155, 184, 196.
" William, 3rd, 297.
" William, 4th, 26, 28, 65.
" William L., 341.
" William W., 40.
Waters, Aaron, 341.
" Alla, 341.
" Ami, 304.
" Elisha, 130, 342.
" Hannah, 341.
" Jacob, 405.
" James, 405.
" Jared, 342.
" John, 93, 167, 341.
" Mary, 341.
" Olive, 167.
" Rachel, 341.
" Sarah, 130, 342.
" Selleck, 341.
" Stephen, 405.
" Zilpah, 341.
Webb, Abigail, 103, 133, 136, 230, 405.
" Albert, 133, 385, 386.
" Alfred, 135, 176, 227, 296, 386.
" Andrew, 133.
" Angeline, 174.
" Ann, 95.
" Anne, 399.
" Augustus, 295, 405.
" Betsy, 114.
" Caroline, 174, 175.
" Catherine, 40, 174.
" Caty, 4, 133.
" Charles H., 386.
" Cornelia, 174.
" Darius, 296.
" David, 4, 40, 174, 386, 405.
" Deborah, 133.
" Ebenezer, 28, 296.
" Ebenezer, Jr., 40, 59, 91.
" Ebenezer T., 345, 348.
" Elisha, 94, 95, 133.
" Eliza, 296.

INDEX TO PERSONS.

W.

Webb, Elizabeth, 174, 227.
" Elizabeth A., 342, 386.
" Elnathan T., 296.
" Epenetus, 296, 303, 304, 405.
" Esther, 9, 174.
" Frances, 174, 386.
" Frances W., 227.
" Frederick, 19, 61, 109, 133, 405.
" George, 296.
" Greenleaf S., 137.
" Hannah, 91, 94, 95, 133, 227, 296.
" Hannah W., 386.
" Harriet, 296.
" Harry, 391.
" Henry, 103, 174, 175, 294, 349.
" Henry, Jr., 97.
" Henry W., 27, 174.
" Hetty, 76, 399.
" Isaac, 227.
" James, 57, 108, 110, 154, 202, 227, 296, 405.
" James A., 174.
" Jerusha, 95, 133.
" John B., 342, 386.
" Joseph, 133.
" Joseph H., 386, 405.
" Josephine, 386.
" Katy, 4, 133.
" Lawson or Nanson, 174.
" Lucy P., 174, 227.
" Mary, 103, 133, 174, 175, 227, 349, 391, 405.
" Mary A., 133.
" Mary V., 296.
" Molly, 27.
" Nancy, 133, 405.
" Naomi, 295, 386.
" Nathaniel, 33, 49, 94, 95, 133, 174.
" Nathaniel, Jr., 9, 29, 67.
" Noah, 157.
" Phebe, 91, 296.
" Philander, 227.
" Polly, 133, 174, 296.

W.

Webb, Rebecca, 95, 133, 296.
" Rheua, 133.
" Rufus, 296.
" Sally, 133.
" Samuel, Dr., 227.
" Samuel, 15, 17, 22, 24, 26, 27, 33, 35, 40, 41, 46, 66, 80, 85, 88, 97, 110, 114, 125, 144, 166, 172, 174, 175, 176, 177, 392, 393, 396, 404.
" Sarah, 23, 40, 135, 176, 386, 406.
" Sarah E., 405.
" Sarah R., 386.
" Seth, 95, 112, 133, 399.
" Susan, 114.
" Thankful, 174, 200.
" Walter, 133.
" Washington, 296.
" White, 76, 399.
" William, 46, 157, 175, 176, 215, 227, 296, 298.
" William A., 174, 175, 405.
" William E., 133.
" William H., 227, 301.
" William S., 174.
" Wilse, 227.
" Woolsey, 23.
Webber, Margaret D., 61.
Weed, Aaron, 175.
" Abigail, 92, 95, 134, 135, 193, 227, 228, 296, 344, 363, 387.
" Abishai, 16, 58, 88, 130, 134, 342.
" Abishai, Jr., 98.
" Abraham, 134, 228.
" Alanson, 343.
" Alexander, 249.
" Alexander X., 406.
" Alfred, 343.
" Alvah, 386, 387.
" Amelia F., 344.
" Amos, 16, 30, 34, 36, 38, 60, 80, 95, 97.
" Ananias, 133, 406.
" Ann, 135, 264, 296, 345.
" Anna, 112, 135, 175, 176, 281

INDEX TO PERSONS.

W.

Weed, Anne, 135.
" Asahel, 16, 175, 227.
" Benjamin, 80, 134, 351, 380, 387.
" Benjamin, Jr., 19, 351, 406.
" Benjamin, 3rd, 25.
" Benjamin M., 134, 135, 254, 304, 342, 344, 347.
" Betsy, 83, 95, 96, 135, 175, 382.
" Caroline E., 344.
" Cary, 313, 314, 363.
" Catherine, 97, 344, 373, 374, 388.
" Catherine W., 343.
" Charles, 73, 266, 343, 390.
" Charles, Jr., 259, 303, 390.
" Charles A., 344.
" Charles E., 212, 228.
" Charles S., 298.
" Charlotte, 98, 348.
" Clarissa, 97, 134, 343, 344.
" Cornelia, 189.
" Cornelia M., 344.
" Cynthia, 133.
" Daniel, 96.
" Daniel A., 44, 101, 229.
" Daniel H., 227.
" Darius, 98, 133, 348.
" Daty, 134, 148, 228, 235, 266.
" David, 95, 96, 228, 405.
" David, Jr., 38.
" Debby, 135.
" Deborah, 41, 97, 98, 135, 398.
" Ebenezer, 44, 96, 97, 106, 263, 277, 342, 343, 344.
" Ebenezer E., 96.
" Ebenezer P., 96, 406.
" Ebenezer S., 313.
" Edward A., 345.
" Elbert, 297.
" Elijah, 281.

W.

Weed, Eliza, 202.
" Elizabeth, 32, 36, 98, 134, 297, 299, 345, 388.
" Enos, 96, 227, 228.
" Erastus H., 44, 101, 116, 120, 125, 140, 144, 149, 166, 176, 202, 228, 229.
" Eunice, 119, 134.
" Frances M., 297, 342, 343.
" Frederick, 10, 21, 297, 343.
" Frederick A., 228, 229, 297.
" George, 98, 131, 228, 387.
" George A., 334.
" George S., 345.
" Gideon, 112, 134, 228, 405.
" Gilbert D., 406.
" Hannah, 16, 44, 51, 60, 94, 95, 96, 125, 134, 165, 175, 228, 297, 312, 386, 387, 406.
" Hannah A., 95.
" Harriet A., 373.
" Harvey, 343, 387.
" Henry, 39, 41, 97, 98, 175, 182, 225, 228, 229, 252, 297, 298, 313, 314, 363.
" Henry, Jr., 108, 175, 283.
" Henry, 3rd, 135, 343.
" Henry D., 293.
" Henry R., 44, 83, 96, 134.
" Hezekiah, 10, 48, 97, 310, 343, 344, 345, 397.
" Hezekiah, Jr., 40.
" Hezekiah, 3rd, 97.
" Holly B., 298.
" Isaac, 2, 9, 134, 228, 294, 391, 386, 387.
" Isaac, Jr., 176, 297, 298, 306, 342.
" I. S., 249.
" Jacob, 134, 228, 249, 297, 343.
" Jacob T., 297, 312.
" James, 12, 41, 96, 97, 284, 343, 344.
" James A., 228, 229, 345.
" James B., 97, 343, 344.
" James E., 297.

INDEX TO PERSONS.

W.

Weed, James H., 134, 176, 362, 386.
" James J., 176, 298.
" James L., 234, 235.
" James R., 387.
" Jarvis, 257, 298, 344.
" Jerusha, 95, 96.
" Jesse, 40, 41, 96, 97.
" Joel, 97.
" John, 10, 84, 134, 135, 142, 172, 175, 228, 298, 334, 344, 387.
" John, Jr., 30, 36, 46, 48, 93, 105, 123, 135, 157, 173, 174, 175, 186, 203, 207, 227, 232, 234, 242, 265, 269, 279, 284, 293, 296, 300, 343, 391.
" John, 2nd, 126, 166.
" John, 3rd, 40, 97, 176, 298.
" John A., 345.
" John P., 388.
" John R., 313.
" Jonas, 41, 134, 135, 176.
" Jonas, Jr., 176.
" Jonas, 3rd, 97, 98, 135.
" Jonathan, 16, 44, 65, 96, 101, 134, 228, 229, 344.
" Jonathan, Jr., 15, 109.
" Jonathan J., 344.
" Joseph, 41, 135, 203, 218, 166, 230, 232, 387.
" Joseph A., 95.
" Julia M., 229, 299.
" Lewis, 215, 266.
" Louisa, 386, 387.
" Lucretia, 134.
" Lucy A., 55, 98.
" Luther, 112, 126, 133, 181, 195, 229, 311, 342, 387.
" Lydia, 97, 229, 263, 284, 343, 344.
" Lydia A., 44.
" Maltbie, 343.
" Maria E., 134, 342, 344.
" Maria L., 252.
" Martha, 98, 134, 176, 228.
" Martin E., 344.

W.

Weed, Mary, 4, 16, 41, 93, 95, 96, 97, 98, 112, 134, 135, 136, 176, 193, 229, 343, 344, 387, 390, 406.
" Mary A., 299.
" Mary E., 174, 297, 343, 344, 388.
" Mary S., 334.
" Matilda, 343.
" Mercy, 95, 112.
" Miles, 84, 98, 125.
" Miles H., 344.
" Nancy, 21, 176.
" Naomi, 98.
" Nathan, 3, 10, 21, 39, 40, 41, 62, 64, 86, 91, 93, 94, 97, 134, 135, 193, 297, 299, 393, 401, 405, 406, 407.
" Nathan, Jr., 42.
" Nathan S., 387.
" Nathaniel, 343, 405.
" Nathaniel B., 345, 351.
" Nelson, 299.
" Noah, 211, 313, 314, 363.
" Noah B., 380.
" Oliver, 83, 382.
" Paul, 135, 176.
" Peter, 41, 51, 98, 406.
" Phebe, 294, 297, 343.
" Philo, 19, 95, 98.
" Polly, 175, 298, 405.
" Prudence, 16.
" Rachel, 25, 73, 96.
" Raymond, 135.
" Raymond K., 345, 405.
" Rebecca, 95, 96, 135, 176, 343, 351, 386, 387.
" Reuama, 193.
" Robert M., 388.
" Rufus, 313, 314, 363, 386, 387.
" Ruth, 134.
" Sally, 10, 17, 95, 96, 98, 133, 174, 225, 231, 263, 343, 388.
" Sally A., 298.
" Samuel, 133, 228, 236, 297,

INDEX TO PERSONS.

W.

Weed, 298,299,344,387,388,406.
" Samuel,Jr.,36,84,91.
" Sarah,12,41,44,64,101, 135,176,229,231,297,299, 344,345,386,387.
" Sarah A., 344.
" Sarah E.,229,299,388, 406.
" Scudder, 98.
" Scudder,Jr., 98.
" Selleck,112,134,228,229, 345,388.
" Seth,5,29,40,55,65,83, 95,96,97,98,135,136,406.
" Seymour, 135.
" Smith,41,95,96,174,343, 361,406.
" Smith,Jr., 41.
" Stephen, 96.
" Susannah,41,58,96,406.
" Sylvanus,41,98,193.
" Sylvanus,Jr., 41.
" Theodore, 299.
" Theodore E.,228,229, 299,406.
" Thaddeus,133,406.
" Thirza,44,229.
" Usual,186,345.
" William,274,296,312, 327,339,356,387,388.
" William B., 373.
" William F.,135,136,176.
" William H.,175,176,212, 298,299,344,406.
" William W., 298.
Weeks, Anne, 41.
" Bartholomew, 41.
" Charles D., 99.
" Elizabeth,27,41.
" Hannah,41,99.
" Hannah M.,345.
" Henry,27,41,58.
" James W.,245,333,345.
" Jane, 406.
" John, 41.
" John V., 99.

W.

Weeks, Jonathan D.,288,307, 318.
" Joseph, 136.
" Joseph H., 299,230.
" Mary, 41.
" Phebe, 245,264.
" Phebe M., 99.
" Samuel, 27.
" William,41,98,99.
" William A., 99.
" William W., 99.
Welch, Mary, 136.
Welles, Benjamin, 41.
" Emeline, 388.
" Emeline W.,375,388.
" John, 41.
" Mary S., 41.
" Melanchton W., 41.
" Noah, 41.
" Rebecca, 41.
" Sarah, 42.
" William, 41,42.
Wells, see Welles.
Wheaton, Eliza A., 299.
" John S., 299.
" Mary,176,299,300.
" Samuel,87,117,176, 177.
Whelpley, Abigail,36,84.
" Amos, 84.
" Ann, 136.
" Charlotte, 136.
" Daniel, 136.
" Deborah, 266.
" Henry,136,214,266.
" Loisa, 136.
" Lucretia, 136.
" Mary, 136.
" Phebe, 136.
Whitcomb, George, 268.
White, Abel, 388.
" Abigail, 230.
" Ann, 136.
" Anna, 300.
" Anne, 42.
" Anson, 230.

INDEX TO PERSONS.

W.

White, Augusta, 138;
" Bartow F., 138,139,214, 238,261,267,275,336,337, 351,352,365,371.
" Benjamin, 230.
" Betsy, 230.
" Daniel, 230.
" Esther, 29,42,300,406.
" Hannah, 42.
" Henry,42,300,383.
" Israel, 135.
" Jacob,20,42,300,388.
" Jacob,Jr., 300.
" Joseph,164,212,230, 405.
" Lavinia, 337.
" Levina, 383.
" Mariah,42,300.
" Mary,135,138,400.
" Nathan,42,53,161,225, 286,288,300,308,402,406.
" Nathaniel, 230.
" Polly, 80.
" Richard H., 300.
" Sarah,42,&c,300.
" Seth W., 334.
" Smith, 230.
" Stephen,80,400.
" Susannah,89,230.
" William,34,36,59,84, 89,230,394.
" William,Jr., 155,165, 173,207.
Whiting, Abigail, 362,391.
" Alice, 230,295.
" Anne, 230.
" Charles,3,30,35,97, 177,401,405.
" Deborah, 14,177.
" Elizabeth, 230.
" Hannah,177,230.
" Harvey,230.
" Isaac, 244.
" Jesse,230,283,289, 295,300,362.
" Maria, 230.
" Mary,177,230,287,391.

W.

Whiting, Molly,163,230.
" Phebe, 230.
" Rachel, 406.
" Samuel,14,45,51,85, 86,88,113,124,126,127, 134,147,163,172,177,212, 230,300,345.
" Samuel F., 136.
" William B., 177.
Whitney, Isaac, 177.
" Josiah, 14.
" Lewis E., 317. (L.)
" Mary, 89.
" Phebe, 394.
" Zeriah, 189.
Wicks, Rebecca,153.
Wilcox, Josiah, 329,351.
" William L.,230,300.
Willets, Amos, 357.
" Daniel T., 357.
" Samuel, 357.
Williams, Abigail W., 176.
Wilmot, Abigail,137,300,346.
" Belinda, 346.
" Cary, 388.
" David, 230.
" David W., 137.
" Eben, 177.
" Enos, 105.
" Esther,42,99.
" Francis,42,99.
" Hannah,137,177.
" Henry, 110.
" James, 300.
" John,177,236,304,346.
" Joseph,137,177,200.
" Mary E.,297,388.
" Polly, 46,388.
" Polly A., 236.
" Sally, 304,346.
" Samuel,346.
" Sarah, 177.
" Stephen M., 34.
" William,137,154,177, 315,388.
Wilson, Ann, 190.
" Arna,181.

INDEX TO PERSONS.

W.

Wilson, Betsy, 178, 214, 278.
" Burrage, 137.
" Charles, 8, 115, 358.
" Daniel, 42, 99.
" Desire, 39, 99, 177, 397.
" Drake, 42.
" Eunice, 99, 177.
" Hannah, 42.
" James, 39, 224, 246, 247, 248, 273, 275, 290, 291, 310, 311, 339, 358, 371, 384.
" Johanna, 99.
" John B., 247, 310, 311, 358.
" Joseph, 42, 99.
" Jotham, 8, 42, 247.
" Jotham, Jr., 8.
" Maria, 214.
" Mary, 8, 42.
" Monmouth, 42, 115.
" Nancy, 247.
" Nathaniel, 358.
" Nehemiah, 8, 29, 39, 42, 44, 68, 74, 99, 177, 397, 402.
" Polly, 247.
" Rachel, 388.
" Ruth, 213.
" Sally, 115, 116, 247, 248, 310.
" Samuel, 247, 310.
" Samuel G., 375.
" Sarah, 44, 99, 145, 177, 178, 247.
" Susannah, 42.
" Thomas, 42, 213, 214, 247, 310.
" Thomas M., 42, 78, 178, 230.
" Urdah, 99.
Winthrop, Catherine R., 300.
" Charles E. R., 300.
" Cornelia, 300.
" Emily R., 301, 346.
" Francis B., 301, 346.
" Harriet, 300.
" Henry R., 301, 346.
" John S., 214, 300, 301.

W.

Winthrop, John S., Jr., 301, 346.
" Susan R., 301, 346.
Wolcott, Alexander S., 389.
" Cynthia L., 389.
Wollis, Amy, 15.
Wood, Betsy, 230.
" Clarissa R., 350.
" David, 8, 13, 51, 52, 53, 61, 63, 67, 81, 87, 99, 100, 104, 144, 150, 230, 231, 301, 393.
" David, Jr., 13, 47.
" Elizabeth, 82, 83.
" Frances, 230.
" Frances A., 301.
" Francis, 159.
" George, 230.
" George S., 285.
" Hannah, 99.
" Henry M., 230.
" Hezekiah, 6, 130.
" Isaac, 346.
" Israel K., 150.
" Jemima, 6.
" John, 231.
" Joseph, 4, 16, 49, 56, 90, 99, 100, 109, 127, 137, 143, 144, 154, 393, 399.
" Julias L., 229, 230.
" Lemuel, 406.
" Martha, 99.
" Rebecca, 99.
" Rhoda, 130.
" Sally, 63.
" Sally V., 63, 159, 230, 231.
" Sarah, 99, 100.
" Silas, 159, 230.
" William, 406.
Wooden, Isaac, 40, 231.
" Mary, 231.
" Sarah, 40, 231.
" Solomon, 231.
Woods, John, 376.
Woolsey, Gilbert, 112.
" Rhoda, 112.
" Theodosia, 88.
Wooster, Ebeneser, 407.
" Elizabeth, 12, 176, 407.

INDEX TO PERSONS.

W.

Wooster, Henry, 407.
" James, 407.
" John, 407.
" William N., 301.
Worden, Hannah, 100.
" Isaac, 100.
" Lucretia, 136.
Wright, Joseph, 71.
Wyant, Sarah, 389.
Wyk, see Wicks.

Y.

Young, Abraham, 42, 43.
" Anna, 300.
" Asahel, 148.
" Daniel, 161.
" Elizabeth, 137, 231, 407.
" Elizabeth E., 172.
Young, Enoch, 31, 70.
" Frederick, 137.
" George W., 22, 355.
" Greenleaf, 249.
" Hannah, 42, 137, 300, 407.
" James, 138, 232.
" Jeremiah, 137.
" John, 138, 195, 342.
" Jonathan, 137.
" Keziah, 137.
" Lewis, 137.
" Phebe, 42, 231, 407.
" Rebecca, 407.
" Richard, 42, 232.
" Ruth, 137.
" Sally, 137.
" Samuel, 137, 194.
" Sarah, 42.
" Susannah, 42.
" William, 110, 172, 244.
" William W., 335.
Youngs, see Young.